THE LAW OF THE SEA

Compendium of Basic Documents

International Seabed Authority
in collaboration with
The Caribbean Law Publishing Company
KINGSTON

Published in Jamaica 2001 by
The International Seabed Authority

in collaboration with

The Caribbean Law Publishing Company
11 Cunningham Avenue, Box 686
Kingston 6

© International Seabed Authority, 2001

National Library of Jamaica Cataloguing-in-Publication Data

The law of the sea : compendium of basic documents. – Kingston : International Seabed
     Authority : Caribbean Law Publishing, 2001

     p. ;   cm.
Includes index

ISBN: 976-610-373-9
ISBN: 976-610-374-7 (pbk)

1. Maritime law   2. United Nations Convention on the Law of the Sea
3. Access to the sea (International law)
341.450262 – dc 20

Cover design by Errol Stennett

Printed and bound in the U.S.A.

Introductory Note

This Compendium of Basic Documents on the Law of the Sea contains the text of the United Nations Convention on the Law of the Sea, signed at Montego Bay, Jamaica, on 10 December 1982, as well as the text of the Agreement relating to the Implementation of Part XI of the United Nations Convention on the Law of the Sea, adopted by the General Assembly on 28 July 1994, and of the Agreement for the Implementation of the Provisions of the United Nations Convention on the Law of the Sea of 10 December 1982 relating to the Conservation and Management of Straddling Fish Stocks and Highly Migratory Fish Stocks of 1995.

In addition, the Compendium includes the official text of the Regulations on Prospecting and Exploration for Polymetallic Nodules in the Area, approved by the Assembly of the International Seabed Authority on 13 July 2000. Also included are the Final Act of the Third United Nations Conference on the Law of the Sea, containing an official account, approved and signed by the participants, of the proceedings leading to the adoption of the Convention (1973-1982), and the four resolutions adopted by the Conference and related to the Convention, and the Final Act of the United Nations Conference on Straddling Fish Stocks and Highly Migratory Fish Stocks (1993-1995). These texts are supplemented by a completely revised subject index to the Convention, its nine annexes and associated resolutions, the two implementing Agreements and the Regulations on Prospecting and Exploration for Polymetallic Nodules in the Area.

Explanatory material consists of an introduction by the Special Representative of the Secretary-General of the United Nations (reproduced from the 1983 edition of the Convention published by the United Nations) and statements delivered at the closing session of the Conference by its President and by the Secretary-General as well as the Report of the Secretary-General on outstanding issues relating to the deep seabed mining provisions of the Convention and statements delivered in the General Assembly upon the adoption of the 1994 Agreement. In addition, relevant General Assembly resolutions have been included.

The main contents of this Compendium are as follows:

Table of contents

Introduction and statements

United Nations Convention on the Law of the Sea

General Assembly resolution 48/263 and the Agreement
relating to the implementation of Part XI of the United Nations
Convention on the Law of the Sea of 10 December 1982

Regulations on prospecting and exploration for polymetallic
nodules in the Area

Agreement for the implementation of the provisions of the
United Nations Convention on the Law of the Sea of
10 December 1982 relating to the conservation and management
of straddling fish stocks and highly migratory fish stocks

Final Act of the Third United Nations Conference on
the Law of the Sea

Final Act of the United Nations Conference on the conservation
and management of straddling fish stocks and highly migratory
fish stocks

Resolutions of the United Nations General Assembly

List of signatories of the Convention

Chronology

Consolidated Index

Table of Contents

UNITED NATIONS CONVENTION ON
THE LAW OF THE SEA

ANNEX

REGULATIONS ON PROSPECTING AND EXPLORATION FOR POLYMETALLIC NODULES IN THE AREA

AGREEMENT FOR THE IMPLEMENTATION OF THE PROVISIONS OF THE UNITED NATIONS CONVENTION ON THE LAW OF THE SEA OF 10 DECEMBER 1982 RELATING TO THE CONSERVATION AND MANAGEMENT OF STRADDLING FISH STOCKS AND HIGHLY MIGRATORY FISH STOCKS

FINAL ACT OF THE THIRD UNITED NATIONS CONFERENCE ON THE LAW OF THE SEA

FINAL ACT OF THE UNITED NATIONS CONFERENCE ON THE CONSERVATION AND MANAGEMENT OF STRADDLING FISH STOCKS AND HIGHLY MIGRAORY FISH STOCKS

ANNEX

GENERAL ASSEMBLY RESOLUTIONS ON THE LAW OF THE SEA

● ● ● ● ● ● ● ● ●

FOREWORD

It is a great pleasure to introduce this Compendium of Basic Documents on the Law of the Sea, which contains for the first time in one volume the 1982 United Nations Convention on the Law of the Sea, the two implementing agreements of 1994 and 1995, the Regulations on Prospecting and Exploration for Polymetallic Nodules in the Area adopted by the International Seabed Authority and selected resolutions of the General Assembly of the United Nations relating to the law of the sea. In addition, the Compendium contains the Final Acts of the Third United Nations Conference on the Law of the Sea and the United Nations Conference on Straddling Fish Stocks and Highly Migratory Fish Stocks, as well as introductory material of great historical significance, some of which has been reproduced by kind permission of the United Nations from the 1983 United Nations' edition of the Convention.

The Compendium has been compiled by the staff of the Office of Legal Affairs of the International Seabed Authority, who also prepared the subject index. Although the text of the Convention itself is widely available and has been published in many forms, the significance of the present Compendium lies in the fact that not only is the Convention reproduced together with all related instruments, but also that the index covers in a comprehensive manner the Convention, its nine annexes and associated resolutions, the two implementing agreements and the Regulations on Prospecting and Exploration for Polymetallic Nodules in the Area.

The 1982 United Nations Convention on the Law of the Sea forms the basis of the modern legal framework for ocean governance. The Convention is an important contribution to the rule of law. It sets out principles and norms for the conduct of relations among States on maritime issues. As such it contributes immensely to the maintenance of global peace and security.

It has been described as a constitution for the oceans and has, without fanfare, but surely and imperceptibly, earned its place as a great achievement of the international community. Its influence goes beyond the confines of the law of the sea. It has established itself as part of the global system for peace and security, of which the Charter of the United Nations is the foundation. The former Secretary-General of the United Nations, Boutros Boutros-Ghali, at the inaugural meeting of the International Seabed Authority in Kingston on 16 November 1994, spoke of the Convention as follows:

> The dream of a comprehensive law of the oceans is an old one. Turning this dream into reality has been one of the greatest achievements of this century. It is one of the decisive contributions of our era. It will be one of our most enduring legacies.

The achievements of the Convention are many. It has resolved a number of critical issues, some of which had eluded agreement for centuries. It reflects a delicate balance between competing interests in the use of the ocean and its resources by taking a functional approach to establishing the various maritime zones and the rights and duties of States in those zones, including in the ocean space beyond national jurisdiction.

It finally settles the breadth of the territorial sea at 12 nautical miles, with a guaranteed right of passage for international navigation in those waters; it ensures unhampered passage of vessels and aircraft through and over archipelagic waters and vital straits used for international navigation around the world; it secures for coastal States resource and environmental jurisdiction in a 200 nautical mile exclusive economic zone without limiting other legitimate activities in that zone by the international community; it imposes a duty on all States to ensure, through proper conservation and management measures, the long-term sustainable use of living resources; it provides for an extended continental shelf jurisdiction, combining scientific and geological criteria with distance criteria for determining precisely its outer limit and makes provision for the sharing of revenues from the resources of the shelf beyond the exclusive economic zone; it guarantees access to and from the sea for land-locked States; it provides for a regime for archipelagic States; it establishes an innovative regime for the development of the mineral resources of the deep seabed which is the common heritage of mankind, and from which eventually mankind as a whole is to benefit; it sets out rules for the conduct of marine scientific research; it contains the most comprehensive rules for the protection and preservation of the marine environment and imposes a duty on all States to protect the oceans from all sources of pollution; and it promotes peaceful settlement of disputes by establishing mechanisms and procedures for compulsory settlement of disputes arising from the interpretation and application of the provisions of the Convention.

Thus the Convention has established certainty in the international law of the sea in place of the chaos that preceded it. In reviewing the old law and revising or replacing it where necessary, and by introducing new concepts and norms to meet the current needs of the international community, the Convention has revolutionized the international law of the sea. It did so through painstaking negotiation on each important issue and through the process of consensus building.

The success of the Convention is determined not only by the number of States Parties – which is already remarkable and beyond all expectations – but also by its tangible achievements. The fundamental provisions of the Convention are consistently and uniformly applied in State practice. This is self-evident from a careful examination of the practice of States in all parts of the world. Those few States who have not become parties so far have certain specific difficulties peculiar to them. These are either internal constitutional problems or bilateral issues which cannot be resolved through a global treaty. On the other hand, in practice, most of these States recognize that the Convention reflects the current international law of the sea. Indeed, the Convention is recognized as the pre-eminent source of international law of the sea by States, the International Court of Justice, the International Tribunal for the Law of the Sea and other judicial or arbitral bodies dealing with marine-related issues and has become the basis for settlement of disputes on marine-related matters.

The Convention has changed the political geography of the world by enclosing large areas of the oceans under the national jurisdiction of sovereign States. With the near-universal acceptance of the Convention, the problem today is not that there is no legal framework for ocean governance but rather how States should act in the discharge of their responsibilities under the Convention and in the exercise of the rights and duties ascribed to them for ocean governance.

It is important to understand that the Convention is not a static instrument. It provides a basic framework for the conduct of relations among States on maritime issues. Its norms are precise but it also establishes principles which lend themselves to further development. In this sense, there is an in-built flexibility which allows for the development of new norms within the framework of the Convention in response to evolving circumstances. We have already seen this happen in the two implementing agreements that have been adopted: the agreement on the implementation of Part XI and the agreement on the implementation of the provisions on straddling fish stocks and highly migratory fish stocks.

The most controversial aspect of the Convention was the regime for deep seabed mining contained in Part XI and Annex III. Indeed, as is well known, it was the outright rejection of certain elements of the Part XI regime which led, in 1982, to the non-acceptance of the Convention on the part of certain important industrialized States, including the United States of America, the United Kingdom and Germany.

However, the other parts of the Convention achieved a broad measure of support from all major interest groups and are widely reflected in State practice. The difficulties with regard to Part XI were eventually resolved during the period from 1990 to 1994 through consultation and negotiation among all interested parties and by taking a creative and flexible approach. The resulting régime is now reflected in Part XI of the Convention and the implementing Agreement, adopted by the General Assembly on 28 July 1995.

The régime set out in the Convention and the Agreement, however, while containing the basic principles for exploration and exploitation of the resources of the deep seabed, also requires further elaboration and implementation through the adoption of regulations for the conduct of exploration and exploitation activities. In July 2000, following negotiations extending over many years, the Assembly of the International Seabed Authority approved the first set of such regulations covering prospecting and exploration for polymetallic nodules. The significance of this achievement lies in the fact that it completes the scheme set out in the Convention and the Agreement for the administration of the resources of the international Area and provides a mechanism for the practical implementation of the legal régime through the issue of contracts to those who wish to explore the deep seabed.

While the focus of the present legal régime is on the exploration of polymetallic nodules in the international seabed area, this is only one kind of resource available from the sea floor. Recent scientific studies have shown the existence of cobalt bearing crusts and polymetallic sulphides as potentially viable economic resources. Regulations governing these resources will be developed in due course within the overall legal framework of the Convention and the Agreement, with due regard to the need to protect the marine environment from potentially harmful effects.

In the area of fisheries, by the early 1990s it was widely recognized that there was over-exploitation of fish resources resulting in dangerous depletion of important fish stocks. It was also recognized that the legal régime for high seas fishing set out in the Geneva Conventions of 1958, and largely incorporated in the 1982 Convention, was inadequate to safeguard the fisheries resources of the high seas, particularly those classed as straddling fish stocks and highly migratory fish stocks. It was therefore not surprising that the United Nations Conference on Environment and Development (UNCED) in 1992 called for a conference to address the problems of high seas fisheries. Such a conference was convened by the United Nations in 1993 and completed its work in 1995 with the adoption of the Agreement for the Implementation of the

Provisions of the United Nations Conference on the Law of the Sea Relating to the Conservation and Management of Straddling Fish Stocks and Highly Migratory Fish Stocks.

In the context of straddling fish stocks and highly migratory fish stocks, the Agreement establishes norms and principles for fisheries management, many of which are of general application to all types of fish stocks and in all jurisdictional areas. Thus, since the conference was dealing with the marine ecosystem in which such stocks are found, it indirectly addressed the problem of fisheries management in general. In particular, the Agreement introduces the concept of the precautionary approach to fisheries management both on the high seas and in areas under national jurisdiction. In this respect, the Agreement is a blueprint for fisheries conservation and management in general and the future of fisheries depends on how this very important agreement on conservation and management of fisheries will be implemented by States.

The Agreement recognizes the importance of a cooperative approach to fisheries management and calls for compatible conservation and management measures. While the Agreement does not in any way affect the concept of sovereign rights as found in the Convention it nevertheless emphasizes the interdependency of stocks and recognizes that, in the final analysis, neither the coastal State nor the distant water fishing State, can manage the stocks in isolation.

The holistic approach to management cannot be left to coastal States or fishing States alone. There must be a framework through which they can cooperate to establish management régimes and agree on problems of allocation and effort limitation. In this regard the provisions of the Convention have been elaborated upon. The roles and responsibilities of regional fisheries management organizations have been clarified and made more meaningful as a forum for management of shared resources. In particular, not only have the requirements for flag State responsibility been further developed and enumerated, but also they have been supplemented by the measures that can be taken by members of regional organizations in cases where the flag State is unable or unwilling to take effective action itself. Thus, through a combination of the mechanisms provided in the Agreement and the measures to be adopted through regional organizations, an important gap in the effective application of conservation and management measures has been filled. This is an important innovation and a major development in international law.

The provisions of the Agreement have been supplemented by the FAO Code of Conduct for Responsible Fisheries and the related Agreement to Promote Compliance with International Conservation and Management Measures by Fishing Vessels on the High Seas.

One of the important features of the Convention is that throughout its many parts, it calls for cooperation between and among States in the implementation of its provisions. It is to be hoped that all future problems arising from the use of the oceans will be resolved through such cooperation.

No system of law would be complete without a mechanism for settling disputes. In most international treaties, it is difficult to get States to agree to such a system. Even in the case of the Charter of the United Nations, which establishes the Statute of the International Court of Justice, there is no compulsory and binding dispute settlement mechanism. One of the most important contributions of the Convention, therefore, is the establishment of mechanisms and procedures for compulsory settlement of disputes arising from the interpretation and application of the provisions of the Convention. For this purpose, the Convention establishes a new international institution, the International Tribunal for the Law of the Sea, in addition to existing mechanisms for settlement of disputes, such as arbitration, conciliation and the International Court of Justice itself.

When we look at the broad spectrum of issues dealt with in the Convention it is more apparent than ever that the problems of ocean space are closely interrelated and need to be considered as a whole. Indeed, this principle is embodied in the Preamble of the Convention and the inter-relationship of the various parts of the Convention is premised on this fundamental principle. It is therefore imperative that this integrated approach to the different uses of the oceans and the development of their resources is adopted in its implementation. It is only through such an approach that the delicate balance between the conflicting interests and activities in the oceans achieved in the Convention can be maintained. Such a balance was seen as a *sine qua non* for the general and widespread acceptance of the Convention.

While the Convention provides the basic framework, the norms for ocean governance go beyond the Convention and are contained in many instruments, declarations and decisions related to the regulation of different uses of the oceans and the development of their resources. Since the Convention was adopted, and especially since the early 1990s, a large number of new international instruments have been put in place, a number of which are within the framework of the Convention. These cover subjects as diverse as navigation and overflight, fisheries, scientific research and the ocean environment in general. In addition, aspects of ocean governance are being discussed by a number of international organizations and technical bodies. These developments, which have taken place within the parameters established by the Convention, represent great progress towards a comprehensive system of ocean governance.

There are other important instruments, such as the London Dumping Convention, the Antarctic Treaty System, the Convention on Biological Diversity, the Framework Convention on Climate Change and related protocols, which also impact upon the system of ocean governance. To these must be added the influence of declarations such as the Stockholm Declaration on the Human Environment, from which the basic principles for protection and preservation of the marine environment were developed for inclusion in Part XII of the Convention, and the UNCED, which produced Agenda 21, in particular Chapter 17 on the seas and oceans, as well as the Global Programme of Action on the Protection of the Marine Environment from Land-Based Activities. While not having the status of treaty law, these instruments contain important principles which apply to the oceans and make an important contribution to the overall system of ocean governance.

There are also a large number of technical regulatory measures that have been established through global and regional organizations. Among these must be included the rules and guidelines adopted by the International Maritime Organization in relation to maritime safety and prevention of pollution from ships, the rules, codes and conventions adopted by the Food and Agriculture Organization of the United Nations in relation to responsible fishing practices, and the regional seas conventions adopted under the auspices of the United Nations Environment Programme.

Undoubtedly, major challenges will continue to arise as we seek to manage the oceans and their resources in the face of increasing pressure from rapid technological development, increased scientific research and concerns for the marine environment as the new millennium progresses. These pressures will come from an ever-growing demand for food resources, rapid growth in communication, trade and transportation as well from the demand for oil, gas and other mineral resources from the sea. It is to be hoped that these challenges will be addressed through increased international cooperation and through a flexible and creative approach to the implementation of the principles and norms embodied in the Convention.

Satya N. Nandan
Secretary-General
International Seabed Authority

Kingston, December 2000

INTRODUCTION*

On 10 December 1982 the United Nations Convention on the Law of the Sea was opened for signature in Montego Bay, Jamaica. This marked the culmination of over 14 years of work involving participation by more than 150 countries representing all regions of the world, all legal and political systems, all degrees of socio-economic development, countries with various dispositions regarding the kinds of minerals that can be found in the sea-bed, coastal States, States described as geographically disadvantaged with regard to ocean space, archipelagic States, island States and land-locked States. These countries convened for the purpose of establishing a comprehensive régime "dealing with all matters relating to the law of the sea, ... bearing in mind that the problems of ocean space are closely interrelated and need to be considered as a whole." The fruits of their labours are embodied in the United Nations Convention on the Law of the Sea.

The Convention is multi-faceted and represents a monument to international co-operation in the treaty-making process: the need to elaborate a new and comprehensive régime for the law of the sea was perceived, and the international community expressed its collective will to co-operate in this effort on a scale the magnitude of which was unprecedented in treaty history. The elaboration of the Convention represents an attempt to establish true universality in the effort to achieve a "just and equitable international economic order" governing ocean space.

These ideals were transformed through the treaty-making process into the substance of the text, which itself is of unique nature. It comprises 320 articles and nine annexes, governing all aspects of ocean space from delimitations to environmental control, scientific research, economic and commercial activities, technology and the settlement of disputes relating to ocean matters. An examination of the character of the individual provisions reveals that the Convention represents not only the codification of customary norms, but also and more significantly the progressive development of international law, and contains the constituent instruments of two major new international organizations.

It is, however, the conceptual underpinnings of the Convention as a "package" which is its most significant quality, and has contributed most distinctly to the remarkable achievement of the Convention. Its quality as a package is a result of the singular nature of the circumstances from which it emerged, which factors included the close interrelationship of the many different issues involved, the large number of participating States, and the vast number of often conflicting interests which

---

* Reproduced by kind permission of the United Nations.

frequently cut across the traditional lines of negotiation by region. In addition, the strong desire that the Convention allow for flexibility of practice in order to ensure durability over time, and so as not to encroach upon the sovereignty of States, was recognized as another important consideration. All of these factors necessitated that every individual provision of the text be weighed within the context of the whole, producing an intricately balanced text to provide a basis for universality.

The concept of the package pervaded all work on the elaboration of the Convention and was not limited to consideration of substance alone. It became the *leit-motiv* of the Conference and in fact permeates the law of the sea as it exists today.

THE HISTORY OF THE CONVENTION

The mammoth task of elaborating this new régime began in 1967, when the concept of the Common Heritage of Mankind was first discussed by the General Assembly in the context of the question of preservation of the sea-bed and ocean floor exclusively for peaceful purposes. The common heritage concept was not a new one (it dates back to the 19th century, and was referred to by the President of the first Law of the Sea Conference in his opening speech in 1958) but it had never before been discussed in an international forum. It is of particular relevance to note that the discussion took place in the First Committee of the General Assembly, as the item was perceived from the very beginning as being of primarily political significance, and not limited to strictly legal or economic concern. This conclusion was based on the same rationale which is the foundation of the package concept, and is the reason that the work of the Third United Nations Conference was not based on draft articles prepared by the International Law Commission, as was the work of the 1958 Conference.

The General Assembly established an *Ad Hoc* Committee to study the Peaceful Uses of the Sea-Bed and the Ocean Floor beyond the Limits of National Jurisdiction, and subsequently created a standing committee, the Committee on the Peaceful Uses of the Sea-Bed and Ocean Floor beyond the Limits of National Jurisdiction (Sea-Bed Committee), for the purpose of shaping and refining the ideas and concepts which were to form the basis of the new international régime. These committees, cognizant of the concerns which were to develop into the concept of the package, worked on the basis of consensus.

In 1970 the General Assembly adopted a Declaration of Principles (General Assembly resolution 2749 (XXV)), following upon negotiations which took place in the Sea-Bed Committee, which resolution solemnly declared that "The sea-bed and ocean floor, and the subsoil thereof, beyond the limits of national jurisdiction ... as well as the resources of the area, are the common heritage of mankind" and "shall not be subject to appropriation by any means by States or persons". In addition, it was declared that this area "shall be open to use exclusively for peaceful purposes by all States ... without discrimination". Thus the common heritage was formally spelled out.

The General Assembly at the same time adopted a related three-part resolution, the preambular paragraphs of which reiterated the recognition of need for a reformed régime and mandated its consideration as a package, as follows:

"*Conscious* that the problems of ocean space are closely inter-related and need to be considered as a whole,

"*Noting* that the political and economic realities, scientific development and rapid technological advances of the last decade have accentuated the need for early and progressive development of the law of the sea in a framework of close international co-operation,

"*Having regard* to the fact that many of the present States Members of the United Nations did not take part in the previous United Nations Conferences on the law of the sea, ..."

The resolution continued, calling upon the Sea-Bed Committee to act as a preparatory committee for the future conference. (For a more detailed history of the pre-conference work on law of the sea, see the Introduction to the Report of the Sea-Bed Committee, A/9021.)

In late 1973 the Third United Nations Conference on the Law of the Sea was convened in accordance with General Assembly resolution 3067 (XXVIII), and set about its task with an organizational session. The first order of business was the question of procedure: procedural practices had to be developed which would foster the cohesiveness of the "package" of law of the sea. Indeed, the procedural innovations of the Conference were at times quite unique and have no doubt contributed to the progressive development of the treaty-making process itself.

As a consequence of the deliberations, the Conference adopted its Rules of Procedure (A/CONF.62/30/Rev.3). Since the earlier committees had worked on the basis of consensus, and due to the widely divergent interests on issues of such paramount importance, it was recognized that resort to traditional voting rules would be unsatisfactory as a method for achieving the desired goals. Consensus was therefore adopted as the principal means by which decisions were to be taken. This notion was embodied in the Declaration incorporating the Gentleman's Agreement, appended to the Rules of Procedure, and provided the context in which the rules themselves were framed. For example, the rules on decision-making require that the Conference in the first instance decide that it has exhausted all efforts to reach consensus before any voting on questions of substance can take place. In order to ensure that this decision is not taken lightly, the rules allow various deferment or "cooling-off" periods before the actual voting may begin. By delaying the voting as long as possible, it was hoped that the divergent positions might be reconciled in the interim, thus obviating the need to vote at all.

The Conference realized at an early stage that negotiations could not be effectively carried out in formal proceedings, and that because of the large number of participants and sensitive issues involved, working groups would be more efficient than plenary meetings. Indeed, much of the elaboration process took place in smaller or more informal meetings, but always on an *ad referendum* basis to larger and/or more formal bodies, and always on the basis of consensus. The working or negotiating groups were generally established on the basis of interest in a particular issue. In this respect States did not coalesce within traditional regional or political alignments. Rather, they grouped themselves to face specific issues and to protect clearly identifiable interests. For example, coastal States wanted a legal régime that would allow them to manage and conserve the biological and mineral resources within their national jurisdiction; archipelagic States wanted to obtain recognition for the new régime of archipelagic waters; landlocked States were seeking general rules of international law that would grant them transit to and from the sea and rights of access to the living resources of their neighbouring States; some industrialized nations wanted to have guaranteed access to the sea-bed mineral resources beyond national jurisdiction within a predictable legal framework; countries that produced the same minerals in their territories wanted assurances that the sea-bed production of these minerals would not undermine their economies or result in a "de facto" monopoly; developing countries wanted to be more than silent witnesses to the acquisition of new knowledge of the oceans so that marine science and technology could be put at the service of all and not only of a limited number of very wealthy countries; States bordering straits wanted to ensure that free passage would not result in damage to their marine environment or threats to their national security; practically all nations wanted to preserve the freedoms of navigation, commerce and communication; and finally, mankind as a whole needed to ensure that a new legal régime would safeguard the marine environment against depredation or irrational use of non-renewable resources, the discharge or dumping of noxious substances into the oceans or the so-called scientific tests that could affect the delicate balance of marine life. These are only a few of the multitude of particular interests which needed consideration at the Conference. Any individual State could fall into any number of different interest groups, depending upon its individual national concerns and the texture of the negotiations on the overall package. The interest groups did not, however, replace regional group consultations, which also took place, thereby enhancing the flow of information and compounding the number of considerations which had to be weighed with respect to any given issue at any given time.

It is understandable in this context, then, that the Rules of Procedure and the Gentleman's Agreement appended to them not only contemplated the application of consensus with regard to the final adoption of the Convention as a whole, but also for its application at each and every step along the way. The consensus principle was in fact applied throughout the work of the Conference and the many revisions of the text which would become the treaty. In some cases specific informal Conference practices were formally introduced, notably in the later stages of the work when only the more thorny issues remained to be resolved, in order to foster agreement and to ensure that there would be no objection to decisions taken.

A significant procedural step in this respect took place in 1977, at the seventh session of the Conference, when the programme of work contained in document A/CONF.62/62 was adopted. This document followed upon the consolidation, at the end of the sixth session of the various parts of the text into a single working paper, the Informal Composite Negotiating Text. The procedural act of consolidation, albeit producing a text not yet refined nor acceptable to the point of constituting a draft text, itself represented a milestone and a significant step towards the realization of a single comprehensive and unified international régime.

The emergence of the Informal Composite Negotiating Text denotes that the negotiations had proceeded to a very delicate stage, and threw into relief the remaining "hard-core" issues which required resolution. Document A/CONF.62/62 acknowledged this situation and mandated the institutionalization of various previously utilized informal Conference practices to promote agreement. One such practice was the establishment of issue-specific negotiating groups. Another was the formal institution of the President's "Collegium", the body of principal officers of the Conference which acted in an advisory capacity to the President. It had been the principal officers who had informally prepared and revised the negotiating texts upon which the work of the Conference had been focused all along. However, the programme of work now established stringent standards to direct the Collegium in its work: it mandated that no revision could be made without prior presentation of the proposed change to the Plenary, wherein it must have received "widespread and substantial support", indicating that it offered a "substantially improved prospect of consensus". By these procedural devices the Conference was able to ensure that the package remained cohesive until such time as all of the pieces fell into place.

Another of the peculiarities of the law of the sea treaty is that it is a major instrument which has equally authentic Arabic, Chinese, English, French, Russian and Spanish texts. Indeed, if the object of the package is to have a Convention which is universally acceptable, then it follows that it must be acceptable in each and every of the six languages to which a State may refer. The achievement of this goal required another innovation in the treaty-making process as applied to the Drafting Committee.

The Drafting Committee of the Conference undertook its work in two stages. The first stage involved the harmonization of recurring words and phrases so as to ensure a sense of a whole, unified text, and to avoid misinterpretation and confusion in instances when an identical meaning was intended by phraseology which was varied. Such discrepancies had arisen because the different parts of the text had been drafted in different committees, with reference to varied existing treaty sources, thus necessitating this first stage. The second stage of the work involved the article-by-article reading of the text for the purpose of ensuring that each provision was identical in meaning in each of the languages.

To facilitate its work in the light of the desired goals, and because the Drafting Committee was the only committee of limited representation in the Conference, it was necessary to devise a procedure to ensure universality of participation in the work of the Committee. The informal language groups of the Conference accordingly developed. These were open-ended groups which grappled with Drafting Committee issues and their co-ordination, and then reported back to the Committee. The role of the Committee itself was reserved to policy and decision-making, with little of the actual deliberations taking place in that forum.

At the close of the tenth session in 1981, the Conference decided to revise the informal text, officially producing a Draft Convention (A/CONF.62/L.78). Virtually all the parts of the package had by now fallen into place — only the most seemingly intractable political questions remained. The shape of the comprehensive package on the law of the sea, as comprising the Convention itself plus a number of resolutions, could by now be foreseen. In conjunction with the issuance of the Draft Convention, the Conference adopted a timetable calling for the final decision-making session to be held in 1982. The five-week plan allowed time for negotiation of the remaining points to be resolved; these points included the mandate of the Preparatory Commission and the rules governing pioneer investors in the sea-bed Area prior to the entry into force of the Convention, that is, questions of the work to succeed the Conference.

After long deliberations marking the culmination of over ninety weeks of work, on 23 April 1982, the Conference, in accordance with its Rules of Procedure, determined that all efforts to reach a consensus had been exhausted. Thus the machinery for the final decision-making was set in motion. The Draft Convention and the four Resolutions that were before the Conference on 30 April 1982 did not include any texts which had not undergone an elaborate structure of negotiations devised by the Conference in order to ensure that all provisions could command widespread and substantial support. On that day the Conference, at the request of one delegation, had to resort to voting on the question of adoption of the whole of the package on the law of the sea. The results of that vote (130 in favour, 4 against, with 17 abstentions) represented the overwhelming reaffirmation of support for the ideals, principles and goals of a new international order for the seas as embodied in the package of the Convention on the Law of the Sea. This reaffirmation of support is further strengthened by the fact that the majority of States which abstained in the voting later became signatories to the Convention.

The final meetings of the Conference were held in Montego Bay, Jamaica, from 6 December to 10 December 1982. The Conference heard closing statements by delegations (see A/CONF.62/PV.185-193), after which the Final Act was signed (for a more detailed history of the Conference, see the Final Act). The Convention was opened for signature in Jamaica on 10 December. On that first day, signatures from 119 delegations comprising 117 States, the Cook Islands (a self-governing associated State) and the United Nations Council for Namibia, were appended to the Convention. In addition, one ratification, that of Fiji, was deposited that day. Never before has such overwhelming support been demonstrated so concretely on the first day that a treaty has been open for signature. The Convention's first achievement in its own right was unprecedented in the history of treaty law.

THE TEXT ITSELF: SOME HIGHLIGHTS

The Convention itself establishes a comprehensive framework for the regulation of all ocean space. It is divided into 17 parts and nine annexes, and contains provisions governing, *inter alia*, the limits of national jurisdiction over ocean space, access to the seas, navigation, protection and preservation of the marine environment, exploitation of living resources and conservation, scientific research, sea-bed mining and other exploitation of non-living resources, and the settlement of disputes. In addition, it establishes new international bodies to carry out functions for the realization of specific objectives.

The touchstone of the package of the Convention is the notion that the enjoyment of rights and benefits involves the concomitant undertaking of duties and obligations, so that an overall equitable order may be created. The paramount duty of all States Parties is to respect the rights of others; however, some duties may entail more executory acts. The duty to give due notice of hazards would be an example of the latter kind of duty. This omnipresent concept of the balance of rights and duties is emphasized by article 300 of the Convention, which mandates good faith in the fulfillment of obligations and proscribes the abuse of rights. The first six parts of the Convention deal generally with the question of areas of national jurisdiction. The General Assembly Declaration of Principles (resolution 2749 (XXV)) established that the Common Heritage of Mankind comprises the area of sea-bed and ocean floor beyond the limits of national jurisdiction, "the precise limits of which are yet to be determined". It is the Convention which sets out the guidelines for the determination of those limits.

The Convention allows for the establishment of a territorial sea of up to 12 nautical miles in breadth, providing various methods for determining baselines and for distinguishing between territorial waters and internal waters. The traditional right of innocent passage through territorial waters is recognized, and some specificity as to what kinds of activities will contravene innocence of passage is included. In the case of the waters of States bordering straits, the concept of transit passage is introduced, which draws more from the concept of necessity than does innocent passage and is somewhat more liberal. The concept of archipelagic waters is introduced for the case of archipelagoes, whereby sovereignty may be recognized over the waters within an island group, and the conditions and modalities for establishment of baselines in such cases are specified. Archipelagic sea-lanes passage is also provided.

Beyond territorial waters, the Convention allows the creation of an exclusive economic zone of up to 200 nautical miles. Traditionally, all areas beyond territorial waters comprised the high seas. In order for coastal States to gain economic benefit from areas further off their shores, it was necessary for them to extend their territorial waters, thus eliminating all freedoms of the high seas in the annexed areas. This imposed upon the interest of other maritime States, which insisted that customary law permitted a territorial sea of only three miles breadth, and that anything beyond that entailed abridgement of their freedoms. This disagreement was one of the major issues facing the Conference when it began its work.

The provisions pertaining to the exclusive economic zone are the manifestation of one of the first "mini-packages" of delicately balanced compromises to emerge from the negotiations. The ubiquitous concept of the balance of rights and duties can be most clearly illustrated in this context. The Convention allows the coastal state certain rights in the exclusive economic zone for the purpose of economic advantage, notably rights over fishing and exploitation of non-living resources, as well as concomitant limited jurisdiction in order to realize those rights. At the same time, however, neighbouring land-locked and geographically disadvantaged States must be allowed access to those resources of the zone that the coastal state does not exploit, and, further, the traditional freedoms of the high seas are to be maintained in this area. The recognition of the rights of others in the zone is, however, without prejudice to the rights of the coastal State. In order to safeguard the protection of so many different interests in the zone, all States must undertake to respect and accommodate the rights and legitimate uses of other States in the zone. The Convention lays a broad framework for the peaceful accomplishment of this purpose.

Beyond the limits of the exclusive economic zone, the determination of which provisions of the Convention are applicable to a given activity depends upon the site of the activity involved. Activities on the surface and in the water column are governed by the provisions on the high seas. These generally follow customary international law allowing the freedoms of the high seas, but augment the law in several important respects, notably with regard to pollution and safety regulations, scientific research, conservation, and prevention of illicit traffic in drugs and psychotropic substances. Activities on the sea-bed and in the subsoil of the continental shelf may fall within the national jurisdiction of the coastal state if the formation of the continental shelf meets specified criteria. The Convention provides for the establishment of a Commission of experts to advise on the delineation of the outer edge of the continental margin, that is, the limit of national jurisdiction over the continental shelf.

Having provided the guidelines for the determination of the limits of national jurisdiction, the Convention then sets out the principles and regulations governing the sea-bed and ocean floor beyond those limits, the common heritage of mankind. The formulation of these provisions was especially difficult since it wholly represents the progressive development of law, and was therefore unaided by the guidance of precedent. The very delicate balance of compromises which emerged represented another "mini-package" within the package, and cannot be divorced from the provisions of resolutions I and II.

The body empowered to administer the common heritage of mankind and to regulate its exploration and exploitation will be the International Sea-Bed Authority, an international organization open to membership by all States as well as international organizations and other entities meeting specified criteria (parties to the Convention are *ipso facto* members of the Authority, article 156). The Authority will have an Assembly, which will be the supreme body and will reflect the balance between the sovereign equality of all States, and a Council with limited representation. The Council will have primary responsibility over sea-bed mining activities, and will be advised by specialized commissions

It is not the structure but the functions of the International Sea-Bed Authority which make it a forerunner in the development of the law of international organizations. Not only will it be entrusted with the power to directly regulate purely commercial activities, but it will also be empowered to engage in sea-bed mining in its own right, through its commercial arm, the Enterprise. This is the essence of the "parallel system", a concept arrived at as a compromise in 1976 after arduous negotiations. The conditions and modalities for financing the Enterprise and for ensuring that it is technologically equipped to carry out activities form an integral part of the package. The Convention also delineates specific provisions regarding how the Authority must go about selecting among applicants for sea-bed mining and on what basis, how much production from the resources of the Area will be allowed in a specified period, and other technical aspects of application, authorization and the conduct of sea-bed activities.

Resolution I creates the Preparatory Commission, the body which will make the arrangements enabling the Authority (and the International Tribunal for the Law of the Sea) to be set up and to operate. The Commission will draft the specific rules, regulations and procedures of the Authority to govern activities in the Area so that the system of sea-bed mining under the Convention can commence. The shape these rules and regulations take may well determine the viability of the system as a whole, and therefore the significance of this task and its place within the overall package cannot be underestimated.

The Preparatory Commission will also be entrusted to carry out functions under resolution II, which governs preparatory investment in pioneer activities. Under this resolution, certain protections are granted to qualifying sea-bed miners who apply to the Commission and are registered by it to conduct exploratory activities. It is the Commission which will be empowered to fulfill certain functions on behalf of the international community as a whole, on the "other" side of the parallel system, prior to the entry into operation of the Authority.

In addition to the enunciation of régimes on a spatial basis, the Convention deals with certain other matters of global concern. Among these are ecological and environmental issues. The general principles and policies governing prevention, reduction and control of pollution throughout the marine environment are established, as are the specific rights and duties of States concerned for the realization of their environmental and ecological goals. The allocation of the rights and the burden of the duties would vary depending upon the location and/or the type of pollution involved, and specific safeguard and enforcement provisions are included. The Convention is intended to be compatible with existing treaties on this question and to provide a broad framework for the conclusion of future, more specific agreements.

The Convention also includes provisions intended to foster the development and facilitate the transfer of all kinds of marine technology, and to encourage the conduct of marine scientific research. The inclusion of such provisions was dependent upon the establishment of adequate safeguards for the holders of rights concerned.

The elaboration of the international régime comes full circle with the stipulation of a comprehensive set of provisions governing the settlement of disputes. It could be foreseen that the effective implementation of the complex new international order under the Convention would be greatly hindered without the creation of an obligation to settle disputes and the designation of means for doing so.

The Convention obliges parties to settle their disputes peacefully, and provides a selection of methods for doing so in the event that they are otherwise unable to reach agreement even with third party intervention. The system under the Convention is a compulsory and binding one in that, with limited exceptions, a party has no choice but to submit to a settlement procedure if requested to do so by the other disputant, and is bound to abide by the findings of the body to which the dispute is submitted. States may make a prior determination of which fora they would be amenable to, and for this purpose the Convention allows a choice from among the International Court of Justice, arbitration, or the International Tribunal for the Law of the Sea, a new and autonomous specialized tribunal established by the Convention. In certain cases where the Convention does not call for a binding method of settlement, the parties are enjoined to submit their dispute to conciliation.

The International Tribunal for the Law of the Sea will have shared competence over all law of the sea matters, but it is its specialized chamber, the Sea-Bed Disputes Chamber, that will have exclusive competence over all disputes involving the international sea-bed Area, even as against the rest of the Tribunal. That is, the Sea-Bed Disputes Chamber alone will have competence to the exclusion of all other fora over sea-bed mining and related activities.

The creation of the International Tribunal for the Law of the Sea marks an advance in the evolution of the law of international institutions of its kind not only because of the structural autonomy of the Sea-Bed Disputes Chamber and the fact that the Chamber has exclusive jurisdiction over sea-bed matters, but also because private and juridical persons will have direct access to the Chamber on an equal footing with States, since these persons will be the ones directly involved in the activities over which the disputes may arise.

These brief descriptions of the main features of the Convention should not be construed as representing any official interpretations on the provisions in question or of implying such.

The Convention is due to enter into force twelve months after the deposit of the sixtieth instrument of ratification or accession. In the meanwhile, it stands as testimony to the way in which the international community would like to structure its relations regarding ocean space: the adopted Convention provides a model, establishing the framework within which States may act, and the package persists.

Bernardo Zuleta
Under-Secretary-General
Special Representative of the Secretary-General
for the Law of the Sea

"INTERNATIONAL LAW IS IRREVOCABLY TRANSFORMED"

Statement by Javier Pérez de Cuéllar, Secretary-General of the United Nations

With the signing of the Final Act of the Third United Nations Conference on the Law of the Sea, and with the opening for signature of the United Nations Convention on the Law of the Sea, the efforts begun almost 14 years ago to establish a new legal order for ocean space are now reaching their culmination. In order to affirm that international law is now irrevocably transformed, so far as the seas are concerned, we need not wait for the process of ratification of the Convention to begin.

Many of those present today in this hall participated in the initial stages of the lengthy negotiations which are ending today. They will remember that there were some who reacted with scepticism when the possibility of embarking upon a fundamental revision of sometimes age-old institutions was first suggested. There were also some who reacted with open hostility to the prospect of going even further in certain fields by establishing completely new legal institutions.

The earlier efforts of the United Nations in connection with the law of the sea, the merits of which it is not for us to judge today, provided little encouragement for this new undertaking, since the international community which decided to convene this Third Conference was, in quantitative terms, much larger than the community which drew up the 1958 Conventions, and the kaleidoscopic diversity of its members made it, in qualitative terms, a new and different entity.

The six years of work done by the Committee on the Peaceful Uses of the Sea-Bed and the Ocean Floor beyond the Limits of National Jurisdiction encompassed negotiations of a scope that constituted a challenge for some and a Utopia for others.

It is easy to understand the state of mind which prevailed when the Conference opened almost nine years ago. It oscillated between hope and fear, between the concern to agree on new ways of peaceful coexistence and the constraints imposed by national interests, by ideological and economic differences, and in some cases by undue attachment to traditional principles and concepts.

In convening this Conference, the General Assembly recognized that all the problems concerning ocean space were closely interrelated and that they should therefore be considered and solved together. The conference complied rigorously with this premise of its mandate. It departed from traditional procedures and sought new working methods which, through patient effort, would gradually lead first to informal texts that brought consensus increasingly closer and finally to the adoption of a draft convention on which all States could decide officially. The rules of procedure of the Conference, which often appeared to be a strait-jacket, turned out in practice to be a helpful factor in the search for consensus on individual parts of the Convention and on the Convention as a whole. These methods were devised in recognition of the indivisibility of the single whole which the law of the sea must constitute; this was the only way of reconciling divergent interests and promoting compromise, thereby ensuring as full participation as possible in the final agreement.

However, the innovative method adopted by the Conference would not in itself have advanced the negotiations had not the various regions of the world been determined vigorously to pursue ways of reconciling interests and harmonizing different legal and political systems.

The convening of the Conference set in motion not only a complex negotiating process at several levels but at the same time an accelerated process of change in the conduct of States vis-à-vis the uses of the sea. The orderly process of change in the legal order of the oceans that took place through the United Nations responded in fact to an urgent need, felt in every region of the world, which manifested itself in a multiplicity of international declarations and agreements bearing the names of the cities of various continents in which they were adopted, thereby testifying to the universal character of this evolutionary process. Every one of those documents represents a new contribution, an attempt at rapprochement and, above all else, an expression of the determination of States to find formulas of collective agreement designed to bring about the peaceful uses of the seas and their resources.

The new law of the sea thus created is not simply the result of a process of action and reaction among the most powerful countries but the product of the will of an overwhelming majority of nations from all parts of the world, at different levels of development and having diverse geographical characteristics in relation to the oceans, which combined to make a wind of change blow at the universal level.

I should like to refer briefly to the nature of the results of the Conference, because it seems to me that such an analysis can provide important lessons for the multilateral negotiating system in general and for treaty-making in particular.

The novel process for the drawing up of this important multilateral treaty met with frequent criticism for being prolonged, slow and cumbersome. However, the fact that 119 countries have signed the Convention today, the very day of its opening for signature, is the most convincing response to such criticism. Never in the history of international relations have such a large number of countries immediately signed the result of their deliberations, thereby committing themselves to act in accordance with their obligations. This is a particularly important lesson to emerge from this Conference.

The Conference has produced agreements which are essentially non-denominational, devoid of partisan doctrine. Its decisions derive in the final analysis from a pragmatic reconciliation of interests rather than from comparisons of doctrines. This work necessarily has had to go beyond declared positions, although these at times appeared to be carved in stone; to venture outside Plato's cavernous spaces in order to endeavour to grapple with and satisfy the basic needs underlying national ideas and at times national laws — which are, after all, made by man.

It is my hope that States, when contemplating in their sovereign capacity the signature and ratification of this Convention, will be guided by this approach of the Conference and will thus disregard all myths in their own decision-making.

The Convention, which was opened for signature today, contains generally acceptable solutions with respect to the maritime spaces under the sovereignty and jurisdiction of States, the rational utilization of living and non-living resources, the rights of land-locked States, the promotion of marine scientific research as an instrument for the economic and social development of all peoples, the conservation of the marine environment, respect for the freedoms which have traditionally been observed in so far as the community as a whole is concerned and the settlement by peaceful means of disputes concerning ocean space.

The effectiveness of these principles, which constitute a balanced and harmonious whole, will be enhanced if States can co-ordinate their action, compare their experience and make the new legal régime an incentive for new forms of international co-operation. This requires equally co-ordinated action by the United Nations and the specialized agencies, an objective which as Secretary-General I shall henceforth promote as part of my functions under the United Nations Charter and the Convention itself.

I must make reference to the very special challenge represented by the inauguration of the régime and machinery that the Convention has established for the administration of the sea-bed and ocean floor beyond national jurisdiction, which constitute the common heritage of mankind. By a happy coincidence this innovative concept, designed to serve mankind, which must be the beneficiary of the law, and embodied in the Declaration of Principles adopted by the General Assembly in 1970, comes to a legal fruition on Human Rights Day.

At the same time as it adopted the Convention the Conference decided to establish a Preparatory Commission, empowered to grant certain rights to persons who have made preparatory investments compatible with the new legal régime, with a view to subsequent exploitation of the resources of the sea-bed, and to take the necessary measures to ensure the entry into operation of the International Sea-Bed Authority and the International Tribunal for the Law of the Sea as soon as the Convention enters into force. This fact alone creates a situation without precedent in the history of international law. The Preparatory Commission now has the opportunity to produce rules and procedures that will remove uncertainties regarding the rights and obligations of all parties concerned and thus facilitate the decision-making process that will promote universal acceptance of the new legal régime.

The international community owes a debt of deep gratitude to you, Mr. President, and to your illustrious predecessor, whose memory is with us on this historic afternoon, to the Chairmen of the three main Committees, to the Chairman of the Drafting Committee, to the Rapporteur-General and to all the representatives who have worked together in the difficult negotiations and whose names are recorded on the Final Act. You and all of them, together with the Secretariat headed by my Special Representative, have set an example of perseverance, of devotion to a cause in which they believe with profound conviction, and of objectivity in the search for solutions acceptable to all.

Today one phase is successfully concluded and a new one, equally demanding and difficult, begins. This Convention is like a breath of fresh air at a time of serious crisis in international co-operation and of decline in the use of international machinery for the solution of world problems. Let us hope that this breath of fresh air presages a warm breeze from North to South, South to North, East to West and West to East, for this will make clear whether the international community is prepared to reaffirm its determination to find, through the United Nations, more satisfactory solutions to the serious problems of a world in which the common denominator is interdependence.

Slightly edited text of a statement made on 10 December 1982 at the final session of the Law of the Sea Conference at Montego Bay, Jamaica, after the Convention was opened for signature. Reproduced by kind permission of the United Nations.

"A CONSTITUTION FOR THE OCEANS"

Remarks by Tommy T.B. Koh, of Singapore
President of the Third United Nations Conference on the Law of the Sea

On 10 December 1982, we created a new record in legal history. Never in the annals of international law had a Convention been signed by 119 countries on the very first day on which it was opened for signature. Not only was the number of signatories a remarkable fact but just as important was the fact that the Convention had been signed by States from every region of the world, from the North and from the South, from the East and from the West, by coastal States as well as land-locked and geographically disadvantaged States.

When we set out on the long and arduous journey to secure a new Convention on the Law of the Sea, covering 25 subjects and issues, there were many who told us that our goal was too ambitious and not attainable. We proved the skeptics wrong, and we succeeded in adopting a Convention covering every aspect of the uses and resources of the sea.

The question is whether we achieved our fundamental objective of producing a comprehensive constitution for the oceans which will stand the test of time. My answer is in the affirmative for the following reasons:

- The Convention will promote the maintenance of international peace and security because it will replace a plethora of conflicting claims by coastal States with universally agreed limits on the territorial sea, on the contiguous zone, on the exclusive economic zone and on the continental shelf.
- The world community's interest in the freedom of navigation will be facilitated by the important compromises on the status of the exclusive economic zone, by the régime of innocent passage through the territorial sea, by the régime of transit passage through straits used for international navigation and by the régime of archipelagic sea-lanes passage.
- The world community's interest in the conservation and optimum utilization of the living resources of the sea will be enhanced by the conscientious implementation of the provisions in the Convention relating to the exclusive economic zone.
- The Convention contains important new rules for the protection and preservation of the marine environment from pollution.
- The Convention contains new rules on marine scientific research which strike an equitable balance between the interests of the research States and the interests of the coastal States in whose economic zones or continental shelves the research is to be carried out.
- The world community's interest in the peaceful settlement of disputes and the prevention of use of force in the settlement of disputes between States have been advanced by the mandatory system of dispute settlement in the Convention.

- The Convention has succeeded in translating the principle that the resources of the deep sea-bed constitute the common heritage of mankind into fair and workable institutions and arrangements.
- Though far from ideal, we can nevertheless find elements of international equity in the Convention, such as revenue sharing on the continental shelf beyond 200 miles, giving land-locked and geographically disadvantaged States access to the living resources of the exclusive economic zones of their neighbouring States, the relationship between coastal fishermen and distant-water fishermen, and the sharing of the benefits derived from the exploitation of the resources of the deep sea-bed.

I would like to highlight the major themes which I found in the statements made by delegations at Montego Bay.

First, delegations said that the Convention does not fully satisfy the interests and objectives of any State. Nevertheless, they were of the view that it represents a monumental achievement of the international community, second only to the Charter of the United Nations. The Convention is the first comprehensive treaty dealing with practically every aspect of the uses and resources of the seas and the oceans. It has successfully accommodated the competing interests of all nations.

The second theme which emerged from the statements is that the provisions of the Convention are closely interrelated and form an integral package. Thus it is not possible for a State to pick what it likes and to disregard what it does not like. It was also said that rights and obligations go hand in hand and it is not permissible to claim rights under the Convention without being willing to shoulder the corresponding obligations.

The third theme I heard was that this Convention is not a codification Convention. The argument that, except for Part XI, the Convention codifies customary law or reflects existing international practice is factually incorrect and legally insupportable. The régime of transit passage through straits used for international navigation and the régime of archipelagic sea lanes passage are two examples of the many new concepts in the Convention. Even in the case of article 76 on the continental shelf, the article contains new law in that it has expanded the concept of the continental shelf to include the continental slope and the continental rise. This concession to the broad margin States was in return for their agreement for revenue-sharing on the continental shelf beyond 200 miles. It is therefore my view that a State which is not a party to this Convention cannot invoke the benefits of article 76.

The fourth theme relates to the lawfulness of any attempt to mine the resources of the international Area of the sea-bed and ocean floor. Speakers from every regional and interest group expressed the view that the doctrine of the freedom of the high seas can provide no legal basis for the grant by any State of exclusive title to a specific mine site in the international Area. Many are of the view that article 137 of the Convention has become as much a part of customary international law as the freedom of navigation. Any attempt by any State to mine the resources of the deep sea-bed outside the Convention will earn the universal condemnation of the international community and will incur grave political and legal consequences. All speakers have addressed an earnest appeal to the United States to reconsider its position. The United States is a country which has, throughout its history, supported the progressive development of international law and has fought for the rule of law in the relations between States. The present position of the United States Government towards this Convention is, therefore, inexplicable in the light of its history, in the light of its specific law of the sea interests and in the light of the leading role which it has played in negotiating the many compromises which have made this treaty possible.

A final theme which emerged from the statements concerns the preparatory Commission. Now that the required number of States have signed the Convention, the Preparatory Commission for the establishment of the International Sea-Bed Authority and the International Tribunal for the Law of the Sea will begin its work. The Commission will have to adopt the rules and procedures for the implementation of resolution II, relating to pioneer investors. It will, *inter alia*, draft the detailed rules, regulations and procedures for the mining of the sea-bed. If it carries out its work in an efficient, objective and business-like manner, we will have a viable system for the mining of the deep sea-bed. This will induce those who are standing on the sidelines to come in and support the Convention. If, on the other hand, the Preparatory Commission does not carry out its tasks in an efficient, objective and practical manner, then all our efforts in the last 14 years will have been in vain.

In the report of the Secretary-General on the work of the United Nations (A/37/1) dated 7 September 1982, he wrote:

"We have seen, in the case of the law of the sea..., what remarkable results can be achieved in well-organized negotiations within the United Nations framework, even on the most complex of issues..."

It may be helpful to identify those features of the negotiating process of this Conference which were productive, and to distil some wisdom from our experience.

I would point, *first* of all, to the importance of reaching agreements on substantive matters on which States have important interests by consensus. The Conference was wise to resist the temptation of putting substantive proposals to the vote, because those who vote against a proposal would naturally not feel bound by it. The consensus procedure, however, requires all delegations, those in the majority as well as those in the minority, to make efforts, in good faith, to accommodate the interests of others.

Second, the Conference took the wise decision that the package deal approach did not preclude it from allocating the 25 different subjects and issues to different negotiating forums, so long as the results were brought together to form an integral whole.

Third, the group system in the Conference contributed to its work by helping delegations to identify their positions and by enabling negotiations to take place between competing interest groups. The group system should, however, be used with flexibility and not be allowed to paralyze the negotiating process with rigidity.

Fourth, the negotiations in this Conference could not have been brought to a successful conclusion if we had failed to progressively miniaturize them. It is obvious that no meaningful negotiations can take place in a forum consisting of 160 delegations.

Fifth, there is a role for the main committees, for formal negotiating groups, for informal negotiating groups and even for privately convened negotiating groups. In general, the more informal a negotiating group, the more likely are we to make progress. Some of the most intractable problems of the Conference were resolved in privately convened negotiating groups, such as the Evensen Group and the Castañeda Group.

Sixth, the Drafting Committee and its language groups played a very important role in the negotiating process. It was due to their hard work that we have one treaty in six languages and not six treaties in six languages.

Seventh, the leaders of a conference can play a significant role in determining the success or failure of a conference. In our case, we were extremely fortunate that the Collegium worked well together. The Conference could well have floundered during its many crises if the Collegium had not been united and if it had failed to provide the Conference with leadership.

Eighth, the Secretariat played an important role in the work of this Conference. The members of the Secretariat, under the able leadership of the Special Representative of the Secretary-General, not only provided the Conference with excellent services but also ably assisted the President and the Chairmen of the various committees and groups in the negotiations. I should like to take this opportunity to thank Mr. Bernardo Zuleta and his loyal Deputy, Mr. David Hall.

Ninth, I should also acknowledge the role played by the non-governmental organizations, such as the Neptune Group. They provided the Conference with three valuable services. They brought independent experts to meet with delegations, thus enabling us to have an independent source of information on technical issues. They assisted representatives from developing countries to narrow the technical gap between them and their counterparts from developed countries. They also provided us with opportunities to meet, away from the Conference, in a more relaxed atmosphere, to discuss some of the most difficult issues confronted by the Conference.

Although the Convention consists of a series of compromises, they form an integral whole. This is why the Convention does not provide for reservations. It is therefore not possible for States to pick what they like and disregard what they do not like. In international law, as in domestic law, rights and duties go hand in hand. It is therefore legally impermissible to claim rights under the Convention without being willing to assume the correlative duties.

Let no nation put asunder this landmark achievement of the international community.

I cannot conclude without recalling, once more, our collective debt to two men, Hamilton Shirley Amerasinghe [former President of the Conference] and

Arvid Pardo [former Permanent Representative of Malta to the United Nations]. Arvid Pardo contributed two seminal ideas to our work: first, that the resources of the deep sea-bed constitute the common heritage of mankind, and second, that all aspects of ocean space are interrelated and should be treated as an integral whole. Shirley Amerasinghe led our efforts from 1968 until his untimely death in 1979.

In the final analysis, I believe that this Conference succeeded because it brought together a "critical mass" of colleagues who were outstanding lawyers and negotiators. We succeeded because we did not regard our counterparts in the negotiations as the enemies to be conquered. We considered the issues under dispute as the common obstacles to be overcome. We worked not only to promote our individual national interests but also in pursuit of our common dream of writing a constitution for the oceans.

We have strengthened the United Nations by proving that with political will, nations can use the Organization as a centre to harmonize their actions. We have shown that with good leadership and management, the United Nations can be an efficient forum for the negotiation of complex issues. We celebrate the victory of the rule of law and of the principle of the peaceful settlement of disputes. Finally, we celebrate human solidarity and the reality of interdependence which is symbolized by the United Nations Convention on the Law of the Sea.

Adapted from statements by the President on 6 and 11 December 1982 at the final session of the Conference at Montego Bay. Reproduced by kind permission of the United Nations.

CONSULTATIONS OF THE SECRETARY-GENERAL ON OUTSTANDING ISSUES RELATING TO THE DEEP SEABED MINING PROVISIONS OF THE UNITED NATIONS CONVENTION ON THE LAW OF THE SEA[*]

Report of the Secretary-General

1.   In July 1990 the Secretary-General, Mr. Javier Pérez de Cuéllar, took the initiative to convene informal consultations aimed at achieving universal participation in the United Nations Convention on the Law of the Sea. The Secretary-General stressed the importance of securing general acceptance of the United Nations Convention on the Law of the Sea, an instrument which represented many years of negotiations and which had already made a significant contribution to the international legal maritime order. He pointed out that though he would continue to encourage all States which had not done so to ratify or accede to the Convention, it had to be acknowledged that there were problems with some aspects of the deep seabed mining provisions of the Convention which had prevented some States from ratifying or acceding to the Convention.

2.   He noted that in the eight years that had elapsed since the Convention was adopted certain significant political and economic changes had occurred which had had a marked effect on the regime for deep seabed mining contained in the Convention. Prospects for commercial mining of deep seabed minerals had receded into the next century, which was not what was envisaged during the negotiations at the Third United Nations Conference on the Law of the Sea. The general economic climate had been transformed as a result of the changing perception with respect to the roles of the public and private sectors. There was a discernible shift towards a more market-oriented economy. In addition, the Secretary-General made mention of the emergence of a new spirit of international cooperation in resolving outstanding problems of regional and global concern. These factors were to be taken into account in considering the problems with respect to deep seabed mining.[1]

3.   Thus began a series of informal consultations under the aegis of the Secretary-General on outstanding issues relating to the deep seabed mining provisions of the United Nations Convention on the Law of the Sea.

4.   These informal consultations took place in the years 1990 to 1994, during which 15 meetings were convened.[2] They can be conveniently divided into two phases. The first phase was devoted to the identification of issues of concern to some States, the approach to be taken in examining them and the search for solu-

---

[*] A/48/950, paragraphs 1 to 28.

tions. During the second phase more precision was given to the results reached so far; additional points were raised for consideration and participants directed their attention to an examination of consolidated texts embodying these solutions and on the procedure whereby they might be adopted.

THE FIRST PHASE

5.   During the initial part of this phase the consultations identified nine issues as representing areas of difficulty: costs to States parties; the Enterprise; decision-making; the Review Conference; transfer of technology; production limitation; compensation fund; financial terms of contract; and environmental considerations. After examining the various approaches that might be taken in the examination of these issues, there was general agreement on an approach which enabled participants to examine all the outstanding issues with a view to resolving them and to decide how to deal with those that might remain unresolved.

6.   Participants then began to review all of these issues *seriatim*. This review was based on information notes compiled by the Secretariat containing background information, questions that needed to be addressed and possible approaches for the resolution of these issues.

7.   In the course of six informal consultations held during the years 1990 and 1991, participants completed the consideration of all the outstanding issues relating to the deep seabed mining provisions of the United Nations Convention on the Law of the Sea. It can fairly be said that a certain measure of general agreement was emerging on these issues.

8.   The results of the Secretary-General's informal consultations held in 1990 and 1991 were set out in the summary of informal consultations conducted by the Secretary-General on the law of the sea during 1990 and 1991, dated 31 January 1992, and in an information note dated 26 May 1992. These results fell under two categories. First, general agreement seemed to have been reached on relatively detailed solutions on: costs to States parties, the Enterprise, decision-making, Review Conference and transfer of technology. Secondly, with respect to production limitation, the compensation fund and financial terms of contract it was generally agreed that it was neither necessary nor prudent to formulate a new set of detailed rules for these items. Accordingly, for those items the information note set out general principles to be applied when commercial production of deep seabed minerals was imminent.

THE SECOND PHASE

9.   In 1992 I continued the informal consultations initiated by my predecessor. During this phase the consultations were open to all delegations. Some 75 to 90 delegations attended these meetings. In the first three rounds of this phase, consideration was given to the nine issues in order to give more precision to the

results reached so far in the consultations. Additional points were submitted for consideration on the following issues: costs to States parties; the Enterprise; decision-making; Review Conference; and transfer of technology. During these consultations it was decided to remove the issue of environmental considerations from the list of issues, since it was no longer considered to be a controversial issue in the context of deep seabed mining.

10. At the informal consultations held on 28 and 29 January 1993, it was generally felt among participants that the stage had been reached when a text based on a more operational approach should be prepared in a form which could be the basis of an agreement.

11. In accordance with this request, an information note dated 8 April 1993 was prepared. This information note contained two parts:

(a) Part A dealt with various procedural approaches with respect to the use to be made of the results of the consultations. The four approaches could be summarized as follows:
(i) A contractual instrument such as a protocol amending the Convention;
(ii) An interpretative agreement consisting of understandings on the interpretation and application of the Convention;
(iii) An interpretative agreement on the establishment of an initial Authority and an initial Enterprise during an interim regime accompanied by a procedural arrangement for the convening of a conference to establish the definitive regime for the commercial production of deep seabed minerals when such production became feasible;
(iv) An agreement additional to the Convention providing for the transition between the initial phase and the definitive regime, in particular, the Authority would be mandated to develop solutions for issues still outstanding on the entry into force of the Convention.
(b) Part B set out an operationally directed formulation of the results reached so far in the consultations. It was divided into two sections:
(i) Arrangements following the entry into force of the Convention;
(ii) Draft texts concerning the definitive deep seabed mining regime.

12. The procedural approaches were reviewed during consultations held on 27 and 28 April 1993. Certain basic elements emerged from the review of these approaches. It was generally agreed that, whatever approach might be adopted, it must be of a legally binding nature. It was also pointed out that a duality of regimes must be avoided. Finally, as the position of States which have ratified or acceded to the Convention must be respected, it was considered useful to examine the role that the notion of implied or tacit consent might play in protecting their positions.

13. For the next round of consultations, held from 2 to 6 August 1993, an information note dated 4 June 1993 was circulated which updated parts A and B (i) of the information note of 8 April 1993 to reflect the observations made during the previous round of consultations. During the course of this round of consultations a paper dated 3 August 1993 prepared by representatives of several developed and developing States was circulated among delegations as a contribution to the process of the consultations. It was understood that the paper, which was commonly known as the "boat paper", did not necessarily reflect the position of any of the delegations involved, but that it was considered to provide a useful basis for negotiation.

14. Thereafter, while addressing the substantive issues contained in the information note dated 4 June 1993, delegations also made cross-references to the relevant portions of the "boat paper". That paper was divided into three parts: (i) a draft resolution for adoption by the General Assembly; (ii) a draft Agreement relating to the Implementation of Part XI of the United Nations Convention on the Law of the Sea; and (iii) two annexes. Annex I contained the agreed conclusions of the Secretary-General's consultations and annex II was entitled "Consequential adjustments".

15. At the last round of consultations held in 1993 (8-12 November), participants had before them three documents: the information note dated 4 June 1993; a new version of the "boat paper" consolidating the two annexes to the original paper into one; and a paper entitled "Agreement on the Implementation of Part XI and Annexes III and IV of the United Nations Convention on the Law of the Sea", submitted by the delegation of Sierra Leone. At this November meeting participants completed the review of all the items contained in the information note dated 4 June 1993. After having completed consideration of those issues, delegations embarked upon a renewed examination of the issue of "Costs to States parties and institutional arrangements", but this time based essentially on the "boat paper".

16. On 16 November 1993, the Convention on the Law of the Sea received its sixtieth instrument of ratification or accession, which means that, in accordance with its terms (article 308), it will enter into force on 16 November 1994. The General Assembly itself invited all States to participate in the consultations and to increase efforts to achieve universal participation in the Convention as early as possible.[3] The imminent entry into force of the Convention introduced a sense of urgency to the informal consultations.

17. During the first round held in 1994 (31 January-4 February), the consultations examined a revised version of the "boat paper", dated November 1993. This revision took into account the discussions which had taken place during the Secretary-General's informal consultations held in November 1993. The work of the current round of consultations focused on some crucial issues:

(a) Decision-making, in particular the question of the relationship between the Assembly and the Council, and the question as to which group of

States in the Council should be considered chambers for the purposes of decision-making in the Council;

(b) Whether the administrative expenses of the Authority should be met by assessed contributions of its members, including the provisional members of the Authority, or through the budget of the United Nations;

(c) The issue of provisional application of the Agreement and of provisional membership in the Authority.

During this round of consultations progress was made on the latter two issues. A revised version of the document submitted by the delegation of Sierra Leone was submitted to this round of consultations.

18. The second round of the Secretary-General's informal consultations in 1994 was held from 4 to 8 April. The meeting had before it a further updated version of the "boat paper" entitled "Draft resolution and draft Agreement relating to the Implementation of Part XI of the 1982 United Nations Convention on the Law of the Sea", dated 14 February 1994.

19. Participants undertook an article-by-article review of the draft Agreement. Attention was then focused on the two most important issues facing the consultations: decision-making in the Council, and the Enterprise. These issues, which lay at the heart of the consultations, proved most difficult to resolve. From the outset of the consultations it was evident that these issues could only be resolved in the final stages of this process, when a clearer picture of the results of the consultations had emerged. With respect to decision-making the debate was directed at the system of chambered voting, in particular whether the categories or groups of States, mainly developing States, should be treated as chambers for the purposes of decision-making in the Council. The discussion on the Enterprise centred on the type of mechanism which would trigger the commencement of its operations as well as its functions.

20. Revisions were made to the draft Agreement in the light of the debates on the various issues. This in fact was a unique feature of this round of consultations, reflecting the urgency of the situation. The revisions related to provisional application of the Agreement; provisional membership in the Authority; the treatment of the registered pioneer investors; and production policy.

21. Based on these revisions, the draft resolution and draft Agreement relating to the Implementation of Part XI of the United Nations Convention on the Law of the Sea were revised in their entirety and a revised text was issued on 8 April 1994, the last day of the meeting.

22. During this round of consultations, according to many delegations, significant progress was achieved. It appeared that solutions were found to several important issues, including decision-making, the Enterprise and the treatment of the registered pioneer investors. However, not all the issues were resolved in this round of consultations.

23. The last meeting of the Secretary-General's consultations was held from 31 May to 3 June 1994. The primary purpose of this final round of consultations was the harmonization of the text in the various language versions of the draft resolution and draft Agreement relating to the Implementation of Part XI of the 1982 United Nations Convention on the Law of the Sea. The meeting had before it the draft resolution and draft Agreement dated 15 April 1994 which was revised on the basis of discussions in the previous round of consultations and a corrigendum to the document dated 23 May 1994. Two documents (SG/LOS/CRP.1 and SG/LOS/CRP.2), containing suggested amendments of a drafting nature prepared by the Secretariat, were also submitted to the meeting in order to facilitate the process of harmonizing the language versions of the text.

24. The first part of the meeting addressed the substantive issues that were still pending, and solutions were found for some of those issues. Delegations, however, continued their search for solutions on matters relating, *inter alia*, to the treatment of the registered pioneer investors and the issue of representation in the Council. The second part of the meeting was devoted to the task of harmonizing the language versions of the draft resolution and draft Agreement. The final part dealt with the decisions to be taken with regard to the convening of a resumed forty-eighth session of the General Assembly to adopt the draft resolution and draft Agreement.

25. At the close of the meeting, delegations were presented with a revised text (SG/LOS/CRP.1/Rev.1), dated 3 June 1994. That document elicited a few drafting comments which are reflected in the text of the draft resolution and draft Agreement relating to the Implementation of Part XI of the United Nations Convention on the Law of the Sea of 10 December 1982, contained in annex I to the present report. A proposed solution to the question of the issue of representation in the Council is to be found in the informal understanding contained in annex II.

26. At the conclusion of the informal consultations the delegation of the Russian Federation made a statement reserving its position in view of the fact that a number of proposals it had made had not been reflected in the draft Agreement. In reply, it was pointed out that all proposals made by delegations or groups had been thoroughly examined without exception but that it had not been possible to accept every one of them.

27. The consultations then indicated that Member States wished to convene a resumed forty-eighth session of the General Assembly of the United Nations from 27 to 29 July 1994, for adoption of the resolution. They further wished that, after the adoption of the resolution, the Agreement would be immediately opened for signature.

28. I wish to recall that the objective of the consultations was to achieve wider participation in the Convention from the major industrialized States in order to reach the goal of universality. Accordingly, it is with satisfaction that I report to

the General Assembly that these consultations, initiated by my predecessor and continued by me, have led to a result which in my view could form the basis of a general agreement on the issues that were the subject of the consultations. In the light of the outcome, I consider that I have fulfilled my mandate.

Notes

[1] See A/45/721 and A/46/724.

[2] Informal consultations were held on the following dates: 19 July 1990; 30 October 1990; 25 March 1991; 23 July 1991; 14 and 15 October 1991; 10 and 11 December 1991; 16 and 17 June 1992; 6 and 7 August 1992; 28 and 29 January 1993; 27 and 28 April 1993; 2-6 August 1993; 8-12 November 1993; 31 January-4 February 1994; 4-8 April 1994; and 31 May-3 June 1994.

[3] General Assembly resolution 48/28.

STATEMENT BY H.E. AMBASSADOR SATYA N. NANDAN

Statement by H.E. Ambassador Satya N. Nandan (Fiji) to the General Assembly on 27 July 1994, introducing draft resolution A/48/L.60 entitled "Agreement relating to the implementation of Part XI of the United Nations Convention on the Law of the Sea of 10 December 1982" *

The adoption in 1982 of the United Nations Convention on the Law of the Sea was a momentous occasion in the history of international law and international relations. That event was all the more significant in that the Convention, for the most part, was the result of consensus or broad agreement among some 160 States which participated in the Third United Nations Conference on the Law of the Sea.

The present session of the General Assembly will establish another milestone in the development of the modern international law of the sea. It will mark the achievement of broad agreement on that part of the Convention which deals with the regime for the mining of minerals from the deep-sea bed, that is Part XI of the Convention, over which differences had persisted since the conclusion of the Third United Nations Conference. Those differences have until now inhibited a number of States from becoming parties to the Convention, a Convention which they otherwise support. Upon the adoption of the draft resolution before the General Assembly in document A/48/L.60 of 22 June 1994 and of the draft agreement appended to it, the international community will be able justifiably to claim that it has at last achieved a consensus or broad agreement on all parts of the Convention and therefore on all aspects of the law of the sea.

Taken as a whole, the Convention provides for an equitable relationship among States in their use of the oceans based on their respective geographical characteristics, economic circumstances, political imperatives and global responsibilities. It establishes certainty in the international law of the sea in place of the chaos and uncertainty created by the proliferation of unilateral claims that caused the General Assembly to convene in 1973 the Third United Nations Conference on the Law of the Sea.

The Convention achieves a delicate balance between competing interests in maritime zones. It establishes 12 nautical miles as the breadth of the territorial sea with a guaranteed right of passage for international navigation in those waters; it ensures unhampered passage of all kinds of vessels through archipelagic sea lanes and vital straits around the world; it secures for coastal States resource

* *Official Records of the General Assembly, Forty-eighth session, agenda item 36, document A/48/PV.99.*

jurisdiction in a 200-nautical-mile exclusive economic zone; it provides for an extended continental shelf jurisdiction of coastal States up to 350 nautical miles; it guarantees access to and from the sea for land-locked States; it provides for a regime for archipelagic States; it establishes a regime for the development of the mineral resources of the deep seabed; it sets out rules for the conduct of marine scientific research; it imposes a duty on all States to ensure, through proper conservation and management measures, the long-term sustainability of fish resources; it contains the most comprehensive rules for the protection and preservation of the marine environment and imposes a duty on States to protect the oceans from all sources of pollution; and it promotes peaceful settlement of disputes arising from the interpretation and application of the provisions of the Convention.

The broad support that the Convention already enjoys in respect of matters relating to the oceans, other than those which relate to the regime for the seabed, is evidenced by the remarkable level of uniformity that has evolved in State practice consistent with the provisions of the Convention. The Convention, even before its entry into force, has become the basis for the settlement of disputes on maritime issues, as is reflected in the decisions of the International Court of Justice and other tribunals. In this sense the Convention, which governs about 70 per cent of the Earth's surface, has already made an immeasurable contribution to international peace and security. It has indeed become an indispensable part of the global system for peace and security of which the Charter of the United Nations is the foundation.

In recognizing the contribution of the Convention to the international community, it is fitting to pay tribute to the many delegations and individuals who worked so arduously at the Third United Nations Convention on the Law of the Sea to weave together the many provisions which ultimately became the 1982 United Nations Convention on the Law of the Sea.

Given the global importance of the Convention, my delegation has always supported the view that its achievements can best be consolidated through universal participation. We firmly believe that the outstanding issues relating to the regime for deep seabed mining could and should be resolved in a practical and pragmatic manner satisfactory to all. We were therefore very grateful to Secretary-General Javier Pérez de Cuéllar when he took the timely step, in July 1990, of promoting dialogue amongst States in order to address the specific areas of difficulties that some States had with Part XI of the Convention and for the approaches that he suggested towards resolving those outstanding issues. These suggestions were summarized in a note dated 31 January 1992 and became the foundation for the Agreement that this Assembly is considering for adoption. We are also grateful to Secretary-General Boutros Boutros-Ghali for continuing to provide a forum for States to resolve the outstanding issues. We also extend our thanks to the members of the Secretariat for their invaluable assistance.

The dialogue to resolve the outstanding issues that ensued since 1990 was based on two fundamental premises: first, the integrity of the Convention must not be eroded – all issues in the Convention are interrelated and must remain part of the whole, there can be no reservation on any part of the Convention, and all parts must be subject to compulsory dispute settlement procedures as provided for in the Convention.

The second premise was that specific issues in Part XI which created difficulties for industrialized countries should be clearly identified and addressed in the context of Part XI. The progress that has been made in the negotiations among States since 1990 is clearly due to adherence to these two premises and is reflected in the Agreement that is before the General Assembly for adoption.

At the Third United Nations Conference on the Law of the Sea, informal private negotiating groups were critical to the resolution of some of the most intractable issues. The negotiations which led to the present Agreement were no exception to this well-established practice. Thus, at a crucial stage in the Secretary-General's informal consultations, when negotiations were heading towards an impasse, a group of representatives from both developed and developing States who held similar views in the discussion on procedural approaches to an agreement developed an informal and anonymous paper which was dated August 1993. The paper came to be known as the "Boat Paper" because of an illustration of a seabed mining vessel on the cover.

This paper, which was presented as a contribution to the process of consultations, soon became the basic paper in the negotiations. It contained a draft resolution for adoption by the General Assembly to which was appended a draft agreement with annexes. Subsequent revisions of the paper were undertaken in an expanded Boat Paper Group in which all key delegations and interest groups were represented. These revisions took into account the discussions in the Secretary-General's consultations and in the Boat Paper Group itself. The final text as developed by the Group is now contained in the annex of the Secretary-General's report (A/48/950) and in document A/48/L.60.

My delegation would like to express its sincere gratitude to our colleagues from developed and developing countries who participated in the original Boat Paper Group and also to those who participated in and contributed to the work of the expanded Group. We believe that the General Assembly also owes a debt of gratitude to the members of the Group of 77 and to representatives of the industrialized countries, all of whom set aside their ideological positions, which had led to an impasse in the negotiations at the Conference, and who in these negotiations approached the issues in a practical and pragmatic manner. The result of this approach can be readily observed in the quality of the Agreement that has been reached.

As a consequence, the regime for the mining of the deep seabed is considerably streamlined and simplified. It takes a functional approach towards the establishment of the administrative institutions under Part XI; it provides for a stable environment for investors in deep-seabed minerals under a market-oriented regime; it guarantees access to the resources of the seabed to all qualified investors; it provides for the establishment of a system of taxation which is fair to the seabed miner and from which the international community as a whole may benefit; and it makes provisions for assistance to developing land-based producers of minerals whose economies may be affected as a consequence of deep seabed mining. Thus the Agreement provides a practical and realistic basis for the realization of the principle of the common heritage of mankind.

My delegation considers it a privilege to introduce on behalf of its sponsors the draft resolution and the Agreement contained in document A/48/L.60 which is before the General Assembly. This draft resolution is being sponsored by the following States: Antigua and Barbuda, Argentina, Australia, Austria, the Bahamas, Chile, Germany, Greece, Grenada, Iceland, India, Indonesia, Jamaica, Japan, Kenya, Malta, the Federated States of Micronesia, Myanmar, the Marshall Islands, the Netherlands, New Zealand, Namibia, the Republic of Korea, Singapore, Sri Lanka, the United Kingdom of Great Britain and Northern Ireland, the United States of America and my own, Fiji.

In adopting the draft resolution, the General Assembly would also adopt the Agreement relating to the Implementation of Part XI of the United Nations Convention on the Law of the Sea of 10 December 1982, which is appended to it. The General Assembly, *inter alia*, would also affirm that the Agreement shall be interpreted and applied together with Part XI of the Convention as a single instrument.

It will express its satisfaction at the entry into force of the Convention on 16 November 1994, and it will decide to fund the administrative expenses of the International Seabed Authority from the budget of the United Nations as a transitional measure. The General Assembly would also request the Secretary-General to transmit immediately certified copies of the Agreement to the States and entities that are entitled to become parties to the Convention and this Agreement, with a view to facilitating universal participation in the Convention.

The Assembly would also request the Secretary-General to open the Agreement for signature immediately after its adoption. It would urge all States and entities to apply the Agreement provisionally and become parties to it at the earliest possible date. In addition, it would urge those who have not already done so to become parties to the Convention as a whole in order to ensure universal participation in it.

Finally, the Assembly will call upon the Preparatory Commission for the International Seabed Authority and for the International Tribunal for the Law of the Sea to take into account the terms of the Agreement when drawing up its final report.

In the Agreement which is appended to the draft resolution, States would, *inter alia*, recognize the important contribution of the 1982 United Nations Convention on the Law of the Sea to the maintenance of peace, justice and progress for all peoples of the world. The Agreement refers to the report of the Secretary-General on the results of the informal consultations among States held from 1990 to 1994 on the outstanding issues relating to Part XI and related provisions of the Convention. It notes that political and economic changes, including market-oriented approaches, have affected the implementation of Part XI since the adoption of the Convention in 1982. It also indicates that States consider that the Agreement relating to the implementation of Part XI – the Agreement appended to the draft resolution – would best meet the objective of facilitating universal participation in the Convention.

The operative part establishes the relationship between this Agreement and Part XI of the Convention, which are to be interpreted and applied together as a single instrument. It states that the Agreement shall remain open for signature for 12 months after the date of its adoption and that any future instrument of ratification or formal confirmation or accession to the Convention shall also represent consent to be bound by the Agreement. It prescribes various methods that States may utilize to establish their consent to be bound by the Agreement. In particular, it provides for a simplified procedure for those States which have already expressed their consent to be bound by the Convention prior to the adoption of this Agreement.

With respect to the entry into force of the Agreement, it provides that entry into force will take place 30 days after the date on which 40 States have established their consent to be bound, provided that such States would include at least seven of the States entitled to become pioneer investors under resolution II of the Third United Nations Conference on the Law of the Sea, and that of these seven, at least five States should be from among developed industrialized States. The entry into force of the Agreement, however, shall not take place before 16 November 1994, which is the date of entry into force of the Convention itself.

The Agreement further provides for its provisional application if it has not entered into force on 16 November 1994, and it sets out procedures for such provisional application. It also states that provisional application shall terminate upon entry into force of the Agreement, or in any event on 16 November 1998, if the requirement that at least five industrialized States referred to in resolution II should have become parties to the Agreement by that date has not been fulfilled. The Secretary-General of the United Nations, as depositary of the Convention, is designated as depositary of the Agreement.

The annex to the instrument contains the substantive terms of the Agreement on the outstanding issues relating to Part XI. The annex contains nine sections.

Section 1 deals with costs to States Parties and institutional arrangements. It provides, *inter alia*, that a cost-effective and evolutionary approach should be taken in the establishment of all organs and subsidiary bodies under the Convention and this Agreement in order to minimize costs to States Parties. Consistent with this approach, it identifies the early functions on which the International Seabed Authority will concentrate. It sets out the procedures for the approval of plans of work, and, in particular, it deals with the plans of work that are to be submitted to the Authority by those identified as being eligible for pioneer investors status under resolution II. It prescribes special procedures to facilitate the integration into the Convention system of the pioneer investors registered by the Preparatory Commission for the International Seabed Authority and for the International Tribunal for the Law of the Sea. It also provides that any plan of work submitted to the Authority shall be accompanied by an assessment of the potential environmental impact of the proposed activities and by a description of a programme for oceanographic and baseline environmental studies in accordance with the rules, regulations and procedures to be adopted by the Authority.

It provides for the continuation of the membership of the Authority on a provisional basis for States which have not become parties to the Convention before the provisional application period terminates. Such membership shall not extend beyond 16 November 1996, unless it is extended for a further period of up to two years if the State concerned is making a good faith effort to become a party to the Convention and the Agreement. Provisional members are to have the same rights and obligations under Part XI and the Agreement as States Parties.

With respect to the administrative budget of the Authority, as a transitional measure it is provided that the administrative expenses of the Authority shall be met from the budget of the United Nations. The transitional period is limited to the end of the year following the year during which the Agreement enters into force. Thereafter, contributions to the administrative budget will be made directly to the Authority by States Parties.

Finally, this section provides that the Authority may, at any time, elaborate and adopt rules, regulations and procedures based on the principles contained in the annex to the Agreement, as well as any additional rules, regulations and procedures necessary to facilitate the approval of plans of work for exploration or exploitation as seabed mining activities develop.

Section 2 of the annex deals with the Enterprise, the operating arm of the Authority. It provides that the initial functions of the Enterprise shall be undertaken by the Secretariat of the Authority. These functions have been identified in this section. More importantly, this section provides that the initial deep-seabed mining operations of the Enterprise shall be through joint ventures. If joint-venture arrangements with the Enterprise accord with sound commercial principles, the Council is required to issue a directive for the independent functioning of the Enterprise from the Secretariat of the Authority. The obligation of States Parties to fund one mine site for the Enterprise as provided for in the Convention shall not apply, and States Parties shall be under no obligation to finance any operation of the Enterprise. The Enterprise shall be subject to the same rules and regulations as any other deep-seabed mining operator.

Section 3 deals with decision-making. The procedure for decision-making in the Council of the Authority has been considerably streamlined and simplified. This section provides that voting shall take place only when all efforts to reach a decision on substantive matters by consensus have been exhausted. This section sets out a system of voting by chambers. The practical effect of the chamber system of voting is to promote decisions by consensus. In cases other than those for which the Convention provides for decisions by consensus, decisions on substantive matters in the Council are to be taken by a two-thirds majority, provided such decisions are not opposed by a majority in any one of the chambers. The Council will have 36 members and will consist of four chambers for this purpose. These chambers will ensure that important interests have assured representation in the Council.

In order to ensure that a duly qualified applicant is assured of a contract with the Authority, a special procedure is prescribed for the approval of an application for a plan of work. Such plans of work can only be disapproved by the Council of the Authority by a two-thirds majority, provided such majority includes a majority of members in each chamber. Further, a plan of work would be deemed to have been approved if the Council did not act within 60 days following the recommendation of its approval by the Legal and Technical Commission, which will be a technical body composed of experts.

Section 4 deals with the Review Conference and provides that such a review may take place at any time, and not after 15 years from the date of the first commercial production, as was stated in the Convention. Furthermore, any amendments arising from such a Review Conference shall be subject to the amendment procedures set out in the Convention.

Section 5 deals with the transfer of technology. In the light of the approach taken for the operations of the Enterprise, the requirement for a possible mandatory transfer of technology by a contractor as provided for originally in the Convention will not apply. The Enterprise and developing States are to obtain the required technology through joint venture arrangements or from the open market. If this is not possible, the Authority may request the cooperation of States whose nationals may have such technology to facilitate their acquisition on fair and reasonable commercial terms and conditions consistent with the protection of intellectual property rights. For this purpose, the cooperation of all States Parties is urged.

Section 6 deals with production policy. The Convention had provided for a mathematical formula to control the level of production of minerals from the seabed. This formula was based on historical data on the growth of consumption of minerals, in particular, nickel. However, the prolonged downturn in the world metal market in the last two decades has rendered the formula inoperative. The Agreement therefore provides that the production policy of the Authority shall be based on market forces and that the provisions of the General Agreement on Tariffs and Trade (GATT), its relevant codes and successor or superseding agreements shall apply to activities in the deep seabed. To ensure that minerals produced from land-based sources and those from the seabed compete on a level field, it is provided that there shall be no subsidization of mining activities in the seabed, except as permitted under the GATT rules. Further, there shall be no discrimination between minerals derived from the deep seabed and from other sources in their access to markets or for imports of commodities produced from such minerals.

Section 7 deals with economic assistance to developing land-based producer countries. It anticipates that some land-based producers of the same minerals that are to be produced from the seabed may suffer serious adverse effects on their export earnings or economies. In cases where such effects may be attributed to mining from the deep seabed, the Authority is required to provide assistance to the affected developing countries. For this purpose, the Authority is to establish an economic assistance fund from a portion of the proceeds from mining in excess of those necessary to cover the administrative expenses of the Authority. This is a significant improvement, in that there is now a clear indication of the source from which such assistance would be provided.

Section 8 deals with the financial terms of contracts. This relates to the system of payment to the Authority for the mineral resources recovered by an operator from the deep seabed. The Agreement sets out the principles on which the financial terms of contract shall be established. In essence, the rates of payment under the system shall be within the range of those prevailing in respect of land-based mining of similar minerals in order to avoid giving deep seabed minerals an artificial competitive advantage or imposing on them a competitive disadvantage. The system, however, must be fair to the operator and to the Authority.

Section 9 establishes a Finance Committee within the Authority which is essentially a technical body charged with the responsibility of overseeing the financial implications of the decisions of the Authority. The Committee will include nationals of the highest contributors in its membership. In particular, the Council and the Assembly are obliged to take into account the recommendations of this technical body. On this issue of finance, it is also prescribed that no decisions having financial implications shall be adopted by the Assembly without first receiving a recommendation on the financial implications from the Council, and in cases where the Assembly does not agree with a recommendation of the Council, the matter shall be referred to the Council for its further consideration and recommendation, taking into account the views expressed in the Assembly.

This summarizes the content of the draft resolution and the Agreement and its annex.

On behalf of the sponsors, my delegation commends this historic draft resolution and the Agreement appended to it for adoption by the Assembly.

Because of the requirements relating to the provisional application of the Agreement, my delegation wishes to request that the draft resolution and the Agreement be adopted by a recorded vote.

Finally, I am pleased to inform the Assembly that the Government of Fiji has decided to sign the Agreement when it opens for signature on Friday, 29 July 1994.

STATEMENT BY U.S. PERMANENT REPRESENTATIVE TO THE UNITED NATIONS MADELEINE ALBRIGHT

Statement by H.E. Ambassador Madeleine Albright, Permanent Representative of the United States of America, to the United Nations General Assembly on 27 July 1994 *

I am particularly pleased to address the General Assembly in support of the draft resolution on the Law of the Sea Convention. In April 1993, I announced a significant change in my Government's policy – that the Clinton Administration had decided to take a more active role in the ongoing search at the United Nations for a way to achieve a widely accepted Convention. The Law of the Sea Convention has been recognized as a remarkable achievement in successfully balancing the maritime interests of all nations. Unfortunately, in one important area, general agreement had to date eluded the international community. Today, thanks to the efforts of a broad spectrum of Member States, this Assembly has before it a draft resolution that completes the long quest.

The work that has been done in the past 16 months validates the Administration's decision to work closely with other Members to resolve the problems with Part XI of the Convention. As someone who has been involved in this issue for many years, both inside and outside my Government, it is especially gratifying for me to be able to share in the international community's final success.

In 1970, this Assembly adopted a resolution which declared the resources of the deep seabed beyond national jurisdiction "the common heritage of mankind" (resolution 2749 (XXV), para. 1). The resolution called for negotiation of an international regime to give effect to the principle that all nations have an interest in, and should benefit from, the development of the resources of the deep seabed. The principle itself was not a new one. It has found expression in many forms over the centuries. Indeed, John Adams, the second President of the United States of America stated that "the oceans and their treasures are the common property of all men".

Similarly, in 1966, President Johnson declared: "We must ensure that the deep seas and the ocean bottoms are, and remain, the legacy of all human beings", and in 1980 the principle was incorporated into United States domestic deep seabed mining legislation.

However, despite the Conference on the Law of the Sea's great success on other contentious maritime issues, it failed in the attempt to give concrete expres-

---

* *Official Records of the General Assembly, Forty-eighth session, agenda item 36, document A/48/PV.99.*

sion to the principle in a legal regime for the deep seabed. As a result, a number of countries, including the United States, refused to sign the Convention; and many States which had signed refused to ratify unless the outstanding problems with the seabed mining provisions of the Convention were solved. It was in an effort to address this failure and achieve a universally applicable treaty that the Secretary-General's informal consultations were conducted.

We now have before us the fruits of those consultations, an implementation Agreement which removes the remaining obstacles to widespread acceptance of the Law of the Sea Convention. With the changes contained in this Agreement, the seabed mining regime established under the Convention will give all States a voice in managing the resources of the ocean.

It recognizes that certain groups such as consumers and producers of minerals, and investors in seabed mining, have particular interests deserving special protection, while at the same time it recognizes the special interests of developing countries. Of fundamental importance, it provides for the application of free-market principles to the development of the deep seabed. Finally, it establishes a lean institution that is both flexible, and efficient, enough to adapt to the needs of the international community as interest in commercial seabed mining emerges.

For the immediate future we will need to be vigilant, however, to ensure that those institutions' spending is compatible with the limited commercial activity on the seabed. We believe this can be done, keeping the budget comparable to what is now spent on the Preparatory Commission. Additionally, we will need to assure the principle of non-discrimination: that all who seek exploration rights on the seabed based on activities before the Convention's entry into force are treated similarly.

Finally, we note that the entry into force of the Agreement establishing the World Trade Organization will require clarification of the provisions of section 6 of the annex to the Agreement.

The decades-long search for a comprehensive and widely supported Convention on the Law of the Sea will be concluded this week. But the evolution of human activities that led to this Convention will continue, as new technologies emerge and our use of marine resources intensifies. These factors highlight the vital importance to our planet's future of protecting the marine environment and conserving ocean resources. The ongoing negotiations on high-seas fisheries here at the United Nations are just one example of the need to respond as mankind continues to define its relationship with the oceans. In this process, however, the United Nations Convention on the Law of the Sea provides an essential framework that will guide developments. The widespread acceptance of the norms and principles it incorporates and the institutions it establishes will greatly increase the likelihood of expeditiously solving problems we cannot foresee today and dramatically reduce the potential for future conflict.

For these reasons, the United States is pleased to co-sponsor the draft resolution by which the Assembly will adopt this Agreement, and it will sign the Agreement, subject to ratification, when it is opened for signature on 29 July. The United States will provisionally apply the Agreement beginning on 16 November

1994, pending its entry into force, in accordance with our laws and regulations. Such provisional application will be based on our signature of the Agreement rather than on our consent to the adoption of the draft resolution.

In conclusion, I would like to acknowledge the contributions by the many dedicated individuals, too numerous to mention by name, who have made this unique achievement possible. I look around this Hall and see many of the negotiators who worked long and diligently at the Conference on the Law of the Sea. My own delegation includes many of the former heads of the United States delegation to the Conference, as well as members of Congress who played an important role. Although their heads may be a bit grayer, their dedication to the quest for a universal convention has lost none of its vigour. With them I see many of the new generation of negotiators who followed in their footsteps and who, encouraged by the achievements of their predecessors, brought renewed dedication, creativity and energy to the task of removing the remaining obstacles to a universal convention. To all, we owe a debt of gratitude.

Finally, I would like to commend the Secretary-General and his predecessor, Javier Pérez de Cuéllar, and their staffs for their dedication to this undertaking. Without their support and prodding, this Agreement would not have been possible. I am firmly convinced that history will judge the negotiation of the Law of the Sea Convention as one to the great achievements of the United Nations and multilateral diplomacy, and I consider it a privilege to have the opportunity to sign the Agreement on behalf of the United States of America.

UNITED NATIONS CONVENTION
ON THE LAW OF THE SEA

The States Parties to this Convention,

Prompted by the desire to settle, in a spirit of mutual understanding and co-operation, all issues relating to the law of the sea and aware of the historic significance of this Convention as an important contribution to the maintenance of peace, justice and progress for all peoples of the world,

Noting that developments since the United Nations Conferences on the Law of the Sea held at Geneva in 1958 and 1960 have accentuated the need for a new and generally acceptable Convention on the law of the sea,

Conscious that the problems of ocean space are closely interrelated and need to be considered as a whole,

Recognizing the desirability of establishing through this Convention, with due regard for the sovereignty of all States, a legal order for the seas and oceans which will facilitate international communication, and will promote the peaceful uses of the seas and oceans, the equitable and efficient utilization of their re-sources, the conservation of their living resources, and the study, protection and preservation of the marine environment,

Bearing in mind that the achievement of these goals will contribute to the realization of a just and equitable international economic order which takes into account the interests and needs of mankind as a whole and, in particular, the spe-cial interests and needs of developing countries, whether coastal or land-locked,

Desiring by this Convention to develop the principles embodied in resolu-tion 2749 (XXV) of 17 December 1970 in which the General Assembly of the United Nations solemnly declared *inter alia* that the area of the seabed and ocean floor and the subsoil thereof, beyond the limits of national jurisdiction, as well as its resources, are the common heritage of mankind, the exploration and exploita-tion of which shall be carried out for the benefit of mankind as a whole, irrespective of the geographical location of States,

Believing that the codification and progressive development of the law of the sea achieved in this Convention will contribute to the strengthening of peace, security, cooperation and friendly relations among all nations in conformity with the principles of justice and equal rights and will promote the economic and social advancement of all peoples of the world, in accordance with the Purposes and Principles of the United Nations as set forth in the Charter,

Affirming that matters not regulated by this Convention continue to be governed by the rules and principles of general international law,

Have agreed as follows:

PART I

INTRODUCTION

Article 1
Use of terms and scope

1. For the purposes of this Convention:

(1) "Area" means the seabed and ocean floor and subsoil thereof, beyond the limits of national jurisdiction;

(2) "Authority" means the International Seabed Authority;

(3) "activities in the Area" means all activities of exploration for, and exploitation of, the resources of the Area;

(4) "pollution of the marine environment" means the introduction by man, directly or indirectly, of substances or energy into the marine environment, including estuaries, which results or is likely to result in such deleterious effects as harm to living resources and marine life, hazards to human health, hindrance to marine activities, including fishing and other legitimate uses of the sea, impairment of quality for use of sea water and reduction of amenities;

(5) (a)   "dumping" means:

(i) any deliberate disposal of wastes or other matter from vessels, aircraft, platforms or other man-made structures at sea;

(ii) any deliberate disposal of vessels, aircraft, platforms or other man-made structures at sea;

(b) "dumping" does not include:

(i) the disposal of wastes or other matter incidental to, or derived from the normal operations of vessels, aircraft, platforms or other man-made structures at sea and their equipment, other than wastes or other matter transported by or to vessels, aircraft, platforms or other man-made structures at sea, operating for the purpose of disposal of such matter or derived from the treatment of such wastes or other matter on such vessels, air-craft, platforms or structures;

(ii) placement of matter for a purpose other than the mere disposal thereof, provided that such placement is not contrary to the aims of this Convention.

2.　(1) "States Parties" means States which have consented to be bound by this Convention and for which this Convention is in force.

(2) This Convention applies *mutatis mutandis* to the entities referred to in article 305, paragraph l(b), (c), (d), (e) and (f), which become Parties to this Convention in accordance with the conditions relevant to each, and to that extent "States Parties" refers to those entities.

PART II
TERRITORIAL SEA AND CONTIGUOUS ZONE
SECTION 1. GENERAL PROVISIONS

Article 2
*Legal status of the territorial sea, of the air space over
the territorial sea and of its bed and subsoil*

1.　The sovereignty of a coastal State extends, beyond its land territory and internal waters and, in the case of an archipelagic State, its archipelagic waters, to an adjacent belt of sea, described as the territorial sea.

2.　This sovereignty extends to the air space over the territorial sea as well as to its bed and subsoil.

3.　The sovereignty over the territorial sea is exercised subject to this Convention and to other rules of international law.

SECTION 2. LIMITS OF THE TERRITORIAL SEA

Article 3
Breadth of the territorial sea

Every State has the right to establish the breadth of its territorial sea up to a limit not exceeding 12 nautical miles, measured from baselines determined in accordance with this Convention.

Article 4
Outer limit of the territorial sea

The outer limit of the territorial sea is the line every point of which is at a distance from the nearest point of the baseline equal to the breadth of the territorial sea.

Article 5
Normal baseline

Except where otherwise provided in this Convention, the normal baseline for measuring the breadth of the territorial sea is the low-water line along the coast as marked on large-scale charts officially recognized by the coastal State.

Article 6
Reefs

In the case of islands situated on atolls or of islands having fringing reefs, the baseline for measuring the breadth of the territorial sea is the seaward low-water line of the reef, as shown by the appropriate symbol on charts officially recognized by the coastal State.

Article 7
Straight baselines

1.   In localities where the coastline is deeply indented and cut into, or if there is a fringe of islands along the coast in its immediate vicinity, the method of straight baselines joining appropriate points may be employed in drawing the baseline from which the breadth of the territorial sea is measured.

2.   Where because of the presence of a delta and other natural conditions the coastline is highly unstable, the appropriate points may be selected along the furthest seaward extent of the low-water line and, notwithstanding subsequent regression of the low-water line, the straight baselines shall remain effective until changed by the coastal State in accordance with this Convention.

3.   The drawing of straight baselines must not depart to any appreciable extent from the general direction of the coast, and the sea areas lying within the lines must be sufficiently closely linked to the land domain to be subject to the regime of internal waters.

4.   Straight baselines shall not be drawn to and from low-tide elevations, unless lighthouses or similar installations which are permanently above sea level have been built on them or except in instances where the drawing of baselines to and from such elevations has received general international recognition.

5.   Where the method of straight baselines is applicable under paragraph 1, account may be taken, in determining particular baselines, of economic interests peculiar to the region concerned, the reality and the importance of which are clearly evidenced by long usage.

6.   The system of straight baselines may not be applied by a State in such a manner as to cut off the territorial sea of another State from the high seas or an exclusive economic zone.

Article 8
Internal waters

1.   Except as provided in Part IV, waters on the landward side of the baseline of the territorial sea form part of the internal waters of the State.

2.   Where the establishment of a straight baseline in accordance with the method set forth in article 7 has the effect of enclosing as internal waters areas which had not previously been considered as such, a right of innocent passage as provided in this Convention shall exist in those waters.

Article 9
Mouths of rivers

If a river flows directly into the sea, the baseline shall be a straight line across the mouth of the river between points on the low-water line of its banks.

Article 10
Bays

1. This article relates only to bays the coasts of which belong to a single State.

2. For the purposes of this Convention, a bay is a well-marked indentation whose penetration is in such proportion to the width of its mouth as to contain land-locked waters and constitute more than a mere curvature of the coast. An indentation shall not, however, be regarded as a bay unless its area is as large as, or larger than, that of the semi-circle whose diameter is a line drawn across the mouth of that indentation.

3. For the purpose of measurement, the area of an indentation is that lying between the low-water mark around the shore of the indentation and a line joining the low-water mark of its natural entrance points. Where, because of the presence of islands, an indentation has more than one mouth, the semi-circle shall be drawn on a line as long as the sum total of the lengths of the lines across the different mouths. Islands within an indentation shall be included as if they were part of the water area of the indentation.

4. If the distance between the low-water marks of the natural entrance points of a bay does not exceed 24 nautical miles, a closing line may be drawn between these two low-water marks, and the waters enclosed thereby shall be considered as internal waters.

5. Where the distance between the low-water marks of the natural entrance points of a bay exceeds 24 nautical miles, a straight baseline of 24 nautical miles shall be drawn within the bay in such a manner as to enclose the maximum area of water that is possible with a line of that length.

6. The foregoing provisions do not apply to so-called "historic" bays, or in any case where the system of straight baselines provided for in article 7 is applied.

Article 11
Ports

For the purpose of delimiting the territorial sea, the outermost permanent harbour works which form an integral part of the harbour system are regarded as forming part of the coast. Off-shore installations and artificial islands shall not be considered as permanent harbour works.

Article 12
Roadsteads

Roadsteads which are normally used for the loading, unloading and anchoring of ships, and which would otherwise be situated wholly or partly outside the outer limit of the territorial sea, are included in the territorial sea.

Article 13
Low-tide elevations

1.   A low-tide elevation is a naturally formed area of land which is surrounded by and above water at low tide but submerged at high tide. Where a low-tide elevation is situated wholly or partly at a distance not exceeding the breadth of the territorial sea from the mainland or an island, the low-water line on that elevation may be used as the baseline for measuring the breadth of the territorial sea.

2.   Where a low-tide elevation is wholly situated at a distance exceeding the breadth of the territorial sea from the mainland or an island, it has no territorial sea of its own.

Article 14
Combination of methods for determining baselines

The coastal State may determine baselines in turn by any of the methods provided for in the foregoing articles to suit different conditions.

Article 15
Delimitation of the territorial sea between States
with opposite or adjacent coasts

Where the coasts of two States are opposite or adjacent to each other, neither of the two States is entitled, failing agreement between them to the contrary, to extend its territorial sea beyond the median line every point of which is equidistant from the nearest points on the baselines from which the breadth of the territorial seas of each of the two States is measured. The above provision does not apply, however, where it is necessary by reason of historic title or other special circumstances to delimit the territorial seas of the two States in a way which is at variance therewith.

Article 16
Charts and lists of geographical co-ordinates

1.   The baselines for measuring the breadth of the territorial sea determined in accordance with articles 7, 9 and 10, or the limits derived therefrom, and the lines of delimitation drawn in accordance with articles 12 and 15 shall be shown on charts of a scale or scales adequate for ascertaining their position. Alternatively, a list of geographical co-ordinates of points, specifying the geodetic datum, may be substituted.

2.   The coastal State shall give due publicity to such charts or lists of geographical co-ordinates and shall deposit a copy of each such chart or list with the Secretary-General of the United Nations.

SECTION 3. INNOCENT PASSAGE IN THE TERRITORIAL SEA

SUBSECTION A. RULES APPLICABLE TO ALL SHIPS

Article 17
Right of innocent passage

Subject to this Convention, ships of all States, whether coastal or land-locked, enjoy the right of innocent passage through the territorial sea.

Article 18
Meaning of passage

1.   Passage means navigation through the territorial sea for the purpose of:
(a)   traversing that sea without entering internal waters or calling at a road-stead or port facility outside internal waters; or
(b)   proceeding to or from internal waters or a call at such roadstead or port facility.

2.   Passage shall be continuous and expeditious. However, passage includes stopping and anchoring, but only in so far as the same are incidental to ordinary navigation or are rendered necessary by *force majeure* or distress or for the purpose of rendering assistance to persons, ships or aircraft in danger or distress.

Article 19
Meaning of innocent passage

1.   Passage is innocent so long as it is not prejudicial to the peace, good order or security of the coastal State. Such passage shall take place in conformity with this Convention and with other rules of international law.

2.   Passage of a foreign ship shall be considered to be prejudicial to the peace, good order or security of the coastal State if in the territorial sea it engages in any of the following activities:
(a)   any threat or use of force against the sovereignty, territorial integrity or political independence of the coastal State, or in any other manner in violation of the principles of international law embodied in the Charter of the United Nations;
(b)   any exercise or practice with weapons of any kind;
(c)   any act aimed at collecting information to the prejudice of the defence or security of the coastal State;
(d)   any act of propaganda aimed at affecting the defence or security of the coastal State;
(e)   the launching, landing or taking on board of any aircraft;
(f)   the launching, landing or taking on board of any military device;
(g)   the loading or unloading of any commodity, currency or person contrary to the customs, fiscal, immigration or sanitary laws and regulations of the coastal State;

(h) any act of wilful and serious pollution contrary to this Convention;
(i) any fishing activities;
(j) the carrying out of research or survey activities;
(k) any act aimed at interfering with any systems of communication or any other facilities or installations of the coastal State;
(l) any other activity not having a direct bearing on passage.

Article 20
Submarines and other underwater vehicles

In the territorial sea, submarines and other underwater vehicles are required to navigate on the surface and to show their flag.

Article 21
Laws and regulations of the coastal State relating to innocent passage

1.   The coastal State may adopt laws and regulations, in conformity with the provisions of this Convention and other rules of international law, relating to innocent passage through the territorial sea, in respect of all or any of the following:
(a) the safety of navigation and the regulation of maritime traffic;
(b) the protection of navigational aids and facilities and other facilities or installations;
(c) the protection of cables and pipelines;
(d) the conservation of the living resources of the sea;
(e) the prevention of infringement of the fisheries laws and regulations of the coastal State;
(f) the preservation of the environment of the coastal State and the prevention, reduction and control of pollution thereof;
(g) marine scientific research and hydrographic surveys;
(h) the prevention of infringement of the customs, fiscal, immigration or sanitary laws and regulations of the coastal State.

2.   Such laws and regulations shall not apply to the design, construction, manning or equipment of foreign ships unless they are giving effect to generally accepted international rules or standards.

3.   The coastal State shall give due publicity to all such laws and regulations.

4.   Foreign ships exercising the right of innocent passage through the territorial sea shall comply with all such laws and regulations and all generally accepted international regulations relating to the prevention of collisions at sea.

Article 22
Sea lanes and traffic separation schemes in the territorial sea

1.   The coastal State may, where necessary having regard to the safety of navigation, require foreign ships exercising the right of innocent passage through

its territorial sea to use such sea lanes and traffic separation schemes as it may designate or prescribe for the regulation of the passage of ships.

2. In particular, tankers, nuclear-powered ships and ships carrying nuclear or other inherently dangerous or noxious substances or materials may be required to confine their passage to such sea lanes.

3. In the designation of sea lanes and the prescription of traffic separation schemes under this article, the coastal State shall take into account:

(a) the recommendations of the competent international organization;

(b) any channels customarily used for international navigation;

(c) the special characteristics of particular ships and channels; and

(d) the density of traffic.

4. The coastal State shall clearly indicate such sea lanes and traffic separation schemes on charts to which due publicity shall be given.

Article 23
Foreign nuclear-powered ships and ships carrying nuclear or other inherently dangerous or noxious substances

Foreign nuclear-powered ships and ships carrying nuclear or other inherently dangerous or noxious substances shall, when exercising the right of innocent passage through the territorial sea, carry documents and observe special precautionary measures established for such ships by international agreements.

Article 24
Duties of the coastal State

1. The coastal State shall not hamper the innocent passage of foreign ships through the territorial sea except in accordance with this Convention. In particular, in the application of this Convention or of any laws or regulations adopted in conformity with this Convention, the coastal State shall not:

(a) impose requirements on foreign ships which have the practical effect of denying or impairing the right of innocent passage; or

(b) discriminate in form or in fact against the ships of any State or against ships carrying cargoes to, from or on behalf of any State.

2. The coastal State shall give appropriate publicity to any danger to navigation, of which it has knowledge, within its territorial sea.

Article 25
Rights of protection of the coastal State

1. The coastal State may take the necessary steps in its territorial sea to prevent passage which is not innocent.

2. In the case of ships proceeding to internal waters or a call at a port facility outside internal waters, the coastal State also has the right to take the necessary steps to prevent any breach of the conditions to which admission of those ships to internal waters or such a call is subject.

3.   The coastal State may, without discrimination in form or in fact among foreign ships, suspend temporarily in specified areas of its territorial sea the innocent passage of foreign ships if such suspension is essential for the protection of its security, including weapons exercises. Such suspension shall take effect only after having been duly published.

Article 26
Charges which may be levied upon foreign ships

1.   No charge may be levied upon foreign ships by reason only of their passage through the territorial sea.

2.   Charges may be levied upon a foreign ship passing through the territorial sea as payment only for specific services rendered to the ship. These charges shall be levied without discrimination.

SUBSECTION B. RULES APPLICABLE TO MERCHANT SHIPS AND GOVERNMENT SHIPS OPERATED FOR COMMERCIAL PURPOSES

Article 27
Criminal jurisdiction on board a foreign ship

1.   The criminal jurisdiction of the coastal State should not be exercised on board a foreign ship passing through the territorial sea to arrest any person or to conduct any investigation in connection with any crime committed on board the ship during its passage, save only in the following cases:
   (a)   if the consequences of the crime extend to the coastal State;
   (b)   if the crime is of a kind to disturb the peace of the country or the good order of the territorial sea;
   (c)   if the assistance of the local authorities has been requested by the master of the ship or by a diplomatic agent or consular officer of the flag State; or
   (d)   if such measures are necessary for the suppression of illicit traffic in narcotic drugs or psychotropic substances.

2.   The above provisions do not affect the right of the coastal State to take any steps authorized by its laws for the purpose of an arrest or investigation on board a foreign ship passing through the territorial sea after leaving internal waters.

3.   In the cases provided for in paragraphs 1 and 2, the coastal State shall, if the master so requests, notify a diplomatic agent or consular officer of the flag State before taking any steps, and shall facilitate contact between such agent or officer and the ship's crew. In cases of emergency this notification may be communicated while the measures are being taken.

4.   In considering whether or in what manner an arrest should be made, the local authorities shall have due regard to the interests of navigation.

5.   Except as provided in Part XII or with respect to violations of laws and regulations adopted in accordance with Part V, the coastal State may not take any

steps on board a foreign ship passing through the territorial sea to arrest any person or to conduct any investigation in connection with any crime committed before the ship entered the territorial sea, if the ship, proceeding from a foreign port, is only passing through the territorial sea without entering internal waters.

Article 28
Civil jurisdiction in relation to foreign ships

1.   The coastal State should not stop or divert a foreign ship passing through the territorial sea for the purpose of exercising civil jurisdiction in relation to a person on board the ship.

2.   The coastal State may not levy execution against or arrest the ship for the purpose of any civil proceedings, save only in respect of obligations or liabilities assumed or incurred by the ship itself in the course or for the purpose of its voyage through the waters of the coastal State.

3.   Paragraph 2 is without prejudice to the right of the coastal State, in accordance with its laws, to levy execution against or to arrest, for the purpose of any civil proceedings, a foreign ship lying in the territorial sea, or passing through the territorial sea after leaving internal waters.

SUBSECTION C. RULES APPLICABLE TO WARSHIPS AND OTHER GOVERNMENT SHIPS OPERATED FOR NON-COMMERCIAL PURPOSES

Article 29
Definition of warships

For the purposes of this Convention, "warship" means a ship belonging to the armed forces of a State bearing the external marks distinguishing such ships of its nationality, under the command of an officer duly commissioned by the government of the State and whose name appears in the appropriate service list or its equivalent, and manned by a crew which is under regular armed forces discipline.

Article 30
Non-compliance by warships with the laws and regulations of the coastal State

If any warship does not comply with the laws and regulations of the coastal State concerning passage through the territorial sea and disregards any request for compliance therewith which is made to it, the coastal State may require it to leave the territorial sea immediately.

Article 31
Responsibility of the flag State for damage caused by a warship or other government ship operated for non-commercial purposes

The flag State shall bear international responsibility for any loss or damage to the coastal State resulting from the non-compliance by a warship or other government ship operated for non-commercial purposes with the laws and regulations of the coastal State concerning passage through the territorial sea or with the provisions of this Convention or other rules of international law.

Article 32
Immunities of warships and other government ships
operated for non-commercial purposes

With such exceptions as are contained in subsection A and in articles 30 and 31, nothing in this Convention affects the immunities of warships and other government ships operated for non-commercial purposes.

SECTION 4. CONTIGUOUS ZONE

Article 33
Contiguous zone

1.   In a zone contiguous to its territorial sea, described as the contiguous zone, the coastal State may exercise the control necessary to:
    (a) prevent infringement of its customs, fiscal, immigration or sanitary laws and regulations within its territory or territorial sea;
    (b) punish infringement of the above laws and regulations committed within its territory or territorial sea.
2.   The contiguous zone may not extend beyond 24 nautical miles from the baselines from which the breadth of the territorial sea is measured.

PART III
STRAITS USED FOR INTERNATIONAL NAVIGATION
SECTION 1. GENERAL PROVISIONS

Article 34
Legal status of waters forming straits used for international navigation

1.   The régime of passage through straits used for international navigation established in this Part shall not in other respects affect the legal status of the waters forming such straits or the exercise by the States bordering the straits of their sovereignty or jurisdiction over such waters and their air space, bed and subsoil.
2.   The sovereignty or jurisdiction of the States bordering the straits is exercised subject to this Part and to other rules of international law.

Article 35
Scope of this Part

Nothing in this Part affects:
    (a) any areas of internal waters within a strait, except where the establishment of a straight baseline in accordance with the method set forth in article 7

has the effect of enclosing as internal waters areas which had not previously been considered as such;

(b) the legal status of the waters beyond the territorial seas of States bordering straits as exclusive economic zones or high seas; or

(c) the legal regime in straits in which passage is regulated in whole or in part by long-standing international conventions in force specifically relating to such straits.

Article 36
High seas routes or routes through exclusive economic zones through straits used for international navigation

This Part does not apply to a strait used for international navigation if there exists through the strait a route through the high seas or through an exclusive economic zone of similar convenience with respect to navigational and hydrographical characteristics; in such routes, the other relevant Parts of this Convention, including the provisions regarding the freedoms of navigation and overflight, apply.

SECTION 2. TRANSIT PASSAGE

Article 37
Scope of this section

This section applies to straits which are used for international navigation between one part of the high seas or an exclusive economic zone and another part of the high seas or an exclusive economic zone.

Article 38
Right of transit passage

1. In straits referred to in article 37, all ships and aircraft enjoy the right of transit passage, which shall not be impeded; except that, if the strait is formed by an island of a State bordering the strait and its mainland, transit passage shall not apply if there exists seaward of the island a route through the high seas or through an exclusive economic zone of similar convenience with respect to navigational and hydrographical characteristics.

2. Transit passage means the exercise in accordance with this Part of the freedom of navigation and overflight solely for the purpose of continuous and expeditious transit of the strait between one part of the high seas or an exclusive economic zone and another part of the high seas or an exclusive economic zone. However, the requirement of continuous and expeditious transit does not preclude passage through the strait for the purpose of entering, leaving or returning from a State bordering the strait, subject to the conditions of entry to that State.

3.   Any activity which is not an exercise of the right of transit passage through a strait remains subject to the other applicable provisions of this Convention.

Article 39
Duties of ships and aircraft during transit passage

1.   Ships and aircraft, while exercising the right of transit passage, shall:
(a) proceed without delay through or over the strait;
(b) refrain from any threat or use of force against the sovereignty, territorial integrity or political independence of States bordering the strait, or in any other manner in violation of the principles of international law embodied in the Charter of the United Nations;
(c) refrain from any activities other than those incident to their normal modes of continuous and expeditious transit unless rendered necessary by *force majeure* or by distress;
(d) comply with other relevant provisions of this Part.
2.   Ships in transit passage shall:
(a) comply with generally accepted international regulations, procedures and practices for safety at sea, including the International Regulations for Preventing Collisions at Sea;
(b) comply with generally accepted international regulations, procedures and practices for the prevention, reduction and control of pollution from ships.
3.   Aircraft in transit passage shall:
(a) observe the Rules of the Air established by the International Civil Aviation Organization as they apply to civil aircraft; state aircraft will normally comply with such safety measures and will at all times operate with due regard for the safety of navigation;
(b) at all times monitor the radio frequency assigned by the competent internationally designated air traffic control authority or the appropriate international distress radio frequency.

Article 40
Research and survey activities

During transit passage, foreign ships, including marine scientific research and hydrographic survey ships, may not carry out any research or survey activities without the prior authorization of the States bordering straits.

Article 41
Sea lanes and traffic separation schemes in straits used for international navigation

1.   In conformity with this Part, States bordering straits may designate sea lanes and prescribe traffic separation schemes for navigation in straits where necessary to promote the safe passage of ships.

2.   Such States may, when circumstances require, and after giving due publicity thereto, substitute other sea lanes or traffic separation schemes for any sea lanes or traffic separation schemes previously designated or prescribed by them.

3.   Such sea lanes and traffic separation schemes shall conform to generally accepted international regulations.

4.   Before designating or substituting sea lanes or prescribing or substituting traffic separation schemes, States bordering straits shall refer proposals to the competent international organization with a view to their adoption. The organization may adopt only such sea lanes and traffic separation schemes as may be agreed with the States bordering the straits, after which the States may designate, prescribe or substitute them.

5.   In respect of a strait where sea lanes or traffic separation schemes through the waters of two or more States bordering the strait are being proposed, the States concerned shall co-operate in formulating proposals in consultation with the competent international organization.

6.   States bordering straits shall clearly indicate all sea lanes and traffic separation schemes designated or prescribed by them on charts to which due publicity shall be given.

7.   Ships in transit passage shall respect applicable sea lanes and traffic separation schemes established in accordance with this article.

Article 42
Laws and regulations of States bordering straits
relating to transit passage

1.   Subject to the provisions of this section, States bordering straits may adopt laws and regulations relating to transit passage through straits, in respect of all or any of the following:

(a)   the safety of navigation and the regulation of maritime traffic, as provided in article 41;

(b)   the prevention, reduction and control of pollution, by giving effect to applicable international regulations regarding the discharge of oil, oily wastes and other noxious substances in the strait;

(c)   with respect to fishing vessels, the prevention of fishing, including the stowage of fishing gear;

(d)   the loading or unloading of any commodity, currency or person in contravention of the customs, fiscal, immigration or sanitary laws and regulations of States bordering straits.

2.   Such laws and regulations shall not discriminate in form or in fact among foreign ships or in their application have the practical effect of denying, hampering or impairing the right of transit passage as defined in this section.

3.   States bordering straits shall give due publicity to all such laws and regulations.

4.   Foreign ships exercising the right of transit passage shall comply with such laws and regulations.

5.   The flag State of a ship or the State of registry of an aircraft entitled to sovereign immunity which acts in a manner contrary to such laws and regulations or other provisions of this Part shall bear international responsibility for any loss or damage which results to States bordering straits.

Article 43
Navigational and safety aids and other improvements and the prevention, reduction and control of pollution

User States and States bordering a strait should by agreement cooperate:
(a)   in the establishment and maintenance in a strait of necessary navigational and safety aids or other improvements in aid of international navigation; and
(b)   for the prevention, reduction and control of pollution from ships.

Article 44
Duties of States bordering straits

States bordering straits shall not hamper transit passage and shall give appropriate publicity to any danger to navigation or overflight within or over the strait of which they have knowledge. There shall be no suspension of transit passage.

SECTION 3. INNOCENT PASSAGE

Article 45
Innocent passage

1.   The regime of innocent passage, in accordance with Part II, section 3, shall apply in straits used for international navigation:
(a)   excluded from the application of the régime of transit passage under article 38, paragraph 1; or
(b)   between a part of the high seas or an exclusive economic zone and the territorial sea of a foreign State.
2.   There shall be no suspension of innocent passage through such straits.

PART IV
ARCHIPELAGIC STATES

Article 46
Use of terms

For the purposes of this Convention:
(a)   "archipelagic State" means a State constituted wholly by one or more archipelagos and may include other islands;

(b) "archipelago" means a group of islands, including parts of islands, interconnecting waters and other natural features which are so closely interrelated that such islands, waters and other natural features form an intrinsic geographical, economic and political entity, or which historically have been regarded as such.

Article 47
Archipelagic baselines

1.   An archipelagic State may draw straight archipelagic baselines joining the outermost points of the outermost islands and drying reefs of the archipelago provided that within such baselines are included the main islands and an area in which the ratio of the area of the water to the area of the land, including atolls, is between 1 to 1 and 9 to 1.

2.   The length of such baselines shall not exceed 100 nautical miles, except that up to 3 per cent of the total number of baselines enclosing any archipelago may exceed that length, up to a maximum length of 125 nautical miles.

3.   The drawing of such baselines shall not depart to any appreciable extent from the general configuration of the archipelago.

4.   Such baselines shall not be drawn to and from low-tide elevations, unless lighthouses or similar installations which are permanently above sea level have been built on them or where a low-tide elevation is situated wholly or partly at a distance not exceeding the breadth of the territorial sea from the nearest island.

5.   The system of such baselines shall not be applied by an archipelagic State in such a manner as to cut off from the high seas or the exclusive economic zone the territorial sea of another State.

6.   If a part of the archipelagic waters of an archipelagic State lies between two parts of an immediately adjacent neighbouring State, existing rights and all other legitimate interests which the latter State has traditionally exercised in such waters and all rights stipulated by agreement between those States shall continue and be respected.

7.   For the purpose of computing the ratio of water to land under paragraph 1, land areas may include waters lying within the fringing reefs of islands and atolls, including that part of a steep-sided oceanic plateau which is enclosed or nearly enclosed by a chain of limestone islands and drying reefs lying on the perimeter of the plateau.

8.   The baselines drawn in accordance with this article shall be shown on charts of a scale or scales adequate for ascertaining their position. Alternatively, lists of geographical co-ordinates of points, specifying the geodetic datum, may be substituted.

9. The archipelagic State shall give due publicity to such charts or lists of geographical co-ordinates and shall deposit a copy of each such chart or list with the Secretary-General of the United Nations.

Article 48
Measurement of the breadth of the territorial sea, the contiguous zone, the exclusive economic zone and the continental shelf

The breadth of the territorial sea, the contiguous zone, the exclusive economic zone and the continental shelf shall be measured from archipelagic baselines drawn in accordance with article 47.

Article 49
Legal status of archipelagic waters, of the air space over archipelagic waters and of their bed and subsoil

1.   The sovereignty of an archipelagic State extends to the waters enclosed by the archipelagic baselines drawn in accordance with article 47, described as archipelagic waters, regardless of their depth or distance from the coast.

2.   This sovereignty extends to the air space over the archipelagic waters, as well as to their bed and subsoil, and the resources contained therein.

3.   This sovereignty is exercised subject to this Part.

4.   The régime of archipelagic sea lanes passage established in this Part shall not in other respects affect the status of the archipelagic waters, including the sea lanes, or the exercise by the archipelagic State of its sovereignty over such waters and their air space, bed and subsoil, and the resources contained therein.

Article 50
Delimitation of internal waters

Within its archipelagic waters, the archipelagic State may draw closing lines for the delimitation of internal waters, in accordance with articles 9, 10 and 11.

Article 51
Existing agreements, traditional fishing rights and existing submarine cables

1.   Without prejudice to article 49, an archipelagic State shall respect existing agreements with other States and shall recognize traditional fishing rights and other legitimate activities of the immediately adjacent neighbouring States in certain areas falling within archipelagic waters. The terms and conditions for the exercise of such rights and activities, including the nature, the extent and the areas to which they apply, shall, at the request of any of the States concerned, be regulated by bilateral agreements between them. Such rights shall not be transferred to or shared with third States or their nationals.

2.   An archipelagic State shall respect existing submarine cables laid by other States and passing through its waters without making a landfall. An archipelagic State shall permit the maintenance and replacement of such cables upon receiving due notice of their location and the intention to repair or replace them.

Article 52
Right of innocent passage

1.   Subject to article 53 and without prejudice to article 50, ships of all States enjoy the right of innocent passage through archipelagic waters, in accordance with Part II, section 3.

2.   The archipelagic State may, without discrimination in form or in fact among foreign ships, suspend temporarily in specified areas of its archipelagic waters the innocent passage of foreign ships if such suspension is essential for the protection of its security. Such suspension shall take effect only after having been duly published.

Article 53
Right of archipelagic sea lanes passage

1.   An archipelagic State may designate sea lanes and air routes thereabove, suitable for the continuous and expeditious passage of foreign ships and aircraft through or over its archipelagic waters and the adjacent territorial sea.

2.   All ships and aircraft enjoy the right of archipelagic sea lanes passage in such sea lanes and air routes.

3.   Archipelagic sea lanes passage means the exercise in accordance with this Convention of the rights of navigation and overflight in the normal mode solely for the purpose of continuous, expeditious and unobstructed transit between one part of the high seas or an exclusive economic zone and another part of the high seas or an exclusive economic zone.

4.   Such sea lanes and air routes shall traverse the archipelagic waters and the adjacent territorial sea and shall include all normal passage routes used as routes for international navigation or overflight through or over archipelagic waters and, within such routes, so far as ships are concerned, all normal navigational channels, provided that duplication of routes of similar convenience between the same entry and exit points shall not be necessary.

5.   Such sea lanes and air routes shall be defined by a series of continuous axis lines from the entry points of passage routes to the exit points. Ships and aircraft in archipelagic sea lanes passage shall not deviate more than 25 nautical miles to either side of such axis lines during passage, provided that such ships and aircraft shall not navigate closer to the coasts than 10 per cent of the distance between the nearest points on islands bordering the sea lane.

6.   An archipelagic State which designates sea lanes under this article may also prescribe traffic separation schemes for the safe passage of ships through narrow channels in such sea lanes.

7.   An archipelagic State may, when circumstances require, after giving due publicity thereto, substitute other sea lanes or traffic separation schemes for any sea lanes or traffic separation schemes previously designated or prescribed by it.

8.   Such sea lanes and traffic separation schemes shall conform to generally accepted international regulations.

9. In designating or substituting sea lanes or prescribing or substituting traffic separation schemes, an archipelagic State shall refer proposals to the competent international organization with a view to their adoption. The organization may adopt only such sea lanes and traffic separation schemes as may be agreed with the archipelagic State, after which the archipelagic State may designate, prescribe or substitute them.

10. The archipelagic State shall clearly indicate the axis of the sea lanes and the traffic separation schemes designated or prescribed by it on charts to which due publicity shall be given.

11. Ships in archipelagic sea lanes passage shall respect applicable sea lanes and traffic separation schemes established in accordance with this article.

12. If an archipelagic State does not designate sea lanes or air routes, the right of archipelagic sea lanes passage may be exercised through the routes normally used for international navigation.

Article 54
Duties of ships and aircraft during their passage,
research and survey activities, duties of the archipelagic State
and laws and regulations of the archipelagic State
relating to archipelagic sea lanes passage

Articles 39, 40, 42 and 44 apply *mutatis mutandis* to archipelagic sea lanes passage.

PART V
EXCLUSIVE ECONOMIC ZONE

Article 55
Specific legal régime of the exclusive economic zone

The exclusive economic zone is an area beyond and adjacent to the territorial sea, subject to the specific legal régime established in this Part, under which the rights and jurisdiction of the coastal State and the rights and freedoms of other States are governed by the relevant provisions of this Convention.

Article 56
Rights, jurisdiction and duties of the coastal State in the exclusive
economic zone

1. In the exclusive economic zone, the coastal State has:
(a) sovereign rights for the purpose of exploring and exploiting, conserving and managing the natural resources, whether living or non-living, of the waters superjacent to the seabed and of the seabed and its subsoil, and with regard to other activities for the economic exploitation and exploration of the zone, such as the production of energy from the water, currents and winds;

(b) jurisdiction as provided for in the relevant provisions of this Convention with regard to:

(i) the establishment and use of artificial islands, installations and structures;

(ii) marine scientific research;

(iii) the protection and preservation of the marine environment;

(c) other rights and duties provided for in this Convention.

2. In exercising its rights and performing its duties under this Convention in the exclusive economic zone, the coastal State shall have due regard to the rights and duties of other States and shall act in a manner compatible with the provisions of this Convention.

3. The rights set out in this article with respect to the seabed and subsoil shall be exercised in accordance with Part VI.

Article 57
Breadth of the exclusive economic zone

The exclusive economic zone shall not extend beyond 200 nautical miles from the baselines from which the breadth of the territorial sea is measured.

Article 58
Rights and duties of other States
in the exclusive economic zone

1. In the exclusive economic zone, all States, whether coastal or land-locked, enjoy, subject to the relevant provisions of this Convention, the freedoms referred to in article 87 of navigation and overflight and of the laying of submarine cables and pipelines, and other internationally lawful uses of the sea related to these freedoms, such as those associated with the operation of ships, aircraft and submarine cables and pipelines, and compatible with the other provisions of this Convention.

2. Articles 88 to 115 and other pertinent rules of international law apply to the exclusive economic zone in so far as they are not incompatible with this Part.

3. In exercising their rights and performing their duties under this Convention in the exclusive economic zone, States shall have due regard to the rights and duties of the coastal State and shall comply with the laws and regulations adopted by the coastal State in accordance with the provisions of this Convention and other rules of international law in so far as they are not incompatible with this Part.

Article 59
Basis for the resolution of conflicts
regarding the attribution of rights and jurisdiction
in the exclusive economic zone

In cases where this Convention does not attribute rights or jurisdiction to the coastal State or to other States within the exclusive economic zone, and a conflict arises between the interests of the coastal State and any other State or States, the conflict should be resolved on the basis of equity and in the light of all the relevant circumstances, taking into account the respective importance of the interests involved to the parties as well as to the international community as a whole.

Article 60
Artificial islands, installations and structures
in the exclusive economic zone

1.   In the exclusive economic zone, the coastal State shall have the exclusive right to construct and to authorize and regulate the construction, operation and use of:

(a)   artificial islands;

(b)   installations and structures for the purposes provided for in article 56 and other economic purposes;

(c)   installations and structures which may interfere with the exercise of the rights of the coastal State in the zone.

2.   The coastal State shall have exclusive jurisdiction over such artificial islands, installations and structures, including jurisdiction with regard to customs, fiscal, health, safety and immigration laws and regulations.

3.   Due notice must be given of the construction of such artificial islands, installations or structures, and permanent means for giving warning of their presence must be maintained. Any installations or structures which are abandoned or disused shall be removed to ensure safety of navigation, taking into account any generally accepted international standards established in this regard by the competent international organization. Such removal shall also have due regard to fishing, the protection of the marine environment and the rights and duties of other States. Appropriate publicity shall be given to the depth, position and dimensions of any installations or structures not entirely removed.

4.   The coastal State may, where necessary, establish reasonable safety zones around such artificial islands, installations and structures in which it may take appropriate measures to ensure the safety both of navigation and of the artificial islands, installations and structures.

5.   The breadth of the safety zones shall be determined by the coastal State, taking into account applicable international standards. Such zones shall be designed to ensure that they are reasonably related to the nature and function of the artificial islands, installations or structures, and shall not exceed a distance of 500 metres around them, measured from each point of their outer edge, except as authorized by generally accepted international standards or as recommended by the competent international organization. Due notice shall be given of the extent of safety zones.

6.   All ships must respect these safety zones and shall comply with generally accepted international standards regarding navigation in the vicinity of artificial islands, installations, structures and safety zones.

7.   Artificial islands, installations and structures and the safety zones around them may not be established where interference may be caused to the use of recognized sea lanes essential to international navigation.

8. Artificial islands, installations and structures do not possess the status of islands. They have no territorial sea of their own, and their presence does not affect the delimitation of the territorial sea, the exclusive economic zone or the continental shelf.

Article 61
Conservation of the living resources

1. The coastal State shall determine the allowable catch of the living resources in its exclusive economic zone.

2. The coastal State, taking into account the best scientific evidence available to it, shall ensure through proper conservation and management measures that the maintenance of the living resources in the exclusive economic zone is not endangered by over-exploitation. As appropriate, the coastal State and competent international organizations, whether subregional, regional or global, shall co-operate to this end.

3. Such measures shall also be designed to maintain or restore populations of harvested species at levels which can produce the maximum sustainable yield, as qualified by relevant environmental and economic factors, including the economic needs of coastal fishing communities and the special requirements of developing States, and taking into account fishing patterns, the interdependence of stocks and any generally recommended international minimum standards, whether subregional, regional or global.

4. In taking such measures the coastal State shall take into consideration the effects on species associated with or dependent upon harvested species with a view to maintaining or restoring populations of such associated or dependent species above levels at which their reproduction may become seriously threatened.

5. Available scientific information, catch and fishing effort statistics, and other data relevant to the conservation of fish stocks shall be contributed and exchanged on a regular basis through competent international organizations, whether subregional, regional or global, where appropriate and with participation by all States concerned, including States whose nationals are allowed to fish in the exclusive economic zone.

Article 62
Utilization of the living resources

1. The coastal State shall promote the objective of optimum utilization of the living resources in the exclusive economic zone without prejudice to article 61.

2. The coastal State shall determine its capacity to harvest the living resources of the exclusive economic zone. Where the coastal State does not have the capacity to harvest the entire allowable catch, it shall, through agreements or other arrangements and pursuant to the terms, conditions, laws and regulations referred to in paragraph 4, give other States access to the surplus of the allowable catch, having particular regard to the provisions of articles 69 and 70, especially in relation to the developing States mentioned therein.

3.   In giving access to other States to its exclusive economic zone under this article, the coastal State shall take into account all relevant factors, including, *inter alia*, the significance of the living resources of the area to the economy of the coastal State concerned and its other national interests, the provisions of articles 69 and 70, the requirements of developing States in the subregion or region in harvesting part of the surplus and the need to minimize economic dislocation in States whose nationals have habitually fished in the zone or which have made substantial efforts in research and identification of stocks.

4.   Nationals of other States fishing in the exclusive economic zone shall comply with the conservation measures and with the other terms and conditions established in the laws and regulations of the coastal State. These laws and regulations shall be consistent with this Convention and may relate, *inter alia*, to the following:

(a) licensing of fishermen, fishing vessels and equipment, including payment of fees and other forms of remuneration, which, in the case of developing coastal States, may consist of adequate compensation in the field of financing, equipment and technology relating to the fishing industry;

(b) determining the species which may be caught, and fixing quotas of catch, whether in relation to particular stocks or groups of stocks or catch per vessel over a period of time or to the catch by nationals of any State during a specified period;

(c) regulating seasons and areas of fishing, the types, sizes and amount of gear, and the types, sizes and number of fishing vessels that may be used;

(d) fixing the age and size of fish and other species that may be caught;

(e) specifying information required of fishing vessels, including catch and effort statistics and vessel position reports;

(f) requiring, under the authorization and control of the coastal State, the conduct of specified fisheries research programmes and regulating the conduct of such research, including the sampling of catches, disposition of samples and reporting of associated scientific data;

(g) the placing of observers or trainees on board such vessels by the coastal State;

(h) the landing of all or any part of the catch by such vessels in the ports of the coastal State;

(i) terms and conditions relating to joint ventures or other cooperative arrangements;

(j) requirements for the training of personnel and the transfer of fisheries technology, including enhancement of the coastal State's capability of undertaking fisheries research;

(k) enforcement procedures.

5.   Coastal States shall give due notice of conservation and management laws and regulations.

Article 63
Stocks occurring within the exclusive economic zones of
two or more coastal States or both within the exclusive economic zone
and in an area beyond and adjacent to it

1.   Where the same stock or stocks of associated species occur within the exclusive economic zones of two or more coastal States, these States shall seek, either directly or through appropriate subregional or regional organizations, to agree upon the measures necessary to co-ordinate and ensure the conservation and development of such stocks without prejudice to the other provisions of this Part.

2.   Where the same stock or stocks of associated species occur both within the exclusive economic zone and in an area beyond and adjacent to the zone, the coastal State and the States fishing for such stocks in the adjacent area shall seek, either directly or through appropriate subregional or regional organizations, to agree upon the measures necessary for the conservation of these stocks in the adjacent area.

Article 64
Highly migratory species

1.   The coastal State and other States whose nationals fish in the region for the highly migratory species listed in Annex I shall cooperate directly or through appropriate international organizations with a view to ensuring conservation and promoting the objective of optimum utilization of such species throughout the region, both within and beyond the exclusive economic zone. In regions for which no appropriate international organization exists, the coastal State and other States whose nationals harvest these species in the region shall co-operate to establish such an organization and participate in its work.

2.   The provisions of paragraph 1 apply in addition to the other provisions of this Part.

Article 65
Marine mammals

Nothing in this Part restricts the right of a coastal State or the competence of an international organization, as appropriate, to prohibit, limit or regulate the exploitation of marine mammals more strictly than provided for in this Part. States shall cooperate with a view to the conservation of marine mammals and in the case of cetaceans shall in particular work through the appropriate international organizations for their conservation, management and study.

Article 66
Anadromous stocks

1.   States in whose rivers anadromous stocks originate shall have the primary interest in and responsibility for such stocks.

2.   The State of origin of anadromous stocks shall ensure their conservation

by the establishment of appropriate regulatory measures for fishing in all waters landward of the outer limits of its exclusive economic zone and for fishing provided for in paragraph 3(b). The State of origin may, after consultations with the other States referred to in paragraphs 3 and 4 fishing these stocks, establish total allowable catches for stocks originating in its rivers.

    3.   (a) Fisheries for anadromous stocks shall be conducted only in waters landward of the outer limits of exclusive economic zones, except in cases where this provision would result in economic dislocation for a State other than the State of origin. With respect to such fishing beyond the outer limits of the exclusive economic zone, States concerned shall maintain consultations with a view to achieving agreement on terms and conditions of such fishing giving due regard to the conservation requirements and the needs of the State of origin in respect of these stocks.

        (b) The State of origin shall cooperate in minimizing economic dislocation in such other States fishing these stocks, taking into account the normal catch and the mode of operations of such States, and all the areas in which such fishing has occurred.

        (c) States referred to in subparagraph (b), participating by agreement with the State of origin in measures to renew anadromous stocks, particularly by expenditures for that purpose, shall be given special consideration by the State of origin in the harvesting of stocks originating in its rivers.

        (d) Enforcement of regulations regarding anadromous stocks beyond the exclusive economic zone shall be by agreement between the State of origin and the other States concerned.

    4.   In cases where anadromous stocks migrate into or through the waters landward of the outer limits of the exclusive economic zone of a State other than the State of origin, such State shall co-operate with the State of origin with regard to the conservation and management of such stocks.

    5.   The State of origin of anadromous stocks and other States fishing these stocks shall make arrangements for the implementation of the provisions of this article, where appropriate, through regional organizations.

Article 67
Catadromous species

    1.   A coastal State in whose waters catadromous species spend the greater part of their life cycle shall have responsibility for the management of these species and shall ensure the ingress and egress of migrating fish.

    2.   Harvesting of catadromous species shall be conducted only in waters landward of the outer limits of exclusive economic zones. When conducted in exclusive economic zones, harvesting shall be subject to this article and the other provisions of this Convention concerning fishing in these zones.

    3.   In cases where catadromous fish migrate through the exclusive economic zone of another State, whether as juvenile or maturing fish, the management, including harvesting, of such fish shall be regulated by agreement between the

State mentioned in paragraph 1 and the other State concerned. Such agreement shall ensure the rational management of the species and take into account the responsibilities of the State mentioned in paragraph 1 for the maintenance of these species.

Article 68
Sedentary species

This Part does not apply to sedentary species as defined in article 77, paragraph 4.

Article 69
Right of land-locked States

1.   Land-locked States shall have the right to participate, on an equitable basis, in the exploitation of an appropriate part of the surplus of the living resources of the exclusive economic zones of coastal States of the same subregion or region, taking into account the relevant economic and geographical circumstances of all the States concerned and in conformity with the provisions of this article and of articles 61 and 62.

2.   The terms and modalities of such participation shall be established by the States concerned through bilateral, subregional or regional agreements taking into account, *inter alia*:

(a)   the need to avoid effects detrimental to fishing communities or fishing industries of the coastal State;

(b)   the extent to which the land-locked State, in accordance with the provisions of this article, is participating or is entitled to participate under existing bilateral, subregional or regional agreements in the exploitation of living resources of the exclusive economic zones of other coastal States;

(c)   the extent to which other land-locked States and geographically disadvantaged States are participating in the exploitation of the living resources of the exclusive economic zone of the coastal State and the consequent need to avoid a particular burden for any single coastal State or a part of it;

(d)   the nutritional needs of the populations of the respective States.

3.   When the harvesting capacity of a coastal State approaches a point which would enable it to harvest the entire allowable catch of the living resources in its exclusive economic zone, the coastal State and other States concerned shall cooperate in the establishment of equitable arrangements on a bilateral, subregional or regional basis to allow for participation of developing land-locked States of the same subregion or region in the exploitation of the living resources of the exclusive economic zones of coastal States of the subregion or region, as may be appropriate in the circumstances and on terms satisfactory to all parties. In the implementation of this provision the factors mentioned in paragraph 2 shall also be taken into account.

4.   Developed land-locked States shall, under the provisions of this article, be entitled to participate in the exploitation of living resources only in the exclusive economic zones of developed coastal States of the same subregion or region having regard to the extent to which the coastal State, in giving access to other States to the living resources of its exclusive economic zone, has taken into account the need to minimize detrimental effects on fishing communities and economic dislocation in States whose nationals have habitually fished in the zone.

5.   The above provisions are without prejudice to arrangements agreed upon in subregions or regions where the coastal States may grant to land-locked States of the same subregion or region equal or preferential rights for the exploitation of the living resources in the exclusive economic zones.

Article 70
Right of geographically disadvantaged States

1.   Geographically disadvantaged States shall have the right to participate, on an equitable basis, in the exploitation of an appropriate part of the surplus of the living resources of the exclusive economic zones of coastal States of the same subregion or region, taking into account the relevant economic and geographical circumstances of all the States concerned and in conformity with the provisions of this article and of articles 61 and 62.

2.   For the purposes of this Part, "geographically disadvantaged States" means coastal States, including States bordering enclosed or semi-enclosed seas, whose geographical situation makes them dependent upon the exploitation of the living resources of the exclusive economic zones of other States in the subregion or region for adequate supplies of fish for the nutritional purposes of their populations or parts thereof, and coastal States which can claim no exclusive economic zones of their own.

3.   The terms and modalities of such participation shall be established by the States concerned through bilateral, subregional or regional agreements taking into account, *inter alia*:

(a)   the need to avoid effects detrimental to fishing communities or fishing industries of the coastal State;

(b)   the extent to which the geographically disadvantaged State, in accordance with the provisions of this article, is participating or is entitled to participate under existing bilateral, subregional or regional agreements in the exploitation of living resources of the exclusive economic zones of other coastal States;

(c)   the extent to which other geographically disadvantaged States and land-locked States are participating in the exploitation of the living resources of the exclusive economic zone of the coastal State and the consequent need to avoid a particular burden for any single coastal State or a part of it;

(d)   the nutritional needs of the populations of the respective States.

4.   When the harvesting capacity of a coastal State approaches a point which would enable it to harvest the entire allowable catch of the living resources in its

exclusive economic zone, the coastal State and other States concerned shall co-operate in the establishment of equitable arrangements on a bilateral, subregional or regional basis to allow for participation of developing geographically disadvantaged States of the same subregion or region in the exploitation of the living resources of the exclusive economic zones of coastal States of the subregion or region, as may be appropriate in the circumstances and on terms satisfactory to all parties. In the implementation of this provision the factors mentioned in paragraph 3 shall also be taken into account.

5.   Developed geographically disadvantaged States shall, under the provisions of this article, be entitled to participate in the exploitation of living resources only in the exclusive economic zones of developed coastal States of the same subregion or region having regard to the extent to which the coastal State, in giving access to other States to the living resources of its exclusive economic zone, has taken into account the need to minimize detrimental effects on fishing communities and economic dislocation in States whose nationals have habitually fished in the zone.

6.   The above provisions are without prejudice to arrangements agreed upon in subregions or regions where the coastal States may grant to geographically disadvantaged States of the same subregion or region equal or preferential rights for the exploitation of the living resources in the exclusive economic zones.

Article 71
Non-applicability of articles 69 and 70

The provisions of articles 69 and 70 do not apply in the case of a coastal State whose economy is overwhelmingly dependent on the exploitation of the living resources of its exclusive economic zone.

Article 72
Restrictions on transfer of rights

1.   Rights provided under articles 69 and 70 to exploit living resources shall not be directly or indirectly transferred to third States or their nationals by lease or licence, by establishing joint ventures or in any other manner which has the effect of such transfer unless otherwise agreed by the States concerned.

2.   The foregoing provision does not preclude the States concerned from obtaining technical or financial assistance from third States or international organizations in order to facilitate the exercise of the rights pursuant to articles 69 and 70, provided that it does not have the effect referred to in paragraph 1.

Article 73
Enforcement of laws and regulations of the coastal State

1.   The coastal State may, in the exercise of its sovereign rights to explore, exploit, conserve and manage the living resources in the exclusive economic zone, take such measures, including boarding, inspection, arrest and judicial proceedings, as may be necessary to ensure compliance with the laws and regulations adopted by it in conformity with this Convention.

2.   Arrested vessels and their crews shall be promptly released upon the posting of reasonable bond or other security.

3.   Coastal State penalties for violations of fisheries laws and regulations in the exclusive economic zone may not include imprisonment, in the absence of agreements to the contrary by the States concerned, or any other form of corporal punishment.

4.   In cases of arrest or detention of foreign vessels the coastal State shall promptly notify the flag State, through appropriate channels, of the action taken and of any penalties subsequently imposed.

Article 74
Delimitation of the exclusive economic zone
between States with opposite or adjacent coasts

1.   The delimitation of the exclusive economic zone between States with opposite or adjacent coasts shall be effected by agreement on the basis of international law, as referred to in Article 38 of the Statute of the International Court of Justice, in order to achieve an equitable solution.

2.   If no agreement can be reached within a reasonable period of time, the States concerned shall resort to the procedures provided for in Part XV.

3.   Pending agreement as provided for in paragraph 1, the States concerned, in a spirit of understanding and co-operation, shall make every effort to enter into provisional arrangements of a practical nature and, during this transitional period, not to jeopardize or hamper the reaching of the final agreement. Such arrangements shall be without prejudice to the final delimitation.

4.   Where there is an agreement in force between the States concerned, questions relating to the delimitation of the exclusive economic zone shall be determined in accordance with the provisions of that agreement.

Article 75
Charts and lists of geographical co-ordinates

1.   Subject to this Part, the outer limit lines of the exclusive economic zone and the lines of delimitation drawn in accordance with article 74 shall be shown on charts of a scale or scales adequate for ascertaining their position. Where appropriate, lists of geographical co-ordinates of points, specifying the geodetic datum, may be substituted for such outer limit lines or lines of delimitation.

2.   The coastal State shall give due publicity to such charts or lists of geographical coordinates and shall deposit a copy of each such chart or list with the Secretary-General of the United Nations.

PART VI
CONTINENTAL SHELF

Article 76
Definition of the continental shelf

1.   The continental shelf of a coastal State comprises the seabed and subsoil of the submarine areas that extend beyond its territorial sea throughout the natural prolongation of its land territory to the outer edge of the continental margin, or to a distance of 200 nautical miles from the baselines from which the breadth of the territorial sea is measured where the outer edge of the continental margin does not extend up to that distance.

2.   The continental shelf of a coastal State shall not extend beyond the limits provided for in paragraphs 4 to 6.

3.   The continental margin comprises the submerged prolongation of the land mass of the coastal State, and consists of the seabed and subsoil of the shelf, the slope and the rise. It does not include the deep ocean floor with its oceanic ridges or the subsoil thereof.

4.   (a) For the purposes of this Convention, the coastal State shall establish the outer edge of the continental margin wherever the margin extends beyond 200 nautical miles from the baselines from which the breadth of the territorial sea is measured, by either:

   (i)   a line delineated in accordance with paragraph 7 by reference to the outermost fixed points at each of which the thickness of sedimentary rocks is at least 1 per cent of the shortest distance from such point to the foot of the continental slope; or

   (ii) a line delineated in accordance with paragraph 7 by reference to fixed points not more than 60 nautical miles from the foot of the continental slope.

(b) In the absence of evidence to the contrary, the foot of the continental slope shall be determined as the point of maximum change in the gradient at its base.

5.   The fixed points comprising the line of the outer limits of the continental shelf on the seabed, drawn in accordance with paragraph 4 (a)(i) and (ii), either shall not exceed 350 nautical miles from the baselines from which the breadth of the territorial sea is measured or shall not exceed 100 nautical miles from the 2,500 metre isobath, which is a line connecting the depth of 2,500 metres.

6.   Notwithstanding the provisions of paragraph 5, on submarine ridges, the outer limit of the continental shelf shall not exceed 350 nautical miles from the baselines from which the breadth of the territorial sea is measured. This paragraph does not apply to submarine elevations that are natural components of the continental margin, such as its plateaux, rises, caps, banks and spurs.

7.   The coastal State shall delineate the outer limits of its continental shelf, where that shelf extends beyond 200 nautical miles from the baselines from which the breadth of the territorial sea is measured, by straight lines not exceeding 60

nautical miles in length, connecting fixed points, defined by co-ordinates of latitude and longitude.

8.   Information on the limits of the continental shelf beyond 200 nautical miles from the baselines from which the breadth of the territorial sea is measured shall be submitted by the coastal State to the Commission on the Limits of the Continental Shelf set up under Annex II on the basis of equitable geographical representation. The Commission shall make recommendations to coastal States on matters related to the establishment of the outer limits of their continental shelf. The limits of the shelf established by a coastal State on the basis of these recommendations shall be final and binding.

9.   The coastal State shall deposit with the Secretary-General of the United Nations charts and relevant information, including geodetic data, permanently describing the outer limits of its continental shelf. The Secretary-General shall give due publicity thereto.

10.   The provisions of this article are without prejudice to the question of delimitation of the continental shelf between States with opposite or adjacent coasts.

Article 77
Rights of the coastal State over the continental shelf

1.   The coastal State exercises over the continental shelf sovereign rights for the purpose of exploring it and exploiting its natural resources.

2.   The rights referred to in paragraph 1 are exclusive in the sense that if the coastal State does not explore the continental shelf or exploit its natural resources, no one may undertake these activities without the express consent of the coastal State.

3.   The rights of the coastal State over the continental shelf do not depend on occupation, effective or notional, or on any express proclamation.

4.   The natural resources referred to in this Part consist of the mineral and other non-living resources of the seabed and subsoil together with living organisms belonging to sedentary species, that is to say, organisms which, at the harvestable stage, either are immobile on or under the seabed or are unable to move except in constant physical contact with the seabed or the subsoil.

Article 78
Legal status of the superjacent waters and air space
and the rights and freedoms of other States

1.   The rights of the coastal State over the continental shelf do not affect the legal status of the superjacent waters or of the air space above those waters.

2.   The exercise of the rights of the coastal State over the continental shelf must not infringe or result in any unjustifiable interference with navigation and other rights and freedoms of other States as provided for in this Convention.

Article 79
Submarine cables and pipelines on the continental shelf

1.   All States are entitled to lay submarine cables and pipelines on the continental shelf, in accordance with the provisions of this article.

2.   Subject to its right to take reasonable measures for the exploration of the continental shelf, the exploitation of its natural resources and the prevention, reduction and control of pollution from pipelines, the coastal State may not impede the laying or maintenance of such cables or pipelines.

3.   The delineation of the course for the laying of such pipelines on the continental shelf is subject to the consent of the coastal State.

4.   Nothing in this Part affects the right of the coastal State to establish conditions for cables or pipelines entering its territory or territorial sea, or its jurisdiction over cables and pipelines constructed or used in connection with the exploration of its continental shelf or exploitation of its resources or the operations of artificial islands, installations and structures under its jurisdiction.

5.   When laying submarine cables or pipelines, States shall have due regard to cables or pipelines already in position. In particular, possibilities of repairing existing cables or pipelines shall not be prejudiced.

Article 80
Artificial islands, installations and structures on the continental shelf

Article 60 applies *mutatis mutandis* to artificial islands, installations and structures on the continental shelf.

Article 81
Drilling on the continental shelf

The coastal State shall have the exclusive right to authorize and regulate drilling on the continental shelf for all purposes.

Article 82
Payments and contributions with respect to the
exploitation of the continental shelf beyond 200 nautical miles

1.   The coastal State shall make payments or contributions in kind in respect of the exploitation of the non-living resources of the continental shelf beyond 200 nautical miles from the baselines from which the breadth of the territorial sea is measured.

2.   The payments and contributions shall be made annually with respect to all production at a site after the first five years of production at that site. For the sixth year, the rate of payment or contribution shall be 1 per cent of the value or volume of production at the site. The rate shall increase by 1 per cent for each subsequent year until the twelfth year and shall remain at 7 per cent thereafter. Production does not include resources used in connection with exploitation.

3.   A developing State which is a net importer of a mineral resource produced from its continental shelf is exempt from making such payments or
contributions in respect of that mineral resource.

4.   The payments or contributions shall be made through the Authority,
which shall distribute them to States Parties to this Convention, on the basis of
equitable sharing criteria, taking into account the interests and needs of developing States, particularly the least developed and the land-locked among them.

Article 83
Delimitation of the continental shelf
between States with opposite or adjacent coasts

1.   The delimitation of the continental shelf between States with opposite
or adjacent coasts shall be effected by agreement on the basis of international
law, as referred to in Article 38 of the Statute of the International Court of Justice, in order to achieve an equitable solution.

2.   If no agreement can be reached within a reasonable period of time, the
States concerned shall resort to the procedures provided for in Part XV.

3.   Pending agreement as provided for in paragraph 1, the States concerned,
in a spirit of understanding and co-operation, shall make every effort to enter
into provisional arrangements of a practical nature and, during this transitional
period, not to jeopardize or hamper the reaching of the final agreement. Such
arrangements shall be without prejudice to the final delimitation.

4.   Where there is an agreement in force between the States concerned,
questions relating to the delimitation of the continental shelf shall be determined in accordance with the provisions of that agreement.

Article 84
Charts and lists of geographical co-ordinates

1.   Subject to this Part, the outer limit lines of the continental shelf and
the lines of delimitation drawn in accordance with article 83 shall be shown on
charts of a scale or scales adequate for ascertaining their position. Where appropriate, lists of geographical co-ordinates of points, specifying the geodetic datum,
may be substituted for such outer limit lines or lines of delimitation.

2.   The coastal State shall give due publicity to such charts or lists of
geographical co-ordinates and shall deposit a copy of each such chart or list
with the Secretary-General of the United Nations and, in the case of those showing
the outer limit lines of the continental shelf, with the Secretary-General of the
Authority.

Article 85
Tunnelling

This Part does not prejudice the right of the coastal State to exploit the
subsoil by means of tunnelling, irrespective of the depth of water above the
subsoil.

PART VII
HIGH SEAS

SECTION 1. GENERAL PROVISIONS

Article 86
Application of the provisions of this Part

The provisions of this Part apply to all parts of the sea that are not included in the exclusive economic zone, in the territorial sea or in the internal waters of a State, or in the archipelagic waters of an archipelagic State. This article does not entail any abridgement of the freedoms enjoyed by all States in the exclusive economic zone in accordance with article 58.

Article 87
Freedom of the high seas

1. The high seas are open to all States, whether coastal or land-locked. Freedom of the high seas is exercised under the conditions laid down by this Convention and by other rules of international law. It comprises, *inter alia*, both for coastal and land-locked States:
    (a) freedom of navigation;
    (b) freedom of overflight;
    (c) freedom to lay submarine cables and pipelines, subject to Part VI;
    (d) freedom to construct artificial islands and other installations permitted under international law, subject to Part VI;
    (e) freedom of fishing, subject to the conditions laid down in section 2;
    (f) freedom of scientific research, subject to Parts VI and XIII.
2. These freedoms shall be exercised by all States with due regard for the interests of other States in their exercise of the freedom of the high seas, and also with due regard for the rights under this Convention with respect to activities in the Area.

Article 88
Reservation of the high seas for peaceful purposes

The high seas shall be reserved for peaceful purposes.

Article 89
Invalidity of claims of sovereignty over the high seas

No State may validly purport to subject any part of the high seas to its sovereignty.

Article 90
Right of navigation

Every State, whether coastal or land-locked, has the right to sail ships flying its flag on the high seas.

Article 91
Nationality of ships

1.   Every State shall fix the conditions for the grant of its nationality to ships, for the registration of ships in its territory, and for the right to fly its flag. Ships have the nationality of the State whose flag they are entitled to fly. There must exist a genuine link between the State and the ship.

2.   Every State shall issue to ships to which it has granted the right to fly its flag documents to that effect.

Article 92
Status of ships

1.   Ships shall sail under the flag of one State only and, save in exceptional cases expressly provided for in international treaties or in this Convention, shall be subject to its exclusive jurisdiction on the high seas. A ship may not change its flag during a voyage or while in a port of call, save in the case of a real transfer of ownership or change of registry.

2.   A ship which sails under the flags of two or more States, using them according to convenience, may not claim any of the nationalities in question with respect to any other State, and may be assimilated to a ship without nationality.

Article 93
Ships flying the flag of the United Nations, its specialized agencies and the International Atomic Energy Agency

The preceding articles do not prejudice the question of ships employed on the official service of the United Nations, its specialized agencies or the International Atomic Energy Agency, flying the flag of the organization.

Article 94
Duties of the flag State

1.   Every State shall effectively exercise its jurisdiction and control in administrative, technical and social matters over ships flying its flag.

2.   In particular every State shall:
(a)   maintain a register of ships containing the names and particulars of ships flying its flag, except those which are excluded from generally accepted international regulations on account of their small size; and
(b)   assume jurisdiction under its internal law over each ship flying its flag and its master, officers and crew in respect of administrative, technical and social matters concerning the ship.

3.   Every State shall take such measures for ships flying its flag as are necessary to ensure safety at sea with regard, *inter alia*, to:
(a)   the construction, equipment and seaworthiness of ships;
(b)   the manning of ships, labour conditions and the training of crews, taking into account the applicable international instruments;

(c) the use of signals, the maintenance of communications and the prevention of collisions.

4. Such measures shall include those necessary to ensure:

(a) that each ship, before registration and thereafter at appropriate intervals, is surveyed by a qualified surveyor of ships, and has on board such charts, nautical publications and navigational equipment and instruments as are appropriate for the safe navigation of the ship;

(b) that each ship is in the charge of a master and officers who possess appropriate qualifications, in particular in seamanship, navigation, communications and marine engineering, and that the crew is appropriate in qualification and numbers for the type, size, machinery and equipment of the ship;

(c) that the master, officers and, to the extent appropriate, the crew are fully conversant with and required to observe the applicable international regulations concerning the safety of life at sea, the prevention of collisions, the prevention, reduction and control of marine pollution, and the maintenance of communications by radio.

5. In taking the measures called for in paragraphs 3 and 4 each State is required to conform to generally accepted international regulations, procedures and practices and to take any steps which may be necessary to secure their observance.

6. A State which has clear grounds to believe that proper jurisdiction and control with respect to a ship have not been exercised may report the facts to the flag State. Upon receiving such a report, the flag State shall investigate the matter and, if appropriate, take any action necessary to remedy the situation.

7. Each State shall cause an inquiry to be held by or before a suitably qualified person or persons into every marine casualty or incident of navigation on the high seas involving a ship flying its flag and causing loss of life or serious injury to nationals of another State or serious damage to ships or installations of another State or to the marine environment. The flag State and the other State shall cooperate in the conduct of any inquiry held by that other State into any such marine casualty or incident of navigation.

Article 95
Immunity of warships on the high seas

Warships on the high seas have complete immunity from the jurisdiction of any State other than the flag State.

Article 96
Immunity of ships used only on government non-commercial service

Ships owned or operated by a State and used only on government non-commercial service shall, on the high seas, have complete immunity from the jurisdiction of any State other than the flag State.

Article 97
Penal jurisdiction in matters of collision
or any other incident of navigation

1.   In the event of a collision or any other incident of navigation concerning a ship on the high seas, involving the penal or disciplinary responsibility of the master or of any other person in the service of the ship, no penal or disciplinary proceedings may be instituted against such person except before the judicial or administrative authorities either of the flag State or of the State of which such person is a national.

2.   In disciplinary matters, the State which has issued a master's certificate or a certificate of competence or licence shall alone be competent, after due legal process, to pronounce the withdrawal of such certificates, even if the holder is not a national of the State which issued them.

3.   No arrest or detention of the ship, even as a measure of investigation, shall be ordered by any authorities other than those of the flag State.

Article 98
Duty to render assistance

1.   Every State shall require the master of a ship flying its flag, in so far as he can do so without serious danger to the ship, the crew or the passengers:
   (a) to render assistance to any person found at sea in danger of being lost;
   (b) to proceed with all possible speed to the rescue of persons in distress, if informed of their need of assistance, in so far as such action may reasonably be expected of him;
   (c) after a collision, to render assistance to the other ship, its crew and its passengers and, where possible, to inform the other ship of the name of his own ship, its port of registry and the nearest port at which it will call.

2.   Every coastal State shall promote the establishment, operation and maintenance of an adequate and effective search and rescue service regarding safety on and over the sea and, where circumstances so require, by way of mutual regional arrangements co-operate with neighbouring States for this purpose.

Article 99
Prohibition of the transport of slaves

Every State shall take effective measures to prevent and punish the transport of slaves in ships authorized to fly its flag and to prevent the unlawful use of its flag for that purpose. Any slave taking refuge on board any ship, whatever its flag, shall *ipso facto* be free.

Article 100
Duty to co-operate in the repression of piracy

All States shall co-operate to the fullest possible extent in the repression of piracy on the high seas or in any other place outside the jurisdiction of any State.

Article 101
Definition of piracy

Piracy consists of any of the following acts:
(a) any illegal acts of violence or detention, or any act of depredation, committed for private ends by the crew or the passengers of a private ship or a private aircraft, and directed:
  (i) on the high seas, against another ship or aircraft, or against persons or property on board such ship or aircraft;
  (ii) against a ship, aircraft, persons or property in a place outside the jurisdiction of any State;
(b) any act of voluntary participation in the operation of a ship or of an aircraft with knowledge of facts making it a pirate ship or aircraft;
(c) any act of inciting or of intentionally facilitating an act described in subparagraph (a) or (b).

Article 102
Piracy by a warship, government ship or government aircraft whose crew has mutinied

The acts of piracy, as defined in article 101, committed by a warship, government ship or government aircraft whose crew has mutinied and taken control of the ship or aircraft are assimilated to acts committed by a private ship or aircraft.

Article 103
Definition of a pirate ship or aircraft

A ship or aircraft is considered a pirate ship or aircraft if it is intended by the persons in dominant control to be used for the purpose of committing one of the acts referred to in article 101. The same applies if the ship or aircraft has been used to commit any such act, so long as it remains under the control of the persons guilty of that act.

Article 104
Retention or loss of the nationality of a pirate ship or aircraft

A ship or aircraft may retain its nationality although it has become a pirate ship or aircraft. The retention or loss of nationality is determined by the law of the State from which such nationality was derived.

Article 105
Seizure of a pirate ship or aircraft

On the high seas, or in any other place outside the jurisdiction of any State, every State may seize a pirate ship or aircraft, or a ship or aircraft taken by piracy and under the control of pirates, and arrest the persons and seize the property on board. The courts of the State which carried out the seizure may decide upon the penalties to be imposed, and may also determine the action to be taken with regard to the ships, aircraft or property, subject to the rights of third parties acting in good faith.

Article 106
Liability for seizure without adequate grounds

Where the seizure of a ship or aircraft on suspicion of piracy has been effected without adequate grounds, the State making the seizure shall be liable to the State the nationality of which is possessed by the ship or aircraft for any loss or damage caused by the seizure.

Article 107
Ships and aircraft which are entitled to seize on account of piracy

A seizure on account of piracy may be carried out only by warships or military aircraft, or other ships or aircraft clearly marked and identifiable as being on government service and authorized to that effect.

Article 108
Illicit traffic in narcotic drugs or psychotropic substances

1.   All States shall co-operate in the suppression of illicit traffic in narcotic drugs and psychotropic substances engaged in by ships on the high seas contrary to international conventions.

2.   Any State which has reasonable grounds for believing that a ship flying its flag is engaged in illicit traffic in narcotic drugs or psychotropic substances may request the co-operation of other States to suppress such traffic.

Article 109
Unauthorized broadcasting from the high seas

1.   All States shall co-operate in the suppression of unauthorized broadcasting from the high seas.

2.   For the purposes of this Convention, "unauthorized broadcasting" means the transmission of sound radio or television broadcasts from a ship or installation on the high seas intended for reception by the general public contrary to international regulations, but excluding the transmission of distress calls.

3.   Any person engaged in unauthorized broadcasting may be prosecuted before the court of:

(a)   the flag State of the ship;

(b)   the State of registry of the installation;

(c)   the State of which the person is a national;

(d)   any State where the transmissions can be received; or

(e)   any State where authorized radio communication is suffering interference.

4.   On the high seas, a State having jurisdiction in accordance with paragraph 3 may, in conformity with article 110, arrest any person or ship engaged in unauthorized broadcasting and seize the broadcasting apparatus.

Article 110
Right of visit

1.   Except where acts of interference derive from powers conferred by treaty, a warship which encounters on the high seas a foreign ship, other than a ship entitled to complete immunity in accordance with articles 95 and 96, is not justified in boarding it unless there is reasonable ground for suspecting that:

(a)   the ship is engaged in piracy;
(b)   the ship is engaged in the slave trade;
(c)   the ship is engaged in unauthorized broadcasting and the flag State of the warship has jurisdiction under article 109;
(d)   the ship is without nationality; or
(e)   though flying a foreign flag or refusing to show its flag, the ship is, in reality, of the same nationality as the warship.

2.   In the cases provided for in paragraph 1, the warship may proceed to verify the ship's right to fly its flag. To this end, it may send a boat under the command of an officer to the suspected ship. If suspicion remains after the documents have been checked, it may proceed to a further examination on board the ship, which must be carried out with all possible consideration.

3.   If the suspicions prove to be unfounded, and provided that the ship boarded has not committed any act justifying them, it shall be compensated for any loss or damage that may have been sustained.

4.   These provisions apply *mutatis mutandis* to military aircraft.

5.   These provisions also apply to any other duly authorized ships or aircraft clearly marked and identifiable as being on government service.

Article 111
Right of hot pursuit

1.   The hot pursuit of a foreign ship may be undertaken when the competent authorities of the coastal State have good reason to believe that the ship has violated the laws and regulations of that State. Such pursuit must be commenced when the foreign ship or one of its boats is within the internal waters, the archipelagic waters, the territorial sea or the contiguous zone of the pursuing State, and may only be continued outside the territorial sea or the contiguous zone if the pursuit has not been interrupted. It is not necessary that, at the time when the foreign ship within the territorial sea or the contiguous zone receives the order to stop, the ship giving the order should likewise be within the territorial sea or the contiguous zone. If the foreign ship is within a contiguous zone, as defined in article 33, the pursuit may only be undertaken if there has been a violation of the rights for the protection of which the zone was established.

2.   The right of hot pursuit shall apply *mutatis mutandis* to violations in the exclusive economic zone or on the continental shelf, including safety zones around continental shelf installations, of the laws and regulations of the coastal State applicable in accordance with this Convention to the exclusive economic zone or the continental shelf, including such safety zones.

3.   The right of hot pursuit ceases as soon as the ship pursued enters the territorial sea of its own State or of a third State.

4.   Hot pursuit is not deemed to have begun unless the pursuing ship has satisfied itself by such practicable means as may be available that the ship pursued or one of its boats or other craft working as a team and using the ship pursued as a mother ship is within the limits of the territorial sea, or, as the case may be, within the contiguous zone or the exclusive economic zone or above the continental shelf. The pursuit may only be commenced after a visual or auditory signal to stop has been given at a distance which enables it to be seen or heard by the foreign ship.

5.   The right of hot pursuit may be exercised only by warships or military aircraft, or other ships or aircraft clearly marked and identifiable as being on government service and authorized to that effect.

6.   Where hot pursuit is effected by an aircraft:

(a)   the provisions of paragraphs 1 to 4 shall apply *mutatis mutandis;*

(b)   the aircraft giving the order to stop must itself actively pursue the ship until a ship or another aircraft of the coastal State, summoned by the aircraft, arrives to take over the pursuit, unless the aircraft is itself able to arrest the ship. It does not suffice to justify an arrest outside the territorial sea that the ship was merely sighted by the aircraft as an offender or suspected offender, if it was not both ordered to stop and pursued by the aircraft itself or other aircraft or ships which continue the pursuit without interruption.

7.   The release of a ship arrested within the jurisdiction of a State and escorted to a port of that State for the purposes of an inquiry before the competent authorities may not be claimed solely on the ground that the ship, in the course of its voyage, was escorted across a portion of the exclusive economic zone or the high seas, if the circumstances rendered this necessary.

8.   Where a ship has been stopped or arrested outside the territorial sea in circumstances which do not justify the exercise of the right of hot pursuit, it shall be compensated for any loss or damage that may have been thereby sustained.

Article 112
Right to lay submarine cables and pipelines

1.   All States are entitled to lay submarine cables and pipelines on the bed of the high seas beyond the continental shelf.

2.   Article 79, paragraph 5, applies to such cables and pipelines.

Article 113
Breaking or injury of a submarine cable or pipeline

Every State shall adopt the laws and regulations necessary to provide that the breaking or injury by a ship flying its flag or by a person subject to its jurisdiction of a submarine cable beneath the high seas done wilfully or through culpable negligence, in such a manner as to be liable to interrupt or obstruct telegraphic or telephonic communications, and similarly the breaking or injury of a submarine pipeline or high-voltage power cable, shall be a punishable offence. This provision shall apply also to conduct calculated or likely to result in such breaking or injury. However, it shall not apply to any break or injury caused by persons who acted merely with the legitimate object of saving their lives or their ships, after having taken all necessary precautions to avoid such break or injury.

Article 114
Breaking or injury by owners of a submarine cable or pipeline
of another submarine cable or pipeline

Every State shall adopt the laws and regulations necessary to provide that, if persons subject to its jurisdiction who are the owners of a submarine cable or pipeline beneath the high seas, in laying or repairing that cable or pipeline, cause a break in or injury to another cable or pipeline, they shall bear the cost of the repairs.

Article 115
Indemnity for loss incurred in avoiding injury
to a submarine cable or pipeline

Every State shall adopt the laws and regulations necessary to ensure that the owners of ships who can prove that they have sacrificed an anchor, a net or any other fishing gear, in order to avoid injuring a submarine cable or pipeline, shall be indemnified by the owner of the cable or pipeline, provided that the owner of the ship has taken all reasonable precautionary measures beforehand.

SECTION 2. CONSERVATION AND MANAGEMENT OF THE LIVING RESOURCES OF THE HIGH SEAS

Article 116
Right to fish on the high seas

All States have the right for their nationals to engage in fishing on the high seas subject to:
- (a) their treaty obligations;
- (b) the rights and duties as well as the interests of coastal States provided for, *inter alia,* in article 63, paragraph 2, and articles 64 to 67; and
- (c) the provisions of this section.

Article 117
Duty of States to adopt with respect to their nationals
measures for the conservation of the living resources of the high seas

All States have the duty to take, or to cooperate with other States in taking, such measures for their respective nationals as may be necessary for the conservation of the living resources of the high seas.

Article 118
Co-operation of States in the conservation and management
of living resources

States shall co-operate with each other in the conservation and management of living resources in the areas of the high seas. States whose nationals exploit identical living resources, or different living resources in the same area, shall enter into negotiations with a view to taking the measures necessary for the conservation of the living resources concerned. They shall, as appropriate, co-operate to establish subregional or regional fisheries organizations to this end.

Article 119
Conservation of the living resources of the high seas

1.   In determining the allowable catch and establishing other conservation measures for the living resources in the high seas, States shall:
   (a)   take measures which are designed, on the best scientific evidence available to the States concerned, to maintain or restore populations of harvested species at levels which can produce the maximum sustainable yield, as qualified by relevant environmental and economic factors, including the special requirements of developing States, and taking into account fishing patterns, the interdependence of stocks and any generally recommended international minimum standards, whether subregional, regional or global;
   (b)   take into consideration the effects on species associated with or dependent upon harvested species with a view to maintaining or restoring populations of such associated or dependent species above levels at which their reproduction may become seriously threatened.
2.   Available scientific information, catch and fishing effort statistics, and other data relevant to the conservation of fish stocks shall be contributed and exchanged on a regular basis through competent international organizations, whether subregional, regional or global, where appropriate and with participation by all States concerned.
3. States concerned shall ensure that conservation measures and their implementation do not discriminate in form or in fact against the fishermen of any State.

Article 120
Marine mammals

Article 65 also applies to the conservation and management of marine mammals in the high seas.

PART VIII
REGIME OF ISLANDS

Article 121
Régime of islands

1.   An island is a naturally formed area of land, surrounded by water, which is above water at high tide.

2.   Except as provided for in paragraph 3, the territorial sea, the contiguous zone, the exclusive economic zone and the continental shelf of an island are determined in accordance with the provisions of this Convention applicable to other land territory.

3.   Rocks which cannot sustain human habitation or economic life of their own shall have no exclusive economic zone or continental shelf.

PART IX
ENCLOSED OR SEMI-ENCLOSED SEAS

Article 122
Definition

For the purposes of this Convention, "enclosed or semi-enclosed sea" means a gulf, basin or sea surrounded by two or more States and connected to another sea or the ocean by a narrow outlet or consisting entirely or primarily of the territorial seas and exclusive economic zones of two or more coastal States.

Article 123
Cooperation of States bordering enclosed or semi-enclosed seas

States bordering an enclosed or semi-enclosed sea should co-operate with each other in the exercise of their rights and in the performance of their duties under this Convention. To this end they shall endeavour, directly or through an appropriate regional organization:

(a)   to co-ordinate the management, conservation, exploration and exploitation of the living resources of the sea;

(b)   to co-ordinate the implementation of their rights and duties with respect to the protection and preservation of the marine environment;

(c)   to co-ordinate their scientific research policies and undertake where appropriate joint programmes of scientific research in the area;

(d)   to invite, as appropriate, other interested States or international organizations to co-operate with them in furtherance of the provisions of this article.

PART X
RIGHT OF ACCESS OF LAND-LOCKED STATES TO AND FROM THE SEA AND FREEDOM OF TRANSIT

Article 124
Use of terms

1.   For the purposes of this Convention:
(a)   "land-locked State" means a State which has no sea-coast;
(b)   "transit State" means a State, with or without a sea-coast, situated between a land-locked State and the sea, through whose territory traffic in transit passes;
(c)   "traffic in transit" means transit of persons, baggage, goods and means of transport across the territory of one or more transit States, when the passage across such territory, with or without trans-shipment, warehousing, breaking bulk or change in the mode of transport, is only a portion of a complete journey which begins or terminates within the territory of the land-locked State;
(d)   "means of transport" means:
    (i)   railway rolling stock, sea, lake and river craft and road vehicles;
    (ii) where local conditions so require, porters and pack animals.

2. Land-locked States and transit States may, by agreement between them, include as means of transport pipelines and gas lines and means of transport other than those included in paragraph 1.

Article 125
Right of access to and from the sea and freedom of transit

1. Land-locked States shall have the right of access to and from the sea for the purpose of exercising the rights provided for in this Convention including those relating to the freedom of the high seas and the common heritage of mankind. To this end, land-locked States shall enjoy freedom of transit through the territory of transit States by all means of transport.

2.   The terms and modalities for exercising freedom of transit shall be agreed between the land-locked States and transit States concerned through bilateral, subregional or regional agreements.

3.   Transit States, in the exercise of their full sovereignty over their territory, shall have the right to take all measures necessary to ensure that the rights and facilities provided for in this Part for land-locked States shall in no way infringe their legitimate interests.

Article 126
Exclusion of application of the most-favoured-nation clause

The provisions of this Convention, as well as special agreements relating to the exercise of the right of access to and from the sea, establishing rights and facilities on account of the special geographical position of land-locked States, are excluded from the application of the most-favoured-nation clause.

Article 127
Customs duties, taxes and other charges

1. Traffic in transit shall not be subject to any customs duties, taxes or other charges except charges levied for specific services rendered in connection with such traffic.

2. Means of transport in transit and other facilities provided for and used by land-locked States shall not be subject to taxes or charges higher than those levied for the use of means of transport of the transit State.

Article 128
Free zones and other customs facilities

For the convenience of traffic in transit, free zones or other customs facilities may be provided at the ports of entry and exit in the transit States, by agreement between those States and the land-locked States.

Article 129
Co-operation in the construction and improvement of means of transport

Where there are no means of transport in transit States to give effect to the freedom of transit or where the existing means, including the port installations and equipment, are inadequate in any respect, the transit States and land-locked States concerned may co-operate in constructing or improving them.

Article 130
Measures to avoid or eliminate delays
or other difficulties of a technical nature in traffic in transit

1. Transit States shall take all appropriate measures to avoid delays or other difficulties of a technical nature in traffic in transit.

2. Should such delays or difficulties occur, the competent authorities of the transit States and land-locked States concerned shall co-operate towards their expeditious elimination.

Article 131
Equal treatment in maritime ports

Ships flying the flag of land-locked States shall enjoy treatment equal to that accorded to other foreign ships in maritime ports.

Article 132
Grant of greater transit facilities

This Convention does not entail in any way the withdrawal of transit facilities which are greater than those provided for in this Convention and which are agreed between States Parties to this Convention or granted by a State Party. This Convention also does not preclude such grant of greater facilities in the future.

PART XI
THE AREA

SECTION 1. GENERAL PROVISIONS

Article 133
Use of terms

For the purposes of this Part:

(a)   "resources" means all solid, liquid or gaseous mineral resources *in situ* in the Area at or beneath the seabed, including polymetallic nodules;

(b)   resources, when recovered from the Area, are referred to as "minerals".

Article 134
Scope of this Part

1.   This Part applies to the Area.

2.   Activities in the Area shall be governed by the provisions of this Part.

3.   The requirements concerning deposit of, and publicity to be given to, the charts or lists of geographical coordinates showing the limits referred to in article 1, paragraph 1 (1), are set forth in Part VI.

4.   Nothing in this article affects the establishment of the outer limits of the continental shelf in accordance with Part VI or the validity of agreements relating to delimitation between States with opposite or adjacent coasts.

Article 135
Legal status of the superjacent waters and air space

Neither this Part nor any rights granted or exercised pursuant thereto shall affect the legal status of the waters superjacent to the Area or that of the air space above those waters.

SECTION 2. PRINCIPLES GOVERNING THE AREA

Article 136
Common heritage of mankind

The Area and its resources are the common heritage of mankind.

Article 137
Legal status of the Area and its resources

1.   No State shall claim or exercise sovereignty or sovereign rights over any part of the Area or its resources, nor shall any State or natural or juridical person

appropriate any part thereof. No such claim or exercise of sovereignty or sovereign rights nor such appropriation shall be recognized.

2.   All rights in the resources of the Area are vested in mankind as a whole, on whose behalf the Authority shall act. These resources are not subject to alienation. The minerals recovered from the Area, however, may only be alienated in accordance with this Part and the rules, regulations and procedures of the Authority.

3.   No State or natural or juridical person shall claim, acquire or exercise rights with respect to the minerals recovered from the Area except in accordance with this Part. Otherwise, no such claim, acquisition or exercise of such rights shall be recognized.

Article 138
General conduct of States in relation to the Area

The general conduct of States in relation to the Area shall be in accordance with the provisions of this Part, the principles embodied in the Charter of the United Nations and other rules of international law in the interests of maintaining peace and security and promoting international co-operation and mutual understanding.

Article 139
Responsibility to ensure compliance and liability for damage

1.   States Parties shall have the responsibility to ensure that activities in the Area, whether carried out by States Parties, or state enterprises or natural or juridical persons which possess the nationality of States Parties or are effectively controlled by them or their nationals, shall be carried out in conformity with this Part. The same responsibility applies to international organizations for activities in the Area carried out by such organizations.

2.   Without prejudice to the rules of international law and Annex III, article 22, damage caused by the failure of a State Party or international organization to carry out its responsibilities under this Part shall entail liability; States Parties or international organizations acting together shall bear joint and several liability. A State Party shall not however be liable for damage caused by any failure to comply with this Part by a person whom it has sponsored under article 153, paragraph 2(b), if the State Party has taken all necessary and appropriate measures to secure effective compliance under article 153, paragraph 4, and Annex III, article 4, paragraph 4.

3.   States Parties that are members of international organizations shall take appropriate measures to ensure the implementation of this article with respect to such organizations.

Article 140
Benefit of mankind

1.   Activities in the Area shall, as specifically provided for in this Part, be carried out for the benefit of mankind as a whole, irrespective of the geographical

location of States, whether coastal or land-locked, and taking into particular consideration the interests and needs of developing States and of peoples who have not attained full independence or other self-governing status recognized by the United Nations in accordance with General Assembly resolution 1514 (XV) and other relevant General Assembly resolutions.

2.   The Authority shall provide for the equitable sharing of financial and other economic benefits derived from activities in the Area through any appropriate mechanism, on a non-discriminatory basis, in accordance with article 160, paragraph 2(f)(i).

Article 141
Use of the Area exclusively for peaceful purposes

The Area shall be open to use exclusively for peaceful purposes by all States, whether coastal or land-locked, without discrimination and without prejudice to the other provisions of this Part.

Article 142
Rights and legitimate interests of coastal States

1.   Activities in the Area, with respect to resource deposits in the Area which lie across limits of national jurisdiction, shall be conducted with due regard to the rights and legitimate interests of any coastal State across whose jurisdiction such deposits lie.

2.   Consultations, including a system of prior notification, shall be maintained with the State concerned, with a view to avoiding infringement of such rights and interests. In cases where activities in the Area may result in the exploitation of resources lying within national jurisdiction, the prior consent of the coastal State concerned shall be required.

3.   Neither this Part nor any rights granted or exercised pursuant thereto shall affect the rights of coastal States to take such measures consistent with the relevant provisions of Part XII as may be necessary to prevent, mitigate or eliminate grave and imminent danger to their coastline, or related interests from pollution or threat thereof or from other hazardous occurrences resulting from or caused by any activities in the Area.

Article 143
Marine scientific research

1.   Marine scientific research in the Area shall be carried out exclusively for peaceful purposes and for the benefit of mankind as a whole, in accordance with Part XIII.

2.   The Authority may carry out marine scientific research concerning the Area and its resources, and may enter into contracts for that purpose. The Authority shall promote and encourage the conduct of marine scientific research in the Area, and shall co-ordinate and disseminate the results of such research and analysis when available.

3.   States Parties may carry out marine scientific research in the Area. States Parties shall promote international co-operation in marine scientific research in the Area by:

(a)   participating in international programmes and encouraging co-operation in marine scientific research by personnel of different countries and of the Authority;

(b)   ensuring that programmes are developed through the Authority or other international organizations as appropriate for the benefit of developing States and technologically less developed States with a view to:

(i)   strengthening their research capabilities;

(ii)   training their personnel and the personnel of the Authority in the techniques and applications of research;

(iii)   fostering the employment of their qualified personnel in research in the Area;

(c)   effectively disseminating the results of research and analysis when available, through the Authority or other international channels when appropriate.

Article 144
Transfer of technology

1.   The Authority shall take measures in accordance with this Convention:

(a)   to acquire technology and scientific knowledge relating to activities in the Area; and

(b)   to promote and encourage the transfer to developing States of such technology and scientific knowledge so that all States Parties benefit therefrom.

2.   To this end the Authority and States Parties shall co-operate in promoting the transfer of technology and scientific knowledge relating to activities in the Area so that the Enterprise and all States Parties may benefit therefrom. In particular they shall initiate and promote:

(a)   programmes for the transfer of technology to the Enterprise and to developing States with regard to activities in the Area, including, *inter alia*, facilitating the access of the Enterprise and of developing States to the relevant technology, under fair and reasonable terms and conditions;

(b)   measures directed towards the advancement of the technology of the Enterprise and the domestic technology of developing States, particularly by providing opportunities to personnel from the Enterprise and from developing States for training in marine science and technology and for their full participation in activities in the Area.

AGREEMENT, ANNEX, SECTION 5
SECTION 5. TRANSFER OF TECHNOLOGY

1.   In addition to the provisions of article 144 of the Convention, transfer of technology for the purposes of Part XI shall be governed by the following principles:

(a) The Enterprise, and developing States wishing to obtain deep seabed mining technology, shall seek to obtain such technology on fair and reasonable commercial terms and conditions on the open market, or through joint-venture arrangements;

(b) If the Enterprise or developing States are unable to obtain deep seabed mining technology, the Authority may request all or any of the contractors and their respective sponsoring State or States to co-operate with it in facilitating the acquisition of deep seabed mining technology by the Enterprise or its joint venture, or by a developing State or States seeking to acquire such technology on fair and reasonable commercial terms and conditions, consistent with the effective protection of intellectual property rights. States Parties undertake to co-operate fully and effectively with the Authority for this purpose and to ensure that contractors sponsored by them also co-operate fully with the Authority;

(c) As a general rule, States Parties shall promote international technical and scientific co-operation with regard to activities in the Area either between the parties concerned or by developing training, technical assistance and scientific co-operation programmes in marine science and technology and the protection and preservation of the marine environment.

Article 145
Protection of the marine environment

Necessary measures shall be taken in accordance with this Convention with respect to activities in the Area to ensure effective protection for the marine environment from harmful effects which may arise from such activities. To this end the Authority shall adopt appropriate rules, regulations and procedures for *inter alia:*

(a) the prevention, reduction and control of pollution and other hazards to the marine environment, including the coastline, and of interference with the ecological balance of the marine environment, particular attention being paid to the need for protection from harmful effects of such activities as drilling, dredging, excavation, disposal of waste, construction and operation or maintenance of installations, pipelines and other devices related to such activities;

(b) the protection and conservation of the natural resources of the Area and the prevention of damage to the flora and fauna of the marine environment.

Article 146
Protection of human life

With respect to activities in the Area, necessary measures shall be taken to ensure effective protection of human life. To this end the Authority shall adopt appropriate rules, regulations and procedures to supplement existing international law as embodied in relevant treaties.

Article 147

Accommodation of activities in the Area and in the marine environment

1.   Activities in the Area shall be carried out with reasonable regard for other activities in the marine environment.

2.   Installations used for carrying out activities in the Area shall be subject to the following conditions:

(a)   such installations shall be erected, emplaced and removed solely in accordance with this Part and subject to the rules, regulations and procedures of the Authority. Due notice must be given of the erection, emplacement and removal of such installations, and permanent means for giving warning of their presence must be maintained;

(b)   such installations may not be established where interference may be caused to the use of recognized sea lanes essential to international navigation or in areas of intense fishing activity;

(c)   safety zones shall be established around such installations with appropriate markings to ensure the safety of both navigation and the installations. The configuration and location of such safety zones shall not be such as to form a belt impeding the lawful access of shipping to particular maritime zones or navigation along international sea lanes;

(d)   such installations shall be used exclusively for peaceful purposes;

(e)   such installations do not possess the status of islands. They have no territorial sea of their own, and their presence does not affect the delimitation of the territorial sea, the exclusive economic zone or the continental shelf.

3.   Other activities in the marine environment shall be conducted with reasonable regard for activities in the Area.

Article 148

Participation of developing States in activities in the Area

The effective participation of developing States in activities in the Area shall be promoted as specifically provided for in this Part, having due regard to their special interests and needs, and in particular to the special need of the land-locked and geographically disadvantaged among them to overcome obstacles arising from their disadvantaged location, including remoteness from the Area and difficulty of access to and from it.

Article 149

Archaeological and historical objects

All objects of an archaeological and historical nature found in the Area shall be preserved or disposed of for the benefit of mankind as a whole, particular regard being paid to the preferential rights of the State or country of origin, or the State of cultural origin, or the State of historical and archaeological origin.

SECTION 3. DEVELOPMENT OF RESOURCES OF THE AREA

Article 150
Policies relating to activities in the Area

Activities in the Area shall, as specifically provided for in this Part, be carried out in such a manner as to foster healthy development of the world economy and balanced growth of international trade, and to promote international co-operation for the over-all development of all countries, especially developing States, and with a view to ensuring:

(a) the development of the resources of the Area;
(b) orderly, safe and rational management of the resources of the Area, includ-ing the efficient conduct of activities in the Area and, in accordance with sound principles of conservation, the avoidance of unnecessary waste;
(c) the expansion of opportunities for participation in such activities consistent in particular with articles 144 and 148;
(d) participation in revenues by the Authority and the transfer of technology to the Enterprise and developing States as provided for in this Convention;
(e) increased availability of the minerals derived from the Area as needed in conjunction with minerals derived from other sources, to ensure supplies to consumers of such minerals;
(f) the promotion of just and stable prices remunerative to producers and fair to consumers for minerals derived both from the Area and from other sources, and the promotion of long-term equilibrium between supply and demand;
(g) the enhancement of opportunities for all States Parties, irrespective of their social and economic systems or geographical location, to participate in the development of the resources of the Area and the prevention of monopoli-zation of activities in the Area;
(h) the protection of developing countries from adverse effects on their econo-mies or on their export earnings resulting from a reduction in the price of an affected mineral, or in the volume of exports of that mineral, to the extent that such reduction is caused by activities in the Area, as provided in article 151;
(i) the development of the common heritage for the benefit of mankind as a whole; and
(j) conditions of access to markets for the imports of minerals produced from the resources of the Area and for imports of commodities produced from such minerals shall not be more favourable than the most favourable ap-plied to imports from other sources.

Article 151
Production policies

[1-7. Do not apply. See Agreement, annex, Section 6, paragraph 7][a]
8. Rights and obligations relating to unfair economic practices under relevant

---
[a] See page 192

multilateral trade agreements shall apply to the exploration for and exploitation of minerals from the Area. In the settlement of disputes arising under this provision, States Parties which are Parties to such multilateral trade agreements shall have recourse to the dispute settlement procedures of such agreements.

[9. Does not apply. See Agreement, annex, Section 6, paragraph 7]

10. Upon the recommendation of the Council on the basis of advice from the Economic Planning Commission, the Assembly shall establish a system of compensation or take other measures of economic adjustment assistance including co-operation with specialized agencies and other international organizations to assist developing countries which suffer serious adverse effects on their export earnings or economies resulting from a reduction in the price of an affected mineral or in the volume of exports of that mineral, to the extent that such reduction is caused by activities in the Area. The Authority on request shall initiate studies on the problems of those States which are likely to be most seriously affected with a view to minimizing their difficulties and assisting them in their economic adjustment.

AGREEMENT, ANNEX, SECTIONS 6 AND 7
SECTION 6. PRODUCTION POLICY

1. The production policy of the Authority shall be based on the following principles:

(a) Development of the resources of the Area shall take place in accordance with sound commercial principles;

(b) The provisions of the General Agreement on Tariffs and Trade, its relevant codes and successor or superseding agreements shall apply with respect to activities in the Area;

(c) In particular, there shall be no subsidization of activities in the Area except as may be permitted under the agreements referred to in subparagraph (b). Subsidization for the purpose of these principles shall be defined in terms of the agreements referred to in subparagraph (b);

(d) There shall be no discrimination between minerals derived from the Area and from other sources. There shall be no preferential access to markets for such minerals or for imports of commodities produced from such minerals, in particular:

(i) By the use of tariff or non-tariff barriers; and

(ii) Given by States Parties to such minerals or commodities produced by their state enterprises or by natural or juridical persons which possess their nationality or are controlled by them or their nationals;

(e) The plan of work for exploitation approved by the Authority in respect of each mining area shall indicate an anticipated production schedule which shall include the estimated maximum amounts of minerals that would be produced per year under the plan of work;

   (f)   The following shall apply to the settlement of disputes concerning the provisions of the agreements referred to in subparagraph (b):

       (i)   Where the States Parties concerned are parties to such agreements, they shall have recourse to the dispute settlement procedures of those agreements;

      (ii)   Where one or more of the States Parties concerned are not parties to such agreements, they shall have recourse to the dispute settlement procedures set out in the Convention;

   (g)   In circumstances where a determination is made under the agreements referred to in subparagraph (b) that a State Party has engaged in subsidization which is prohibited or has resulted in adverse effects on the interests of another State Party and appropriate steps have not been taken by the relevant State Party or States Parties, a State Party may request the Council to take appropriate measures.

2.   The principles contained in paragraph 1 shall not affect the rights and obligations under any provision of the agreements referred to in paragraph 1 (b), as well as the relevant free trade and customs union agreements, in relations between States Parties which are parties to such agreements.

3.   The acceptance by a contractor of subsidies other than those which may be permitted under the agreements referred to in paragraph 1 (b) shall constitute a violation of the fundamental terms of the contract forming a plan of work for the carrying out of activities in the Area.

4.   Any State Party which has reason to believe that there has been a breach of the requirements of paragraphs 1 (b) to (d) or 3 may initiate dispute settlement procedures in conformity with paragraph 1 (f) or (g).

5.   A State Party may at any time bring to the attention of the Council activities which in its view are inconsistent with the requirements of paragraph 1 (b) to (d).

6.   The Authority shall develop rules, regulations and procedures which ensure the implementation of the provisions of this section, including relevant rules, regulations and procedures governing the approval of plans of work.

7.   The provisions of article 151, paragraphs 1 to 7 and 9, article 162, paragraph 2 (q), article 165, paragraph 2 (n), and Annex III, article 6, paragraph 5, and article 7, of the Convention shall not apply.

SECTION 7. ECONOMIC ASSISTANCE

1.   The policy of the Authority of assisting developing countries which suffer serious adverse effects on their export earnings or economies resulting from a reduction in the price of an affected mineral or in the volume of exports of that mineral, to the extent that such reduction caused by activities in the Area, shall be based on the following principles:

   (a)   The Authority shall establish an economic assistance fund from a portion of the funds of the Authority which exceeds those necessary to cover the administrative expenses of the Authority. The amount set aside for this purpose shall be determined by the Council from time to time, upon the recommendation of the Finance Committee. Only funds from payments received from contractors, including the Enterprise, and voluntary contributions shall be used for the establishment of the economic assistance fund;

(b) Developing land-based producer States whose economies have been determined to be seriously affected by the production of minerals from the deep seabed shall be assisted from the economic assistance fund of the Authority;

(c) The Authority shall provide assistance from the fund to affected developing land-based producer States, where appropriate, in co-operation with existing global or regional development institutions which have the infrastructure and expertise to carry out such assistance programmes;

(d) The extent and period of such assistance shall be determined on a case-by-case basis. In doing so, due consideration shall be given to the nature and magnitude of the problems encountered by affected developing land-based producer States.

2.   Article 151, paragraph 10, of the Convention shall be implemented by means of measures of economic assistance referred to in paragraph 1. Article 160, paragraph 2 (l), article 162, paragraph 2 (n), article 164, paragraph 2 (d), article 171, subparagraph (f), and article 173, paragraph 2 (c), of the Convention shall be interpreted accordingly.

Article 152
Exercise of powers and functions by the Authority

1.   The Authority shall avoid discrimination in the exercise of its powers and functions, including the granting of opportunities for activities in the Area.

2.   Nevertheless, special consideration for developing States, including particular consideration for the land-locked and geographically disadvantaged among them, specifically provided for in this Part shall be permitted.

Article 153
System of exploration and exploitation

1.   Activities in the Area shall be organized, carried out and controlled by the Authority on behalf of mankind as a whole in accordance with this article as well as other relevant provisions of this Part and the relevant Annexes, and the rules, regulations and procedures of the Authority.

2.   Activities in the Area shall be carried out as prescribed in paragraph 3:

(a) by the Enterprise, and

(b) in association with the Authority by States Parties, or state enterprises or natural or juridical persons which possess the nationality of States Parties or are effectively controlled by them or their nationals, when sponsored by such States, or any group of the foregoing which meets the requirements provided in this Part and in Annex III.

3.   Activities in the Area shall be carried out in accordance with a formal written plan of work drawn up in accordance with Annex III and approved by the Council after review by the Legal and Technical Commission.   In the case of activities in the Area carried out as authorized by the Authority by the entities specified in paragraph 2(b), the plan of work shall, in accordance with Annex III, article 3, be in the form of a contract.   Such contracts may provide for joint arrangements in accordance with Annex III, article 11.

AGREEMENT, ANNEX, SECTION 2, PARAGRAPH 4

4.   The obligations applicable to contractors shall apply to the Enterprise. Notwithstanding the provisions of article 153, paragraph 3, and Annex III, article 3, paragraph 5, of the Convention, a plan of work for the Enterprise upon its approval shall be in the form of a contract concluded between the Authority and the Enterprise.

---

4.   The Authority shall exercise such control over activities in the Area as is necessary for the purpose of securing compliance with the relevant provisions of this Part and the Annexes relating thereto, and the rules, regulations and procedures of the Authority, and the plans of work approved in accordance with paragraph 3.   States Parties shall assist the Authority by taking all measures necessary to ensure such compliance in accordance with article 139.

5.   The Authority shall have the right to take at any time any measures provided for under this Part to ensure compliance with its provisions and the exercise of the functions of control and regulation assigned to it thereunder or under any contract. The Authority shall have the right to inspect all installations in the Area used in connection with activities in the Area.

6.   A contract under paragraph 3 shall provide for security of tenure. Accordingly, the contract shall not be revised, suspended or terminated except in accordance with Annex III, articles 18 and 19.

Article 154
Periodic review

Every five years from the entry into force of this Convention, the Assembly shall undertake a general and systematic review of the manner in which the international régime of the Area established in this Convention has operated in practice. In the light of this review the Assembly may take, or recommend that other organs take, measures in accordance with the provisions and procedures of this Part and the Annexes relating thereto which will lead to the improvement of the operation of the régime.

Article 155
The Review Conference

[1.   Does not apply. See Agreement, annex, Section 4][b]

2.   The Review Conference shall ensure the maintenance of the principle of the common heritage of mankind, the international régime designed to ensure equitable exploitation of the resources of the Area for the benefit of all countries, especially the developing States, and an Authority to organize, conduct and control activities in the Area. It shall also ensure the maintenance of the principles laid down in this Part with regard to the exclusion of claims or exercise of sovereignty over any part of the Area, the rights of States and their general conduct in relation to the Area, and their participation in activities in the Area in conformity with this Convention, the prevention of monopolization of activities in the Area, the use of the Area exclusively for peaceful purposes, economic aspects of activities in the Area, marine scientific research, transfer of technology, protection of the marine environment, protection of human life, rights of coastal States, the legal status of the waters superjacent to the Area and that of the air space above those waters and accommodation between activities in the Area and other activities in the marine environment.

[3.   Does not apply. See Agreement, annex, Section 4]

[4.   Does not apply. See Agreement, annex, Section 4]

5.   Amendments adopted by the Review Conference pursuant to this article shall not affect rights acquired under existing contracts.

AGREEMENT, ANNEX, SECTION 4
SECTION 4.   REVIEW CONFERENCE

The provisions relating to the Review Conference in article 155, paragraphs 1, 3 and 4, of the Convention shall not apply. Notwithstanding the provisions of article 314, paragraph 2, of the Convention, the Assembly, on the recommendation of the Council, may undertake at any time a review of the matters referred to in article 155, paragraph 1, of the Convention. Amendments relating to this Agreement and Part XI shall be subject to the procedures contained in articles 314, 315 and 316 of the Convention, provided that the principles, régime and other terms referred to in article 155, paragraph 2, of the Convention shall be maintained and the rights referred to in paragraph 5 of that article shall not be affected.

---

b See page 194.

SECTION 4. THE AUTHORITY
SUBSECTION A. GENERAL PROVISIONS

AGREEMENT, ANNEX, SECTION 1, PARAGRAPH 17

17. The relevant provisions of Part XI, section 4, of the Convention shall be interpreted and applied in accordance with this Agreement.

Article 156
Establishment of the Authority

1. There is hereby established the International Seabed Authority, which shall function in accordance with this Part.

2. All States Parties are *ipso facto* members of the Authority.

3. Observers at the Third United Nations Conference on the Law of the Sea who have signed the Final Act and who are not referred to in article 305, paragraph 1(c), (d), (e) or (f), shall have the right to participate in the Authority as observers, in accordance with its rules, regulations and procedures.

4. The seat of the Authority shall be in Jamaica.

5. The Authority may establish such regional centres or offices as it deems necessary for the exercise of its functions.

AGREEMENT, ANNEX, SECTION 1, PARAGRAPH 12

12. Upon the entry into force of this Agreement, States and entities referred to in article 3 of this Agreement which have been applying it provisionally in accordance with article 7 and for which it is not in force may continue to be members of the Authority on a provisional basis pending its entry into force for such States and entities, in accordance with the following subparagraphs:

(a) If this Agreement enters into force before 16 November 1996, such States and entities shall be entitled to continue to participate as members of the Authority on a provisional basis upon notification to the depositary of the Agreement by such a State or entity of its intention to participate as a member on a provisional basis. Such membership shall terminate either on 16 November 1996 or upon the entry into force of this Agreement and the Convention for such member, whichever is earlier. The Council may, upon the request of the State or entity concerned, extend such membership beyond 16 November 1996 for a further period or periods not exceeding a total of two years provided that the Council is satisfied that the State or entity concerned has been making efforts in good faith to become a party to the Agreement and the Convention;

(b) If this Agreement enters into force after 15 November 1996, such States and entities may request the Council to grant continued membership in the Authority on a provisional basis for a period or periods not extending beyond 16 November 1998. The Council shall grant such membership with effect from the date of the request if it is satisfied that the State or entity concerned has been making efforts in good faith to become a party to the Agreement and the Convention;

(c) States and entities which are members of the Authority on a provisional basis in accordance with subparagraph (a) or (b) shall apply the terms of Part XI and this Agreement in accordance with their national or internal laws, regulations and annual budgetary appropriations and shall have the same rights and obligations as other members, including:

    (i) The obligation to contribute to the administrative budget of the Authority in accordance with the scale of assessed contributions;

    (ii) The right to sponsor an application for approval of a plan of work for exploration. In the case of entities whose components are natural or juridical persons possessing the nationality of more than one State, a plan of work for exploration shall not be approved unless all the States whose natural or juridical persons comprise those entities are States Parties or members on a provisional basis;

(d) Notwithstanding the provisions of paragraph 9, an approved plan of work in the form of a contract for exploration which was sponsored pursuant to subparagraph (c) (ii) by a State which was a member on a provisional basis shall terminate if such membership ceases and the State or entity has not become a State Party;

(e) If such a member has failed to make its assessed contributions or otherwise failed to comply with its obligations in accordance with this paragraph, its membership on a provisional basis shall be terminated.

Article 157
Nature and fundamental principles of the Authority

1.   The Authority is the organization through which States Parties shall, in accordance with this Part, organize and control activities in the Area, particularly with a view to administering the resources of the Area.

2.   The powers and functions of the Authority shall be those expressly conferred upon it by this Convention. The Authority shall have such incidental powers consistent with this Convention, as are implicit in and necessary for the exercise of those powers and functions with respect to activities in the Area.

3.   The Authority is based on the principle of the sovereign equality of all its members.

4.   All members of the Authority shall fulfil in good faith the obligations assumed by them in accordance with this Part in order to ensure to all of them the rights and benefits resulting from membership.

AGREEMENT, ANNEX, SECTION 1, PARAGRAPH 1

1.   The International Seabed Authority (hereinafter referred to as "the Authority") is the organization through which States Parties to the Convention shall, in accordance with the régime for the Area established in Part XI and this Agreement, organize and control activities in the Area, particularly with a view to administering the resources of the Area. The powers and functions of the Authority shall be those expressly conferred upon it by the Convention. The Authority shall have such incidental powers, consistent with the Convention, as are implicit in, and necessary for, the exercise of those powers and functions with respect to activities in the Area.

Article 158
Organs of the Authority

1.   There are hereby established, as the principal organs of the Authority, an Assembly, a Council and a Secretariat.

2.   There is hereby established the Enterprise, the organ through which the Authority shall carry out the functions referred to in article 170, paragraph 1.

3.   Such subsidiary organs as may be found necessary may be established in accordance with this Part.

4.   Each principal organ of the Authority and the Enterprise shall be responsible for exercising those powers and functions which are conferred upon it. In exercising such powers and functions each organ shall avoid taking any action which may derogate from or impede the exercise of specific powers and functions conferred upon another organ.

AGREEMENT, ANNEX, SECTION 1, PARAGRAPHS 2 TO 5

2.   In order to minimize costs to States Parties, all organs and subsidiary bodies to be established under the Convention and this Agreement shall be cost-effective. This principle shall also apply to the frequency, duration and scheduling of meetings.

3.   The setting up and the functioning of the organs and subsidiary bodies of the Authority shall be based on an evolutionary approach, taking into account the functional needs of the organs and subsidiary bodies concerned in order that they may discharge effectively their respective responsibilities at various stages of the development of activities in the Area.

4.   The early functions of the Authority upon entry into force of the Convention shall be carried out by the Assembly, the Council, the Secretariat, the Legal and Technical Commission and the Finance Committee. The functions of

the Economic Planning Commission shall be performed by the Legal and Technical Commission until such time as the Council decides otherwise or until the approval of the first plan of work for exploitation.

5.   Between the entry into force of the Convention and the approval of the first plan of work for exploitation, the Authority shall concentrate on:

(a) Processing of applications for approval of plans of work for exploration in accordance with Part XI and this Agreement;

(b) Implementation of decisions of the Preparatory Commission for the International Seabed Authority and for the International Tribunal for the Law of the Sea (hereinafter referred to as "the Preparatory Commission") relating to the registered pioneer investors and their certifying States, including their rights and obligations, in accordance with article 308, paragraph 5, of the Convention and resolution II, paragraph 13;

(c) Monitoring of compliance with plans of work for exploration approved in the form of contracts;

(d) Monitoring and review of trends and developments relating to deep seabed mining activities, including regular analysis of world metal market conditions and metal prices, trends and prospects;

(e) Study of the potential impact of mineral production from the Area on the economies of developing land-based producers of those minerals which are likely to be most seriously affected, with a view to minimizing their difficulties and assisting them in their economic adjustment, taking into account the work done in this regard by the Preparatory Commission;

(f) Adoption of rules, regulations and procedures necessary for the conduct of activities in the Area as they progress. Notwithstanding the provisions of Annex III, article 17, paragraph 2 (b) and (c), of the Convention, such rules, regulations and procedures shall take into account the terms of this Agreement, the prolonged delay in commercial deep seabed mining and the likely pace of activities in the Area;

(g) Adoption of rules, regulations and procedures incorporating applicable standards for the protection and preservation of the marine environment;

(h) Promotion and encouragement of the conduct of marine scientific research with respect to activities in the Area and the collection and dissemination of the results of such research and analysis, when available, with particular emphasis on research related to the environmental impact of activities in the Area;

(i) Acquisition of scientific knowledge and monitoring of the development of marine technology relevant to activities in the Area, in particular technology relating to the protection and preservation of the marine environment;

(j) Assessment of available data relating to prospecting and exploration;

(k) Timely elaboration of rules, regulations and procedures for exploitation, including those relating to the protection and preservation of the marine environment.

SUBSECTION B. THE ASSEMBLY

AGREEMENT, ANNEX, SECTION 3, PARAGRAPH 14

14.   Part XI, section 4, subsections B and C, of the Convention shall be interpreted and applied in accordance with this section.

Article 159
Composition, procedure and voting

1.   The Assembly shall consist of all the members of the Authority. Each member shall have one representative in the Assembly, who may be accompanied by alternates and advisers.

2.   The Assembly shall meet in regular annual sessions and in such special sessions as may be decided by the Assembly, or convened by the Secretary-General at the request of the Council or of a majority of the members of the Authority.

3.   Sessions shall take place at the seat of the Authority unless otherwise decided by the Assembly.

4.   The Assembly shall adopt its rules of procedure. At the beginning of each regular session, it shall elect its President and such other officers as may be required. They shall hold office until a new President and other officers are elected at the next regular session.

5.   A majority of the members of the Assembly shall constitute a quorum.

6.   Each member of the Assembly shall have one vote.

7.   Decisions on questions of procedure, including decisions to convene special sessions of the Assembly, shall be taken by a majority of the members present and voting.

8.   Decisions on questions of substance shall be taken by a two-thirds majority of the members present and voting, provided that such majority includes a majority of the members participating in the session. When the issue arises as to whether a question is one of substance or not, that question shall be treated as one of substance unless otherwise decided by the Assembly by the majority required for decisions on questions of substance.

AGREEMENT, ANNEX, SECTION 3, PARAGRAPHS 2, 3, 4 AND 7

2.   As a general rule, decision-making in the organs of the Authority should be by consensus.

3.   If all efforts to reach a decision by consensus have been exhausted, decisions by voting in the Assembly on questions of procedure shall be taken by a majority of members present and voting, and decisions on questions of substance

shall be taken by a two-thirds majority of members present and voting, as provided for in article 159, paragraph 8, of the Convention.

4.   Decisions of the Assembly on any matter for which the Council also has competence or on any administrative, budgetary or financial matter shall be based on the recommendations of the Council. If the Assembly does not accept the recommendation of the Council on any matter, it shall return the matter to the Council for further consideration. The Council shall reconsider the matter in the light of the views expressed by the Assembly.

...

7.   Decisions by the Assembly or the Council having financial or budgetary implications shall be based on the recommendations of the Finance Committee.

---

9.   When a question of substance comes up for voting for the first time, the President may, and shall, if requested by at least one fifth of the members of the Assembly, defer the issue of taking a vote on that question for a period not exceeding five calendar days. This rule may be applied only once to any question and shall not be applied so as to defer the question beyond the end of the session.

10.   Upon a written request addressed to the President and sponsored by at least one fourth of the members of the Authority for an advisory opinion on the conformity with this Convention of a proposal before the Assembly on any matter, the Assembly shall request the Seabed Disputes Chamber of the International Tribunal for the Law of the Sea to give an advisory opinion thereon and shall defer voting on that proposal pending receipt of the advisory opinion by the Chamber. If the advisory opinion is not received before the final week of the session in which it is requested, the Assembly shall decide when it will meet to vote upon the deferred proposal.

Article 160
Powers and functions

1.   The Assembly as the sole organ of the Authority consisting of all the members, shall be considered the supreme organ of the Authority to which the other principal organs shall be accountable as specifically provided for in this Convention. The Assembly shall have the power to establish general policies in conformity with the relevant provisions of this Convention on any question or matter within the competence of the Authority.

AGREEMENT, ANNEX, SECTION 3, PARAGRAPH 1

1.   The general policies of the Authority shall be established by the Assembly in collaboration with the Council.

---

2.   In addition, the powers and functions of the Assembly shall be:
(a)   to elect the members of the Council in accordance with article 161;

(b) to elect the Secretary-General from among the candidates proposed by the Council;

(c) to elect, upon the recommendation of the Council, the members of the Governing Board of the Enterprise and the Director-General of the Enterprise;

(d) to establish such subsidiary organs as it finds necessary for the exercise of its functions in accordance with this Part. In the composition of these subsidiary organs due account shall be taken of the principle of equitable geographical distribution and of special interests and the need for members qualified and competent in the relevant technical questions dealt with by such organs;

(e) to assess the contributions of members to the administrative budget of the Authority in accordance with an agreed scale of assessment based upon the scale used for the regular budget of the United Nations until the Authority shall have sufficient income from other sources to meet its administrative expenses;

AGREEMENT, ANNEX, SECTION 9, PARAGRAPH 7

7.   Decisions by the Assembly and the Council on the following issues shall take into account recommendations of the Finance Committee:

...

(b) Assessment of contributions of members to the administrative budget of the Authority in accordance with article 160, paragraph 2 (e), of the Convention;

(f) (i)   to consider and approve, upon the recommendation of the Council, the rules, regulations and procedures on the equitable sharing of financial and other economic benefits derived from activities in the Area and the payments and contributions made pursuant to article 82, taking into particular consideration the interests and needs of developing States and peoples who have not attained full independence or other self-governing status. If the Assembly does not approve the recommendations of the Council, the Assembly shall return them to the Council for reconsideration in the light of the views expressed by the Assembly;

(ii) to consider and approve the rules, regulations and procedures of the Authority, and any amendments thereto, provisionally adopted by the Council pursuant to article 162, paragraph 2 (o)(ii). These rules, regulations and procedures shall relate to prospecting, exploration and exploitation in the Area, the financial management and internal administration of the Authority, and, upon the recommendation of the Governing Board of the Enterprise, to the transfer of funds from the Enterprise to the Authority;

(g) to decide upon the equitable sharing of financial and other economic benefits derived from activities in the Area, consistent with this Convention and the rules, regulations and procedures of the Authority;

(h) to consider and approve the proposed annual budget of the Authority submitted by the Council;

(i) to examine periodic reports from the Council and from the Enterprise and special reports requested from the Council or any other organ of the Authority;

(j) to initiate studies and make recommendations for the purpose of promoting international co-operation concerning activities in the Area and encouraging the progressive development of international law relating thereto and its codification;

(k) to consider problems of a general nature in connection with activities in the Area arising in particular for developing States, as well as those problems for States in connection with activities in the Area that are due to their geographical location, particularly for land-locked and geographically disadvantaged States;

(l) to establish, upon the recommendation of the Council, on the basis of advice from the Economic Planning Commission, a system of compensation or other measures of economic adjustment assistance as provided in article 151, paragraph 10;

AGREEMENT, ANNEX, SECTION 7, PARAGRAPH 2

2. Article 151, paragraph 10, of the Convention shall be implemented by means of measures of economic assistance referred to in paragraph 1. Article 160, paragraph 2 (l) ... of the Convention shall be interpreted accordingly.

...

(m) to suspend the exercise of rights and privileges of membership pursuant to article 185;

(n) to discuss any question or matter within the competence of the Authority and to decide as to which organ of the Authority shall deal with any such question or matter not specifically entrusted to a particular organ, consistent with the distribution of powers and functions among the organs of the Authority.

SUBSECTION C. THE COUNCIL

Article 161
Composition, procedure and voting

[1. Does not apply. See Agreement, annex, Section 3, paragraph 16][c]

---

[c] See page 195

AGREEMENT, ANNEX, SECTION 3, PARAGRAPHS 15, 16, 9 AND 10

15. The Council shall consist of 36 members of the Authority elected by the Assembly in the following order:

(a) Four members from among those States Parties which, during the last five years for which statistics are available, have either consumed more than 2 per cent in value terms of total world consumption or have had net imports of more than 2 per cent in value terms of total world imports of the commodities produced from the categories of minerals to be derived from the Area, provided that the four members shall include one State from the Eastern European region having the largest economy in that region in terms of gross domestic product and the State, on the date of entry into force of the Convention, having the largest economy in terms of gross domestic product, if such States wish to be represented in this group;

(b) Four members from among the eight States Parties which have made the largest investments in preparation for and in the conduct of activities in the Area, either directly or through their nationals;

(c) Four members from among States Parties which, on the basis of production in areas under their jurisdiction, are major net exporters of the categories of minerals to be derived from the Area, including at least two developing States whose exports of such minerals have a substantial bearing upon their economies;

(d) Six members from among developing States Parties, representing special interests. The special interests to be represented shall include those of States with large populations, States which are land-locked or geographically disadvantaged, island States, States which are major importers of the categories of minerals to be derived from the Area, States which are potential producers of such minerals and least developed States;

(e) Eighteen members elected according to the principle of ensuring an equitable geographical distribution of seats in the Council as a whole, provided that each geographical region shall have at least one member elected under this subparagraph. For this purpose, the geographical regions shall be Africa, Asia, Eastern Europe, Latin America and the Caribbean and Western Europe and Others.

16. The provisions of article 161, paragraph 1, of the Convention shall not apply.

...

9.(a) Each group of States elected under paragraph 15 (a) to (c) shall be treated as a chamber for the purposes of voting in the Council. The developing States elected under paragraph 15 (d) and (e) shall be treated as a single chamber for the purposes of voting in the Council.

(b) Before electing the members of the Council, the Assembly shall establish lists of countries fulfilling the criteria for membership in the groups of

States in paragraph 15 (a) to (d). If a State fulfils the criteria for membership in more than one group, it may only be proposed by one group for election to the Council and it shall represent only that group in voting in the Council.

10.   Each group of States in paragraph 15 (a) to (d) shall be represented in the Council by those members nominated by that group. Each group shall nominate only as many candidates as the number of seats required to be filled by that group. When the number of potential candidates in each of the groups referred to in paragraph 15 (a) to (e) exceeds the number of seats available in each of those respective groups, as a general rule, the principle of rotation shall apply. States members of each of those groups shall determine how this principle shall apply in those groups.

2.   In electing the members of the Council in accordance with paragraph 1,[1] the Assembly shall ensure that:

(a)   land-locked and geographically disadvantaged States are represented to a degree which is reasonably proportionate to their representation in the Assembly;

(b)   coastal States, especially developing States, which do not qualify under paragraph 1(a), (b) (c) or (d) are represented to a degree which is reasonably proportionate to their representation in the Assembly;

(c)   each group of States Parties to be represented on the Council is represented by those members, if any, which are nominated by that group.

3.   Elections shall take place at regular sessions of the Assembly. Each member of the Council shall be elected for four years. At the first election however, the term of one half of the members of each group referred to in paragraph 1 shall be two years.[2]

4.   Members of the Council shall be eligible for re-election, but due regard should be paid to the desirability of rotation of membership.

5.   The Council shall function at the seat of the Authority, and shall meet as often as the business of the Authority may require, but not less than three times a year.

---

[1] Paragraph 1 of article 161 does not apply. However, an equivalent provision occurs in the Agreement, annex, Section 3, paragraph 15. In accordance with article 2 of the Agreement, the provisions of the Agreement and Part XI shall be interpreted and applied together as a single instrument. In the event of any inconsistency between the Agreement and Part XI, the provisions of the Agreement shall prevail.

[2] Paragraph 1 of article 161 does not apply. However, an equivalent provision occurs in the Agreement, annex, Section 3, paragraph 15. In accordance with article 2 of the Agreement, the provisions of the Agreement and Part XI shall be interpreted and applied together as a single instrument. In the event of any inconsistency between the Agreement and Part XI, the provisions of the Agreement shall prevail.

6.   A majority of the members of the Council shall constitute a quorum.

7.   Each member of the Council shall have one vote.

8.   (a) Decisions on questions of procedure shall be taken by a majority of the members present and voting.

[(b) Does not apply. See Agreement, annex, Section 3, paragraph 8]

[(c) Does not apply. See Agreement, annex, Section 3, paragraph 8]

AGREEMENT, ANNEX, SECTION 3, PARAGRAPH 8

8.   The provisions of article 161, paragraph 8 (b) and (c), of the Convention shall not apply.

(d)   Decisions on questions of substance arising under the following provisions shall be taken by consensus: article 162, paragraph 2(m) and (o); adoption of amendments to Part XI.

(e)   For the purposes of subparagraphs (d), (f) and (g), "consensus" means the absence of any formal objection. Within 14 days of the submission of a proposal to the Council, the President of the Council shall determine whether there would be a formal objection to the adoption of the proposal. If the President determines that there would be such an objection, the President shall establish and convene, within three days following such determination, a conciliation committee consisting of not more than nine members of the Council, with the President as chairman, for the purpose of reconciling the differences and producing a proposal which can be adopted by consensus. The committee shall work expeditiously and report to the Council within 14 days following its establishment. If the committee is unable to recommend a proposal which can be adopted by consensus, it shall set out in its report the grounds on which the proposal is being opposed.

(f)   Decisions on questions not listed above which the Council is authorized to take by the rules, regulations and procedures of the Authority or otherwise shall be taken pursuant to the subparagraphs of this paragraph specified in the rules, regulations and procedures or, if not specified therein, then pursuant to the subparagraph determined by the Council if possible in advance, by consensus.

(g)   When the issue arises as to whether a question is within subparagraph (a), (b), (c) or (d), the question shall be treated as being within the subparagraph requiring the higher or highest majority or consensus as the case may be, unless otherwise decided by the Council by the said majority or by consensus.

AGREEMENT, ANNEX, SECTION 3, PARAGRAPHS 2, 5 TO 7

2.   As a general rule, decision-making in the organs of the Authority should be by consensus.

...

5.   If all efforts to reach a decision by consensus have been exhausted, decisions by voting in the Council on questions of procedure shall be taken by a majority of members present and voting, and decisions on questions of substance, except where the Convention provides for decisions by consensus in the Council, shall be taken by a two-thirds majority of members present and voting, provided that such decisions are not opposed by a majority in any one of the chambers referred to in paragraph 9. In taking decisions the Council shall seek to promote the interests of all the members of the Authority.

6.   The Council may defer the taking of a decision in order to facilitate further negotiation whenever it appears that all efforts at achieving consensus on a question have not been exhausted.

7.   Decisions by the Assembly or the Council having financial or budgetary implications shall be based on the recommendations of the Finance Committee.

---

9.   The Council shall establish a procedure whereby a member of the Authority not represented on the Council may send a representative to attend a meeting of the Council when a request is made by such member, or a matter particularly affecting it is under consideration. Such a representative shall be entitled to participate in the deliberations but not to vote.

Article 162
Powers and functions

1.   The Council is the executive organ of the Authority. The Council shall have the power to establish, in conformity with this Convention and the general policies established by the Assembly, the specific policies to be pursued by the Authority on any question or matter within the competence of the Authority.

2.   In addition, the Council shall:

(a)   supervise and co-ordinate the implementation of the provisions of this Part on all questions and matters within the competence of the Authority and invite the attention of the Assembly to cases of non-compliance;

(b)   propose to the Assembly a list of candidates for the election of the Secretary-General;

(c)   recommend to the Assembly candidates for the election of the members of the Governing Board of the Enterprise and the Director-General of the Enterprise;

(d) establish, as appropriate, and with due regard to economy and efficiency, such subsidiary organs as it finds necessary for the exercise of its functions in accordance with this Part. In the composition of subsidiary organs, emphasis shall be placed on the need for members qualified and competent in relevant technical matters dealt with by those organs provided that due account shall be taken of the principle of equitable geographical distribution and of special interests;

(e) adopt its rules of procedure including the method of selecting its president;

(f) enter into agreements with the United Nations or other international organizations on behalf of the Authority and within its competence, subject to approval by the Assembly;

(g) consider the reports of the Enterprise and transmit them to the Assembly with its recommendations;

(h) present to the Assembly annual reports and such special reports as the Assembly may request;

(i) issue directives to the Enterprise in accordance with article 170;

[(j) Does not apply. See Agreement, annex, Section 3, paragraph 11(b)][d]

AGREEMENT, ANNEX, SECTION 3, PARAGRAPHS 11 AND 12

11. (a) The Council shall approve a recommendation by the Legal and Technical Commission for approval of a plan of work unless by a two-thirds majority of its members present and voting, including a majority of members present and voting in each of the chambers of the Council, the Council decides to disapprove a plan of work. If the Council does not take a decision on a recommendation for approval of a plan of work within a prescribed period, the recommendation shall be deemed to have been approved by the Council at the end of that period. The prescribed period shall normally be 60 days unless the Council decides to provide for a longer period. If the Commission recommends the disapproval of a plan of work or does not make a recommendation, the Council may nevertheless approve the plan of work in accordance with its rules of procedure for decision-making on questions of substance.

(b) The provisions of article 162, paragraph 2 (j), of the Convention shall not apply.

12. Where a dispute arises relating to the disapproval of a plan of work, such dispute shall be submitted to the dispute settlement procedures set out in the Convention.

---

[d] See page 196.

(k) approve plans of work submitted by the Enterprise in accordance with Annex IV, article 12, applying, *mutatis mutandis*, the procedures set forth in subparagraphs (j);

(l) exercise control over activities in the Area in accordance with article 153, paragraph 4, and the rules, regulations and procedures of the Authority;

(m) take, upon the recommendation of the Economic Planning Commission, necessary and appropriate measures in accordance with article 150, sub-paragraph (h), to provide protection from the adverse economic effects specified therein;

(n) make recommendations to the Assembly, on the basis of advice from the Economic Planning Commission, for a system of compensation or other measures of economic adjustment assistance as provided in article 151, paragraph 10;

AGREEMENT, ANNEX, SECTION 7, PARAGRAPH 2

2. Article 151, paragraph 10, of the Convention shall be implemented by means of measures of economic assistance referred to in paragraph 1. Article 160, paragraph 2 (l), article 162, paragraph 2 (n), article 164, paragraph 2 (d), article 171, subparagraph (f), and article 173, paragraph 2 (c), of the Convention shall be interpreted accordingly.

(o) (i) recommend to the Assembly rules, regulations and procedures on the equitable sharing of financial and other economic benefits derived from activities in the Area and the payments and contributions made pursuant to article 82, taking into particular consideration the interests and needs of the developing States and peoples who have not attained full independence or other self-governing status;

(ii) adopt and apply provisionally, pending approval by the Assembly, the rules, regulations and procedures of the Authority, and any amendments thereto, taking into account the recommendations of the Legal and Technical Commission or other subordinate organ concerned. These rules, regulations and procedures shall relate to prospecting, exploration and exploitation in the Area and the financial management and internal administration of the Authority. Priority shall be given to the adoption of rules, regulations and procedures for the exploration for and exploitation of polymetallic nodules. Rules, regulations and procedures for the exploration for and exploitation of any resource other than polymetallic nodules shall be adopted within three years from the date of a request to the Authority by any of its members to adopt such rules, regulations and procedures in respect of such resource. All rules, regulations and procedures shall remain in effect on a provisional basis until approved by the Assembly or until amended by the Council in the light of any views expressed by the Assembly;

AGREEMENT, ANNEX, SECTION 1, PARAGRAPHS 15 AND 16

15.   The Authority shall elaborate and adopt, in accordance with article 162, paragraph 2 (o) (ii), of the Convention, rules, regulations and procedures based on the principles contained in sections 2, 5, 6, 7 and 8 of this Annex, as well as any additional rules, regulations and procedures necessary to facilitate the approval of plans of work for exploration or exploitation, in accordance with the following subparagraphs:

(a)   The Council may undertake such elaboration any time it deems that all or any of such rules, regulations or procedures are required for the conduct of activities in the Area, or when it determines that commercial exploitation is imminent, or at the request of a State whose national intends to apply for approval of a plan of work for exploitation;

(b)   If a request is made by a State referred to in subparagraph (a) the Council shall, in accordance with article 162, paragraph 2 (o), of the Convention, complete the adoption of such rules, regulations and procedures within two years of the request;

(c)   If the Council has not completed the elaboration of the rules, regulations and procedures relating to exploitation within the prescribed time and an application for approval of a plan of work for exploitation is pending, it shall none the less consider and provisionally approve such plan of work based on the provisions of the Convention and any rules, regulations and procedures that the Council may have adopted provisionally, or on the basis of the norms contained in the Convention and the terms and principles contained in this Annex as well as the principle of non-discrimination among contractors.

16.   The draft rules, regulations and procedures and any recommendations relating to the provisions of Part XI, as contained in the reports and recommendations of the Preparatory Commission, shall be taken into account by the Authority in the adoption of rules, regulations and procedures in accordance with Part XI of this Agreement.

(p)   review the collection of all payments to be made by or to the Authority in connection with operations pursuant to this Part;

[(q)   Does not apply. See Agreement, annex, Section 6, paragraph 7]

AGREEMENT, ANNEX, SECTION 6, PARAGRAPH 7

7.   The provisions of ... article 162, paragraph 2 (q) ... of the Convention shall not apply.

(r) submit the proposed annual budget of the Authority to the Assembly for its approval;

(s) make recommendations to the Assembly concerning policies on any question or matter within the competence of the Authority;

(t) make recommendations to the Assembly concerning suspension of the exercise of the rights and privileges of membership pursuant to article 185;

(u) institute proceedings on behalf of the Authority before the Seabed Disputes Chamber in cases of non-compliance;

(v) notify the Assembly upon a decision by the Seabed Disputes Chamber in proceedings instituted under subparagraph (u), and make any recommendations which it may find appropriate with respect to measures to be taken;

(w) issue emergency orders which may include orders for the suspension or adjustment of operations, to prevent serious harm to the marine environment arising out of activities in the Area;

(x) disapprove areas for exploitation by contractors or the Enterprise in cases where substantial evidence indicates the risk of serious harm to the marine environment;

(y) establish a subsidiary organ for the elaboration of draft financial rules, regulations and procedures relating to:
   (i) financial management in accordance with articles 171 to 175; and
   (ii) financial arrangements in accordance with Annex III, article 13 and article 17, paragraph 1(c);

AGREEMENT, ANNEX, SECTION 9, PARAGRAPH 9

9.   The requirement of article 162, paragraph 2 (y), of the Convention to establish a subsidiary organ to deal with financial matters shall be deemed to have been fulfilled by the establishment of the Finance Committee in accordance with this section.

(z) establish appropriate mechanisms for directing and supervising a staff of inspectors who shall inspect activities in the Area to determine whether this Part, the rules, regulations and procedures of the Authority, and the terms and conditions of any contract with the Authority are being complied with.

Article 163
Organs of the Council

1.   There are hereby established the following organs of the Council:

(a) an Economic Planning Commission;

(b)   a Legal and Technical Commission.

2.   Each Commission shall be composed of 15 members, elected by the Council from among the candidates nominated by the States Parties. However, if necessary, the Council may decide to increase the size of either Commission giving due regard to economy and efficiency.

3.   Members of a Commission shall have appropriate qualifications in the area of competence of that Commission. States Parties shall nominate candidates of the highest standards of competence and integrity with qualifications in relevant fields so as to ensure the effective exercise of the functions of the Commissions.

4.   In the election of members of the Commissions, due account shall be taken of the need for equitable geographical distribution and the representation of special interests.

5.   No State Party may nominate more than one candidate for the same Commission. No person shall be elected to serve on more than one Commission.

6.   Members of the Commissions shall hold office for a term of five years. They shall be eligible for re-election for a further term.

7.   In the event of the death, incapacity or resignation of a member of a Commission prior to the expiration of the term of office, the Council shall elect for the remainder of the term, a member from the same geographical region or area of interest.

8.   Members of Commissions shall have no financial interest in any activity relating to exploration and exploitation in the Area. Subject to their responsibilities to the Commissions upon which they serve, they shall not disclose, even after the termination of their functions, any industrial secret, proprietary data which are transferred to the Authority in accordance with Annex III, article 14, or any other confidential information coming to their knowledge by reason of their duties for the Authority.

9.   Each Commission shall exercise its functions in accordance with such guidelines and directives as the Council may adopt.

10.   Each Commission shall formulate and submit to the Council for approval such rules and regulations as may be necessary for the efficient conduct of the Commission's functions.

11.   The decision-making procedures of the Commissions shall be established by the rules, regulations and procedures of the Authority. Recommendations to the Council shall, where necessary, be accompanied by a summary on the divergencies of opinion in the Commission.

AGREEMENT, ANNEX, SECTION 3, PARAGRAPHS 2 AND 13

2.   As a general rule, decision-making in the organs of the Authority should be by consensus.

...

13. Decisions by voting in the Legal and Technical Commission shall be by a majority of members present and voting.

---

12. Each Commission shall normally function at the seat of the Authority and shall meet as often as is required for the efficient exercise of its functions.

13. In the exercise of its functions, each Commission may, where appropriate, consult another commission, any competent organ of the United Nations or of its specialized agencies or any international organizations with competence in the subject-matter of such consultation.

Article 164
The Economic Planning Commission

1. Members of the Economic Planning Commission shall have appropriate qualifications such as those relevant to mining, management of mineral resource activities, international trade or international economics. The Council shall endeavour to ensure that the membership of the Commission reflects all appropriate qualifications. The Commission shall include at least two members from developing States whose exports of the categories of minerals to be derived from the Area have a substantial bearing upon their economies.

AGREEMENT, ANNEX, SECTION 1, PARAGRAPH 4

4. ...The functions of the Economic Planning Commission shall be performed by the Legal and Technical Commission until such time as the Council decides otherwise or until the approval of the first plan of work for exploitation.

---

2. The Commission shall:
(a) propose, upon the request of the Council, measures to implement decisions relating to activities in the Area taken in accordance with this Convention;
(b) review the trends of and the factors affecting supply, demand and prices of materials which may be derived from the Area, bearing in mind the interests of both importing and exporting countries, and in particular of the developing States among them;
(c) examine any situation likely to lead to the adverse effects referred to in article 150, subparagraph (h), brought to its attention by the State Party or States Parties concerned, and make appropriate recommendations to the Council;
(d) propose to the Council for submission to the Assembly, as provided in article 151, paragraph 10, a system of compensation or other measures of economic adjustment assistance for developing States which suffer ad-

verse effects caused by activities in the Area. The Commission shall make the recommendations to the Council that are necessary for the application of the system or other measures adopted by the Assembly in specific cases.

AGREEMENT, ANNEX, SECTION 7, PARAGRAPH 2

2.   Article 151, paragraph 10, of the Convention shall be implemented by means of measures of economic assistance referred to in paragraph 1. ... article 164, paragraph 2 (d) ... of the Convention shall be interpreted accordingly.

Article 165
The Legal and Technical Commission

1.   Members of the Legal and Technical Commission shall have appropriate qualifications such as those relevant to exploration for and exploitation and processing of mineral resources, oceanology, protection of the marine environment, or economic or legal matters relating to ocean mining and related fields of expertise. The Council shall endeavour to ensure that the membership of the Commission reflects all appropriate qualifications.

2.   The Commission shall:

(a)   make recommendations with regard to the exercise of the Authority's functions upon the request of the Council;

(b)   review formal written plans of work for activities in the Area in accordance with article 153, paragraph 3, and submit appropriate recommendations to the Council. The Commission shall base its recommendations solely on the grounds stated in Annex III and shall report fully thereon to the Council;

(c)   supervise, upon the request of the Council, activities in the Area, where appropriate, in consultation and collaboration with any entity carrying out such activities or State or States concerned and report to the Council;

(d)   prepare assessments of the environmental implications of activities in the Area;

(e)   make recommendations to the Council on the protection of the marine environment, taking into account the views of recognized experts in that field;

(f)   formulate and submit to the Council the rules, regulations and procedures referred to in article 162, paragraph 2(o), taking into account all relevant factors including assessments of the environmental implications of activities in the Area;

(g)   keep such rules, regulations and procedures under review and recommend to the Council from time to time such amendments thereto as it may deem necessary or desirable;

(h) make recommendations to the Council regarding the establishment of a monitoring programme to observe, measure, evaluate and analyse, by recognized scientific methods, on a regular basis, the risks or effects of pollution of the marine environment resulting from activities in the Area, ensure that existing regulations are adequate and are complied with and co-ordinate the implementation of the monitoring programme approved by the Council;

(i) recommend to the Council that proceedings be instituted on behalf of the Authority before the Seabed Disputes Chamber, in accordance with this Part and the relevant Annexes taking into account particularly article 187;

(j) make recommendations to the Council with respect to measures to be taken, upon a decision by the Seabed Disputes Chamber in proceedings instituted in accordance with subparagraph (i);

(k) make recommendations to the Council to issue emergency orders, which may include orders for the suspension or adjustment of operations, to prevent serious harm to the marine environment arising out of activities in the Area. Such recommendations shall be taken up by the Council on a priority basis;

(l) make recommendations to the Council to disapprove areas for exploitation by contractors or the Enterprise in cases where substantial evidence indicates the risk of serious harm to the marine environment;

(m) make recommendations to the Council regarding the direction and supervision of a staff of inspectors who shall inspect activities in the Area to determine whether the provisions of this Part, the rules, regulations and procedures of the Authority, and the terms and conditions of any contract with the Authority are being complied with;

[(n) Does not apply. See Agreement, annex, Section 6, paragraph 7][e]

AGREEMENT, ANNEX, SECTION 6, PARAGRAPH 7

7. The provisions of ... article 165, paragraph 2 (n) ... of the Convention shall not apply.

3. The members of the Commission shall, upon request by any State Party or other party concerned, be accompanied by a representative of such State or other party concerned when carrying out their function of supervision and inspection.

[e] See page 196.

AGREEMENT, ANNEX, SECTION 9
SECTION 9. THE FINANCE COMMITTEE

1.   There is hereby established a Finance Committee. The Committee shall be composed of 15 members with appropriate qualifications relevant to financial matters. States Parties shall nominate candidates of the highest standards of competence and integrity.

2.   No two members of the Finance Committee shall be nationals of the same State Party.

3.   Members of the Finance Committee shall be elected by the Assembly and due account shall be taken of the need for equitable geographical distribution and the representation of special interests. Each group of States referred to in section 3, paragraph 15 (a), (b), (c) and (d), of this Annex shall be represented on the Committee by at least one member. Until the Authority has sufficient funds other than assessed contributions to meet its administrative expenses, the membership of the Committee shall include representatives of the five largest financial contributors to the administrative budget of the Authority. Thereafter, the election of one member from each group shall be on the basis of nomination by the members of the respective group, without prejudice to the possibility of further members being elected from each group.

4.   Members of the Finance Committee shall hold office for a term of five years. They shall be eligible for re-election for a further term.

5.   In the event of the death, incapacity or resignation of a member of the Finance Committee prior to the expiration of the term of office, the Assembly shall elect for the remainder of the term a member from the same geographical region or group of States.

6.   Members of the Finance Committee shall have no financial interest in any activity relating to matters upon which the Committee has the responsibility to make recommendations. They shall not disclose, even after the termination of their functions, any confidential information coming to their knowledge by reason of their duties for the Authority.

7.   Decisions by the Assembly and the Council on the following issues shall take into account recommendations of the Finance Committee:

(a) Draft financial rules, regulations and procedures of the organs of the Authority and the financial management and internal financial administration of the Authority;

(b) Assessment of contributions of members to the administrative budget of the Authority in accordance with article 160, paragraph 2 (e), of the Convention;

(c) All relevant financial matters, including the proposed annual budget prepared by the Secretary-General of the Authority in accordance with article 172 of the Convention and the financial aspects of the implementation of the programmes of work of the Secretariat;

(d)   The administrative budget;

(e)   Financial obligations of States Parties arising from the implementation of this Agreement and Part XI as well as the administrative and budgetary implications of proposals and recommendations involving expenditure from the funds of the Authority;

(f)   Rules, regulations and procedures on the equitable sharing of financial and other economic benefits derived from activities in the Area and the decisions to be made thereon.

8.   Decisions in the Finance Committee on questions of procedure shall be taken by a majority of members present and voting. Decisions on questions of substance shall be taken by consensus.

9.   The requirement of article 162, paragraph 2 (y), of the Convention to establish a subsidiary organ to deal with financial matters shall be deemed to have been fulfilled by the establishment of the Finance Committee in accordance with this section.

SUBSECTION D. THE SECRETARIAT

Article 166
The Secretariat

1.   The Secretariat of the Authority shall comprise a Secretary-General and such staff as the Authority may require.

2.   The Secretary-General shall be elected for four years by the Assembly from among the candidates proposed by the Council and may be re-elected.

3.   The Secretary-General shall be the chief administrative officer of the Authority, and shall act in that capacity in all meetings of the Assembly, of the Council and of any subsidiary organ, and shall perform such other administrative functions as are entrusted to the Secretary-General by these organs.

4.   The Secretary-General shall make an annual report to the Assembly on the work of the Authority.

Article 167
The staff of the Authority

1.   The Staff of the Authority shall consist of such qualified scientific and technical and other personnel as may be required to fulfil the administrative functions of the Authority.

2.   The paramount consideration in the recruitment and employment of the staff and in the determination of their conditions of service shall be the necessity of securing the highest standards of efficiency, competence and integrity. Subject to this consideration, due regard shall be paid to the importance of recruiting the staff on as wide a geographical basis as possible.

3.   The staff shall be appointed by the Secretary-General. The terms and conditions on which they shall be appointed, remunerated and dismissed shall be in accordance with the rules, regulations and procedures of the Authority.

Article 168
International character of the Secretariat

1.   In the performance of their duties the Secretary-General and the staff shall not seek or receive instructions from any government or from other source external to the Authority. They shall refrain from any action which might reflect on their position as international officials responsible only to the Authority. Each State Party undertakes to respect the exclusively international character of the responsibilities of the Secretary-General and the staff and not to seek to influence them in the discharge of their responsibilities. Any violation of responsibilities by a staff member shall be submitted to the appropriate administrative tribunal as provided in the rules, regulations and procedures of the Authority.

2.   The Secretary-General and the staff shall have no financial interest in any activity relating to exploration and exploitation in the Area. Subject to their responsibilities to the Authority, they shall not disclose, even after the termination of their functions, any industrial secret, proprietary data which are transferred to the Authority in accordance with Annex III, article 14, or any other confidential information coming to their knowledge by reason of their employment with the Authority.

3.   Violations of the obligations of a staff member of the Authority set forth in paragraph 2 shall, on the request of a State Party affected by such violation, or a natural or juridical person, sponsored by a State Party as provided in article 153, paragraph 2(b), and affected by such violation, be submitted by the Authority against the staff member concerned to a tribunal designated by the rules, regulations and procedures of the Authority. The Party affected shall have the right to take part in the proceedings. If the tribunal so recommends, the Secretary-General shall dismiss the staff member concerned.

4.   The rules, regulations and procedures of the Authority shall contain such provisions as are necessary to implement this article.

Article 169
Consultation and co-operation with international and
non-governmental organizations

1.   The Secretary-General shall, on matters within the competence of the Authority, make suitable arrangements, with the approval of the Council, for consultation and co-operation with international and non-governmental organizations recognized by the Economic and Social Council of the United Nations.

2.   Any organization with which the Secretary-General has entered into an arrangement under paragraph 1 may designate representatives to attend meetings of the organs of the Authority as observers in accordance with the rules of procedure of these organs. Procedures shall be established for obtaining the views of such organizations in appropriate cases.

3.   The Secretary-General may distribute to States Parties written reports submitted by the non-governmental organizations referred to in paragraph 1 on subjects in which they have special competence and which are related to the work of the Authority.

SUBSECTION E. THE ENTERPRISE

Article 170
The Enterprise

1.   The Enterprise shall, be the organ of the Authority which shall carry out activities in the Area directly, pursuant to article 153, paragraph 2(a), as well as the transporting, processing and marketing of minerals recovered from the Area.

2.   The Enterprise shall, within the framework of the international legal personality of the Authority, have such legal capacity as is provided for in the Statute set forth in Annex IV. The Enterprise shall act in accordance with this Convention and the rules, regulations and procedures of the Authority, as well as the general policies established by the Assembly, and shall be subject to the directives and control of the Council.

3.   The Enterprise shall have its principal place of business at the seat of the Authority.

4.   The Enterprise shall, in accordance with article 173, paragraph 2, and Annex IV, article 11, be provided with such funds as it may require to carry out its functions, and shall receive technology as provided in article 144 and other relevant provisions of this Convention.

AGREEMENT, ANNEX, SECTION 2

SECTION 2. THE ENTERPRISE

1.   The Secretariat of the Authority shall perform the functions of the Enterprise until it begins to operate independently of the Secretariat. The Secretary-General of the Authority shall appoint from within the staff of the Authority an interim Director-General to oversee the performance of these functions by the Secretariat.

These functions shall be:

(a) Monitoring and review of trends and developments relating to deep seabed mining activities, including regular analysis of world metal market conditions and metal prices, trends and prospects;

(b) Assessment of the results of the conduct of marine scientific research with respect to activities in the Area, with particular emphasis on research related to the environmental impact of activities in the Area;

(c) Assessment of available data relating to prospecting and exploration, including the criteria for such activities;

(d) Assessment of technological developments relevant to activities in the Area, in particular technology relating to the protection and preservation of the marine environment;

(e) Evaluation of information and data relating to areas reserved for the Authority;

(f) Assessment of approaches to joint-venture operations;

(g) Collection of information on the availability of trained manpower;

(h) Study of managerial policy options for the administration of the Enterprise at different stages of its operations.

2.   The Enterprise shall conduct its initial deep seabed mining operations through joint ventures. Upon the approval of a plan of work for exploitation for an entity other than the Enterprise, or upon receipt by the Council of an application for a joint-venture operation with the Enterprise, the Council shall take up the issue of the functioning of the Enterprise independently of the Secretariat of the Authority. If joint-venture operations with the Enterprise accord with sound commercial principles, the Council shall issue a directive pursuant to article 170, paragraph 2, of the Convention providing for such independent functioning.

3.   The obligation of States Parties to fund one mine site of the Enterprise as provided for in Annex IV, article 11, paragraph 3, of the Convention shall not apply and States Parties shall be under no obligation to finance any of the operations in any mine site of the Enterprise or under its joint-venture arrangements.

4.   The obligations applicable to contractors shall apply to the Enterprise. Notwithstanding the provisions of article 153, paragraph 3, and Annex III, article 3, paragraph 5, of the Convention, a plan of work for the Enterprise upon its approval shall be in the form of a contract concluded between the Authority and the Enterprise.

5.   A contractor which has contributed a particular area to the Authority as a reserved area has the right of first refusal to enter into a joint-venture arrangement with the Enterprise for exploration and exploitation of that area. If the Enterprise does not submit an application for a plan of work for activities in respect of such a reserved area within 15 years of the commencement of its functions independent of the Secretariat of the Authority or within 15 years of the date on which that area is reserved for the Authority, whichever is the later, the contractor which contributed the area shall be entitled to apply for a plan of work for that area provided it offers in good faith to include the Enterprise as a joint-venture partner.

6.   Article 170, paragraph 4, Annex IV and other provisions of the Convention relating to the Enterprise shall be interpreted and applied in accordance with this section.

SUBSECTION F. FINANCIAL ARRANGEMENTS OF
THE AUTHORITY

Article 171
Funds of the Authority

The funds of the Authority shall include:

(a) assessed contributions made by members of the Authority in accordance with article 160, paragraph 2(e);

(b) funds received by the Authority pursuant to Annex III, article 13, in connection with activities in the Area;

(c) funds transferred from the Enterprise in accordance with Annex IV, article 10;

(d) funds borrowed pursuant to article 174;

(e) voluntary contributions made by members or other entities; and

(f) payments to a compensation fund, in accordance with article 151, paragraph 10, whose sources are to be recommended by the Economic Planning Commission.

AGREEMENT, ANNEX, SECTION 7, PARAGRAPH 2

2. Article 151, paragraph 10, of the Convention shall be implemented by means of measures of economic assistance referred to in paragraph 1. ... article 171, subparagraph (f) ... of the Convention shall be interpreted accordingly.

Article 172
Annual budget of the Authority

The Secretary-General shall draft the proposed annual budget of the Authority and submit it to the Council. The Council shall consider the proposed annual budget and submit it to the Assembly, together with any recommendations thereon. The Assembly shall consider and approve the proposed annual budget in accordance with article 160, paragraph 2(h).

AGREEMENT, ANNEX, SECTION 1, PARAGRAPH 14

14. The Authority shall have its own budget. Until the end of the year following the year during which this Agreement enters into force, the administrative expenses of the Authority shall be met through the budget of the United Nations. Thereafter, the administrative expenses of the Authority shall be met by assessed contributions of its members, including any members on a provisional basis, in accordance with articles 171, subparagraph (a), and 173 of the Convention and

this Agreement, until the Authority has sufficient funds from other sources to meet those expenses. The Authority shall not exercise the power referred to in article 174, paragraph 1, of the Convention to borrow funds to finance its administrative budget.

AGREEMENT, ANNEX, SECTION 9, PARAGRAPH 7

7.   Decisions by the Assembly and the Council on the following issues shall take into account recommendations of the Finance Committee:

...

(c)   All relevant financial matters, including the proposed annual budget prepared by the Secretary-General of the Authority in accordance with article 172 of the Convention and the financial aspects of the implementation of the programmes of work of the Secretariat;

(d)   The administrative budget;

Article 173
Expenses of the Authority

1.   The contributions referred to in article 171, subparagraph (a), shall be paid into a special account to meet the administrative expenses of the Authority until the Authority has sufficient funds from other sources to meet those expenses.

2.   The administrative expenses of the Authority shall be a first call upon the funds of the Authority. Except for the assessed contributions referred to in article 171, subparagraph (a), the funds which remain after payment of administrative expenses may, *inter alia:*

(a)   be shared in accordance with article 140 and article 160, paragraph 2(g);

(b)   be used to provide the Enterprise with funds in accordance with article 170, paragraph 4;

(c)   be used to compensate developing States in accordance with article 151, paragraph 10, and article 160, paragraph 2(1).

AGREEMENT, ANNEX, SECTION 7, PARAGRAPH 2

2.   Article 151, paragraph 10, of the Convention shall be implemented by means of measures of economic assistance referred to in paragraph 1. ... article 173, paragraph 2 (c), of the Convention shall be interpreted accordingly.

Article 174
Borrowing power of the Authority

1.   The Authority shall have the power to borrow funds.

2. The Assembly shall prescribe the limits on the borrowing power of the Authority in the financial regulations adopted pursuant to article 160, paragraph 2(f).

3. The Council shall exercise the borrowing power of the Authority.

4. States Parties shall not be liable for the debts of the Authority.

AGREEMENT, ANNEX, SECTION 1, PARAGRAPH 14

14. The Authority shall not exercise the power referred to in article 174, paragraph 1, of the Convention to borrow funds to finance its administrative budget.

Article 175
Annual audit

The records, books and accounts of the Authority, including its annual financial statements, shall be audited annually by an independent auditor appointed by the Assembly.

SUBSECTION G. LEGAL STATUS, PRIVILEGES AND IMMUNITIES

Article 176
Legal status

The Authority shall have international legal personality and such legal capacity as may be necessary for the exercise of its functions and the fulfilment of its purposes.

Article 177
Privileges and immunities

To enable the Authority to exercise its functions, it shall enjoy in the territory of each State Party the privileges and immunities set forth in this subsection. The privileges and immunities relating to the Enterprise shall be those set forth in Annex IV, article 13.

Article 178
Immunity from legal process

The Authority, its property and assets, shall enjoy immunity from legal process except to the extent that the Authority expressly waives this immunity in a particular case.

Article 179
Immunity from search and any form of seizure

The property and assets of the Authority, wherever located and by whomsoever held, shall be immune from search, requisition, confiscation, expropriation or any other form of seizure by executive or legislative action.

Article 180
Exemption from restrictions, regulations, controls and moratoria

The property and assets of the Authority shall be exempt from restrictions, regulations, controls and moratoria of any nature.

Article 181
Archives and official communications of the Authority

1.   The archives of the Authority, wherever located, shall be inviolable.
2.   Proprietary data, industrial secrets or similar information and personnel records shall not be placed in archives which are open to public inspection.
3.   With regard to its official communications, the Authority shall be accorded by each State Party treatment no less favourable than that accorded by that State to other international organizations.

Article 182
Privileges and immunities of certain persons connected with the Authority

Representatives of States Parties attending meetings of the Assembly, the Council or organs of the Assembly or the Council, and the Secretary-General and staff of the Authority, shall enjoy in the territory of each State Party:
   (a)   immunity from legal process with respect to acts performed by them in the exercise of their functions, except to the extent that the State which they represent or the Authority, as appropriate, expressly waives this immunity in a particular case;
   (b)   if they are not nationals of that State Party, the same exemptions from immigration restrictions, alien registration requirements and national service obligations, the same facilities as regards exchange restrictions and the same treatment in respect of travelling facilities as are accorded by that State to the representatives, officials and employees of comparable rank of other States Parties.

Article 183
Exemption from taxes and customs duties

1.   Within the scope of its official activities, the Authority, its assets and property, its income, and its operations and transactions, authorized by this Convention, shall be exempt from all direct taxation and goods imported or exported for its official use shall be exempt from all customs duties. The Authority shall not claim exemption from taxes which are no more than charges for services rendered.

2.   When purchases of goods or services of substantial value necessary for the official activities of the Authority are made by or on behalf of the Authority, and when the price of such goods or services includes taxes or duties, appropriate measures shall, to the extent practicable, be taken by States Parties to grant exemption from such taxes or duties or provide for their reimbursement. Goods imported or purchased under an exemption provided for in this article shall not be sold or otherwise disposed of in the territory of the State Party which granted the exemption, except under conditions agreed with that State Party.

3.   No tax shall be levied by States Parties on or in respect of salaries and emoluments paid or any other form of payment made by the Authority to the Secretary-General and staff of the Authority, as well as experts performing missions for the Authority, who are not their nationals.

SUBSECTION H. SUSPENSION OF THE EXERCISE OF RIGHTS AND PRIVILEGES OF MEMBERS

Article 184
Suspension of the exercise of voting rights

A State Party which is in arrears in the payment of its financial contributions to the Authority shall have no vote if the amount of its arrears equals or exceeds the amount of the contributions due from it for the preceding two full years. The Assembly may nevertheless, permit such a member to vote if it is satisfied that the failure to pay is due to conditions beyond the control of the member.

Article 185
Suspension of exercise of rights and privileges of membership

1.   A State Party which has grossly and persistently violated the provisions of this Part may be suspended from the exercise of the rights and privileges of membership by the Assembly upon the recommendation of the Council.

2.   No action may be taken under paragraph 1 until the Seabed Disputes Chamber has found that a State Party has grossly and persistently violated the provisions of this Part.

SECTION 5. SETTLEMENT OF DISPUTES AND ADVISORY OPINIONS

Article 186
Seabed Disputes Chamber of the International Tribunal for the Law of the Sea

The establishment of the Seabed Disputes Chamber and the manner in which it shall exercise its jurisdiction shall be governed by the provisions of this section, of Part XV and of Annex VI.

Article 187
Jurisdiction of the Seabed Disputes Chamber

The Seabed Disputes Chamber shall have jurisdiction under this Part and the Annexes relating thereto in disputes with respect to activities in the Area falling within the following categories:

(a) disputes between States Parties concerning the interpretation or application of this Part and the Annexes relating thereto;

(b) disputes between a State Party and the Authority concerning:

(i) acts or omissions of the Authority or of a State Party alleged to be in violation of this Part or the Annexes relating thereto or of rules, regulations and procedures of the Authority adopted in accordance therewith; or

(ii) acts of the Authority alleged to be in excess of jurisdiction or a misuse of power;

(c) disputes between parties to a contract, being States Parties, the Authority or the Enterprise, state enterprises and natural or juridical persons referred to in article 153, paragraph 2(b), concerning:

(i) the interpretation or application of a relevant contract or a plan of work; or

(ii) acts or omissions of a party to the contract relating to activities in the Area and directed to the other party or directly affecting its legitimate interests;

(d) disputes between the Authority and a prospective contractor who has been sponsored by a State as provided in article 153, paragraph 2 (b), and has duly fulfilled the conditions referred to in Annex III, article 4, paragraph 6, and article 13, paragraph 2, concerning the refusal of a contract or a legal issue arising in the negotiation of the contract;

(e) disputes between the Authority and a State Party, a state enterprise or a natural or juridical person sponsored by a State Party as provided for in article 153, paragraph 2(b), where it is alleged that the Authority has incurred liability as provided in Annex III, article 22;

(f) any other disputes for which the jurisdiction of the Chamber is specifically provided in this Convention.

Article 188
Submission of disputes to a special chamber of the International Tribunal for the Law of the Sea or an ad hoc chamber of the Seabed Disputes Chamber or to binding commercial arbitration

1. Disputes between States Parties referred to in article 187, subparagraph (a), may be submitted:

(a) at the request of the parties to the dispute, to a special chamber of the International Tribunal for the Law of the Sea to be formed in accordance with Annex VI, articles 15 and 17; or

(b) at the request of any party to the dispute, to an *ad hoc* chamber of the Seabed Disputes Chamber to be formed in accordance with Annex VI, article 36.

2. (a) Disputes concerning the interpretation or application of a contract referred to in article 187, subparagraph (c)(i), shall be submitted, at the request of any party to the dispute, to binding commercial arbitration, unless the parties otherwise agree. A commercial arbitral tribunal to which the dispute is submitted shall have no jurisdiction to decide any question of interpretation of this Convention. When the dispute also involves a question of the interpretation of Part XI and the Annexes relating thereto, with respect to activities in the Area, that question shall be referred to the Seabed Disputes Chamber for a ruling.

(b) If, at the commencement of or in the course of such arbitration, the arbitral tribunal determines, either at the request of any party to the dispute or *proprio motu,* that its decision depends upon a ruling of the Seabed Disputes Chamber, the arbitral tribunal shall refer such question to the Seabed Disputes Chamber for such ruling. The arbitral tribunal shall then proceed to render its award in conformity with the ruling of the Seabed Disputes Chamber.

(c) In the absence of a provision in the contract on the arbitration procedure to be applied in the dispute, the arbitration shall be conducted in accordance with the UNCITRAL Arbitration Rules or such other arbitration rules as may be prescribed in the rules, regulations and procedures of the Authority, unless the parties to the dispute otherwise agree.

Article 189
Limitation on jurisdiction with regard to decisions of the Authority

The Seabed Disputes Chamber shall have no jurisdiction with regard to the exercise by the Authority of its discretionary powers in accordance with this Part; in no case shall it substitute its discretion for that of the Authority. Without prejudice to article 191, in exercising its jurisdiction pursuant to article 187, the Seabed Disputes Chamber shall not pronounce itself on the question of whether any rules, regulations and procedures of the Authority are in conformity with this Convention, nor declare invalid any such rules, regulations and procedures. Its jurisdiction in this regard shall be confined to deciding claims that the application of any rules, regulations and procedures of the Authority in individual cases would be in conflict with the contractual obligations of the parties to the dispute or their obligations under this Convention, claims concerning excess of jurisdiction or misuse of power, and to claims for damages to be paid or other remedy to be given to the party concerned for the failure of the other party to comply with its contractual obligations or its obligations under this Convention.

Article 190
Participation and appearance of sponsoring States Parties in proceedings

1.   If a natural or juridical person is a party to a dispute referred to in article 187, the sponsoring State shall be given notice thereof and shall have the right to participate in the proceedings by submitting written or oral statements.

2.   If an action is brought against a State Party by a natural or juridical person sponsored by another State Party in a dispute referred to in article 187, subparagraph (c), the respondent State may request the State sponsoring that person to appear in the proceedings on behalf of that person. Failing such appearance, the respondent State may arrange to be represented by a juridical person of its nationality.

Article 191
Advisory opinions

The Seabed Disputes Chamber shall give advisory opinions at the request of the Assembly or the Council on legal questions arising within the scope of their activities. Such opinions shall be given as a matter of urgency.

PART XII
PROTECTION AND PRESERVATION
OF THE MARINE ENVIRONMENT
SECTION 1. GENERAL PROVISIONS

Article 192
General obligation

States have the obligation to protect and preserve the marine environment.

Article 193
Sovereign right of States
to exploit their natural resources

States have the sovereign right to exploit their natural resources pursuant to their environmental policies and in accordance with their duty to protect and preserve the marine environment.

Article 194
Measures to prevent, reduce and control pollution
of the marine environment

1.   States shall take, individually or jointly as appropriate, all measures consistent with this Convention that are necessary to prevent, reduce and control

pollution of the marine environment from any source, using for this purpose the best practicable means at their disposal and in accordance with their capabilities, and they shall endeavour to harmonize their policies in this connection.

2.   States shall take all measures necessary to ensure that activities under their jurisdiction or control are so conducted as not to cause damage by pollution to other States and their environment, and that pollution arising from incidents or activities under their jurisdiction or control does not spread beyond the areas where they exercise sovereign rights in accordance with this Convention.

3.   The measures taken pursuant to this Part shall deal with all sources of pollution of the marine environment. These measures shall include, inter alia, those designed to minimize to the fullest possible extent:

   (a) the release of toxic, harmful or noxious substances, especially those which are persistent, from land-based sources, from or through the atmosphere or by dumping;

   (b) pollution from vessels, in particular measures for preventing accidents and dealing with emergencies, ensuring the safety of operations at sea, preventing intentional and unintentional discharges, and regulating the design, construction, equipment, operation and manning of vessels;

   (c) pollution from installations and devices used in exploration or exploitation of the natural resources of the seabed and subsoil, in particular measures for preventing accidents and dealing with emergencies, ensuring the safety of operations at sea, and regulating the design, construction, equipment, operation and manning of such installations or devices;

   (d) pollution from other installations and devices operating in the marine environment, in particular measures for preventing accidents and dealing with emergencies, ensuring the safety of operations at sea, and regulating the design, construction, equipment, operation and manning of such installations or devices.

4.   In taking measures to prevent, reduce or control pollution of the marine environment, States shall refrain from unjustifiable interference with activities carried out by other States in the exercise of their rights and in pursuance of their duties in conformity with this Convention.

5.   The measures taken in accordance with this Part shall include those necessary to protect and preserve rare or fragile ecosystems as well as the habitat of depleted, threatened or endangered species and other forms of marine life.

Article 195
Duty not to transfer damage or hazards
or transform one type of pollution into another

In taking measures to prevent, reduce and control pollution of the marine environment, States shall act so as not to transfer, directly or indirectly, damage or hazards from one area to another or transform one type of pollution into another.

Article 196
Use of technologies or introduction of alien or new species

1.   States shall take all measures necessary to prevent, reduce and control pollution of the marine environment resulting from the use of technologies under their jurisdiction or control, or the intentional or accidental introduction of species, alien or new, to a particular part of the marine environment, which may cause significant and harmful changes thereto.

2.   This article does not affect the application of this Convention regarding the prevention, reduction and control of pollution of the marine environment.

SECTION 2. GLOBAL AND REGIONAL CO-OPERATION

Article 197
Co-operation on a global or regional basis

States shall co-operate on a global basis and, as appropriate, on a regional basis, directly or through competent international organizations, in formulating and elaborating international rules, standards and recommended practices and procedures consistent with this Convention, for the protection and preservation of the marine environment, taking into account characteristic regional features.

Article 198
Notification of imminent or actual damage

When a State becomes aware of cases in which the marine environment is in imminent danger of being damaged or has been damaged by pollution, it shall immediately notify other States it deems likely to be affected by such damage, as well as the competent international organizations.

Article 199
Contingency plans against pollution

In the cases referred to in article 198, States in the area affected, in accordance with their capabilities, and the competent international organizations shall co-operate, to the extent possible, in eliminating the effects of pollution and preventing or minimizing the damage. To this end, States shall jointly develop and promote contingency plans for responding to pollution incidents in the marine environment.

Article 200
Studies, research programmes and exchange of information and data

States shall co-operate, directly or through competent international organizations, for the purpose of promoting studies, undertaking programmes of scientific research and encouraging the exchange of information and data acquired about pollution of the marine environment. They shall endeavour to participate actively in regional and global programmes to acquire knowledge for the assessment of the nature and extent of pollution, exposure to it, and its pathways, risks and remedies.

Article 201
Scientific criteria for regulations

In the light of the information and data acquired pursuant to article 200, States shall co-operate, directly or through competent international organizations, in establishing appropriate scientific criteria for the formulation and elaboration of rules, standards and recommended practices and procedures for the prevention, reduction and control of pollution of the marine environment.

SECTION 3. TECHNICAL ASSISTANCE

Article 202
Scientific and technical assistance to developing States

States shall, directly or through competent international organizations:
(a) promote programmes of scientific, educational, technical and other assistance to developing States for the protection and preservation of the marine environment and the prevention, reduction and control of marine pollution. Such assistance shall include, inter alia:
   (i) training of their scientific and technical personnel;
   (ii) facilitating their participation in relevant international programmes;
   (iii) supplying them with necessary equipment and facilities;
   (iv) enhancing their capacity to manufacture such equipment;
   (v) advice on and developing facilities for research, monitoring, educational and other programmes;
(b) provide appropriate assistance, especially to developing States, for the minimization of the effects of major incidents which may cause serious pollution of the marine environment;
(c) provide appropriate assistance, especially to developing States, concerning the preparation of environmental assessments.

Article 203
Preferential treatment for developing States

Developing States shall, for the purposes of prevention, reduction and control of pollution of the marine environment or minimization of its effects, be granted preference by international organizations in:
(a) the allocation of appropriate funds and technical assistance; and
(b) the utilization of their specialized services.

SECTION 4. MONITORING AND ENVIRONMENTAL ASSESSMENT

Article 204
Monitoring of the risks or effects of pollution

1.   States shall, consistent with the rights of other States, endeavour, as far as practicable, directly or through the competent international organizations, to observe, measure, evaluate and analyse, by recognized scientific methods, the risks or effects of pollution of the marine environment.

2.   In particular, States shall keep under surveillance the effects of any activities which they permit or in which they engage in order to determine whether these activities are likely to pollute the marine environment.

Article 205
Publication of reports

States shall publish reports of the results obtained pursuant to article 204 or provide such reports at appropriate intervals to the competent international organizations, which should make them available to all States.

Article 206
Assessment of potential effects of activities

When States have reasonable grounds for believing that planned activities under their jurisdiction or control may cause substantial pollution of or significant and harmful changes to the marine environment, they shall, as far as practicable, assess the potential effects of such activities on the marine environment and shall communicate reports of the results of such assessments in the manner provided in article 205.

SECTION 5. INTERNATIONAL RULES AND NATIONAL LEGISLATION TO PREVENT, REDUCE AND CONTROL POLLUTION OF THE MARINE ENVIRONMENT

Article 207
Pollution from land-based sources

1.   States shall adopt laws and regulations to prevent, reduce and control pollution of the marine environment from land-based sources, including rivers, estuaries, pipelines and outfall structures, taking into account internationally agreed rules, standards and recommended practices and procedures.

2.   States shall take other measures as may be necessary to prevent, reduce and control such pollution.

3.   States shall endeavour to harmonize their policies in this connection at the appropriate regional level.

4.   States, acting especially through competent international organizations or diplomatic conference, shall endeavour to establish global and regional rules,

standards and recommended practices and procedures to prevent, reduce and control pollution of the marine environment from land-based sources, taking into account characteristic regional features, the economic capacity of developing States and their need for economic development. Such rules, standards and recommended practices and procedures shall be re-examined from time to time as necessary.

5.   Laws, regulations, measures, rules, standards and recommended practices and procedures referred to in paragraphs 1, 2 and 4 shall include those designed to minimize, to the fullest extent possible, the release of toxic, harmful or noxious substances, especially those which are persistent, into the marine environment.

Article 208
Pollution from seabed activities subject to national jurisdiction

1.   Coastal States shall adopt laws and regulations to prevent, reduce and control pollution of the marine environment arising from or in connection with seabed activities subject to their jurisdiction and from artificial islands, installations and structures under their jurisdiction, pursuant to articles 60 and 80.

2.   States shall take other measures as may be necessary to prevent, reduce and control such pollution.

3.   Such laws, regulations and measures shall be no less effective than international rules, standards and recommended practices and procedures.

4.   States shall endeavour to harmonize their policies in this connection at the appropriate regional level.

5.   States, acting especially through competent international organizations or diplomatic conference, shall establish global and regional rules, standards and recommended practices and procedures to prevent, reduce and control pollution of the marine environment referred to in paragraph l. Such rules, standards and recommended practices and procedures shall be re-examined from time to time as necessary.

Article 209
Pollution from activities in the Area

1. International rules, regulations and procedures shall be established in accordance with Part XI to prevent, reduce and control pollution of the marine environment from activities in the Area. Such rules, regulations and procedures shall be re-examined from time to time as necessary.

2. Subject to the relevant provisions of this section, States shall adopt laws and regulations to prevent, reduce and control pollution of the marine environment from activities in the Area undertaken by vessels, installations, structures and other devices flying their flag or of their registry or operating under their authority, as the case may be. The requirements of such laws and regulations shall be no less effective than the international rules, regulations and procedures referred to in paragraph 1.

Article 210
Pollution by dumping

1.   States shall adopt laws and regulations to prevent, reduce and control pollution of the marine environment by dumping.

2.   States shall take other measures as may be necessary to prevent, reduce and control such pollution.

3.   Such laws, regulations and measures shall ensure that dumping is not carried out without the permission of the competent authorities of States.

4.   States, acting especially through competent international organizations or diplomatic conference, shall endeavour to establish global and regional rules, standards and recommended practices and procedures to prevent, reduce and control such pollution. Such rules, standards and recommended practices and procedures shall be re-examined from time to time as necessary.

5.   Dumping within the territorial sea and the exclusive economic zone or onto the continental shelf shall not be carried out without the express prior approval of the coastal State, which has the right to permit, regulate and control such dumping after due consideration of the matter with other States which by reason of their geographical situation may be adversely affected thereby.

6.   National laws, regulations and measures shall be no less effective in preventing, reducing and controlling such pollution than the global rules and standards.

Article 211
Pollution from vessels

1.   States, acting through the competent international organization or general diplomatic conference, shall establish international rules and standards to prevent, reduce and control pollution of the marine environment from vessels and promote the adoption, in the same manner, wherever appropriate, of routeing systems designed to minimize the threat of accidents which might cause pollution of the marine environment, including the coastline, and pollution damage to the related interests of coastal States. Such rules and standards shall, in the same manner, be re-examined from time to time as necessary.

2.   States shall adopt laws and regulations for the prevention, reduction and control of pollution of the marine environment from vessels flying their flag or of their registry. Such laws and regulations shall at least have the same effect as that of generally accepted international rules and standards established through the competent international organization or general diplomatic conference.

3.   States which establish particular requirements for the prevention, reduction and control of pollution of the marine environment as a condition for the entry of foreign vessels into their ports or internal waters or for a call at their offshore terminals shall give due publicity to such requirements and shall communicate them to the competent international organization. Whenever such requirements are established in identical form by two or more coastal States in an endeavour to harmonize policy, the communication shall indicate which States are participating

in such cooperative arrangements. Every State shall require the master of a vessel flying its flag or of its registry, when navigating within the territorial sea of a State participating in such cooperative arrangements, to furnish, upon the request of that State, information as to whether it is proceeding to a State of the same region participating in such cooperative arrangements and, if so, to indicate whether it complies with the port entry requirements of that State. This article is without prejudice to the continued exercise by a vessel of its right of innocent passage or to the application of article 25, paragraph 2.

4.   Coastal States may, in the exercise of their sovereignty within their territorial sea, adopt laws and regulations for the prevention, reduction and control of marine pollution from foreign vessels, including vessels exercising the right of innocent passage. Such laws and regulations shall, in accordance with Part II, section 3, not hamper innocent passage of foreign vessels.

5.   Coastal States, for the purpose of enforcement as provided for in section 6, may in respect of their exclusive economic zones adopt laws and regulations for the prevention, reduction and control of pollution from vessels conforming to and giving effect to generally accepted international rules and standards established through the competent international organization or general diplomatic conference.

6.   (a) Where the international rules and standards referred to in paragraph 1 are inadequate to meet special circumstances and coastal States have reasonable grounds for believing that a particular, clearly defined area of their respective exclusive economic zones is an area where the adoption of special mandatory measures for the prevention of pollution from vessels is required for recognized technical reasons in relation to its oceanographical and ecological conditions, as well as its utilization or the protection of its resources and the particular character of its traffic, the coastal States, after appropriate consultations through the competent international organization with any other States concerned, may, for that area, direct a communication to that organization, submitting scientific and technical evidence in support and information on necessary reception facilities. Within 12 months after receiving such a communication, the organization shall determine whether the conditions in that area correspond to the requirements set out above. If the organization so determines, the coastal States may, for that area, adopt laws and regulations for the prevention, reduction and control of pollution from vessels implementing such international rules and standards or navigational practices as are made applicable, through the organization, for special areas. These laws and regulations shall not become applicable to foreign vessels until 15 months after the submission of the communication to the organization.

(b)   The coastal States shall publish the limits of any such particular, clearly defined area.

(c)   If the coastal States intend to adopt additional laws and regulations for the same area for the prevention, reduction and control of pollution from vessels, they shall, when submitting the aforesaid communication, at the same time notify the organization thereof. Such additional laws and regulations may relate to discharges or navigational practices but shall not require foreign vessels to observe design, construction, manning or equipment standards other than generally accepted international rules and standards; they shall become applicable to foreign vessels 15 months after the submission of the communication to the organization, provided that the organization agrees within 12 months after the submission of the communication.

7.   The international rules and standards referred to in this article should include *inter alia* those relating to prompt notification to coastal States, whose coastline or related interests may be affected by incidents, including maritime casualties, which involve discharges or probability of discharges.

Article 212
Pollution from or through the atmosphere

1.   States shall adopt laws and regulations to prevent, reduce and control pollution of the marine environment from or through the atmosphere, applicable to the air space under their sovereignty and to vessels flying their flag or vessels or aircraft of their registry, taking into account internationally agreed rules, standards and recommended practices and procedures and the safety of air navigation.

2.   States shall take other measures as may be necessary to prevent, reduce and control such pollution.

3.   States, acting especially through competent international organizations or diplomatic conference, shall endeavour to establish global and regional rules, standards and recommended practices and procedures to prevent, reduce and control such pollution.

SECTION 6. ENFORCEMENT

Article 213
Enforcement with respect to pollution from land-based sources

States shall enforce their laws and regulations adopted in accordance with article 207 and shall adopt laws and regulations and take other measures necessary to implement applicable international rules and standards established through competent international organizations or diplomatic conference to prevent, reduce and control pollution of the marine environment from land-based sources.

Article 214
Enforcement with respect to pollution from seabed activities

States shall enforce their laws and regulations adopted in accordance with article 208 and shall adopt laws and regulations and take other measures necessary to implement applicable international rules and standards established through

competent international organizations or diplomatic conference to prevent, reduce and control pollution of the marine environment arising from or in connection
with seabed activities subject to their jurisdiction and from artificial islands, installations and structures under their jurisdiction, pursuant to articles 60 and 80.

Article 215
Enforcement with respect to pollution from activities in the Area

Enforcement of international rules, regulations and procedures established
in accordance with Part XI to prevent, reduce and control pollution of the marine
environment from activities in the Area shall be governed by that Part.

Article 216
Enforcement with respect to pollution by dumping

1.   Laws and regulations adopted in accordance with this Convention and
applicable international rules and standards established through competent international organizations or diplomatic conference for the prevention, reduction and
control of pollution of the marine environment by dumping shall be enforced:
   (a) by the coastal State with regard to dumping within its territorial sea or
        its exclusive economic zone or onto its continental shelf;
   (b) by the flag State with regard to vessels flying its flag or vessels or air-
        craft of its registry;
   (c) by any State with regard to acts of loading of wastes or other matter
        occurring within its territory or at its off-shore terminals.
2.   No State shall be obliged by virtue of this article to institute proceedings when another State has already instituted proceedings in accordance with
this article.

Article 217
Enforcement by flag States

1.   States shall ensure compliance by vessels flying their flag or of their
registry with applicable international rules and standards, established through the
competent international organization or general diplomatic conference, and with
their laws and regulations adopted in accordance with this Convention for the
prevention, reduction and control of pollution of the marine environment from
vessels and shall accordingly adopt laws and regulations and take other measures
necessary for their implementation. Flag States shall provide for the effective enforcement of such rules, standards, laws and regulations, irrespective of where a
violation occurs.
2.   States shall, in particular, take appropriate measures in order to ensure
that vessels flying their flag or of their registry are prohibited from sailing, until
they can proceed to sea in compliance with the requirements of the international
rules and standards referred to in paragraph 1, including requirements in respect
of design, construction, equipment and manning of vessels.

3.   States shall ensure that vessels flying their flag or of their registry carry on board certificates required by and issued pursuant to international rules and standards referred to in paragraph 1. States shall ensure that vessels flying their flag are periodically inspected in order to verify that such certificates are in conformity with the actual condition of the vessels. These certificates shall be accepted by other States as evidence of the condition of the vessels and shall be regarded as having the same force as certificates issued by them, unless there are clear grounds for believing that the condition of the vessel does not correspond substantially with the particulars of the certificates.

4.   If a vessel commits a violation of rules and standards established through the competent international organization or general diplomatic conference, the flag State, without prejudice to articles 218, 220 and 228, shall provide for immediate investigation and where appropriate institute proceedings in respect of the alleged violation irrespective of where the violation occurred or where the pollution caused by such violation has occurred or has been spotted.

5.   Flag States conducting an investigation of the violation may request the assistance of any other State whose co-operation could be useful in clarifying the circumstances of the case. States shall endeavour to meet appropriate requests of flag States.

6.   States shall, at the written request of any State, investigate any violation alleged to have been committed by vessels flying their flag. If satisfied that sufficient evidence is available to enable proceedings to be brought in respect of the alleged violation, flag States shall without delay institute such proceedings in accordance with their laws.

7.   Flag States shall promptly inform the requesting State and the competent international organization of the action taken and its outcome. Such information shall be available to all States.

8.   Penalties provided for by the laws and regulations of States for vessels flying their flag shall be adequate in severity to discourage violations wherever they occur.

Article 218
Enforcement by port States

1.   When a vessel is voluntarily within a port or at an off-shore terminal of a State, that State may undertake investigations and, where the evidence so warrants, institute proceedings in respect of any discharge from that vessel outside the internal waters, territorial sea or exclusive economic zone of that State in violation of applicable international rules and standards established through the competent international organization or general diplomatic conference.

2.   No proceedings pursuant to paragraph 1 shall be instituted in respect of a discharge violation in the internal waters, territorial sea or exclusive economic zone of another State unless requested by that State, the flag State, or a State damaged or threatened by the discharge violation, or unless the violation has caused

or is likely to cause pollution in the internal waters, territorial sea or exclusive economic zone of the State instituting the proceedings.

3. When a vessel is voluntarily within a port or at an off-shore terminal of a State, that State shall, as far as practicable, comply with requests from any State for investigation of a discharge violation referred to in paragraph 1, believed to have occurred in, caused, or threatened damage to the internal waters, territorial sea or exclusive economic zone of the requesting State. It shall likewise, as far as practicable, comply with requests from the flag State for investigation of such a violation, irrespective of where the violation occurred.

4. The records of the investigation carried out by a port State pursuant to this article shall be transmitted upon request to the flag State or to the coastal State. Any proceedings instituted by the port State on the basis of such an investigation may, subject to section 7, be suspended at the request of the coastal State when the violation has occurred within its internal waters, territorial sea or exclusive economic zone. The evidence and records of the case, together with any bond or other financial security posted with the authorities of the port State, shall in that event be transmitted to the coastal State. Such transmittal shall preclude the continuation of proceedings in the port State.

Article 219
Measures relating to seaworthiness of vessels to avoid pollution

Subject to section 7, States which, upon request or on their own initiative, have ascertained that a vessel within one of their ports or at one of their off-shore terminals is in violation of applicable international rules and standards relating to seaworthiness of vessels and thereby threatens damage to the marine environment shall, as far as practicable, take administrative measures to prevent the vessel from sailing. Such States may permit the vessel to proceed only to the nearest appropriate repair yard and, upon removal of the causes of the violation, shall permit the vessel to continue immediately.

Article 220
Enforcement by coastal States

1. When a vessel is voluntarily within a port or at an off-shore terminal of a State, that State may, subject to section 7, institute proceedings in respect of any violation of its laws and regulations adopted in accordance with this Convention or applicable international rules and standards for the prevention, reduction and control of pollution from vessels when the violation has occurred within the territorial sea or the exclusive economic zone of that State.

2. Where there are clear grounds for believing that a vessel navigating in the territorial sea of a State has, during its passage therein, violated laws and regulations of that State adopted in accordance with this Convention or applicable international rules and standards for the prevention, reduction and control of pollution from vessels, that State, without prejudice to the application of the relevant provisions of Part II, section 3, may undertake physical inspection of the

vessel relating to the violation and may, where the evidence so warrants, institute proceedings, including detention of the vessel, in accordance with its laws, subject to the provisions of section 7.

3.   Where there are clear grounds for believing that a vessel navigating in the exclusive economic zone or the territorial sea of a State has, in the exclusive economic zone, committed a violation of applicable international rules and standards for the prevention, reduction and control of pollution from vessels or laws and regulations of that State conforming and giving effect to such rules and standards, that State may require the vessel to give information regarding its identity and port of registry, its last and its next port of call and other relevant information required to establish whether a violation has occurred.

4.   States shall adopt laws and regulations and take other measures so that vessels flying their flag comply with requests for information pursuant to paragraph 3.

5.   Where there are clear grounds for believing that a vessel navigating in the exclusive economic zone or the territorial sea of a State has, in the exclusive economic zone, committed a violation referred to in paragraph 3 resulting in a substantial discharge causing or threatening significant pollution of the marine environment, that State may undertake physical inspection of the vessel for matters relating to the violation if the vessel has refused to give information or if the information supplied by the vessel is manifestly at variance with the evident factual situation and if the circumstances of the case justify such inspection.

6.   Where there is clear objective evidence that a vessel navigating in the exclusive economic zone or the territorial sea of a State has, in the exclusive economic zone, committed a violation referred to in paragraph 3 resulting in a discharge causing major damage or threat of major damage to the coastline or related interests of the coastal State, or to any resources of its territorial sea or exclusive economic zone, that State may, subject to section 7, provided that the evidence so warrants, institute proceedings, including detention of the vessel, in accordance with its laws.

7.   Notwithstanding the provisions of paragraph 6, whenever appropriate procedures have been established, either through the competent international organization or as otherwise agreed, whereby compliance with requirements for bonding or other appropriate financial security has been assured, the coastal State if bound by such procedures shall allow the vessel to proceed.

8.   The provisions of paragraphs 3, 4, 5, 6 and 7 also apply in respect of national laws and regulations adopted pursuant to article 211, paragraph 6.

Article 221
Measures to avoid pollution arising from maritime casualties

1.   Nothing in this Part shall prejudice the right of States, pursuant to international law, both customary and conventional, to take and enforce measures beyond the territorial sea proportionate to the actual or threatened damage to protect their coastline or related interests, including fishing, from pollution or threat

of pollution following upon a maritime casualty or acts relating to such a casualty, which may reasonably be expected to result in major harmful consequences.

2.   For the purposes of this article, "maritime casualty" means a collision of vessels, stranding or other incident of navigation, or other occurrence on board a vessel or external to it resulting in material damage or imminent threat of material damage to a vessel or cargo.

Article 222
Enforcement with respect to pollution from or through the atmosphere

States shall enforce, within the air space under their sovereignty or with regard to vessels flying their flag or vessels or aircraft of their registry, their laws and regulations adopted in accordance with article 212, paragraph 1, and with other provisions of this Convention and shall adopt laws and regulations and take other measures necessary to implement applicable international rules and standards established through competent international organizations or diplomatic conference to prevent, reduce and control pollution of the marine environment from or through the atmosphere, in conformity with all relevant international rules and standards concerning the safety of air navigation.

SECTION 7. SAFEGUARDS

Article 223
Measures to facilitate proceedings

In proceedings instituted pursuant to this Part, States shall take measures to facilitate the hearing of witnesses and the admission of evidence submitted by authorities of another State, or by the competent international organization, and shall facilitate the attendance at such proceedings of official representatives of the competent international organization, the flag State and any State affected by pollution arising out of any violation. The official representatives attending such proceedings shall have such rights and duties as may be provided under national laws and regulations or international law.

Article 224
Exercise of powers of enforcement

The powers of enforcement against foreign vessels under this Part may only be exercised by officials or by warships, military aircraft, or other ships or aircraft clearly marked and identifiable as being on government service and authorized to that effect.

Article 225
Duty to avoid adverse consequences
in the exercise of the powers of enforcement

In the exercise under this Convention of their powers of enforcement against foreign vessels, States shall not endanger the safety of navigation or otherwise create any hazard to a vessel, or bring it to an unsafe port or anchorage, or expose the marine environment to an unreasonable risk.

Article 226
Investigation of foreign vessels

1. (a) States shall not delay a foreign vessel longer than is essential for purposes of the investigations provided for in articles 216, 218 and 220. Any physical inspection of a foreign vessel shall be limited to an examination of such certificates, records or other documents as the vessel is required to carry by generally accepted international rules and standards or of any similar documents which it is carrying; further physical inspection of the vessel may be undertaken only after such an examination and only when:

    (i)   there are clear grounds for believing that the condition of the vessel or its equipment does not correspond substantially with the particulars of those documents;

    (ii) the contents of such documents are not sufficient to confirm or verify a suspected violation; or

    (iii) the vessel is not carrying valid certificates and records.

  (b) If the investigation indicates a violation of applicable laws and regulations or international rules and standards for the protection and preservation of the marine environment, release shall be made promptly subject to reasonable procedures such as bonding or other appropriate financial security.

  (c) Without prejudice to applicable international rules and standards relating to the seaworthiness of vessels, the release of a vessel may, whenever it would present an unreasonable threat of damage to the marine environment, be refused or made conditional upon proceeding to the nearest appropriate repair yard. Where release has been refused or made conditional, the flag State of the vessel must be promptly notified, and may seek release of the vessel in accordance with Part XV.

2. States shall co-operate to develop procedures for the avoidance of unnecessary physical inspection of vessels at sea.

Article 227
Non-discrimination with respect to foreign vessels

In exercising their rights and performing their duties under this Part, States shall not discriminate in form or in fact against vessels of any other State.

Article 228
Suspension and restrictions on institution of proceedings

1. Proceedings to impose penalties in respect of any violation of applicable laws and regulations or international rules and standards relating to the

prevention, reduction and control of pollution from vessels committed by a foreign vessel beyond the territorial sea of the State instituting proceedings shall be suspended upon the taking of proceedings to impose penalties in respect of corresponding charges by the flag State within six months of the date on which proceedings were first instituted, unless those proceedings relate to a case of major damage to the coastal State or the flag State in question has repeatedly disregarded its obligation to enforce effectively the applicable international rules and standards in respect of violations committed by its vessels. The flag State shall in due course make available to the State previously instituting proceedings a full dossier of the case and the records of the proceedings, whenever the flag State has requested the suspension of proceedings in accordance with this article. When proceedings instituted by the flag State have been brought to a conclusion, the suspended proceedings shall be terminated. Upon payment of costs incurred in respect of such proceedings, any bond posted or other financial security provided in connection with the suspended proceedings shall be released by the coastal State.

2.   Proceedings to impose penalties on foreign vessels shall not be instituted after the expiry of three years from the date on which the violation was committed, and shall not be taken by any State in the event of proceedings having been instituted by another State subject to the provisions set out in paragraph 1.

3. The provisions of this article are without prejudice to the right of the flag State to take any measures, including proceedings to impose penalties, according to its laws irrespective of prior proceedings by another State.

Article 229
Institution of civil proceedings

Nothing in this Convention affects the institution of civil proceedings in respect of any claim for loss or damage resulting from pollution of the marine environment.

Article 230
Monetary penalties and the observance of recognized rights of the accused

1.   Monetary penalties only may be imposed with respect to violations of national laws and regulations or applicable international rules and standards for the prevention, reduction and control of pollution of the marine environment, committed by foreign vessels beyond the territorial sea.

2.   Monetary penalties only may be imposed with respect to violations of national laws and regulations or applicable international rules and standards for the prevention, reduction and control of pollution of the marine environment, committed by foreign vessels in the territorial sea, except in the case of a wilful and serious act of pollution in the territorial sea.

3.   In the conduct of proceedings in respect of such violations committed by a foreign vessel which may result in the imposition of penalties, recognized rights of the accused shall be observed.

Article 231
Notification to the flag State and other States concerned

States shall promptly notify the flag State and any other State concerned of any measures taken pursuant to section 6 against foreign vessels, and shall submit to the flag State all official reports concerning such measures. However, with respect to violations committed in the territorial sea, the foregoing obligations of the coastal State apply only to such measures as are taken in proceedings. The diplomatic agents or consular officers and where possible the maritime authority of the flag State, shall be immediately informed of any such measures taken pursuant to section 6 against foreign vessels.

Article 232
Liability of States arising from enforcement measures

States shall be liable for damage or loss attributable to them arising from measures taken pursuant to section 6 when such measures are unlawful or exceed those reasonably required in the light of available information. States shall provide for recourse in their courts for actions in respect of such damage or loss.

Article 233
Safeguards with respect to straits used for international navigation

Nothing in sections 5, 6 and 7 affects the legal régime of straits used for international navigation. However, if a foreign ship other than those referred to in section 10 has committed a violation of the laws and regulations referred to in article 42, paragraph 1(a) and (b), causing or threatening major damage to the marine environment of the straits, the States bordering the straits may take appropriate enforcement measures and if so shall respect *mutatis mutandis* the provisions of this section.

SECTION 8. ICE-COVERED AREAS

Article 234
Ice-covered areas

Coastal States have the right to adopt and enforce non-discriminatory laws and regulations for the prevention, reduction and control of marine pollution from vessels in ice-covered areas within the limits of the exclusive economic zone, where particularly severe climatic conditions and the presence of ice covering such areas for most of the year create obstructions or exceptional hazards to navigation, and pollution of the marine environment could cause major harm to or irreversible disturbance of the ecological balance. Such laws and regulations shall have due regard to navigation and the protection and preservation of the marine environment based on the best available scientific evidence.

SECTION 9. RESPONSIBILITY AND LIABILITY

Article 235
Responsibility and liability

1.   States are responsible for the fulfilment of their international obligations concerning the protection and preservation of the marine environment. They shall be liable in accordance with international law.

2.   States shall ensure that recourse is available in accordance with their legal systems for prompt and adequate compensation or other relief in respect of damage caused by pollution of the marine environment by natural or juridical persons under their jurisdiction.

3.   With the objective of assuring prompt and adequate compensation in respect of all damage caused by pollution of the marine environment, States shall co-operate in the implementation of existing international law and the further development of international law relating to responsibility and liability for the assessment of and compensation for damage and the settlement of related disputes, as well as, where appropriate, development of criteria and procedures for payment of adequate compensation, such as compulsory insurance or compensation funds.

SECTION 10. SOVEREIGN IMMUNITY

Article 236
Sovereign immunity

The provisions of this Convention regarding the protection and preservation of the marine environment do not apply to any warship, naval auxiliary, other vessels or aircraft owned or operated by a State and used, for the time being, only on government non-commercial service. However, each State shall ensure, by the adoption of appropriate measures not impairing operations or operational capabilities of such vessels or aircraft owned or operated by it, that such vessels or aircraft act in a manner consistent, so far as is reasonable and practicable, with this Convention.

SECTION 11. OBLIGATIONS UNDER OTHER CONVENTIONS ON THE PROTECTION AND PRESERVATION OF THE MARINE ENVIRONMENT

Article 237
Obligations under other conventions on the protection and preservation of the marine environment

1.   The provisions of this Part are without prejudice to the specific obligations assumed by States under special conventions and agreements concluded previously which relate to the protection and preservation of the marine environment and to agreements which may be concluded in furtherance of the general principles set forth in this Convention.

2.   Specific obligations assumed by States under special conventions, with respect to the protection and preservation of the marine environment, should be carried out in a manner consistent with the general principles and objectives of this Convention.

PART XIII
MARINE SCIENTIFIC RESEARCH
SECTION 1. GENERAL PROVISIONS

Article 238
Right to conduct marine scientific research

All States, irrespective of their geographical location, and competent international organizations have the right to conduct marine scientific research subject to the rights and duties of other States as provided for in this Convention.

Article 239
Promotion of marine scientific research

States and competent international organizations shall promote and facilitate the development and conduct of marine scientific research in accordance with this Convention.

Article 240
General principles for the conduct of marine scientific research

In the conduct of marine scientific research the following principles shall apply:
  (a) marine scientific research shall be conducted exclusively for peaceful purposes;
  (b) marine scientific research shall be conducted with appropriate scientific methods and means compatible with this Convention;
  (c) marine scientific research shall not unjustifiably interfere with other legitimate uses of the sea compatible with this Convention and shall be duly respected in the course of such uses;
  (d) marine scientific research shall be conducted in compliance with all relevant regulations adopted in conformity with this Convention including those for the protection and preservation of the marine environment.

Article 241
Non-recognition of marine scientific research activities
as the legal basis for claims

Marine scientific research activities shall not constitute the legal basis for any claim to any part of the marine environment or its resources.

SECTION 2. INTERNATIONAL CO-OPERATION

Article 242
Promotion of international co-operation

1.   States and competent international organizations shall, in accordance with the principle of respect for sovereignty and jurisdiction and on the basis of mutual benefit, promote international co-operation in marine scientific research for peaceful purposes.

2.   In this context, without prejudice to the rights and duties of States under this Convention, a State, in the application of this Part, shall provide, as appropriate, other States with a reasonable opportunity to obtain from it, or with its co-operation, information necessary to prevent and control damage to the health and safety of persons and to the marine environment.

Article 243
Creation of favourable conditions

States and competent international organizations shall co-operate, through the conclusion of bilateral and multilateral agreements, to create favourable conditions for the conduct of marine scientific research in the marine environment and to integrate the efforts of scientists in studying the essence of phenomena and processes occurring in the marine environment and the interrelations between them.

Article 244
Publication and dissemination of information and knowledge

1.   States and competent international organizations shall, in accordance with this Convention, make available by publication and dissemination through appropriate channels information on proposed major programmes and their objectives as well as knowledge resulting from marine scientific research.

2.   For this purpose, States, both individually and in co-operation with other States and with competent international organizations, shall actively promote the flow of scientific data and information and the transfer of knowledge resulting from marine scientific research, especially to developing States, as well as the strengthening of the autonomous marine scientific research capabilities of developing States through, *inter alia,* programmes to provide adequate education and training of their technical and scientific personnel.

SECTION 3. CONDUCT AND PROMOTION OF MARINE SCIENTIFIC RESEARCH

Article 245
Marine scientific research in the territorial sea

Coastal States, in the exercise of their sovereignty, have the exclusive right to regulate, authorize and conduct marine scientific research in their territorial sea.

Marine scientific research therein shall be conducted only with the express consent of and under the conditions set forth by the coastal State.

Article 246
Marine scientific research in the exclusive economic zone
and on the continental shelf

1.   Coastal States, in the exercise of their jurisdiction, have the right to regulate, authorize and conduct marine scientific research in their exclusive economic zone and on their continental shelf in accordance with the relevant provisions of this Convention.

2.   Marine scientific research in the exclusive economic zone and on the continental shelf shall be conducted with the consent of the coastal State.

3.   Coastal States shall, in normal circumstances, grant their consent for marine scientific research projects by other States or competent international organizations in their exclusive economic zone or on their continental shelf to be carried out in accordance with this Convention exclusively for peaceful purposes and in order to increase scientific knowledge of the marine environment for the benefit of all mankind. To this end, coastal States shall establish rules and procedures ensuring that such consent will not be delayed or denied unreasonably.

4.   For the purposes of applying paragraph 3, normal circumstances may exist in spite of the absence of diplomatic relations between the coastal State and the researching State.

5.   Coastal States may however in their discretion withhold their consent to the conduct of a marine scientific research project of another State or competent international organization in the exclusive economic zone or on the continental shelf of the coastal State if that project:

(a) is of direct significance for the exploration and exploitation of natural resources, whether living or non-living;

(b) involves drilling into the continental shelf, the use of explosives or the introduction of harmful substances into the marine environment;

(c) involves the construction, operation or use of artificial islands, installations and structures referred to in articles 60 and 80;

(d) contains information communicated pursuant to article 248 regarding the nature and objectives of the project which is inaccurate or if the researching State or competent international organization has outstanding obligations to the coastal State from a prior research project.

6.   Notwithstanding the provisions of paragraph 5, coastal States may not exercise their discretion to withhold consent under subparagraph (a) of that paragraph in respect of marine scientific research projects to be undertaken in accordance with the provisions of this Part on the continental shelf, beyond 200 nautical miles from the baselines from which the breadth of the territorial sea is measured, outside those specific areas which coastal States may at any time publicly designate as areas in which exploitation or detailed exploratory operations focused on those areas are occurring or will occur within a reasonable period of time. Coastal States shall give reasonable notice of the designation of such areas, as well as any modifications thereto, but shall not be obliged to give details of the operations therein.

7.   The provisions of paragraph 6 are without prejudice to the rights of coastal States over the continental shelf as established in article 77.

8.   Marine scientific research activities referred to in this article shall not unjustifiably interfere with activities undertaken by coastal States in the exercise of their sovereign rights and jurisdiction provided for in this Convention.

Article 247
Marine scientific research projects undertaken
by or under the auspices of international organizations

A coastal State which is a member of or has a bilateral agreement with an international organization, and in whose exclusive economic zone or on whose continental shelf that organization wants to carry out a marine scientific research project, directly or under its auspices, shall be deemed to have authorized the project to be carried out in conformity with the agreed specifications if that State approved the detailed project when the decision was made by the organization for the undertaking of the project, or is willing to participate in it, and has not expressed any objection within four months of notification of the project by the organization to the coastal State.

Article 248
Duty to provide information to the coastal State

States and competent international organizations which intend to undertake marine scientific research in the exclusive economic zone or on the continental shelf of a coastal State shall, not less than six months in advance of the expected starting date of the marine scientific research project, provide that State with a full description of:

(a)   the nature and objectives of the project;

(b)   the method and means to be used, including name, tonnage, type and class of vessels and a description of scientific equipment;

(c)   the precise geographical areas in which the project is to be conducted;

(d)   the expected date of first appearance and final departure of the research vessels, or deployment of the equipment and its removal, as appropriate;

(e)   the name of the sponsoring institution, its director, and the person in charge of the project; and

(f)   the extent to which it is considered that the coastal State should be able to participate or to be represented in the project.

Article 249
Duty to comply with certain conditions

1. States and competent international organizations when undertaking marine scientific research in the exclusive economic zone or on the continental shelf of a coastal State shall comply with the following conditions:

(a)   ensure the right of the coastal State, if it so desires, to participate or be represented in the marine scientific research project, especially on board research vessels and other craft or scientific research installations, when practicable, without payment of any remuneration to the scientists of the coastal State and without obligation to contribute towards the costs of the project;

(b) provide the coastal State, at its request, with preliminary reports, as soon as practicable, and with the final results and conclusions after the completion of the research;

(c) undertake to provide access for the coastal State, at its request, to all data and samples derived from the marine scientific research project and likewise to furnish it with data which may be copied and samples which may be divided without detriment to their scientific value;

(d) if requested, provide the coastal State with an assessment of such data, samples and research results or provide assistance in their assessment or interpretation;

(e) ensure, subject to paragraph 2, that the research results are made internationally available through appropriate national or international channels, as soon as practicable;

(f) inform the coastal State immediately of any major change in the research programme;

(g) unless otherwise agreed, remove the scientific research installations or equipment once the research is completed.

2.   This article is without prejudice to the conditions established by the laws and regulations of the coastal State for the exercise of its discretion to grant or withhold consent pursuant to article 246, paragraph 5, including requiring prior agreement for making internationally available the research results of a project of direct significance for the exploration and exploitation of natural resources.

Article 250
Communications concerning marine scientific research projects

Communications concerning the marine scientific research projects shall be made through appropriate official channels, unless otherwise agreed.

Article 251
General criteria and guidelines

States shall seek to promote through competent international organizations the establishment of general criteria and guidelines to assist States in ascertaining the nature and implications of marine scientific research.

Article 252
Implied consent

States or competent international organizations may proceed with a marine scientific research project six months after the date upon which the information required pursuant to article 248 was provided to the coastal State unless within four months of the receipt of the communication containing such information the coastal State has informed the State or organization conducting the research that:

(a) it has withheld its consent under the provisions of article 246; or

(b) the information given by that State or competent international organiza- tion regarding the nature or objectives of the project does not conform to the manifestly evident facts; or

(c) it requires supplementary information relevant to conditions and the in- formation provided for under articles 248 and 249; or

(d) outstanding obligations exist with respect to a previous marine scien- tific research project carried out by that State or organization, with regard to conditions established in article 249.

Article 253
Suspension or cessation of marine scientific research activities

1. A coastal State shall have the right to require the suspension of any marine scientific research activities in progress within its exclusive economic zone or on its continental shelf if:

(a) the research activities are not being conducted in accordance with the information communicated as provided under article 248 upon which the consent of the coastal State was based; or

(b) the State or competent international organization conducting the research activities fails to comply with the provisions of article 249 concerning the rights of the coastal State with respect to the marine scientific re- search project.

2. A coastal State shall have the right to require the cessation of any marine scientific research activities in case of any non-compliance with the provisions of article 248 which amounts to a major change in the research project or the re- search activities.

3. A coastal State may also require cessation of marine scientific research activities if any of the situations contemplated in paragraph 1 are not rectified within a reasonable period of time.

4. Following notification by the coastal State of its decision to order sus- pension or cessation, States or competent international organizations authorized to conduct marine scientific research activities shall terminate the research activi- ties that are the subject of such a notification.

5. An order of suspension under paragraph 1 shall be lifted by the coastal State and the marine scientific research activities allowed to continue once the researching State or competent international organization has complied with the conditions required under articles 248 and 249.

Article 254
Rights of neighbouring land-locked
and geographically disadvantaged States

1. States and competent international organizations which have submitted to a coastal State a project to undertake marine scientific research referred to in

article 246, paragraph 3, shall give notice to the neighbouring land-locked and geographically disadvantaged States of the proposed research project, and shall notify the coastal State thereof.

2.   After the consent has been given for the proposed marine scientific research project by the coastal State concerned, in accordance with article 246 and other relevant provisions of this Convention, States and competent international organizations undertaking such a project shall provide to the neighbouring land-locked and geographically disadvantaged States, at their request and when appropriate, relevant information as specified in article 248 and article 249, paragraph 1(f).

3.   The neighbouring land-locked and geographically disadvantaged States referred to above shall, at their request, be given the opportunity to participate, whenever feasible, in the proposed marine scientific research project through qualified experts appointed by them and not objected to by the coastal State, in accordance with the conditions agreed for the project, in conformity with the provisions of this Convention, between the coastal State concerned and the State or competent international organizations conducting the marine scientific research.

4.   States and competent international organizations referred to in paragraph 1 shall provide to the above-mentioned land-locked and geographically disadvantaged States, at their request, the information and assistance specified in article 249, paragraph 1(d), subject to the provisions of article 249, paragraph 2.

Article 255
Measures to facilitate marine scientific research and assist research vessels

States shall endeavour to adopt reasonable rules, regulations and procedures to promote and facilitate marine scientific research conducted in accordance with this Convention beyond their territorial sea and, as appropriate, to facilitate, subject to the provisions of their laws and regulations, access to their harbours and promote assistance for marine scientific research vessels which comply with the relevant provisions of this Part.

Article 256
Marine scientific research in the Area

All States, irrespective of their geographical location, and competent international organizations have the right, in conformity with the provisions of Part XI, to conduct marine scientific research in the Area.

Article 257
Marine scientific research in the water column beyond the exclusive economic zone

All States, irrespective of their geographical location, and competent international organizations have the right, in conformity with this Convention, to conduct marine scientific research in the water column beyond the limits of the exclusive economic zone.

SECTION 4. SCIENTIFIC RESEARCH INSTALLATIONS OR EQUIPMENT IN THE MARINE ENVIRONMENT

Article 258
Deployment and use

The deployment and use of any type of scientific research installations or equipment in any area of the marine environment shall be subject to the same conditions as are prescribed in this Convention for the conduct of marine scientific research in any such area.

Article 259
Legal status

The installations or equipment referred to in this section do not possess the status of islands. They have no territorial sea of their own, and their presence does not affect the delimitation of the territorial sea, the exclusive economic zone or the continental shelf.

Article 260
Safety zones

Safety zones of a reasonable breadth not exceeding a distance of 500 metres may be created around scientific research installations in accordance with the relevant provisions of this Convention. All States shall ensure that such safety zones are respected by their vessels.

Article 261
Non-interference with shipping routes

The deployment and use of any type of scientific research installations or equipment shall not constitute an obstacle to established international shipping routes.

Article 262
Identification markings and warning signals

Installations or equipment referred to in this section shall bear identification markings indicating the State of registry or the international organization to which they belong and shall have adequate internationally agreed warning signals to ensure safety at sea and the safety of air navigation, taking into account rules and standards established by competent international organizations.

SECTION 5. RESPONSIBILITY AND LIABILITY

Article 263
Responsibility and liability

1.   States and competent international organizations shall be responsible for ensuring that marine scientific research, whether undertaken by them or on their behalf, is conducted in accordance with this Convention.

2.   States and competent international organizations shall be responsible and liable for the measures they take in contravention of this Convention in respect of marine scientific research conducted by other States, their natural or juridical persons or by competent international organizations, and shall provide compensation for damage resulting from such measures.

3.   States and competent international organizations shall be responsible and liable pursuant to article 235 for damage caused by pollution of the marine environment arising out of marine scientific research undertaken by them or on their behalf.

SECTION 6. SETTLEMENT OF DISPUTES
AND INTERIM MEASURES

Article 264
Settlement of disputes

Disputes concerning the interpretation or application of the provisions of this Convention with regard to marine scientific research shall be settled in accordance with Part XV, sections 2 and 3.

Article 265
Interim measures

Pending settlement of a dispute in accordance with Part XV, sections 2 and 3, the State or competent international organization authorized to conduct a marine scientific research project shall not allow research activities to commence or continue without the express consent of the coastal State concerned.

PART XIV
DEVELOPMENT AND TRANSFER OF MARINE TECHNOLOGY

SECTION 1. GENERAL PROVISIONS

Article 266
Promotion of the development and transfer of marine technology

1.   States, directly or through competent international organizations, shall co-operate in accordance with their capabilities to promote actively the develop-

ment and transfer of marine science and marine technology on fair and reasonable terms and conditions.

2.   States shall promote the development of the marine scientific and technological capacity of States which may need and request technical assistance in this field, particularly developing States, including land-locked and geographically disadvantaged States, with regard to the exploration, exploitation, conservation and management of marine resources, the protection and preservation of the marine environment, marine scientific research and other activities in the marine environment compatible with this Convention, with a view to accelerating the social and economic development of the developing States.

3.   States shall endeavour to foster favourable economic and legal conditions for the transfer of marine technology for the benefit of all parties concerned on an equitable basis.

Article 267
Protection of legitimate interests

States, in promoting co-operation pursuant to article 266, shall have due regard for all legitimate interests including, *inter alia*, the rights and duties of holders, suppliers and recipients of marine technology.

Article 268
Basic objectives

States, directly or through competent international organizations, shall promote:
  (a)   the acquisition, evaluation and dissemination of marine technological knowledge and facilitate access to such information and data;
  (b)   the development of appropriate marine technology;
  (c)   the development of the necessary technological infrastructure to facilitate the transfer of marine technology;
  (d)   the development of human resources through training and education of nationals of developing States and countries and especially the nationals of the least developed among them;
  (e)   international co-operation at all levels, particularly at the regional, sub-regional and bilateral levels.

Article 269
Measures to achieve the basic objectives

In order to achieve the objectives referred to in article 268, States, directly or through competent international organizations, shall endeavour, *inter alia*, to:
  (a)   establish programmes of technical co-operation for the effective transfer of all kinds of marine technology to States which may need and request technical assistance in this field, particularly the developing land-locked and geographically disadvantaged States, as well as other developing States which have not been able either to establish or develop their own tech-

nological capacity in marine science and in the exploration and exploitation of marine resources or to develop the infrastructure of such technology;

(b) promote favourable conditions for the conclusion of agreements, contracts and other similar arrangements, under equitable and reasonable conditions;

(c) hold conferences, seminars and symposia on scientific and technological subjects, in particular on policies and methods for the transfer of marine technology;

(d) promote the exchange of scientists and of technological and other experts;

(e) undertake projects and promote joint ventures and other forms of bilateral and multilateral co-operation.

SECTION 2. INTERNATIONAL CO-OPERATION

Article 270
Ways and means of international co-operation

International co-operation for the development and transfer of marine technology shall be carried out, where feasible and appropriate, through existing bilateral, regional or multilateral programmes, and also through expanded and new programmes in order to facilitate marine scientific research, the transfer of marine technology, particularly in new fields, and appropriate international funding for ocean research and development.

Article 271
Guidelines, criteria and standards

States, directly or through competent international organizations, shall promote the establishment of generally accepted guidelines, criteria and standards for the transfer of marine technology on a bilateral basis or within the framework of international organizations and other fora, taking into account, in particular, the interests and needs of developing States.

Article 272
Co-ordination of international programmes

In the field of transfer of marine technology, States shall endeavour to ensure that competent international organizations co-ordinate their activities, including any regional or global programmes, taking into account the interests and needs of developing States, particularly land-locked and geographically disadvantaged States.

Article 273
Co-operation with international organizations and the Authority

States shall co-operate actively with competent international organizations and the Authority to encourage and facilitate the transfer to developing States, their nationals and the Enterprise of skills and marine technology with regard to activities in the Area.

Article 274
Objectives of the Authority

Subject to all legitimate interests including, *inter alia*, the rights and duties of holders, suppliers and recipients of technology, the Authority, with regard to activities in the Area, shall ensure that:

(a) on the basis of the principle of equitable geographical distribution, nationals of developing States, whether coastal, land-locked or geographically disadvantaged, shall be taken on for the purposes of training as members of the managerial, research and technical staff constituted for its undertakings;

(b) the technical documentation on the relevant equipment, machinery, devices and processes is made available to all States, in particular developing States which may need and request technical assistance in this field;

(c) adequate provision is made by the Authority to facilitate the acquisition of technical assistance in the field of marine technology by States which may need and request it, in particular developing States, and the acquisition by their nationals of the necessary skills and know-how, including professional training;

(d) States which may need and request technical assistance in this field, in particular developing States, are assisted in the acquisition of necessary equipment, processes, plant and other technical know-how through any financial arrangements provided for in this Convention.

SECTION 3. NATIONAL AND REGIONAL MARINE SCIENTIFIC AND TECHNOLOGICAL CENTRES

Article 275
Establishment of national centres

1.   States, directly or through competent international organizations and the Authority, shall promote the establishment, particularly in developing coastal States, of national marine scientific and technological research centres and the strengthening of existing national centres, in order to stimulate and advance the conduct of marine scientific research by developing coastal States and to enhance their national capabilities to utilize and preserve their marine resources for their economic benefit.

2.   States, through competent international organizations and the Authority, shall give adequate support to facilitate the establishment and strengthening of such national centres so as to provide for advanced training facilities and necessary equipment, skills and know-how as well as technical experts to such States which may need and request such assistance.

Establishment of regional centres

1.   States, in co-ordination with the competent international organizations, the Authority and national marine scientific and technological research institutions, shall promote the establishment of regional marine scientific and technological research centres, particularly in developing States, in order to stimulate and advance the conduct of marine scientific research by developing States and foster the transfer of marine technology.

2.   All States of a region shall co-operate with the regional centres therein to ensure the more effective achievement of their objectives.

Article 277
Functions of regional centres

The functions of such regional centres shall include, *inter alia:*

(a) training and educational programmes at all levels on various aspects of marine scientific and technological research, particularly marine biology, including conservation and management of living resources, oceanography, hydrography, engineering, geological exploration of the seabed, mining and desalination technologies;

(b) management studies;

(c) study programmes related to the protection and preservation of the marine environment and the prevention, reduction and control of pollution;

(d) organization of regional conferences, seminars and symposia;

(e) acquisition and processing of marine scientific and technological data and information;

(f) prompt dissemination of results of marine scientific and technological research in readily available publications;

(g) publicizing national policies with regard to the transfer of marine technology and systematic comparative study of those policies;

(h) compilation and systematization of information on the marketing of technology and on contracts and other arrangements concerning patents;

(i) technical co-operation with other States of the region.

SECTION 4. CO-OPERATION AMONG INTERNATIONAL ORGANIZATIONS

Article 278
Cooperation among international organizations

The competent international organizations referred to in this Part and in Part XIII shall take all appropriate measures to ensure, either directly or in close co-operation among themselves, the effective discharge of their functions and responsibilities under this Part.

PART XV
SETTLEMENT OF DISPUTES
SECTION 1. GENERAL PROVISIONS

Article 279
Obligation to settle disputes by peaceful means

States Parties shall settle any dispute between them concerning the interpretation or application of this Convention by peaceful means in accordance with Article 2, paragraph 3, of the Charter of the United Nations and, to this end, shall seek a solution by the means indicated in Article 33, paragraph 1, of the Charter.

Article 280
Settlement of disputes by any peaceful means chosen by the parties

Nothing in this Part impairs the right of any States Parties to agree at any time to settle a dispute between them concerning the interpretation or application of this Convention by any peaceful means of their own choice.

Article 281
Procedure where no settlement has been reached by the parties

1.   If the States Parties which are parties to a dispute concerning the interpretation or application of this Convention have agreed to seek settlement of the dispute by a peaceful means of their own choice, the procedures provided for in this Part apply only where no settlement has been reached by recourse to such means and the agreement between the parties does not exclude any further procedure.

2.   If the parties have also agreed on a time-limit, paragraph 1 applies only upon the expiration of that time-limit.

Article 282
Obligations under general, regional or bilateral agreements

If the States Parties which are parties to a dispute concerning the interpretation or application of this Convention have agreed, through a general, regional or bilateral agreement or otherwise, that such dispute shall, at the request of any party to the dispute, be submitted to a procedure that entails a binding decision, that procedure shall apply in lieu of the procedures provided for in this Part, unless the parties to the dispute otherwise agree.

Article 283
Obligation to exchange views

1.   When a dispute arises between States Parties concerning the interpretation or application of this Convention, the parties to the dispute shall proceed expeditiously to an exchange of views regarding its settlement by negotiation or other peaceful means.

2.   The parties shall also proceed expeditiously to an exchange of views where a procedure for the settlement of such a dispute has been terminated without a settlement or where a settlement has been reached and the circumstances require consultation regarding the manner of implementing the settlement.

Article 284
Conciliation

1.   A State Party which is a party to a dispute concerning the interpretation or application of this Convention may invite the other party or parties to submit the dispute to conciliation in accordance with the procedure under Annex V, section 1, or another conciliation procedure.

2.   If the invitation is accepted and if the parties agree upon the conciliation procedure to be applied, any party may submit the dispute to that procedure.

3.   If the invitation is not accepted or the parties do not agree upon the procedure, the conciliation proceedings shall be deemed to be terminated.

4. Unless the parties otherwise agree, when a dispute has been submitted to conciliation, the proceedings may be terminated only in accordance with the agreed conciliation procedure.

Article 285
Application of this section to disputes submitted pursuant to Part XI

This section applies to any dispute which pursuant to Part XI, section 5, is to be settled in accordance with procedures provided for in this Part. If an entity other than a State Party is a party to such a dispute, this section applies *mutatis mutandis.*

SECTION 2. COMPULSORY PROCEDURES ENTAILING BINDING DECISIONS

Article 286
Application of procedures under this section

Subject to section 3, any dispute concerning the interpretation or application of this Convention shall, where no settlement has been reached by recourse to section 1, be submitted at the request of any party to the dispute to the court or tribunal having jurisdiction under this section.

Article 287
Choice of procedure

1.   When signing, ratifying or acceding to this Convention or at any time thereafter, a State shall be free to choose, by means of a written declaration, one or

more of the following means for the settlement of disputes concerning the interpretation or application of this Convention:

    (a) the International Tribunal for the Law of the Sea established in accordance with Annex VI;

    (b) the International Court of Justice;

    (c) an arbitral tribunal constituted in accordance with Annex VII;

    (d) a special arbitral tribunal constituted in accordance with Annex VIII for one or more of the categories of disputes specified therein.

2.   A declaration made under paragraph 1 shall not affect or be affected by the obligation of a State Party to accept the jurisdiction of the Seabed Disputes Chamber of the International Tribunal for the Law of the Sea to the extent and in the manner provided for in Part XI, section 5.

3.   A State Party, which is a party to a dispute not covered by a declaration in force, shall be deemed to have accepted arbitration in accordance with Annex VII.

4.   If the parties to a dispute have accepted the same procedure for the settlement of the dispute, it may be submitted only to that procedure, unless the parties otherwise agree.

5.   If the parties to a dispute have not accepted the same procedure for the settlement of the dispute, it may be submitted only to arbitration in accordance with Annex VII, unless the parties otherwise agree.

6.   A declaration made under paragraph 1 shall remain in force until three months after notice of revocation has been deposited with the Secretary-General of the United Nations.

7.   A new declaration, a notice of revocation or the expiry of a declaration does not in any way affect proceedings pending before a court or tribunal having jurisdiction under this article, unless the parties otherwise agree.

8.   Declarations and notices referred to in this article shall be deposited with the Secretary-General of the United Nations, who shall transmit copies thereof to the States Parties.

Article 288
Jurisdiction

1.   A court or tribunal referred to in article 287 shall have jurisdiction over any dispute concerning the interpretation or application of this Convention which is submitted to it in accordance with this Part.

2.   A court or tribunal referred to in article 287 shall also have jurisdiction over any dispute concerning the interpretation or application of an international agreement related to the purposes of this Convention, which is submitted to it in accordance with the agreement.

3.   The Seabed Disputes Chamber of the International Tribunal for the Law of the Sea established in accordance with Annex VI, and any other chamber or arbitral tribunal referred to in Part XI, section 5, shall have jurisdiction in any matter which is submitted to it in accordance therewith.

4.   In the event of a dispute as to whether a court or tribunal has jurisdiction, the matter shall be settled by decision of that court or tribunal.

Article 289
Experts

In any dispute involving scientific or technical matters, a court or tribunal exercising jurisdiction under this section may, at the request of a party or *proprio motu*, select in consultation with the parties no fewer than two scientific or technical experts chosen preferably from the relevant list prepared in accordance with Annex VIII, article 2, to sit with the court or tribunal but without the right to vote.

Article 290
Provisional measures

1.   If a dispute has been duly submitted to a court or tribunal which considers that *prima facie* it has jurisdiction under this Part or Part XI, section 5, the court or tribunal may prescribe any provisional measures which it considers appropriate under the circumstances to preserve the respective rights of the parties to the dispute or to prevent serious harm to the marine environment, pending the final decision.

2.   Provisional measures may be modified or revoked as soon as the circumstances justifying them have changed or ceased to exist.

3.   Provisional measures may be prescribed, modified or revoked under this article only at the request of a party to the dispute and after the parties have been given an opportunity to be heard.

4.   The court or tribunal shall forthwith give notice to the parties to the dispute, and to such other States Parties as it considers appropriate, of the prescription, modification or revocation of provisional measures.

5.   Pending the constitution of an arbitral tribunal to which a dispute is being submitted under this section, any court or tribunal agreed upon by the parties or, failing such agreement within two weeks from the date of the request for provisional measures, the International Tribunal for the Law of the Sea or, with respect to activities in the Area, the Seabed Disputes Chamber, may prescribe, modify or revoke provisional measures in accordance with this article if it considers that *prima facie* the tribunal which is to be constituted would have jurisdiction and that the urgency of the situation so requires. Once constituted, the tribunal to which the dispute has been submitted may modify, revoke or affirm those provisional measures, acting in conformity with paragraphs 1 to 4.

6.   The parties to the dispute shall comply promptly with any provisional measures prescribed under this article.

Article 291
Access

1.   All the dispute settlement procedures specified in this Part shall be open to States Parties.

2.   The dispute settlement procedures specified in this Part shall be open to entities other than States Parties only as specifically provided for in this Convention.

Article 292
Prompt release of vessels and crews

1.   Where the authorities of a State Party have detained a vessel flying the flag of another State Party and it is alleged that the detaining State has not complied with the provisions of this Convention for the prompt release of the vessel or its crew upon the posting of a reasonable bond or other financial security, the question of release from detention may be submitted to any court or tribunal agreed upon by the parties or, failing such agreement within 10 days from the time of detention, to a court or tribunal accepted by the detaining State under article 287 or to the International Tribunal for the Law of the Sea, unless the parties otherwise agree.

2.   The application for release may be made only by or on behalf of the flag State of the vessel.

3.   The court or tribunal shall deal without delay with the application for release and shall deal only with the question of release, without prejudice to the merits of any case before the appropriate domestic forum against the vessel, its owner or its crew. The authorities of the detaining State remain competent to release the vessel or its crew at any time.

4.   Upon the posting of the bond or other financial security determined by the court or tribunal, the authorities of the detaining State shall comply promptly with the decision of the court or tribunal concerning the release of the vessel or its crew.

Article 293
Applicable law

1.   A court or tribunal having jurisdiction under this section shall apply this Convention and other rules of international law not incompatible with this Convention.

2.   Paragraph 1 does not prejudice the power of the court or tribunal having jurisdiction under this section to decide a case *ex aequo et bono*, if the parties so agree.

Article 294
Preliminary proceedings

1.   A court or tribunal provided for in article 287 to which an application is made in respect of a dispute referred to in article 297 shall determine at the request of a party, or may determine *proprio motu*, whether the claim constitutes an abuse of legal process or whether *prima facie* it is well founded. If the court or tribunal determines that the claim constitutes an abuse of legal process or is *prima facie* unfounded, it shall take no further action in the case.

2.   Upon receipt of the application, the court or tribunal shall immediately notify the other party or parties of the application, and shall fix a reasonable time-limit within which they may request it to make a determination in accordance with paragraph 1.

3.   Nothing in this article affects the right of any party to a dispute to make preliminary objections in accordance with the applicable rules of procedure.

Article 295
Exhaustion of local remedies

Any dispute between States Parties concerning the interpretation or application of this Convention may be submitted to the procedures provided for in this section only after local remedies have been exhausted where this is required by international law.

Article 296
Finality and binding force of decisions

1.   Any decision rendered by a court or tribunal having jurisdiction under this section shall be final and shall be complied with by all the parties to the dispute.

2.   Any such decision shall have no binding force except between the parties and in respect of that particular dispute.

SECTION 3. LIMITATIONS AND EXCEPTIONS TO APPLICABILITY OF SECTION 2

Article 297
Limitations on applicability of section 2

1.   Disputes concerning the interpretation or application of this Convention with regard to the exercise by a coastal State of its sovereign rights or jurisdiction provided for in this Convention shall be subject to the procedures provided for in section 2 in the following cases:

(a)   when it is alleged that a coastal State has acted in contravention of the provisions of this Convention in regard to the freedoms and rights of navigation, overflight or the laying of submarine cables and pipelines, or in regard to other internationally lawful uses of the sea specified in article 58;

(b)   when it is alleged that a State in exercising the aforementioned freedoms, rights or uses has acted in contravention of this Convention or of laws or regulations adopted by the coastal State in conformity with this Convention and other rules of international law not incompatible with this Convention; or

(c)   when it is alleged that a coastal State has acted in contravention of specified international rules and standards for the protection and preservation of the marine environment which are applicable to the coastal State and which have been established by this Convention or through a competent international organization or diplomatic conference in accordance with this Convention.

2.   (a) Disputes concerning the interpretation or application of the provisions of this Convention with regard to marine scientific research shall be settled in accordance with section 2, except that the coastal State shall not be obliged to accept the submission to such settlement of any dispute arising out of:

       (i) the exercise by the coastal State of a right or discretion in accordance with article 246; or

      (ii) a decision by the coastal State to order suspension or cessation of a research project in accordance with article 253.

    (b) A dispute arising from an allegation by the researching State that with respect to a specific project the coastal State is not exercising its rights under articles 246 and 253 in a manner compatible with this Convention shall be submitted, at the request of either party, to conciliation under Annex V, section 2, provided that the conciliation commission shall not call in question the exercise by the coastal State of its discretion to designate specific areas as referred to in article 246, paragraph 6, or of its discretion to withhold consent in accordance with article 246, paragraph 5.

3.   (a) Disputes concerning the interpretation or application of the provisions of this Convention with regard to fisheries shall be settled in accordance with section 2, except that the coastal State shall not be obliged to accept the submission to such settlement of any dispute relating to its sovereign rights with respect to the living resources in the exclusive economic zone or their exercise, including its discretionary powers for determining the allowable catch, its harvesting capacity, the allocation of surpluses to other States and the terms and conditions established in its conservation and management laws and regulations.

    (b) Where no settlement has been reached by recourse to section 1 of this Part, a dispute shall be submitted to conciliation under Annex V, section 2, at the request of any party to the dispute, when it is alleged that:

       (i) a coastal State has manifestly failed to comply with its obligations to ensure through proper conservation and management measures that the maintenance of the living resources in the exclusive economic zone is not seriously endangered;

      (ii) a coastal State has arbitrarily refused to determine, at the request of another State, the allowable catch and its capacity to harvest living resources with respect to stocks which that other State is interested in fishing; or

     (iii) a coastal State has arbitrarily refused to allocate to any State, under articles 62, 69 and 70 and under the terms and conditions established by the coastal State consistent with this Convention, the whole or part of the surplus it has declared to exist.

(c) In no case shall the conciliation commission substitute its discretion for that of the coastal State.

(d) The report of the conciliation commission shall be communicated to the appropriate international organizations.

(e) In negotiating agreements pursuant to articles 69 and 70, States Parties, unless they otherwise agree, shall include a clause on measures which they shall take in order to minimize the possibility of a disagreement concerning the interpretation or application of the agreement, and on how they should proceed if a disagreement nevertheless arises.

Article 298
Optional exceptions to applicability of section 2

1.   When signing, ratifying or acceding to this Convention or at any time thereafter, a State may, without prejudice to the obligations arising under section 1, declare in writing that it does not accept any one or more of the procedures provided for in section 2 with respect to one or more of the following categories of disputes:

(a)   (i)   disputes concerning the interpretation or application of articles 15, 74 and 83 relating to sea boundary delimitations, or those involving historic bays or titles, provided that a State having made such a declaration shall, when such a dispute arises subsequent to the entry into force of this Convention and where no agreement within a reasonable period of time is reached in negotiations between the parties, at the request of any party to the dispute, accept submission of the matter to conciliation under Annex V, section 2; and provided further that any dispute that necessarily involves the concurrent consideration of any unsettled dispute concerning sovereignty or other rights over continental or insular land territory shall be excluded from such submission;

(ii) after the conciliation commission has presented its report, which shall state the reasons on which it is based, the parties shall negotiate an agreement on the basis of that report; if these negotiations do not result in an agreement, the parties shall, by mutual consent, submit the question to one of the procedures provided for in section 2, unless the parties otherwise agree;

(iii) this subparagraph does not apply to any sea boundary dispute finally settled by an arrangement between the parties, or to any such dispute which is to be settled in accordance with a bilateral or multilateral agreement binding upon those parties;

(b)   disputes concerning military activities, including military activities by government vessels and aircraft engaged in non-commercial service, and disputes concerning law enforcement activities in regard to the exercise of sovereign rights or jurisdiction excluded from the jurisdiction of a court or tribunal under article 297, paragraph 2 or 3;

(c)   disputes in respect of which the Security Council of the United Nations is exercising the functions assigned to it by the Charter of the United

Nations, unless the Security Council decides to remove the matter from its agenda or calls upon the parties to settle it by the means provided for in this Convention.

2.   A State Party which has made a declaration under paragraph 1 may at any time withdraw it, or agree to submit a dispute excluded by such declaration to any procedure specified in this Convention.

3.   A State Party which has made a declaration under paragraph 1 shall not be entitled to submit any dispute falling within the excepted category of disputes to any procedure in this Convention as against another State Party, without the consent of that party.

4.   If one of the States Parties has made a declaration under paragraph 1(a), any other State Party may submit any dispute falling within an excepted category against the declarant party to the procedure specified in such declaration.

5.   A new declaration, or the withdrawal of a declaration, does not in any way affect proceedings pending before a court or tribunal in accordance with this article, unless the parties otherwise agree.

6.   Declarations and notices of withdrawal of declarations under this article shall be deposited with the Secretary-General of the United Nations, who shall transmit copies thereof to the States Parties.

Article 299
Right of the parties to agree upon a procedure

1.   A dispute excluded under article 297 or excepted by a declaration made under article 298 from the dispute settlement procedures provided for in section 2 may be submitted to such procedures only by agreement of the parties to the dispute.

2.   Nothing in this section impairs the right of the parties to the dispute to agree to some other procedure for the settlement of such dispute or to reach an amicable settlement.

PART XVI
GENERAL PROVISIONS

Article 300
Good faith and abuse of rights

States Parties shall fulfil in good faith the obligations assumed under this Convention and shall exercise the rights, jurisdiction and freedoms recognized in this Convention in a manner which would not constitute an abuse of right.

Article 301
Peaceful uses of the seas

In exercising their rights and performing their duties under this Convention, States Parties shall refrain from any threat or use of force against the territorial integrity or political independence of any State, or in any other manner inconsistent with the principles of international law embodied in the Charter of the United Nations.

Article 302
Disclosure of information

Without prejudice to the right of a State Party to resort to the procedures for the settlement of disputes provided for in this Convention, nothing in this Convention shall be deemed to require a State Party, in the fulfilment of its obligations under this Convention, to supply information the disclosure of which is contrary to the essential interests of its security.

Article 303
Archaeological and historical objects found at sea

1.   States have the duty to protect objects of an archaeological and historical nature found at sea and shall co-operate for this purpose.

2.   In order to control traffic in such objects, the coastal State may, in applying article 33, presume that their removal from the seabed in the zone referred to in that article without its approval would result in an infringement within its territory or territorial sea of the laws and regulations referred to in that article.

3.   Nothing in this article affects the rights of identifiable owners, the law of salvage or other rules of admiralty, or laws and practices with respect to cultural exchanges.

4.   This article is without prejudice to other international agreements and rules of international law regarding the protection of objects of an archaeological and historical nature.

Article 304
Responsibility and liability for damage

The provisions of this Convention regarding responsibility and liability for damage are without prejudice to the application of existing rules and the development of further rules regarding responsibility and liability under international law.

PART XVII
FINAL PROVISIONS

Article 305
Signature

1.   This Convention shall be open for signature by:

(a)   all States;

(b)   Namibia, represented by the United Nations Council for Namibia;

(c)   all self-governing associated States which have chosen that status in an act of self-determination supervised and approved by the United Nations in accordance with General Assembly resolution 1514 (XV) and which have competence over the matters governed by this Convention, including the competence to enter into treaties in respect of those matters;

(d) all self-governing associated States which, in accordance with their respective instruments of association, have competence over the matters governed by this Convention, including the competence to enter into treaties in respect of those matters;

(e) all territories which enjoy full internal self-government, recognized as such by the United Nations, but have not attained full independence in accordance with General Assembly resolution 1514 (XV) and which have competence over the matters governed by this Convention, including the competence to enter into treaties in respect of those matters;

(f) international organizations, in accordance with Annex IX.

2. This Convention shall remain open for signature until 9 December 1984 at the Ministry of Foreign Affairs of Jamaica and also, from 1 July 1983 until 9 December 1984, at United Nations Headquarters in New York.

Article 306
Ratification and formal confirmation

This Convention is subject to ratification by States and the other entities referred to in article 305, paragraph 1 (b), (c), (d) and (e), and to formal confirmation, in accordance with Annex IX, by the entities referred to in article 305, paragraph 1 (f). The instruments of ratification and of formal confirmation shall be deposited with the Secretary-General of the United Nations.

Article 307
Accession

This Convention shall remain open for accession by States and the other entities referred to in article 305. Accession by the entities referred to in article 305, paragraph 1 (f), shall be in accordance with Annex IX. The instruments of accession shall be deposited with the Secretary-General of the United Nations.

Article 308
Entry into force

1. This Convention shall enter into force 12 months after the date of deposit of the sixtieth instrument of ratification or accession.

2. For each State ratifying or acceding to this Convention after the deposit of the sixtieth instrument of ratification or accession, the Convention shall enter into force on the thirtieth day following the deposit of its instrument of ratification or accession, subject to paragraph 1.

3. The Assembly of the Authority shall meet on the date of entry into force of this Convention and shall elect the Council of the Authority. The first Council

shall be constituted in a manner consistent with the purpose of article 161 if the provisions of that article cannot be strictly applied.

4. The rules, regulations and procedures drafted by the Preparatory Commission shall apply provisionally pending their formal adoption by the Authority in accordance with Part XI.

5. The Authority and its organs shall act in accordance with resolution II of the Third United Nations Conference on the Law of the Sea relating to preparatory investment and with decisions of the Preparatory Commission taken pursuant to that resolution.

Article 309
Reservations and exceptions

No reservations or exceptions may be made to this Convention unless expressly permitted by other articles of this Convention.

Article 310
Declarations and statements

Article 309 does not preclude a State, when signing, ratifying or acceding to this Convention, from making declarations or statements, however phrased or named, with a view, *inter alia*, to the harmonization of its laws and regulations with the provisions of this Convention, provided that such declarations or statements do not purport to exclude or to modify the legal effect of the provisions of this Convention in their application to that State.

Article 311
Relation to other conventions and international agreements

1. This Convention shall prevail, as between States Parties, over the Geneva Conventions on the Law of the Sea of 29 April 1958.

2. This Convention shall not alter the rights and obligations of States Parties which arise from other agreements compatible with this Convention and which do not affect the enjoyment by other States Parties of their rights or the performance of their obligations under this Convention.

3. Two or more States Parties may conclude agreements modifying or suspending the operation of provisions of this Convention, applicable solely to the relations between them, provided that such agreements do not relate to a provision derogation from which is incompatible with the effective execution of the object and purpose of this Convention, and provided further that such agreements shall not affect the application of the basic principles embodied herein, and that the provisions of such agreements do not affect the enjoyment by other States Parties of their rights or the performance of their obligations under this Convention.

4. States Parties intending to conclude an agreement referred to in paragraph 3 shall notify the other States Parties through the depositary of this

Convention of their intention to conclude the agreement and of the modification or suspension for which it provides.

5.   This article does not affect international agreements expressly permitted or preserved by other articles of this Convention.

6.   States Parties agree that there shall be no amendments to the basic principle relating to the common heritage of mankind set forth in article 136 and that they shall not be party to any agreement in derogation thereof.

Article 312
Amendment

1.   After the expiry of a period of 10 years from the date of entry into force of this Convention, a State Party may, by written communication addressed to the Secretary-General of the United Nations, propose specific amendments to this Convention, other than those relating to activities in the Area, and request the convening of a conference to consider such proposed amendments. The Secretary-General shall circulate such communication to all States Parties. If, within 12 months from the date of the circulation of the communication, not less than one half of the States Parties reply favourably to the request, the Secretary-General shall convene the conference.

2.   The decision-making procedure applicable at the amendment conference shall be the same as that applicable at the Third United Nations Conference on the Law of the Sea unless otherwise decided by the conference. The conference should make every effort to reach agreement on any amendments by way of consensus and there should be no voting on them until all efforts at consensus have been exhausted.

Article 313
Amendment by simplified procedure

1.   A State Party may, by written communication addressed to the Secretary-General of the United Nations, propose an amendment to this Convention, other than an amendment relating to activities in the Area, to be adopted by the simplified procedure set forth in this article without convening a conference. The Secretary-General shall circulate the communication to all States Parties.

2.   If, within a period of 12 months from the date of the circulation of the communication, a State Party objects to the proposed amendment or to the proposal for its adoption by the simplified procedure, the amendment shall be considered rejected. The Secretary-General shall immediately notify all States Parties accordingly.

3.   If, 12 months from the date of the circulation of the communication, no State Party has objected to the proposed amendment or to the proposal for its adoption by the simplified procedure, the proposed amendment shall be considered adopted. The Secretary-General shall notify all States Parties that the proposed amendment has been adopted.

Article 314
Amendments to the provisions of this Convention
relating exclusively to activities in the Area

1.   A State Party may, by written communication addressed to the Secretary-General of the Authority, propose an amendment to the provisions of this Convention relating exclusively to activities in the Area, including Annex VI, section 4. The Secretary-General shall circulate such communication to all States Parties. The proposed amendment shall be subject to approval by the Assembly following its approval by the Council. Representatives of States Parties in those organs shall have full powers to consider and approve the proposed amendment. The proposed amendment as approved by the Council and the Assembly shall be considered adopted.

2.   Before approving any amendment under paragraph 1, the Council and the Assembly shall ensure that it does not prejudice the system of exploration for and exploitation of the resources of the Area, pending the Review Conference in accordance with article 155.

Article 315
Signature, ratification of, accession to
and authentic texts of amendments

1.   Once adopted, amendments to this Convention shall be open for signature by States Parties for 12 months from the date of adoption, at United Nations Headquarters in New York, unless otherwise provided in the amendment itself.

2.   Articles 306, 307 and 320 apply to all amendments to this Convention.

Article 316
Entry into force of amendments

1.   Amendments to this Convention, other than those referred to in paragraph 5, shall enter into force for the States Parties ratifying or acceding to them on the thirtieth day following the deposit of instruments of ratification or accession by two thirds of the States Parties or by 60 States Parties, whichever is greater. Such amendments shall not affect the enjoyment by other States Parties of their rights or the performance of their obligations under this Convention.

2.   An amendment may provide that a larger number of ratifications or accessions shall be required for its entry into force than are required by this article.

3.   For each State Party ratifying or acceding to an amendment referred to in paragraph 1 after the deposit of the required number of instruments of ratification or accession, the amendment shall enter into force on the thirtieth day following the deposit of its instrument of ratification or accession.

4.   A State which becomes a Party to this Convention after the entry into force of an amendment in accordance with paragraph 1 shall, failing an expression of a different intention by that State:

(a)   be considered as a Party to this Convention as so amended; and

(b) be considered as a Party to the unamended Convention in relation to any State Party not bound by the amendment.

5.   Any amendment relating exclusively to activities in the Area and any amendment to Annex VI shall enter into force for all States Parties one year following the deposit of instruments of ratification or accession by three fourths of the States Parties.

6.   A State which becomes a Party to this Convention after the entry into force of amendments in accordance with paragraph 5 shall be considered as a Party to this Convention as so amended.

Article 317
Denunciation

1.   A State Party may, by written notification addressed to the Secretary-General of the United Nations, denounce this Convention and may indicate its reasons. Failure to indicate reasons shall not affect the validity of the denunciation. The denunciation shall take effect one year after the date of receipt of the notification, unless the notification specifies a later date.

2.   A State shall not be discharged by reason of the denunciation from the financial and contractual obligations which accrued while it was a Party to this Convention, nor shall the denunciation affect any right, obligation or legal situation of that State created through the execution of this Convention prior to its termination for that State.

3.   The denunciation shall not in any way affect the duty of any State Party to fulfil any obligation embodied in this Convention to which it would be subject under international law independently of this Convention.

Article 318
Status of Annexes

The Annexes form an integral part of this Convention and, unless expressly provided otherwise, a reference to this Convention or to one of its Parts includes a reference to the Annexes relating thereto.

Article 319
Depositary

1.   The Secretary-General of the United Nations shall be the depositary of this Convention and amendments thereto.

2.   In addition to his functions as depositary, the Secretary-General shall:

(a) report to all States Parties, the Authority and competent international organizations on issues of a general nature that have arisen with respect to this Convention;

(b) notify the Authority of ratifications and formal confirmations of and accessions to this Convention and amendments thereto, as well as of denunciations of this Convention;

    (c)   notify States Parties of agreements in accordance with article 311, paragraph 4;

    (d)   circulate amendments adopted in accordance with this Convention to States Parties for ratification or accession;

    (e)   convene necessary meetings of States Parties in accordance with this Convention.

3.   (a)   The Secretary-General shall also transmit to the observers referred to in article 156:

        (i)   reports referred to in paragraph 2(a);

        (ii)   notifications referred to in paragraph 2(b) and (c); and

        (iii)   texts of amendments referred to in paragraph 2(d), for their information.

    (b)   The Secretary-General shall also invite those observers to participate as observers at meetings of States Parties referred to in paragraph 2(e).

Article 320
Authentic texts

The original of this Convention, of which the Arabic, Chinese, English, French, Russian and Spanish texts are equally authentic, shall, subject to article 305, paragraph 2, be deposited with the Secretary-General of the United Nations.

IN WITNESS WHEREOF, the undersigned Plenipotentiaries, being duly authorized thereto, have signed this Convention.

DONE AT MONTEGO BAY, this tenth day of December, one thousand nine hundred and eighty-two.

ANNEX I. HIGHLY MIGRATORY SPECIES

1. Albacore tuna: *Thunnus alalunga.*
2. Bluefin tuna: *Thunnus thynnus.*
3. Bigeye tuna: *Thunnus obesus.*
4. Skipjack tuna: *Katsuwonus pelamis.*
5. Yellowfin tuna: *Thunnus albacares.*
6. Blackfin tuna: *Thunnus atlanticus.*
7. Little tuna: *Euthynnus alletteratus; Euthynnus affinis.*
8. Southern bluefin tuna: *Thunnus maccoyii.*
9. Frigate mackerel: *Auxis thazard; Auxis rochei.*
10. Pomfrets: Family *Bramidae.*
11. Marlins: *Tetrapturus angustirostris; Tetrapturus belone; Tetrapturus pfluegeri; Tetrapturus albidus; Tetrapturus audax; Tetrapturus georgei; Makaira mazara; Makaira indica; Makaira nigricans.*
12. Sail-fishes: *Istiophorus platypterus; Istiophorus albicans.*
13. Swordfish: *Xiphias gladius.*
14. Sauries: *Scomberesox saurus; Cololabis saira; Cololabis adocetus; Scomberesox saurus scombroides.*
15. Dolphin: Coryphaena hippurus; *Coryphaena equiselis.*
16. Oceanic sharks: *Hexanchus griseus; Cetorhinus maximus;* Family *Alopiidae; Rhincodon typus;* Family *Carcharhinidae;* Family *Sphyrnidae;* Family *Isurida.*
17. Cetaceans: Family *Physeteridae;* Family *Balaenopteridae;* Family *Balaenidae;* Family *Eschrichtiidae;* Family *Monodontidae;* Family *Ziphiidae;* Family *Delphinidae.*

ANNEX II. COMMISSION ON THE LIMITS OF THE CONTINENTAL SHELF

Article 1

In accordance with the provisions of article 76, a Commission on the Limits of the Continental Shelf beyond 200 nautical miles shall be established in conformity with the following articles.

Article 2

1. The Commission shall consist of 21 members who shall be experts in the field of geology, geophysics or hydrography, elected by States Parties to this Convention from among their nationals, having due regard to the need to ensure equitable geographical representation, who shall serve in their personal capacities.

2. The initial election shall be held as soon as possible but in any case within 18 months after the date of entry into force of this Convention. At least

three months before the date of each election, the Secretary-General of the United Nations shall address a letter to the States Parties, inviting the submission of nominations, after appropriate regional consultations, within three months. The Secretary-General shall prepare a list in alphabetical order of all persons thus nominated and shall submit it to all the States Parties.

3.   Elections of the members of the Commission shall be held at a meeting of States Parties convened by the Secretary-General at United Nations Headquarters. At that meeting, for which two thirds of the States Parties shall constitute a quorum, the persons elected to the Commission shall be those nominees who obtain a two-thirds majority of the votes of the representatives of States Parties present and voting. Not less than three members shall be elected from each geographical region.

4.   The members of the Commission shall be elected for a term of five years. They shall be eligible for re-election.

5.   The State Party which submitted the nomination of a member of the Commission shall defray the expenses of that member while in performance of Commission duties. The coastal State concerned shall defray the expenses incurred in respect of the advice referred to in article 3, paragraph 1(b), of this Annex. The secretariat of the Commission shall be provided by the Secretary-General of the United Nations.

Article 3

1.   The functions of the Commission shall be:
(a)   to consider the data and other material submitted by coastal States concerning the outer limits of the continental shelf in areas where those limits extend beyond 200 nautical miles, and to make recommendations in accordance with article 76 and the Statement of Understanding adopted on 29 August 1980 by the Third United Nations Conference on the Law of the Sea;
(b)   to provide scientific and technical advice, if requested by the coastal State concerned during the preparation of the data referred to in subparagraph (a).
2.   The Commission may co-operate, to the extent considered necessary and useful, with the Intergovernmental Oceanographic Commission of UNESCO, the International Hydrographic Organization and other competent international organizations with a view to exchanging scientific and technical information which might be of assistance in discharging the Commission's responsibilities.

Article 4

Where a coastal State intends to establish, in accordance with article 76, the outer limits of its continental shelf beyond 200 nautical miles, it shall submit particulars of such limits to the Commission along with supporting scientific and technical data as soon as possible but in any case within 10 years of the entry into force of this Convention for that State. The coastal State shall at the same time give the names of any Commission members who have provided it with scientific and technical advice.

Article 5

Unless the Commission decides otherwise, the Commission shall function by way of sub-commissions composed of seven members, appointed in a balanced manner taking into account the specific elements of each submission by a coastal State. Nationals of the coastal State making the submission who are members of the Commission and any Commission member who has assisted a coastal State by providing scientific and technical advice with respect to the delineation shall not be a member of the sub-commission dealing with that submission but has the right to participate as a member in the proceedings of the Commission concerning the said submission. The coastal State which has made a submission to the Commission may send its representatives to participate in the relevant proceedings without the right to vote.

Article 6

1. The sub-commission shall submit its recommendations to the Commission.
2. Approval by the Commission of the recommendations of the sub-commission shall be by a majority of two thirds of Commission members present and voting.
3. The recommendations of the Commission shall be submitted in writing to the coastal State which made the submission and to the Secretary-General of the United Nations.

Article 7

Coastal States shall establish the outer limits of the continental shelf in conformity with the provisions of article 76, paragraph 8, and in accordance with the appropriate national procedures.

Article 8

In the case of disagreement by the coastal State with the recommendations of the Commission, the coastal State shall, within a reasonable time, make a revised or new submission to the Commission.

Article 9

The actions of the Commission shall not prejudice matters relating to delimitation of boundaries between States with opposite or adjacent coasts.

ANNEX III. BASIC CONDITIONS OF PROSPECTING, EXPLORATION AND EXPLOITATION

Article 1
Title to minerals

Title to minerals shall pass upon recovery in accordance with this Convention.

Article 2
Prospecting

1. (a) The Authority shall encourage prospecting in the Area.
   (b) Prospecting shall be conducted only after the Authority has received a satisfactory written undertaking that the proposed prospector will comply with this Convention and the relevant rules, regulations and procedures of the Authority concerning co-operation in the training programmes referred to in articles 143 and 144 and the protection of the marine environment, and will accept verification by the Authority of compliance therewith. The proposed prospector shall, at the same time, notify the Authority of the approximate area or areas in which prospecting is to be conducted.
   (c) Prospecting may be conducted simultaneously by more than one prospector in the same area or areas.
   2. Prospecting shall not confer on the prospector any rights with respect to resources. A prospector may, however, recover a reasonable quantity of minerals to be used for testing.

Article 3
Exploration and exploitation

1. The Enterprise, States Parties, and the other entities referred to in article 153, paragraph 2(b), may apply to the Authority for approval of plans of work for activities in the Area.
   2. The Enterprise may apply with respect to any part of the Area, but applications by others with respect to reserved areas are subject to the additional requirements of article 9 of this Annex.
   3. Exploration and exploitation shall be carried out only in areas specified in plans of work referred to in article 153, paragraph 3, and approved by the Authority in accordance with this Convention and the relevant rules, regulations and procedures of the Authority.
   4. Every approved plan of work shall:
   (a) be in conformity with this Convention and the rules, regulations and procedures of the Authority;
   (b) provide for control by the Authority of activities in the Area in accordance with article 153, paragraph 4;

(c) confer on the operator, in accordance with the rules, regulations and procedures of the Authority, the exclusive right to explore for and exploit the specified categories of resources in the area covered by the plan of work. If, however, the applicant presents for approval a plan of work covering only the stage of exploration or the stage of exploitation, the approved plan of work shall confer such exclusive right with respect to that stage only.

5.   Upon its approval by the Authority, every plan of work, except those presented by the Enterprise, shall be in the form of a contract concluded between the Authority and the applicant or applicants.

AGREEMENT, ANNEX, SECTION 2, PARAGRAPH 4

4.   ... Notwithstanding the provisions of article 153, paragraph 3, and Annex III, article 3, paragraph 5, of the Convention, a plan of work for the Enterprise upon its approval shall be in the form of a contract concluded between the Authority and the Enterprise.

Article 4
Qualifications of applicants

1.   Applicants, other than the Enterprise, shall be qualified if they have the nationality or control and sponsorship required by article 153, paragraph 2(b), and if they follow the procedures and meet the qualification standards set forth in the rules, regulations and procedures of the Authority.

2.   Except as provided in paragraph 6, such qualification standards shall relate to the financial and technical capabilities of the applicant and his performance under any previous contracts with the Authority.

3.   Each applicant shall be sponsored by the State Party of which it is a national unless the applicant has more than one nationality, as in the case of a partnership or consortium of entities from several States, in which event all States Parties involved shall sponsor the application, or unless the applicant is effectively controlled by another State Party or its nationals, in which event both States Parties shall sponsor the application. The criteria and procedures for implementation of the sponsorship requirements shall be set forth in the rules, regulations and procedures of the Authority.

4.   The sponsoring State or States shall, pursuant to article 139, have the responsibility to ensure, within their legal systems, that a contractor so sponsored shall carry out activities in the Area in conformity with the terms of its contract and its obligations under this Convention. A sponsoring State shall not, however, be liable for damage caused by any failure of a contractor sponsored by it to comply with its obligations if that State Party has adopted laws and regulations and taken administrative measures which are, within the framework of its legal

system, reasonably appropriate for securing compliance by persons under its jurisdiction.

5.   The procedures for assessing the qualifications of States Parties which are applicants shall take into account their character as States.

6.   The qualification standards shall require that every applicant, without exception, shall as part of his application undertake:

(a)   to accept as enforceable and comply with the applicable obligations created by the provisions of Part XI, the rules, regulations and procedures of the Authority, the decisions of the organs of the Authority and terms of his contracts with the Authority;

(b)   to accept control by the Authority of activities in the Area, as authorized by this Convention;

(c)   to provide the Authority with a written assurance that his obligations under the contract will be fulfilled in good faith;

(d)   to comply with the provisions on the transfer of technology set forth in article 5 of this Annex.

Article 5
Transfer of technology

[Does not apply. See Agreement, annex, Section 5, paragraph 2][f]

AGREEMENT, ANNEX, SECTION 5, PARAGRAPH 2

2.   The provisions of Annex III, article 5, of the Convention shall not apply.

Article 6
Approval of plans of work

1.   Six months after the entry into force of this Convention, and thereafter each fourth month, the Authority shall take up for consideration proposed plans of work.

2.   When considering an application for approval of a plan of work in the form of a contract, the Authority shall first ascertain whether:

(a)   the applicant has complied with the procedures established for applications in accordance with article 4 of this Annex and has given the Authority the undertakings and assurances required by the article. In cases of non-compliance with these procedures or in the absence of any of these undertakings and assurances, the applicant shall be given 45 days to remedy these defects;

(b)   the applicant possesses the requisite qualifications provided for in article 4 of this Annex.

---

[f] See page 196.

3.   All proposed plans of work shall be taken up in the order in which they are received. The proposed plans of work shall comply with and be governed by the relevant provisions of this Convention and the rules, regulations and procedures of the Authority, including those on operational requirements, financial contributions and the undertakings concerning the transfer of technology. If the proposed plans of work conform to these requirements, the Authority shall approve them provided that they are in accordance with the uniform and non-discriminatory requirements set forth in the rules, regulations and procedures of the Authority, unless:

   (a)   part or all of the area covered by the proposed plan of work is included in an approved plan of work or a previously submitted proposed plan of work which has not yet been finally acted on by the Authority;

   (b)   part or all of the area covered by the proposed plan of work is disapproved by the Authority pursuant to article 162, paragraph 2(x); or

   (c)   the proposed plan of work has been submitted or sponsored by a State Party which already holds:

      (i)   plans of work for exploration and exploitation of polymetallic nodules in non-reserved areas that, together with either part of the area covered by the application for a plan of work, exceed in size 30 per cent of a circular area of 400,000 square kilometres surrounding the centre of either part of the area covered by the proposed plan of work;

      (ii)   plans of work for the exploration and exploitation of polymetallic nodules in non-reserved areas which, taken together, constitute 2 per cent of the total seabed area which is not reserved or disapproved for exploitation pursuant to article 162, paragraph (2)(x).

4.   For the purpose of the standard set forth in paragraph 3(c), a plan of work submitted by a partnership or consortium shall be counted on a *pro rata* basis among the sponsoring States Parties involved in accordance with article 4, paragraph 3, of this Annex. The Authority may approve plans of work covered by paragraph 3(c) if it determines that such approval would not permit a State Party or entities sponsored by it to monopolize the conduct of activities in the Area or to preclude other States Parties from activities in the Area.

   [5.   Does not apply. See Agreement, annex, Section 6, paragraph 7][g]

Article 7
Selection among applicants for production authorizations

[Does not apply. See Agreement, annex, Section 6, paragraph 7]

AGREEMENT, ANNEX, SECTION 6, PARAGRAPH 7

7.   The provisions of ... Annex III, article 6, paragraph 5, and article 7, of the Convention, shall not apply.

---

[g] See page 199.

AGREEMENT, ANNEX, SECTION 1, PARAGRAPHS 6 TO 11

6.   (a) An application for approval of a plan of work for exploration shall be considered by the Council following the receipt of a recommendation on the application from the Legal and Technical Commission. The processing of an application for approval of a plan of work for exploration shall be in accordance with the provisions of the Convention, including Annex III thereof, and this Agreement, and subject to the following:

   (i) A plan of work for exploration submitted on behalf of a State or entity, or any component of such entity, referred to in resolution II, paragraph 1 (a) (ii) or (iii), other than a registered pioneer investor, which had already undertaken substantial activities in the Area prior to the entry into force of the Convention, or its successor in interest, shall be considered to have met the financial and technical qualifications necessary for approval of a plan of work if the sponsoring State or States certify that the applicant has expended an amount equivalent to at least US$30 million in research and exploration activities and has expended no less than 10 per cent of that amount in the location, survey and evaluation of the area referred to in the plan of work. If the plan of work otherwise satisfies the requirements of the Convention and any rules, regulations and procedures adopted pursuant thereto, it shall be approved by the Council in the form of a contract. The provisions of section 3, paragraph 11, of this Annex shall be interpreted and applied accordingly;

   (ii) Notwithstanding the provisions of resolution II, paragraph 8 (a), a registered pioneer investor may request approval of a plan of work for exploration within 36 months of the entry into force of the Convention. The plan of work for exploration shall consist of documents, reports and other data submitted to the Preparatory Commission both before and after registration and shall be accompanied by a certificate of compliance, consisting of a factual report describing the status of fulfilment of obligations under the pioneer investor regime, issued by the Preparatory Commission in accordance with resolution II, paragraph 11 (a). Such a plan of work shall be considered to be approved. Such an approved plan of work shall be in the form of a contract concluded between the Authority and the registered pioneer investor in accordance with Part XI and this Agreement. The fee of US$ 250,000 paid pursuant to resolution II, paragraph 7 (a), shall be deemed to be the fee relating to the exploration phase pursuant to section 8, paragraph 3, of this Annex. Section 3, paragraph 11, of this Annex shall be interpreted and applied accordingly;

   (iii) In accordance with the principle of non-discrimination, a contract with a State or entity or any component of such entity referred to in subparagraph (a) (i) shall include arrangements which shall be similar to and no less favourable than those agreed with any registered pioneer investor referred to in subparagraph (a) (ii). If any of the States or entities or any components of such entities referred to in subparagraph (a) (i) are granted more favourable arrangements, the Council shall make similar and no less favourable arrangements with regard to the rights and obligations assumed by the registered pioneer investors referred to in subparagraph (a) (ii), provided that such arrangements do not affect or prejudice the interests of the Authority;

(iv) A State sponsoring an application for a plan of work pursuant to the provisions of subparagraph (a) (i) or (ii) may be a State Party or a State which is applying this Agreement provisionally in accordance with article 7, or a State which is a member of the Authority on a provisional basis in accordance with paragraph 12;

(v) Resolution II, paragraph 8 (c), shall be interpreted and applied in accordance with subparagraph (a) (iv).

(b) The approval of a plan of work for exploration shall be in accordance with article 153, paragraph 3, of the Convention.

7. An application for approval of a plan of work shall be accompanied by an assessment of the potential environmental impacts of the proposed activities and by a description of a programme for oceanographic and baseline environmental studies in accordance with the rules, regulations and procedures adopted by the Authority.

8. An application for approval of a plan of work for exploration, subject to paragraph 6 (a) (i) or (ii), shall be processed in accordance with the procedures set out in section 3, paragraph 11, of this annex.

9. A plan of work for exploration shall be approved for a period of 15 years. Upon the expiration of a plan of work for exploration, the contractor shall apply for a plan of work for exploitation unless the contractor has already done so or has obtained an extension for the plan of work for exploration. Contractors may apply for such extensions for periods of not more than five years each. Such extensions shall be approved if the contractor has made efforts in good faith to comply with the requirements of the plan of work but for reasons beyond the contractor's control has been unable to complete the necessary preparatory work for proceeding to the exploitation stage or if the prevailing economic circumstances do not justify proceeding to the exploitation stage.

10. Designation of a reserved area for the Authority in accordance with Annex III, article 8, of the Convention shall take place in connection with approval of an application for a plan of work for exploration or approval of an application for a plan of work for exploration and exploitation.

11. Notwithstanding the provisions of paragraph 9, an approved plan of work for exploration which is sponsored by at least one State provisionally applying this Agreement shall terminate if such a State ceases to apply this Agreement provisionally and has not become a member on a provisional basis in accordance with paragraph 12 or has not become a State Party.

Article 8
Reservation of areas

Each application, other than those submitted by the Enterprise or by any other entities for reserved areas, shall cover a total area, which need not be a single continuous area, sufficiently large and of sufficient estimated commercial value to allow two mining operations. The applicant shall indicate the coordinates dividing the area into two parts of equal estimated commercial value and submit all the data obtained by him with respect to both parts. Without prejudice to the powers of the Authority pursuant to article 17 of this Annex, the data to be submitted concerning polymetallic nodules shall relate to mapping, sampling, the abundance of nodules, and their metal content. Within 45 days of receiving such data, the Authority shall designate which part is to be reserved solely for the conduct of activities by the Authority through the Enterprise or in association with developing States. This designation may be deferred for a further period of 45 days if the Authority requests an independent expert to assess whether all data required by this article has been submitted. The area designated shall become a reserved area as soon as the plan of work for the non-reserved area is approved and the contract is signed.

AGREEMENT, ANNEX, SECTION 1, PARAGRAPH 10

10. Designation of a reserved area for the Authority in accordance with Annex III, article 8, of the Convention shall take place in connection with approval of an application for a plan of work for exploration or approval of an application for a plan of work for exploration and exploitation.

Article 9
Activities in reserved areas

1.   The Enterprise shall be given an opportunity to decide whether it intends to carry out activities in each reserved area. This decision may be taken at any time, unless a notification pursuant to paragraph 4 is received by the Authority, in which event the Enterprise shall take its decision within a reasonable time. The Enterprise may decide to exploit such areas in joint ventures with the interested State or entity.

2.   The Enterprise may conclude contracts for the execution of part of its activities in accordance with Annex IV, article 12. It may also enter into joint ventures for the conduct of such activities with any entities which are eligible to carry out activities in the Area pursuant to article 153, paragraph 2(b). When considering such joint ventures, the Enterprise shall offer to States Parties which are developing States and their nationals the opportunity of effective participation.

3.   The Authority may prescribe, in its rules, regulations and procedures, substantive and procedural requirements and conditions with respect to such contracts and joint ventures.

4.   Any State Party which is a developing State or any natural or juridical person sponsored by it and effectively controlled by it or by other developing State which is a qualified applicant, or any group of the foregoing, may notify the Authority that it wishes to submit a plan of work pursuant to article 6 of this Annex with respect to a reserved area. The plan of work shall be considered if the Enterprise decides, pursuant to paragraph 1, that it does not intend to carry out activities in that area.

AGREEMENT, ANNEX, SECTION 2, PARAGRAPH 5

5.   A contractor which has contributed a particular area to the Authority as a reserved area has the right of first refusal to enter into a joint-venture arrangement with the Enterprise for exploration and exploitation of that area. If the Enterprise does not submit an application for a plan of work for activities in respect of such a reserved area within 15 years of the commencement of its functions independent of the Secretariat of the Authority or within 15 years of the date on which that area is reserved for the Authority, whichever is the later, the contractor which contributed the area shall be entitled to apply for a plan of work for that area provided it offers in good faith to include the Enterprise as a joint-venture partner.

Article 10
Preference and priority among applicants

An operator who has an approved plan of work for exploration only, as provided in article 3, paragraph 4(c), of this Annex shall have a preference and a priority among applicants for a plan of work covering exploitation of the same area and resources. However, such preference or priority may be withdrawn if the operator's performance has not been satisfactory.

AGREEMENT, ANNEX, SECTION 1, PARAGRAPH 13

13.   The reference in Annex III, article 10, of the Convention to performance which has not been satisfactory shall be interpreted to mean that the contractor has failed to comply with the requirements of an approved plan of work in spite of a written warning or warnings from the Authority to the contractor to comply therewith.

Article 11
Joint arrangements

1.   Contracts may provide for joint arrangements between the contractor and the Authority through the Enterprise, in the form of joint ventures or produc-

tion sharing, as well as any other form of joint arrangement, which shall have the same protection against revision, suspension or termination as contracts with the Authority.

2.   Contractors entering into such joint arrangements with the Enterprise may receive financial incentives as provided for in article 13 of this Annex.

3.   Partners in joint ventures with the Enterprise shall be liable for the payments required by article 13 of this Annex to the extent of their share in the joint ventures, subject to financial incentives as provided for in that article.

Article 12
Activities carried out by the Enterprise

1.   Activities in the Area carried out by the Enterprise pursuant to article 153, paragraph 2(a), shall be governed by Part XI, the rules, regulations and procedures of the Authority and its relevant decisions.

2.   Any plan of work submitted by the Enterprise shall be accompanied by evidence supporting its financial and technical capabilities.

AGREEMENT, ANNEX, SECTION 2, PARAGRAPH 4

4.   The obligations applicable to contractors shall apply to the Enterprise. Notwithstanding the provisions of article 153, paragraph 3, and Annex III, article 3, paragraph 5, of the Convention, a plan of work for the Enterprise upon its approval shall be in the form of a contract concluded between the Authority and the Enterprise.

Article 13
Financial terms of contracts

1.   In adopting rules, regulations and procedures concerning the financial terms of a contract between the Authority and the entities referred to in article 153, paragraph 2(b), and in negotiating those financial terms in accordance with Part XI and those rules, regulations and procedures, the Authority shall be guided by the following objectives:

   (a)   to ensure optimum revenues for the Authority from the proceeds of commercial production;

   (b)   to attract investments and technology to the exploration and exploitation of the Area;

   (c)   to ensure equality of financial treatment and comparable financial obligations for contractors;

   (d)   to provide incentives on a uniform and non-discriminatory basis for contractors to undertake joint arrangements with the Enterprise and developing States or their nationals, to stimulate the transfer of technology thereto, and to train the personnel of the Authority and of developing States;

(e) to enable the Enterprise to engage in seabed mining effectively at the same time as the entities referred to in article 153, paragraph 2(b); and

(f) to ensure that, as a result of the financial incentives provided to contractors under paragraph 14, under the terms of contracts reviewed in accordance with article 19 of this Annex or under the provisions of article 11 of this Annex with respect to joint ventures, contractors are not subsidized so as to be given an artificial competitive advantage with respect to land-based miners.

2.   A fee shall be levied for the administrative cost of processing an application for approval of a plan of work in the form of a contract and shall be fixed at an amount of $US500,000 per application.[1] The amount of the fee shall be reviewed from time to time by the Council in order to ensure that it covers the administrative cost incurred. If such administrative cost incurred by the Authority in processing an application is less than the fixed amount, the Authority shall refund the difference to the applicant.

[3-10. Do not apply. See Agreement, annex, Section 8, paragraph 2][h]

11.   All costs, expenditures, proceeds and revenues, and all prices and values referred to in this article, shall be determined in accordance with generally recognized accounting principles and the financial rules, regulations and procedures of the Authority.

12.   Payments to the Authority under paragraphs 5 and 6[2] shall be made in freely usable currencies or currencies which are freely available and effectively usable on the major foreign exchange markets or, at the contractor's option, in the equivalents of processed metals at market value. The market value shall be determined in accordance with paragraph 5(b).[3] The freely usable currencies and

---

[1] The Agreement, annex, Section 8, paragraph 3 provides that with regard to the implementation of Annex III, article 13, paragraph 2, of the Convention, the fee for processing applications for approval of a plan of work limited to one phase, either the exploration phase or the exploitation phase, shall be US$ 250,000. In accordance with article 2 of the Agreement, the provisions of the Agreement and Part XI shall be interpreted and applied together as a single instrument. In the event of any inconsistency between the Agreement and Part XI, the provisions of the Agreement shall prevail.

[2] Paragraphs 5 and 6 of article 13 do not apply. However, provisions relating to Financial Terms of Contracts occur in the Agreement, annex, Section 8. In accordance with article 2 of the Agreement, the provisions of the Agreement and Part XI shall be interpreted and applied together as a single instrument. In the event of any inconsistency between the Agreement and Part XI, the provisions of the Agreement shall prevail.

[3] Paragraph 5(b) of article 13 does not apply. However, provisions relating to Financial Terms of Contracts occur in the Agreement, annex, Section 8. In accordance with article 2 of the Agreement, the provisions of the Agreement and Part XI shall be interpreted and applied together as a single instrument. In the event of any inconsistency between the Agreement and Part XI, the provisions of the Agreement shall prevail.

---

[h] See page 200

currencies which are freely available and effectively usable on the major foreign exchange markets shall be defined in the rules, regulations and procedures of the Authority in accordance with prevailing international monetary practice.

13.   All financial obligations of the contractor to the Authority, as well as all his fees, costs, expenditures, proceeds and revenues referred to in this article, shall be adjusted by expressing them in constant terms relative to a base year.

14.   The Authority may, taking into account any recommendations of the Economic Planning Commission and the Legal and Technical Commission, adopt rules, regulations and procedures that provide for incentives, on a uniform and non-discriminatory basis, to contractors to further the objectives set out in paragraph 1.

15.   In the event of a dispute between the Authority and a contractor over the interpretation or application of the financial terms of a contract, either party may submit the dispute to binding commercial arbitration, unless both parties agree to settle the dispute by other means, in accordance with article 188, paragraph 2.

AGREEMENT, ANNEX, SECTION 8

SECTION 8. FINANCIAL TERMS OF CONTRACTS

1.   The following principles shall provide the basis for establishing rules, regulations and procedures for financial terms of contracts:

(a)   The system of payments to the Authority shall be fair both to the contractor and to the Authority and shall provide adequate means of determining compliance by the contractor with such system;

(b)   The rates of payments under the system shall be within the range of those prevailing in respect of land-based mining of the same or similar minerals in order to avoid giving deep seabed miners an artificial competitive advantage or imposing on them a competitive disadvantage;

(c)   The system should not be complicated and should not impose major administrative costs on the Authority or on a contractor. Consideration should be given to the adoption of a royalty system or a combination of a royalty and profit-sharing system. If alternative systems are decided upon, the contractor has the right to choose the system applicable to its contract. Any subsequent change in choice between alternative systems, however, shall be made by agreement between the Authority and the contractor;

(d)   An annual fixed fee shall be payable from the date of commencement of commercial production. This fee may be credited against other payments due under the system adopted in accordance with subparagraph (c). The amount of the fee shall be established by the Council;

(e)   The system of payments may be revised periodically in the light of changing circumstances. Any changes shall be applied in a non-discriminatory manner. Such changes may apply to existing contracts only at the election of the contractor. Any subsequent change in choice between alternative systems shall be made by agreement between the Authority and the contractor;

(f)   Disputes concerning the interpretation or application of the rules and regulations based on these principles shall be subject to the dispute settlement procedures set out in the Convention.

2.   The provisions of Annex III, article 13, paragraphs 3 to 10, of the Convention shall not apply.

3.   With regard to the implementation of Annex III, article 13, paragraph 2, of the Convention, the fee for processing applications for approval of a plan of work limited to one phase, either the exploration phase or the exploitation phase, shall be US$ 250,000.

Article 14
Transfer of data

1.   The operator shall transfer to the Authority, in accordance with its rules, regulations and procedures and the terms and conditions of the plan of work, at time intervals determined by the Authority all data which are both necessary for and relevant to the effective exercise of the powers and functions of the principal organs of the Authority in respect of the area covered by the plan of work.

2.   Transferred data in respect of the area covered by the plan of work, deemed proprietary, may only be used for the purposes set forth in this article. Data necessary for the formulation by the Authority of rules, regulations and procedures concerning protection of the marine environment and safety, other than equipment design data, shall not be deemed proprietary.

3.   Data transferred to the Authority by prospectors, applicants for contracts or contractors, deemed proprietary, shall not be disclosed by the Authority to the Enterprise or to anyone external to the Authority, but data on the reserved areas may be disclosed to the Enterprise. Such data transferred by such persons to the Enterprise shall not be disclosed by the Enterprise to the Authority or to anyone external to the Authority.

Article 15
Training programmes

The contractor shall draw up practical programmes for the training of personnel of the Authority and developing States, including the participation of such personnel in all activities in the Area which are covered by the contract, in accordance with article 144, paragraph 2.

Article 16
Exclusive right to explore and exploit

The Authority shall, pursuant to Part XI and its rules, regulations and procedures, accord the operator the exclusive right to explore and exploit the area covered by the plan of work in respect of a specified category of resources and shall ensure that no other entity operates in the same area for a different category of resources in a manner which might interfere with the operations of the operator. The operator shall have security of tenure in accordance with article 153, paragraph 6.

Article 17
Rules, regulations and procedures of the Authority

1.   The Authority shall adopt and uniformly apply rules, regulations and procedures in accordance with Article 160, paragraph 2(f)(ii), and article 162, paragraph 2(o)(ii), for the exercise of its functions as set forth in Part XI on, *inter alia*, the following matters:
   (a) administrative procedures relating to prospecting, exploration and exploitation in the Area;
   (b) operations:
      (i)   size of area;
      (ii)   duration of operations;
      (iii) performance requirements including assurances pursuant to article 4, paragraph 6(c), of this Annex;
      (iv)   categories of resources;
      (v)   renunciation of areas;
      (vi)   progress reports;
      (vii) submission of data;
      (viii) inspection and supervision of operations;
      (ix)   prevention of interference with other activities in the marine environment;
      (x)   transfer of rights and obligations by a contractor;
      (xi)   procedures for transfer of technology to developing States in accordance with article 144 and for their direct participation;
      (xii) mining standards and practices, including those relating to operational safety, conservation of the resources and the protection of the marine environment;
      (xiii) definition of commercial production;
      (xiv) qualification standards for applicants;
   (c) financial matters:
      (i)   establishment of uniform and non-discriminatory costing and accounting rules and the method of selection of auditors;
      (ii)   apportionment of proceeds of operations;
      (iii) the incentives referred to in article 13 of this Annex;
   (d) implementation of decisions taken pursuant to article 151, paragraph 10, and article 164, paragraph 2(d).
2.   Rules, regulations and procedures on the following items shall fully reflect the objective criteria set out below:
   (a) Size of areas:
        The Authority shall determine the appropriate size of areas for exploration which may be up to twice as large as those for exploitation in order to permit intensive exploration operations. The size of area shall be calcu-

lated to satisfy the requirements of article 8 of this Annex on reservation of areas as well as stated production requirements consistent with article 151 in accordance with the terms of the contract taking into account the state of the art of technology then available for seabed mining and the relevant physical characteristics of the areas. Areas shall be neither smaller nor larger than are necessary to satisfy this objective.

(b) Duration of operations:

    (i) Prospecting shall be without time-limit;

    (ii) Exploration should be of sufficient duration to permit a thorough survey of the specific area, the design and construction of mining equipment for the area and the design and construction of small and medium-size processing plants for the purpose of testing mining and processing systems;

    (iii) The duration of exploitation should be related to the economic life of the mining project, taking into consideration such factors as the depletion of the ore, the useful life of mining equipment and processing facilities and commercial viability. Exploitation should be of sufficient duration to permit commercial extraction of minerals of the area and should include a reasonable time period for construction of commercial-scale mining and processing systems, during which period commercial production should not be required. The total duration of exploitation, however, should also be short enough to give the Authority an opportunity to amend the terms and conditions of the plan of work at the time it considers renewal in accordance with rules, regulations and procedures which it has adopted subsequent to approving the plan of work.

(c) Performance requirements:

The Authority shall require that during the exploration stage periodic expenditures be made by the operator which are reasonably related to the size of the area covered by the plan of work and the expenditures which would be expected of a *bona fide* operator who intended to bring the area into commercial production within the time-limits established by the Authority. The required expenditures should not be established at a level which would discourage prospective operators with less costly technology than is prevalently in use. The Authority shall establish a maximum time interval, after the exploration stage is completed and the exploitation stage begins, to achieve commercial production. To determine this interval, the Authority should take into consideration that construction of large-scale mining and processing systems cannot be initiated until after the termination of the exploration stage and the commencement of the exploitation stage. Accordingly, the interval to bring an area into commercial production should take into account the time necessary for this construction after the completion of the exploration stage and reasonable allowance should be made for unavoidable delays in the construction schedule. Once commercial production is achieved, the Authority shall within reasonable limits and taking into consideration all relevant factors require the operator to maintain commercial production throughout the period of the plan of work.

AGREEMENT, ANNEX, SECTION 1, PARAGRAPH 5

5.   Between the entry into force of the Convention and the approval of the first plan of work for exploitation, the Authority shall concentrate on:

    …

(f) Adoption of rules, regulations and procedures necessary for the conduct of activities in the Area as they progress. Notwithstanding the provisions of Annex III, article 17, paragraph 2 (b) and (c), of the Convention, such rules, regulations and procedures shall take into account the terms of this Agreement, the prolonged delay in commercial deep seabed mining and the likely pace of activities in the Area;

(d) Categories of resources:
In determining the category of resources in respect of which a plan of work may be approved, the Authority shall give emphasis *inter alia* to the following characteristics:
(i)   that certain resources require the use of similar mining methods; and
(ii) that some resources can be developed simultaneously without undue interference between operators developing different resources in the same area.
Nothing in this subparagraph shall preclude the Authority from approving a plan of work with respect to more than one category of resources in the same area to the same applicant.

(e) Renunciation of areas:
The operator shall have the right at any time to renounce without penalty the whole or part of his rights in the area covered by a plan of work.

(f) Protection of the marine environment:
Rules, regulations and procedures shall be drawn up in order to secure effective protection of the marine environment from harmful effects directly resulting from activities in the Area or from shipboard processing immediately above a mine site of minerals derived from that mine site, taking into account the extent to which such harmful effects may directly result from drilling, dredging, coring and excavation and from disposal, dumping and discharge into the marine environment of sediment, wastes or other effluents.

(g) Commercial production:
Commercial production shall be deemed to have begun if an operator engages in sustained large-scale recovery operations which yield a quantity of materials sufficient to indicate clearly that the principal purpose is large-scale production rather than production intended for information gathering, analysis or the testing of equipment or plant.

Article 18
Penalties

1. A contractor's rights under the contract may be suspended or terminated only in the following cases:

(a) if, in spite of warnings by the Authority, the contractor has conducted his activities in such a way as to result in serious, persistent and wilful violations of the fundamental terms of the contract, Part XI and the rules, regulations and procedures of the Authority; or

(b) if the contractor has failed to comply with a final binding decision of the dispute settlement body applicable to him.

2. In the case of any violation of the contract not covered by paragraph 1(a), or in lieu of suspension or termination under paragraph 1(a), the Authority may impose upon the contractor monetary penalties proportionate to the seriousness of the violation.

3. Except for emergency orders under article 162, paragraph 2(w), the Authority may not execute a decision involving monetary penalties, suspension or termination until the contractor has been accorded a reasonable opportunity to exhaust the judicial remedies available to him pursuant to Part XI, section 5.

Article 19
Revision of contract

1. When circumstances have arisen or are likely to arise which, in the opinion of either party, would render the contract inequitable or make it impracticable or impossible to achieve the objectives set out in the contract or in Part XI, the parties shall enter into negotiations to revise it accordingly.

2. Any contract entered into in accordance with article 153, paragraph 3, may be revised only with the consent of the parties.

Article 20
Transfer of rights and obligations

The rights and obligations arising under a contract may be transferred only with the consent of the Authority, and in accordance with its rules, regulations and procedures. The Authority shall not unreasonably withhold consent to the transfer if the proposed transferee is in all respects a qualified applicant and assumes all of the obligations of the transferor and if the transfer does not confer to the transferee a plan of work, the approval of which would be forbidden by article 6, paragraph 3(c), of this Annex.

Article 21
Applicable law

1. The contract shall be governed by the terms of the contract, the rules, regulations and procedures of the Authority, Part XI and other rules of international law not incompatible with this Convention.

2.   Any final decision rendered by a court or tribunal having jurisdiction under this Convention relating to the rights and obligations of the Authority and of the contractor shall be enforceable in the territory of each State Party.

3.   No State Party may impose conditions on a contractor that are inconsistent with Part XI. However, the application by a State Party to contractors sponsored by it, or to ships flying its flag, of environmental or other laws and regulations more stringent than those in the rules, regulations and procedures of the Authority adopted pursuant to article 17, paragraph 2(f), of this Annex shall not be deemed inconsistent with Part XI.

Article 22
Responsibility

The contractor shall have responsibility or liability for any damage arising out of wrongful acts in the conduct of its operations, account being taken of contributory acts or omissions by the Authority. Similarly, the Authority shall have responsibility or liability for any damage arising out of wrongful acts in the exercise of its powers and functions, including violations under article 168, paragraph 2, account being taken of contributory acts or omissions by the contractor. Liability in every case shall be for the actual amount of damage.

ANNEX IV. STATUTE OF THE ENTERPRISE

Article 1
Purpose

1.   The Enterprise is the organ of the Authority which shall carry out activities in the Area directly, pursuant to article 153, paragraph 2(a), as well as the transporting, processing and marketing of minerals recovered from the Area.

2.   In carrying out its purposes and in the exercise of its functions, the Enterprise shall act in accordance with this Convention and the rules, regulations and procedures of the Authority.

3.   In developing the resources of the Area pursuant to paragraph 1, the Enterprise shall, subject to this Convention, operate in accordance with sound commercial principles.

AGREEMENT, ANNEX, SECTION 2

SECTION 2. THE ENTERPRISE

1.   The Secretariat of the Authority shall perform the functions of the Enterprise until it begins to operate independently of the Secretariat. The Secretary-General of the Authority shall appoint from within the staff of the Authority an interim Director-General to oversee the performance of these functions by the Secretariat.

These functions shall be:

(a) Monitoring and review of trends and developments relating to deep seabed mining activities, including regular analysis of world metal market conditions and metal prices, trends and prospects;

(b) Assessment of the results of the conduct of marine scientific research with respect to activities in the Area, with particular emphasis on research related to the environmental impact of activities in the Area;

(c) Assessment of available data relating to prospecting and exploration, including the criteria for such activities;

(d) Assessment of technological developments relevant to activities in the Area, in particular technology relating to the protection and preservation of the marine environment;

(e) Evaluation of information and data relating to areas reserved for the Authority;

(f) Assessment of approaches to joint venture operations;

(g) Collection of information on the availability of trained manpower;

(h) Study of managerial policy options for the administration of the Enterprise at different stages of its operations.

2.   The Enterprise shall conduct its initial deep seabed mining operations through joint ventures. Upon the approval of a plan of work for exploitation for an entity other than the Enterprise, or upon receipt by the Council of an application for a joint venture operation with the Enterprise, the Council shall take up the issue of the functioning of the Enterprise independently of the Secretariat of the Authority. If joint venture operations with the Enterprise accord with sound commercial principles, the Council shall issue a directive pursuant to article 170, paragraph 2, of the Convention providing for such independent functioning.

...

6.   Article 170, paragraph 4, Annex IV and other provisions of the Convention relating to the Enterprise shall be interpreted and applied in accordance with this section.

Article 2
Relationship to the Authority

1.   Pursuant to article 170, the Enterprise shall act in accordance with the general policies of the Assembly and the directives of the Council.

2.   Subject to paragraph 1, the Enterprise shall enjoy autonomy in the conduct of its operations.

3.   Nothing in this Convention shall make the Enterprise liable for the acts or obligations of the Authority, or make the Authority liable for the acts or obligations of the Enterprise.

Article 3
Limitation of liability

Without prejudice to article 11, paragraph 3, of this Annex, no member of the Authority shall be liable by reason only of its membership for the acts or obligations of the Enterprise.

Article 4
Structure

The Enterprise shall have a Governing Board, a Director-General and the staff necessary for the exercise of its functions.

Article 5
Governing Board

1.   The Governing Board shall be composed of 15 members elected by the Assembly in accordance with article 160, paragraph 2(c). In the election of the members of the Board, due regard shall be paid to the principle of equitable geographical distribution. In submitting nominations of candidates for election to the Board, members of the Authority shall bear in mind the need to nominate candidates of the highest standard of competence, with qualifications in relevant fields, so as to ensure the viability and success of the Enterprise.

2.   Members of the Board shall be elected for four years and may be re-elected; and due regard shall be paid to the principle of rotation of membership.

3.   Members of the Board shall continue in office until their successors are elected. If the office of a member of the Board becomes vacant, the Assembly shall, in accordance with Article 160, paragraph 2(c), elect a new member for the remainder of his predecessor's term.

4.   Members of the Board shall act in their personal capacity. In the performance of their duties they shall not seek or receive instructions from any government or from any other source. Each member of the Authority shall respect the independent character of the members of the Board and shall refrain from all attempts to influence any of them in the discharge of their duties.

5.   Each member of the Board shall receive remuneration to be paid out of the funds of the Enterprise. The amount of remuneration shall be fixed by the Assembly, upon the recommendation of the Council.

6.   The Board shall normally function at the principal office of the Enterprise and shall meet as often as the business of the Enterprise may require.

7.   Two thirds of the members of the Board shall constitute a quorum.

8.   Each member of the Board shall have one vote. All matters before the Board shall be decided by a majority of its members. If a member has a conflict of interest on a matter before the Board he shall refrain from voting on that matter.

9.   Any member of the Authority may ask the Board for information in respect of its operations which particularly affect that member. The Board shall endeavour to provide such information.

Article 6
Powers and functions of the Governing Board

The Governing Board shall direct the operations of the Enterprise. Subject to this Convention, the Governing Board shall exercise the powers necessary to fulfil the purposes of the Enterprise, including powers:

(a) to elect a Chairman from among its members;

(b) to adopt its rules of procedure;

(c) to draw up and submit formal written plans of work to the Council in accordance with article 153, paragraph 3, and article 162, paragraph 2(j);

AGREEMENT, ANNEX, SECTION 3, PARAGRAPH 11(b)

11. (b) The provisions of article 162, paragraph 2 (j), of the Convention shall not apply.

(d) to develop plans of work and programmes for carrying out the activities specified in article 170;

(e) to prepare and submit to the Council applications for production authorizations in accordance with article 151, paragraphs 2 to 7;

AGREEMENT, ANNEX, SECTION 6, PARAGRAPH 7

2. The provisions of article 151, paragraphs 1 to 7 of the Convention shall not apply.

(f) to authorize negotiations concerning the acquisition of technology, including those provided for in Annex III, article 5, paragraph 3(a), (c), and (d), and to approve the results of those negotiations;

AGREEMENT, ANNEX, SECTION 5, PARAGRAPH 2

2. The provisions of Annex III, article 5, of the Convention shall not apply.

(g) to establish terms and conditions, and to authorize negotiations, concerning joint ventures and other forms of joint arrangements referred to in Annex III, articles 9 and 11, and to approve the results of such negotiations;

(h) to recommend to the Assembly what portion of the net income of the Enterprise should be retained as its reserves in accordance with article 160, paragraph 2(f), and article 10 of this Annex;

(i) to approve the annual budget of the Enterprise;

(j) to authorize the procurement of goods and services in accordance with article 12, paragraph 3, of this Annex;

(k) to submit an annual report to the Council in accordance with article 9 of this Annex;

(l)   to submit to the Council for the approval of the Assembly draft rules in respect of the organization, management, appointment and dismissal of the staff of the Enterprise and to adopt regulations to give effect to such rules;

(m) to borrow funds and to furnish such collateral or other security as it may determine in accordance with article 11, paragraph 2, of this Annex;

(n)   to enter into any legal proceedings, agreements and transactions and to take any other actions in accordance with article 13 of this Annex;

(o)   to delegate, subject to the approval of the Council, any non-discretionary powers to the Director-General and to its committees.

Article 7
Director-General and staff of the Enterprise

1.   The Assembly shall, upon the recommendation of the Council and the nomination of the Governing Board, elect the Director-General of the Enterprise who shall not be a member of the Board. The Director-General shall hold office for a fixed term, not exceeding five years, and may be re-elected for further terms.

2.   The Director-General shall be the legal representative and chief executive of the Enterprise and shall be directly responsible to the Board for the conduct of the operations of the Enterprise. He shall be responsible for the organization, management, appointment and dismissal of the staff of the Enterprise in accordance with the rules and regulations referred to in article 6, subparagraph (1), of this Annex. He shall participate, without the right to vote, in the meetings of the Board and may participate, without the right to vote, in the meetings of the Assembly and the Council when these organs are dealing with matters concerning the Enterprise.

3.   The paramount consideration in the recruitment and employment of the staff and in the determination of their conditions of service shall be the necessity of securing the highest standards of efficiency and of technical competence. Subject to this consideration, due regard shall be paid to the importance of recruiting the staff on an equitable geographical basis.

4.   In the performance of their duties the Director-General and the staff shall not seek or receive instructions from any government or from any other source external to the Enterprise. They shall refrain from any action which might reflect on their position as international officials of the Enterprise responsible only to the Enterprise. Each State Party undertakes to respect the exclusively international character of the responsibilities of the Director-General and the staff and not to seek to influence them in the discharge of their responsibilities.

5.   The responsibilities set forth in article 168, paragraph 2, are equally applicable to the staff of the Enterprise.

Article 8
Location

The Enterprise shall have its principal office at the seat of the Authority. The Enterprise may establish other offices and facilities in the territory of any State Party with the consent of that State Party.

Article 9
Reports and financial statements

1.   The Enterprise shall, not later than three months after the end of each financial year, submit to the Council for its consideration an annual report containing an audited statement of its accounts and shall transmit to the Council at appropriate intervals a summary statement of its financial position and a profit and loss statement showing the results of its operations.

2.   The Enterprise shall publish its annual report and such other reports as it finds appropriate.

3.   All reports and financial statements referred to in this article shall be distributed to the members of the Authority.

Article 10
Allocation of net income

1.   Subject to paragraph 3, the Enterprise shall make payments to the Authority under Annex III, article 13, or their equivalent.

2.   The Assembly shall, upon the recommendation of the Governing Board, determine what portion of the net income of the Enterprise shall be retained as reserves of the Enterprise. The remainder shall be transferred to the Authority.

3.   During an initial period required for the Enterprise to become self-supporting, which shall not exceed 10 years from the commencement of commercial production by it, the Assembly shall exempt the Enterprise from the payments referred to in paragraph 1, and shall leave all of the net income of the Enterprise in its reserves.

Article 11
Finances

1.   The funds of the Enterprise shall include:
(a)   amounts received from the Authority in accordance with article 173, paragraph 2(b);
(b)   voluntary contributions made by States Parties for the purpose of financing activities of the Enterprise;
(c)   amounts borrowed by the Enterprise in accordance with paragraphs 2 and 3;
(d)   income of the Enterprise from its operations;
(e)   other funds made available to the Enterprise to enable it to commence operations as soon as possible and to carry out its functions.

2.   (a)   The Enterprise shall have the power to borrow funds and to furnish such collateral or other security as it may determine. Before making a public sale of its obligations in the financial markets or currency of a State Party, the Enterprise shall obtain the approval of that State Party. The total amount of borrowings shall be approved by the Council upon the recommendation of the Governing Board.

(b) States Parties shall make every reasonable effort to support applications by the Enterprise for loans on capital markets and from international financial institutions.

3. (a) The Enterprise shall be provided with the funds necessary to explore and exploit one mine site, and to transport, process and market the minerals recovered therefrom and the nickel, copper, cobalt and manganese obtained, and to meet its initial administrative expenses. The amount of the said funds, and the criteria and factors for its adjustment, shall be included by the Preparatory Commission in the draft rules, regulations and procedures of the Authority.

(b) All States Parties shall make available to the Enterprise an amount equivalent to one half of the funds referred to in subparagraph (a) by way of long-term interest-free loans in accordance with the scale of assessments for the United Nations regular budget in force at the time when the assessments are made, adjusted to take into account the States which are not members of the United Nations. Debts incurred by the Enterprise in raising the other half of the funds shall be guaranteed by all States Parties in accordance with the same scale.

(c) If the sum of the financial contributions of States Parties is less than the funds to be provided to the Enterprise under subparagraph (a), the Assembly shall, at its first session, consider the extent of the shortfall and adopt by consensus measures for dealing with this shortfall, taking into account the obligation of State Parties under subparagraphs (a) and (b) and any recommendations of the Preparatory Commission.

(d) (i) Each State Party shall, within 60 days after the entry into force of this Convention, or within 30 days after the deposit of its instrument of ratification or accession, whichever is later, deposit with the Enterprise irrevocable, non-negotiable, non-interest-bearing promissory notes in the amount of the share of such State Party of interest-free loans pursuant to subparagraph (b).

(ii) The Board shall prepare, at the earliest practicable date after this Convention enters into force, and thereafter at annual or other appropriate intervals, a schedule of the magnitude and timing of its requirements for the funding of its administrative expenses and for activities carried out by the Enterprise in accordance with article 170 and article 12 of this Annex.

(iii) The States Parties shall, thereupon, be notified by the Enterprise, through the Authority, of their respective shares of the funds in accordance with subparagraph (b), required for such expenses. The Enterprise shall encash such amounts of the promissory notes as may be required to meet the expenditure referred to in the schedule with respect to interest-free loans.

(iv) States Parties shall, upon receipt of the notification, make available their respective shares of debt guarantees for the Enterprise in accordance with subparagraph (b).

(e) (i) If the Enterprise so requests, States Parties may provide debt guarantees in addition to those provided in accordance with the scale referred to in subparagraph (b).

    (ii) In lieu of debt guarantees, a State Party may make a voluntary contribution to the Enterprise in an amount equivalent to that portion of the debts which it would otherwise be liable to guarantee.

(f) Repayment of the interest-bearing loans shall have priority over the repayment of the interest-free loans. Repayment of interest-free loans shall be in accordance with a schedule adopted by the Assembly, upon the recommendation of the Council and the advice of the Board. In the exercise of this function the Board shall be guided by the relevant provisions of the rules, regulations and procedures of the Authority, which shall take into account the paramount importance of ensuring the effective functioning of the Enterprise and, in particular, ensuring its financial independence.

(g) Funds made available to the Enterprise shall be in freely usable currencies or currencies which are freely available and effectively usable in the major foreign exchange markets. These currencies shall be defined in the rules, regulations and procedures of the Authority in accordance with prevailing international monetary practice. Except as provided in paragraph 2, no State Party shall maintain or impose restrictions on the holding, use or exchange by the Enterprise of these funds.

(h) "Debt guarantee" means a promise of a State Party to creditors of the Enterprise to pay, *pro rata* in accordance with the appropriate scale, the financial obligations of the Enterprise covered by the guarantee following notice by the creditors to the State Party of a default by the Enterprise. Procedures for the payment of those obligations shall be in conformity with the rules, regulations and procedures of the Authority.

AGREEMENT, ANNEX, SECTION 2, PARAGRAPH 3

3. The obligation of States Parties to fund one mine site of the Enterprise as provided for in Annex IV, article 11, paragraph 3, of the Convention shall not apply and States Parties shall be under no obligation to finance any of the operations in any mine site of the Enterprise or under its joint venture arrangements.

4. The funds, assets and expenses of the Enterprise shall be kept separate from those of the Authority. This article shall not prevent the Enterprise from making arrangements with the Authority regarding facilities, personnel and services and arrangements for reimbursement of administrative expenses paid by either on behalf of the other.

5. The records, books and accounts of the Enterprise, including its annual financial statements, shall be audited annually by an independent auditor appointed by the Council.

Article 12
Operations

1.   The Enterprise shall propose to the Council projects for carrying out activities in accordance with article 170. Such proposals shall include a formal written plan of work for activities in the Area in accordance with article 153, paragraph 3, and all such other information and data as may be required from time to time for its appraisal by the Legal and Technical Commission and approval by the Council.

2.   Upon approval by the Council, the Enterprise shall execute the project on the basis of the formal written plan of work referred to in paragraph 1.

3.   (a) If the Enterprise does not possess the goods and services required for its operations it may procure them. For that purpose, it shall issue invitations to tender and award contracts to bidders offering the best combination of quality, price and delivery time.

(b)   If there is more than one bid offering such a combination, the contract shall be awarded in accordance with:

   (i)   the principle of non-discrimination on the basis of political or other considerations not relevant to the carrying out of operations with due diligence and efficiency; and

   (ii) guidelines approved by the Council with regard to the preferences to be accorded to goods and services originating in developing States, including the land-locked and geographically disadvantaged among them.

(c)   The Governing Board may adopt rules determining the special circumstances in which the requirement of invitations to bid may, in the best interests of the Enterprise, be dispensed with.

4.   The Enterprise shall have title to all minerals and processed substances produced by it.

5.   The Enterprise shall sell its products on a non-discriminatory basis. It shall not give non-commercial discounts.

6.   Without prejudice to any general or special power conferred on the Enterprise under any other provision of this Convention, the Enterprise shall exercise such powers incidental to its business as shall be necessary.

7.   The Enterprise shall not interfere in the political affairs of any State Party; nor shall it be influenced in its decisions by the political character of the State Party concerned. Only commercial considerations shall be relevant to its decisions, and these considerations shall be weighed impartially in order to carry out the purposes specified in article 1 of this Annex.

Article 13
Legal status, privileges and immunities

1.   To enable the Enterprise to exercise its functions, the status, privileges and immunities set forth in this article shall be accorded to the Enterprise in the territories of States Parties. To give effect to this principle the Enterprise and States Parties may, where necessary, enter into special agreements.

2.   The Enterprise shall have such legal capacity as is necessary for the exercise of its functions and the fulfilment of its purposes and, in particular, the capacity:

(a)   to enter into contracts, joint arrangements or other arrangements, including agreements with States and international organizations;

(b)   to acquire, lease, hold and dispose of immovable and movable property;

(c)   to be a party to legal proceedings.

3.   (a) Actions may be brought against the Enterprise only in a court of competent jurisdiction in the territory of a State Party in which the Enterprise:

(i)   has an office or facility;

(ii) has appointed an agent for the purpose of accepting service or notice of process;

(iii) has entered into a contract for goods or services;

(iv) has issued securities; or

(v)   is otherwise engaged in commercial activity.

(b)   The property and assets of the Enterprise, wherever located and by whomsoever held, shall be immune from all forms of seizure, attachment or execution before the delivery of final judgment against the Enterprise.

4.   (a) The property and assets of the Enterprise, wherever located and by whomsoever held, shall be immune from requisition, confiscation, expropriation or any other form of seizure by executive or legislative action.

(b)   The property and assets of the Enterprise, wherever located and by whomsoever held, shall be free from discriminatory restrictions, regulations, controls and moratoria of any nature.

(c)   The Enterprise and its employees shall respect local laws and regulations in any State or territory in which the Enterprise or its employees may do business or otherwise act.

(d)   States Parties shall ensure that the Enterprise enjoys all rights, privileges and immunities accorded by them to entities conducting commercial activities in their territories. These rights, privileges and immunities shall be accorded to the Enterprise on no less favourable a basis than that on which they are accorded to entities engaged in similar commercial activities. If special privileges are provided by States Parties for developing States or their commercial entities, the Enterprise shall enjoy those privileges on a similarly preferential basis.

(e)   States Parties may provide special incentives, rights, privileges and immunities to the Enterprise without the obligation to provide such incentives, rights, privileges and immunities to other commercial entities.

5.   The Enterprise shall negotiate with the host countries in which its offices and facilities are located for exemption from direct and indirect taxation.

6.   Each State Party shall take such action as is necessary for giving effect in terms of its own law to the principles set forth in this Annex and shall inform the Enterprise of the specific action which it has taken.

7.   The Enterprise may waive any of the privileges and immunities conferred under this article or in the special agreements referred to in paragraph 1 to
such extent and upon such conditions as it may determine.

ANNEX V. CONCILIATION

SECTION 1. CONCILIATION PROCEDURE
PURSUANT TO SECTION 1 OF PART XV

Article 1
Institution of proceedings

If the parties to a dispute have agreed, in accordance with article 284, to
submit it to conciliation under this section, any such party may institute the proceedings by written notification addressed to the other party or parties to the dispute.

Article 2
List of conciliators

A list of conciliators shall be drawn up and maintained by the Secretary-
General of the United Nations. Every State Party shall be entitled to nominate
four conciliators, each of whom shall be a person enjoying the highest reputation
for fairness, competence and integrity. The names of the persons so nominated
shall constitute the list. If at any time the conciliators nominated by a State Party
in the list so constituted shall be fewer than four, that State Party shall be entitled
to make further nominations as necessary. The name of a conciliator shall remain
on the list until withdrawn by the State Party which made the nomination, provided that such conciliator shall continue to serve on any conciliation commission
to which that conciliator has been appointed until the completion of the proceedings before that commission.

Article 3
Constitution of conciliation commission

The conciliation commission shall, unless the parties otherwise agree, be constituted as follows:

  (a) Subject to subparagraph (g), the conciliation commission shall consist
       of five members.
  (b) The party instituting the proceedings shall appoint two conciliators to be
       chosen preferably from the list referred to in article 2 of this Annex, one
       of whom may be its national, unless the parties otherwise agree. Such
       appointments shall be included in the notification referred to in article 1
       of this Annex.
  (c) The other party to the dispute shall appoint two conciliators in the man-
       ner set forth in subparagraph (b) within 21 days of receipt of the
       notification referred to in article 1 of this Annex. If the appointments are

not made within that period, the party instituting the proceedings may, within one week of the expiration of that period, either terminate the proceedings by notification addressed to the other party or request the Secretary-General of the United Nations to make the appointments in accordance with subparagraph (e).

(d) Within 30 days after all four conciliators have been appointed, they shall appoint a fifth conciliator chosen from the list referred to in article 2 of this Annex, who shall be chairman. If the appointment is not made within that period, either party may, within one week of the expiration of that period, request the Secretary-General of the United Nations to make the appointment in accordance with subparagraph (e).

(e) Within 30 days of the receipt of a request under subparagraph (c) or (d), the Secretary-General of the United Nations shall make the necessary appointments from the list referred to in article 2 of this Annex in consultation with the parties to the dispute.

(f) Any vacancy shall be filled in the manner prescribed for the initial appointment.

(g) Two or more parties which determine by agreement that they are in the same interest shall appoint two conciliators jointly. Where two or more parties have separate interests or there is a disagreement as to whether they are of the same interest, they shall appoint conciliators separately.

(h) In disputes involving more than two parties having separate interests, or where there is disagreement as to whether they are of the same interest, the parties shall apply subparagraphs (a) to (f) in so far as possible.

Article 4
Procedure

The conciliation commission shall, unless the parties otherwise agree, determine its own procedure. The commission may, with the consent of the parties to the dispute, invite any State Party to submit to it its views orally or in writing. Decisions of the commission regarding procedural matters, the report and recommendations shall be made by a majority vote of its members.

Article 5
Amicable settlement

The commission may draw the attention of the parties to any measures which might facilitate an amicable settlement of the dispute.

Article 6
Functions of the commission

The commission shall hear the parties, examine their claims and objections, and make proposals to the parties with a view to reaching an amicable settlement.

Article 7
Report

1.   The commission shall report within 12 months of its constitution. Its report shall record any agreements reached and, failing agreement, its conclusions on all questions of fact or law relevant to the matter in dispute and such recommendations as the commission may deem appropriate for an amicable settlement. The report shall be deposited with the Secretary-General of the United Nations and shall immediately be transmitted by him to the parties to the dispute.

2.   The report of the commission, including its conclusions or recommendations, shall not be binding upon the parties.

Article 8
Termination

The conciliation proceedings are terminated when a settlement has been reached, when the parties have accepted or one party has rejected the recommendations of the report by written notification addressed to the Secretary-General of the United Nations, or when a period of three months has expired from the date of transmission of the report to the parties.

Article 9
Fees and expenses

The fees and expenses of the commission shall be borne by the parties to the dispute.

Article 10
Right of parties to modify procedure

The parties to the dispute may by agreement applicable solely to that dispute modify any provision of this Annex.

SECTION 2. COMPULSORY SUBMISSION
TO CONCILIATION PROCEDURE
PURSUANT TO SECTION 3 OF PART XV

Article 11
Institution of proceedings

1.   Any party to a dispute which, in accordance with Part XV, section 3, may be submitted to conciliation under this section, may institute the proceedings by written notification addressed to the other party or parties to the dispute.

2.   Any party to the dispute, notified under paragraph 1, shall be obliged to submit to such proceedings.

Article 12
Failure to reply or to submit to conciliation

The failure of a party or parties to the dispute to reply to notification of institution of proceedings or to submit to such proceedings shall not constitute a bar to the proceedings.

Article 13
Competence

A disagreement as to whether a conciliation commission acting under this section has competence shall be decided by the commission.

Article 14
Application of section 1

Articles 2 to 10 of section 1 of this Annex apply subject to this section.

ANNEX VI. STATUTE OF THE INTERNATIONAL TRIBUNAL FOR THE LAW OF THE SEA

Article 1
General provisions

1.   The International Tribunal for the Law of the Sea is constituted and shall function in accordance with the provisions of this Convention and this Statute.

2.   The seat of the Tribunal shall be in the Free and Hanseatic City of Hamburg in the Federal Republic of Germany.

3.   The Tribunal may sit and exercise its functions elsewhere whenever it considers this desirable.

4.   A reference of a dispute to the Tribunal shall be governed by the provisions of Parts XI and XV.

SECTION 1. ORGANIZATION OF THE TRIBUNAL

Article 2
Composition

1. The Tribunal shall be composed of a body of 21 independent members, elected from among persons enjoying the highest reputation for fairness and integrity and of recognized competence in the field of the law of the sea.

2.   In the Tribunal as a whole the representation of the principal legal systems of the world and equitable geographical distribution shall be assured.

Article 3
Membership

1.   No two members of the Tribunal may be nationals of the same State. A person who for the purposes of membership in the Tribunal could be regarded as a national of more than one State shall be deemed to be a national of the one in which he ordinarily exercises civil and political rights.

2.   There shall be no fewer than three members from each geographical group as established by the General Assembly of the United Nations.

Article 4
Nominations and elections

1. Each State Party may nominate not more than two persons having the qualifications prescribed in article 2 of this Annex. The members of the Tribunal shall be elected from the list of persons thus nominated.

2.   At least three months before the date of the election, the Secretary-General of the United Nations in the case of the first election and the Registrar of the Tribunal in the case of subsequent elections shall address a written invitation to the States Parties to submit their nominations for members of the Tribunal within two months. He shall prepare a list in alphabetical order of all the persons thus nominated, with an indication of the States Parties which have nominated them, and shall submit it to the States Parties before the seventh day of the last month before the date of each election.

3.   The first election shall be held within six months of the date of entry into force of this Convention.

4.   The members of the Tribunal shall be elected by secret ballot. Elections shall be held at a meeting of the States Parties convened by the Secretary-General of the United Nations in the case of the first election and by a procedure agreed to by the States Parties in the case of subsequent elections. Two thirds of the States Parties shall constitute a quorum at that meeting. The persons elected to the Tribunal shall be those nominees who obtain the largest number of votes and a two-thirds majority of the States Parties present and voting, provided that such majority includes a majority of the States Parties.

Article 5
Term of office

1.   The members of the Tribunal shall be elected for nine years and may be re-elected; provided, however, that of the members elected at the first election, the terms of seven members shall expire at the end of three years and the terms of seven more members shall expire at the end of six years.

2.   The members of the Tribunal whose terms are to expire at the end of the above-mentioned initial periods of three and six years shall be chosen by lot to be drawn by the Secretary-General of the United Nations immediately after the first election.

3.   The members of the Tribunal shall continue to discharge their duties until their places have been filled. Though replaced, they shall finish any proceedings which they may have begun before the date of their replacement.

4.   In the case of the resignation of a member of the Tribunal, the letter of resignation shall be addressed to the President of the Tribunal. The place becomes vacant on the receipt of that letter.

Article 6
Vacancies

1.   Vacancies shall be filled by the same method as that laid down for the first election, subject to the following provision: the Registrar shall, within one month of the occurrence of the vacancy, proceed to issue the invitations provided for in article 4 of this Annex, and the date of the election shall be fixed by the President of the Tribunal after consultation with the States Parties.

2.   A member of the Tribunal elected to replace a member whose term of office has not expired shall hold office for the remainder of his predecessor's term.

Article 7
Incompatible activities

1.   No member of the Tribunal may exercise any political or administrative function, or associate actively with or be financially interested in any of the operations of any enterprise concerned with the exploration for or exploitation of the resources of the sea or the seabed or other commercial use of the sea or the seabed.

2.   No member of the Tribunal may act as agent, counsel or advocate in any case.

3.   Any doubt on these points shall be resolved by decision of the majority of the other members of the Tribunal present.

Article 8
Conditions relating to participation of members in a particular case

1.   No member of the Tribunal may participate in the decision of any case in which he has previously taken part as agent, counsel or advocate for one of the parties, or as a member of a national or international court or tribunal, or in any other capacity.

2.   If, for some special reason, a member of the Tribunal considers that he should not take part in the decision of a particular case, he shall so inform the President of the Tribunal.

3.   If the President considers that for some special reason one of the members of the Tribunal should not sit in a particular case, he shall give him notice accordingly.

4.   Any doubt on these points shall be resolved by decision of the majority of the other members of the Tribunal present.

Article 9
Consequence of ceasing to fulfil required conditions

If, in the unanimous opinion of the other members of the Tribunal, a member has ceased to fulfil the required conditions, the President of the Tribunal shall declare the seat vacant.

Article 10
Privileges and immunities

The members of the Tribunal, when engaged on the business of the Tribunal, shall enjoy diplomatic privileges and immunities.

Article 11
Solemn declaration by members

Every member of the Tribunal shall, before taking up his duties, make a solemn declaration in open session that he will exercise his powers impartially and conscientiously.

Article 12
President, Vice-President and Registrar

1.   The Tribunal shall elect its President and Vice-President for three years; they may be re-elected.
2.   The Tribunal shall appoint its Registrar and may provide for the appointment of such other officers as may be necessary.
3.   The President and the Registrar shall reside at the seat of the Tribunal.

Article 13
Quorum

1.   All available members of the Tribunal shall sit; a quorum of 11 elected members shall be required to constitute the Tribunal.
2.   Subject to article 17 of this Annex, the Tribunal shall determine which members are available to constitute the Tribunal for the consideration of a particular dispute, having regard to the effective functioning of the chambers as provided for in articles 14 and 15 of this Annex.
3.   All disputes and applications submitted to the Tribunal shall be heard and determined by the Tribunal, unless article 14 of this Annex applies, or the parties request that it shall be dealt with in accordance with article 15 of this Annex.

Article 14
Seabed Disputes Chamber

A Seabed Disputes Chamber shall be established in accordance with the provisions of section 4 of this Annex. Its jurisdiction, powers and functions shall be as provided for in Part XI, section 5.

Article 15
Special chambers

1.   The Tribunal may form such chambers, composed of three or more of its elected members, as it considers necessary for dealing with particular categories of disputes.

2.   The Tribunal shall form a chamber for dealing with a particular dispute submitted to it if the parties so request. The composition of such a chamber shall be determined by the Tribunal with the approval of the parties.

3.   With a view to the speedy dispatch of business, the Tribunal shall form annually a chamber composed of five of its elected members which may hear and determine disputes by summary procedure. Two alternative members shall be selected for the purpose of replacing members who are unable to participate in a particular proceeding.

4.   Disputes shall be heard and determined by the chambers provided for in this article if the parties so request.

5.   A judgment given by any of the chambers provided for in this article and in article 14 of this Annex shall be considered as rendered by the Tribunal.

Article 16
Rules of the Tribunal

The Tribunal shall frame rules for carrying out its functions. In particular it shall lay down rules of procedure.

Article 17
Nationality of members

1.   Members of the Tribunal of the nationality of any of the parties to a dispute shall retain their right to participate as members of the Tribunal.

2.   If the Tribunal, when hearing a dispute, includes upon the bench a member of the nationality of one of the parties, any other party may choose a person to participate as a member of the Tribunal.

3.   If the Tribunal, when hearing a dispute, does not include upon the bench a member of the nationality of the parties, each of those parties may choose a person to participate as a member of the Tribunal.

4.   This article applies to the chambers referred to in articles 14 and 15 of this Annex. In such cases, the President, in consultation with the parties, shall request specified members of the Tribunal forming the chamber, as many as necessary, to give place to the members of the Tribunal of the nationality of the parties concerned, and, failing such, or if they are unable to be present, to the members specially chosen by the parties.

5.   Should there be several parties in the same interest, they shall, for the purpose of the preceding provisions, be considered as one party only. Any doubt on this point shall be settled by the decision of the Tribunal.

6.   Members chosen in accordance with paragraphs 2, 3 and 4 shall fulfil the conditions required by articles 2, 8 and 11 of this Annex. They shall participate in the decision on terms of complete equality with their colleagues.

Article 18
Remuneration of members

1.   Each elected member of the Tribunal shall receive an annual allowance and, for each day on which he exercises his functions, a special allowance, provided that in any year the total sum payable to any member as special allowance shall not exceed the amount of the annual allowance.

2.   The President shall receive a special annual allowance.

3.   The Vice-President shall receive a special allowance for each day on which he acts as President.

4.   The members chosen under article 17 of this Annex, other than elected members of the Tribunal, shall receive compensation for each day on which they exercise their functions.

5.   The salaries, allowances and compensation shall be determined from time to time at meetings of the States Parties, taking into account the workload of the Tribunal. They may not be decreased during the term of office.

6.   The salary of the Registrar shall be determined at meetings of the States Parties, on the proposal of the Tribunal.

7.   Regulations adopted at meetings of the States Parties shall determine the conditions under which retirement pensions may be given to members of the Tribunal and to the Registrar, and the conditions under which members of the Tribunal and Registrar shall have their travelling expenses refunded.

8.   The salaries, allowances, and compensation shall be free of all taxation.

Article 19
Expenses of the Tribunal

1.   The expenses of the Tribunal shall be borne by the States Parties and by the Authority on such terms and in such a manner as shall be decided at meetings of the States Parties.

2.   When an entity other than a State Party or the Authority is a party to a case submitted to it, the Tribunal shall fix the amount which that party is to contribute towards the expenses of the Tribunal.

SECTION 2. COMPETENCE

Article 20
Access to the Tribunal

1.   The Tribunal shall be open to States Parties.

2.   The Tribunal shall be open to entities other than States Parties in any case expressly provided for in Part XI or in any case submitted pursuant to any

other agreement conferring jurisdiction on the Tribunal which is accepted by all the parties to that case.

Article 21
Jurisdiction

The jurisdiction of the Tribunal comprises all disputes and all applications submitted to it in accordance with this Convention and all matters specifically provided for in any other agreement which confers jurisdiction on the Tribunal.

Article 22
Reference of disputes subject to other agreements

If all the parties to a treaty or convention already in force and concerning the subject-matter covered by this Convention so agree, any disputes concerning the interpretation or application of such treaty or convention may, in accordance with such agreement, be submitted to the Tribunal.

Article 23
Applicable law

The Tribunal shall decide all disputes and applications in accordance with article 293.

SECTION 3. PROCEDURE

Article 24
Institution of proceedings

1.   Disputes are submitted to the Tribunal, as the case may be, either by notification of a special agreement or by written application, addressed to the Registrar. In either case, the subject of the dispute and the parties shall be indicated.

2.   The Registrar shall forthwith notify the special agreement or the application to all concerned.

3.   The Registrar shall also notify all States Parties.

Article 25
Provisional measures

1.   In accordance with article 290, the Tribunal and its Seabed Disputes Chamber shall have the power to prescribe provisional measures.

2.   If the Tribunal is not in session or a sufficient number of members is not available to constitute a quorum, the provisional measures shall be prescribed by the chamber of summary procedure formed under article 15, paragraph 3, of this Annex. Notwithstanding article 15, paragraph 4, of this Annex, such provisional measures may be adopted at the request of any party to the dispute. They shall be subject to review and revision by the Tribunal.

Article 26
Hearing

1.   The hearing shall be under the control of the President or, if he is unable to preside, of the Vice-President. If neither is able to preside, the senior judge present of the Tribunal shall preside.

2.   The hearing shall be public, unless the Tribunal decides otherwise or unless the parties demand that the public be not admitted.

Article 27
Conduct of case

The Tribunal shall make orders for the conduct of the case, decide the form and time in which each party must conclude its arguments, and make all arrangements connected with the taking of evidence.

Article 28
Default

When one of the parties does not appear before the Tribunal or fails to defend its case, the other party may request the Tribunal to continue the proceedings and make its decision. Absence of a party or failure of a party to defend its case shall not constitute a bar to the proceedings. Before making its decision, the Tribunal must satisfy itself not only that it has jurisdiction over the dispute, but also that the claim is well founded in fact and law.

Article 29
Majority for decision

1.   All questions shall be decided by a majority of the members of the Tribunal who are present.

2.   In the event of an equality of votes, the President or the member of the Tribunal who acts in his place shall have a casting vote.

Article 30
Judgment

1.   The judgment shall state the reasons on which it is based.

2.   It shall contain the names of the members of the Tribunal who have taken part in the decision.

3.   If the judgment does not represent in whole or in part the unanimous opinion of the members of the Tribunal, any member shall be entitled to deliver a separate opinion.

4.   The judgment shall be signed by the President and by the Registrar. It shall be read in open court, due notice having been given to the parties to the dispute.

Article 31
Request to intervene

1.   Should a State Party consider that it has an interest of a legal nature which may be affected by the decision in any dispute, it may submit a request to the Tribunal to be permitted to intervene.

2.   It shall be for the Tribunal to decide upon this request.

3.   If a request to intervene is granted, the decision of the Tribunal in respect of the dispute shall be binding upon the intervening State Party in so far as it relates to matters in respect of which that State Party intervened.

Article 32
Right to intervene in cases of interpretation or application

1.   Whenever the interpretation or application of this Convention is in question, the Registrar shall notify all States Parties forthwith.

2.   Whenever pursuant to article 21 or 22 of this Annex the interpretation or application of an international agreement is in question, the Registrar shall notify all the parties to the agreement.

3.   Every party referred to in paragraphs 1 and 2 has the right to intervene in the proceedings; if it uses this right, the interpretation given by the judgment will be equally binding upon it.

Article 33
Finality and binding force of decisions

1.   The decision of the Tribunal is final and shall be complied with by all the parties to the dispute.

2.   The decision shall have no binding force except between the parties in respect of that particular dispute.

3.   In the event of dispute as to the meaning or scope of the decision, the Tribunal shall construe it upon the request of any party.

Article 34
Costs

Unless otherwise decided by the Tribunal, each party shall bear its own costs.

SECTION 4. SEABED DISPUTES CHAMBER

Article 35
Composition

1.   The Seabed Disputes Chamber referred to in article 14 of this Annex shall be composed of 11 members, selected by a majority of the elected members of the Tribunal from among them.

2.   In the selection of the members of the Chamber, the representation of the principal legal systems of the world and equitable geographical distribution

shall be assured. The Assembly of the Authority may adopt recommendations of a general nature relating to such representation and distribution.

3.   The members of the Chamber shall be selected every three years and may be selected for a second term.

4.   The Chamber shall elect its President from among its members, who shall serve for the term for which the Chamber has been selected.

5.   If any proceedings are still pending at the end of any three-year period for which the Chamber has been selected, the Chamber shall complete the proceedings in its original composition.

6.   If a vacancy occurs in the Chamber, the Tribunal shall select a successor from among its elected members, who shall hold office for the remainder of his predecessor's term.

7.   A quorum of seven of the members selected by the Tribunal shall be required to constitute the Chamber.

Article 36
Ad hoc chambers

1.   The Seabed Disputes Chamber shall form an *ad hoc* chamber, composed of three of its members, for dealing with a particular dispute submitted to it in accordance with article 188, paragraph 1(b). The composition of such a chamber shall be determined by the Seabed Disputes Chamber with the approval of the parties.

2.   If the parties do not agree on the composition of an *ad hoc* chamber, each party to the dispute shall appoint one member, and the third member shall be appointed by them in agreement. If they disagree, or if any party fails to make an appointment, the President of the Seabed Disputes Chamber shall promptly make the appointment or appointments from among its members, after consultation with the parties.

3.   Members of the *ad hoc* chamber must not be in the service of, or nationals of, any of the parties to the dispute.

Article 37
Access

The Chamber shall be open to the States Parties, the Authority and the other entities referred to in Part XI, section 5.

Article 38
Applicable law

In addition to the provisions of article 293, the Chamber shall apply:

(a) the rules, regulations and procedures of the Authority adopted in accordance with this Convention; and

(b) the terms of contracts concerning activities in the Area in matters relating to those contracts.

Article 39
Enforcement of decisions of the Chamber

The decisions of the Chamber shall be enforceable in the territories of the States Parties in the same manner as judgments or orders of the highest court of the State Party in whose territory the enforcement is sought.

Article 40
Applicability of other sections of this Annex

1.   The other sections of this Annex which are not incompatible with this section apply to the Chamber.

2.   In the exercise of its functions relating to advisory opinions, the Chamber shall be guided by the provisions of this Annex relating to procedure before the Tribunal to the extent to which it recognizes them to be applicable.

SECTION 5. AMENDMENTS

Article 41
Amendments

1.   Amendments to this Annex, other than amendments to section 4, may be adopted only in accordance with article 313 or by consensus at a conference convened in accordance with this Convention.

2.   Amendments to section 4 may be adopted only in accordance with article 314.

3.   The Tribunal may propose such amendments to this Statute as it may consider necessary, by written communications to the States Parties for their consideration in conformity with paragraphs 1 and 2.

ANNEX VII. ARBITRATION

Article 1
Institution of proceedings

Subject to the provisions of Part XV, any party to a dispute may submit the dispute to the arbitral procedure provided for in this Annex by written notification addressed to the other party or parties to the dispute. The notification shall be accompanied by a statement of the claim and the grounds on which it is based.

Article 2
List of arbitrators

1.   A list of arbitrators shall be drawn up and maintained by the Secretary-General of the United Nations. Every State Party shall be entitled to nominate four arbitrators, each of whom shall be a person experienced in maritime affairs

and enjoying the highest reputation for fairness, competence and integrity. The names of the persons so nominated shall constitute the list.

2.   If at any time the arbitrators nominated by a State Party in the list so constituted shall be fewer than four, that State Party shall be entitled to make further nominations as necessary.

3.   The name of an arbitrator shall remain on the list until withdrawn by the State Party which made the nomination, provided that such arbitrator shall continue to serve on any arbitral tribunal to which that arbitrator has been appointed until the completion of the proceedings before that arbitral tribunal.

Article 3
Constitution of arbitral tribunal

For the purpose of proceedings under this Annex, the arbitral tribunal shall, unless the parties otherwise agree, be constituted as follows:

(a)   Subject to subparagraph (g), the arbitral tribunal shall consist of five members.

(b)   The party instituting the proceedings shall appoint one member to be chosen preferably from the list referred to in article 2 of this Annex, who may be its national. The appointment shall be included in the notification referred to in article 1 of this Annex.

(c)   The other party to the dispute shall, within 30 days of receipt of the notification referred to in article 1 of this Annex, appoint one member to be chosen preferably from the list, who may be its national. If the appointment is not made within that period, the party instituting the proceedings may, within two weeks of the expiration of that period, request that the appointment be made in accordance with subparagraph (e).

(d)   The other three members shall be appointed by agreement between the parties. They shall be chosen preferably from the list and shall be nationals of third States unless the parties otherwise agree. The parties to the dispute shall appoint the President of the arbitral tribunal from among those three members. If, within 60 days of receipt of the notification referred to in article 1 of this Annex, the parties are unable to reach agreement on the appointment of one or more of the members of the tribunal to be appointed by agreement, or on the appointment of the President, the remaining appointment or appointments shall be made in accordance with subparagraph (e), at the request of a party to the dispute. Such request shall be made within two weeks of the expiration of the aforementioned 60-day period.

(e)   Unless the parties agree that any appointment under subparagraphs (c) and (d) be made by a person or a third State chosen by the parties, the President of the International Tribunal for the Law of the Sea shall make the necessary appointments. If the President is unable to act under this subparagraph or is a national of one of the parties to the dispute, the appointment shall be made by the next senior member of the International Tribunal for the Law of the

Sea who is available and is not a national of one of the parties. The appointments referred to in this subparagraph shall be made from the list referred to in article 2 of this Annex within a period of 30 days of the receipt of the request and in consultation with the parties. The members so appointed shall be of different nationalities and may not be in the service of, ordinarily resident in the territory of, or nationals of, any of the parties to the dispute.

(f) Any vacancy shall be filled in the manner prescribed for the initial appointment.

(g) Parties in the same interest shall appoint one member of the tribunal jointly by agreement. Where there are several parties having separate interests or where there is disagreement as to whether they are of the same interest, each of them shall appoint one member of the tribunal. The number of members of the tribunal appointed separately by the parties shall always be smaller by one than the number of members of the tribunal to be appointed jointly by the parties.

(h) In disputes involving more than two parties, the provisions of subparagraphs (a) to (f) shall apply to the maximum extent possible.

Article 4
Functions of arbitral tribunal

An arbitral tribunal constituted under article 3 of this Annex shall function in accordance with this Annex and the other provisions of this Convention.

Article 5
Procedure

Unless the parties to the dispute otherwise agree, the arbitral tribunal shall determine its own procedure, assuring to each party a full opportunity to be heard and to present its case.

Article 6
Duties of parties to a dispute

The parties to the dispute shall facilitate the work of the arbitral tribunal and, in particular, in accordance with their law and using all means at their disposal, shall:

(a) provide it with all relevant documents, facilities and information; and

(b) enable it when necessary to call witnesses or experts and receive their evidence and to visit the localities to which the case relates.

Article 7
Expenses

Unless the arbitral tribunal decides otherwise because of the particular circumstances of the case, the expenses of the tribunal, including the remuneration of its members, shall be borne by the parties to the dispute in equal shares.

Article 8
Required majority for decisions

Decisions of the arbitral tribunal shall be taken by a majority vote of its members. The absence or abstention of less than half of the members shall not constitute a bar to the tribunal reaching a decision. In the event of an equality of votes, the President shall have a casting vote.

Article 9
Default of appearance

If one of the parties to the dispute does not appear before the arbitral tribunal or fails to defend its case, the other party may request the tribunal to continue the proceedings and to make its award. Absence of a party or failure of a party to defend its case shall not constitute a bar to the proceedings. Before making its award, the arbitral tribunal must satisfy itself not only that it has jurisdiction over the dispute but also that the claim is well founded in fact and law.

Article 10
Award

The award of the arbitral tribunal shall be confined to the subject-matter of the dispute and state the reasons on which it is based. It shall contain the names of the members who have participated and the date of the award. Any member of the tribunal may attach a separate or dissenting opinion to the award.

Article 11
Finality of award

The award shall be final and without appeal, unless the parties to the dispute have agreed in advance to an appellate procedure. It shall be complied with by the parties to the dispute.

Article 12
Interpretation or implementation of award

1.   Any controversy which may arise between the parties to the dispute as regards the interpretation or manner of implementation of the award may be submitted by either party for decision to the arbitral tribunal which made the award. For this purpose, any vacancy in the tribunal shall be filled in the manner provided for in the original appointments of the members of the tribunal.

2.   Any such controversy may be submitted to another court or tribunal under article 287 by agreement of all the parties to the dispute.

Article 13
Application to entities other than States Parties

The provisions of this Annex shall apply *mutatis mutandis* to any dispute involving entities other than States Parties.

ANNEX VIII. SPECIAL ARBITRATION

Article 1
Institution of proceedings

Subject to Part XV, any party to a dispute concerning the interpretation or application of the articles of this Convention relating to (1) fisheries, (2) protection and preservation of the marine environment, (3) marine scientific research, or (4) navigation, including pollution from vessels and by dumping, may submit the dispute to the special arbitral procedure provided for in this Annex by written notification addressed to the other party or parties to the dispute. The notification shall be accompanied by a statement of the claim and the grounds on which it is based.

Article 2
Lists of experts

1.   A list of experts shall be established and maintained in respect of each of the fields of (1) fisheries, (2) protection and preservation of the marine environment, (3) marine scientific research, and (4) navigation, including pollution from vessels and by dumping.

2.   The lists of experts shall be drawn up and maintained, in the field of fisheries by the Food and Agriculture Organization of the United Nations, in the field of protection and preservation of the marine environment by the United Nations Environment Programme, in the field of marine scientific research by the Intergovernmental Oceanographic Commission, in the field of navigation, including pollution from vessels and by dumping, by the International Maritime Organization, or in each case by the appropriate subsidiary body concerned to which such organization, programme or commission has delegated this function.

3.   Every State Party shall be entitled to nominate two experts in each field whose competence in the legal, scientific or technical aspects of such field is established and generally recognized and who enjoy the highest reputation for fairness and integrity. The names of the persons so nominated in each field shall constitute the appropriate list.

4.   If at any time the experts nominated by a State Party in the list so constituted shall be fewer than two, that State Party shall be entitled to make further nominations as necessary.

5.   The name of an expert shall remain on the list until withdrawn by the State Party which made the nomination, provided that such expert shall continue to serve on any special arbitral tribunal to which that expert has been appointed until the completion of the proceedings before that special arbitral tribunal.

Article 3
Constitution of special arbitral tribunal

For the purpose of proceedings under this Annex, the special arbitral tribunal shall, unless the parties otherwise agree, be constituted as follows:

(a) Subject to subparagraph (g), the special arbitral tribunal shall consist of five members.

(b) The party instituting the proceedings shall appoint two members to be chosen preferably from the appropriate list or lists referred to in article 2 of this Annex relating to the matters in dispute, one of whom may be its national. The appointments shall be included in the notification referred to in article 1 of this Annex.

(c) The other party to the dispute shall, within 30 days of receipt of the notification referred to in article 1 of this Annex, appoint two members to be chosen preferably from the appropriate list or lists relating to the matters in dispute, one of whom may be its national. If the appointments are not made within that period, the party instituting the proceedings may, within two weeks of the expiration of that period, request that the appointments be made in accordance with subparagraph (e).

(d) The parties to the dispute shall by agreement appoint the President of the special arbitral tribunal, chosen preferably from the appropriate list, who shall be a national of a third State, unless the parties otherwise agree. If, within 30 days of receipt of the notification referred to in article 1 of this Annex, the parties are unable to reach agreement on the appointment of the President, the appointment shall be made in accordance with subparagraph (e), at the request of a party to the dispute. Such request shall be made within two weeks of the expiration of the aforementioned 30-day period.

(e) Unless the parties agree that the appointment be made by a person or a third State chosen by the parties, the Secretary-General of the United Nations shall make the necessary appointments within 30 days of receipt of a request under subparagraphs (c) and (d). The appointments referred to in this subparagraph shall be made from the appropriate list or lists of experts referred to in article 2 of this Annex and in consultation with the parties to the dispute and the appropriate international organization. The members so appointed shall be of different nationalities and may not be in the service of, ordinarily resident in the territory of, or nationals of, any of the parties to the dispute.

(f) Any vacancy shall be filled in the manner prescribed for the initial appointment.

(g) Parties in the same interest shall appoint two members of the tribunal jointly by agreement. Where there are several parties having separate interests or where there is disagreement as to whether they are of the same interest, each of them shall appoint one member of the tribunal.

(h) In disputes involving more than two parties, the provisions of subparagraphs (a) to (f) shall apply to the maximum extent possible.

Article 4
General provisions

Annex VII, articles 4 to 13, apply *mutatis mutandis* to the special arbitration proceedings in accordance with this Annex.

Article 5
Fact finding

1.   The parties to a dispute concerning the interpretation or application of the provisions of this Convention relating to (1) fisheries, (2) protection and preservation of the marine environment, (3) marine scientific research, or (4) navigation, including pollution from vessels and by dumping, may at any time agree to request a special arbitral tribunal constituted in accordance with article 3 of this Annex to carry out an inquiry and establish the facts giving rise to the dispute.

2.   Unless the parties otherwise agree, the findings of fact of the special arbitral tribunal acting in accordance with paragraph 1, shall be considered as conclusive as between the parties.

3.   If all the parties to the dispute so request, the special arbitral tribunal may formulate recommendations which, without having the force of a decision, shall only constitute the basis for a review by the parties of the questions giving rise to the dispute.

4.   Subject to paragraph 2, the special arbitral tribunal shall act in accordance with the provisions of this Annex, unless the parties otherwise agree.

ANNEX IX. PARTICIPATION BY INTERNATIONAL ORGANIZATIONS

Article 1
Use of terms

For the purposes of article 305 and of this Annex, "international organization" means an intergovernmental organization constituted by States to which its member States have transferred competence over matters governed by this Convention, including the competence to enter into treaties in respect of those matters.

Article 2
Signature

An international organization may sign this Convention if a majority of its member States are signatories of this Convention. At the time of signature an international organization shall make a declaration specifying the matters governed by this Convention in respect of which competence has been transferred to that organization by its member States which are signatories, and the nature and extent of that competence.

Article 3
Formal confirmation and accession

1.   An international organization may deposit its instrument of formal confirmation or of accession if a majority of its member States deposit or have deposited their instruments of ratification or accession.

2.   The instruments deposited by the international organization shall contain the undertakings and declarations required by articles 4 and 5 of this Annex.

Article 4
Extent of participation and rights and obligations

1.   The instrument of formal confirmation or of accession of an international organization shall contain an undertaking to accept the rights and obligations of States under this Convention in respect of matters relating to which competence has been transferred to it by its member States which are Parties to this Convention.

2.   An international organization shall be a Party to this Convention to the extent that it has competence in accordance with the declarations, communications of information or notifications referred to in article 5 of this Annex.

3.   Such an international organization shall exercise the rights and perform the obligations which its member States which are Parties would otherwise have under this Convention, on matters relating to which competence has been transferred to it by those member States. The member States of that international organization shall not exercise competence which they have transferred to it.

4.   Participation of such an international organization shall in no case entail an increase of the representation to which its member States which are States Parties would otherwise be entitled, including rights in decision-making.

5.   Participation of such an international organization shall in no case confer any rights under this Convention on member States of the organization which are not States Parties to this Convention.

6. In the event of a conflict between the obligations of an international organization under this Convention and its obligations under the agreement establishing the organization or any acts relating to it, the obligations under this Convention shall prevail.

Article 5
Declarations, notifications and communications

1.   The instrument of formal confirmation or of accession of an international organization shall contain a declaration specifying the matters governed by this Convention in respect of which competence has been transferred to the organization by its member States which are Parties to this Convention.

2.   A member State of an international organization shall, at the time it ratifies or accedes to this Convention or at the time when the organization deposits its instrument of formal confirmation or of accession, whichever is later, make a declaration specifying the matters governed by this Convention in respect of which it has transferred competence to the organization.

3.   States Parties which are member States of an international organization which is a Party to this Convention shall be presumed to have competence over all matters governed by this Convention in respect of which transfers of competence

to the organization have not been specifically declared, notified or communicated by those States under this article.

4.   The international organization and its member States which are States Parties shall promptly notify the depositary of this Convention of any changes to the distribution of competence, including new transfers of competence, specified in the declarations under paragraphs 1 and 2.

5.   Any State Party may request an international organization and its member States which are States Parties to provide information as to which, as between the organization and its member States, has competence in respect of any specific question which has arisen. The organization and the member States concerned shall provide this information within a reasonable time. The international organization and the member States may also, on their own initiative, provide this information.

6.   Declarations, notifications and communications of information under this article shall specify the nature and extent of the competence transferred.

Article 6
Responsibility and liability

1.   Parties which have competence under article 5 of this Annex shall have responsibility for failure to comply with obligations or for any other violation of this Convention.

2.   Any State Party may request an international organization or its member States which are States Parties for information as to who has responsibility in respect of any specific matter. The organization and the member States concerned shall provide this information. Failure to provide this information within a reasonable time or the provision of contradictory information shall result in joint and several liability.

Article 7
Settlement of disputes

1.   At the time of deposit of its instrument of formal confirmation or of accession, or at any time thereafter, an international organization shall be free to choose, by means of a written declaration, one or more of the means for the settlement of disputes concerning the interpretation or application of this Convention, referred to in article 287, paragraph 1(a), (c) or (d).

2.   Part XV applies *mutatis mutandis* to any dispute between Parties to this Convention, one or more of which are international organizations.

3.   When an international organization and one or more of its member States are joint parties to a dispute, or parties in the same interest, the organization shall be deemed to have accepted the same procedures for the settlement of disputes as the member States; when, however, a member State has chosen only the International Court of Justice under article 287, the organization and the member State concerned shall be deemed to have accepted arbitration in accordance with Annex VII, unless the parties to the dispute otherwise agree.

Article 8
Applicability of Part XVII

Part XVII applies *mutatis mutandis* to an international organization, except in respect of the following:

(a)   the instrument of formal confirmation or of accession of an international organization shall not be taken into account in the application of article 308, paragraph 1;

(b)   (i)   an international organization shall have exclusive capacity with respect to the application of articles 312 to 315, to the extent that it has competence under article 5 of this Annex over the entire subject-matter of the amendment;

(ii)   the instrument of formal confirmation or of accession of an international organization to an amendment, the entire subject-matter over which the international organization has competence under article 5 of this Annex, shall be considered to be the instrument of ratification or accession of each of the member States which are States Parties, for the purposes of applying article 316, paragraphs 1, 2 and 3;

(iii) the instrument of formal confirmation or of accession of the international organization shall not be taken into account in the application of article 316, paragraphs 1 and 2, with regard to all other amendments;

(c)   (i)   an international organization may not denounce this Convention in accordance with article 317 if any of its member States is a State Party and if it continues to fulfil the qualifications specified in article 1 of this Annex;

(ii)   an international organization shall denounce this Convention when none of its member States is a State Party or if the international organization no longer fulfils the qualifications specified in article 1 of this Annex. Such denunciation shall take effect immediately.

NOTE ON THE CONSOLIDATION OF PART XI AND ANNEX III OF THE CONVENTION AND THE AGREEMENT RELATING TO THE IMPLEMENTATION OF PART XI OF THE CONVENTION

In this Compendium, Part XI, and Annex III, of the Convention have been consolidated with the relevant provisions of the Agreement relating to the implementation of Part XI of the United Nations Convention on the Law of the Sea. This unofficial consolidation of Part XI and the Agreement has been prepared by the Office of Legal Affairs of the International Seabed Authority and was originally published by the Authority in 1998 (ISA/98/04). It in no way replaces the official texts of the Convention and the Agreement published by the United Nations (UN Publication, Sales No. E.97.V.10).

In accordance with article 2 of the Agreement, the provisions of the Agreement and Part XI shall be interpreted and applied together as a single instrument. In the event of any inconsistency between the Agreement and Part XI, the provisions of the Agreement shall prevail.

The text of the consolidation follows the order of Part XI of the Convention. Relevant provisions of the Agreement are inserted in the appropriate places in the text. Certain provisions of the Agreement affect more than one provision of Part XI and are therefore repeated in several places.

In a number of instances, the Agreement states that a particular provision of Part XI "does not apply". In such cases, so as not to interrupt the flow of the text, the provisions of Part XI which, pursuant to the Agreement, do not apply are indicated by an endnote reference and omitted from the main body of the text. For reference purposes, those provisions are, however, set out in full at the end of this note.

In a number of cases, provisions contained in Part XI include cross-references to other provisions of Part XI which, pursuant to the Agreement, no longer apply. Where this occurs, reference is made by means of a footnote to the equivalent, or parallel, provision of the Agreement. The applicability, or otherwise, of the equivalent, or parallel, provision would be subject to article 2 of the Agreement.

The annex to the Agreement does not follow the same order as Part XI of the Convention. Accordingly, in consolidating the provisions of the annex to the Agreement with the provisions of Part XI, it is not possible to set out the provisions of the annex to the Agreement sequentially. The entire text of the Agreement, in its original form as an annex to General Assembly resolution 48/263, is also reproduced in this Compendium.

^a   The relevant parts of article 151 which, pursuant to Section 6, paragraph 7 of the annex to the Agreement, shall not apply, formerly read as follows:

1.   (a) Without prejudice to the objectives set forth in article 150 and for the purpose of implementing subparagraph (h) of that article, the Authority, acting through existing forums or such new arrangements or agreements as may be appropriate, in which all interested parties, including both producers and consumers, participate, shall take measures necessary to promote the growth, efficiency and stability of markets for those commodities produced from the minerals derived from the Area, at prices remunerative to producers and fair to consumers. All States Parties shall co-operate to this end.

(b)   The Authority shall have the right to participate in any commodity conference dealing with those commodities and in which all interested parties including both producers and consumers participate. The Authority shall have the right to become a party to any arrangement or agreement resulting from such conferences. Participation of the Authority in any organs established under those arrangements or agreements shall be in respect of production in the Area and in accordance with the relevant rules of those organs.

(c)   The Authority shall carry out its obligations under the arrangements or agreements referred to in this paragraph in a manner which assures a uniform and non-discriminatory implementation in respect of all production in the Area of the minerals concerned. In doing so, the Authority shall act in a manner consistent with the terms of existing contracts and approved plans of work of the Enterprise.

2.   (a) During the interim period specified in paragraph 3, commercial production shall not be undertaken pursuant to an approved plan of work until the operator has applied for and has been issued a production authorization by the Authority. Such production authorizations may not be applied for or issued more than five years prior to the planned commencement of commercial production under the plan of work unless, having regard to the nature and timing of project development, the rules, regulations and procedures of the Authority prescribe another period.

(b)   In the application for the production authorization, the operator shall specify the annual quantity of nickel expected to be recovered under the approved plan of work. The application shall include a schedule of expenditures to be made by the operator after he has received the authorization which are reasonably calculated to allow him to begin commercial production on the date planned.

(c)   For the purposes of subparagraphs (a) and (b), the Authority shall establish appropriate performance requirements in accordance with Annex III, article 17.

(d)   The Authority shall issue a production authorization for the level of production applied for unless the sum of that level and the levels already authorized exceeds the nickel production ceiling, as calculated pursuant to paragraph 4 in the year of issuance of the authorization, during any year of planned production falling within the interim period.

(e)   When issued, the production authorization and approved application shall become a part of the approved plan of work.

(f)   If the operator's application for a production authorization is denied pursuant to subparagraph (d), the operator may apply again to the Authority at any time.

3.   The interim period shall begin five years prior to 1 January of the year in which the earliest commercial production is planned to commence under an approved plan of work. If the earliest commercial production is delayed beyond the year originally planned, the beginning of the interim period and the production ceiling originally calculated shall be adjusted accordingly. The interim period shall last 25 years or until the end of the Review Conference referred to in article 155 or until the day when such new arrangements or agreements as are referred to in paragraph 1 enter into force, whichever is earliest. The Authority shall resume the power provided in this article for the remainder of the interim period if the said arrangements or agreements should lapse or become ineffective for any reason whatsoever.

4.   (a) The production ceiling for any year of the interim period shall be the sum of:

    (i)   the difference between the trend line values for nickel consumption, as calculated pursuant to subparagraph (b), for the year immediately prior to the year of the earliest commercial production and the year immediately prior to the commencement of the interim period; and

    (ii)   sixty per cent of the difference between the trend line values for nickel consumption, as calculated pursuant to subparagraph (b), for the year for which the production authorization is being applied for and the year immediately prior to the year of the earliest commercial production.

(b)   For the purposes of subparagraph (a):

    (i)   trend line values used for computing the nickel production ceiling shall be those annual nickel consumption values on a trend line computed during the year in which a production authorization is issued. The trend line shall be derived from a linear regression of the logarithms of actual nickel consumption for the most recent 15-year period for which such data are available, time being the independent variable. This trend line shall be referred to as the original trend line;

    (ii)   if the annual rate of increase of the original trend line is less than 3 per cent, then the trend line used to determine the quantities referred to in subparagraph (a) shall instead be one passing through the original trend line at the value for the first year of the relevant 15-year period, and increasing at 3 per cent annually; provided however that the production ceiling established for any year of the interim period may not in any case exceed the difference between the original trend line value for that year the original trend line value for the year immediately prior to the commencement of the interim period.

5.   The Authority shall reserve to the Enterprise for its initial production a quantity of 38,000 metric tonnes of nickel from the available production ceiling calculated pursuant to paragraph 4.

6.   (a) An operator may in any year produce less than or up to 8 per cent more than the level of annual production of minerals from polymetallic

nodules specified in his production authorization, provided that the overall amount of production shall not exceed that specified in the authorization. Any excess over 8 per cent and up to 20 per cent in any year, or any excess in the first and subsequent years following two consecutive years in which excesses occur, shall be negotiated with the Authority, which may require the operator to obtain a supplementary production authorization to cover additional production.

(b) Applications for such supplementary production authorizations shall be considered by the Authority only after all pending applications by operators who have not yet received production authorizations have been acted upon and due account has been taken of other likely applicants. The Authority shall be guided by the principle of not exceeding the total production allowed under the production ceiling in any year of the interim period. It shall not authorize the production under any plan of work of a quantity in excess of 46,500 metric tonnes of nickel per year.

7. The levels of production of other metals such as copper, cobalt and manganese extracted from the polymetallic nodules that are recovered pursuant to a production authorization should not be higher than those which would have been produced had the operator produced the maximum level of nickel from those nodules pursuant to this article. The Authority shall establish rules, regulations and procedures pursuant to Annex III, article 17, to implement this paragraph.

...

9. The Authority shall have the power to limit the level of production of minerals from the Area other than minerals from polymetallic nodules, under such conditions and applying such methods as may be appropriate by adopting regulations in accordance with article 161, paragraph 8.

---

[b]   The relevant parts of Article 155 which, pursuant to Section 4 of the annex to the Agreement, shall not apply, formerly read as follows:

1. Fifteen years from 1 January of the year in which the earliest commercial production commences under an approved plan of work, the Assembly shall convene a conference for the review of those provisions of this Part and the relevant Annexes which govern the system of exploration and exploitation of the resources of the Area. The Review Conference shall consider in detail, in the light of the experience acquired during that period:

(a) whether the provisions of this Part which govern the system of exploration and exploitation of the resources of the Area have achieved their aims in all respects, including whether they have benefited mankind as a whole;

(b) whether during the 15-year period, reserved areas have been exploited in an effective and balanced manner in comparison with non-reserved areas;

(c) whether the development and use of the Area and its resources have been undertaken in such a manner as to foster healthy development of the world economy and balanced growth of international trade;

(d) whether monopolization of activities in the Area has been prevented;

   (e)   whether the policies set forth in articles 150 and 151 have been fulfilled; and

   (f)   whether the system has resulted in the equitable sharing of benefits derived from activities in the Area, taking into particular consideration the interests and needs of the developing States.

       ...

3.   The decision-making procedure applicable at the Review Conference shall be the same as that applicable at the Third United Nations Conference on the Law of the Sea. The Conference shall make every effort to reach agreement on any amendments by way of consensus and there should be no voting on such matters until all efforts at achieving consensus have been exhausted.

4.   If, five years after its commencement, the Review Conference has not reached agreement on the system of exploration and exploitation of the resources of the Area, it may decide during the ensuing 12 months, by a three-fourths majority of the States Parties, to adopt and submit to the States Parties for ratification or accession such amendments changing or modifying the system as it determines necessary and appropriate. Such amendments shall enter into force for all States Parties 12 months after the deposit of instruments of ratification or accession by three fourths of the States Parties.

---

   ^c   The relevant provisions of article 161 which, pursuant to Section 3, paragraph 8 of the annex to the Agreement, shall not apply, formerly read as follows:

1.   The Council shall consist of 36 members of the Authority elected by the Assembly in the following order:

   (a)   four members from among those States Parties which, during the last five years for which statistics are available, have either consumed more than 2 per cent of total world consumption or have had net imports of more than 2 per cent of total world imports of the commodities produced from the categories of minerals to be derived from the Area, and in any case one State from the Eastern European (Socialist) region, as well as the largest consumer;

   (b)   four members from among the eight States Parties which have the largest investments in preparation for and in the conduct of activities in the Area, either directly or through their nationals, including at least one State from the Eastern European (Socialist) region;

   (c)   Four members from among States Parties which on the basis of production in areas under their jurisdiction are major net exporters of the categories of minerals to be derived from the Area, including at least two developing States whose exports of such minerals have a substantial bearing upon their economies;

   (d)   six members from among developing States Parties, representing special interests. The special interests to be represented shall include those of States with large populations, States which are land-locked or geographically disadvantaged, States which are major importers of the categories of minerals to be derived from the Area, States which are potential producers of such minerals, and least developed States;

(e)   eighteen members elected according to the principle of ensuring an eq-
       uitable geographical distribution of seats in the Council as a whole
       provided that each geographical region shall have at least one member
       elected under this subparagraph. For this purpose, the geographical
       regions shall be Africa, Asia, Eastern European (Socialist), Latin America
       and Western European and Others....

8.   ...

(b)   Decisions on questions of substance arising under the following provi-
       sions shall be taken by a two-thirds majority of the members present and
       voting, provided that such majority includes a majority of the members of
       the Council: article 162, paragraph 2, subparagraphs (f); (g); (h); (i); (n);
       (p); (v); article 191.

(c)   Decisions on questions of substance arising under the following provi-
       sions shall be taken by a three-fourths majority of the members present
       and voting, provided that such majority includes a majority of the mem-
       bers of the Council: article 162, paragraph 1; article 162, paragraph 2,
       subparagraphs (a); (b); (c); (d); (e); (l); (q); (r); (s); (t); (u) in cases of
       non-compliance by a contractor or a sponsor; (w) provided that orders
       issued thereunder may be binding for not more than 30 days unless
       confirmed by a decision taken in accordance with subparagraph (d);
       article 162, paragraph 2, subparagraphs (x); (y); (z); article 163, para-
       graph 2; article 174, paragraph 3; Annex IV, article 11.

---

[d]   The relevant provisions of article 162 which, pursuant to Section 9, paragraphs 7 and 9 of the annex to the Agreement, shall not apply, formerly read as
follows:

2.   ...

(j)   approve plans of work in accordance with Annex III, article 6. The Council
       shall act upon each plan of work within 60 days of its submission by the
       Legal and Technical Commission at a session of the Council in accor-
       dance with the following procedures:

       (i)   if the Commission recommends the approval of a plan of work, it
             shall be deemed to have been approved by the Council if no mem-
             ber of the Council submits in writing to the President within 14 days
             a specific objection alleging non-compliance with the requirements
             of Annex III, article 6. If there is an objection, the conciliation proce-
             dure set forth in article 161, paragraph 8(e) shall apply. If at the end
             of the conciliation procedure, the objection is still maintained, the
             plan of work shall be deemed to have been approved by the Council
             unless the Council disapproves it by consensus among its mem-
             bers excluding any State or States making the application or
             sponsoring the applicant;

       (ii) if the Commission recommends the disapproval of a plan of work or
             does not make a recommendation, the Council may approve the
             plan of work by a three-fourths majority of the members present and
             voting, provided that such majority includes a majority of the mem-
             bers participating in the session;

       ...

(q)   make the selection from among applicants for production authorizations pursuant to Annex III, article 7, where such selection is required by that provision.

ᵉ   The relevant provisions of article 165 which, pursuant to Section 6 of the annex to the Agreement, shall not apply, formerly read as follows:

2.   ...
n)   calculate the production ceiling and issue production authorizations on behalf of the Authority pursuant to article 151, paragraphs 2 to 7, following any necessary selection among applicants for production authorizations by the Council in accordance with Annex III, article 7.

ᶠ   Article 5 of Annex III which, pursuant to Section 5, paragraph 2 of the annex to the Agreement, shall not apply, formerly read as follows:

1.   When submitting a plan of work, every applicant shall make available to the Authority a general description of the equipment and methods to be used in carrying out activities in the Area, and other relevant non-proprietary information about the characteristics of such technology and information as to where such technology is available.

2.   Every operator shall inform the Authority of revisions in the description and information made available pursuant to paragraph 1 whenever a substantial technological change or innovation is introduced.

3.   Every contract for carrying out activities in the Area shall contain the following undertakings by the contractor:

(a)   to make available to the Enterprise on fair and reasonable commercial terms and conditions, whenever the Authority so requests, the technology which he uses in carrying out activities in the Area under the contract, which the contractor is legally entitled to transfer. This shall be done by means of licences or other appropriate arrangements which the contractor shall negotiate with the Enterprise and which shall be set forth in a specific agreement supplementary to the contract. This undertaking may be invoked only if the Enterprise finds that it is unable to obtain the same or equally efficient and useful technology on the open market on fair and reasonable commercial terms and conditions;

(b)   to obtain a written assurance from the owner of any technology used in carrying out activities in the Area under the contract, which is not generally available on the open market and which is not covered by subparagraph (a), that the owner will, whenever the Authority so requests, make that technology available to the Enterprise under licence or other appropriate arrangements and on fair and reasonable commercial terms and conditions, to the same extent as made available to the contractor. If this assurance is not obtained, the technology in question shall not be used by the contractor in carrying out activities in the Area;

(c) to acquire from the owner by means of an enforceable contract, upon the request of the Enterprise and if it is possible to do so without substantial cost to the contractor, the legal right to transfer to the Enterprise any technology used by the contractor, in carrying out activities in the Area under the contract, which the contractor is otherwise not legally entitled to transfer and which is not generally available on the open market. In cases where there is a substantial corporate relationship between the contractor and the owner of the technology, the closeness of this relationship and the degree of control or influence shall be relevant to the determination whether all feasible measures have been taken to acquire such a right. In cases where the contractor exercises effective control over the owner, failure to acquire from the owner the legal right shall be considered relevant to the contractor's qualification for any subsequent application for approval of a plan of work;

(d) to facilitate, upon the request of the Enterprise, the acquisition by the Enterprise of any technology covered by subparagraph (b), under licence or other appropriate arrangements and on fair and reasonable commercial terms and conditions, if the Enterprise decides to negotiate directly with the owner of the technology;

(e) to take the same measures as are prescribed in subparagraphs (a), (b), (c) and (d) for the benefit of a developing State or group of developing States which has applied for a contract under article 9 of this Annex, provided that these measures shall be limited to the exploitation of the part of the area proposed by the contractor which has been reserved pursuant to article 8 of this Annex and provided that activities under the contract sought by the developing State or group of developing States would not involve transfer of technology to a third State or the nationals of a third State. The obligation under this provision shall only apply with respect to any given contractor where technology has not been requested by the Enterprise or transferred by that contractor to the Enterprise.

4.   Disputes concerning undertakings required by paragraph 3, like other provisions of the contracts, shall be subject to compulsory settlement in accordance with Part XI and, in cases of violation of these undertakings, suspension or termination of the contract or monetary penalties may be ordered in accordance with article 18 of this Annex. Disputes as to whether offers made by the contractor are within the range of fair and reasonable commercial terms and conditions may be submitted by either party to binding commercial arbitration in accordance with the UNCITRAL Arbitration Rules or such other arbitration rules as may be prescribed in the rules, regulations and procedures of the Authority. If the finding is that the offer made by the contractor is not within the range of fair and reasonable commercial terms and conditions, the contractor shall be given 45 days to revise his offer to bring it within that range before the Authority takes any action in accordance with article 18 of this Annex.

5.   If the Enterprise is unable to obtain on fair and reasonable commercial terms and conditions appropriate technology to enable it to commence in a timely manner the recovery and processing of minerals from the Area, either the Council or the Assembly may convene a group of States Parties composed of those which are engaged in activities in the Area, those which have sponsored entities which are engaged in activities in the Area and other States Parties having access to such

technology. This group shall consult together and shall take effective measures to ensure that such technology is made available to the Enterprise on fair and reasonable commercial terms and conditions. Each such State Party shall take all feasible measures to this end within its own legal system.

6.   In the case of joint ventures with the Enterprise, transfer of technology will be in accordance with the terms of the joint venture agreement.

7.   The undertakings required by paragraph 3 shall be included in each contract for the carrying out of activities in the Area until 10 years after the commencement of commercial production by the Enterprise, and may be invoked during that period.

8.   For the purposes of this article, "technology" means the specialized equipment and technical know-how, including manuals, designs, operating instructions, training and technical advice and assistance, necessary to assemble, maintain and operate a viable system and the legal right to use these items for that purpose on a non-exclusive basis.

------

g   The relevant provisions of articles 6 and 7 of Annex III, which, pursuant to Section 6, paragraph 7 of the annex to the Agreement shall not apply, formerly read as follows:

Article 6
Approval of plans of work

...

5.   Notwithstanding paragraph 3(a), after the end of the interim period specified in article 151, paragraph 3, the Authority may adopt by means of rules, regulations and procedures other procedures and criteria consistent with this Convention for deciding which applicants shall have plans of work approved in cases of selection among applicants for a proposed area. These procedures and criteria shall ensure approval of plans of work on an equitable and non-discriminatory basis.

Article 7
Selection among applicants for production authorizations

1.   Six months after the entry into force of this Convention, and thereafter each fourth month, the Authority shall take up for consideration applications for production authorizations submitted during the immediately preceding period. The Authority shall issue the authorizations applied for if all such applications can be approved without exceeding the production limitation or contravening the obligations of the Authority under a commodity agreement or arrangement to which it has become a party, as provided in article 151.

2.   When a selection must be made among applicants for production authorizations because of the production limitation set forth in article 151, paragraphs 2 to 7, or because of the obligations of the Authority under a commodity agreement or arrangement to which it has become a party, as provided for in article 151, paragraph 1, the Authority shall make the selection on the basis of objective and non-discriminatory standards set forth in its rules, regulations and procedures.

3.   In the application of paragraph 2, the Authority shall give priority to those applicants which:
   (a)   give better assurance of performance, taking into account their financial and technical qualifications and their performance, if any, under previously approved plans of work;
   (b)   provide earlier prospective financial benefits to the Authority, taking into account when commercial production is scheduled to begin;
   (c)   have already invested the most resources and effort in prospecting or exploration.
4.   Applicants which are not selected in any period shall have priority in subsequent periods until they receive a production authorization.
5.   Selection shall be made taking into account the need to enhance opportunities for all States Parties, irrespective of their social and economic systems or geographical locations so as to avoid discrimination against any State or system, to participate in activities in the Area and to prevent monopolization of those activities.
6.   Whenever fewer reserved areas than non-reserved areas are under exploitation, applications for production authorizations with respect to reserved areas shall have priority.
7.   The decisions referred to in this article shall be taken as soon as possible after the close of each period.

---

[h]   The relevant provisions of Article 13 of Annex III which, pursuant to Section 8, paragraph 2 of the annex to the Agreement, shall not apply, formerly read as follows:
   ...
3.   A contractor shall pay an annual fixed fee of $US 1 million from the date of entry into force of the contract. If the approved date of commencement of commercial production is postponed because of a delay in issuing the production authorization, in accordance with article 151, the annual fixed fee shall be waived for the period of postponement. From the date of commencement of commercial production, the contractor shall pay either the production charge or the annual fixed fee, whichever is greater.
4.   Within a year of the date of commencement of commercial production, in conformity with paragraph 3, a contractor shall choose to make his financial contribution to the Authority by either:
   (a)   paying a production charge only; or
   (b)   paying a combination of a production charge and a share of net proceeds.
5.   (a) If a contractor chooses to make his financial contribution to the Authority by paying a production charge only, it shall be fixed at a percentage of the market value of the processed metals produced from the polymetallic nodules recovered from the area covered by the contract. This percentage shall be fixed as follows:
      (i)   years 1-10 of commercial production   5 per cent
      (ii)   years 11 to the end of commercial production   12 per cent
   (b)   The said market value shall be the product of the quantity of the processed metals produced from the polymetallic nodules extracted from the area

covered by the contract and the average price for those metals during the relevant accounting year, as defined in paragraphs 7 and 8.

6.   If a contractor chooses to make his financial contribution to the Authority by paying a combination of a production charge and a share of net proceeds, such payments shall be determined as follows:

(a)   The production charge shall be fixed at a percentage of the market value, determined in accordance with subparagraph (b), of the processed metals produced from the polymetallic nodules recovered from the area covered by the contract. This percentage shall be fixed as follows:

(i)   first period of commercial production   2 per cent
(ii)   second period of commercial production   4 per cent

If, in the second period of commercial production, as defined in subparagraph (d), the return on investment in any accounting year as defined in subparagraph (m) falls below 15 per cent as a result of the payment of the production charge at 4 per cent, the production charge shall be 2 per cent instead of 4 per cent in that accounting year.

(b)   The said market value shall be the product of the quantity of the processed metals produced from the polymetallic nodules recovered from the area covered by the contract and the average price for those metals during the relevant accounting year as defined in paragraphs 7 and 8.

(c)   (i)   The Authority's share of net proceeds shall be taken out of that portion of the contractor's net proceeds which is attributable to the mining of the resources of the area covered by the contract, referred to hereinafter as attributable net proceeds.

(ii) The Authority's share of attributable net proceeds shall be determined in accordance with following incremental schedule:

Portion of attributable Net proceeds Share of the Authority	Share of the Authority	
	First period of commercial production	Second period of commercial production
That portion representing a return on investment which is greater than 0 per cent, but less than 10 per cent	35 per cent	40 per cent
That portion representing a return on investment which is 10 per cent or greater, but less than 20 per cent	42.5 per cent	50 per cent
That portion representing a return on investment which is 20 per cent or greater	50 per cent	70 per cent

(d) (i) The first period of commercial production referred to in subparagraphs (a) and (c) shall commence in the first accounting year of commercial production and terminate in the accounting year in which the contractor's development costs with interest on the unrecovered portion thereof are fully recovered by his cash surplus, as follows:

In the first accounting year during which development costs are incurred, unrecovered development costs shall equal the development cost less cash surplus in that year. In each subsequent accounting year, unrecovered development costs shall equal the unrecovered development costs at the end of the preceding accounting year, plus interest thereon at the rate of 10 per cent per annum, plus development costs incurred in the current accounting year and less contractor's cash surplus in the current accounting year. The accounting year in which unrecovered development costs become zero for the first time shall be the accounting year in which the contractor's development costs with interest on the unrecovered portion thereof are fully recovered by his cash surplus. The contractor's cash surplus in any accounting year shall be his gross proceeds less his operating costs and less his payments to the Authority under subparagraph (c).

(ii) The second period of commercial production shall commence in the accounting year following the termination of the first period of commercial production and shall continue until the end of the contract.

(e) "Attributable net proceeds" means the product of the contractor's net proceeds and the ratio of development costs in the mining sector to the contractor's development costs. If the contractor engages in mining, transporting polymetallic nodules and production primarily of three processed metals, namely, cobalt, copper and nickel, the amount of attributable net proceeds shall not be less than 25 per cent of the contractor's net proceeds. Subject to subparagraph (n), in all other cases, including those where the contractor engages in mining, transporting polymetallic nodules, and production primarily of four processed metals, namely, cobalt, copper, manganese and nickel, the Authority may, in its rules, regulations and procedures, prescribe appropriate floors which shall bear the same relationship to each case as the 25 per cent floor does to the three-metal case.

(f) "Contractor's net proceeds" means the contractor's gross proceeds less his operating costs and less the recovery of his development costs as set out in subparagraph (j).

(g) (i) If the contractor engages in mining, transporting polymetallic nodules and production of processed metals, "contractor's gross proceeds" means the gross revenues from the sale of the processed metals and any other monies deemed reasonably attributable to operations under the contract in accordance with the financial rules, regulations and procedures of the Authority.

(ii) In all cases other than those specified in subparagraphs (g)(i) and (n)(iii), "contractor's gross proceeds" means the gross revenues from the sale of the semi-processed metals from the polymetallic nodules recovered from the area covered by the contract, and any other monies deemed reasonably attributable to operations under the contract in accordance with the financial rules, regulations and procedures of the Authority.

(h) "Contractor's development costs" means:

   (i) all expenditures incurred prior to the commencement of commercial production which are directly related to the development of the productive capacity of the area covered by the contract and the activities related thereto for operations under the contract in all cases other than that specified in subparagraph (n), in conformity with generally recognized accounting principles, including, *inter alia*, costs of machinery, equipment, ships, processing plant, construction, buildings, land, roads, prospecting and exploration of the area covered by the contract, research and development, interest, required leases, licences and fees; and

   (ii) expenditures similar to those set forth in (i) above incurred subsequent to the commencement of commercial production and necessary to carry out the plan of work, except those chargeable to operating costs.

(i) The proceeds from the disposal of capital assets and the market value of those capital assets which are no longer required for operations under the contract and which are not sold shall be deducted from the contractor's development costs during the relevant accounting year. When these deductions exceed the contractor's development costs the excess shall be added to the contractor's gross proceeds.

(j) The contractor's development costs incurred prior to the commencement of commercial production referred to subparagraphs (h)(i) and (n)(iv) shall be recovered in 10 equal annual instalments from the date of commencement of commercial production. The contractor's development costs incurred subsequent to the commencement of commercial production referred to in subparagraphs (h)(ii) and (n)(iv) shall be recovered in 10 or fewer equal annual installments so as to ensure their complete recovery by the end of the contract.

(k) "Contractor's operating costs" means all expenditures incurred after the commencement of commercial production in the operation of the productive capacity of the area covered by the contract and the activities related thereto for operations under the contract, in conformity with generally recognized accounting principles, including, *inter alia*, the annual fixed fee or the production charge, whichever is greater, expenditures for wages, salaries, employee benefits, materials, services, transporting, processing and marketing costs, interest, utilities, preservation of the marine environment, overhead and administrative costs specifically related to operations under the contract, and any net operating losses carried forward or backward as specified herein. Net operating losses may be carried forward for two consecutive years except in the last two years of the contract in which case they may be carried backward to the two preceding years.

(l) If the contractor engages in mining, transporting of polymetallic nodules, and production of processed and semi-processed metals, "development costs of the mining sector" means the portion of the contractor's development costs which is directly related to the mining of the resources of the area covered by the contract, in conformity with generally recognized accounting principles, and the financial rules, regulations and procedures of the Authority, including, *inter alia,* application fee, annual fixed fee and, where applicable, costs of prospecting and exploration of the area covered by the contract, and a portion of research and development costs.

(m) "Return on investment" in any accounting year means ratio of attributable net proceeds in that year to the development costs of the mining sector. For the purpose of computing this ratio the development costs of the mining sector shall include expenditures on new or replacement equipment in the mining sector less the original cost of the equipment replaced.

(n) If the contractor engages in mining only:

  (i) "attributable net proceeds" means the whole of the contractor's net proceeds;

  (ii) "contractor's net proceeds" shall be as defined in subparagraph (f);

  (iii) "contractor's gross proceeds" means the gross revenues from the sale of the polymetallic nodules, and any other monies deemed reasonably attributable to operations under the contract in accordance with the financial rules, regulations and procedures of the Authority;

  (iv) "contractor's development costs" means all expenditures incurred prior to the commencement of commercial production as set forth in subparagraph (h)(i), and all expenditures incurred subsequent to the commencement of commercial production as set forth in subparagraph (h)(ii), which are directly related to the mining of the resources of the area covered by the contract, in conformity with generally recognized accounting principles;

  (v) "contractor's operating costs" means the contractor's operating costs as in subparagraph (k) which are directly related to the mining of the resources of the area covered by the contract in conformity with generally recognized accounting principles;

  (vi) "return on investment" in any accounting year means the ratio of the contractor's net proceeds in that year to the contractor's development costs. For the purpose of computing this ratio, the contractor's development costs shall include expenditures on new or replacement equipment less the original cost of the equipment replaced.

(o) The costs referred to in subparagraphs (h), (k), (l) and (n) in respect of interest paid by the contractor shall be allowed to the extent that, in all the circumstances, the Authority approves, pursuant to article 4, paragraph 1, of this Annex, the debt-equity ratio and the rates of interest as reasonable, having regard to existing commercial practice.

(p) The costs referred to in this paragraph shall not be interpreted as including payments of corporate income taxes or similar charges levied by States in respect of the operations of the contractor.

7. (a) "Processed metals", referred to in paragraphs 5 and 6, means the metals in the most basic form in which they are customarily traded on international terminal markets. For this purpose, the Authority shall specify, in its

financial rules, regulations and procedures, the relevant international terminal market. For the metals which are not traded on such markets, "processed metals" means the metals in the most basic form in which they are customarily traded in representative arm's length transactions.

(b) If the Authority cannot otherwise determine the quantity of the processed metals produced from the polymetallic nodules recovered from the area covered by the contract referred to in paragraphs 5(b) and 6 (b), the quantity shall be determined on the basis of the metal content of the nodules, processing recovery efficiency and other relevant factors, in accordance with the rules, regulations and procedures of the Authority and in conformity with generally recognized accounting principles.

8. If an international terminal market provides a representative pricing mechanism for processed metals, polymetallic nodules and semi-processed metals from the nodules, the average price on that market shall be used. In all other cases, the Authority shall, after consulting the contractor, determine a fair price for the said products in accordance with paragraph 9.

9. (a) All costs, expenditures, proceeds and revenues and all determinations of price and value referred to in this article shall be the result of free market or arm's length transactions. In the absence thereof, they shall be determined by the Authority, after consulting the contractor, as though they were the result of free market or arm's length transactions, taking into account relevant transactions in other markets.

(b) In order to ensure compliance with and enforcement of the provisions of this paragraph, the Authority shall be guided by the principles adopted for, and the interpretation given to, arm's length transactions by the Commission on Transnational Corporations of the United Nations, the Group of Experts on Tax Treaties between Developing and Developed Countries and other international organizations, and shall, in its rules, regulations and procedures, specify uniform and internationally acceptable accounting rules and procedures, and the means of selection by the contractor of certified independent accountants acceptable to the Authority for the purpose of carrying out auditing in compliance with those rules, regulations and procedures.

10. The contractor shall make available to the accountants, in accordance with the financial rules, regulations and procedures of the Authority, such financial data as are required to determine compliance with this article.

...

●●●●●●●●●●

GENERAL ASSEMBLY RESOLUTION ON THE AGREEMENT RELATING TO THE IMPLEMENTATION OF PART XI OF THE UNITED NATIONS CONVENTION ON THE LAW OF THE SEA OF 10 DECEMBER 1982

(RESOLUTION 48/263)

The General Assembly,

Prompted by the desire to achieve universal participation in the United Nations Convention on the Law of the Sea of 10 December 1982 (hereinafter referred to as "the Convention") and to promote appropriate representation in the institutions established by it,

Reaffirming that the seabed and ocean floor and subsoil thereof, beyond the limits of national jurisdiction (hereinafter referred to as the "Area"), as well as the resources of the Area, are the common heritage of mankind,

Recalling that the Convention in its Part XI and related provisions (hereinafter referred to as "Part XI") established a regime for the Area and its resources,

Taking note of the consolidated provisional final report of the Preparatory Commission for the International Seabed Authority and for the International Tribunal for the Law of the Sea,

Recalling its resolution 48/28 of 9 December 1993 on the law of the sea,

Recognizing that political and economic changes, including in particular a growing reliance on market principles, have necessitated the re-evaluation of some aspects of the regime for the Area and its resources,

Noting the initiative of the Secretary-General which began in 1990 to promote dialogue aimed at achieving universal participation in the Convention,

Welcoming the report of the Secretary-General on the outcome of his informal consultations, including the draft of an agreement relating to the implementation of Part XI,

Considering that the objective of universal participation in the Convention may best be achieved by the adoption of an agreement relating to the implementation of Part XI,

Recognizing the need to provide for the provisional application of such an agreement from the date of entry into force of the Convention on 16 November 1994,

1. *Expresses* its appreciation to the Secretary-General for his report on the informal consultations;

2. *Reaffirms* the unified character of the United Nations Convention on the Law of the Sea of 10 December 1982;

3.   *Adopts* the Agreement relating to the Implementation of Part XI of the United Nations Convention on the Law of the Sea of 10 December 1982 (hereinafter referred to as "the Agreement"), the text of which is annexed to the present resolution;

4.   *Affirms* that the Agreement shall be interpreted and applied together with Part XI as a single instrument;

5.   *Considers* that future ratifications or formal confirmations of or accessions to the Convention shall represent also consent to be bound by the Agreement and that no State or entity may establish its consent to be bound by the Agreement unless it has previously established or establishes at the same time its consent to be bound by the Convention;

6.   *Calls upon* States which consent to the adoption of the Agreement to refrain from any act which would defeat its object and purpose;

7.   *Expresses* its satisfaction at the entry into force of the Convention on 16 November 1994;

8.   *Decides* to fund the administrative expenses of the International Seabed Authority in accordance with section 1, paragraph 14, of the annex to the Agreement;

9.   *Requests* the Secretary-General to transmit immediately certified copies of the Agreement to the States and entities referred to in article 3 thereof, with a view to facilitating universal participation in the Convention and the Agreement, and to draw attention to articles 4 and 5 of the Agreement;

10.   *Also requests* the Secretary-General to open the Agreement for signature in accordance with article 3 thereof immediately after its adoption;

11.   *Urges* all States and entities referred to in article 3 of the Agreement to consent to its provisional application as from 16 November 1994 and to establish their consent to be bound by the Agreement at the earliest possible date;

12.   *Also urges* all such States and entities that have not already done so to take all appropriate steps to ratify, formally confirm or accede to the Convention at the earliest possible date in order to ensure universal participation in the Convention;

13.   *Calls upon* the Preparatory Commission for the International Seabed Authority and for the International Tribunal for the Law of the Sea to take into account the terms of the Agreement when drawing up its final report.

101st plenary meeting*
28 July 1994

———————————

* **Informal Understanding to be read by the President of the General Assembly at the time of the adoption of the resolution**
Once there is a widespread participation in the International Seabed Authority and the number of members of each regional group participating in the Authority is substantially similar to its membership in the United Nations, it is understood that each regional group would be represented in the Council of the Authority as a whole by at least three members.
[A/48/950, Annex II.]

ANNEX

AGREEMENT RELATING TO THE IMPLEMENTATION OF PART XI OF THE UNITED NATIONS CONVENTION ON THE LAW OF THE SEA OF 10 DECEMBER 1982

The States Parties to this Agreement,

Recognizing the important contribution of the United Nations Convention on the Law of the Sea of 10 December 1982 (hereinafter referred to as "the Convention") to the maintenance of peace, justice and progress for all peoples of the world,

Reaffirming that the seabed and ocean floor and subsoil thereof, beyond the limits of national jurisdiction (hereinafter referred to as "the Area"), as well as the resources of the Area, are the common heritage of mankind,

Mindful of the importance of the Convention for the protection and preservation of the marine environment and of the growing concern for the global environment,

Having considered the report of the Secretary-General of the United Nations on the results of the informal consultations among States held from 1990 to 1994 on outstanding issues relating to Part XI and related provisions of the Convention (hereinafter referred to as "Part XI"),

Noting the political and economic changes, including market-oriented approaches, affecting the implementation of Part XI,

Wishing to facilitate universal participation in the Convention,

Considering that an agreement relating to the implementation of Part XI would best meet that objective,

Have agreed as follows:

Article 1
Implementation of Part XI

1.   The States Parties to this Agreement undertake to implement Part XI in accordance with this Agreement.

2.   The Annex forms an integral part of this Agreement.

Article 2
Relationship between this Agreement and Part XI

1.   The provisions of this Agreement and Part XI shall be interpreted and applied together as a single instrument. In the event of any inconsistency between this Agreement and Part XI, the provisions of this Agreement shall prevail.

2.   Articles 309 to 319 of the Convention shall apply to this Agreement as they apply to the Convention.

Article 3
Signature

This Agreement shall remain open for signature at United Nations Head-quarters by the States and entities referred to in article 305, paragraph 1 (a), (c) , (d), (e) and (f), of the Convention for 12 months from the date of its adoption.

Article 4
Consent to be bound

1.   After the adoption of this Agreement, any instrument of ratification or formal confirmation of or accession to the Convention shall also represent consent to be bound by this Agreement.

2.   No State or entity may establish its consent to be bound by this Agreement unless it has previously established or establishes at the same time its consent to be bound by the Convention.

3.   A State or entity referred to in article 3 may express its consent to be bound by this Agreement by:
   (a) Signature not subject to ratification, formal confirmation or the procedure set out in article 5;
   (b) Signature subject to ratification or formal confirmation, followed by ratification or formal confirmation;
   (c) Signature subject to the procedure set out in article 5; or
   (d) Accession.

4.   Formal confirmation by the entities referred to in article 305, paragraph 1 (f), of the Convention shall be in accordance with Annex IX of the Convention.

5.   The instruments of ratification, formal confirmation or accession shall be deposited with the Secretary-General of the United Nations.

Article 5
Simplified procedure

1.   A State or entity which has deposited before the date of the adoption of this Agreement an instrument of ratification or formal confirmation of or accession to the Convention and which has signed this Agreement in accordance with article 4, paragraph 3 (c), shall be considered to have established its consent to be bound by this Agreement 12 months after the date of its adoption, unless that State or entity notifies the depositary in writing before that date that it is not availing itself of the simplified procedure set out in this article.

2.   In the event of such notification, consent to be bound by this Agreement shall be established in accordance with article 4, paragraph 3 (b).

Article 6
Entry into force

1.   This Agreement shall enter into force 30 days after the date on which 40 States have established their consent to be bound in accordance with articles 4

and 5, provided that such States include at least seven of the States referred to in paragraph 1 (a) of resolution II of the Third United Nations Conference on the Law of the Sea (hereinafter referred to as "resolution II") and that at least five of those States are developed States. If these conditions for entry into force are fulfilled before 16 November 1994, this Agreement shall enter into force on 16 November 1994.

2.   For each State or entity establishing its consent to be bound by this Agreement after the requirements set out in paragraph 1 have been fulfilled, this Agreement shall enter into force on the thirtieth day following the date of establishment of its consent to be bound.

Article 7
Provisional application

1.   If on 16 November 1994 this Agreement has not entered into force, it shall be applied provisionally pending its entry into force by:

(a)   States which have consented to its adoption in the General Assembly of the United Nations, except any such State which before 16 November 1994 notifies the depositary in writing either that it will not so apply this Agreement or that it will consent to such application only upon subsequent signature or notification in writing;

(b)   States and entities which sign this Agreement, except any such State or entity which notifies the depositary in writing at the time of signature that it will not so apply this Agreement;

(c)   States and entities which consent to its provisional application by so notifying the depositary in writing;

(d)   States which accede to this Agreement.

2.   All such States and entities shall apply this Agreement provisionally in accordance with their national or internal laws and regulations, with effect form 16 November 1994 or the date of signature, notification of consent or accession, if later.

3.   Provisional application shall terminate upon the date of entry into force of this Agreement. In any event, provisional application shall terminate on 16 November 1998 if at that date the requirement in article 6, paragraph 1, of consent to be bound by this Agreement by at least seven of the States (of which at least five must be developed States) referred to in paragraph 1 (a) of resolution II has not been fulfilled.

Article 8
States Parties

1.   For the purposes of this Agreement, "States Parties" means States which have consented to be bound by this Agreement and for which this Agreement is in force.

2.   This Agreement applies *mutatis mutandis* to the entities referred to in article 305, paragraph 1 (c), (d), (e) and (f), of the Convention which become

Parties to this Agreement in accordance with the conditions relevant to each, and to that extent "States Parties" refers to those entities.

Article 9
Depositary

The Secretary-General of the United Nations shall be the depositary of this Agreement.

Article 10
Authentic texts

The original of this Agreement, of which the Arabic, Chinese, English, French, Russian and Spanish texts are equally authentic, shall be deposited with the Secretary-General of the United Nations.

IN WITNESS WHEREOF, the undersigned Plenipotentiaries, being duly authorized thereto, have signed this Agreement.

DONE AT NEW YORK, this 28th day of July, one thousand nine hundred and ninety-four.

ANNEX

SECTION 1. COSTS TO STATES PARTIES AND INSTITUTIONAL ARRANGEMENTS

1.   The International Seabed Authority (hereinafter referred to as "the Authority") is the organization through which States Parties to the Convention shall, in accordance with the regime for the Area established in Part XI and this Agreement, organize and control activities in the Area, particularly with a view to administering the resources of the Area. The powers and functions of the Authority shall be those expressly conferred upon it by the Convention. The Authority shall have such incidental powers, consistent with the Convention, as are implicit in, and necessary for, the exercise of those powers and functions with respect to activities in the Area.

2.   In order to minimize costs to States Parties, all organs and subsidiary bodies to be established under the Convention and this Agreement shall be cost-effective. This principle shall also apply to the frequency, duration and scheduling of meetings.

3.   The setting up and the functioning of the organs and subsidiary bodies of the Authority shall be based on an evolutionary approach, taking into account the functional needs of the organs and subsidiary bodies concerned in order that they may discharge effectively their respective responsibilities at various stages of the development of activities in the Area.

4.   The early functions of the Authority upon entry into force of the Convention shall be carried out by the Assembly, the Council, the Secretariat, the Legal and Technical Commission and the Finance Committee. The functions of

the Economic Planning Commission shall be performed by the Legal and Technical Commission until such time as the Council decides otherwise or until the approval of the first plan of work for exploitation.

5.   Between the entry into force of the Convention and the approval of the first plan of work for exploitation, the Authority shall concentrate on:

(a) Processing of applications for approval of plans of work for exploration in accordance with Part XI and this Agreement;

(b) Implementation of decisions of the Preparatory Commission for the International Seabed Authority and for the International Tribunal for the Law of the Sea (hereinafter referred to as "the Preparatory Commission") relating to the registered pioneer investors and their certifying States, including their rights and obligations, in accordance with article 308, paragraph 5, of the Convention and resolution II, paragraph 13;

(c) Monitoring of compliance with plans of work for exploration approved in the form of contracts;

(d) Monitoring and review of trends and developments relating to deep seabed mining activities, including regular analysis of world metal market conditions and metal prices, trends and prospects;

(e) Study of the potential impact of mineral production from the Area on the economies of developing land-based producers of those minerals which are likely to be most seriously affected, with a view to minimizing their difficulties and assisting them in their economic adjustment, taking into account the work done in this regard by the Preparatory Commission;

(f) Adoption of rules, regulations and procedures necessary for the conduct of activities in the Area as they progress. Notwithstanding the provisions of Annex III, article 17, paragraph 2 (b) and (c), of the Convention, such rules, regulations and procedures shall take into account the terms of this Agreement, the prolonged delay in commercial deep seabed mining and the likely pace of activities in the Area;

(g) Adoption of rules, regulations and procedures incorporating applicable standards for the protection and preservation of the marine environment;

(h) Promotion and encouragement of the conduct of marine scientific research with respect to activities in the Area and the collection and dissemination of the results of such research and analysis, when available, with particular emphasis on research related to the environmental impact of activities in the Area;

(i) Acquisition of scientific knowledge and monitoring of the development of marine technology relevant to activities in the Area, in particular technology relating to the protection and preservation of the marine environment;

(j) Assessment of available data relating to prospecting and exploration;

(k) Timely elaboration of rules, regulations and procedures for exploitation, including those relating to the protection and preservation of the marine environment.

6.   (a) An application for approval of a plan of work for exploration shall be considered by the Council following the receipt of a recommendation on the application from the Legal and Technical Commission. The processing of an application for approval of a plan of work for exploration shall be in accordance with the provisions of the Convention, including Annex III thereof, and this Agreement, and subject to the following:

    (i) A plan of work for exploration submitted on behalf of a State or entity, or any component of such entity, referred to in resolution II, paragraph 1 (a) (ii) or (iii), other than a registered pioneer investor, which had already undertaken substantial activities in the Area prior to the entry into force of the Convention, or its successor in interest, shall be considered to have met the financial and technical qualifications necessary for approval of a plan of work if the sponsoring State or States certify that the applicant has expended an amount equivalent to at least US$30 million in research and exploration activities and has expended no less than 10 per cent of that amount in the location, survey and evaluation of the area referred to in the plan of work. If the plan of work otherwise satisfies the requirements of the Convention and any rules, regulations and procedures adopted pursuant thereto, it shall be approved by the Council in the form of a contract. The provisions of section 3, paragraph 11, of this Annex shall be interpreted and applied accordingly;

    (ii) Notwithstanding the provisions of resolution II, paragraph 8 (a), a registered pioneer investor may request approval of a plan of work for exploration within 36 months of the entry into force of the Convention. The plan of work for exploration shall consist of documents, reports and other data submitted to the Preparatory Commission both before and after registration and shall be accompanied by a certificate of compliance, consisting of a factual report describing the status of fulfilment of obligations under the pioneer investor regime, issued by the Preparatory Commission in accordance with resolution II, paragraph 11 (a). Such a plan of work shall be considered to be approved. Such an approved plan of work shall be in the form of a contract concluded between the Authority and the registered pioneer investor in accordance with Part XI and this Agreement. The fee of US$ 250,000 paid pursuant to resolution II, paragraph 7 (a), shall be deemed to be the fee relating to the exploration phase pursuant to section 8, paragraph 3, of this Annex. Section 3, paragraph 11, of this Annex shall be interpreted and applied accordingly;

    (iii) In accordance with the principle of non-discrimination, a contract with a State or entity or any component of such entity referred to in subparagraph (a) (i) shall include arrangements which shall be similar to and no less favorable than those agreed with any registered pioneer investor referred to in subparagraph (a) (ii). If any of the States or entities or any components of such entities referred to in subparagraph (a) (i) are granted more favorable arrangements, the Council shall make similar and no less favorable arrangements with regard to the rights and obligations assumed by the registered pioneer investors referred to in subparagraph (a) (ii), provided that such arrangements do not affect or prejudice the interests of the Authority;

(iv) A State sponsoring an application for a plan of work pursuant to the provisions of subparagraph (a) (i) or (ii) may be a State Party or a State which is applying this Agreement provisionally in accordance with article 7, or a State which is a member of the Authority on a provisional basis in accordance with paragraph 12;

(v) Resolution II, paragraph 8 (c), shall be interpreted and applied in accordance with subparagraph (a) (iv).

(b) The approval of a plan of work for exploration shall be in accordance with article 153, paragraph 3, of the Convention.

7. An application for approval of a plan of work shall be accompanied by an assessment of the potential environmental impacts of the proposed activities and by a description of a programme for oceanographic and baseline environmental studies in accordance with the rules, regulations and procedures adopted by the Authority.

8. An application for approval of a plan of work for exploration, subject to paragraph 6 (a) (i) or (ii), shall be processed in accordance with the procedures set out in section 3, paragraph 11, of this annex.

9. A plan of work for exploration shall be approved for a period of 15 years. Upon the expiration of a plan of work for exploration, the contractor shall apply for a plan of work for exploitation unless the contractor has already done so or has obtained an extension for the plan of work for exploration. Contractors may apply for such extensions for periods of not more than five years each. Such extensions shall be approved if the contractor has made efforts in good faith to comply with the requirements of the plan of work but for reasons beyond the contractor's control has been unable to complete the necessary preparatory work for proceeding to the exploitation stage or if the prevailing economic circumstances do not justify proceeding to the exploitation stage.

10. Designation of a reserved area for the Authority in accordance with Annex III, article 8, of the Convention shall take place in connection with approval of an application for a plan of work for exploration or approval of an application for a plan of work for exploration and exploitation.

11. Notwithstanding the provisions of paragraph 9, an approved plan of work for exploration which is sponsored by at least one State provisionally applying this Agreement shall terminate if such a State ceases to apply this Agreement provisionally and has not become a member on a provisional basis in accordance with paragraph 12 or has not become a State Party.

12. Upon the entry into force of this Agreement, States and entities referred to in article 3 of this Agreement which have been applying it provisionally in accordance with article 7 and for which it is not in force may continue to be members of the Authority on a provisional basis pending its entry into force for such States and entities, in accordance with the following subparagraphs:

(a) If this Agreement enters into force before 16 November 1996, such States and entities shall be entitled to continue to participate as members of the Authority on a provisional basis upon notification to the depositary of the Agreement by such a State or entity of its intention to participate as a member on a provisional basis. Such membership shall terminate either on 16 November 1996 or upon the entry into force of this Agreement and the Convention for such member, whichever is earlier. The Council may, upon the request of the State or entity concerned, extend such membership beyond 16 November 1996 for a further period or periods not exceeding a total of two years provided that the Council is satisfied that the State or entity concerned has been making efforts in good faith to become a party to the Agreement and the Convention;

(b) If this Agreement enters into force after 15 November 1996, such States and entities may request the Council to grant continued membership in the Authority on a provisional basis for a period or periods not extending beyond 16 November 1998. The Council shall grant such membership with effect from the date of the request if it is satisfied that the State or entity has been making efforts in good faith to become a party to the Agreement and the Convention;

(c) States and entities which are members of the Authority on a provisional basis in accordance with subparagraph (a) or (b) shall apply the terms of Part XI and this Agreement in accordance with their national or internal laws, regulations and annual budgetary appropriations and shall have the same rights and obligations as other members, including:

(i) The obligation to contribute to the administrative budget of the Authority in accordance with the scale of assessed contributions;

(ii) The right to sponsor an application for approval of a plan of work for exploration. In the case of entities whose components are natural or juridical persons possessing the nationality of more than one State, a plan of work for exploration shall not be approved unless all the States whose natural or juridical persons comprise those entities are States Parties or members on a provisional basis;

(d) Notwithstanding the provisions of paragraph 9, an approved plan of work in the form of a contract for exploration which was sponsored pursuant to subparagraph (c) (ii) by a State which was a member on a provisional basis shall terminate if such membership ceases and the State or entity has not become a State Party;

(e) If such a member has failed to make its assessed contributions or otherwise failed to comply with its obligations in accordance with this paragraph, its membership on a provisional basis shall be terminated.

13. The reference in Annex III, article 10, of the Convention to performance which has not been satisfactory shall be interpreted to mean that the contractor has failed to comply with the requirements of an approved plan of work in spite of a written warning or warnings from the Authority to the contractor to comply therewith.

14. The Authority shall have its own budget. Until the end of the year following the year during which this Agreement enters into force, the administrative expenses of the Authority shall be met through the budget of the United Nations. Thereafter, the administrative expenses of the Authority shall be met by assessed contributions of its members, including any members on a provisional basis, in accordance with articles 171, subparagraph (a), and 173 of the Convention and this Agreement, until the Authority has sufficient funds from other sources to meet those expenses. The Authority shall not exercise the power referred to in article 174, paragraph 1, of the Convention to borrow funds to finance its administrative budget.

15. The Authority shall elaborate and adopt, in accordance with article 162, paragraph 2 (o) (ii), of the Convention, rules, regulations and procedures based on the principles contained in sections 2, 5, 6, 7 and 8 of this Annex, as well as any additional rules, regulations and procedures necessary to facilitate the approval of plans of work for exploration or exploitation, in accordance with the following subparagraphs:

    (a)   The Council may undertake such elaboration any time it deems that all or any of such rules, regulations or procedures are required for the conduct of activities in the Area, or when it determines that commercial exploitation is imminent, or at the request of a State whose national intends to apply for approval of a plan of work for exploitation;

    (b)   If a request is made by a State referred to in subparagraph (a) the Council shall, in accordance with article 162, paragraph 2 (o), of the Convention, complete the adoption of such rules, regulations and procedures within two years of the request;

    (c)   If the Council has not completed the elaboration of the rules, regulations and procedures relating to exploitation within the prescribed time and an application for approval of a plan of work for exploitation is pending, it shall none the less consider and provisionally approve such plan of work based on the provisions of the Convention and any rules, regulations and procedures that the Council may have adopted provisionally, or on the basis of the norms contained in the Convention and the terms and principles contained in this Annex as well as the principle of non-discrimination among contractors.

16. The draft rules, regulations and procedures and any recommendations relating to the provisions of Part XI, as contained in the reports and recommendations of the Preparatory Commission, shall be taken into account by the Authority in the adoption of rules, regulations and procedures in accordance with Part XI and this Agreement.

17. The relevant provisions of Part XI, section 4, of the Convention shall be interpreted and applied in accordance with this Agreement.

SECTION 2. THE ENTERPRISE

1. The Secretariat of the Authority shall perform the functions of the Enterprise until it begins to operate independently of the Secretariat. The Secretary-General of the Authority shall appoint from within the staff of the Authority an interim Director-General to oversee the performance of these functions by the Secretariat.

These functions shall be:

(a) Monitoring and review of trends and developments relating to deep seabed mining activities, including regular analysis of world metal market conditions and metal prices, trends and prospects;

(b) Assessment of the results of the conduct of marine scientific research with respect to activities in the Area, with particular emphasis on research related to the environmental impact of activities in the Area;

(c) Assessment of available data relating to prospecting and exploration, including the criteria for such activities;

(d) Assessment of technological developments relevant to activities in the Area, in particular technology relating to the protection and preservation of the marine environment;

(e) Evaluation of information and data relating to areas reserved for the Authority;

(f) Assessment of approaches to joint venture operations;

(g) Collection of information on the availability of trained manpower;

(h) Study of managerial policy options for the administration of the Enterprise at different stages of its operations.

2. The Enterprise shall conduct its initial deep seabed mining operations through joint ventures. Upon the approval of a plan of work for exploitation for an entity other than the Enterprise, or upon receipt by the Council of an application for a joint venture operation with the Enterprise, the Council shall take up the issue of the functioning of the Enterprise independently of the Secretariat of the Authority. If joint venture operations with the Enterprise accord with sound commercial principles, the Council shall issue a directive pursuant to article 170, paragraph 2, of the Convention providing for such independent functioning.

3. The obligation of States Parties to fund one mine site of the Enterprise as provided for in Annex IV, article 11, paragraph 3, of the Convention shall not apply and States Parties shall be under no obligation to finance any of the operations in any mine site of the Enterprise or under its joint venture arrangements.

4. The obligations applicable to contractors shall apply to the Enterprise. Notwithstanding the provisions of article 153, paragraph 3, and Annex III, article 3, paragraph 5, of the Convention, a plan of work for the Enterprise upon its approval shall be in the form of a contract concluded between the Authority and the Enterprise.

5.   A contractor which has contributed a particular area to the Authority as a reserved area has the right of first refusal to enter into a joint venture arrangement with the Enterprise for exploration and exploitation of that area. If the Enterprise does not submit an application for a plan of work for activities in respect of such a reserved area within 15 years of the commencement of its functions independent of the Secretariat of the Authority or within 15 years of the date on which that area is reserved for the Authority, whichever is the later, the contractor which contributed the area shall be entitled to apply for a plan of work for that area provided it offers in good faith to include the Enterprise as a joint venture partner.

6.   Article 170, paragraph 4, Annex IV and other provisions of the Convention relating to the Enterprise shall be interpreted and applied in accordance with this section.

SECTION 3. DECISION-MAKING

1.   The general policies of the Authority shall be established by the Assembly in collaboration with the Council.

2.   As a general rule, decision-making in the organs of the Authority should be by consensus.

3.   If all efforts to reach a decision by consensus have been exhausted, decisions by voting in the Assembly on questions of procedure shall be taken by a majority of members present and voting, and decisions on questions of substance shall be taken by a two-thirds majority of members present and voting, as provided for in article 159, paragraph 8, of the Convention.

4.   Decisions of the Assembly on any matter for which the Council also has competence or on any administrative, budgetary or financial matter shall be based on the recommendations of the Council. If the Assembly does not accept the recommendation of the Council on any matter, it shall return the matter to the Council for further consideration. The Council shall reconsider the matter in the light of the views expressed by the Assembly.

5.   If all efforts to reach a decision by consensus have been exhausted, decisions by voting in the Council on questions of procedure shall be taken by a majority of members present and voting, and decisions on questions of substance, except where the Convention provides for decisions by consensus in the Council, shall be taken by a two-thirds majority of members present and voting, provided that such decisions are not opposed by a majority in any one of the Chambers referred to in paragraph 9. In taking decisions the Council shall seek to promote the interests of all the members of the Authority.

6.   The Council may defer the taking of a decision in order to facilitate further negotiation whenever it appears that all efforts at achieving consensus on a question have not been exhausted.

7.   Decisions by the Assembly or the Council having financial or budgetary implications shall be based on the recommendations of the Finance Committee.

8.   The provisions of article 161, paragraph 8 (b) and (c), of the Convention shall not apply.

9. (a) Each group of States elected under paragraph 15 (a) to (c) shall be treated as a chamber for the purposes of voting in the Council. The developing States elected under paragraph 15 (d) and (e) shall be treated as a single chamber for the purposes of voting in the Council.

(b) Before electing the members of the Council, the Assembly shall establish lists of countries fulfilling the criteria for membership in the groups of States in paragraph 15 (a) to (d). If a State fulfils the criteria for membership in more than one group, it may only be proposed by one group for election to the Council and it shall represent only that group in voting in the Council.

10. Each group of States in paragraph 15 (a) to (d) shall be represented in the Council by those members nominated by that group. Each group shall nominate only as many candidates as the number of seats required to be filled by that group. When the number of potential candidates in each of the groups referred to in paragraph 15 (a) to (e) exceeds the number of seats available in each of those respective groups, as a general rule, the principle of rotation shall apply. States members of each of those groups shall determine how this principle shall apply in those groups.

11. (a) The Council shall approve a recommendation by the Legal and Technical Commission for approval of a plan of work unless by a two-thirds majority of its members present and voting, including a majority of members present and voting in each of the chambers of the Council, the Council decides to disapprove a plan of work. If the Council does not take a decision on a recommendation for approval of a plan of work within a prescribed period, the recommendation shall be deemed to have been approved by the Council at the end of that period. The prescribed period shall normally be 60 days unless the Council decides to provide for a longer period. If the Commission recommends the disapproval of a plan of work or does not make a recommendation, the Council may nevertheless approve the plan of work in accordance with its rules of procedure for decision-making on questions of substance.

(b) The provisions of article 162, paragraph 2 (j), of the Convention shall not apply.

12. Where a dispute arises relating to the disapproval of a plan of work, such dispute shall be submitted to the dispute settlement procedures set out in the Convention.

13. Decisions by voting in the Legal and Technical Commission shall be by a majority of members present and voting.

14. Part XI, section 4, subsections B and C, of the Convention shall be interpreted and applied in accordance with this section.

15. The Council shall consist of 36 members of the Authority elected by the Assembly in the following order:

(a) Four members from among those States Parties which, during the last five years for which statistics are available, have either consumed more than 2 per cent in value terms of total world consumption or have had net imports of more than 2 per cent in value terms of total world imports of the commodities produced from the categories of minerals to be derived from the Area, provided that the four members shall include one State from the Eastern European region having the largest economy in that region in terms of gross domestic product and the State, on the date of entry into force of the Convention, having the largest economy in terms of gross domestic product, if such States wish to be represented in this group;

(b) Four members from among the eight States Parties which have made the largest investments in preparation for and in the conduct of activities in the Area, either directly or through their nationals;

(c) Four members from among States Parties which, on the basis of production in areas under their jurisdiction, are major net exporters of the categories of minerals to be derived from the Area, including at least two developing States whose exports of such minerals have a substantial bearing upon their economies;

(d) Six members from among developing States Parties, representing special interests. The special interests to be represented shall include those of States with large populations, States which are land-locked or geographically disadvantaged, island States, States which are major importers of the categories of minerals to be derived from the Area, States which are potential producers of such minerals and least developed States;

(e) Eighteen members elected according to the principle of ensuring an equitable geographical distribution of seats in the Council as a whole, provided that each geographical region shall have at least one member elected under this subparagraph. For this purpose, the geographical regions shall be Africa, Asia, Eastern Europe, Latin America and the Caribbean and Western Europe and Others.

16. The provisions of article 161, paragraph 1, of the Convention shall not apply.

SECTION 4. REVIEW CONFERENCE

The provisions relating to the Review Conference in article 155, paragraphs 1, 3 and 4, of the Convention shall not apply. Notwithstanding the provisions of article 314, paragraph 2, of the Convention, the Assembly, on the recommendation of the Council, may undertake at any time a review of the matters referred to in article 155, paragraph 1, of the Convention. Amendments relating to this Agreement and Part XI shall be subject to the procedures contained in articles 314, 315 and 316 of the Convention, provided that the principles, regime and other terms referred to in article 155, paragraph 2, of the Convention shall be maintained and the rights referred to in paragraph 5 of that article shall not be affected.

SECTION 5. TRANSFER OF TECHNOLOGY

1.   In addition to the provisions of article 144 of the Convention, transfer of technology for the purposes of Part XI shall be governed by the following principles:

(a) The Enterprise, and developing States wishing to obtain deep seabed mining technology, shall seek to obtain such technology on fair and reasonable commercial terms and conditions on the open market, or through joint venture arrangements;

(b) If the Enterprise or developing States are unable to obtain deep seabed mining technology, the Authority may request all or any of the contractors and their respective sponsoring State or States to cooperate with it in facilitating the acquisition of deep seabed mining technology by the Enterprise or its joint venture, or by a developing State or States seeking to acquire such technology on fair and reasonable commercial terms and conditions, consistent with the effective protection of intellectual property rights. States Parties undertake to cooperate fully and effectively with the Authority for this purpose and to ensure that contractors sponsored by them also cooperate fully with the Authority;

(c) As a general rule, States Parties shall promote international technical and scientific cooperation with regard to activities in the Area either between the parties concerned or by developing training, technical assistance and scientific cooperation programmes in marine science and technology and the protection and preservation of the marine environment.

2. The provisions of Annex III, article 5, of the Convention shall not apply.

SECTION 6. PRODUCTION POLICY

1. The production policy of the Authority shall be based on the following principles:

(a) Development of the resources of the Area shall take place in accordance with sound commercial principles;

(b) The provisions of the General Agreement on Tariffs and Trade, its relevant codes and successor or superseding agreements shall apply with respect to activities in the Area;

(c) In particular, there shall be no subsidization of activities in the Area except as may be permitted under the agreements referred to in subparagraph (b). Subsidization for the purpose of these principles shall be defined in terms of the agreements referred to in subparagraph (b);

(d) There shall be no discrimination between minerals derived from the Area and from other sources. There shall be no preferential access to markets for such minerals or for imports of commodities produced from such minerals, in particular:

    (i) By the use of tariff or non-tariff barriers; and

    (ii) Given by States Parties to such minerals or commodities produced by their state enterprises or by natural or juridical persons which possess their nationality or are controlled by them or their nationals;

(e) The plan of work for exploitation approved by the Authority in respect of each mining area shall indicate an anticipated production schedule

which shall include the estimated maximum amounts of minerals that
would be produced per year under the plan of work;

(f) The following shall apply to the settlement of disputes concerning the
provisions of the agreements referred to in subparagraph (b):

(i) Where the States Parties concerned are parties to such agreements,
they shall have recourse to the dispute settlement procedures of those
agreements;

(ii) Where one or more of the States Parties concerned are not parties to
such agreements, they shall have recourse to the dispute settlement
procedures set out in the Convention;

(g) In circumstances where a determination is made under the agreements
referred to in subparagraph (b) that a State Party has engaged in subsidization which is prohibited or has resulted in adverse effects on the interests
of another State Party and appropriate steps have not been taken by the
relevant State Party or States Parties, a State Party may request the Council
to take appropriate measures.

2.   The principles contained in paragraph 1 shall not affect the rights and
obligations under any provision of the agreements referred to in paragraph 1 (b),
as well as the relevant free trade and customs union agreements, in relations between States Parties which are parties to such agreements.

3.   The acceptance by a contractor of subsidies other than those which may
be permitted under the agreements referred to in paragraph 1 (b) shall constitute a
violation of the fundamental terms of the contract forming a plan of work for the
carrying out of activities in the Area.

4.   Any State Party which has reason to believe that there has been a breach
of the requirements of paragraphs 1 (b) to (d) or 3 may initiate dispute settlement
procedures in conformity with paragraph 1 (f) or (g).

5.   A State Party may at any time bring to the attention of the Council activities
which in its view are inconsistent with the requirements of paragraph 1 (b) to (d).

6.   The Authority shall develop rules, regulations and procedures which
ensure the implementation of the provisions of this section, including relevant
rules, regulations and procedures governing the approval of plans of work.

7.   The provisions of article 151, paragraphs 1 to 7 and 9, article 162, paragraph 2 (q), article 165, paragraph 2 (n), and Annex III, article 6, paragraph 5, and
article 7, of the Convention shall not apply.

SECTION 7. ECONOMIC ASSISTANCE

1.   The policy of the Authority of assisting developing countries which suffer serious adverse effects on their export earnings or economies resulting from a
reduction in the price of an affected mineral or in the volume of exports of that
mineral, to the extent that such reduction is caused by activities in the Area, shall
be based on the following principles:

(a) The Authority shall establish an economic assistance fund from a portion of the funds of the Authority which exceeds those necessary to cover

the administrative expenses of the Authority. The amount set aside for this purpose shall be determined by the Council from time to time, upon the recommendation of the Finance Committee. Only funds from payments received from contractors, including the Enterprise, and voluntary contributions shall be used for the establishment of the economic assistance fund;

(b) Developing land-based producer States whose economies have been determined to be seriously affected by the production of minerals from the deep seabed shall be assisted from the economic assistance fund of the Authority;

(c) The Authority shall provide assistance from the fund to affected developing land-based producer States, where appropriate, in cooperation with existing global or regional development institutions which have the infrastructure and expertise to carry out such assistance programmes;

(d) The extent and period of such assistance shall be determined on a case-by-case basis. In doing so, due consideration shall be given to the nature and magnitude of the problems encountered by affected developing land-based producer States.

2.   Article 151, paragraph 10, of the Convention shall be implemented by means of measures of economic assistance referred to in paragraph 1. Article 160, paragraph 2 (l), article 162, paragraph 2 (n), article 164, paragraph 2 (d), article 171, subparagraph (f), and article 173, paragraph 2 (c), of the Convention shall be interpreted accordingly.

SECTION 8. FINANCIAL TERMS OF CONTRACTS

1.   The following principles shall provide the basis for establishing rules, regulations and procedures for financial terms of contracts:

(a) The system of payments to the Authority shall be fair both to the contractor and to the Authority and shall provide adequate means of determining compliance by the contractor with such system;

(b) The rates of payments under the system shall be within the range of those prevailing in respect of land-based mining of the same or similar minerals in order to avoid giving deep seabed miners an artificial competitive advantage or imposing on them a competitive disadvantage;

(c) The system should not be complicated and should not impose major administrative costs on the Authority or on a contractor. Consideration should be given to the adoption of a royalty system or a combination of a royalty and profit-sharing system. If alternative systems are decided upon, the contractor has the right to choose the system applicable to its contract. Any subsequent change in choice between alternative systems, however, shall be made by agreement between the Authority and the contractor;

(d) An annual fixed fee shall be payable from the date of commencement of commercial production. This fee may be credited against other payments due under the system adopted in accordance with subparagraph (c). The amount of the fee shall be established by the Council;

(e) The system of payments may be revised periodically in the light of changing circumstances. Any changes shall be applied in a non-discriminatory manner. Such changes may apply to existing contracts only at the election of the contractor. Any subsequent change in choice between alternative systems shall be made by agreement between the Authority and the contractor;

(f) Disputes concerning the interpretation or application of the rules and regulations based on these principles shall be subject to the dispute settlement procedures set out in the Convention.

2.   The provisions of Annex III, article 13, paragraph 3 to 10, of the Convention shall not apply.

3.   With regard to the implementation of Annex III, article 13, paragraph 2, of the Convention, the fee for processing applications for approval of a plan of work limited to one phase, either the exploration phase or the exploitation phase, shall be US$ 250,000.

SECTION 9. THE FINANCE COMMITTEE

1.   There is hereby established a Finance Committee. The Committee shall be composed of 15 members with appropriate qualifications relevant to financial matters. States Parties shall nominate candidates of the highest standards of competence and integrity.

2.   No two members of the Finance Committee shall be nationals of the same State Party.

3.   Members of the Finance Committee shall be elected by the Assembly and due account shall be taken of the need for equitable geographical distribution and the representation of special interests. Each group of States referred to in section 3, paragraph 15 (a), (b), (c) and (d), of this Annex shall be represented on the Committee by at least one member. Until the Authority has sufficient funds other than assessed contributions to meet its administrative expenses, the membership of the Committee shall include representatives of the five largest financial contributors to the administrative budget of the Authority. Thereafter, the election of one member from each group shall be on the basis of nomination by the members of the respective group, without prejudice to the possibility of further members being elected from each group.

4.   Members of the Finance Committee shall hold office for a term of five years. They shall be eligible for re-election for a further term.

5.   In the event of the death, incapacity or resignation of a member of the Finance Committee prior to the expiration of the term of office, the Assembly shall elect for the remainder of the term a member from the same geographical region or group of States.

6.   Members of the Finance Committee shall have no financial interest in any activity relating to matters upon which the Committee has the responsibility

to make recommendations. They shall not disclose, even after the termination of their functions, any confidential information coming to their knowledge by reason of their duties for the Authority.

7. Decisions by the Assembly and the Council on the following issues shall take into account recommendations of the Finance Committee:

(a) Draft financial rules, regulations and procedures of the organs of the Authority and the financial management and internal financial administration of the Authority;

(b) Assessment of contributions of members to the administrative budget of the Authority in accordance with article 160, paragraph 2 (e), of the Convention;

(c) All relevant financial matters, including the proposed annual budget prepared by the Secretary-General of the Authority in accordance with article 172 of the Convention and the financial aspects of the implementation of the programmes of work of the Secretariat;

(d) The administrative budget;

(e) Financial obligations of States Parties arising from the implementation of this Agreement and Part XI as well as the administrative and budgetary implications of proposals and recommendations involving expenditure from the funds of the Authority;

(f) Rules, regulations and procedures on the equitable sharing of financial and other economic benefits derived from activities in the Area and the decisions to be made thereon.

8. Decisions in the Finance Committee on questions of procedure shall be taken by a majority of members present and voting. Decisions on questions of substance shall be taken by consensus.

9. The requirement of article 162, paragraph 2 (y), of the Convention to establish a subsidiary organ to deal with financial matters shall be deemed to have been fulfilled by the establishment of the Finance Committee in accordance with this section.

REGULATIONS ON PROSPECTING AND EXPLORATION FOR POLYMETALLIC NODULES IN THE AREA

PREAMBLE

In accordance with the United Nations Convention on the Law of the Sea ("the Convention"), the seabed and ocean floor and the subsoil thereof beyond the limits of national jurisdiction, as well as its resources, are the common heritage of mankind, the exploration and exploitation of which shall be carried out for the benefit of mankind as a whole, on whose behalf the International Seabed Authority acts. The objective of this first set of Regulations is to provide for prospecting and exploration for polymetallic nodules.

PART I
INTRODUCTION

Regulation 1
Use of terms and scope

1. Terms used in the Convention shall have the same meaning in these Regulations.
2. In accordance with the Agreement relating to the Implementation of Part XI of the United Nations Convention on the Law of the Sea of 10 December 1982 ("the Agreement"), the provisions of the Agreement and Part XI of the United Nations Convention on the Law of the Sea of 10 December 1982 shall be interpreted and applied together as a single instrument. These Regulations and references in these Regulations to the Convention are to be interpreted and applied accordingly.
3. For the purposes of these Regulations:
    (a) "exploitation" means the recovery for commercial purposes of polymetallic nodules in the Area and the extraction of minerals therefrom, including the construction and operation of mining, processing and transportation systems, for the production and marketing of metals;
    (b) "exploration" means searching for deposits of polymetallic nodules in the Area with exclusive rights, the analysis of such deposits, the testing of collecting systems and equipment, processing facilities and transportation systems, and the carrying out of studies of the environmental, technical, economic, commercial and other appropriate factors that must be taken into account in exploitation;
    (c) "marine environment" includes the physical, chemical, geological and biological components, conditions and factors which interact and determine the productivity, state, condition and quality of the marine ecosystem, the waters of the seas and oceans and the airspace above those waters, as well as the seabed and ocean floor and subsoil thereof;

(d) "polymetallic nodules" means one of the resources of the Area consisting of any deposit or accretion of nodules, on or just below the surface of the deep seabed, which contain manganese, nickel, cobalt and copper;

(e) "prospecting" means the search for deposits of polymetallic nodules in the Area, including estimation of the composition, sizes and distributions of polymetallic nodule deposits and their economic values, without any exclusive rights;

(f) "serious harm to the marine environment" means any effect from activities in the Area on the marine environment which represents a significant adverse change in the marine environment determined according to the rules, regulations and procedures adopted by the Authority on the basis of internationally recognized standards and practices.

4.   These Regulations shall not in any way affect the freedom of scientific research, pursuant to article 87 of the Convention, or the right to conduct marine scientific research in the Area pursuant to articles 143 and 256 of the Convention. Nothing in these Regulations shall be construed in such a way as to restrict the exercise by States of the freedom of the high seas as reflected in article 87 of the Convention.

5.   These Regulations may be supplemented by further rules, regulations and procedures, in particular on the protection and preservation of the marine environment. These Regulations shall be subject to the provisions of the Convention and the Agreement and other rules of international law not incompatible with the Convention.

PART II
PROSPECTING

Regulation 2
Prospecting

1.   Prospecting shall be conducted in accordance with the Convention and these Regulations and may commence only after the prospector has been informed by the Secretary-General that its notification has been recorded pursuant to regulation 4, paragraph 2.

2.   Prospecting shall not be undertaken if substantial evidence indicates the risk of serious harm to the marine environment.

3.   Prospecting shall not be undertaken in an area covered by an approved plan of work for exploration for polymetallic nodules or in a reserved area; nor may there be prospecting in an area which the Council has disapproved for exploitation because of the risk of serious harm to the marine environment.

4.   Prospecting shall not confer on the prospector any rights with respect to resources. A prospector may, however, recover a reasonable quantity of minerals, being the quantity necessary for testing, and not for commercial use.

5.   There shall be no time limit on prospecting except that prospecting in a particular area shall cease upon written notification to the prospector by the Secretary-General that a plan of work for exploration has been approved with regard to that area.

6.   Prospecting may be conducted simultaneously by more than one prospector in the same area or areas.

Regulation 3
Notification of prospecting

1.   A proposed prospector shall notify the Authority of its intention to engage in prospecting.

2.   Each notification of prospecting shall be in the form prescribed in Annex 1 to these Regulations, addressed to the Secretary-General, and shall conform to the requirements of these Regulations.

3.   Each notification shall be submitted:

(a)   in the case of a State, by the authority designated for that purpose by it;

(b)   in the case of an entity, by its designated representative; and

(c)   in the case of the Enterprise, by its competent authority.

4.   Each notification shall be in one of the languages of the Authority and shall contain:

(a)   the name, nationality and address of the proposed prospector and its designated representative;

(b)   the coordinates of the broad area or areas within which prospecting is to be conducted, in accordance with the most recent generally accepted international standard used by the Authority;

(c)   a general description of the prospecting programme, including the proposed date of commencement and its approximate duration;

(d)   a satisfactory written undertaking that the proposed prospector will:

    (i)   comply with the Convention and the relevant rules, regulations and procedures of the Authority concerning:

        a.   cooperation in the training programmes in connection with marine scientific research and transfer of technology referred to in articles 143 and 144 of the Convention; and

        b.   protection and preservation of the marine environment; and

    (ii) accept verification by the Authority of compliance therewith.

Regulation 4
Consideration of notifications

1.   The Secretary-General shall acknowledge in writing receipt of each notification submitted under regulation 3, specifying the date of receipt.

2.   The Secretary-General shall review and act on the notification within 45 days of its receipt. If the notification conforms with the requirements of the Convention and these Regulations, the Secretary-General shall record the particulars of the notification in a register maintained for that purpose and shall inform the prospector in writing that the notification has been so recorded.

3.   The Secretary-General shall, within 45 days of receipt of the notification, inform the proposed prospector in writing if the notification includes any part of an area included in an approved plan of work for exploration or exploitation of any category of resources, or any part of a reserved area, or any part of an area which has been disapproved by the Council for exploitation because of the risk of serious harm to the marine environment, or if the written undertaking is not satisfactory, and shall provide the proposed prospector with a written statement of reasons. In such cases, the proposed prospector may, within 90 days, submit an amended notification. The Secretary-General shall, within 45 days, review and act upon such amended notification.

4.   A prospector shall inform the Secretary-General in writing of any change in the information contained in the notification.

5.   The Secretary-General shall not release any particulars contained in the notification except with the written consent of the prospector. The Secretary-General shall, however, from time to time inform all members of the Authority of the identity of prospectors and the general areas in which prospecting is being conducted.

Regulation 5
Annual report

1.   A prospector shall, within 90 days of the end of each calendar year, submit a report to the Authority on the status of prospecting. Such reports shall be submitted by the Secretary-General to the Legal and Technical Commission. Each such report shall contain:

(a)   a general description of the status of prospecting and of the results obtained; and

(b)   information on compliance with the undertakings referred to in regulation 3, paragraph (4)(d).

2.   If the prospector intends to claim expenditures for prospecting as part of the development costs incurred prior to the commencement of commercial production, the prospector shall submit an annual statement, in conformity with internationally accepted accounting principles and certified by a duly qualified firm of public accountants, of the actual and direct expenditures incurred by the prospector in carrying out prospecting.

Regulation 6
Confidentiality of data and information from prospecting contained in the annual report

1.   The Secretary-General shall ensure the confidentiality of all data and information contained in the reports submitted under regulation 5 in accordance with the provisions of regulations 35 and 36.

2.   The Secretary-General may, at any time, with the consent of the prospector concerned, release data and information relating to prospecting in an area

in respect of which a notification has been submitted. If the Secretary-General determines that the prospector no longer exists or cannot be located, the Secretary-General may release such data and information.

Regulation 7
Notification of incidents causing serious harm to the marine environment

A prospector shall immediately notify the Secretary-General in writing, using the most effective means, of any incident arising from prospecting which causes serious harm to the marine environment. Upon receipt of such notification the Secretary-General shall act in a manner consistent with regulation 32.

Regulation 8
Objects of an archaeological or historical nature

A prospector shall immediately notify the Secretary-General in writing of any finding in the Area of an object of an archaeological or historical nature and its location. The Secretary-General shall transmit such information to the Director-General of the United Nations Educational, Scientific and Cultural Organization.

PART III
APPLICATIONS FOR APPROVAL OF PLANS OF WORK FOR EXPLORATION IN THE FORM OF CONTRACTS

SECTION 1. GENERAL PROVISIONS

Regulation 9
General

Subject to the provisions of the Convention, the following may apply to the Authority for approval of plans of work for exploration:
  (a) the Enterprise, on its own behalf or in a joint arrangement;
  (b) States Parties, state enterprises or natural or juridical persons which possess the nationality of States Parties or are effectively controlled by them or their nationals, when sponsored by such States, or any group of the foregoing which meets the requirements of these Regulations. [1]

---

[1] A request by a registered pioneer investor for approval of a plan of work for exploration under paragraph 6(a)(ii) of section 1 of the annex to the Agreement shall be submitted within 36 months of the entry into force of the Convention.

SECTION 2. CONTENT OF APPLICATIONS

Regulation 10
Form of applications

1.   Each application for approval of a plan of work for exploration shall be in the form prescribed in Annex 2 to these Regulations, shall be addressed to the Secretary-General, and shall conform to the requirements of these Regulations.[2]

2.   Each application shall be submitted:

(a)   in the case of a State Party, by the authority designated for that purpose by it;

(b)   in the case of an entity, by its designated representative or the authority designated for that purpose by the sponsoring State or States; and

(c)   in the case of the Enterprise, by its competent authority.

3.   Each application by a state enterprise or one of the entities referred to in subparagraph (b) of regulation 9 shall also contain:

(a)   sufficient information to determine the nationality of the applicant or the identity of the State or States by which, or by whose nationals, the applicant is effectively controlled; and

(b)   the principal place of business or domicile and, if applicable, place of registration of the applicant.

4.   Each application submitted by a partnership or consortium of entities shall contain the required information in respect of each member of the partnership or consortium.

Regulation 11
Certificate of sponsorship

1.   Each application by a state enterprise or one of the entities referred to in subparagraph (b) of regulation 9 shall be accompanied by a certificate of sponsorship issued by the State of which it is a national or by which or by whose nationals it is effectively controlled.[3]   If the applicant has more than one nationality, as in

---

[2] A request by a registered pioneer investor for approval of a plan of work for exploration under paragraph 6(a)(ii) of section 1 of the annex to the Agreement shall consist of documents, reports and other data submitted to the Preparatory Commission both before and after registration and shall be accompanied by a certificate of compliance, consisting of a factual report describing the status of fulfilment of obligations under the registered pioneer investor regime, issued by the Preparatory Commission in accordance with resolution II, paragraph 11(a). The registered pioneer investor shall, where such information has not already been provided, update the information, using, as far as possible, the provisions of regulation 18 as a guide, and submit its programme of activities for the immediate future, including a general assessment of the potential environmental impacts of the proposed activities.

[3] In the case of a request by a registered pioneer investor for approval of a plan of work for exploration, the certifying State or States at the time of registration or their successors shall be deemed to be the sponsoring State or States provided such State or States are States Parties to the Convention or are provisional members of the Authority at the time of the request.

the case of a partnership or consortium of entities from more than one State, each State involved shall issue a certificate of sponsorship.

2.   Where the applicant has the nationality of one State but is effectively controlled by another State or its nationals, each State involved shall issue a certificate of sponsorship.

3.   Each certificate of sponsorship shall be duly signed on behalf of the State by which it is submitted and shall contain:

(a) the name of the applicant;

(b) the name of the sponsoring State;

(c) a statement that the applicant is:

    (i)   a national of the sponsoring State; or

    (ii) subject to the effective control of the sponsoring State or its nationals;

(d) a statement by the sponsoring State that it sponsors the applicant;

(e) the date of deposit by the sponsoring State of its instrument of ratification of, or accession or succession to, the Convention;

(f) a declaration that the sponsoring State assumes responsibility in accordance with article 139, article 153, paragraph 4, and Annex III, article 4, paragraph 4, of the Convention.

4.   States or entities in a joint arrangement with the Enterprise shall also comply with this regulation.

Regulation 12
Financial and technical capabilities

1.   Each application for approval of a plan of work for exploration shall contain specific and sufficient information to enable the Council to determine whether the applicant is financially and technically capable of carrying out the proposed plan of work for exploration and of fulfilling its financial obligations to the Authority. [4]

2.   An application for approval of a plan of work for exploration submitted on behalf of a State or entity, or any component of such entity, referred to in resolution II, paragraph 1(a)(ii) or (iii), other than a registered pioneer investor, which has already undertaken substantial activities in the Area prior to the entry into force of the Convention, or its successor in interest, shall be considered to have met the financial and technical qualifications necessary for approval of a plan of work for exploration if the sponsoring State or States certify that the applicant has expended an amount equivalent to at least US$ 30 million in research and exploration activities and has expended no less than 10 per cent of that amount in the location, survey and evaluation of the area referred to in the plan of work for exploration.

---

[4] A registered pioneer investor requesting approval of a plan of work for exploration under paragraph 6(a)(ii) of section 1 of the annex to the Agreement shall be considered to have satisfied the financial and technical qualifications necessary for approval of a plan of work.

3.   An application for approval of a plan of work for exploration by the Enterprise shall include a statement by its competent authority certifying that the Enterprise has the necessary financial resources to meet the estimated costs of the proposed plan of work for exploration.

4.   An application for approval of a plan of work for exploration by a State or a state enterprise, other than a registered pioneer investor or an entity referred to in resolution II, paragraph 1(a)(ii) or (iii), shall include a statement by the State or the sponsoring State certifying that the applicant has the necessary financial resources to meet the estimated costs of the proposed plan of work for exploration.

5.   An application for approval of a plan of work for exploration by an entity, other than a registered pioneer investor or an entity referred to in resolution II, paragraph 1(a)(ii) or (iii), shall include copies of its audited financial statements, including balance sheets and profit-and-loss statements, for the most recent three years, in conformity with internationally accepted accounting principles and certified by a duly qualified firm of public accountants; and

(a)   if the applicant is a newly organised entity and a certified balance sheet is not available, a pro forma balance sheet certified by an appropriate official of the applicant;

(b)   if the applicant is a subsidiary of another entity, copies of such financial statements of that entity and a statement from that entity, in conformity with internationally accepted accounting principles and certified by a duly qualified firm of public accountants, that the applicant will have the financial resources to carry out the plan of work for exploration;

(c)   if the applicant is controlled by a State or a state enterprise, a statement from the State or state enterprise certifying that the applicant will have the financial resources to carry out the plan of work for exploration.

6.   Where an applicant referred to in paragraph 5 intends to finance the proposed plan of work for exploration by borrowings, its application shall include the amount of such borrowings, the repayment period and the interest rate.

7.   Except as provided for in paragraph 2, all applications shall include:

(a)   a general description of the applicant's previous experience, knowledge, skills, technical qualifications and expertise relevant to the proposed plan of work for exploration;

(b)   a general description of the equipment and methods expected to be used in carrying out the proposed plan of work for exploration and other relevant non-proprietary information about the characteristics of such technology; and

(c)   a general description of the applicant's financial and technical capability to respond to any incident or activity which causes serious harm to the marine environment.

8.   Where the applicant is a partnership or consortium of entities in a joint arrangement, each member of the partnership or consortium shall provide the information required by this regulation.

Regulation 13
Previous contracts with the Authority

Where the applicant or, in the case of an application by a partnership or consortium of entities in a joint arrangement, any member of the partnership or consortium, has previously been awarded any contract with the Authority, the application shall include:

(a)   the date of the previous contract or contracts;

(b)   the dates, reference numbers and titles of each report submitted to the Authority in connection with the contract or contracts; and

(c)   the date of termination of the contract or contracts, if applicable.

Regulation 14
Undertakings

Each applicant, including the Enterprise, shall, as part of its application for approval of a plan of work for exploration, provide a written undertaking to the Authority that it will:

(a)   accept as enforceable and comply with the applicable obligations created by the provisions of the Convention and the rules, regulations and procedures of the Authority, the decisions of the relevant organs of the Authority and the terms of its contracts with the Authority;

(b)   accept control by the Authority of activities in the Area, as authorized by the Convention; and

(c)   provide the Authority with a written assurance that its obligations under the contract will be fulfilled in good faith.[5]

Regulation 15
Total area covered by the application

Each application for approval of a plan of work for exploration shall define the boundaries of the area under application by a list of coordinates in accordance with the most recent generally accepted international standard used by the Authority. Applications other than those under regulation 17 shall cover a total area, which need not be a single continuous area, sufficiently large and of sufficient estimated commercial value to allow two mining operations. The applicant shall indicate the coordinates dividing the area into two parts of equal estimated commercial value. The area to be allocated to the applicant shall be subject to the provisions of regulation 25.

Regulation 16
Data and information to be submitted before the designation of a reserved area

1.   Each application shall contain sufficient data and information, as prescribed in Section II of Annex 2 to these Regulations, with respect to the area under applica-

---

[5] Such undertaking shall also be provided by a registered pioneer investor requesting approval of a plan of work for exploration under paragraph 6(a)(ii) of section 1 of the annex to the Agreement.

tion to enable the Council, on the recommendation of the Legal and Technical Commission, to designate a reserved area based on the estimated commercial value of each part. Such data and information shall consist of data available to the applicant with respect to both parts of the area under application, including the data used to determine their commercial value.

2.   The Council, on the basis of the data and information submitted by the applicant pursuant to Section II of Annex 2 to these Regulations, if found satisfactory, and taking into account the recommendation of the Legal and Technical Commission, shall designate the part of the area under application which is to be a reserved area. The area so designated shall become a reserved area as soon as the plan of work for exploration for the non-reserved area is approved and the contract is signed. If the Council determines that additional information, consistent with these Regulations and Annex 2, is needed to designate the reserved area, it shall refer the matter back to the Commission for further consideration, specifying the additional information required.

3.   Once the plan of work for exploration is approved and a contract has been issued, the data and information transferred to the Authority by the applicant in respect of the reserved area may be disclosed by the Authority in accordance with article 14, paragraph 3, of Annex III to the Convention.

Regulation 17
Applications for approval of plans of work with respect to a reserved area

1.   Any State which is a developing State or any natural or juridical person sponsored by it and effectively controlled by it or by any other developing State, or any group of the foregoing, may notify the Authority that it wishes to submit a plan of work for exploration with respect to a reserved area. The Secretary-General shall forward such notification to the Enterprise, which shall inform the Secretary-General in writing within six months whether or not it intends to carry out activities in that area. If the Enterprise intends to carry out activities in that area, it shall, pursuant to paragraph 4, also inform in writing the contractor whose application for approval of a plan of work for exploration originally included that area.

2.   An application for approval of a plan of work for exploration in respect of a reserved area may be submitted at any time after such an area becomes available following a decision by the Enterprise that it does not intend to carry out activities in that area or where the Enterprise has not, within six months of the notification by the Secretary-General, either taken a decision on whether it intends to carry out activities in that area or notified the Secretary-General in writing that it is engaged in discussions regarding a potential joint venture. In the latter instance, the Enterprise shall have one year from the date of such notification in which to decide whether to conduct activities in that area.

3.   If the Enterprise or a developing State or one of the entities referred to in paragraph 1 does not submit an application for approval of a plan of work for exploration for activities in a reserved area within 15 years of the commencement

by the Enterprise of its functions independent of the Secretariat of the Authority or within 15 years of the date on which that area is reserved for the Authority, whichever is the later, the contractor whose application for approval of a plan of work for exploration originally included that area shall be entitled to apply for a plan of work for exploration for that area provided it offers in good faith to include the Enterprise as a joint-venture partner.

4.   A contractor has the right of first refusal to enter into a joint venture arrangement with the Enterprise for exploration of the area which was included in its application for approval of a plan of work for exploration and which was designated by the Council as a reserved area.

Regulation 18
Data and information to be submitted for approval of the plan of work for exploration[6]

After the Council has designated the reserved area, the applicant, if it has not already done so, shall submit, with a view to receiving approval of the plan of work for exploration in the form of a contract, the following information:

(a)   a general description and a schedule of the proposed exploration programme, including the programme of activities for the immediate five-year period, such as studies to be undertaken in respect of the environmental, technical, economic and other appropriate factors that must be taken into account in exploration;

(b)   a description of the programme for oceanographic and environmental baseline studies in accordance with these Regulations and any environmental rules, regulations and procedures established by the Authority that would enable an assessment of the potential environmental impact of the proposed exploration activities, taking into account any recommendations issued by the Legal and Technical Commission;

(c)   a preliminary assessment of the possible impact of the proposed exploration activities on the marine environment;

(d)   a description of proposed measures for the prevention, reduction and control of pollution and other hazards, as well as possible impacts, to the marine environment;

(e)   data necessary for the Council to make the determination it is required to make in accordance with regulation 12, paragraph 1; and

(f)   a schedule of anticipated yearly expenditures in respect of the programme of activities for the immediate five-year period.

---

[6] In the case of a request by a registered pioneer investor for approval of a plan of work for exploration under paragraph 6(a)(ii) of section 1 of the annex to the Agreement, this Regulation shall be implemented in the light of regulation 10.

SECTION 3. FEES

Regulation 19
Fee for applications

1.   The fee for processing applications for approval of a plan of work for exploration shall be US$ 250,000 or its equivalent in a freely convertible currency. The fee shall be paid to the Authority by the applicant at the time of submitting an application.[7]

2.   The amount of the fee shall be reviewed from time to time by the Council in order to ensure that it covers the administrative costs incurred by the Authority in processing the application.

3.   If the administrative costs incurred by the Authority in processing the application are less than the fixed amount, the Authority shall refund the difference to the applicant.

SECTION 4. PROCESSING OF APPLICATIONS

Regulation 20
Receipt, acknowledgement and safe custody of applications

1.   The Secretary-General shall:

(a)   acknowledge in writing receipt of every application for approval of a plan of work for exploration submitted under this Part, specifying the date of receipt;

(b)   place the application together with the attachments and annexes thereto in safe custody and ensure the confidentiality of all confidential data and information contained in the application; and

(c)   notify the members of the Authority of the receipt of such application and circulate to them information of a general nature which is not confidential regarding the application.

Regulation 21
Consideration by the Legal and Technical Commission[8]

1.   Upon receipt of an application for approval of a plan of work for exploration, the Secretary-General shall notify the members of the Legal and Technical

---

[7] In the case of a registered pioneer investor requesting approval for a plan of work for exploration under paragraph 6(a)(ii) of section 1 of the annex to the Agreement, the fee of US$ 250,000 paid pursuant to resolution II, paragraph 7(a), shall be deemed to be the fee referred to under paragraph 1 relating to the exploration phase.

[8] In the case of a request by a registered pioneer investor for approval of a plan of work for exploration under paragraph 6(a)(ii) of section 1 of the annex to the Agreement, the Secretary-General shall ascertain whether:

Contd.

Commission and place consideration of the application as an item on the agenda for the next meeting of the Commission.

2.   The Commission shall examine applications in the order in which they are received.

3.   The Commission shall determine if the applicant:

(a) has complied with the provisions of these Regulations;

(b) has given the undertakings and assurances specified in regulation 14;

(c) possesses the financial and technical capability to carry out the proposed plan of work for exploration; and

(d) has satisfactorily discharged its obligations in relation to any previous contract with the Authority.

4.   The Commission shall, in accordance with the requirements set forth in these Regulations and its procedures, determine whether the proposed plan of work for exploration will:

(a) provide for effective protection of human health and safety;

(b) provide for effective protection and preservation of the marine environment;

(c) ensure that installations are not established where interference may be caused to the use of recognized sea lanes essential to international navigation or in areas of intense fishing activity.

5.   If the Commission makes the determinations specified in paragraph 3 and determines that the proposed plan of work for exploration meets the requirements of paragraph 4, the Commission shall recommend approval of the plan of work for exploration to the Council.

6.   The Commission shall not recommend approval of the plan of work for exploration if part or all of the area covered by the proposed plan of work for exploration is included in:

(a) a plan of work for exploration approved by the Council for polymetallic nodules; or

---

Contd.

(a) the documents, reports and other data submitted to the Preparatory Commission both before and after registration are available;

(b) the certificate of compliance, consisting of a factual report describing the status of fulfilment of obligations under the registered pioneer investor regime, issued by the Preparatory Commission in accordance with resolution II, paragraph 11(a), has been produced;

(c) the registered pioneer investor has updated the information provided in the documents, reports and other data submitted to the Preparatory Commission both before and after registration and has submitted its programme of activities for the immediate future, including a general assessment of the potential environmental impacts of the proposed activities; and

(d) the registered pioneer investor has given the undertakings and assurances specified in regulation 14.

If the Secretary-General informs the Commission that the provisions of (a), (b), (c) and (d) have been satisfied by a registered pioneer investor, the Commission shall recommend approval of the plan of work.

(b) a plan of work approved by the Council for exploration for or exploitation of other resources if such proposed plan of work for exploration for polymetallic nodules might cause undue interference with activities under such an approved plan of work for such other resources; or

(c) an area disapproved for exploitation by the Council in cases where substantial evidence indicates the risk of serious harm to the marine environment; or

(d) if the proposed plan of work for exploration has been submitted or sponsored by a State that already holds:

   (i) plans of work for exploration and exploitation or exploitation only in non-reserved areas that, together with either part of the area covered by the application, exceed in size 30 per cent of a circular area of 400,000 square kilometres surrounding the centre of either part of the area covered by the proposed plan of work;

   (ii) plans of work for exploration and exploitation or exploitation only in non-reserved areas which, taken together, constitute 2 per cent of that part of the Area which is not reserved or disapproved for exploitation pursuant to article 162, paragraph (2)(x), of the Convention.

7. Except in the case of applications by the Enterprise, on its own behalf or in a joint venture, and applications under regulation 17, the Commission shall not recommend approval of the plan of work for exploration if part or all of the area covered by the proposed plan of work for exploration is included in a reserved area or an area designated by the Council to be a reserved area.

8. If the Commission finds that an application does not comply with these Regulations, it shall notify the applicant in writing, through the Secretary-General, indicating the reasons. The applicant may, within 45 days of such notification, amend its application. If the Commission after further consideration is of the view that it should not recommend approval of the plan of work for exploration, it shall so inform the applicant and provide the applicant with a further opportunity to make representations within 30 days of such information. The Commission shall consider any such representations made by the applicant in preparing its report and recommendation to the Council.

9. In considering a proposed plan of work for exploration, the Commission shall have regard to the principles, policies and objectives relating to activities in the Area as provided for in Part XI and Annex III of the Convention and the Agreement.

10. The Commission shall consider applications expeditiously and shall submit its report and recommendations to the Council on the designation of the areas and on the plan of work for exploration at the first possible opportunity, taking into account the schedule of meetings of the Authority.

11. In discharging its duties, the Commission shall apply these Regulations and the rules, regulations and procedures of the Authority in a uniform and non-discriminatory manner.

Regulation 22
Consideration and approval of plans of work for exploration by the Council[9]

The Council shall consider the reports and recommendations of the Commission relating to approval of plans of work for exploration in accordance with paragraphs 11 and 12 of section 3 of the annex to the Agreement.

PART IV
CONTRACTS FOR EXPLORATION

Regulation 23
The contract

1.   After a plan of work for exploration has been approved by the Council, it shall be prepared in the form of a contract between the Authority and the applicant as prescribed in Annex 3 to these Regulations. Each contract shall incorporate the standard clauses set out in Annex 4 in effect at the date of entry into force of the contract.

2.   The contract shall be signed by the Secretary-General on behalf of the Authority and by the applicant. The Secretary-General shall notify all members of the Authority in writing of the conclusion of each contract.

3.   In accordance with the principle of non-discrimination, a contract with a State or entity or any component of such entity referred to in paragraph 6 (a) (i) of section 1 of the annex to the Agreement shall include arrangements that shall be similar to and no less favourable than those agreed with any registered pioneer investor. If any of the States or entities or any components of such entities referred to in paragraph 6 (a) (i) of section 1 of the annex to the Agreement are granted more favourable arrangements, the Council shall make similar and no less favourable arrangements with regard to the rights and obligations assumed by the registered pioneer investors provided that such arrangements do not affect or prejudice the interests of the Authority.

Regulation 24
Rights of the contractor

1.   The contractor shall have the exclusive right to explore an area covered by a plan of work for exploration in respect of polymetallic nodules. The Authority shall ensure that no other entity operates in the same area for resources other than polymetallic nodules in a manner that might interfere with the operations of the contractor.

---

[9] In the case of a request by a registered pioneer investor for approval of a plan of work for exploration under paragraph 6(a)(ii) of section 1 of the Agreement, once the Commission recommends approval of the plan of work and submits its recommendation to the Council, the plan of work shall be considered approved by the Council in accordance with paragraph 6(a)(ii) of section 1 of the annex to the Agreement.

2.   A contractor who has an approved plan of work for exploration only shall have a preference and a priority among applicants submitting plans of work for exploitation of the same area and resources. Such preference or priority may be withdrawn by the Council if the contractor has failed to comply with the requirements of its approved plan of work for exploration within the time period specified in a written notice or notices from the Council to the contractor indicating which requirements have not been complied with by the contractor. The time period specified in any such notice shall not be unreasonable. The contractor shall be accorded a reasonable opportunity to be heard before the withdrawal of such preference or priority becomes final. The Council shall provide the reasons for its proposed withdrawal of preference or priority and shall consider any contractor's response. The decision of the Council shall take account of that response and shall be based on substantial evidence.

3.   A withdrawal of preference or priority shall not become effective until the contractor has been accorded a reasonable opportunity to exhaust the judicial remedies available to it pursuant to Part XI, section 5, of the Convention.

Regulation 25
Size of area and relinquishment

1.   The total area allocated to the contractor under the contract shall not exceed 150,000 square kilometres. The contractor shall relinquish portions of the area allocated to it to revert to the Area, in accordance with the following schedule:

(a)   20 per cent of the area allocated by the end of the third year from the date of the contract;

(b)   an additional 10 per cent of the area allocated by the end of the fifth year from the date of the contract; and

(c)   an additional 20 per cent of the area allocated or such larger amount as would exceed the exploitation area decided upon by the Authority, after eight years from the date of the contract, provided that a contractor shall not be required to relinquish any portion of such area when the total area allocated to it does not exceed 75,000 square kilometres.

2.   In the case of a registered pioneer investor, the contract shall take into account the schedule of relinquishment, where applicable, in accordance with the terms of its registration as a registered pioneer investor.

3.   The Council may, at the request of the contractor, and on the recommendation of the Commission, in exceptional circumstances, defer the schedule of relinquishment. Such exceptional circumstances shall be determined by the Council and shall include, inter alia, consideration of prevailing economic circumstances or other unforeseen exceptional circumstances arising in connection with the operational activities of the Contractor.

Regulation 26
Duration of contracts

1.   A plan of work for exploration shall be approved for a period of 15 years. Upon expiration of a plan of work for exploration, the contractor shall

apply for a plan of work for exploitation unless the contractor has already done so, has obtained an extension for the plan of work for exploration or decides to renounce its rights in the area covered by the plan of work for exploration.

2.   Not later than six months before the expiration of a plan of work for exploration, a contractor may apply for extensions for the plan of work for exploration for periods of not more than five years each. Such extensions shall be approved by the Council, on the recommendation of the Commission, if the contractor has made efforts in good faith to comply with the requirements of the plan of work but for reasons beyond the contractor's control has been unable to complete the necessary preparatory work for proceeding to the exploitation stage or if the prevailing economic circumstances do not justify proceeding to the exploitation stage.

Regulation 27
Training

1.   Pursuant to article 15 of Annex III to the Convention, each contract shall include as a schedule a practical programme for the training of personnel of the Authority and developing States and drawn up by the contractor in cooperation with the Authority and the sponsoring State or States. Training programmes shall focus on training in the conduct of exploration, and shall provide for full participation by such personnel in all activities covered by the contract. Such training programmes may be revised and developed from time to time as necessary by mutual agreement.

2.   In the case of a registered pioneer investor, the contract shall take into account the training provided in accordance with the terms of its registration as a registered pioneer investor.

Regulation 28
Periodic review of the implementation of the plan of work for exploration

1.   The contractor and the Secretary-General shall jointly undertake a periodic review of the implementation of the plan of work for exploration at intervals of five years. The Secretary-General may request the contractor to submit such additional data and information as may be necessary for the purposes of the review.

2.   In the light of the review, the contractor shall indicate its programme of activities for the following five-year period, making such adjustments to its previous programme of activities as are necessary.

3.   The Secretary-General shall report on the review to the Commission and to the Council. The Secretary-General shall indicate in the report whether any observations transmitted to him by States Parties to the Convention concerning the manner in which the contractor has discharged its obligations under these Regulations relating to the protection and preservation of the marine environment were taken into account in the review.

Regulation 29
Termination of sponsorship

1.   Each contractor shall have the required sponsorship throughout the period of the contract.

2.   If a State terminates its sponsorship it shall promptly notify the Secretary-General in writing. The sponsoring State should also inform the Secretary-General of the reasons for terminating its sponsorship. Termination of sponsorship shall take effect six months after the date of receipt of the notification by the Secretary-General, unless the notification specifies a later date.

3.   In the event of termination of sponsorship the contractor shall, within the period referred to in paragraph 2, obtain another sponsor. Such sponsor shall submit a certificate of sponsorship in accordance with regulation 11. Failure to obtain a sponsor within the required period shall result in the termination of the contract.

4.   A sponsoring State shall not be discharged by reason of the termination of its sponsorship from any obligations accrued while it was a sponsoring State, nor shall such termination affect any legal rights and obligations created during such sponsorship.

5.   The Secretary-General shall notify the members of the Authority of the termination or change of sponsorship.

Regulation 30
Responsibility and liability

Responsibility and liability of the contractor and of the Authority shall be in accordance with the Convention. The contractor shall continue to have responsibility for any damage arising out of wrongful acts in the conduct of its operations, in particular damage to the marine environment, after the completion of the exploration phase.

PART V - PROTECTION AND PRESERVATION OF THE MARINE ENVIRONMENT

Regulation 31
Protection and preservation of the marine environment

1.   The Authority shall, in accordance with the Convention and the Agreement, establish and keep under periodic review environmental rules, regulations and procedures to ensure effective protection for the marine environment from harmful effects which may arise from activities in the Area.

2.   In order to ensure effective protection for the marine environment from harmful effects which may arise from activities in the Area, the Authority and sponsoring States shall apply a precautionary approach, as reflected in Principle

15 of the Rio Declaration,[10] to such activities. The Legal and Technical Commission shall make recommendations to the Council on the implementation of this paragraph.

3.   Pursuant to article 145 of the Convention and paragraph 2 of this regulation, each contractor shall take necessary measures to prevent, reduce and control pollution and other hazards to the marine environment arising from its activities in the Area as far as reasonably possible using the best technology available to it.

4.   Each contract shall require the contractor to gather environmental baseline data and to establish environmental baselines, taking into account any recommendations issued by the Legal and Technical Commission pursuant to regulation 38, against which to assess the likely effects of its programme of activities under the plan of work for exploration on the marine environment and a programme to monitor and report on such effects. The recommendations issued by the Commission may, inter alia, list those exploration activities which may be considered to have no potential for causing harmful effects on the marine environment. The contractor shall cooperate with the Authority and the sponsoring State or States in the establishment and implementation of such monitoring programme.

5.   The contractor shall report annually in writing to the Secretary-General on the implementation and results of the monitoring programme referred to in paragraph 4 and shall submit data and information, taking into account any recommendations issued by the Commission pursuant to regulation 38. The Secretary-General shall transmit such reports to the Commission for its consideration pursuant to article 165 of the Convention.

6.   Contractors, sponsoring States and other interested States or entities shall cooperate with the Authority in the establishment and implementation of programmes for monitoring and evaluating the impacts of deep seabed mining on the marine environment.

7.   If the Contractor applies for exploitation rights, it shall propose areas to be set aside and used exclusively as impact reference zones and preservation reference zones. "Impact reference zones" means areas to be used for assessing the effect of each contractor's activities in the Area on the marine environment and which are representative of the environmental characteristics of the Area. "Preservation reference zones" means areas in which no mining shall occur to ensure representative and stable biota of the seabed in order to assess any changes in the flora and fauna of the marine environment.

Regulation 32
Emergency orders

1.   When the Secretary-General has been notified by a contractor or otherwise becomes aware of an incident resulting from or caused by a contractor's activities in

---

[10] Report of the United Nations Conference on Environment and Development, Rio de Janeiro, 3-14 June 1991 (United Nations publication, Sales No. E.91.I.8 and corrigenda), vol. I: Resolutions adopted by the Conference, resolution 1, Annex I.

the Area that has caused, or is likely to cause, serious harm to the marine environment, the Secretary-General shall issue a general notification of the incident, shall notify in writing the contractor and the sponsoring State or States, and shall report immediately to the Legal and Technical Commission and to the Council. A copy of the report shall be circulated to all members of the Authority, to competent international organizations and to concerned subregional, regional and global organizations and bodies. The Secretary-General shall monitor developments with respect to all such incidents and shall report on them as appropriate to the Commission and to the Council.

2.   Pending any action by the Council, the Secretary-General shall take such immediate measures of a temporary nature as are practical and reasonable in the circumstances to prevent, contain and minimize serious harm to the marine environment. Such temporary measures shall remain in effect for no longer than 90 days, or until the Council decides what measures, if any, to take pursuant to paragraph 5 of this regulation, whichever is the earlier.

3.   After having received the report of the Secretary-General, the Commission shall determine, based on the evidence provided to it and taking into account the measures already taken by the contractor, which measures are necessary to respond effectively to the incident in order to prevent, contain and minimize the serious harm, and shall make its recommendations to the Council.

4.   The Council shall consider the recommendations of the Commission.

5.   The Council, taking into account the recommendations of the Commission and any information provided by the Contractor, may issue emergency orders, which may include orders for the suspension or adjustment of operations, as may be reasonably necessary to prevent, contain and minimize serious harm to the marine environment arising out of activities in the Area.

6.   If a contractor does not promptly comply with an emergency order to prevent serious harm to the marine environment arising out of its activities in the Area, the Council shall take by itself or through arrangements with others on its behalf, such practical measures as are necessary to prevent, contain and minimize any such serious harm to the marine environment.

7.   In order to enable the Council, when necessary, to take immediately the practical measures to prevent, contain and minimize serious harm to the marine environment referred to in paragraph 6, the contractor, prior to the commencement of testing of collecting systems and processing operations, will provide the Council with a guarantee of its financial and technical capability to comply promptly with emergency orders or to assure that the Council can take such emergency measures. If the contractor does not provide the Council with such a guarantee, the sponsoring State or States shall, in response to a request by the Secretary-General and pursuant to articles 139 and 235 of the Convention, take necessary measures to ensure that the contractor provides such a guarantee or shall take measures to ensure that assistance is provided to the Authority in the discharge of its responsibilities under paragraph 6.[11]

---

[11] See ISBA/6/C/12 (Decision of the Council relating to the regulations on prospecting and exploration for polymetallic nodules in the Area).

Regulation 33
Rights of coastal States

1.   Nothing in these Regulations shall affect the rights of coastal States in accordance with article 142 and other relevant provisions of the Convention.

2.   Any coastal State which has grounds for believing that any activity in the Area by a contractor is likely to cause serious harm to the marine environment under its jurisdiction or sovereignty may notify the Secretary-General in writing of the grounds upon which such belief is based. The Secretary-General shall provide the Contractor and its sponsoring State or States with a reasonable opportunity to examine the evidence, if any, provided by the coastal State as the basis for its belief. The contractor and its sponsoring State or States may submit their observations thereon to the Secretary-General within a reasonable time.

3.   If there are clear grounds for believing that serious harm to the marine environment is likely to occur, the Secretary-General shall act in accordance with regulation 32 and, if necessary, shall take immediate measures of a temporary nature as provided for in paragraph 2 of regulation 32.

Regulation 34
Objects of an archaelogical or historical nature

The contractor shall immediately notify the Secretary-General in writing of any finding in the exploration area of an object of an archaeological or historical nature and its location. The Secretary-General shall transmit such information to the Director-General of the United Nations Educational, Scientific and Cultural Organization. Following the finding of any such object of an archaeological or historical nature in the exploration area, the contractor shall take all reasonable measures to avoid disturbing such object.

PART VI - CONFIDENTIALITY

Regulation 35
Proprietary data and information and confidentiality

1.   Data and information submitted or transferred to the Authority or to any person participating in any activity or programme of the Authority pursuant to these Regulations or a contract issued under these Regulations, and designated by the contractor, in consultation with the Secretary-General, as being of a confidential nature, shall be considered confidential unless it is data and information which:

(a)   is generally known or publicly available from other sources;

(b)   has been previously made available by the owner to others without an obligation concerning its confidentiality; or

(c)   is already in the possession of the Authority with no obligation concerning its confidentiality.

2.   Confidential data and information may only be used by the Secretary-General and staff of the Secretariat, as authorized by the Secretary-General, and

by the members of the Legal and Technical Commission as necessary for and relevant to the effective exercise of their powers and functions. The Secretary-General shall authorize access to such data and information only for limited use in connection with the functions and duties of the staff of the Secretariat and the functions and duties of the Legal and Technical Commission.

3. Ten years after the date of submission of confidential data and information to the Authority or the expiration of the contract for exploration, whichever is the later, and every five years thereafter, the Secretary-General and the contractor shall review such data and information to determine whether they should remain confidential. Such data and information shall remain confidential if the contractor establishes that there would be a substantial risk of serious and unfair economic prejudice if the data and information were to be released. No such data and information shall be released until the contractor has been accorded a reasonable opportunity to exhaust the judicial remedies available to it pursuant to Part XI, section 5, of the Convention.

4. If, at any time following the expiration of the contract for exploration, the contractor enters into a contract for exploitation in respect of any part of the exploration area, confidential data and information relating to that part of the area shall remain confidential in accordance with the contract for exploitation.

5. The contractor may at any time waive confidentiality of data and information.

Regulation 36
Procedures to ensure confidentiality

1. The Secretary-General shall be responsible for maintaining the confidentiality of all confidential data and information and shall not, except with the prior written consent of the contractor, release such data and information to any person external to the Authority. To ensure the confidentiality of such data and information, the Secretary-General shall establish procedures, consistent with the provisions of the Convention, governing the handling of confidential information by members of the Secretariat, members of the Legal and Technical Commission and any other person participating in any activity or programme of the Authority. Such procedures shall include:

   (a) maintenance of confidential data and information in secure facilities and development of security procedures to prevent unauthorized access to or removal of such data and information;

   (b) development and maintenance of a classification, log and inventory system of all written data and information received, including its type and source and routing from the time of receipt until final disposition.

2. A person who is authorized pursuant to these Regulations to have access to confidential data and information shall not disclose such data and information except as permitted under the Convention and these Regulations. The Secretary-General shall require any person who is authorized to have access to confidential data and information to make a written declaration witnessed by the Secretary-

General or his or her authorized representative to the effect that the person so authorized:

(a) acknowledges his or her legal obligation under the Convention and these Regulations with respect to the non-disclosure of confidential data and information;

(b) agrees to comply with the applicable regulations and procedures established to ensure the confidentiality of such data and information.

3.   The Legal and Technical Commission shall protect the confidentiality of confidential data and information submitted to it pursuant to these Regulations or a contract issued under these Regulations. In accordance with the provisions of article 163, paragraph 8, of the Convention, members of the Commission shall not disclose, even after the termination of their functions, any industrial secret, proprietary data which are transferred to the Authority in accordance with Annex III, article 14, of the Convention, or any other confidential information coming to their knowledge by reason of their duties for the Authority.

4.   The Secretary-General and staff of the Authority shall not disclose, even after the termination of their functions with the Authority, any industrial secret, proprietary data which are transferred to the Authority in accordance with Annex III, article 14, of the Convention, or any other confidential information coming to their knowledge by reason of their employment with the Authority.

5.   Taking into account the responsibility and liability of the Authority pursuant to Annex III, article 22, of the Convention, the Authority may take such action as may be appropriate against any person who, by reason of his or her duties for the Authority, has access to any confidential data and information and who is in breach of the obligations relating to confidentiality contained in the Convention and these Regulations.

PART VII – GENERAL PROCEDURES

Regulation 37
Notice and general procedures

1.   Any application, request, notice, report, consent, approval, waiver, direction or instruction hereunder shall be made by the Secretary-General or by the designated representative of the prospector, applicant or contractor, as the case may be, in writing. Service shall be by hand, or by telex, facsimile or registered airmail to the Secretary-General at the headquarters of the Authority or to the designated representative.

2.   Delivery by hand shall be effective when made. Delivery by telex shall be deemed to be effective on the business day following the day when the "answer back" appears on the sender's telex machine. Delivery by facsimile shall be effective when the "transmit confirmation report" confirming the transmission to the recipient's published facsimile number is received by the transmitter. Delivery by registered airmail shall be deemed to be effective 21 days after posting.

3.   Notice to the designated representative of the prospector, applicant or contractor shall constitute effective notice to the prospector, applicant or contractor for all purposes under these Regulations, and the designated representative shall be the agent of the prospector, applicant or contractor for the service of process or notification in any proceeding of any court or tribunal having jurisdiction.

4.   Notice to the Secretary-General shall constitute effective notice to the Authority for all purposes under these Regulations, and the Secretary-General shall be the Authority's agent for the service of process or notification in any proceeding of any court or tribunal having jurisdiction.

Regulation 38
Recommendations for the guidance of contractors

1.   The Legal and Technical Commission may from time to time issue recommendations of a technical or administrative nature for the guidance of contractors to assist them in the implementation of the rules, regulations and procedures of the Authority.

2.   The full text of such recommendations shall be reported to the Council. Should the Council find that a recommendation is inconsistent with the intent and purpose of these Regulations, it may request that the recommendation be modified or withdrawn.

PART VIII - SETTLEMENT OF DISPUTES

Regulation 39
Disputes

1.   Disputes concerning the interpretation or application of these Regulations shall be settled in accordance with Part XI, section 5, of the Convention.

2.   Any final decision rendered by a court or tribunal having jurisdiction under the Convention relating to the rights and obligations of the Authority and of the Contractor shall be enforceable in the territory of each State Party to the Convention.

PART IX - RESOURCES OTHER THAN POLYMETALLIC NODULES

Regulation 40
Resources other than polymetallic nodules

If a prospector or contractor finds resources in the Area other than polymetallic nodules, the prospecting and exploration for and exploitation of such resources shall be subject to the rules, regulations and procedures of the Authority relating to such resources in accordance with the Convention and the Agreement.

ANNEX 1. NOTIFICATION OF INTENTION TO ENGAGE IN PROSPECTING

1. Name of prospector:
2. Street address of prospector:
3. Postal address (if different from above):
4. Telephone number:
5. Facsimile number:
6. Electronic mail address:
7. Nationality of prospector:
8. If prospector is a juridical person, identify prospector's
   (a) place of registration; and
   (b) principal place of business/domicile.
   and attach a copy of the prospector's certificate of registration.
9. Name of prospector's designated representative:
10. Street address of prospector's designated representative (if different from above):
11. Postal address (if different from above):
12. Telephone number:
13. Facsimile number:
14. Electronic mail address:
15. Attach the coordinates of the broad area or areas in which prospecting is to be conducted (in accordance with the World Geodetic System WGS 84).
16. Attach a general description of the prospecting programme, including the date of commencement and the approximate duration of the programme.
17. Attach a written undertaking that the prospector will:
    (a) comply with the Convention and the relevant rules, regulations and procedures of the Authority concerning:
        (i) cooperation in the training programmes in connection with marine scientific research and transfer of technology referred to in articles 143 and 144 of the Convention; and
        (ii) protection and preservation of the marine environment; and
    (b) accept verification by the Authority of compliance therewith.
18. List hereunder all the attachments and annexes to this notification (all data and information should be submitted in hard copy and in a digital format specified by the Authority):

Date:_____   _____

                              Signature of prospector's designated representative

ATTESTATION:

_____

Signature of person attesting

_____

Name of person attesting

_____

Title of person attesting

ANNEX 2. APPLICATION FOR APPROVAL OF A PLAN OF WORK FOR EXPLORATION TO OBTAIN A CONTRACT

SECTION I. INFORMATION CONCERNING THE APPLICANT

1. Name of applicant:
2. Street address of applicant:
3. Postal address (if different from above):
4. Telephone number:
5. Facsimile number:
6. Electronic mail address:
7. Name of applicant's designated representative:
8. Street address of applicant's designated representative (if different from above):
9. Postal address (if different from above):
10. Telephone number:
11. Facsimile number:
12. Electronic mail address:
13. If the applicant is a juridical person, identify applicant's
(a) place of registration; and
(b) principal place of business/domicile.
    and attach a copy of the applicant's certificate of registration.
14. Identify the sponsoring State or States.
15. In respect of each sponsoring State, provide the date of deposit of its instrument of ratification of, or accession or succession to, the 1982 United Nations Convention on the Law of the Sea and the date of its consent to be bound by the Agreement relating to the Implementation of Part XI of the United Nations Convention on the Law of the Sea of 10 December 1982.
16. A certificate of sponsorship issued by the sponsoring State must be attached with this application. If the applicant has more than one national-

ity, as in the case of a partnership or consortium of entities from more than one State, certificates of sponsorship issued by each of the States involved must be attached.

SECTION II. INFORMATION RELATING TO THE AREA UNDER APPLICATION

17. Define the boundaries of the area under application by attaching a list of geographical coordinates (in accordance with the World Geodetic System WGS 84).

18. Attach a chart (on a scale and projection specified by the Authority) and a list of the coordinates dividing the total area into two parts of equal estimated commercial value.

19. Include in an attachment sufficient information to enable the Council to designate a reserved area based on the estimated commercial value of each part of the area under application. Such attachment must include the data available to the applicant with respect to both parts of the area under application, including:

(a) data on the location, survey and evaluation of the polymetallic nodules in the areas, including:
   (i) a description of the technology related to the recovery and processing of polymetallic nodules that is necessary for making the designation of a reserved area;
   (ii) a map of the physical and geological characteristics, such as seabed topography, bathymetry and bottom currents and information on the reliability of such data;
   (iii) data showing the average density (abundance) of polymetallic nodules in kg/m2 and an associated abundance map showing the location of sampling sites;
   (iv) data showing the average elemental content of metals of economic interest (grade) based on chemical assays in (dry) weight per cent and an associated grade map;
   (v) combined maps of abundance and grade of polymetallic nodules;
   (vi) a calculation based on standard procedures, including statistical analysis, using the data submitted and assumptions made in the calculations that the two areas could be expected to contain polymetallic nodules of equal estimated commercial value expressed as recoverable metals in mineable areas;
   (vii) a description of the techniques used by the applicant.
(b) information concerning environmental parameters (seasonal and during test period) including, inter alia, wind speed and direction, wave height, period and direction, current speed and direction, water salinity, temperature and biological communities.

20. If the area under application includes any part of a reserved area, attach a list of coordinates of the area which forms part of the reserved area and indicate the applicant's qualifications in accordance with regulation 17 of the Regulations.

SECTION III. FINANCIAL AND TECHNICAL INFORMATION [a]

21. Attach sufficient information to enable the Council to determine whether the applicant is financially capable of carrying out the proposed plan of work for exploration and of fulfilling its financial obligations to the Authority.

(a) If the application is made by the Enterprise, attach certification by its competent authority that the Enterprise has the necessary financial resources to meet the estimated costs of the proposed plan of work for exploration.

(b) If the application is made by a State or a state enterprise, attach a statement by the State or the sponsoring State certifying that the applicant has the necessary financial resources to meet the estimated costs of the proposed plan of work for exploration.

(c) If the application is made by an entity, attach copies of the applicant's audited financial statements, including balance sheets and profit-and-loss statements, for the most recent three years in conformity with internationally accepted accounting principles and certified by a duly qualified firm of public accountants; and

   (i)   if the applicant is a newly organized entity and a certified balance sheet is not available, a pro forma balance sheet certified by an appropriate official of the applicant;

   (ii) if the applicant is a subsidiary of another entity, copies of such financial statements of that entity and a statement from that entity in conformity with internationally accepted accounting practices and certified by a duly qualified firm of public accountants that the applicant will have the financial resources to carry out the plan of work for exploration;

   (iii) if the applicant is controlled by a State or a state enterprise, a statement from the State or state enterprise certifying that the applicant will have the financial resources to carry out the plan of work for exploration.

22. If it is intended to finance the proposed plan of work for exploration by borrowings, attach a statement of the amount of such borrowings, the repayment period and the interest rate.

---

[a] An application for approval of a plan of work for exploration submitted on behalf of a State or entity, or any component of such entity, referred to in resolution II, paragraph 1(a)(ii) or (iii), other than a registered pioneer investor, which has already undertaken substantial activities in the Area prior to the entry into force of the Convention, or its successor in interest, shall be considered to have met the financial and technical qualifications necessary for approval of a plan of work if the sponsoring State or States certify that the applicant has expended an amount equivalent to at least US$ 30 million in research and exploration activities and has expended no less than 10 per cent of that amount in the location, survey and evaluation of the area referred to in the plan of work.

23. Attach sufficient information to enable the Council to determine whether the applicant is technically capable of carrying out the proposed plan of work for exploration, including:

(a) a general description of the applicant's previous experience, knowledge, skills, technical qualifications and expertise relevant to the proposed plan of work for exploration;

(b) a general description of the equipment and methods expected to be used in carrying out the proposed plan of work for exploration and other relevant non-proprietary information about the characteristics of such technology; and

(c) a general description of the applicant's financial and technical capability to respond to any incident or activity which causes serious harm to the marine environment.

SECTION IV. THE PLAN OF WORK FOR EXPLORATION

24. Attach the following information relating to the plan of work for exploration:

(a) a general description and a schedule of the proposed exploration programme, including the programme of activities for the immediate five-year period, such as studies to be undertaken in respect of the environmental, technical, economic and other appropriate factors which must be taken into account in exploration;

(b) a description of a programme for oceanographic and environmental baseline studies in accordance with the Regulations and any environmental rules, regulations and procedures established by the Authority that would enable an assessment of the potential environmental impact of the proposed exploration activities, taking into account any recommendations issued by the Legal and Technical Commission;

(c) a preliminary assessment of the possible impact of the proposed exploration activities on the marine environment;

(d) a description of proposed measures for the prevention, reduction and control of pollution and other hazards, as well as possible impacts, to the marine environment;

(e) a schedule of anticipated yearly expenditures in respect of the programme of activities for the immediate five-year period.

SECTION V. UNDERTAKINGS

25. Attach a written undertaking that the applicant will:

(a) accept as enforceable and comply with the applicable obligations created by the provisions of the Convention and the rules, regulations and procedures of the Authority, the decisions of the relevant organs of the Authority and the terms of its contracts with the Authority;

(b) accept control by the Authority of activities in the Area as authorized by the Convention;

(c) provide the Authority with a written assurance that its obligations under the contract will be fulfilled in good faith.

SECTION VI. PREVIOUS CONTRACTS

26. Has the applicant or, in the case of an application by a partnership or consortium of entities in a joint arrangement, any member of the partnership or consortium previously been awarded any contract with the Authority?

27. If the answer to 26 is "yes", the application must include:

(a) the date of the previous contract or contracts;

(b) the dates, reference numbers and titles of each report submitted to the Authority in connection with the contract or contracts; and

(c) the date of termination of the contract or contracts, if applicable.

SECTION VII. ATTACHMENTS

28. List all the attachments and annexes to this application (all data and information should be submitted in hard copy and in a digital format specified by the Authority):

Date:_____   _____

Signature of applicant's designated representative

ATTESTATION:

_____

Signature of person attesting

_____

Name of person attesting

_____

Title of person attesting

ANNEX 3. CONTRACT FOR EXPLORATION

THIS CONTRACT made the   day of   between the INTERNA-TIONAL SEABED AUTHORITY represented by its SECRETARY-GENERAL (hereinafter referred to as "the Authority") and   represented by (hereinafter referred to as "the Contractor") WITNESSETH as follows:

Incorporation of clauses

A.   The standard clauses set out in Annex 4 to the Regulations on Prospecting and Exploration for Polymetallic Nodules in the Area shall be incorporated herein and shall have effect as if herein set out at length.

Exploration area

B.   For the purposes of this contract, the "exploration area" means that part of the Area allocated to the Contractor for exploration, defined by the coordinates listed in schedule 1 hereto, as reduced from time to time in accordance with the standard clauses and the Regulations.

Grant of rights

C.   In consideration of:

(1)   their mutual interest in the conduct of exploration activities in the exploration area pursuant to the Convention and the Agreement;

(2)   the responsibility of the Authority to organize and control activities in the Area, particularly with a view to administering the resources of the Area, in accordance with the legal regime established in Part XI of the Convention and the Agreement and Part XII of the Convention respectively; and

(3)   the interest and financial commitment of the Contractor in conducting activities in the exploration area and the mutual covenants made herein, the Authority hereby grants to the Contractor the exclusive right to explore for polymetallic nodules in the exploration area in accordance with the terms and conditions of this contract.

Entry into force and contract term

D.   This contract shall enter into force on signature by both parties and, subject to the standard clauses, shall remain in force for a period of fifteen years thereafter unless:

(1)   the Contractor obtains a contract for exploitation in the exploration area which enters into force before the expiration of such period of fifteen years; or

(2)   the contract is sooner terminated, provided that the term of the contract may be extended in accordance with standard clauses 3.2 and 17.2.

Schedules

E.   The schedules referred to in the standard clauses, namely section 4 and section 8, are for the purposes of this contract schedules 2 and 3 respectively.

Entire agreement

F.   This contract expresses the entire agreement between the parties, and no oral understanding or prior writing shall modify the terms hereof.

IN WITNESS WHEREOF the undersigned, being duly authorized thereto by the respective parties, have signed this contract at ...., this .... day of ... .

SCHEDULE 1

[Coordinates and illustrative chart of the exploration area]

SCHEDULE 2

[The current five-year programme of activities as revised from time to time]

SCHEDULE 3

[The training programme shall become a schedule to the contract when approved by the Authority in accordance with section 8 of the standard clauses.]

ANNEX 4. STANDARD CLAUSES FOR EXPLORATION CONTRACT

SECTION 1. DEFINITIONS

1.1 In the following clauses:

(a) "exploration area" means that part of the Area allocated to the Contractor for exploration, described in schedule 1 hereto, as the same may be reduced from time to time in accordance with this contract and the Regulations;

(b) "programme of activities" means the programme of activities which is set out in schedule 2 hereto as the same may be adjusted from time to time in accordance with sections 4.3 and 4.4 hereof;

(c) "Regulations" means the Regulations for Prospecting and Exploration for Polymetallic Nodules in the Area, adopted by the Authority.

1.2 Terms and phrases defined in the Regulations shall have the same meaning in these standard clauses.

1.3 In accordance with the Agreement relating to the Implementation of Part XI of the United Nations Convention of the Law of the Sea of 10 December 1982, its provisions and Part XI of the Convention are to be interpreted and applied together as a single instrument; this contract and references in this contract to the Convention are to be interpreted and applied accordingly.

1.4 This contract includes the schedules to this contract, which shall be an integral part hereof.

SECTION 2. SECURITY OF TENURE

2.1 The Contractor shall have security of tenure and this contract shall not be suspended, terminated or revised except in accordance with sections 20, 21 and 24 hereof.

2.2 The Contractor shall have the exclusive right to explore for polymetallic nodules in the exploration area in accordance with the terms and conditions of this contract. The Authority shall ensure that no other entity operates in the exploration area for a different category of resources in a manner that might unreasonably interfere with the operations of the Contractor.

2.3 The Contractor, by notice to the Authority, shall have the right at any time to renounce without penalty the whole or part of its rights in the exploration area, provided that the Contractor shall remain liable for all obligations accrued prior to the date of such renunciation in respect of the area renounced.

2.4 Nothing in this contract shall be deemed to confer any right on the Contractor other than those rights expressly granted herein. The Authority reserves the right to enter into contracts with respect to resources other than polymetallic nodules with third parties in the area covered by this contract.

SECTION 3. CONTRACT TERM

3.1 This contract shall enter into force on signature by both parties and shall remain in force for a period of fifteen years thereafter unless:

  (a) the Contractor obtains a contract for exploitation in the exploration area which enters into force before the expiration of such period of fifteen years; or

  (b) the contract is sooner terminated, provided that the term of the contract may be extended in accordance with sections 3.2 and 17.2 hereof.

3.2 Upon application by the Contractor, not later than six months before the expiration of this contract, this contract may be extended for periods of not more than five years each on such terms and conditions as the Authority and the Contractor may then agree in accordance with the Regulations. Such extensions shall be approved if the Contractor has made efforts in good faith to comply with the requirements of this contract but for reasons beyond the Contractor's control has been unable to complete the necessary preparatory work for proceeding to the exploitation stage or if the prevailing economic circumstances do not justify proceeding to the exploitation stage.

3.3 Notwithstanding the expiration of this contract in accordance with section 3.1 hereof, if the Contractor has, at least 90 days prior to the date of expiration, applied for a contract for exploitation, the Contractor's rights and obligations under this contract shall continue until such time as the application has been considered and a contract for exploitation has been issued or refused.

SECTION 4. EXPLORATION

4.1 The Contractor shall commence exploration in accordance with the time schedule stipulated in the programme of activities set out in schedule 2 hereto and shall adhere to such time periods or any modification thereto as provided for by this contract.

4.2 The Contractor shall carry out the programme of activities set out in schedule 2 hereto. In carrying out such activities the Contractor shall spend in each contract year not less than the amount specified in such programme, or any agreed review thereof, in actual and direct exploration expenditures.

4.3 The Contractor, with the consent of the Authority, which consent shall not be unreasonably withheld, may from time to time make such changes in the programme of activities and the expenditures specified therein as may be necessary and prudent in accordance with good mining industry practice, and taking into account the market conditions for the metals contained in polymetallic nodules and other relevant global economic conditions.

4.4 Not later than 90 days prior to the expiration of each five-year period from the date on which this contract enters into force in accordance with section 3 hereof, the Contractor and the Secretary-General shall jointly undertake a review of the implementation of the plan of work for exploration under this contract. The Secretary-General may require the Contractor to submit such additional data and information as may be necessary for the purposes of the review. In the light of the review, the Contractor shall indicate its programme of activities for the following five-year period, including a revised schedule of anticipated yearly expenditures, making such adjustments to its previous programme of activities as are necessary. Schedule 2 hereto shall be adjusted accordingly.

SECTION 5. ENVIRONMENTAL MONITORING

5.1 The Contractor shall take necessary measures to prevent, reduce and control pollution and other hazards to the marine environment arising from its activities in the Area as far as reasonably possible using the best technology available to it.

5.2 The Contractor shall, in accordance with the Regulations, gather environmental baseline data as exploration activities progress and develop and shall establish environmental baselines against which to assess the likely effects of the Contractor's activities on the marine environment.

5.3 The Contractor shall, in accordance with the Regulations, establish and carry out a programme to monitor and report on such effects on the marine environment. The Contractor shall cooperate with the Authority in the implementation of such monitoring.

5.4 The Contractor shall, within 90 days of the end of each calendar year, report to the Secretary-General on the implementation and results of the monitoring programme referred to in section 5.3 hereof and shall submit data and information in accordance with the Regulations.

5.5 Prior to the commencement of testing of collecting systems and processing operations, the Contractor shall submit to the Authority:

(a) a site-specific environmental impact statement based on available meteorological, oceanographic and environmental data collected during the preceding phases of exploration and containing data that could be used to establish an environmental baseline against which to assess the likely effect of the mining tests;

(b) an assessment of the effects on the marine environment of the proposed tests of collecting systems;

(c) a proposal for a monitoring programme to determine the effect on the marine environment of the equipment that will be used during the proposed mining tests.

SECTION 6. CONTINGENCY PLANS AND EMERGENCIES

6.1 The Contractor shall, prior to the commencement of its programme of activities under this contract, submit to the Secretary-General a contingency plan to respond effectively to incidents that are likely to cause serious harm to the marine environment arising from the Contractor's activities at sea in the exploration area. Such contingency plan shall establish special procedures and provide for adequate and appropriate equipment to deal with such incidents and, in particular, shall include arrangements for:

(a) the immediate raising of a general alarm in the area of the exploration activities;

(b) immediate notification to the Secretary-General;

(c) the warning of ships which might be about to enter the immediate vicinity;

(d) a continuing flow of full information to the Secretary-General relating to particulars of the contingency measures already taken and further actions required;

(e) the removal, as appropriate, of polluting substances;

(f) the reduction and, so far as reasonably possible, prevention of serious harm to the marine environment, as well as mitigation of such effects;

(g) as appropriate, cooperation with other contractors with the Authority to respond to an emergency; and

(h) periodic emergency response exercises.

6.2 The Contractor shall promptly report to the Secretary-General any incident arising from its activities that has caused or is likely to cause serious harm to the marine environment. Each such report shall contain the details of such incident, including, *inter alia*:

(a) the coordinates of the area affected or which can reasonably be anticipated to be affected;

(b) the description of the action being taken by the Contractor to prevent, contain, minimize and repair the serious harm to the marine environment;

(c) a description of the action being taken by the Contractor to monitor the effects of the incident on the marine environment; and

(d) such supplementary information as may reasonably be required by the Secretary-General.

6.3 The Contractor shall comply with emergency orders issued by the Council and immediate measures of a temporary nature issued by the Secretary-General in accordance with the Regulations, to prevent, contain, minimize or repair serious harm to the marine environment, which may include orders to the Contractor to immediately suspend or adjust any activities in the exploration area.

6.4 If the Contractor does not promptly comply with such emergency orders or immediate measures of a temporary nature, the Council may take such reasonable measures as are necessary to prevent, contain, minimize or repair any such serious harm to the marine environment at the Contractor's expense. The Contractor shall promptly reimburse the Authority the amount of such expenses. Such expenses shall be in addition to any monetary penalties which may be imposed on the Contractor pursuant to the terms of this contract or the Regulations.

SECTION 7. OBJECTS OF AN ARCHAELOGICAL OR HISTORICAL NATURE

The Contractor shall immediately notify the Secretary-General in writing of any finding in the exploration area of an object of an archaeological or historical nature and its location. Following the finding of any such object of an archaeological or historical nature in the exploration area, the Contractor shall take all reasonable measures to avoid disturbing such object.

SECTION 8. TRAINING

8.1 In accordance with the Regulations, the Contractor shall, prior to the commencement of exploration under this contract, submit to the Authority for approval proposed training programmes for the training of personnel of the Authority and developing States, including the participation of such personnel in all of the Contractor's activities under this contract.

8.2. The scope and financing of the training programme shall be subject to negotiation between the Contractor, the Authority and the sponsoring State or States.

8.3 The Contractor shall conduct training programmes in accordance with the specific programme for the training of personnel referred to in section 8.1 hereof approved by the Authority in accordance with the Regulations, which programme, as revised and developed from time to time, shall become a part of this contract as schedule 3.

SECTION 9. BOOKS AND RECORDS

The Contractor shall keep a complete and proper set of books, accounts and financial records, consistent with internationally accepted accounting principles. Such books, accounts and financial records shall include information which will fully disclose the actual and direct expenditures for exploration and such other information as will facilitate an effective audit of such expenditures.

SECTION 10. ANNUAL REPORTS

10.1 The Contractor shall, within 90 days of the end of each calendar year, submit a report to the Secretary-General covering its programme of activities in the exploration area and containing, as applicable, information in sufficient detail on:

(a) the exploration work carried out during the calendar year, including maps, charts and graphs illustrating the work that has been done and the results obtained;

(b) the equipment used to carry out the exploration work, including the results of tests conducted of proposed mining technologies, but not equipment design data; and

(c) the implementation of training programmes, including any proposed revisions to or developments of such programmes.

10.2 Such reports shall also contain:

(a) the results obtained from environmental monitoring programmes, including observations, measurements, evaluations and analyses of environmental parameters;

(b) a statement of the quantity of polymetallic nodules recovered as samples or for the purpose of testing;

(c) a statement, in conformity with internationally accepted accounting principles and certified by a duly qualified firm of public accountants, or, where the Contractor is a State or a state enterprise, by the sponsoring State, of the actual and direct exploration expenditures of the Contractor in carrying out the programme of activities during the Contractor's accounting year. Such expenditures may be claimed by the contractor as part of the contractor's development costs incurred prior to the commencement of commercial production; and

(d) details of any proposed adjustments to the programme of activities and the reasons for such adjustments.

10.3 The Contractor shall also submit such additional information to supplement the reports referred to in sections 10.1 and 10.2 hereof as the Secretary-General may from time to time reasonably require in order to carry out the Authority's functions under the Convention, the Regulations and this contract.

10.4 The Contractor shall keep, in good condition, a representative portion of samples of the polymetallic nodules obtained in the course of exploration until the expiration of this contract. The Authority may request the Contractor in writing to deliver to it for analysis a portion of any such sample obtained during the course of exploration.

SECTION 11. DATA AND INFORMATION TO BE SUBMITTED ON EXPIRATION OF THE CONTRACT

11.1 The Contractor shall transfer to the Authority all data and information that are both necessary for and relevant to the effective exercise of the powers and functions of the Authority in respect of the exploration area in accordance with the provisions of this section.

11.2 Upon expiration or termination of this contract the Contractor, if it has not already done so, shall submit the following data and information to the Secretary-General:

(a) copies of geological, environmental, geochemical and geophysical data acquired by the Contractor in the course of carrying out the programme of activities that are necessary for and relevant to the effective exercise of the powers and functions of the Authority in respect of the exploration area;

(b) the estimation of mineable areas, when such areas have been identified, which shall include details of the grade and quantity of the proven, probable and possible polymetallic nodule reserves and the anticipated mining conditions;

(c) copies of geological, technical, financial and economic reports made by or for the Contractor that are necessary for and relevant to the effective exercise of the powers and functions of the Authority in respect of the exploration area;

(d) information in sufficient detail on the equipment used to carry out the exploration work, including the results of tests conducted of proposed mining technologies, but not equipment design data; and

(e) a statement of the quantity of polymetallic nodules recovered as samples or for the purpose of testing.

11.3 The data and information referred to in section 11.2 hereof shall also be submitted to the Secretary-General if, prior to the expiration of this contract, the Contractor applies for approval of a plan of work for exploitation or if the Contractor renounces its rights in the exploration area to the extent that such data and information relates to the renounced area.

SECTION 12. CONFIDENTIALITY

Data and information transferred to the Authority in accordance with this contract shall be treated as confidential in accordance with the provisions of the Regulations.

SECTION 13. UNDERTAKINGS

13.1 The Contractor shall carry out exploration in accordance with the terms and conditions of this contract, the Regulations, Part XI of the Convention, the Agreement and other rules of international law not incompatible with the Convention.

13.2 The Contractor undertakes:

(a) to accept as enforceable and comply with the terms of this contract;

(b) to comply with the applicable obligations created by the provisions of the Convention, the rules, regulations and procedures of the Authority and the decisions of the relevant organs of the Authority;

(c) to accept control by the Authority of activities in the Area as authorized by the Convention;

(d) to fulfil its obligations under this contract in good faith; and

(e) to observe, as far as reasonably practicable, any recommendations which may be issued from time to time by the Legal and Technical Commission.

13.3 The Contractor shall actively carry out the programme of activities:

(a) with due diligence, efficiency and economy;

(b) with due regard to the impact of its activities on the marine environment; and

(c)   with reasonable regard for other activities in the marine environment.

13.4 The Authority undertakes to fulfil in good faith its powers and functions under the Convention and the Agreement in accordance with article 157 of the Convention.

SECTION 14. INSPECTION

14.1 The Contractor shall permit the Authority to send its inspectors on board vessels and installations used by the Contractor to carry out activities in the exploration area to:

(a)   monitor the Contractor's compliance with the terms and conditions of this contract and the Regulations; and

(b)   monitor the effects of such activities on the marine environment.

14.2 The Secretary-General shall give reasonable notice to the Contractor of the projected time and duration of inspections, the name of the inspectors and any activities the inspectors are to perform that are likely to require the availability of special equipment or special assistance from personnel of the Contractor.

14.3 Such inspectors shall have the authority to inspect any vessel or installation, including its log, equipment, records, facilities, all other recorded data and any relevant documents which are necessary to monitor the Contractor's compliance.

14.4 The Contractor, its agents and employees shall assist the inspectors in the performance of their duties and shall:

(a)   accept and facilitate prompt and safe boarding of vessels and installations by inspectors;

(b)   cooperate with and assist in the inspection of any vessel or installation conducted pursuant to these procedures;

(c)   provide access to all relevant equipment, facilities and personnel on vessels and installations at all reasonable times;

(d)   not obstruct, intimidate or interfere with inspectors in the performance of their duties;

(e)   provide reasonable facilities, including, where appropriate, food and accommodation, to inspectors; and

(f)   facilitate safe disembarkation by inspectors.

14.5 Inspectors shall avoid interference with the safe and normal operations on board vessels and installations used by the Contractor to carry out activities in the area visited and shall act in accordance with the Regulations and the measures adopted to protect confidentiality of data and information.

14.6 The Secretary-General and any duly authorized representatives of the Secretary-General, shall have access, for purposes of audit and examination, to any books, documents, papers and records of the Contractor which are necessary and directly pertinent to verify the expenditures referred to in section 10.2 (c).

14.7 The Secretary-General shall provide relevant information contained in the reports of inspectors to the Contractor and its sponsoring State or States where action is necessary.

14.8 If for any reason the contractor does not pursue exploration and does not request a contract for exploitation, it shall, before withdrawing from the exploration area, notify the Secretary-General in writing in order to permit the Authority, if it so decides, to carry out an inspection pursuant to this section.

SECTION 15. SAFETY, LABOUR AND HEALTH STANDARDS

15.1 The Contractor shall comply with the generally accepted international rules and standards established by competent international organizations or general diplomatic conferences concerning the safety of life at sea, and the prevention of collisions and such rules, regulations and procedures as may be adopted by the Authority relating to safety at sea. Each vessel used for carrying out activities in the Area shall possess current valid certificates required by and issued pursuant to such international rules and standards.

15.2 The Contractor shall, in carrying out exploration under this contract, observe and comply with such rules, regulations and procedures as may be adopted by the Authority relating to protection against discrimination in employment, occupational safety and health, labour relations, social security, employment security and living conditions at the work site. Such rules, regulations and procedures shall take into account conventions and recommendations of the International Labour Organization and other competent international organizations.

SECTION 16. RESPONSIBILITY AND LIABILITY

16.1 The Contractor shall be liable for the actual amount of any damage, including damage to the marine environment, arising out of its wrongful acts or omissions, and those of its employees, subcontractors, agents and all persons engaged in working or acting for them in the conduct of its operations under this contract, including the costs of reasonable measures to prevent or limit damage to the marine environment, account being taken of any contributory acts or omissions by the Authority.

16.2 The Contractor shall indemnify the Authority, its employees, subcontractors and agents against all claims and liabilities of any third party arising out of any wrongful acts or omissions of the Contractor and its employees, agents and subcontractors, and all persons engaged in working or acting for them in the conduct of its operations under this contract.

16.3 The Authority shall be liable for the actual amount of any damage to the Contractor arising out of its wrongful acts in the exercise of its powers and functions, including violations under article 168, paragraph 2, of the Convention, account being taken of contributory acts or omissions by the Contractor, its employees, agents and subcontractors, and all persons engaged in working or acting for them in the conduct of its operations under this contract.

16.4 The Authority shall indemnify the Contractor, its employees, subcontractors, agents and all persons engaged in working or acting for them in the conduct of its operations under this contract, against all claims and liabilities of any third party arising out of any wrongful acts or omissions in the exercise of its powers and functions hereunder, including violations under article 168, paragraph 2, of the Convention.

16.5 The Contractor shall maintain appropriate insurance policies with internationally recognized carriers, in accordance with generally accepted international maritime practice.

SECTION 17. FORCE MAJEURE

17.1 The Contractor shall not be liable for an unavoidable delay or failure to perform any of its obligations under this contract due to force majeure. For the purposes of this contract, force majeure shall mean an event or condition that the Contractor could not reasonably be expected to prevent or control; provided that the event or condition was not caused by negligence or by a failure to observe good mining industry practice.

17.2 The Contractor shall, upon request, be granted a time extension equal to the period by which performance was delayed hereunder by force majeure and the term of this contract shall be extended accordingly.

17.3 In the event of force majeure, the Contractor shall take all reasonable measures to remove its inability to perform and comply with the terms and conditions of this contract with a minimum of delay; provided that the Contractor shall not be obligated to resolve or terminate any labour dispute or any other disagreement with a third party except on terms satisfactory to it or pursuant to a final decision of any agency having jurisdiction to resolve the dispute.

17.4 The Contractor shall give notice to the Authority of the occurrence of an event of force majeure as soon as reasonably possible, and similarly give notice to the Authority of the restoration of normal conditions.

SECTION 18. DISCLAIMER

Neither the Contractor nor any affiliated company or subcontractor shall in any manner claim or suggest, whether expressly or by implication, that the Authority or any official thereof has, or has expressed, any opinion with respect to polymetallic nodules in the exploration area and a statement to that effect shall not be included in or endorsed on any prospectus, notice, circular, advertisement, press release or similar document issued by the Contractor, any affiliated company or any subcontractor that refers directly or indirectly to this contract. For the purposes of this section, an "affiliated company" means any person, firm or company or State-owned entity controlling, controlled by, or under common control with, the Contractor.

SECTION 19. RENUNCIATION OF RIGHTS

The Contractor, by notice to the Authority, shall have the right to renounce its rights and terminate this contract without penalty, provided that the Contractor shall remain liable for all obligations accrued prior to the date of such renunciation and those obligations required to be fulfilled after termination in accordance with the Regulations.

SECTION 20. TERMINATION OF SPONSORSHIP

20.1 If the nationality or control of the Contractor changes or the Contractor's sponsoring State, as defined in the Regulations, terminates its sponsorship, the Contractor shall promptly notify the Authority forthwith.

20.2 In either such event, if the Contractor does not obtain another sponsor meeting the requirements prescribed in the Regulations which submits to the Authority a certificate of sponsorship for the Contractor in the prescribed form within the time specified in the Regulations, this contract shall terminate forthwith.

SECTION 21. SUSPENSION AND TERMINATION OF CONTRACT AND PENALTIES

21.1 The Council may suspend or terminate this contract, without prejudice to any other rights that the Authority may have, if any of the following events should occur:

(a) if, in spite of written warnings by the Authority, the Contractor has conducted its activities in such a way as to result in serious persistent and wilful violations of the fundamental terms of this contract, Part XI of the Convention, the Agreement and the rules, regulations and procedures of the Authority; or

(b) if the Contractor has failed to comply with a final binding decision of the dispute settlement body applicable to it; or

(c) if the Contractor becomes insolvent or commits an act of bankruptcy or enters into any agreement for composition with its creditors or goes into liquidation or receivership, whether compulsory or voluntary, or petitions or applies to any tribunal for the appointment of a receiver or a trustee or receiver for itself or commences any proceedings relating to itself under any bankruptcy, insolvency or readjustment of debt law, whether now or hereafter in effect, other than for the purpose of reconstruction.

21.2 Any suspension or termination shall be by notice, through the Secretary-General, which shall include a statement of the reasons for taking such action. The suspension or termination shall be effective 60 days after such notice, unless the Contractor within such period disputes the Authority's right to suspend or terminate this contract in accordance with Part XI, section 5, of the Convention.

21.3 If the Contractor takes such action, this contract shall only be suspended or terminated in accordance with a final binding decision in accordance with Part XI, section 5, of the Convention.

21.4 If the Council has suspended this contract, the Council may by notice require the Contractor to resume its operations and comply with the terms and conditions of this contract, not later than 60 days after such notice.

21.5 In the case of any violation of this contract not covered by section 21.1(a) hereof, or in lieu of suspension or termination under section 21.1 hereof, the Council may impose upon the Contractor monetary penalties proportionate to the seriousness of the violation.

21.6 The Council may not execute a decision involving monetary penalties until the Contractor has been accorded a reasonable opportunity to exhaust the judicial remedies available to it pursuant to Part XI, section 5, of the Convention.

21.7 In the event of termination or expiration of this contract, the Contractor shall comply with the Regulations and shall remove all installations, plant, equipment and materials in the exploration area and shall make the area safe so as not to constitute a danger to persons, shipping or to the marine environment.

SECTION 22. TRANSFER OF RIGHTS AND OBLIGATIONS

22.1 The rights and obligations of the Contractor under this contract may be transferred in whole or in part only with the consent of the Authority and in accordance with the Regulations.

22.2 The Authority shall not unreasonably withhold consent to the transfer if the proposed transferee is in all respects a qualified applicant in accordance with the Regulations and assumes all of the obligations of the Contractor and if the transfer does not confer to the transferee a plan of work, the approval of which would be forbidden by Annex 3, article 6, paragraph 3(c), of the Convention.

22.3 The terms, undertakings and conditions of this contract shall inure to the benefit of and be binding upon the parties hereto and their respective successors and assigns.

SECTION 23. NO WAIVER

No waiver by either party of any rights pursuant to a breach of the terms and conditions of this contract to be performed by the other party shall be construed as a waiver by the party of any succeeding breach of the same or any other term or condition to be performed by the other party.

SECTION 24. REVISION

24.1 When circumstances have arisen or are likely to arise which, in the opinion of the Authority or the Contractor, would render this contract inequitable or make it impracticable or impossible to achieve the objectives set out in this contract or in Part XI of the Convention or the Agreement, the parties shall enter into negotiations to revise it accordingly.

24.2 This contract may also be revised by agreement between the Contractor and the Authority to facilitate the application of any rules, regulations and procedures adopted by the Authority subsequent to the entry into force of this contract.

24.3 This contract may be revised, amended or otherwise modified only with the consent of the Contractor and the Authority by an appropriate instrument signed by the authorized representatives of the parties.

SECTION 25. DISPUTES

25.1 Any dispute between the parties concerning the interpretation or application of this contract shall be settled in accordance with Part XI, section 5, of the Convention.

25.2 Any final decision rendered by a court or tribunal having jurisdiction under the Convention relating to the rights and obligations of the Authority and of the Contractor shall be enforceable in the territory of each State Party to the Convention.

SECTION 26. NOTICE

26.1 Any application, request, notice, report, consent, approval, waiver, direction or instruction hereunder shall be made by the Secretary-General or by the designated representative of the Contractor, as the case may be, in writing. Service shall be by hand, or by telex, facsimile or registered airmail to the Secretary-General at the headquarters of the Authority or to the designated representative.

26.2 Either party shall be entitled to change any such address to any other address by not less than ten days' notice to the other party.

26.3 Delivery by hand shall be effective when made. Delivery by telex shall be deemed to be effective on the business day following the day when the "answer back" appears on the sender's telex machine. Delivery by facsimile shall be effective when the "transmit confirmation report" confirming the transmission to the recipient's published facsimile number is received by the transmitter. Delivery by registered airmail shall be deemed to be effective 21 days after posting.

26.4 Notice to the designated representative of the Contractor shall constitute effective notice to the Contractor for all purposes under this contract, and the designated representative shall be the Contractor's agent for the service of process or notification in any proceeding of any court or tribunal having jurisdiction.

26.5 Notice to the Secretary-General shall constitute effective notice to the Authority for all purposes under this contract, and the Secretary-General shall be the Authority's agent for the service of process or notification in any proceeding of any court or tribunal having jurisdiction.

SECTION 27. APPLICABLE LAW

27.1 This contract shall be governed by the terms of this contract, the rules, regulations and procedures of the Authority, Part XI of the Convention, the Agreement and other rules of international law not incompatible with the Convention.

27.2 The Contractor, its employees, subcontractors, agents and all persons engaged in working or acting for them in the conduct of its operations under this contract shall observe the applicable law referred to in section 27.1 hereof and shall not engage in any transaction, directly or indirectly, prohibited by the applicable law.

27.3 Nothing contained in this contract shall be deemed an exemption from the necessity of applying for and obtaining any permit or authority that may be required for any activities under this contract.

SECTION 28. INTERPRETATION

The division of this contract into sections and subsections and the insertion of headings are for convenience of reference only and shall not affect the construction or interpretation hereof.

SECTION 29. ADDITIONAL DOCUMENTS

Each party hereto agrees to execute and deliver all such further instruments, and to do and perform all such further acts and things as may be necessary or expedient to give effect to the provisions of this contract.

AGREEMENT FOR THE IMPLEMENTATION OF THE PROVISIONS OF THE UNITED NATIONS CONVENTION ON THE LAW OF THE SEA OF 10 DECEMBER 1982 RELATING TO THE CONSERVATION AND MANAGEMENT OF STRADDLING FISH STOCKS AND HIGHLY MIGRATORY FISH STOCKS

The States Parties to this Agreement,

Recalling the relevant provisions of the United Nations Convention on the Law of the Sea of 10 December 1982,

Determined to ensure the long-term conservation and sustainable use of straddling fish stocks and highly migratory fish stocks,

Resolved to improve co-operation between States to that end,

Calling for more effective enforcement by flag States, port States and coastal States of the conservation and management measures adopted for such stocks,

Seeking to address in particular the problems identified in chapter 17, programme area C, of Agenda 21 adopted by the United Nations Conference on Environment and Development, namely, that the management of high seas fisheries is inadequate in many areas and that some resources are overutilized; noting that there are problems of unregulated fishing, over-capitalization, excessive fleet size, vessel reflagging to escape controls, insufficiently selective gear, unreliable databases and lack of sufficient co-operation between States,

Committing themselves to responsible fisheries,

Conscious of the need to avoid adverse impacts on the marine environment, preserve biodiversity, maintain the integrity of marine ecosystems and minimize the risk of long-term or irreversible effects of fishing operations,

Recognizing the need for specific assistance, including financial, scientific and technological assistance, in order that developing States can participate effectively in the conservation, management and sustainable use of straddling fish stocks and highly migratory fish stocks,

Convinced that an agreement for the implementation of the relevant provisions of the Convention would best serve these purposes and contribute to the maintenance of international peace and security,

Affirming that matters not regulated by the Convention or by this Agreement continue to be governed by the rules and principles of general international law,

Have agreed as follows:

PART I
GENERAL PROVISIONS

Article 1
Use of terms and scope

1.   For the purposes of this Agreement:

(a)   "Convention" means the United Nations Convention on the Law of the Sea of 10 December 1982;

(b)   "conservation and management measures" means measures to conserve and manage one or more species of living marine resources that are adopted and applied consistent with the relevant rules of international law as reflected in the Convention and this Agreement;

(c)   "fish" includes molluscs and crustaceans except those belonging to sedentary species as defined in article 77 of the Convention; and

(d)   "arrangement" means a co-operative mechanism established in accordance with the Convention and this Agreement by two or more States for the purpose, *inter alia*, of establishing conservation and management measures in a subregion or region for one or more straddling fish stocks or highly migratory fish stocks.

2.   (a)   "States Parties" means States which have consented to be bound by this Agreement and for which the Agreement is in force.

(b)   This Agreement applies *mutatis mutandis*:

(i)   to any entity referred to in article 305, paragraph 1 (c), (d) and (e), of the Convention and

(ii)   subject to article 47, to any entity referred to as an "international organization" in Annex IX, article 1, of the Convention which becomes a Party to this Agreement, and to that extent "States Parties" refers to those entities.

3.   This Agreement applies *mutatis mutandis* to other fishing entities whose vessels fish on the high seas.

Article 2
Objective

The objective of this Agreement is to ensure the long-term conservation and sustainable use of straddling fish stocks and highly migratory fish stocks through effective implementation of the relevant provisions of the Convention.

Article 3
Application

1.   Unless otherwise provided, this Agreement applies to the conservation and management of straddling fish stocks and highly migratory fish stocks beyond areas under national jurisdiction, except that articles 6 and 7 apply also to the conservation and management of such stocks within areas under national jurisdiction,

subject to the different legal regimes that apply within areas under national jurisdiction and in areas beyond national jurisdiction as provided for in the Convention.

2.   In the exercise of its sovereign rights for the purpose of exploring and exploiting, conserving and managing straddling fish stocks and highly migratory fish stocks within areas under national jurisdiction, the coastal State shall apply *mutatis mutandis* the general principles enumerated in article 5.

3.   States shall give due consideration to the respective capacities of developing States to apply articles 5, 6 and 7 within areas under national jurisdiction and their need for assistance as provided for in this Agreement. To this end, Part VII applies *mutatis mutandis* in respect of areas under national jurisdiction.

Article 4
Relationship between this Agreement and the Convention

Nothing in this Agreement shall prejudice the rights, jurisdiction and duties of States under the Convention. This Agreement shall be interpreted and applied in the context of and in a manner consistent with the Convention.

PART II
CONSERVATION AND MANAGEMENT OF STRADDLING FISH STOCKS AND HIGHLY MIGRATORY FISH STOCKS

Article 5
General principles

In order to conserve and manage straddling fish stocks and highly migratory fish stocks, coastal States and States fishing on the high seas shall, in giving effect to their duty to co-operate in accordance with the Convention:

(a)   adopt measures to ensure long-term sustainability of straddling fish stocks and highly migratory fish stocks and promote the objective of their optimum utilization;

(b)   ensure that such measures are based on the best scientific evidence available and are designed to maintain or restore stocks at levels capable of producing maximum sustainable yield, as qualified by relevant environmental and economic factors, including the special requirements of developing States, and taking into account fishing patterns, the interdependence of stocks and any generally recommended international minimum standards, whether subregional, regional or global;

(c)   apply the precautionary approach in accordance with article 6;

(d)   assess the impacts of fishing, other human activities and environmental factors on target stocks and species belonging to the same ecosystem or associated with or dependent upon the target stocks;

(e) adopt, where necessary, conservation and management measures for species belonging to the same ecosystem or associated with or dependent upon the target stocks, with a view to maintaining or restoring populations of such species above levels at which their reproduction may become seriously threatened;

(f) minimize pollution, waste, discards, catch by lost or abandoned gear, catch of non-target species, both fish and non-fish species, (hereinafter referred to as non-target species) and impacts on associated or dependent species, in particular endangered species, through measures including, to the extent practicable, the development and use of selective, environmentally safe and cost-effective fishing gear and techniques;

(g) protect biodiversity in the marine environment;

(h) take measures to prevent or eliminate overfishing and excess fishing capacity and to ensure that levels of fishing effort do not exceed those commensurate with the sustainable use of fishery resources;

(i) take into account the interests of artisanal and subsistence fishers;

(j) collect and share, in a timely manner, complete and accurate data concerning fishing activities on, *inter alia*, vessel position, catch of target and non-target species and fishing effort, as set out in Annex I, as well as information from national and international research programmes;

(k) promote and conduct scientific research and develop appropriate technologies in support of fishery conservation and management; and

(l) implement and enforce conservation and management measures through effective monitoring, control and surveillance.

Article 6
Application of the precautionary approach

1.   States shall apply the precautionary approach widely to conservation, management and exploitation of straddling fish stocks and highly migratory fish stocks in order to protect the living marine resources and preserve the marine environment.

2.   States shall be more cautious when information is uncertain, unreliable or inadequate. The absence of adequate scientific information shall not be used as a reason for postponing or failing to take conservation and management measures.

3.   In implementing the precautionary approach, States shall:

(a) improve decision-making for fishery resource conservation and management by obtaining and sharing the best scientific information available and implementing improved techniques for dealing with risk and uncertainty;

(b) apply the guidelines set out in Annex II and determine, on the basis of the best scientific information available, stock-specific reference points and the action to be taken if they are exceeded;

(c) take into account, *inter alia*, uncertainties relating to the size and productivity of the stocks, reference points, stock condition in relation to such reference points, levels and distribution of fishing mortality and the impact of fishing activities on non-target and associated or dependent species, as well as existing and predicted oceanic, environmental and socio-economic conditions; and

(d) develop data collection and research programmes to assess the impact of fishing on non-target and associated or dependent species and their environment, and adopt plans which are necessary to ensure the conservation of such species and to protect habitats of special concern.

4.   States shall take measures to ensure that, when reference points are approached, they will not be exceeded. In the event that they are exceeded, States shall, without delay, take the action determined under paragraph 3 (b) to restore the stocks.

5.   Where the status of target stocks or non-target or associated or dependent species is of concern, States shall subject such stocks and species to enhanced monitoring in order to review their status and the efficacy of conservation and management measures. They shall revise those measures regularly in the light of new information.

6.   For new or exploratory fisheries, States shall adopt as soon as possible cautious conservation and management measures, including, *inter alia*, catch limits and effort limits. Such measures shall remain in force until there are sufficient data to allow assessment of the impact of the fisheries on the long-term sustainability of the stocks, whereupon conservation and management measures based on that assessment shall be implemented. The latter measures shall, if appropriate, allow for the gradual development of the fisheries.

7.   If a natural phenomenon has a significant adverse impact on the status of straddling fish stocks or highly migratory fish stocks, States shall adopt conservation and management measures on an emergency basis to ensure that fishing activity does not exacerbate such adverse impact. States shall also adopt such measures on an emergency basis where fishing activity presents a serious threat to the sustainability of such stocks. Measures taken on an emergency basis shall be temporary and shall be based on the best scientific evidence available.

Article 7
Compatibility of conservation and management measures

1.   Without prejudice to the sovereign rights of coastal States for the purpose of exploring and exploiting, conserving and managing the living marine resources within areas under national jurisdiction as provided for in the Convention, and the right of all States for their nationals to engage in fishing on the high seas in accordance with the Convention:

(a) with respect to straddling fish stocks, the relevant coastal States and the States whose nationals fish for such stocks in the adjacent high seas area shall seek, either directly or through the appropriate mechanisms for cooperation provided for in Part III, to agree upon the measures necessary for the conservation of these stocks in the adjacent high seas area;

(b)   with respect to highly migratory fish stocks, the relevant coastal States and other States whose nationals fish for such stocks in the region shall co-operate, either directly or through the appropriate mechanisms for co-operation provided for in Part III, with a view to ensuring conservation and promoting the objective of optimum utilization of such stocks throughout the region, both within and beyond the areas under national jurisdiction.

2.   Conservation and management measures established for the high seas and those adopted for areas under national jurisdiction shall be compatible in order to ensure conservation and management of the straddling fish stocks and highly migratory fish stocks in their entirety. To this end, coastal States and States fishing on the high seas have a duty to co-operate for the purpose of achieving compatible measures in respect of such stocks. In determining compatible conservation and management measures, States shall:

(a)   take into account the conservation and management measures adopted and applied in accordance with article 61 of the Convention in respect of the same stocks by coastal States within areas under national jurisdiction and ensure that measures established in respect of such stocks for the high seas do not undermine the effectiveness of such measures;

(b)   take into account previously agreed measures established and applied for the high seas in accordance with the Convention in respect of the same stocks by relevant coastal States and States fishing on the high seas;

(c)   take into account previously agreed measures established and applied in accordance with the Convention in respect of the same stocks by a subregional or regional fisheries management organization or arrangement;

(d)   take into account the biological unity and other biological characteristics of the stocks and the relationships between the distribution of the stocks, the fisheries and the geographical particularities of the region concerned, including the extent to which the stocks occur and are fished in areas under national jurisdiction;

(e)   take into account the respective dependence of the coastal States and the States fishing on the high seas on the stocks concerned; and

(f)   ensure that such measures do not result in harmful impact on the living marine resources as a whole.

3.   In giving effect to their duty to co-operate, States shall make every effort to agree on compatible conservation and management measures within a reasonable period of time.

4.   If no agreement can be reached within a reasonable period of time, any of the States concerned may invoke the procedures for the settlement of disputes provided for in Part VIII.

5.   Pending agreement on compatible conservation and management measures, the States concerned, in a spirit of understanding and cooperation, shall make every effort to enter into provisional arrangements of a practical nature. In the event that they are unable to agree on such arrangements, any of the States

concerned may, for the purpose of obtaining provisional measures, submit the dispute to a court or tribunal in accordance with the procedures for the settlement of disputes provided for in Part VIII.

6.   Provisional arrangements or measures entered into or prescribed pursuant to paragraph 5 shall take into account the provisions of this Part, shall have due regard to the rights and obligations of all States concerned, shall not jeopardize or hamper the reaching of final agreement on compatible conservation and management measures and shall be without prejudice to the final outcome of any dispute settlement procedure.

7.   Coastal States shall regularly inform States fishing on the high seas in the subregion or region, either directly or through appropriate subregional or regional fisheries management organizations or arrangements, or through other appropriate means, of the measures they have adopted for straddling fish stocks and highly migratory fish stocks within areas under their national jurisdiction.

8.   States fishing on the high seas shall regularly inform other interested States, either directly or through appropriate subregional or regional fisheries management organizations or arrangements, or through other appropriate means, of the measures they have adopted for regulating the activities of vessels flying their flag which fish for such stocks on the high seas.

PART III
MECHANISMS FOR INTERNATIONAL COOPERATION CONCERNING STRADDLING FISH STOCKS AND HIGHLY MIGRATORY FISH STOCKS

Article 8
Cooperation for conservation and management

1.   Coastal States and States fishing on the high seas shall, in accordance with the Convention, pursue co-operation in relation to straddling fish stocks and highly migratory fish stocks either directly or through appropriate subregional or regional fisheries management organizations or arrangements, taking into account the specific characteristics of the subregion or region, to ensure effective conservation and management of such stocks.

2.   States shall enter into consultations in good faith and without delay, particularly where there is evidence that the straddling fish stocks and highly migratory fish stocks concerned may be under threat of over-exploitation or where a new fishery is being developed for such stocks. To this end, consultations may be initiated at the request of any interested State with a view to establishing appropriate arrangements to ensure conservation and management of the stocks. Pending agreement on such arrangements, States shall observe the provisions of this Agreement and shall act in good faith and with due regard to the rights, interests and duties of other States.

3.   Where a subregional or regional fisheries management organization or arrangement has the competence to establish conservation and management measures for particular straddling fish stocks or highly migratory fish stocks, States fishing for the stocks on the high seas and relevant coastal States shall give effect to their duty to co-operate by becoming members of such organization or participants in such arrangement, or by agreeing to apply the conservation and management measures established by such organization or arrangement. States having a real interest in the fisheries concerned may become members of such organization or participants in such arrangement. The terms of participation in such organization or arrangement shall not preclude such States from membership or participation; nor shall they be applied in a manner which discriminates against any State or group of States having a real interest in the fisheries concerned.

4.   Only those States which are members of such an organization or participants in such an arrangement, or which agree to apply the conservation and management measures established by such organization or arrangement, shall have access to the fishery resources to which those measures apply.

5.   Where there is no subregional or regional fisheries management organization or arrangement to establish conservation and management measures for a particular straddling fish stock or highly migratory fish stock, relevant coastal States and States fishing on the high seas for such stock in the subregion or region shall co-operate to establish such an organization or enter into other appropriate arrangements to ensure conservation and management of such stock and shall participate in the work of the organization or arrangement.

6.   Any State intending to propose that action be taken by an intergovernmental organization having competence with respect to living resources should, where such action would have a significant effect on conservation and management measures already established by a competent subregional or regional fisheries management organization or arrangement, consult through that organization or arrangement with its members or participants. To the extent practicable, such consultation should take place prior to the submission of the proposal to the intergovernmental organization.

Article 9
Subregional and regional fisheries management organizations
and arrangements

1.   In establishing subregional or regional fisheries management organizations or in entering into subregional or regional fisheries management arrangements for straddling fish stocks and highly migratory fish stocks, States shall agree, *inter alia*, on:

    (a)   the stocks to which conservation and management measures apply, taking into account the biological characteristics of the stocks concerned and the nature of the fisheries involved;

    (b)   the area of application, taking into account article 7, paragraph 1, and the characteristics of the subregion or region, including socio-economic, geographical and environmental factors;

(c) the relationship between the work of the new organization or arrangement and the role, objectives and operations of any relevant existing fisheries management organizations or arrangements; and

(d) the mechanisms by which the organization or arrangement will obtain scientific advice and review the status of the stocks, including, where appropriate, the establishment of a scientific advisory body.

2. States cooperating in the formation of a subregional or regional fisheries management organization or arrangement shall inform other States which they are aware have a real interest in the work of the proposed organization or arrangement of such cooperation.

Article 10
Functions of subregional and regional fisheries management
organizations and arrangements

In fulfilling their obligation to co-operate through subregional or regional fisheries management organizations or arrangements, States shall:

(a) agree on and comply with conservation and management measures to ensure the long-term sustainability of straddling fish stocks and highly migratory fish stocks;

(b) agree, as appropriate, on participatory rights such as allocations of allowable catch or levels of fishing effort;

(c) adopt and apply any generally recommended international minimum standards for the responsible conduct of fishing operations;

(d) obtain and evaluate scientific advice, review the status of the stocks and assess the impact of fishing on non-target and associated or dependent species;

(e) agree on standards for collection, reporting, verification and exchange of data on fisheries for the stocks;

(f) compile and disseminate accurate and complete statistical data, as described in Annex I, to ensure that the best scientific evidence is available, while maintaining confidentiality where appropriate;

(g) promote and conduct scientific assessments of the stocks and relevant research and disseminate the results thereof;

(h) establish appropriate co-operative mechanisms for effective monitoring, control, surveillance and enforcement;

(i) agree on means by which the fishing interests of new members of the organization or new participants in the arrangement will be accommodated;

(j) agree on decision-making procedures which facilitate the adoption of conservation and management measures in a timely and effective manner;

(k) promote the peaceful settlement of disputes in accordance with Part VIII;

(l) ensure the full co-operation of their relevant national agencies and industries in implementing the recommendations and decisions of the organization or arrangement; and

(m) give due publicity to the conservation and management measures estab-
     lished by the organization or arrangement.

Article 11
New members or participants

In determining the nature and extent of participatory rights for new members
of a subregional or regional fisheries management organization, or for new participants in a subregional or regional fisheries management arrangement, States
shall take into account, *inter alia*:

(a) the status of the straddling fish stocks and highly migratory fish stocks
     and the existing level of fishing effort in the fishery;

(b) the respective interests, fishing patterns and fishing practices of new
     and existing members or participants;

(c) the respective contributions of new and existing members or partici-
     pants to conservation and management of the stocks, to the collection
     and provision of accurate data and to the conduct of scientific research
     on the stocks;

(d) the needs of coastal fishing communities which are dependent mainly
     on fishing for the stocks;

(e) the needs of coastal States whose economies are overwhelmingly
     dependent on the exploitation of living marine resources; and

(f) the interests of developing States from the subregion or region in whose
     areas of national jurisdiction the stocks also occur.

Article 12
Transparency in activities of subregional and regional fisheries management organizations and arrangements

1.   States shall provide for transparency in the decision-making process and
other activities of subregional and regional fisheries management organizations
and arrangements.

2.   Representatives from other intergovernmental organizations and representatives from non-governmental organizations concerned with straddling fish
stocks and highly migratory fish stocks shall be afforded the opportunity to take
part in meetings of subregional and regional fisheries management organizations
and arrangements as observers or otherwise, as appropriate, in accordance with
the procedures of the organization or arrangement concerned. Such procedures
shall not be unduly restrictive in this respect. Such intergovernmental organizations and non-governmental organizations shall have timely access to the records
and reports of such organizations and arrangements, subject to the procedural
rules on access to them.

Article 13
Strengthening of existing organizations and arrangements

States shall co-operate to strengthen existing subregional and regional fisheries management organizations and arrangements in order to improve their

effectiveness in establishing and implementing conservation and management measures for straddling fish stocks and highly migratory fish stocks.

Article 14
Collection and provision of information and co-operation
in scientific research

1.   States shall ensure that fishing vessels flying their flag provide such information as may be necessary in order to fulfil their obligations under this Agreement. To this end, States shall in accordance with Annex I:

   (a) collect and exchange scientific, technical and statistical data with respect to fisheries for straddling fish stocks and highly migratory fish stocks;
   (b) ensure that data are collected in sufficient detail to facilitate effective stock assessment and are provided in a timely manner to fulfil the requirements of subregional or regional fisheries management organizations or arrangements; and
   (c) take appropriate measures to verify the accuracy of such data.

2. States shall co-operate, either directly or through subregional or regional fisheries management organizations or arrangements:

   (a) to agree on the specification of data and the format in which they are to be provided to such organizations or arrangements, taking into account the nature of the stocks and the fisheries for those stocks; and
   (b) to develop and share analytical techniques and stock assessment methodologies to improve measures for the conservation and management of straddling fish stocks and highly migratory fish stocks.

3.   Consistent with Part XIII of the Convention, States shall co-operate, either directly or through competent international organizations, to strengthen scientific research capacity in the field of fisheries and promote scientific research related to the conservation and management of straddling fish stocks and highly migratory fish stocks for the benefit of all. To this end, a State or the competent international organization conducting such research beyond areas under national jurisdiction shall actively promote the publication and dissemination to any interested States of the results of that research and information relating to its objectives and methods and, to the extent practicable, shall facilitate the participation of scientists from those States in such research.

Article 15
Enclosed and semi-enclosed seas

In implementing this Agreement in an enclosed or semi-enclosed sea, States shall take into account the natural characteristics of that sea and shall also act in a manner consistent with Part IX of the Convention and other relevant provisions thereof.

Article 16
Areas of high seas surrounded entirely by an area under
the national jurisdiction of a single State

1.   States fishing for straddling fish stocks and highly migratory fish stocks in an area of the high seas surrounded entirely by an area under the national jurisdiction of a single State and the latter State shall co-operate to establish conservation and management measures in respect of those stocks in the high seas area. Having regard to the natural characteristics of the area, States shall pay special attention to the establishment of compatible conservation and management measures for such stocks pursuant to article 7. Measures taken in respect of the high seas shall take into account the rights, duties and interests of the coastal State under the Convention, shall be based on the best scientific evidence available and shall also take into account any conservation and management measures adopted and applied in respect of the same stocks in accordance with article 61 of the Convention by the coastal State in the area under national jurisdiction. States shall also agree on measures for monitoring, control, surveillance and enforcement to ensure compliance with the conservation and management measures in respect of the high seas.

2.   Pursuant to article 8, States shall act in good faith and make every effort to agree without delay on conservation and management measures to be applied in the carrying out of fishing operations in the area referred to in paragraph 1. If, within a reasonable period of time, the fishing States concerned and the coastal State are unable to agree on such measures, they shall, having regard to paragraph 1, apply article 7, paragraphs 4, 5 and 6, relating to provisional arrangements or measures. Pending the establishment of such provisional arrangements or measures, the States concerned shall take measures in respect of vessels flying their flag in order that they not engage in fisheries which could undermine the stocks concerned.

PART IV
NON-MEMBERS AND NON-PARTICIPANTS

Article 17
Non-members of organizations and non-participants
in arrangements

1.   A State which is not a member of a subregional or regional fisheries management organization or is not a participant in a subregional or regional fisheries management arrangement, and which does not otherwise agree to apply the conservation and management measures established by such organization or arrangement, is not discharged from the obligation to co-operate, in accordance with the Convention and this Agreement, in the conservation and management of the relevant straddling fish stocks and highly migratory fish stocks.

2.   Such State shall not authorize vessels flying its flag to engage in fishing operations for the straddling fish stocks or highly migratory fish stocks which are subject to the conservation and management measures established by such organization or arrangement.

3.   States which are members of a subregional or regional fisheries management organization or participants in a subregional or regional fisheries management arrangement shall, individually or jointly, request the fishing entities referred to in article 1, paragraph 3, which have fishing vessels in the relevant area to co-operate fully with such organization or arrangement in implementing the conservation and management measures it has established, with a view to having such measures applied de facto as extensively as possible to fishing activities in the relevant area. Such fishing entities shall enjoy benefits from participation in the fishery commensurate with their commitment to comply with conservation and management measures in respect of the stocks.

4.   States which are members of such organization or participants in such arrangement shall exchange information with respect to the activities of fishing vessels flying the flags of States which are neither members of the organization nor participants in the arrangement and which are engaged in fishing operations for the relevant stocks. They shall take measures consistent with this Agreement and international law to deter activities of such vessels which undermine the effectiveness of subregional or regional conservation and management measures.

PART V
DUTIES OF THE FLAG STATE

Article 18
Duties of the flag State

1.   A State whose vessels fish on the high seas shall take such measures as may be necessary to ensure that vessels flying its flag comply with subregional and regional conservation and management measures and that such vessels do not engage in any activity which undermines the effectiveness of such measures.

2.   A State shall authorize the use of vessels flying its flag for fishing on the high seas only where it is able to exercise effectively its responsibilities in respect of such vessels under the Convention and this Agreement.

3.   Measures to be taken by a State in respect of vessels flying its flag shall include:

(a)   control of such vessels on the high seas by means of fishing licences, authorizations or permits, in accordance with any applicable procedures agreed at the subregional, regional or global level;

(b)   establishment of regulations:

(i)   to apply terms and conditions to the licence, authorization or permit sufficient to fulfil any subregional, regional or global obligations of the flag State;

(ii) to prohibit fishing on the high seas by vessels which are not duly licensed or authorized to fish, or fishing on the high seas by vessels otherwise than in accordance with the terms and conditions of a licence, authorization or permit;

(iii) to require vessels fishing on the high seas to carry the licence, authorization or permit on board at all times and to produce it on demand for inspection by a duly authorized person; and

(iv) to ensure that vessels flying its flag do not conduct unauthorized fishing within areas under the national jurisdiction of other States;

(c) establishment of a national record of fishing vessels authorized to fish on the high seas and provision of access to the information contained in that record on request by directly interested States, taking into account any national laws of the flag State regarding the release of such information;

(d) requirements for marking of fishing vessels and fishing gear for identification in accordance with uniform and internationally recognizable vessel and gear marking systems, such as the Food and Agriculture Organization of the United Nations Standard Specifications for the Marking and Identification of Fishing Vessels;

(e) requirements for recording and timely reporting of vessel position, catch of target and non-target species, fishing effort and other relevant fisheries data in accordance with subregional, regional and global standards for collection of such data;

(f) requirements for verifying the catch of target and non-target species through such means as observer programmes, inspection schemes, unloading reports, supervision of transshipment and monitoring of landed catches and market statistics;

(g) monitoring, control and surveillance of such vessels, their fishing operations and related activities by, *inter alia*:

(i)   the implementation of national inspection schemes and subregional and regional schemes for co-operation in enforcement pursuant to articles 21 and 22, including requirements for such vessels to permit access by duly authorized inspectors from other States;

(ii) the implementation of national observer programmes and subregional and regional observer programmes in which the flag State is a participant, including requirements for such vessels to permit access by observers from other States to carry out the functions agreed under the programmes; and

(iii) the development and implementation of vessel monitoring systems, including, as appropriate, satellite transmitter systems, in accordance with any national programmes and those which have been subregionally, regionally or globally agreed among the States concerned;

(h) regulation of transshipment on the high seas to ensure that the effectiveness of conservation and management measures is not undermined; and

(i) regulation of fishing activities to ensure compliance with subregional, regional or global measures, including those aimed at minimizing catches of non-target species.

4.   Where there is a subregionally, regionally or globally agreed system of monitoring, control and surveillance in effect, States shall ensure that the measures they impose on vessels flying their flag are compatible with that system.

PART VI
COMPLIANCE AND ENFORCEMENT

Article 19
Compliance and enforcement by the flag State

1.   A State shall ensure compliance by vessels flying its flag with subregional and regional conservation and management measures for straddling fish stocks and highly migratory fish stocks. To this end, that State shall:

(a) enforce such measures irrespective of where violations occur;

(b) investigate immediately and fully any alleged violation of subregional or regional conservation and management measures, which may include the physical inspection of the vessels concerned, and report promptly to the State alleging the violation and the relevant subregional or regional organization or arrangement on the progress and outcome of the investigation;

(c) require any vessel flying its flag to give information to the investigating authority regarding vessel position, catches, fishing gear, fishing operations and related activities in the area of an alleged violation;

(d) if satisfied that sufficient evidence is available in respect of an alleged violation, refer the case to its authorities with a view to instituting proceedings without delay in accordance with its laws and, where appropriate, detain the vessel concerned; and

(e) ensure that, where it has been established, in accordance with its laws, a vessel has been involved in the commission of a serious violation of such measures, the vessel does not engage in fishing operations on the high seas until such time as all outstanding sanctions imposed by the flag State in respect of the violation have been complied with.

2.   All investigations and judicial proceedings shall be carried out expeditiously. Sanctions applicable in respect of violations shall be adequate in severity to be effective in securing compliance and to discourage violations wherever they occur and shall deprive offenders of the benefits accruing from

their illegal activities. Measures applicable in respect of masters and other officers of fishing vessels shall include provisions which may permit, *inter alia*, refusal, withdrawal or suspension of authorizations to serve as masters or officers on such vessels.

Article 20
International co-operation in enforcement

1.   States shall co-operate, either directly or through subregional or regional fisheries management organizations or arrangements, to ensure compliance with and enforcement of subregional and regional conservation and management measures for straddling fish stocks and highly migratory fish stocks.

2.   A flag State conducting an investigation of an alleged violation of conservation and management measures for straddling fish stocks or highly migratory fish stocks may request the assistance of any other State whose co-operation may be useful in the conduct of that investigation. All States shall endeavour to meet reasonable requests made by a flag State in connection with such investigations.

3.   A flag State may undertake such investigations directly, in co-operation with other interested States or through the relevant subregional or regional fisheries management organization or arrangement. Information on the progress and outcome of the investigations shall be provided to all States having aninterest in, or affected by, the alleged violation.

4.   States shall assist each other in identifying vessels reported to have engaged in activities undermining the effectiveness of subregional, regional or global conservation and management measures.

5.   States shall, to the extent permitted by national laws and regulations, establish arrangements for making available to prosecuting authorities in other States evidence relating to alleged violations of such measures.

6.   Where there are reasonable grounds for believing that a vessel on the high seas has been engaged in unauthorized fishing within an area under the jurisdiction of a coastal State, the flag State of that vessel, at the request of the coastal State concerned, shall immediately and fully investigate the matter. The flag State shall co-operate with the coastal State in taking appropriate enforcement action in such cases and may authorize the relevant authorities of the coastal State to board and inspect the vessel on the high seas. This paragraph is without prejudice to article 111 of the Convention.

7.   States Parties which are members of a subregional or regional fisheries management organization or participants in a subregional or regional fisheries management arrangement may take action in accordance with international law, including through recourse to subregional or regional procedures established for this purpose, to deter vessels which have engaged in activities which undermine the effectiveness of or otherwise violate the conservation and management measures established by that organization or arrangement from fishing on the high seas in the subregion or region until such time as appropriate action is taken by the flag State.

Article 21
Subregional and regional co-operation in enforcement

1.   In any high seas area covered by a subregional or regional fisheries management organization or arrangement, a State Party which is a member of such organization or a participant in such arrangement may, through its duly authorized inspectors, board and inspect, in accordance with paragraph 2, fishing vessels flying the flag of another State Party to this Agreement, whether or not such State Party is also a member of the organization or a participant in the arrangement, for the purpose of ensuring compliance with conservation and management measures for straddling fish stocks and highly migratory fish stocks established by that organization or arrangement.

2.   States shall establish, through subregional or regional fisheries management organizations or arrangements, procedures for boarding and inspection pursuant to paragraph 1, as well as procedures to implement other provisions of this article. Such procedures shall be consistent with this article and the basic procedures set out in article 22 and shall not discriminate against non-members of the organization or non-participants in the arrangement. Boarding and inspection as well as any subsequent enforcement action shall be conducted in accordance with such procedures. States shall give due publicity to procedures established pursuant to this paragraph.

3.   If, within two years of the adoption of this Agreement, any organization or arrangement has not established such procedures, boarding and inspection pursuant to paragraph 1, as well as any subsequent enforcement action, shall, pending the establishment of such procedures, be conducted in accordance with this article and the basic procedures set out in article 22.

4.   Prior to taking action under this article, inspecting States shall, either directly or through the relevant subregional or regional fisheries management organization or arrangement, inform all States whose vessels fish on the high seas in the subregion or region of the form of identification issued to their duly authorized inspectors. The vessels used for boarding and inspection shall be clearly marked and identifiable as being on government service. At the time of becoming a Party to this Agreement, a State shall designate an appropriate authority to receive notifications pursuant to this article and shall give due publicity of such designation through the relevant subregional or regional fisheries management organization or arrangement.

5.   Where, following a boarding and inspection, there are clear grounds for believing that a vessel has engaged in any activity contrary to the conservation and management measures referred to in paragraph 1, the inspecting State shall, where appropriate, secure evidence and shall promptly notify the flag State of the alleged violation.

6.   The flag State shall respond to the notification referred to in paragraph 5 within three working days of its receipt, or such other period as may be prescribed in procedures established in accordance with paragraph 2, and shall either:

    (a) fulfil, without delay, its obligations under article 19 to investigate and, if evidence so warrants, take enforcement action with respect to the vessel, in which case it shall promptly inform the inspecting State of the results of the investigation and of any enforcement action taken; or

(b) authorize the inspecting State to investigate.

7.   Where the flag State authorizes the inspecting State to investigate an alleged violation, the inspecting State shall, without delay, communicate the results of that investigation to the flag State. The flag State shall, if evidence so warrants, fulfil its obligations to take enforcement action with respect to the vessel. Alternatively, the flag State may authorize the inspecting State to take such enforcement action as the flag State may specify with respect to the vessel, consistent with the rights and obligations of the flag State under this Agreement.

8.   Where, following boarding and inspection, there are clear grounds for believing that a vessel has committed a serious violation, and the flag State has either failed to respond or failed to take action as required under paragraphs 6 or 7, the inspectors may remain on board and secure evidence and may require the master to assist in further investigation including, where appropriate, by bringing the vessel without delay to the nearest appropriate port, or to such other port as may be specified in procedures established in accordance with paragraph 2. The inspecting State shall immediately inform the flag State of the name of the port to which the vessel is to proceed. The inspecting State and the flag State and, as appropriate, the port State shall take all necessary steps to ensure the well-being of the crew regardless of their nationality.

9.   The inspecting State shall inform the flag State and the relevant organization or the participants in the relevant arrangement of the results of any further investigation.

10. The inspecting State shall require its inspectors to observe generally accepted international regulations, procedures and practices relating to the safety of the vessel and the crew, minimize interference with fishing operations and, to the extent practicable, avoid action which would adversely affect the quality of the catch on board. The inspecting State shall ensure that boarding and inspection is not conducted in a manner that would constitute harassment of any fishing vessel.

11. For the purposes of this article, a serious violation means:

(a) fishing without a valid licence, authorization or permit issued by the flag State in accordance with article 18, paragraph 3 (a);

(b) failing to maintain accurate records of catch and catch-related data, as required by the relevant subregional or regional fisheries management organization or arrangement, or serious misreporting of catch, contrary to the catch reporting requirements of such organization or arrangement;

(c) fishing in a closed area, fishing during a closed season or fishing without, or after attainment of, a quota established by the relevant subregional or regional fisheries management organization or arrangement;

(d) directed fishing for a stock which is subject to a moratorium or for hich fishing is prohibited;

(e) using prohibited fishing gear;

(f) falsifying or concealing the markings, identity or registration of a ishing vessel;

(g) concealing, tampering with or disposing of evidence relating to an investigation;

(h) multiple violations which together constitute a serious disregard of conservation and management measures; or

(i) such other violations as may be specified in procedures established by the relevant subregional or regional fisheries management organization or arrangement.

12. Notwithstanding the other provisions of this article, the flag State may, at any time, take action to fulfil its obligations under article 19 with respect to an alleged violation. Where the vessel is under the direction of the inspecting State, the inspecting State shall, at the request of the flag State, release the vessel to the flag State along with full information on the progress and outcome of its investigation.

13. This article is without prejudice to the right of the flag State to take any measures, including proceedings to impose penalties, according to its laws.

14. This article applies *mutatis mutandis* to boarding and inspection by a State Party which is a member of a subregional or regional fisheries management organization or a participant in a subregional or regional fisheries management arrangement and which has clear grounds for believing that a fishing vessel flying the flag of another State Party has engaged in any activity contrary to relevant conservation and management measures referred to in paragraph 1 in the high seas area covered by such organization or arrangement, and such vessel has subsequently, during the same fishing trip, entered into an area under the national jurisdiction of the inspecting State.

15. Where a subregional or regional fisheries management organization or arrangement has established an alternative mechanism which effectively discharges the obligation under this Agreement of its members or participants to ensure compliance with the conservation and management measures established by the organization or arrangement, members of such organization or participants in such arrangement may agree to limit the application of paragraph 1 as between themselves in respect of the conservation and management measures which have been established in the relevant high seas area.

16. Action taken by States other than the flag State in respect of vessels having engaged in activities contrary to subregional or regional conservation and management measures shall be proportionate to the seriousness of the violation.

17. Where there are reasonable grounds for suspecting that a fishing vessel on the high seas is without nationality, a State may board and inspect the vessel. Where evidence so warrants, the State may take such action as may be appropriate in accordance with international law.

18. States shall be liable for damage or loss attributable to them arising from action taken pursuant to this article when such action is unlawful or exceeds that reasonably required in the light of available information to implement the provisions of this article.

Article 22
*Basic procedures for boarding and inspection pursuant
to article 21*

1. The inspecting State shall ensure that its duly authorized inspectors:

(a) present credentials to the master of the vessel and produce a copy of the text of the relevant conservation and management measures or rules and regulations in force in the high seas area in question pursuant to those measures;

(b) initiate notice to the flag State at the time of the boarding and inspection;

(c) do not interfere with the master's ability to communicate with the authorities of the flag State during the boarding and inspection;

(d) provide a copy of a report on the boarding and inspection to the master and to the authorities of the flag State, noting therein any objection or statement which the master wishes to have included in the report;

(e) promptly leave the vessel following completion of the inspection if they find no evidence of a serious violation; and

(f) avoid the use of force except when and to the degree necessary to ensure the safety of the inspectors and where the inspectors are obstructed in the execution of their duties. The degree of force used shall not exceed that reasonably required in the circumstances.

2. The duly authorized inspectors of an inspecting State shall have the authority to inspect the vessel, its licence, gear, equipment, records, facilities, fish and fish products and any relevant documents necessary to verify compliance with the relevant conservation and management measures.

3. The flag State shall ensure that vessel masters:

(a) accept and facilitate prompt and safe boarding by the inspectors;

(b) co-operate with and assist in the inspection of the vessel conducted pursuant to these procedures;

(c) do not obstruct, intimidate or interfere with the inspectors in the performance of their duties;

(d) allow the inspectors to communicate with the authorities of the flag State and the inspecting State during the boarding and inspection;

(e) provide reasonable facilities, including, where appropriate, food and accommodation, to the inspectors; and

(f) facilitate safe disembarkation by the inspectors.

4. In the event that the master of a vessel refuses to accept boarding and inspection in accordance with this article and article 21, the flag State shall, except in circumstances where, in accordance with generally accepted

international regulations, procedures and practices relating to safety at sea, it is necessary to delay the boarding and inspection, direct the master of the vessel to submit immediately to boarding and inspection and, if the master does

not comply with such direction, shall suspend the vessel's authorization to fish and order the vessel to return immediately to port. The flag State shall advise the inspecting State of the action it has taken when the circumstances referred to in this paragraph arise.

Article 23
Measures taken by a port State

1. A port State has the right and the duty to take measures, in accordance with international law, to promote the effectiveness of subregional, regional and global conservation and management measures. When taking such measures a port State shall not discriminate in form or in fact against the vessels of any State.

2. A port State may, *inter alia*, inspect documents, fishing gear and catch on board fishing vessels, when such vessels are voluntarily in its ports or at its offshore terminals.

3. States may adopt regulations empowering the relevant national authorities to prohibit landings and transshipments where it has been established that the catch has been taken in a manner which undermines the effectiveness of subregional, regional or global conservation and management measures on the high seas.

4. Nothing in this article affects the exercise by States of their sovereignty over ports in their territory in accordance with international law.

PART VII
REQUIREMENTS OF DEVELOPING STATES

Article 24
Recognition of the special requirements of developing States

1. States shall give full recognition to the special requirements of developing States in relation to conservation and management of straddling fish stocks and highly migratory fish stocks and development of fisheries for such stocks. To this end, States shall, either directly or through the United Nations Development Programme, the Food and Agriculture Organization of the United Nations and other specialized agencies, the Global Environment Facility, the Commission on Sustainable Development and other appropriate international and regional organizations and bodies, provide assistance to developing States.

2. In giving effect to the duty to co-operate in the establishment of conservation and management measures for straddling fish stocks and highly migratory fish stocks, States shall take into account the special requirements of developing States, in particular:

(a) the vulnerability of developing States which are dependent on the exploitation of living marine resources, including for meeting the nutritional requirements of their populations or parts thereof;

(b) the need to avoid adverse impacts on, and ensure access to fisheries by, subsistence, small-scale and artisanal fishers and women fishworkers, as well as indigenous people in developing States, particularly small island developing States; and

(c) the need to ensure that such measures do not result in transferring, directly or indirectly, a disproportionate burden of conservation action onto developing States.

Article 25
Forms of co-operation with developing States

1.   States shall co-operate, either directly or through subregional, regional or global organizations:
  (a)   to enhance the ability of developing States, in particular the least-developed among them and small island developing States, to conserve and manage straddling fish stocks and highly migratory fish stocks and to develop their own fisheries for such stocks;
  (b)   to assist developing States, in particular the least-developed among them and small island developing States, to enable them to participate in high seas fisheries for such stocks, including facilitating access to such fisheries subject to articles 5 and 11; and
  (c)   to facilitate the participation of developing States in subregional and regional fisheries management organizations and arrangements.

2.   Cooperation with developing States for the purposes set out in this article shall include the provision of financial assistance, assistance relating to human resources development, technical assistance, transfer of technology, including through joint venture arrangements, and advisory and consultative services.

3.   Such assistance shall, *inter alia*, be directed specifically towards:
  (a)   improved conservation and management of straddling fish stocks and highly migratory fish stocks through collection, reporting, verification, exchange and analysis of fisheries data and related information;
  (b)   stock assessment and scientific research; and
  (c)   monitoring, control, surveillance, compliance and enforcement, including training and capacity-building at the local level, development and funding of national and regional observer programmes and access to technology and equipment.

Article 26
Special assistance in the implementation of this Agreement

1.   States shall co-operate to establish special funds to assist developing States in the implementation of this Agreement, including assisting developing States to meet the costs involved in any proceedings for the settlement of disputes to which they may be parties.

2.   States and international organizations should assist developing States in establishing new subregional or regional fisheries management organizations or arrangements, or in strengthening existing organizations or arrangements, for the conservation and management of straddling fish stocks and highly migratory fish stocks.

PART VIII
PEACEFUL SETTLEMENT OF DISPUTES

Article 27

Obligation to settle disputes by peaceful means

States have the obligation to settle their disputes by negotiation, inquiry, mediation, conciliation, arbitration, judicial settlement, resort to regional agencies or arrangements, or other peaceful means of their own choice.

Article 28
Prevention of disputes

States shall co-operate in order to prevent disputes. To this end, States shall agree on efficient and expeditious decision-making procedures within subregional and regional fisheries management organizations and arrangements and shall strengthen existing decision-making procedures as necessary.

Article 29
Disputes of a technical nature

Where a dispute concerns a matter of a technical nature, the States concerned may refer the dispute to an *ad hoc* expert panel established by them. The panel shall confer with the States concerned and shall endeavour to resolve the dispute expeditiously without recourse to binding procedures for the settlement of disputes.

Article 30
Procedures for the settlement of disputes

1.   The provisions relating to the settlement of disputes set out in Part XV of the Convention apply *mutatis mutandis* to any dispute between States Parties to this Agreement concerning the interpretation or application of this Agreement, whether or not they are also Parties to the Convention.

2.   The provisions relating to the settlement of disputes set out in Part XV of the Convention apply *mutatis mutandis* to any dispute between States Parties to this Agreement concerning the interpretation or application of a subregional, regional or global fisheries agreement relating to straddling fish stocks or highly migratory fish stocks to which they are parties, including any dispute concerning the conservation and management of such stocks, whether or not they are also Parties to the Convention.

3.   Any procedure accepted by a State Party to this Agreement and the Convention pursuant to article 287 of the Convention shall apply to the settlement of

disputes under this Part, unless that State Party, when signing, ratifying or acceding to this Agreement, or at any time thereafter, has accepted another procedure pursuant to article 287 for the settlement of disputes under this Part.

4.   A State Party to this Agreement which is not a Party to the Convention, when signing, ratifying or acceding to this Agreement, or at any time thereafter, shall be free to choose, by means of a written declaration, one or more of the means set out in article 287, paragraph 1, of the Convention for the settlement of disputes under this Part. Article 287 shall apply to such a declaration, as well as to any dispute to which such State is a party which is not covered by a declaration in force. For the purposes of conciliation and arbitration in accordance with Annexes V, VII and VIII to the Convention, such State shall be entitled to nominate conciliators, arbitrators and experts to be included in the lists referred to in Annex V, article 2, Annex VII, article 2, and Annex VIII, article 2, for the settlement of disputes under this Part.

5.   Any court or tribunal to which a dispute has been submitted under this Part shall apply the relevant provisions of the Convention, of this Agreement and of any relevant subregional, regional or global fisheries agreement, as well as generally accepted standards for the conservation and management of living marine resources and other rules of international law not incompatible with the Convention, with a view to ensuring the conservation of the straddling fish stocks and highly migratory fish stocks concerned.

Article 31
Provisional measures

1.   Pending the settlement of a dispute in accordance with this Part, the parties to the dispute shall make every effort to enter into provisional arrangements of a practical nature.

2.   Without prejudice to article 290 of the Convention, the court or tribunal to which the dispute has been submitted under this Part may prescribe any provisional measures which it considers appropriate under the circumstances to preserve the respective rights of the parties to the dispute or to prevent damage to the stocks in question, as well as in the circumstances referred to in article 7, paragraph 5, and article 16, paragraph 2.

3.   A State Party to this Agreement which is not a Party to the Convention may declare that, notwithstanding article 290, paragraph 5, of the Convention, the International Tribunal for the Law of the Sea shall not be entitled to prescribe, modify or revoke provisional measures without the agreement of such State.

Article 32
Limitations on applicability of procedures for the
settlement of disputes

Article 297, paragraph 3, of the Convention applies also to this Agreement.

PART IX
NON-PARTIES TO THIS AGREEMENT

Article 33
Non-parties to this Agreement

1.   States Parties shall encourage non-parties to this Agreement to become parties thereto and to adopt laws and regulations consistent with its provisions.

2.   States Parties shall take measures consistent with this Agreement and international law to deter the activities of vessels flying the flag of non-parties which undermine the effective implementation of this Agreement.

PART X
GOOD FAITH AND ABUSE OF RIGHTS

Article 34
Good faith and abuse of rights

States Parties shall fulfil in good faith the obligations assumed under this Agreement and shall exercise the rights recognized in this Agreement in a manner which would not constitute an abuse of right.

PART XI
RESPONSIBILITY AND LIABILITY

Article 35
Responsibility and liability

States Parties are liable in accordance with international law for damage or loss attributable to them in regard to this Agreement.

PART XII
REVIEW CONFERENCE

Article 36
Review conference

1.   Four years after the date of entry into force of this Agreement, the Secretary-General of the United Nations shall convene a conference with a view to assessing the effectiveness of this Agreement in securing the conservation and management of straddling fish stocks and highly migratory fish stocks. The Secretary-General shall invite to the conference all States Parties and those States and entities which are entitled to become parties to this Agreement as well as those intergovernmental and non-governmental organizations entitled to participate as observers.

2.   The conference shall review and assess the adequacy of the provisions of this Agreement and, if necessary, propose means of strengthening the substance and methods of implementation of those provisions in order better to address any continuing problems in the conservation and management of straddling fish stocks and highly migratory fish stocks.

PART XIII
FINAL PROVISIONS

Article 37
Signature

This Agreement shall be open for signature by all States and the other entities referred to in article 1, paragraph 2(b), and shall remain open for signature at United Nations Headquarters for twelve months from the fourth of December 1995.

Article 38
Ratification

This Agreement is subject to ratification by States and the other entities referred to in article 1, paragraph 2(b). The instruments of ratification shall be deposited with the Secretary-General of the United Nations.

Article 39
Accession

This Agreement shall remain open for accession by States and the other entities referred to in article 1, paragraph 2(b). The instruments of accession shall be deposited with the Secretary-General of the United Nations.

Article 40
Entry into force

1.   This Agreement shall enter into force 30 days after the date of deposit of the thirtieth instrument of ratification or accession.

2.   For each State or entity which ratifies the Agreement or accedes thereto after the deposit of the thirtieth instrument of ratification or accession, this Agreement shall enter into force on the thirtieth day following the deposit of its instrument of ratification or accession.

Article 41
Provisional application

1.   This Agreement shall be applied provisionally by a State or entity which consents to its provisional application by so notifying the depositary in writing. Such provisional application shall become effective from the date of receipt of the notification.

2.   Provisional application by a State or entity shall terminate upon the entry into force of this Agreement for that State or entity or upon notification by that State or entity to the depositary in writing of its intention to terminate provisional application.

Article 42
Reservations and exceptions

No reservations or exceptions may be made to this Agreement.

Article 43
Declarations and statements

Article 42 does not preclude a State or entity, when signing, ratifying or acceding to this Agreement, from making declarations or statements, however phrased or named, with a view, *inter alia*, to the harmonization of its laws and regulations with the provisions of this Agreement, provided that such declarations or statements do not purport to exclude or to modify the legal effect of the provisions of this Agreement in their application to that State or entity.

Article 44
Relation to other agreements

1.   This Agreement shall not alter the rights and obligations of States Parties which arise from other agreements compatible with this Agreement and which do not affect the enjoyment by other States Parties of their rights or the performance of their obligations under this Agreement.

2.   Two or more States Parties may conclude agreements modifying or suspending the operation of provisions of this Agreement, applicable solely to the relations between them, provided that such agreements do not relate to a provision derogation from which is incompatible with the effective execution of the object and purpose of this Agreement, and provided further that such agreements shall not affect the application of the basic principles embodied herein, and that the provisions of such agreements do not affect the enjoyment by other States Parties of their rights or the performance of their obligations under this Agreement.

3.   States Parties intending to conclude an agreement referred to in paragraph 2 shall notify the other States Parties through the depositary of this Agreement of their intention to conclude the agreement and of the modification or suspension for which it provides.

Article 45
Amendment

1.   A State Party may, by written communication addressed to the Secretary-General of the United Nations, propose amendments to this Agreement and

request the convening of a conference to consider such proposed amendments. The Secretary-General shall circulate such communication to all States Parties. If, within six months from the date of the circulation of the communication, not less than one half of the States Parties reply favourably to the request, the Secretary-General shall convene the conference.

2.   The decision-making procedure applicable at the amendment conference convened pursuant to paragraph 1 shall be the same as that applicable at the United Nations Conference on Straddling Fish Stocks and Highly Migratory Fish Stocks, unless otherwise decided by the conference. The conference should make every effort to reach agreement on any amendments by way of consensus and there should be no voting on them until all efforts at consensus have been exhausted.

3.   Once adopted, amendments to this Agreement shall be open for signature at United Nations Headquarters by States Parties for twelve months from the date of adoption, unless otherwise provided in the amendment itself.

4.   Articles 38, 39, 47 and 50 apply to all amendments to this Agreement.

5.   Amendments to this Agreement shall enter into force for the States Parties ratifying or acceding to them on the thirtieth day following the deposit of instruments of ratification or accession by two thirds of the States Parties.

Thereafter, for each State Party ratifying or acceding to an amendment after the deposit of the required number of such instruments, the amendment shall enter into force on the thirtieth day following the deposit of its instrument of ratification or accession.

6.   An amendment may provide that a smaller or a larger number of ratifications or accessions shall be required for its entry into force than are required by this article.

7.   A State which becomes a Party to this Agreement after the entry into force of amendments in accordance with paragraph 5 shall, failing an expression of a different intention by that State:

(a)   be considered as a Party to this Agreement as so amended; and

(b)   be considered as a Party to the unamended Agreement in relation to any State Party not bound by the amendment.

Article 46
Denunciation

1.   A State Party may, by written notification addressed to the Secretary-General of the United Nations, denounce this Agreement and may indicate its reasons. Failure to indicate reasons shall not affect the validity of the denunciation. The denunciation shall take effect one year after the date of receipt of the notification, unless the notification specifies a later date.

2.   The denunciation shall not in any way affect the duty of any State Party to fulfil any obligation embodied in this Agreement to which it would be subject under international law independently of this Agreement.

Article 47
Participation by international organizations

1.   In cases where an international organization referred to in Annex IX, article 1, of the Convention does not have competence over all the matters governed by this Agreement, Annex IX to the Convention shall apply *mutatis mutandis* to participation by such international organization in this Agreement, except that the following provisions of that Annex shall not apply:

(a)   article 2, first sentence; and

(b)   article 3, paragraph 1.

2.   In cases where an international organization referred to in Annex IX, article 1, of the Convention has competence over all the matters governed by this Agreement, the following provisions shall apply to participation by such international organization in this Agreement:

(a)   at the time of signature or accession, such international organization shall make a declaration stating:

(i)   that it has competence over all the matters governed by this Agreement;

(ii)   that, for this reason, its member States shall not become States Parties, except in respect of their territories for which the international organization has no responsibility; and

(iii) that it accepts the rights and obligations of States under this Agreement;

(b)   participation of such an international organization shall in no case confer any rights under this Agreement on member States of the international organization;

(c)   in the event of a conflict between the obligations of an international organization under this Agreement and its obligations under the agreement establishing the international organization or any acts relating to it, the obligations under this Agreement shall prevail.

Article 48
Annexes

1.   The Annexes form an integral part of this Agreement and, unless expressly provided otherwise, a reference to this Agreement or to one of its Parts includes a reference to the Annexes relating thereto.

2.   The Annexes may be revised from time to time by States Parties. Such revisions shall be based on scientific and technical considerations. Notwithstanding the provisions of article 45, if a revision to an Annex is adopted by consensus at a meeting of States Parties, it shall be incorporated in this Agreement and shall take effect from the date of its adoption or from such other date as may be specified in the revision. If a revision to an Annex is not adopted by consensus at such a meeting, the amendment procedures set out in article 45 shall apply.

Article 49
Depositary

The Secretary-General of the United Nations shall be the depositary of this Agreement and any amendments or revisions thereto.

Article 50
Authentic texts

The Arabic, Chinese, English, French, Russian and Spanish texts of this Agreement are equally authentic.

IN WITNESS WHEREOF, the undersigned Plenipotentiaries, being duly authorized thereto, have signed this Agreement.

OPENED FOR SIGNATURE at New York, this fourth day of December, one thousand nine hundred and ninety-five, in a single original, in the Arabic, Chinese, English, French, Russian and Spanish languages.

ANNEX I

STANDARD REQUIREMENTS FOR THE COLLECTION AND SHARING OF DATA

Article 1
General principles

1.   The timely collection, compilation and analysis of data are fundamental to the effective conservation and management of straddling fish stocks and highly migratory fish stocks. To this end, data from fisheries for these stocks on the high seas and those in areas under national jurisdiction are required and should be collected and compiled in such a way as to enable statistically meaningful analysis for the purposes of fishery resource conservation and management. These data include catch and fishing effort statistics and other fishery-related information, such as vessel-related and other data for standardizing fishing effort. Data collected should also include information on non-target and associated or dependent species. All data should be verified to ensure accuracy. Confidentiality of non-aggregated data shall be maintained. The dissemination of such data shall be subject to the terms on which they have been provided.

2.   Assistance, including training as well as financial and technical assistance, shall be provided to developing States in order to build capacity in the field of conservation and management of living marine resources. Assistance should focus on enhancing capacity to implement data collection and verification, observer programmes, data analysis and research projects supporting stock assessments. The fullest possible involvement of developing State scientists and managers in conservation and management of straddling fish stocks and highly migratory fish stocks should be promoted.

Article 2
Principles of data collection, compilation and exchange

The following general principles should be considered in defining the parameters for collection, compilation and exchange of data from fishing operations for straddling fish stocks and highly migratory fish stocks:

(a)   States should ensure that data are collected from vessels flying their flag on fishing activities according to the operational characteristics of each fishing method (e.g., each individual tow for trawl, each set for longline and purse-seine, each school fished for pole-and-line and each day fished for troll) and in sufficient detail to facilitate effective stock assessment;

(b)   States should ensure that fishery data are verified through an appropriate system;

(c)   States should compile fishery-related and other supporting scientific data and provide them in an agreed format and in a timely manner to the relevant subregional or regional fisheries management organization or arrangement where one exists. Otherwise, States should co-operate to exchange data either directly or through such other co-operative mechanisms as may be agreed among them;

(d) States should agree, within the framework of subregional or regional fisheries management organizations or arrangements, or otherwise, on the specification of data and the format in which they are to be provided, in accordance with this Annex and taking into account the nature of the stocks and the fisheries for those stocks in the region. Such organizations or arrangements should request non-members or non-participants to provide data concerning relevant fishing activities by vessels flying their flag;

(e) such organizations or arrangements shall compile data and make them available in a timely manner and in an agreed format to all interested States under the terms and conditions established by the organization or arrangement; and

(f) scientists of the flag State and from the relevant subregional or regional fisheries management organization or arrangement should analyse the data separately or jointly, as appropriate.

Article 3
Basic fishery data

1.   States shall collect and make available to the relevant subregional or regional fisheries management organization or arrangement the following types of data in sufficient detail to facilitate effective stock assessment in accordance with agreed procedures:

(a) time series of catch and effort statistics by fishery and fleet;

(b) total catch in number, nominal weight, or both, by species (both target and non-target) as is appropriate to each fishery. [Nominal weight is defined by the Food and Agriculture Organization of the United Nations as the live-weight equivalent of the landings];

(c) discard statistics, including estimates where necessary, reported as number or nominal weight by species, as is appropriate to each fishery;

(d) effort statistics appropriate to each fishing method; and

(e) fishing location, date and time fished and other statistics on fishing operations as appropriate.

2.   States shall also collect where appropriate and provide to the relevant subregional or regional fisheries management organization or arrangement information to support stock assessment, including:

(a) composition of the catch according to length, weight and sex;

(b) other biological information supporting stock assessments, such as information on age, growth, recruitment, distribution and stock identity; and

(c) other relevant research, including surveys of abundance, biomass surveys, hydro-acoustic surveys, research on environmental factors affecting stock abundance, and oceanographic and ecological studies.

Article 4
Vessel data and information

1. States should collect the following types of vessel-related data for standardizing fleet composition and vessel fishing power and for converting between different measures of effort in the analysis of catch and effort data:

(a) vessel identification, flag and port of registry;

(b) vessel type;

(c) vessel specifications (e.g., material of construction, date built, registered length, gross registered tonnage, power of main engines, hold capacity and catch storage methods); and

(d) fishing gear description (e.g., types, gear specifications and quantity).

2. The flag State will collect the following information:

(a) navigation and position fixing aids;

(b) communication equipment and international radio call sign; and

(c) crew size.

Article 5
Reporting

A State shall ensure that vessels flying its flag send to its national fisheries administration and, where agreed, to the relevant subregional or regional fisheries management organization or arrangement, logbook data on catch and effort, including data on fishing operations on the high seas, at sufficiently frequent intervals to meet national requirements and regional and international obligations. Such data shall be transmitted, where necessary, by radio, telex, facsimile or satellite transmission or by other means.

Article 6
Data verification

States or, as appropriate, subregional or regional fisheries management organizations or arrangements should establish mechanisms for verifying fishery data, such as:

(a) position verification through vessel monitoring systems;

(b) scientific observer programmes to monitor catch, effort, catch composition (target and non-target) and other details of fishing operations;

(c) vessel trip, landing and transshipment reports; and

(d) port sampling.

Article 7
Data exchange

1. Data collected by flag States must be shared with other flag States and relevant coastal States through appropriate subregional or regional fisheries management organizations or arrangements. Such organizations or arrangements shall

compile data and make them available in a timely manner and in an agreed format to all interested States under the terms and conditions established by the organization or arrangement, while maintaining confidentiality of non-aggregated data, and should, to the extent feasible, develop database systems which provide efficient access to data.

2.   At the global level, collection and dissemination of data should be effected through the Food and Agriculture Organization of the United Nations. Where a subregional or regional fisheries management organization or arrangement does not exist, that organization may also do the same at the subregional or regional level by arrangement with the States concerned.

ANNEX II

GUIDELINES FOR THE APPLICATION OF PRECAUTIONARY REFERENCE POINTS IN CONSERVATION AND MANAGEMENT OF STRADDLING FISH STOCKS AND HIGHLY MIGRATORY FISH STOCKS

1.   A precautionary reference point is an estimated value derived through an agreed scientific procedure, which corresponds to the state of the resource and of the fishery, and which can be used as a guide for fisheries management.

2.   Two types of precautionary reference points should be used: conservation, or limit, reference points and management, or target, reference points. Limit reference points set boundaries which are intended to constrain harvesting within safe biological limits within which the stocks can produce maximum sustainable yield. Target reference points are intended to meet management objectives.

3.   Precautionary reference points should be stock-specific to account, *inter alia*, for the reproductive capacity, the resilience of each stock and the characteristics of fisheries exploiting the stock, as well as other sources of mortality and major sources of uncertainty.

4.   Management strategies shall seek to maintain or restore populations of harvested stocks, and where necessary associated or dependent species, at levels consistent with previously agreed precautionary reference points. Such reference points shall be used to trigger pre-agreed conservation and management action. Management strategies shall include measures which can be implemented when precautionary reference points are approached.

5.   Fishery management strategies shall ensure that the risk of exceeding limit reference points is very low. If a stock falls below a limit reference point or is at risk of falling below such a reference point, conservation and management action should be initiated to facilitate stock recovery. Fishery management strategies shall ensure that target reference points are not exceeded on average.

6.   When information for determining reference points for a fishery is poor or absent, provisional reference points shall be set. Provisional reference points

may be established by analogy to similar and better-known stocks. In such situations, the fishery shall be subject to enhanced monitoring so as to enable revision of provisional reference points as improved information becomes available.

7. The fishing mortality rate which generates maximum sustainable yield should be regarded as a minimum standard for limit reference points. For stocks which are not overfished, fishery management strategies shall ensure that fishing mortality does not exceed that which corresponds to maximum sustainable yield, and that the biomass does not fall below a predefined threshold. For overfished stocks, the biomass which would produce maximum sustainable yield can serve as a rebuilding target.

• • • • • • • •

FINAL ACT OF THE THIRD UNITED NATIONS CONFERENCE ON THE LAW OF THE SEA

INTRODUCTION

1.   The General Assembly of the United Nations on 17 December 1970 adopted resolution 2749 (XXV) containing the Declaration of Principles Governing the Seabed and the Ocean Floor, and the Subsoil Thereof, beyond the Limits of National Jurisdiction and resolution 2750 C (XXV) on the same date, wherein it decided to convene, in 1973, a Conference on the Law of the Sea, which would deal with the establishment of an equitable international régime—including an international machinery—for the area and the resources of the seabed and ocean floor, and the subsoil thereof, beyond the limits of national jurisdiction, with a precise definition of that area and with a broad range of related issues including those concerning the regimes of the high seas, the continental shelf, the territorial sea (including the question of its breadth and the question of international straits) and contiguous zone, fishing and conservation of the living resources of the high seas (including the question of the preferential rights of coastal States) , the preservation of the marine environment (including, *inter alia*, the prevention of pollution) and scientific research.

2.   Prior to the adoption of these resolutions, the General Assembly had considered the item introduced in 1967 on the initiative of the Government of Malta[1] and had subsequently adopted the following resolutions on the question of the reservation exclusively for peaceful purposes of the seabed and the ocean floor, and the subsoil thereof, underlying the high seas beyond the limits of present national jurisdiction, and the use of their resources in the interests of mankind:

Resolution 2340 (XXII) on 18 December 1967,

Resolution 2467 (XXIII) on 21 December 1968, and

Resolution 2574 (XXIV) on 15 December 1969.

3.   The General Assembly, by resolution 2340 (XXII), established an *Ad Hoc* Committee to Study the Peaceful Uses of the Seabed and the Ocean Floor beyond the Limits of National Jurisdiction and, having considered its report,[2] established by resolution 2467 A (XXIII) the Committee on the Peaceful Uses of the Seabed and the Ocean Floor beyond the Limits of National Jurisdiction. The General Assembly, by resolution 2750 C (XXV), enlarged that Committee and requested it to prepare draft treaty articles and a comprehensive list of items and matters for the Conference on the Law of the Sea. The Committee as thus constituted held six sessions, and a number of additional meetings, between 1971 and

1973 at United Nations Headquarters in New York and at the Office of the United Nations in Geneva. Having considered its report,[3] the General Assembly requested the Secretary-General by resolution 2574 A (XXIV) to ascertain the views of Member States on the desirability of convening, at an early date, a Conference on the Law of the Sea.

4.   Subsequent to the adoption of resolutions 2749 (XXV) and 2750 (XXV), the General Assembly, having considered the relevant reports of the Committee,[4] adopted the following resolutions on the same question:

Resolution 2881 (XXVI) on 21 December 1971,

Resolution 3029 (XXVII) on 18 December 1972, and

Resolution 3067 (XXVIII) on 16 November 1973.

5.   By resolution 3029 A (XXVII) the General Assembly requested the Secretary-General to convene the first and second sessions of the Third United Nations Conference on the Law of the Sea. The Secretary-General was authorized, in consultation with the Chairman of the Committee, to make such arrangements as might be necessary for the efficient organization and administration of the Conference and the Committee, and to provide the assistance that might be required in legal, economic, technical and scientific matters. The specialized agencies, the International Atomic Energy Agency and other intergovernmental organizations were invited to co-operate fully with the Secretary-General in the preparations for the Conference and to send observers to the Conference.[5] The Secretary-General was requested, subject to approval by the Conference, to invite interested non-governmental organizations having consultative status with the Economic and Social Council to send observers to the Conference.

6.   By resolution 3067 (XXVIII) the General Assembly decided that the mandate of the Conference was the adoption of a Convention dealing with all matters relating to the Law of the Sea, taking into account the subject matter listed in paragraph 2 of General Assembly resolution 2750 C (XXV) and the list of subjects and issues relating to the Law of the Sea formally approved by the Committee, and bearing in mind that the problems of ocean space were closely interrelated and needed to be considered as a whole. By the same resolution, the General Assembly also decided to convene the first session of the Conference in New York from 3 to 14 December 1973 for the purpose of dealing with organizational matters, including the election of officers, the adoption of the agenda and rules of procedure of the Conference, the establishment of subsidiary organs and the allocation of work to these organs, and any other purpose within its mandate. The second session was to be held in Caracas, at the invitation of the Government of Venezuela, from 20 June to 29 August 1974 to deal with the substantive work of the Conference and, if necessary, any subsequent session, or sessions, were to be convened as might be decided upon by the Conference and approved by the Assembly.

I. SESSIONS

7.   In accordance with that decision and subsequently either on the recommendation of the Conference as approved by the General Assembly, or in

accordance with decisions of the Conferences, the sessions of the Third United Nations Conference on the Law of the Sea were held as follows:

- First session held at United Nations Headquarters in New York, 3 to 15 December 1973;
- Second session held at Parque Central, Caracas, 20 June to 29 August 1974;
- Third session held at the Office of the United Nations in Geneva, 17 March to 9 May 1975;[6]
- Fourth session held at United Nations Headquarters in New York, 15 March to 7 May 1976;[7]
- Fifth session held at United Nations Headquarters in New York, 2 August to 17 September 1976;[8]
- Sixth session held at United Nations Headquarters in New York, 23 May to 15 July 1977;[9]
- Seventh session held at the Office of the United Nations in Geneva, 28 March to 19 May 1978;[10]
- Resumed seventh session held at United Nations Headquarters in New York, 21 August to 15 September 1978;[11]
- Eighth session held at the Office of the United Nations in Geneva, 19 March to 27 April 1979;[12]
- Resumed eighth session held at United Nations Headquarters in New York, 19 July to 24 August 1979;[13]
- Ninth session held at United Nations Headquarters in New York, 3 March to 4 April 1980;[14]
- Resumed ninth session held at the Office of the United Nations in Geneva, 28 July to 29 August 1980;[15]
- Tenth session, held at United Nations Headquarters in New York, 9 March to 24 April 1981;[16]
- Resumed tenth session held at the Office of the United Nations in Geneva, 3 to 28 August 1981;[17]
- Eleventh session held at United Nations Headquarters in New York, 8 March to 30 April 1982;[18]
- Resumed eleventh session held at United Nations Headquarters in New York, 22 to 24 September 1982.[19, 19 bis]

II. PARTICIPATION IN THE CONFERENCE

8.   Having regard to the desirability of achieving universality of participation in the Conference, the General Assembly decided by resolution 3067 (XXVIII) to request the Secretary-General to invite States Members of the United Nations or members of the specialized agencies or the International Atomic Energy Agency and States parties to the Statute of the International Court of Justice, as well as the following States, to participate in the Conference: the Republic of Guinea-Bissau and the Democratic Republic of Viet Nam.

Participating at the sessions of the Conference were the delegations of: Afghanistan, Albania, Algeria, Angola, Antigua and Barbuda, Argentina, Australia, Austria, Bahamas, Bahrain, Bangladesh, Barbados, Belgium, Benin, Bhutan, Bolivia, Botswana, Brazil, Bulgaria, Burma, Burundi, Byelorussian Soviet Socialist Republic, Canada, Cape Verde, Central African Republic, Chad, Chile, China, Colombia, Comoros, Congo, Costa Rica, Cuba, Cyprus, Czechoslovakia, Democratic Kampuchea, Democratic People's Republic of Korea, Democratic Yemen, Denmark, Djibouti, Dominica, Dominican Republic, Ecuador, Egypt, El Salvador, Equatorial Guinea, Ethiopia, Fiji, Finland, France, Gabon, Gambia, German Democratic Republic, Germany, Federal Republic of, Ghana, Greece, Grenada, Guatemala, Guinea, Guinea-Bissau, Guyana, Haiti, Holy See, Honduras, Hungary, Iceland, India, Indonesia, Iran, Iraq, Ireland, Israel, Italy, Ivory Coast, Jamaica, Japan, Jordan, Kenya, Kuwait, Lao People's Democratic Republic, Lebanon, Lesotho, Liberia, Libyan Arab Jamahiriya, Liechtenstein, Luxembourg, Madagascar, Malawi, Malaysia, Maldives, Mali, Malta, Mauritania, Mauritius, Mexico, Monaco, Mongolia, Morocco, Mozambique, Nauru, Nepal, Netherlands, New Zealand, Nicaragua, Niger, Nigeria, Norway, Oman, Pakistan, Panama, Papua New Guinea, Paraguay, Peru, Philippines, Poland, Portugal, Qatar, Republic of Korea, Romania, Rwanda, Saint Lucia, Saint Vincent and the Grenadines, Samoa, San Marino, Sao Tome and Principe, Saudi Arabia, Senegal, Seychelles, Sierra Leone, Singapore, Solomon Islands, Somalia, South Africa, Spain, Sri Lanka, Sudan, Suriname, Swaziland, Sweden, Switzerland, Syrian Arab Republic, Thailand, Togo, Tonga, Trinidad and Tobago, Tunisia, Turkey, Uganda, Ukrainian Soviet Socialist Republic, Union of Soviet Socialist Republics, United Arab Emirates, United Kingdom of Great Britain and Northern Ireland, United Republic of Cameroon, United Republic of Tanzania, United States of America, Upper Volta, Uruguay, Venezuela, Viet Nam, Yemen, Yugoslavia, Zaire, Zambia and Zimbabwe.[20]

9.   The Secretary-General was also requested by resolution 3067 (XXVIII) to invite interested intergovernmental and non-governmental organizations, as well as the United Nations Council for Namibia, to participate in the Conference as observers.

The specialized agencies and inter-governmental organizations participating as observers at the several sessions or the Conference are listed in the appendix hereto.

10.   On the recommendation of the Conference, by resolution 3334 (XXIX), adopted on 17 December 1974, the General Assembly requested the Secretary-General to invite Papua New Guinea, the Cook Islands, the Netherlands Antilles, Niue, Suriname, the West Indies Associated States and the Trust Territory of the Pacific Islands to attend future sessions or the Conference as observers or, if any of them became independent, to attend as a participating State.

The States and Territories participating as observers at the several sessions of the Conference are also listed in the appendix hereto.

11.   The Conference decided on 11 July 1974 to extend invitations to national liberation movements, recognized by the Organization or African Unity and the League or Arab States in their respective regions, to participate in its proceedings as observers.[21]

The national liberation movements participating as observers at the several sessions of the Conference are also listed in the appendix hereto.

12. Consequent upon General Assembly resolution 34/92, the Conference decided on 6 March 1980[22] that Namibia, represented by the United Nations Council for Namibia, should participate in the Conference in accordance with the relevant decisions of the General Assembly.

III. OFFICERS AND COMMITTEES

13. The Conference elected Hamilton Shirley Amerasinghe (Sri Lanka) as its President. Subsequently, at its seventh session, the Conference confirmed that he was, and continued to be the President of the Conference although he was no longer a member of his national delegation.[23] On the death of Hamilton Shirley Amerasinghe on 4 December 1980, the Conference paid tribute to his memory at a special commemorative meeting on 17 March 1981 at its tenth session (A/CONF.62/SR.144).[24]

14. The Secretary-General of the United Nations opened the tenth session as temporary President. The Conference elected Tommy T. B. Koh (Singapore) as President on 13 March 1981.[25]

15. The Conference decided that the Chairmen and Rapporteurs of the three Main Committees, the Chairman of the Drafting Committee, and the Rapporteur-General of the Conference would be elected in a personal capacity and that the Vice-Presidents, the Vice-Chairmen of the Main Committees and the members of the Drafting Committee should be elected by country.[26]

16. The Conference elected as Vice-Presidents, the representatives of the following States: Algeria; Belgium, replaced by Ireland during alternate sessions (by agreement of the regional group concerned); Bolivia; Chile; China; Dominican Republic; Egypt; France; Iceland; Indonesia; Iran; Iraq; Kuwait; Liberia; Madagascar; Nepal; Nigeria; Norway; Pakistan; Peru; Poland; Singapore, replaced by Sri Lanka at the tenth session (by agreement of the regional group concerned); Trinidad and Tobago; Tunisia; Uganda; Union of Soviet Socialist Republics; United Kingdom of Great Britain and Northern Ireland; United States of America; Yugoslavia; Zaire and Zambia.

17. The following Committees were set up by the Conference: the General Committee; the three Main Committees; the Drafting Committee and the Credentials Committee. The assignment of subjects to the plenary and each of the Main Committees was set out in section III of document A/CONF.62/29.

The General Committee consisted of the President of the Conference as its Chairman, the Vice-Presidents, the officers of the Main Committees, and the Rapporteur-General. The Chairman of the Drafting Committee had the right to participate in the meeting of the General Committee without the right to vote.[27]

The Conference elected the following officers for the three Main Committees which were constituted by all States represented at the Conference:

First Committee
    Chairman — Paul Bamela Engo (United Republic of Cameroon)

    Vice-Chairmen — The representatives of Brazil, the German Democratic Republic and Japan

    Rapporteur

First and second sessions	H. C. Mott (Australia)
Third to tenth sessions	John Bailey (Australia)
Eleventh session	Keith Brennan (Australia)

Second Committee
    Chairman

First and second sessions	Andrés Aguilar (Venezuela)
Third session	Reynaldo Galindo Pohl (El Salvador) (by agreement of the regional group concerned)
Fourth to eleventh sessions	Andrés Aguilar (Venezuela)
Vice-Chairmen	The representatives of Czechoslovakia, Kenya and Turkey
Rapporteur	Satya Nandan (Fiji)

Third Committee
Chairman	Alexander Yankov (Bulgaria)
Vice-Chairmen	The representatives of Colombia, Cyprus and the Federal Republic of Germany

    Rapporteur

First and second sessions	Abdel Magied A. Hassan (Sudan)
Third session	Manyang d' Awol (Sudan)
Fourth and fifth sessions	Abdel Magied A. Hassan (Sudan)
Fifth to eleventh sessions	Manyang d' Awol (Sudan)

The Conference elected the following officer and members of the Drafting Committee:

Drafting Committee
Chairman	J. Alan Beesley (Canada)
Members	The representatives of: Afghanistan; Argentina; Bangladesh (alternating with Thailand every year) ; Ecuador; El Salvador (replaced by Venezuela for the duration of the third session by agreement of the regional group

concerned) ; Ghana; India; Italy; Lesotho; Malaysia; Mauritania; Mauritius; Mexico; Netherlands (alternating with Austria every session) ; Philippines; Romania; Sierra Leone; Spain; Syrian Arab Republic; Union of Soviet Socialist Republics; United Republic of Tanzania and United States of America.

The Conference elected the following officers and members of the Credentials Committee:

Credentials Committee
    Chairman

First session	Heinrich Gleissner (Austria)
Second and third sessions	Franz Weidinger (Austria)
Fourth to eleventh sessions	Karl Wolf (Austria)
Members	The representatives of:
	Austria; Chad; China; Costa Rica;
	Hungary; Ireland; Ivory Coast;
	Japan and Uruguay.

Kenneth Rattray (Jamaica) was elected Rapporteur-General of the Conference.

18. The Secretary-General of the United Nations as Secretary-General of the Conference was represented by Constantin Stavropoulos, Under-Secretary-General, at the first and second sessions. Thereafter Bernardo Zuleta, Under-Secretary-General, represented the Secretary-General. David L. D. Hall was Executive Secretary of the Conference.

19. The General Assembly, by its resolution 3067 (XXVIII) convening the Conference, referred to it the reports and documents of the Committee on the Peaceful Uses of the Seabed and the Ocean Floor beyond the Limits of National Jurisdiction and the relevant documentation of the General Assembly. At the commencement of the Conference the following documentation was also before it:

(a) The provisional agenda or the first session of the Conference (A/ CONF.62/1);

(b) The draft rules of procedure prepared by the Secretary-General (A/ CONF.62/2 and Add.1-3), containing an appendix which embodied the "Gentleman's Agreement", approved by the General Assembly at its twenty-eighth session on 16 November 1973.

Subsequently, the Conference also had before it the following documentation:

(i) The proposals submitted by the delegations participating in the Conference, as shown in the *Official Records* of the Conference;

    (ii) The reports and studies prepared by the Secretary-General;[28]

    (iii) The informal negotiating texts and the draft Convention on the Law of the Sea and related draft resolutions and decision drawn up by the Conference as hereafter set out.

IV. DRAFTING COMMITTEE

20. The Drafting Committee commenced its work at the seventh session of the Conference with the informal examination of negotiating texts, for the purposes of refining drafts, harmonizing recurring words and expressions and achieving, through textual review, concordance of the text of the Convention in the six languages. The Committee was assisted in its informal work by six language groups comprising both members and non-members of the Drafting committee, representing the six official languages of the Conference each group being chaired by a co-ordinator[29] and assisted by Secretariat linguistic experts. The co-ordinators, under the direction of the Chairman of the Drafting Committee, performed the major task of harmonizing the views of the language groups and of preparing proposals for the Drafting Committee, through meetings open to both members and non-members of the Drafting Committee. In addition to the meetings held during the regular sessions of the Conference, the Committee held intersessional meetings as follows:

— At United Nations Headquarters In New York, from 9 to 27 June 1980;
— At United Nations Headquarters in New York, from 12 January to 27 February 1981;
— At the Office of the United Nations in Geneva, from 29 June to 31 July 1981;
— At United Nations Headquarters in New York, from 18 January to 26 February 1982;
— At the Office of the United Nations in Geneva, from 12 July to 25 August 1982.

The Drafting Committee presented a first series of reports concerning the harmonization of recurring words and expressions.[30] The Committee presented a second series of reports containing recommendations arising out of the textual review of the Convention.[31]

V. RULES OF PROCEDURE AND CONDUCT OF NEGOTIATIONS

21. The Conference adopted its rules of procedure (A/CONF.62/30) at its second session.[32] The declaration incorporating the "Gentleman's Agreement" approved by the General Assembly,[33] made by the President and endorsed by the Conference,[34] was appended to the rules of procedure. The declaration provided that:

"Bearing in mind that the problems of ocean space are closely interrelated and need to be considered as a whole and the desirability of adopting a Convention on the Law of the Sea which will secure the widest possible acceptance,

"The Conference should make every effort to reach agreement on substantive matters by way of consensus and there should be no voting on such matters until all efforts at consensus have been exhausted."

22. The rules of procedure were subsequently amended by the Conference on 12 July 1974,[35] on 17 March 1975[36] and on 6 March 1980.[37]

23. At its second session,[38] the Conference determined the competence of the three Main Committees by allocating to the plenary or the Committees the subjects and issues on the list prepared in accordance with General Assembly resolution 2750 C (XXV) (A/CONF.62/29). The Main Committees established informal working groups or other subsidiary bodies which assisted the Committees in their work.[39]

24. At the third session, at the request of the Conference, the Chairmen of the three Main Committees each prepared a single negotiating text covering the subjects entrusted to the respective Committee which together constituted the Informal Single Negotiating Text (A/CONF.62/WP.8, Parts I, II and III), the nature of which is described in the introductory note by the President. Subsequently, the President of the Conference, taking into consideration the allocation of subjects and issues to the plenary and the Main Committees submitted a single negotiating text on the subject of settlement of disputes (A/CONF.62/WP.9).

25. At the fourth session of the Conference, following a general debate in the plenary on the subject, as recorded in A/CONF.62/SR.58 to SR.65, at the request of the Conference[40] the President prepared a revised text on the settlement of disputes (A/CONF.62/WP.9/Rev.1) which constituted Part IV of the Informal Single Negotiating Text in document A/CONF.62/WP.8. At the same session, the Chairmen of the Main Committees each prepared a revised Single Negotiating Text (A/CONF.62/WP.8/Rev.1, Parts I to III) and the note by the President which is attached to the text describes its nature.

26. During the fifth session, at the request of the Conference,[41] the President prepared a revised single negotiating text on the settlement of disputes (A/CONF.62/WP.9/Rev.2), which constituted the fourth part of the Revised Single Negotiating Text (A/CONF.62/WP.8/Rev .1) .

27. At its sixth session,[42] the Conference requested the President and the Chairmen of the Main Committees, working under the President's leadership as a team with which the Chairman of the Drafting Committee and the Rapporteur-General were associated,[43] which was subsequently referred to as "the Collegium",[44] to prepare an Informal Composite Negotiating Text (A/CONF.62/WP.10), covering the entire range of subjects and issues contained in Parts I to IV of the Revised Single Negotiating Text. The nature of the composite text so prepared was described in the President's memorandum (A/CONF.62/WP.10 Add.1).

28. At its seventh session, the Conference identified certain outstanding core issues and established seven negotiating groups (as recorded in A/CONF.62/62) for the purpose of resolving these issues.[45] Each group comprised a nucleus of countries principally concerned with the outstanding core issue, but was open-ended.

The Chairmen of the Negotiating Groups were:

Negotiating Group on item 1	Francis X. Njenga (Kenya)
Negotiating Group on item 2	Tommy T. B. Koh (Singapore)
Negotiating Group on item 3	Paul Bamela Engo (United Republic of Cameroon), Chairman of the First Committee

Negotiating Group on item 4	Satya N. Nandan (Fiji)
Negotiating Group on item 5	Constantin A. Stavropoulos (Greece)
Negotiating Group on item 6	Andrés Aguilar (Venezuela) , Chairman of the Second Committee
Negotiating Group on item 7	E. J. Manner (Finland)

The Chairmen of the Negotiating Groups were to report on the results of their negotiations to the Committee or the plenary functioning as a Committee, as appropriate, before they were presented to the plenary.

29. The negotiations carried out at the seventh session and resumed seventh session of the Conference were reported on by the President concerning the work of the plenary functioning as a Main Committee, and by the Chairmen of the Main Committees and the Negotiating Groups. These reports, together with the report of the Chairman of the Drafting Committee, were incorporated in documents A/CONF.62/RCNG.1 and 2.[46] The Conference also laid down criteria for any modifications or revisions of the Informal Composite Negotiating Text, which are set out in document A/CONF.62/62.

30. At the eighth session a group of Legal Experts was set up with Harry Wuensche (German Democratic Republic) as its Chairman.[47]

31. On the basis of the deliberations of the Conference (A/CONF.62/SR.111-SR.116) concerning the reports of the President, the Chairmen of the Main Committees, the Chairmen of the Negotiating Groups and the Chairman of the Group of Legal Experts on consultations conducted by them, a revision of the Informal Composite Negotiating Text (A/CONF.62/WP.10/Rev.1) was prepared by the Collegium referred to in paragraph 27. The nature of the text was described in the explanatory memorandum by the President attached to the text.

32. At the resumed eighth session a further Group of Legal Experts was set up with Jens Evensen (Norway) as its Chairman.[48]

33. The reports on the negotiations conducted at the resumed eighth session by the President, the Chairmen of the Main Committees, the Chairmen of the Negotiating Groups and the Chairmen of the two Groups of Legal Experts together with the report of the Chairman of the Drafting Committee were incorporated in a memorandum by the President (A/CONF.62/91).

34. At its ninth session, on the basis of the report of the President concerning consultations conducted in the plenary acting as a Main Committee (A/CONF.62/L.49/ Add.1 and 2) , the Conference considered the draft Preamble prepared by the President (A/CONF.62/L.49) for incorporation in the next revision of the Informal Composite Negotiating Text (A/CONF.62/WP.10/Rev .1). On the basis of the deliberations of the Conference (A/CONF.62/ SR.125-SR.128) concerning the reports of the President, the Chairmen of the Main Committees, the Chairmen of the Negotiating Groups and the Chairmen of the Groups of Legal Experts on the consultations conducted by them, and the report of the Chairman of the Drafting Committee on its work, the Collegium[49] undertook a second revision of the Informal Composite Negotiating Text presented as the Informal Composite Negotiating Text/Rev.2 (in document A/CONF.62/WP.10/Rev .2), the nature of which was described in the President's explanatory memorandum attached to it.

35. At its resumed ninth session, on the basis of the deliberations of the Conference (A/CONF.62/SR.134-SR.140) concerning the reports of the President and the Chairmen of the Main Committees on the consultations conducted by them, the Collegium prepared a further revision of the Informal Composite Negotiating Text. The revised text, titled "Draft Convention on the Law of the Sea (Informal Text)" (A/CONF.62/WP.10/Rev.3), was issued together with the explanatory memorandum of the President (A/CONF.62/WP.10/ Rev.3/Add.1), which described the nature of the text.

36. The Conference also decided that the statement of understanding on an exceptional method of delimitation of the Continental Shelf applicable to certain specific geological and geomorphological conditions would be incorporated in an annex to the Final Act.[50]

37. The Conference decided that the tenth session was to determine the status to be given to the draft Convention (Informal Text).[51]

38. Following the deliberations of the Conference at its tenth and resumed tenth sessions (A/CONF.62/SR.142-SR.155), the Collegium prepared a revision of the draft Convention on the Law of the Sea (Informal Text). The Conference decided that the text as revised (A/CONF .62/L.78) was the official draft Convention of the Conference, subject only to the specific conditions recorded in document A/CONF.62/114. At the resumed tenth session, the Conference decided that the decisions taken in the informal plenary concerning the seats of the International Seabed Authority (Jamaica) and the International Tribunal for the Law of the Sea (the Free and Hanseatic City of Hamburg in the Federal Republic of Germany) should be incorporated in the revision of the draft Convention; and that the introductory note to that revision should record the requirements agreed upon when the decision concerning the two seats was taken (A/CONF.62/L.78).

39. Following consideration by the plenary[52] of the final clauses and in particular the question of entry into force of the Convention, the question of establishing a Preparatory Commission for the International Seabed Authority and the convening of the International Tribunal for the Law of the Sea was considered by the plenary at the ninth session. The President, on the basis of the deliberations of the informal plenary, prepared a draft resolution to be adopted by the Conference concerning interim arrangements, which was annexed to his report (A/CONF.62/L.55 and Corr.1). On the basis of the further consideration of the subject jointly by the plenary and the First Committee at the tenth, resumed tenth and eleventh sessions of the Conference, the President and the Chairman of the First Committee presented a draft resolution (A/CONF.62/C.1/L.30, annex I).

40. Following consideration at the eleventh session of the question of the treatment to be accorded to preparatory investments made before the Convention enters into force, provided that such investments are compatible with the Convention and would not defeat its object and purpose, the President and the Chairman of the First Committee presented a draft resolution contained in annex II to their report A/CONF.62/C.1/L.30. The question of participation in the Convention was considered by the plenary of the Conference during the eighth to eleventh ses-

sions, and the President presented a report on the consultations at the eleventh session in document A/CONF.62/L.86.

41. The eleventh session had been declared as the final decision-making session of the Conference.[53] During that session, on the basis of the deliberations of the Conference (A/CONF.62/SR.157-SR.166) concerning the report of the President (A/CONF.62/L.86) and the reports of the Chairmen of the Main Committees (A/CONF.62/L.87, L.91 and L.92), on the negotiations conducted by them and the report of the Chairman of the Drafting Committee on its work (A/CONF.62/L.85 and L.89), the Collegium issued a memorandum (A/CONF.62/L.93 and Corr.1) containing changes to be incorporated in the Draft Convention on the Law of the Sea (A/CONF.62/L.78), and document A/CONF.62/L.94 setting out three draft resolutions and a draft decision of the Conference which were to be adopted at the same time as the draft Convention.

The Conference determined that all efforts at reaching general agreement had been exhausted.[54] Throughout the preceding eight years of its work the Conference had taken all decisions by consensus although it had exceptionally resorted to a vote only on procedural questions, on questions concerning the appointment of officials and on invitations to be extended to participants in the Conference as observers.

42. On the basis of the deliberations recorded in the records of the Conference (A/CONF .62/SR.167-SR.182), the Conference drew up:

THE UNITED NATIONS CONVENTION ON THE LAW OF THE SEA

RESOLUTION I on the establishment of the Preparatory Commission for the International Seabed Authority and for the International Tribunal for the Law of the Sea

RESOLUTION II governing Preparatory Investment in Pioneer Activities relating to Polymetallic Nodules

RESOLUTION III relating to territories whose people have not obtained either full independence or some other self-governing status recognized by the United Nations or territories under colonial domination

RESOLUTION IV relating to national liberation movements.

The foregoing Convention together with resolutions I to IV, forming an integral whole, was adopted on 30 April 1982, by a recorded vote taken at the request of one delegation.[55] The Convention together with resolution I to IV were adopted subject to drafting changes thereafter approved by the Conference[56] which were incorporated in the Convention and in resolutions I to IV, which are annexed to this Final Act (annex I). The Convention is subject to ratification and is opened for signature from 10 December 1982 until 9 December 1984 at the Ministry of Foreign Affairs of Jamaica and also from 1 July 1983 until 9 December 1984 at United Nations Headquarters. The same instrument is opened for accession in accordance with its provisions.

After 9 December 1984, the closing date for signature at United Nations Headquarters, the Convention will be deposited with the Secretary-General of the United Nations.

There are annexed to this Final Act:

The Statement of Understanding referred to in paragraph 36 above (annex II); and the following resolutions adopted by the Conference:

Resolution paying tribute to Simón Bolívarthe Liberator (annex III);[57]

Resolution expressing gratitude to the President, the Government and officials of Venezuela (annex IV);[58]

Tribute to the Amphictyonic Congress of Panama (annex V);[59]

Resolution on Development of National Marine Science, Technology and Ocean Service Infrastructures (annex VI) ;[60, 60 bis]

IN WITNESS WHEREOF the representatives have signed this Final Act.

DONE AT MONTEGO BAY this tenth day of December, one thousand nine hundred and eighty-two in a single copy in the Arabic, Chinese, English, French, Russian and Spanish languages, each text being equally authentic. The original texts shall be deposited in the archives of the United Nations Secretariat.

The President of the Conference:
   T.T. B. KOH
The Special Representative of the
Secretary-General to the Conference:
   BERNARDO ZULETA
The Executive Secretary of the Conference:
   DAVID HALL

Notes to the Final Act

[1] *Official Records of the General Assembly, Twenty-second Session, Annexes,* agenda item 92, document A/6695.

[2] *Ibid., Twenty-third Session, Annexes,* agenda item 26, document A/7230.

[3] *Ibid., Twenty-fourth Session, Supplement Nos. 22 and* 22A (A/7622 and Corr.1 and A/7622/Add.1).

[4] *Ibid., Twenty-sixth Session, Supplement No. 21* (A/8421) ; *ibid., Twenty-seventh Session, Supplement No. 21* (A/8721 and Corr.l); and *ibid., Twenty-eighth Session, Supplement No. 21* (A/9021 and Corr.1-3) , vols. I- VI.

[5] In addition it may be noted that the Conference was attended and assisted by observers from the United Nations Programmes and Conferences.

[6] General Assembly resolution 3334 (XXIX) of 17 December 1974.

[7] General Assembly resolution 3483 (XXX) of 12 December 1975.

[8] Decision taken at the 69th meeting of the plenary Conference on 7 May 1976 (see *Official*

Records of the Third United Nations Conference on the Law of the Sea, vol. V, A/CONF.62/ SR.69) .

[9] General Assembly resolution 31/63 of 10 December 1976.

[10] General Assembly resolution 32/194 of 20 December 1977.

[11] Decision taken at the 106th meeting of the plenary on 19 May 1978 (see *Official Records of the Third United Nations Conference on the Law of the Sea*, vol. IX, A/CONF.62/SR.106).

[12] General Assembly resolution 33/17 of 10 November 1978.

[13] Decision taken at the 115th meeting of the plenary on 27 April 1979 (see *Official Records of the Third United Nations Conference on the Law of the Sea*, vol. XI, A/CONF.62/SR.115).

[14] General Assembly resolution 34/20 of 9 November 1979.

[15] *Ibid.*

[16] General Assembly resolution 35/116 of 10 December 1980, and decision taken at the 147th meeting of the plenary Conference on 20 April 1981 (A/CONF.62/SR.147).

[17] General Assembly resolution 35/452 of 11 May 1981.

[18] General Assembly resolution 36/79 of 9 December 1981.

[19] Decision taken at the 182nd meeting of the plenary Conference on 30 April 1982 (A/ CONF.62/SR.182) .

[19 bis] Final part of the eleventh session held at Montego Bay, Jamaica from 6 to 10 December 1982: decision taken at the 184th meeting of the plenary on 24 September 1982.

[20] The list of States participating at each session is recorded in the appropriate report of the Credentials Committee.

[21] Decision taken at the 38th meeting of the plenary Conference on 11 July 1974, *Official Records of the Third United Nations Conference on the Law of the Sea*, vol. I, A/CONF.62/ SR.38.

[22] Ibid., vol. XIII, A/CONF.62/SR.122.

[23] 86th closed meeting of the plenary Conference held on 5 April 1978, in adopting resolution A/CONF.62/R.1 proposed by Nepal on behalf of the Asian Group; *ibid.*, vol. IX, footnote on page 3.

[24] The General Assembly of the United Nations paid tribute to the memory of Ambassador Hamilton Shirley Amerasinghe, President of the Conference since its inception, and prior to that, Chairman of the Committee on the Peaceful Uses of the Seabed and the Ocean Floor beyond the Limits of National Jurisdiction (A/35/PV.82) .The General Assembly thereafter established a memorial fellowship in his name (resolution 35/116, paragraphs 1 and 2 of 10 December 1980 and resolution 36/79, third preambular paragraph and paragraph 6, of 9 December 1981). See also A/36/697.

[25] A/CONF.62/SR.143.

[26] *Ibid.*, vol. I, A/CONF.62/SR.2.

[27] Decision taken at the 3rd meeting of the plenary Conference on 10 December 1973 (see *Official Records of the Third United Nations Conference on the Law of the Sea*, vol. I, p. 9).

[28] Economic implications of seabed mineral development in the international area: *ibid.*, vol.III (A/CONF.62/25 dated 22 May 1974).

Economic implications of seabed mining in the international area: *ibid.*, vol. IV (A/ CONF.62/37 dated 18 February 1975).

Description of some types of marine technology and possible methods for their transfer: *ibid.*, vol. IV (A/CONF.62/C.3/L.22) dated 27 February 1975.

Draft alternative texts of the preamble and final clauses: *ibid.*, vol. VI (A/CONF.62/L.13) dated 26 July 1976.

Annotated directory of inter-governmental organizations concerned with ocean affairs (A/ CONF.62/L.14) dated 10 August 1976.

Alternative means of financing the Enterprise: *ibid.*, vol. VI (A/CONF.62/C.1/L.17) dated 3 September 1976.

Costs of the Authority and contractual means of financing its activities, *ibid.*, vol.VII (A/CONF.62/C.1/L.19) dated 18 May 1977.

Manpower requirements of the Authority and related training needs, *ibid.*, vol. XII (A/CONF.62/82) dated 17 August 1979.

Potential financial implications for States Parties to the future Convention on the Law of the Sea (A/CONF.62/L.65) dated 20 February 1981.

Effects of the production limitation formula under certain specified assumptions (A/CONF.62/L.66) dated 24 February 1981 and (A/CONF.62/L.66/Corr.l) dated 3 March 1981.

Preliminary study illustrating various formulae for the definition of the continental shelf: *ibid.*, vol. IX (A/CONF.62/C.2/L.98) dated 18 April 1978; map illustrating various formulae for the definition of the continental shelf (A/CONF .62/C.2/L. 98/Add.1); calculation of areas illustrated beyond 200 miles in document A/CONF.62/C.2/L.98/Add.1, *ibid.*, vol. IX, (A/CONF.62/C.2/L.98/Add.2) dated 3 May 1978; communication received from the Secretary of the Intergovernmental Oceanographic Commission: *ibid.*, vol. IX (A/CONF.62/C.2/L.98/Add.3) dated 28 August 1978.

Study of the implications of preparing large-scale maps for the Third United Nations Conference on the Law of the Sea: *ibid.*, vol. XI (A/CONF.62/C.2/L.99) dated 9 April 1979.

Study on the future functions of the Secretary-General under the draft Convention and on the needs of countries, especially developing countries, for information, advice, and assistance under the new legal regime (A/CONF.62/L.76) dated 18 August 1981.

[29] The co-ordinators of the language groups were as follows:

Arabic language group: Mustafa Kamil Yasseen (United Arab Emirates), and Mohammad Al-Haj Hamoud (Iraq) .

Chinese language group: Wang Tieya (China), Ni Zhengyu (China), and Zhang Hongzeng (China).

English language group: Bernard H. Oxman (United States) and Thomas A. Clingan (United States) .

Alternates: Steven Asher (United States) and Milton Drucker (United States).

French language group: Tullio Treves (Italy) .

Alternate: Lucius Caflisch (Switzerland).

Russian language group: F. N. Kovalev (USSR), P. N. Evseev (USSR), Yevgeny N. Nasinovsky (USSR) and Georgy G. Ivanov (USSR).

Spanish language group: José Antonio Yturriaga Barbarán (Spain), José Manuel Lacleta Muñoz (Spain) , José Antonio Pastor Ridruejo (Spain) and Luis Valencia Rodriguez (Ecuador) .

[30] A/CONF.62/L.56, A/CONF.62/L.57/Rev.1 and A/CONF/62/L.63/Rev.l. See *Official Records of the Third United Nations Conference on the Law of the Sea*, vols. XIII and XIV.

[31] A/CONF.62/L.67/Add.1-16, A/CONF.62/L.75/Add.1-13, A/CONF.62/L.85/Add.1-9, A/CONF.62/L.142/Rev.1/Add.l and A/CONF.62/L.152/Add.1-27.

[32] *Ibid.*, vol. I, A/CONF.62/SR.20.

[33] *Official Records of the General Assembly, Twenty-eighth Session, Plenary Meetings*, 2169th meeting.

[34] *Official Records of the Third United Nations Conference on the Law of the Sea*, vol. I, A/CONF.62/SR.19.

[35] *Ibid.*, vol. I, A/CONF.62/SR.40.

[36] *Ibid.*, vol. IV, A/CONF.62/SR.52.

[37] *Ibid.*, vol. XIII, A/CONF.62/SR.122.

[38] *Ibid.*, vol. I, A/CONF.62/SR.15.

[39] The First Committee appointed the following officers of the informal working groups set up by it between the second and eleventh sessions:

Christopher W. Pinto (Sri Lanka): Chairman of the informal body of the whole (decision of the first meeting of the First Committee) *Official Records of the Third United Nations Conference on the Law of the Sea*, vol. II; Chairman of the negotiating group on the system of operations, the régime and the conditions of exploration and exploitation of the Area, with a membership of 50 States, but open-ended (decision of the 14th to 16th meetings of the First Committee, *ibid.*).

S. P. Jagota (India) and H. H. M. Sondaal (Netherlands): Co-chairmen of the open-ended working group (decision of the 26th meeting of the First Committee, *ibid.*, vol. VI) .

Jens Evensen (Norway) : Special Co-ordinator of the Chairman's informal working group of the whole on the system of exploitation (decision of the 38th meeting of the First Committee, *ibid.*, vol. VII).

Satya N. Nandan (Fiji): Chairman of the informal group on the question of production policies, established under the auspices of Negotiating Group 1 referred to in paragraph 28 hereunder (see 114th meeting of the General Committee on 26 April 1979, *ibid.*, vol. IX) .

Paul Bamela Engo (United Republic of Cameroon): Chairman of the First Committee, Francis X. Njenga (Kenya), Tommy T. B. Koh (Singapore) and Harry Wuensche (German Democratic Republic): Co-chairmen of the Working Group of 21 on First Committee issues with the Chairman of the First Committee as principal co-ordinator. The Working Group consisted of 10 members nominated by the Group of 77, China, and 10 members nominated by the principal industrialized countries with alternates for each group. The Group was constituted with members and alternates as necessary to represent the interests of the issue under consideration (decision of the 45th meeting of the General Committee on 9 April 1979, *ibid.*, vol. XI; see also 114th meeting of the plenary on 26 April 1979, *ibid.*, vol. XI).

The Second Committee set up informal consultative groups, at different stages, chaired by the three Vice-Chairmen, the representatives of Czechoslovakia, Kenya and Turkey and by the Rapporteur of the Committee, Satya N. Nandan (Fiji). (See statement by the Chairman of the Second Committee, A/CONF.62/C.2/L.87 (*ibid.*, vol. IV). See also statement on the work of the Committee prepared by the Rapporteur, A/CONF.62/C.2/L.89/Rev.1, *ibid.*).

The Third Committee appointed the following officers of its informal meetings:

José Luis Vallarta (Mexico): Chairman of the informal meetings on Protection and preservation of the marine environment (decision of the second meeting of the Third Committee, *ibid.*, vol. II).

Cornel A. Metternich (delegate of the Federal Republic of Germany): Chairman of the informal meetings on Scientific Research and the Development and Transfer of Technology (decision of the second meeting of the Third Committee, *ibid.*, vol. II; see also A/CONF.62/C.3/L.16, *ibid.*, vol. III).

[40] Decision taken at the 65th meeting of the plenary Conference on 12 April 1976, *ibid.*, vol. V, A/CONF .62/SR.65.

[41] *Ibid.*, vol. VI, A/CONF.62/SR.71.

[42] *Ibid.*, vol. VII, A/CONF.62/SR.77-SR.79.

[43] Decision taken at the 79th meeting of the plenary Conference on 28 June 1977, *ibid.*,vol.VII.

[44] President's explanatory memorandum attached to A/CONF.62/WP.10/Rev.2, dated 11 April 1980.

[45] *Official Records of the Third United Nations Conference on the Law of the Sea*, vol. IX, A/CONF.62/SR.89 and 90. The descriptions of the items are recorded in A/CONF.62/62, *ibid.*, vol. X.

[46] *Ibid*, vol. X.

[47] The Group of Legal Experts on the Settlement of Disputes relating to Part XI of the Informal Composite Negotiating Text was established by the Chairman or the First Committee in consultation with the President as reflected at the 114th meeting of the plenary and in A/CONF.62/C.1/L.25 and L.36, *ibid.*, vol. XI.

[48] The Group of Legal Experts on the Final Clauses was established by the President to deal with the technical aspects of the Final Clauses after their preliminary consideration in the informal plenary as recorded at the 120th meeting of the plenary of 24 August 1979, *ibid.*, vol. XII.

[49] As referred to in paragraph 27 above and in the President's explanatory memorandum attached to A/CONF.62/WP.10/Rev.2.

[50] Decision taken at the 141st meeting of the plenary on 29 August 1980, *ibid.*, vol. XIV, A/CONF.62/SR.141.

[51] *Ibid.*, also referred to in A/CONF.62/BUR.13/Rev.1.

[52] At the resumed eighth session.

[53] In adopting the programme of work (A/CONF.62/116), *ibid.*, A/CONF/62/SR.154.

[54] A/CONF.62/SR.174.

[55] Recorded vote taken at the request of the delegation of the U nited States of America, with two delegations not participating in the vote. The result was 130 in favour, 4 against with 17 abstentions.

[56] Decision taken by the Conference at the 182nd meeting of the plenary Conference on 30 April 1982 as well as its decision taken at the 184th meeting on 24 September 1982.

[57] Draft resolution A/CONF.62/L.3 and Add.1-4 adopted by the Conference at the 43rd meeting of the plenary on 22 July 1974, *ibid.*, vol. I.

[58] Draft resolution A/CONF/62/L.9 adopted by the Conference at the 51st meeting of the plenary on 28 August 1974, *ibid.*, vol. I.

[59] Draft Tribute A/CONF .62/L.15 adopted by the Conference at the 76th meeting of the plenary on 17 September 1976, *ibid.*, vol. VI.

[60] Draft resolution A/CONF .62/L.127 adopted by the Conference at the 182nd meeting of the plenary on 30 April 1982.

[60 bis] Annex VII

RESOLUTION EXPRESSING GRATITUDE TO THE PRIME MINISTER; FOREIGN MINISTER AND DEPUTY PRIME MINISTER, THE GOVERNMENT AND OFFICIALS OF JAMAICA

The Third United Nations Conference on the Law of the Sea,

Bearing in mind that the Conference accepted with gratitude the invitation of the Government of Jamaica and held the final part of its eleventh session for the purpose of signing the Final Act of the Conference and opening the United Nations Convention on the Law of the Sea for signature, in the city of Montego Bay in Jamaica,

Acknowledging with grateful appreciation the generosity of the Government and the people of Jamaica, which enabled the Conference to meet in a congenial atmosphere under excellent conditions,

Decides to express to their Excellencies the Prime Minister and the Deputy Prime Minister and Minister for Foreign Affairs and Government and people of Jamaica, its profound gratitude for the exceptional hospitality extended to it.

— Resolution proposed by the President and adopted by the Conference at the 192nd meeting of the plenary on 9 December 1982.

Additions to the Final Act, in the form in which it was presented to the Conference, are given in footnotes 19 *bis* and 60 *bis*.

ANNEX I

RESOLUTION I

ESTABLISHMENT OF THE PREPARATORY COMMISSION FOR THE INTERNATIONAL SEA-BED AUTHORITY AND FOR THE INTERNATIONAL TRIBUNAL FOR THE LAW OF THE SEA

The Third United Nations Conference on the Law of the Sea,

Having adopted the Convention on the Law of the Sea which provides for the establishment of the International Seabed Authority and the International Tribunal for the Law of the Sea,

Having decided to take all possible measures to ensure the entry into effective operation without undue delay of the Authority and the Tribunal and to make the necessary arrangements for the commencement of their functions,

Having decided that a Preparatory Commission should be established for the fulfilment of these purposes,

Decides as follows:

1.   There is hereby established the Preparatory Commission for the International Seabed Authority and for the International Tribunal for the Law of the Sea. Upon signature of or accession to the Convention by 50 States, the Secretary-General of the United Nations shall convene the Commission, and it shall meet no sooner than 60 days and no later than 90 days thereafter.

2.   The Commission shall consist of the representatives of States and of Namibia, represented by the United Nations Council for Namibia, which have signed the Convention or acceded to it. The representatives of signatories of the Final Act may participate fully in the deliberations of the Commission as observers but shall not be entitled to participate in the taking of decisions.

3.   The Commission shall elect its Chairman and other officers.

4.   The Rules of Procedure of the Third United Nations Conference on the Law of the Sea shall apply *mutatis mutandis* to the adoption of the rules of procedure of the Commission.

5.   The Commission shall:

(a) prepare the provisional agenda for the first session of the Assembly and of the Council and, as appropriate, make recommendations relating to items thereon;

(b) prepare draft rules of procedure of the Assembly and of the Council;

(c) make recommendations concerning the budget for the first financial period of the Authority;

(d) make recommendations concerning the relationship between the Authority and the United Nations and other international organizations;

(e) make recommendations concerning the Secretariat of the Authority in accordance with the relevant provisions of the Convention;

(f) undertake studies, as necessary, concerning the establishment of the headquarters of the Authority, and make recommendations relating thereto;

(g) prepare draft rules, regulations and procedures, as necessary, to enable the Authority to commence its functions, including draft regulations concerning the financial management and the internal administration of the Authority;

(h) exercise the powers and functions assigned to it by resolution II of the Third United Nations Conference on the Law of the Sea relating to preparatory investment;

(i) undertake studies on the problems which would be encountered by developing land-based producer States likely to be most seriously affected by the production of minerals derived from the Area with a view to minimizing their difficulties and helping them to make the necessary economic adjustment, including studies on the establishment of a compensation fund, and submit recommendations to the Authority thereon.

6.   The Commission shall have such legal capacity as may be necessary for the exercise of its functions and the fulfilment of its purposes as set forth in this resolution.

7.   The Commission may establish such subsidiary bodies as are necessary for the exercise of its functions and shall determine their functions and rules of procedure. It may also make use, as appropriate, of outside sources of expertise in accordance with United Nations practice to facilitate the work of bodies so established.

8.   The Commission shall establish a special commission for the Enterprise and entrust to it the functions referred to in paragraph 12 of resolution II of the Third United Nations Conference on the Law of the Sea relating to preparatory investment. The special commission shall take all measures necessary for the early entry into effective operation of the Enterprise.

9.   The Commission shall establish a special commission on the problems which would be encountered by developing land-based producer States likely to be most seriously affected by the production of minerals derived from the Area and entrust to it the functions referred to in paragraph 5(i).

10.   The Commission shall prepare a report containing recommendations for submission to the meeting of the States Parties to be convened in accordance with Annex VI, article 4, of the Convention regarding practical arrangements for the establishment of the International Tribunal for the Law of the Sea.

11.   The Commission shall prepare a final report on all matters within its mandate, except as provided in paragraph 10, for the presentation to the Assembly at its first session. Any action which may be taken on the basis of the report must be in conformity with the provisions of the Convention concerning the powers and functions entrusted to the respective organs of the Authority.

12.   The Commission shall meet at the seat of the Authority if facilities are available; it shall meet as often as necessary for the expeditious exercise of its functions.

13.   The Commission shall remain in existence until the conclusion of the first session of the Assembly, at which time its property and records shall be transferred to the Authority.

14. The expenses of the Commission shall be met from the regular budget of the United Nations, subject to the approval of the General Assembly of the United Nations.

15. The Secretary-General of the United Nations shall make available to the Commission such secretariat services as may be required.

16. The Secretary-General of the United Nations shall bring this resolution, in particular paragraphs 14 and 15, to the attention of the General Assembly for necessary action.

RESOLUTION II

GOVERNING PREPARATORY INVESTMENT IN PIONEER ACTIVITIES RELATING TO POLYMETALLIC NODULES

The Third United Nations Conference on the Law of the Sea,

Having adopted the Convention on the Law of the Sea (the "Convention"),

Having established by resolution I the Preparatory Commission for the International Seabed Authority and for the International Tribunal for the Law of the Sea (the "Commission") and directed it to prepare draft rules, regulations and procedures, as necessary to enable the Authority to commence its functions, as well as to make recommendations for the early entry into effective operation of the Enterprise,

Desirous of making provision for investments by States and other entities made in a manner compatible with the international régime set forth in Part XI of the Convention and the Annexes relating thereto, before the entry into force of the Convention,

Recognizing the need to ensure that the Enterprise will be provided with the funds, technology and expertise necessary to enable it to keep pace with the States and other entities referred to in the preceding paragraph with respect to activities in the Area,

Decides as follows:

1. For the purposes of this resolution:

(a) "pioneer investor" refers to:

   (i) France, India, Japan and the Union of Soviet Socialist Republics, or a state enterprise of each of those States or one natural or juridical person which possesses the nationality of or is effectively controlled by each of those States, or their nationals, provided that the State concerned signs the Convention and the State or state enterprise or natural or juridical person has expended, before 1 January 1983, an amount equivalent to at least $US 30 million (United States dollars calculated in constant dollars relative to 1982) in pioneer activities and has expended no less than 10 per cent of that amount in the location, survey and evaluation of the area referred to in paragraph 3(a);

    (ii) four entities, whose components being natural or juridical persons[1] possess the nationality of one or more of the following States, or are effectively controlled by one or more of them or their nationals: Belgium, Canada, the Federal Republic of Germany, Italy, Japan, The Netherlands, the United Kingdom of Great Britain and Northern Ireland, and the United States of America, provided that the certifying State or States sign the Convention and the entity concerned has expended, before 1 January 1983, the levels of expenditure for the purpose stated in subparagraph (i);

    (iii) any developing State which signs the Convention or any state enterprise or natural or juridical person which possesses the nationality of such State or is effectively controlled by it or its nationals, or any group of the foregoing, which, before 1 January 1985, has expended the levels of expenditure for the purpose stated in subparagraph (i);

The rights of the pioneer investor may devolve upon its successor in interest.

(b)   "pioneer activities" means undertakings, commitments of financial and other assets, investigations, findings, research, engineering development and other activities relevant to the identification, discovery, and systematic analysis and evaluation of polymetallic nodules and to the determination of the technical and economic feasibility of exploitation. Pioneer activities include:

    (i) any at-sea observation and evaluation activity which has as its objective the establishment and documentation of the nature, shape, concentration, location and grade of polymetallic nodules and of the environmental, technical and other appropriate factors which must be taken into account before exploitation;

    (ii) the recovery from the Area of polymetallic nodules with a view to the designing, fabricating and testing of equipment which is intended to be used in the exploitation of polymetallic nodules;

(c)   "certifying State" means a State which signs the Convention, standing in the same relation to a pioneer investor as would a sponsoring State pursuant to Annex III, article 4, of the Convention and which certifies the levels of expenditure specified in subparagraph (a);

(d)   "polymetallic nodules" means one of the resources of the Area consisting of any deposit or accretion of nodules, on or just below the surface of the deep seabed, which contain manganese, nickel, cobalt and copper;

(e)   "pioneer area" means an area allocated by the Commission to a pioneer investor for pioneer activities pursuant to this resolution. A pioneer area shall not exceed 150,000 square kilometres. The pioneer investor

---

[1] For their identity and composition see "Seabed mineral resource development: recent activities of the International Consortia" and addendum, published by the Department of International Economic and Social Affairs of the United Nations (ST/ESA/107 and Add.l).

shall relinquish portions of the pioneer area to revert to the Area, in accordance with the following schedule:

(i) 20 per cent of the area allocated by the end of the third year from the date of the allocation;

(ii) an additional 10 per cent of the area allocated by the end of the fifth year from the date of the allocation;

(iii) an additional 20 per cent of the area allocated or such larger amount as would exceed the exploitation area decided upon by the Authority in its rules, regulations and procedures, after eight years from the date of the allocation of the area or the date of the award of a production authorization, whichever is earlier;

(f) "Area", "Authority", "activities in the Area" and "resources" have the meanings assigned to those terms in the Convention.

2.   As soon as the Commission begins to function, any State which has signed the Convention may apply to the Commission on its behalf or on behalf of any state enterprise or entity or natural or juridical person specified in paragraph 1(a) for registration as a pioneer investor. The Commission shall register the applicant as a pioneer investor if the application:

(a) is accompanied, in the case of a State which has signed the Convention, by a statement certifying the level of expenditure made in accordance with paragraph 1(a), and, in all other cases, a certificate concerning such level of expenditure issued by a certifying State or States; and

(b) is in conformity with the other provisions of this resolution, including paragraph 5.

3.   (a) Every application shall cover a total area which need not be a single continuous area, sufficiently large and of sufficient estimated commercial value to allow two mining operations. The application shall indicate the co-ordinates of the area defining the total area and dividing it into two parts of equal estimated commercial value and shall contain all the data available to the applicant with respect to both parts of the area. Such data shall include, *inter alia*, information relating to mapping, testing, the density of polymetallic nodules and their metal content. In dealing with such data, the Commission and its staff shall act in accordance with the relevant provisions of the Convention and its Annexes concerning the confidentiality of data.

(b) Within 45 days of receiving the data required by subparagraph (a), the Commission shall designate the part of the area which is to be reserved in accordance with the Convention for the conduct of activities in the Area by the Authority through the Enterprise or in association with developing States. The other part of the area shall be allocated to the pioneer investor as a pioneer area.

4. No pioneer investor may be registered in respect of more than one pioneer area. In the case of a pioneer investor which is made up of two or more components, none of such components may apply to be registered as a pioneer investor in its own right or under paragraph 1 (a) (iii).

5. (a) Any State which has signed the Convention and which is a prospective certifying State shall ensure, before making applications to the Commission under paragraph 2, that areas in respect of which applications are made do not overlap one another or areas previously allocated as pioneer areas. The States concerned shall keep the Commission currently and fully informed of any efforts to resolve conflicts with respect to overlapping claims and of the results thereof.

(b) Certifying States shall ensure, before the entry into force of the Convention, that pioneer activities are conducted in a manner compatible with it.

(c) The prospective certifying States, including all potential claimants, shall resolve their conflicts as required under subparagraph (a) by negotiations within a reasonable period. If such conflicts have not been resolved by 1 March 1983, the prospective certifying States shall arrange for the submission of all such claims to binding arbitration in accordance with UNCITRAL Arbitration Rules to commence not later than 1 May 1983 and to be completed by 1 December 1984. If one of the States concerned does not wish to participate in the arbitration, it shall arrange for a juridical person of its nationality to represent it in the arbitration. The arbitral tribunal may, for good cause, extend the deadline for the making of the award for one or more 30-day periods.

(d) In determining the issue as to which applicant involved in a conflict shall be awarded all or part of each area in conflict, the arbitral tribunal shall find a solution which is fair and equitable, having regard, with respect to each applicant involved in the conflict, to the following factors:

(i) the deposit of the list of relevant co-ordinates with the prospective certifying State or States not later than the date of adoption of the Final Act or 1 January 1983, whichever is earlier;

(ii) the continuity and extent of past activities relevant to each area in conflict and to the application area of which it is a part;

(iii) the date on which each pioneer investor concerned or predecessor in interest or component organization thereof commenced activities at sea in the application area;

(iv) the financial cost of activities measured in constant United States dollars relevant to each area in conflict and to the application area of which it is a part; and

(v) the time when those activities were carried out and the quality of activities.

6. A pioneer investor registered pursuant to this resolution shall, from the date of registration, have the exclusive right to carry out pioneer activities in the pioneer area allocated to it.

7. (a) Every applicant for registration as a pioneer investor shall pay to the Commission a fee of $US 250,000. When the pioneer investor ap-

plies to the Authority for a plan of work for exploration and exploitation the fee referred to in Annex III, article 13, paragraph 2, of the Convention shall be $US 250,000.

(b) Every registered pioneer investor shall pay an annual fixed fee of $US 1 million commencing from the date of the allocation of the pioneer area. The payments shall be made by the pioneer investor to the Authority upon the approval of its plan of work for exploration and exploitation. The financial arrangements undertaken pursuant to such plan of work shall be adjusted to take account of the payments made pursuant to this paragraph.

(c) Every registered pioneer investor shall agree to incur periodic expenditures, with respect to the pioneer area allocated to it, until approval of its plan of work pursuant to paragraph 8, of an amount to be determined by the Commission. The amount should be reasonably related to the size of the pioneer area and the expenditures which would be expected of a bona fide operator who intends to bring that area into commercial production within a reasonable time.

8. (a) Within six months of the entry into force of the Convention and certification by the Commission in accordance with paragraph 11, of compliance with this resolution, the pioneer investor so registered shall apply to the Authority for approval of a plan of work for exploration and exploitation, in accordance with the Convention. The plan of work in respect of such application shall comply with and be governed by the relevant provisions of the Convention and the rules, regulations and procedures of the Authority, including those on the operational requirements, the financial requirements and the undertakings concerning the transfer of technology. Accordingly, the Authority shall approve such application.

(b) When an application for approval of a plan of work is submitted by an entity other than a State, pursuant to subparagraph (a), the certifying State or States shall be deemed to be the sponsoring State for the purposes of Annex III, article 4, of the Convention, and shall thereupon assume such obligations.

(c) No plan of work for exploration and exploitation shall be approved unless the certifying State is a Party to the Convention. In the case of the entities referred to in paragraph 1(a) (ii), the plan of work for exploration and exploitation shall not be approved unless all the States whose natural or juridical persons comprise those entities are Parties to the Convention. If any such State fails to ratify the Convention within six months after it has received a notification from the Authority that an application by it, or sponsored by it, is pending, its status as a pioneer investor or certifying State, as the case may be, shall terminate, unless the Council, by a majority of three fourths of its members present and voting, decides to postpone the terminal date for a period not exceeding six months.

9. (a) In the allocation of production authorizations, in accordance with article 151 and Annex III, article 7, of the Convention, the pioneer investors who have obtained approval of plans of work for exploration and exploitation shall have priority over all applicants other than the Enterprise which shall be entitled to production authorizations for two mine sites including that referred to in article 151, paragraph 5, of the Convention. After each of the pioneer investors has obtained production authorization for its first mine site, the priority for the Enterprise contained in Annex III, article 7, paragraph 6, of the Convention shall apply.

(b) Production authorizations shall be issued to each pioneer investor within 30 days of the date on which that pioneer investor notifies the Authority that it will commence commercial production within five years. If a pioneer investor is unable to begin production within the period of five years for reasons beyond its control, it shall apply to the Legal and Technical Commission for an extension of time. That Commission shall grant the extension of time, for a period not exceeding five years and not subject to further extension, if it is satisfied that the pioneer investor cannot begin on an economically viable basis at the time originally planned. Nothing in this subparagraph shall prevent the Enterprise or any other pioneer applicant, who has notified the Authority that it will commence commercial production within five years, from being given a priority over any applicant who has obtained an extension of time under this subparagraph.

(c) If the Authority, upon being given notice, pursuant to subparagraph (b), determines that the commencement of commercial production within five years would exceed the production ceiling in article 151, paragraphs 2 to 7, of the Convention, the applicant shall hold a priority over any other applicant for the award of the next production authorization allowed by the production ceiling.

(d) If two or more pioneer investors apply for production authorizations to begin commercial production at the same time and article 151, paragraphs 2 to 7, of the Convention, would not permit all such production to commence simultaneously, the Authority shall notify the pioneer investors concerned. Within three months of such notification, they shall decide whether and, if so, to what extent they wish to apportion the allowable tonnage among themselves.

(e) If, pursuant to subparagraph (d), the pioneer investors concerned decide not to apportion the available production among themselves they shall agree on an order of priority for production authorizations and all subsequent applications for production authorizations will be granted after those referred to in this subparagraph have been approved.

(f) If, pursuant to subparagraph (d), the pioneer investors concerned decide to apportion the available production among themselves, the Authority shall award each of them a production authorization for such lesser quantity as they have agreed. In each case the stated production requirements of the applicant will be approved and their full production will be allowed as soon as the production ceiling admits of additional capacity sufficient for the applicants involved in the competition. All subsequent applications for production authorizations will only be granted after the requirements of this subparagraph have been met and the applicant is no longer subject to the reduction of production provided for in this subparagraph.

(g) If the parties fail to reach agreement within the stated time period, the matter shall be decided immediately by the means provided for in paragraph 5(c) in accordance with the criteria set forth in Annex III, article 7, paragraphs 3 and 5, of the Convention.

10. (a) Any rights acquired by entities or natural or juridical persons which possess the nationality of or are effectively controlled by a State or States whose status as certifying State has been terminated, shall lapse unless the pioneer investor changes its nationality and sponsorship within six months of the date of such termination, as provided for in subparagraph (c).

(b) A pioneer investor may change its nationality and sponsorship from that existing at the time of its registration as a pioneer investor to that of any State Party to the Convention which has effective control over the pioneer investor in terms of paragraph 1 (a).

(c) Changes of nationality and sponsorship pursuant to this paragraph shall not affect any right or priority conferred on a pioneer investor pursuant to paragraphs 6 and 8.

11. The Commission shall:

(a) provide each pioneer investor with the certificate of compliance with the provisions of this resolution referred to in paragraph 8; and

(b) include in its final report required by paragraph 11 of resolution I of the Conference details of all registrations of pioneer investors and allocations of pioneer areas pursuant to this resolution.

12. In order to ensure that the Enterprise is able to carry out activities in the Area in such a manner as to keep pace with States and other entities:

(a) every registered pioneer investor shall:

(i) carry out exploration, at the request of the Commission, in the area reserved, pursuant to paragraph 3 in connection with its application, for activities in the Area by the Authority through the Enterprise or in association with developing States, on the basis that the costs so incurred plus interest thereon at the rate of 10 per cent per annum shall be reimbursed;

(ii) provide training at all levels for personnel designated by the Commission;

(iii) undertake before the entry into force of the Convention, to perform the obligations prescribed in the Convention relating to transfer of technology;

(b) every certifying State shall:
  (i) ensure that the necessary funds are made available to the Enterprise in a timely manner in accordance with the Convention, upon its entry into force; and
  (ii) report periodically to the Commission on the activities carried out by it, by its entities or natural or juridical persons.

13. The Authority and its organs shall recognize and honour the rights and obligations arising from this resolution and the decisions of the Commission taken pursuant to it.

14. Without prejudice to paragraph 13, this resolution shall have effect until the entry into force of the Convention.

15. Nothing in this resolution shall derogate from Annex III, article 6, paragraph 3(c), of the Convention.

RESOLUTION III

The Third United Nations Conference on the Law of the Sea,
Having regard to the Convention on the Law of the Sea,
Bearing in mind the Charter of the United Nations, in particular Article 73,
1. *Declares* that:
  (a) In the case of a territory whose people have not attained full independence or other self-governing status recognized by the United Nations, or a territory under colonial domination, provisions concerning rights and interests under the Convention shall be implemented for the benefit of the people of the territory with a view to promoting their well-being and development.
  (b) Where a dispute exists between States over the sovereignty of a territory to which this resolution applies, in respect of which the United Nations has recommended specific means of settlement, there shall be consultations between the parties to that dispute regarding the exercise of the rights referred to in subparagraph (a). In such consultations the interests of the people of the territory concerned shall be a fundamental consideration. Any exercise of those rights shall take into account the relevant resolutions of the United Nations and shall be without prejudice to the position of any party to the dispute. The States concerned shall make every effort to enter into provisional arrangements of a practical nature and shall not jeopardize or hamper the reaching of a final settlement of the dispute.

2. *Requests* the Secretary-General of the United Nations to bring this resolution to the attention of all Members of the United Nations and the other participants in the Conference, as well as the principal organs of the United Nations, and to request their compliance with it.

RESOLUTION IV

The Third United Nations Conference on the Law of the Sea,

Bearing in mind that national liberation movements have been invited to participate in the Conference as observers in accordance with rule 62 of its rules of procedure,

Decides that the national liberation movements, which have been participating in the Third United Nations Conference on the Law of the Sea, shall be entitled to sign the Final Act of the Conference, in their capacity as observers.

ANNEX II

STATEMENT OF UNDERSTANDING CONCERNING A SPECIFIC METHOD TO BE USED IN ESTABLISHING THE OUTER EDGE OF THE CONTINENTAL MARGIN

The Third United Nations Conference on the Law of the Sea,

Considering the special characteristics of a State's continental margin where: (1) the average distance at which the 200 metre isobath occurs is not more than 20 nautical miles; (2) the greater proportion of the sedimentary rock of the continental margin lies beneath the rise; and

Taking into account the inequity that would result to that State from the application to its continental margin of article 76 of the Convention, in that, the mathematical average of the thickness of sedimentary rock along a line established at the maximum distance permissible in accordance with the provisions of paragraph 4 (a) (i) and (ii) of that article as representing the entire outer edge of the continental margin would not be less than 3.5 kilometres; and that more than half of the margin would be excluded thereby;

Recognizes that such State may, notwithstanding the provisions of article 76, establish the outer edge of its continental margin by straight lines not exceeding 60 nautical miles in length connecting fixed points, defined by latitude and longitude, at each of which the thickness of sedimentary rock is not less than 1 kilometre,

Where a State establishes the outer edge of its continental margin by applying the method set forth in the preceding paragraph of this statement, this method may also be utilized by a neighbouring State for delineating the outer edge of its continental margin on a common geological feature, where its outer edge would lie on such feature on a line established at the maximum distance permissible in accordance with article 76, paragraph 4 (a) (i) and (ii), along which the mathematical average of the thickness of sedimentary rock is not less than 3.5 kilometres,

The Conference requests the Commission on the Limits of the Continental Shelf set up pursuant to Annex II of the Convention, to be governed by the terms of this Statement when making its recommendations on matters related to the establishment of the outer edge of the continental margins of these States in the southern part of the Bay of Bengal.

ANNEX III

TRIBUTE TO SIMON BOLIVAR THE LIBERATOR

The Third United Nations Conference on the Law of the Sea,

Considering that 24 July 1974 marks a further anniversary of the birth of Simón Bolívar, the Liberator, a man of vision and early champion of international organization, and a historic figure of universal dimensions,

Considering further that the work of Simón Bolívar the Liberator, based on the concepts of liberty and justice as foundations for the peace and progress of peoples, has left an indelible mark on history and constitutes a source of constant inspiration,

Decides to pay a public tribute of admiration and respect to Simón Bolívar the Liberator, in the plenary meeting of the Third United Nations Conference on the Law of the Sea.

ANNEX IV

RESOLUTION EXPRESSING GRATITUDE TO THE PRESIDENT , THE GOVERNMENT AND OFFICIALS OF VENEZUELA

The Third United Nations Conference on the Law of the Sea,

Bearing in mind that its second session was held in the city of Caracas, cradle of Simón Bolívar, Liberator of five nations, who devoted his life to fighting for the self-determination of peoples, equality among States and justice as the expression of their common destiny,

Acknowledging with keen appreciation the extraordinary effort made by the Government and the people of Venezuela, which enabled the Conference to meet in the most favourable spirit of brotherhood and in unparalleled material conditions,

Decides

1. To express to His Excellency the President of the Republic of Venezuela, the President and members of the Organizing Committee of the Conference and the Government and people of Venezuela its deepest gratitude for the unforgettable hospitality which they have offered it;

2. To give voice to its hope that the ideals of social justice, equality among nations and solidarity among peoples advocated by the Liberator Simón Bolívar will serve to guide the future work of the Conference.

ANNEX V

TRIBUTE TO THE AMPHICTYONIC CONGRESS OF PANAMA

The Third United Nations Conference on the Law of the Sea, at its fifth session,

Considering that the current year 1976 marks the one hundred and fiftieth anniversary of the Amphictyonic Congress of Panama, convoked by the Liberator

Simón Bolívar for the laudable and visionary purpose of uniting the Latin American peoples,

Considering likewise that a spirit of universality prevailed at the Congress of Panama, which was ahead of its time and which foresaw that only on the basis of union and reciprocal co-operation is it possible to guarantee peace and promote the development of nations,

Considering further that the Congress of Panama evoked the prestigious and constructive Greek Amphictyony and anticipated the ecumenical and creative image of the United Nations,

Decides to render to the Amphictyonic Congress of Panama, in a plenary meeting of the Third United Nations Conference on the Law of the Sea, at its fifth session, a public tribute acknowledging its expressive historic significance.

ANNEX VI

RESOLUTION ON DEVELOPMENT OF NATIONAL MARINE SCIENCE, TECHNOLOGY AND OCEAN SERVICE INFRASTRUCTURES

The Third United Nations Conference on the Law of the Sea,

Recognizing that the Convention on the Law of the Sea is intended to establish a new régime for the seas and oceans which will contribute to the realization of a just and equitable international economic order through making provision for the peaceful use of ocean space, the equitable and efficient management and utilization of its resources, and the study, protection and preservation of the marine environment,

Bearing in mind, that the new régime must take into account, in particular, the special needs and interests of the developing countries, whether coastal, land-locked, or geographically disadvantaged,

Aware of the rapid advances being made in the field of marine science and technology, and the need for the developing countries, whether coastal, land-locked or geographically disadvantaged, to share in these achievements if the aforementioned goals are to be met,

Convinced that, unless urgent measures are taken, the marine scientific and technological gap between the developed and the developing countries will widen further and thus endanger the very foundations of the new régime,

Believing that optimum utilization of the new opportunities for social and economic development offered by the new régime will be facilitated through action at the national and international level aimed at strengthening national capabilities in marine science, technology and ocean services, particularly in the developing countries, with a view to ensuring the rapid absorption and efficient application of technology and scientific knowledge available to them,

Considering that national and regional marine scientific and technological centres would be the principal institutions through which States and, in particular, the developing countries, foster and conduct marine scientific research, and receive and disseminate marine technology.

Recognizing the special role of the competent international organizations en-visaged by the Convention on the Law of the Sea, especially in relation to the establishment and development of national and regional marine scientific and technological centres,

Noting that present efforts undertaken within the United Nations system in training, education and assistance in the field of marine science and technology and ocean services are far below current requirements and would be particularly inadequate to meet the demands generated through operation of the Convention on the Law of the Sea,

Welcoming recent initiatives within international organizations to promote and co-ordinate their major international assistance programmes aimed at strength-ening marine science infrastructures in developing countries,

1. *Calls upon* all Member States to determine appropriate priorities in their development plans for the strengthening of their marine science, technology and ocean services;

2. *Calls upon* the developing countries to establish programmes for the pro-motion of technical co-operation among themselves in the field of marine science, technology and ocean service development;

3. *Urges* the industrialized countries to assist the developing countries in the preparation and implementation of their marine science, technology and ocean service development programmes;

4. *Recommends* that the World Bank, the regional banks, the United Nations Development Programme, the United Nations Financing System for Science and Technology and other multilateral funding agencies augment and co-ordinate their operations for the provision of funds to developing countries for the preparation and implementation of major programmes of assistance in strengthening their marine science, technology and ocean services;

5. *Recommends* that all competent international organizations within the United Nations system expand programmes within their respective fields of com-petence for assistance to developing countries in the field of marine science technology and ocean services and co-ordinate their efforts on a system-wide ba-sis in the implementation of such programmes, paying particular attention to the special needs of the developing countries, whether coastal, land-locked or geo-graphically disadvantaged;

6. *Requests* the Secretary-General of the United Nations to transmit this reso-lution to the General Assembly at its thirty-seventh session.

Appendix

OBSERVERS THAT PARTICIPATED AT SESSIONS OF THE CONFERENCE

States and territories

Cook Islands (third and tenth sessions)
Netherlands Antilles (third to resumed seventh sessions, resumed eighth session, ninth and eleventh sessions)
Papua New Guinea (third session)
Seychelles (fifth session)
Suriname (third session)
Trust Territory of the Pacific Islands (third to eleventh sessions)

Liberation movements

African National Congress (South Africa)
African National Council (Zimbabwe)
African Party for the Independence of Guinea and Cape Verde Islands (PAIGC)
Palestine Liberation Organization
Pan Africanist Congress of Azania (South Africa)
Patriotic Front (Zimbabwe)
Seychelles People's United Party (SPUP)
South West Africa People's Organization (SWAPO)

Specialized agencies and other organizations

International Labour Organisation (ILO)
Food and Agriculture Organization of the United Nations (FAO)
United Nations Educational, Scientific and Cultural Organization (UNESCO)
Intergovernmental Oceanographic Commission (IOC)
International Civil Aviation Organization (ICAO)
World Health Organization (WHO)

World Bank

International Telecommunication Union (ITU)
World Meteorological Organization (WMO)
International Maritime Organization (IMO)
World Intellectual Property Organization (WIPO)

International Atomic Energy Agency (IAEA)

Intergovernmental organizations

Andes Development Corporation
Asian-African Legal Consultative Committee

Commonwealth Secretariat
Council of Arab Economic Unity
Council of Europe
European Communities
Inter-American Development Bank
International Hydrographic Bureau
International Oil Pollution Compensation Fund
League of Arab States
Organization of African Unity
Organization of American States
Organization of Arab Petroleum Exporting Countries
Organization of the Islamic Conference
Organization for Economic Co-operation and Development
Organization of Petroleum Exporting Countries
Permanent Commission for the South Pacific
Saudi-Sudanese Red Sea Joint Commission
West African Economic Community

Non-governmental organizations

Category I

International Chamber of Commerce
International Confederation of Free Trade Unions
International Co-operative Alliance
International Council of Voluntary Agencies
International Council of Women
International Youth and Student Movement for the United Nations
United Towns Organization
World Confederation of Labour
World Federation of United Nations Associations
World Muslim Congress

Category II

Arab Lawyers Union
Bahá'i International Community
Baptist World Alliance
Carnegie Endowment for International Peace
Commission of the Churches on International Affairs
Foundation for the Peoples of the South Pacific, Inc., The
Friends World Committee for Consultation
Inter-American Council of Commerce and Production
International Air Transport Association
International Association for Religious Freedom
International Bar Association
International Chamber of Shipping

International Commission of Jurists
International Co-operation for Socio-Economic Development
International Council of Environmental Law
International Council of Scientific Unions
International Federation for Human Rights
International Hotel Association
International Law Association
International Movement for Fraternal Union among Races and Peoples (UFER)
International Organization of Consumers' Unions
International Union for Conservation of Nature and Natural Resources
Latin American Association of Finance Development Institutions (ALIDE)
Mutual Assistance of the Latin American Government Oil Companies (ARPEL)
Pan American Federation of Engineering Societies (UPADI)
Pax Christi, International Catholic Peace Movement
Society for International Development (SID)
Women's International League for Peace and Freedom
World Alliance of Young Men's Christian Associations
World Association of World Federalists
World Conference on Religion and Peace
World Peace Through Law Centre
World Young Women's Christian Association

Roster

Asian Environmental Society
Center for Inter-American Relations
Commission to Study the Organization of Peace
Foresta Institute for Ocean and Mountain Studies
Friends of the Earth (F.O.E.)
International Institute for Environment and Development
International Ocean Institute
International Studies Association
National Audubon Society
Population Institute
Sierra Club
United Seamen's Service
World Federation of Scientific Workers
World Society of Ekistics

FINAL ACT OF THE UNITED NATIONS CONFERENCE ON STRADDLING FISH STOCKS AND HIGHLY MIGRATORY FISH STOCKS

I. INTRODUCTION

1.   The United Nations Conference on Straddling Fish Stocks and Highly Migratory Fish Stocks was convened pursuant to paragraph 1 of General Assembly resolution 47/192 of 22 December 1992 in accordance with the mandate agreed upon at the United Nations Conference on Environment and Development.

2.   The United Nations Conference on Environment and Development, held at Rio de Janeiro from 3 to 14 June 1992, adopted Agenda 21, paragraph 17.49 of which reads as follows:

"States should take effective action, including bilateral and multilateral co-operation, where appropriate at the subregional, regional and global levels, to ensure that high seas fisheries are managed in accordance with the provisions of the United Nations Convention on the Law of the Sea. In particular, they should:

(e)   Convene, as soon as possible, an intergovernmental conference under United Nations auspices, taking into account relevant activities at the subregional, regional and global levels, with a view to promoting effective implementation of the provisions of the United Nations Convention on the Law of the Sea on straddling fish stocks and highly migratory fish stocks. The conference, drawing, *inter alia,* on scientific and technical studies by FAO, should identify and assess existing problems related to the conservation and management of such fish stocks, and consider means of improving cooperation on fisheries among States, and formulate appropriate recommendations. The work and results of the conference should be fully consistent with the provisions of the United Nations Convention on the Law of the Sea, in particular the rights and obligations of coastal States and States fishing on the high seas."[1]

3.   The General Assembly, in its resolution 47/192, recalled Agenda 21, in particular chapter 17, programme area C, relating to the sustainable use and conservation of marine living resources of the high seas, and decided that the Conference, in accordance with the mandate quoted above, should take into account relevant activities at the subregional, regional and global levels, with a view to promoting effective implementation of the provisions of the United Nations Convention on the Law of the Sea on straddling fish stocks and highly migratory fish stocks. The Assembly further decided that the Conference, drawing, *inter alia,* on scientific and technical studies by the Food and Agriculture Organization

of the United Nations, should: (a) identify and assess existing problems related to the conservation and management of such fish stocks; (b) consider means of improving fisheries cooperation among States; and (c) formulate appropriate recommendations.

4.   The General Assembly also reaffirmed that the work and results of the Conference should be fully consistent with the provisions of the United Nations Convention on the Law of the Sea, in particular the rights and obligations of coastal States and States fishing on the high seas, and that States should give full effect to the high seas fisheries provisions of the Convention with regard to fisheries populations whose ranges lie both within and beyond exclusive economic zones (straddling fish stocks) and highly migratory fish stocks.

5.   By the same resolution, the General Assembly invited relevant specialized agencies, particularly the Food and Agriculture Organization of the United Nations, and other appropriate organs, organizations and programmes of the United Nations system, as well as regional and subregional fisheries organizations, to contribute relevant scientific and technical studies and reports. It also invited relevant non-governmental organizations from developed and developing countries to contribute to the Conference within the areas of their competence and expertise.

II. SESSIONS OF THE CONFERENCE

6.   Pursuant to General Assembly resolutions 47/192, 48/194 of 21 December 1993 and 49/121 of 19 December 1994, the following sessions of the United Nations Conference on Straddling Fish Stocks and Highly Migratory Fish Stocks were held at United Nations Headquarters in New York:[2]
- First session: 19 to 23 April 1993;
- Second session: 12 to 30 July 1993;
- Third session: 14 to 31 March 1994;
- Fourth session: 15 to 26 August 1994;
- Fifth session: 27 March to 12 April 1995;
- Sixth session: 24 July to 4 August 1995.[3]

III. PARTICIPATION IN THE CONFERENCE

7.   Pursuant to paragraph 4 of General Assembly resolution 47/192, the following were invited to the Conference:
- (a) States Members of the United Nations or members of the specialized agencies and the International Atomic Energy Agency;
- (b) Representatives of organizations that have received a standing invitation from the General Assembly to participate, in the capacity of observers, in the sessions and work of all international conferences convened under its auspices;
- (c) Associate members of regional commissions;
- (d) Representatives of the national liberation movements recognized by the Organization of African Unity in its region;

(e) Specialized agencies and the International Atomic Energy Agency, as well as other organs, organizations and programmes of the United Nations system;

(f) Relevant intergovernmental organizations that had been invited to participate in the work of the Preparatory Committee for the United Nations Conference on Environment and Development;

(g) Regional and subregional fisheries organizations;

(h) Relevant non-governmental organizations.

8. The representatives of the following States participated in the sessions of the Conference: Albania, Algeria, Angola, Antigua and Barbuda, Argentina, Australia, Austria, Bahamas, Bahrain, Bangladesh, Barbados, Belarus, Belgium, Belize, Benin, Brazil, Bulgaria, Burundi, Cameroon, Canada, Cape Verde, Chile, China, Colombia, Congo, Cook Islands, Costa Rica, Côte d'Ivoire, Cuba, Cyprus, Democratic People's Republic of Korea, Denmark, Djibouti, Ecuador, Egypt, El Salvador, Eritrea, Estonia, Fiji, Finland, France, Gabon, Gambia, Germany, Ghana, Greece, Grenada, Guatemala, Guinea, Guinea-Bissau, Guyana, Honduras, Hungary, Iceland, India, Indonesia, Iran (Islamic Republic of), Ireland, Israel, Italy, Jamaica, Japan, Kazakstan, Kenya, Kiribati, Latvia, Lebanon, Lesotho, Libyan Arab Jamahiriya, Liechtenstein, Lithuania, Luxembourg, Madagascar, Malaysia, Maldives, Mali, Malta, Marshall Islands, Mauritania, Mauritius, Mexico, Micronesia (Federated States of), Morocco, Myanmar, Namibia, Netherlands, New Zealand, Nicaragua, Niger, Nigeria, Niue, Norway, Pakistan, Palau, Panama, Papua New Guinea, Peru, Philippines, Poland, Portugal, Qatar, Republic of Korea, Romania, Russian Federation, Saint Lucia, Samoa, Saudi Arabia, Senegal, Seychelles, Sierra Leone, Singapore, Solomon Islands, South Africa, Spain, Sri Lanka, Suriname, Sweden, Switzerland, Syrian Arab Republic, Thailand, Togo, Tonga, Trinidad and Tobago, Tunisia, Turkey, Tuvalu, Uganda, Ukraine, United Arab Emirates, United Kingdom of Great Britain and Northern Ireland, United Republic of Tanzania, United States of America, Uruguay, Vanuatu, Venezuela, Viet Nam, Zambia and Zimbabwe.

9. The representative of the European Community[4] participated in the sessions without the right to vote.

10. The following associate members of a regional commission were represented as observers at the sessions: Montserrat and United States Virgin Islands.

11. The following national liberation movement was represented as observer at the first session: Pan Africanist Congress of Azania.

12. The following specialized agencies were represented as observers at the sessions: Food and Agriculture Organization of the United Nations (FAO), United Nations Educational, Scientific and Cultural Organization (UNESCO) and World Bank.

13. The Intergovernmental Oceanographic Commission (IOC) of UNESCO, the United Nations Development Programme (UNDP) and the United Nations Environment Programme (UNEP) were also present as observers at the sessions.

14. The following intergovernmental organizations were represented as observers at the sessions: Asian-African Legal Consultative Committee, Commission

on the Indian Ocean, Inter-American Tropical Tuna Commission, International Commission for the Conservation of Atlantic Tunas, International Council for the Exploration of the Sea, International Maritime Satellite Organization, International Whaling Commission, Latin American Organization for the Development of Fisheries, Ministerial Conference on Fisheries Cooperation among African States bordering the Atlantic Ocean, North Atlantic Salmon Conservation Organization, Northwest Atlantic Fisheries Organization, Organization of African Unity, Organisation for Economic Cooperation and Development, South Pacific Commission, South Pacific Permanent Commission and South Pacific Forum Fisheries Agency.

15. The following non-governmental organizations were represented as observers at the sessions: Alaska Marine Conservation Council, Alaska Public Interest Research Group, American Oceans Campaign, American Society of International Law, Association Algérienne pour la Protection de la Nature et de l'Environnement, Association Tunisienne pour la Protection de la Nature et de l'Environnement, Association of the Bar of the City of New York, Atlantic Salmon Federation, Bering Sea Fisherman's Association, Both Ends, Canadian Oceans Caucus, Center for Development of International Law, Center for Marine Conservation, Centre de Recherches pour le Développement des Technologies Intermédiares de Pêche, Comité Catholique Contre la Faim et pour le Développement, Confederación de Trabajadores Portuarios, Gente de Mar y Pesqueros de Chile, Confederación Nacional de Pescadores Artesanales de Chile, Coordinadora de Tripulantes Pesqueros Industriales del Cono Sur de América Latina, Council on Ocean Law, Earth Council, Earth Island Institute, Earthtrust, Environmental Defense Fund, Federación Nacional de Cooperativas Pesqueras del Ecuador, Federation of Japan Tuna Fisheries Cooperative Associations, Fish, Food and Allied Workers, Fisheries Council of Canada, Four Directions Council, Friends of the Earth International, Friends World Committee for Consultations (Quaker United Nations Office), Fundación Hernandiana, Global Education Associates, Greenpeace International, Groupement d'Intérêt Économique, International Coalition of Fisheries Associations, International Coastal and Ocean Organization, International Collective in Support of Fishworkers, International Confederation of Free Trade Unions, International Institute for Sustainable Development, International Law Association, International Ocean Institute, International Union for the Conservation of Nature and Natural Resources (IUCN), Japan Fisheries Association, Kandune Self Help Water Project, Marine Environmental Research Institute, Namibian Food and Allied Workers Union, National Audubon Society, National Wildlife Federation, Nationwide Coalition of Fisherfolks for Aquatic Reform, Natural Resources Defense Council, Netherlands National Committee for IUCN, Newfoundland and Labrador Environmental Association, Newfoundland Inshore Fisheries Association, Oceans Institute of Canada, Ocean Trust, Overseas Fishery Cooperation Foundation, Pamalakaya (National United Movement of Fisherfolk - Philippines), Red Mexicana de Acción frente al Libre Comercio, Réserve Internationale Maritime en Mediterranée Occidentale, Samoan Association of Non-governmental Organizations, Sindicato de Obreros Marítimos Unidos, SONAR (Save Our

Northwest Atlantic Resources), Trickle Up Program, United Nations Association in Canada, United Nations Association-United Kingdom, United Nations Environment and Development-United Kingdom Committee, Wildlife Conservation Society, Women and Fisheries Network, World Wide Fund for Nature, World Wide Fund Suisse.

16. Pursuant to paragraph 9 of General Assembly resolution 47/192, a voluntary fund was established in the Secretariat for the purpose of assisting developing countries, especially those most concerned by the subject-matter of the Conference, in particular the least developed among them, to participate in the Conference. Contributions to the Fund were made by the Governments of Canada, Japan, Norway and the Republic of Korea.

IV. OFFICERS AND COMMITTEES

17. At its first meeting, the Conference elected Mr. Satya N. Nandan (Fiji) as its Chairman.

18. The Conference also elected as Vice-Chairmen the representatives of the following States: Chile, Italy and Mauritania.

19. The Conference appointed the representatives of the following States as members of the Credentials Committee: Antigua and Barbuda, Argentina, Burundi, China, Kenya, New Zealand, Papua New Guinea, Russian Federation and United States of America. At its first meeting, on 28 July 1993, the Credentials Committee elected Mr. Alberto Luis Daverede (Argentina) as its Chairman.

20. At the first and second sessions, Mr. Carl-August Fleischhauer, Under-Secretary-General for Legal Affairs, the Legal Counsel, and thereafter Mr. Hans Corell, served as Secretary-General of the Conference, representing the Secretary-General of the United Nations. For the first four sessions, Mr. Dolliver L. Nelson, and thereafter Mr. Moritaka Hayashi, served as Secretary of the Conference.

21. In accordance with paragraph 11 of General Assembly resolution 47/192, the Food and Agriculture Organization of the United Nations provided an officer, Mr. David J. Doulman, to serve as Scientific and Technical Adviser to the Conference.

V. DOCUMENTATION OF THE CONFERENCE

22. The Conference documentation[5] included, inter alia, the following:
(a) Rules of procedure;[6]
(b) Proposals and other communications submitted by delegations;[7]
(c) Reports and studies submitted by the Secretariat, FAO and IOC;[8]
(d) Reports and comments submitted by intergovernmental organizations, regional and subregional fisheries organizations and arrangements;[9]
(e) Statements by the Chairman of the Conference;[10]
(f) A guide to the issues before the Conference, the negotiating texts and the draft agreement prepared by the Chairman of the Conference.[11]

VI. WORK OF THE CONFERENCE

23. The Conference adopted its agenda (A/CONF.164/5) and rules of procedure (A/CONF.164/6) at its first session.

24. At the second session, the Conference devoted the first three days to general debate, following which the Chairman outlined the key issues on which there was general agreement.[12]

25. At the same session, the Conference proceeded to examine the issues relating to straddling fish stocks and highly migratory fish stocks as contained in the document entitled "A guide to the issues before the Conference prepared by the Chairman" (A/CONF.164/10).

26. At the end of the second session, the Chairman prepared a negotiating text (A/CONF.164/13), which the Conference considered at the third session.

27. Also at the third session, the Conference established two open-ended working groups to consider the information papers, prepared by FAO at the request of the Conference, on the precautionary approach to fisheries management and on management reference points. Mr. Andrés Couve (Chile) and Mr. Andrew Rosenberg (United States of America) served as chairmen of the working groups. The results of the work of the two working groups are contained in documents A/CONF.164/WP.1 and WP.2. At the end of the third session, the Chairman submitted a revision of his negotiating text (A/CONF.164/13/Rev.1), which reflected the work of the Working Groups.

28. At the fourth session, the Chairman prepared a new revision of his negotiating text in the form of a binding instrument, entitled "Draft Agreement for the Implementation of the Provisions of the United Nations Convention on the Law of the Sea of 10 December 1982 relating to the Conservation and Management of Straddling Fish Stocks and Highly Migratory Fish Stocks" (A/CONF.164/22). At the end of the fifth session, the Chairman prepared a revised text of the Draft Agreement (A/CONF.164/22/Rev.1).

29. At the sixth session, the Conference considered the revised text of the Draft Agreement (A/CONF.164/22/Rev.1), as well as suggested drafting changes and editorial improvements (A/CONF.164/CRP.7). Following the deliberations of the Conference, the Chairman proposed for adoption a "Draft Agreement for the Implementation of the Provisions of the United Nations Convention on the Law of the Sea of 10 December 1982 relating to the Conservation and Management of Straddling Fish Stocks and Highly Migratory Fish Stocks" (A/CONF.164/33).

30. On 4 August 1995, the Conference adopted without a vote the Agreement for the Implementation of the Provisions of the United Nations Convention on the Law of the Sea of 10 December 1982 relating to the Conservation and Management of Straddling Fish Stocks and Highly Migratory Fish Stocks, as well as resolutions I and II (A/CONF.164/32, annex). The two resolutions are annexed to this Final Act. In doing so, the Conference discharged the mandate given to it by the General Assembly in its resolution 47/192.

31. The Conference decided to resume its sixth session on 4 December 1995 for a ceremony of signature of the Agreement and this Final Act. The Conference

requested the Secretariat to prepare the final text of the Agreement, incorporating necessary editing and drafting changes and ensuring concordance among the six language versions.[13]

IN WITNESS WHEREOF the undersigned have signed this Final Act.

DONE AT UNITED NATIONS HEADQUARTERS in New York this fourth day of December, one thousand nine hundred ninety-five, in a single copy in the Arabic, Chinese, English, French, Russian and Spanish languages, each text being equally authentic. The original texts shall be deposited in the archives of the United Nations Secretariat.

The Chairman of the Conference:
Satya N. NANDAN

The Under-Secretary-General for Legal Affairs, The Legal Counsel:
Hans CORELL

The Secretary of the Conference:
Moritaka HAYASHI

Notes to the Final Act

[1] *Official Records of the General Assembly, Twenty-second Session, Annexes*, agenda item 92, document A/6695.

[2] *Ibid., Twenty-third Session, Annexes*, agenda item 26, document A/7230.

[3] *Ibid., Twenty-fourth Session, Supplement Nos. 22 and* 22A (A/7622 and Corr.1 and A/7622/Add.1).

[4] *Ibid., Twenty-sixth Session, Supplement No. 21* (A/8421) ; *ibid., Twenty-seventh Session, Supplement No. 21* (A/8721 and Corr.1); and *ibid., Twenty-eighth Session, Supplement No. 21* (A/9021 and Corr.1-3) , vols. I- VI.

[5] In addition it may be noted that the Conference was attended and assisted by observers from the United Nations Programmes and Conferences.

[6] General Assembly resolution 3334 (XXIX) of 17 December 1974.

[7] General Assembly resolution 3483 (XXX) of 12 December 1975.

[8] Decision taken at the 69th meeting of the plenary Conference on 7 May 1976 (see *Official Records of the Third United Nations Conference on the Law of the Sea*, vol. V, A/CONF.62/SR.69) .

[9] General Assembly resolution 31/63 of 10 December 1976.

[10] General Assembly resolution 32/194 of 20 December 1977.

[11] Decision taken at the 106th meeting of the plenary on 19 May 1978 (see *Official Records of the Third United Nations Conference on the Law of the Sea*, vol. IX, A/CONF.62/SR.106).

[12] General Assembly resolution 33/17 of 10 November 1978.

[13] Decision taken at the 115th meeting of the plenary on 27 April 1979 (see *Official Records of the Third United Nations Conference on the Law of the Sea*, vol. XI, A/CONF.62/SR.115).

ANNEX

RESOLUTION I

EARLY AND EFFECTIVE IMPLEMENTATION OF THE AGREEMENT FOR THE IMPLEMENTATION OF THE PROVISIONS OF THE UNITED NATIONS CONVENTION ON THE LAW OF THE SEA OF 10 DECEMBER 1982 RELATING TO THE CONSERVATION AND MANAGEMENT OF STRADDLING FISH STOCKS AND HIGHLY MIGRATORY FISH STOCKS

The United Nations Conference on Straddling Fish Stocks and Highly Migratory Fish Stocks,

Having adopted the Agreement for the Implementation of the Provisions of the United Nations Convention on the Law of the Sea of 10 December 1982 relating to the Conservation and Management of Straddling Fish Stocks and Highly Migratory Fish Stocks,

Underlining the importance of early and effective implementation of the Agreement,

Recognizing, therefore, the need to provide for the provisional application of the Agreement,

Emphasizing the importance of rapid entry into force of the Agreement and early achievement of universal participation,

1. *Requests* the Secretary-General of the United Nations to open the Agreement for signature in New York on 4 December 1995;

2. *Urges* all States and other entities referred to in article 1, paragraph 2 (b), of the Agreement to sign it on 4 December 1995 or at the earliest subsequent opportunity and thereafter to ratify, or accede to it;

3. *Calls upon* States and other entities referred to in paragraph 2 of the present resolution to apply the Agreement provisionally.

RESOLUTION II

REPORTS ON DEVELOPMENTS BY THE SECRETARY-GENERAL OF THE UNITED NATIONS

The United Nations Conference on Straddling Fish Stocks and Highly Migratory Fish Stocks,

Having adopted the Agreement for the Implementation of the Provisions of the United Nations Convention on the Law of the Sea of 10 December 1982 relating to the Conservation and Management of Straddling Fish Stocks and Highly Migratory Fish Stocks,

Recognizing the importance of periodic consideration and review of developments relating to the conservation and management of straddling fish stocks and highly migratory fish stocks,

Recalling General Assembly resolution 49/28 of 6 December 1994, in which the Assembly underlined the importance of consideration and review of the overall developments relating to the law of the sea by the Assembly, as the global institution having the competence to undertake such a review,

Recalling also the responsibility of the Secretary-General under the United Nations Convention on the Law of the Sea to report on developments pertaining to the implementation of the Convention,

Recognizing the importance of exchange of information among States, and relevant intergovernmental and non-governmental organizations concerning the implementation of the Agreement,

1.   *Recommends* to the General Assembly that it review developments relating to the conservation and management of straddling fish stocks and highly migratory fish stocks, on the basis of a report to be submitted by the Secretary-General at the second session following the adoption of the Agreement and biennially thereafter;

2.   *Requests* the Secretary-General of the United Nations, in preparing such report, to take into account information provided by States, the Food and Agriculture Organization of the United Nations and its fisheries bodies and subregional and regional organizations and arrangements for the conservation and management of straddling fish stocks and highly migratory fish stocks, as well as other relevant intergovernmental bodies and relevant non-governmental organizations;

3.   *Also requests* the Secretary-General to cooperate with the Food and Agriculture Organization of the United Nations in order to ensure that reporting on all major fisheries instruments and activities is coordinated and the required scientific and technical analysis standardized to minimize duplication and to reduce the reporting burden for national administrations.

RESOLUTIONS OF THE UNITED NATIONS GENERAL ASSEMBLY CONCERNING THE PEACEFUL USES OF THE SEABED AND OCEAN FLOOR BEYOND THE LIMITS OF NATIONAL JURISDICTION, THE THIRD UNITED NATIONS CONVENTION ON THE LAW OF THE SEA

2340 (XXII). Examination of the question of the reservation exclusively for peaceful purposes of seabed and the ocean floor, and the subsoil thereof, underlying the high seas beyond the limits of present national jurisdiction, and the use of their resources in the interests of mankind

The General Assembly,

Having considered the item, entitled "Examination of the question of the reservation exclusively for peaceful purposes of the seabed and the ocean floor, and the subsoil thereof, underlying the high seas beyond the limits of present national jurisdiction, and the use of their resources in the interests of mankind",

Noting that developing technology is making the seabed and the ocean floor, and the subsoil thereof, accessible and exploitable for scientific, economic, military and other purposes,

Recognizing the common interest of mankind in the seabed and the ocean floor, which constitute the major portion of the area of this planet,

Recognizing further that the exploration and use of the seabed and the ocean floor and the subsoil thereof, as contemplated in the title of the item, should be conducted in accordance with the purposes and principles of the Charter of the United Nations, in the interest of maintaining international peace and security and for the benefit of all mankind,

Mindful of the provisions and practice of the law of the sea relating to this question,

Mindful also of the importance of preserving the seabed and the ocean floor, and the subsoil thereof, as contemplated in the title of the item, from actions and uses which might be detrimental to the common interests of mankind,

Desiring to foster greater international co-operation and co-ordination in the further peaceful exploration and use of the seabed and the ocean floor, and the subsoil thereof, as contemplated in the title of the item.

Recalling the past and continuing valuable work on questions relating to this matter carried out by the competent organs of the United Nations, the specialized agencies, the International Atomic Energy Agency and other intergovernmental organizations,

Recalling further that surveys are being prepared by the Secretary-General in response to General Assembly resolution 2172 (XXI) of 6 December 1966 and Economic and Social Council resolution 1112 (XL) of 7 March 1966,

1.   *Decides* to establish an Ad Hoc Committee to Study the Peaceful Uses of the Seabed and the Ocean Floor beyond the Limits of National Jurisdiction, composed of Argentina, Australia, Austria, Belgium, Brazil, Bulgaria, Canada, Ceylon, Chile, Czechoslovakia, Ecuador, El Salvador, France, Iceland, India, Italy, Japan, Kenya, Liberia, Libya, Malta, Norway, Pakistan, Peru, Poland, Romania, Senegal, Somalia, Thailand, the Union of Soviet Socialist Republics, the United Arab Republic, the United Kingdom of Great Britain and Northern Ireland, the United Republic of Tanzania, the United States of America and Yugoslavia, to study the scope and various aspects of this item;

2.   *Requests* the Ad Hoc Committee, in co-operation with the Secretary-General, to prepare, for consideration by the General Assembly at its twenty-third session, a study which would include:

(a)   Survey of the past and present activities of the United Nations, the specialized agencies, the International Atomic Energy Agency and other intergovernmental bodies with regard to the seabed and the ocean floor, and of existing international agreements concerning these areas:

(b)   An account of the scientific, technical, economic, legal and other aspects of this item;

(c)   An indication regarding practical means of promoting international co-operation in the exploration, conservation and use of the seabed and the ocean floor, and the subsoil thereof, as contemplated in the title of the item, and of their resources, having regard to the views expressed and the suggestions put forward by Member States during the consideration of this item at the twenty-second session of the General Assembly;

3.   *Requests* the Secretary-General:

(a)   To transmit the text of the present resolution to the Governments of all Member States in order to seek their views on the subject;

(b)   To transmit to the Ad Hoc Committee the records of the First Committee relating to the discussion of this item;

(c)   To render all appropriate assistance to the Ad Hoc Committee, including the submission to it of the results of the studies being undertaken in pursuance of General Assembly resolution 2172 (XXI) and Economic and Social Council resolution 1112 (XL), and such documentation pertinent to this item as may be provided by the United Nations Educational, Scientific and Cultural Organization and its Intergovernmental Oceanographic Commission, the Inter-Governmental Maritime Consultative Organization, the Food and Agriculture Organization of the United Nations, the World Meteorological Organization, the World Health Organization, the International Atomic Energy Agency and other intergovernmental bodies;

4.   *Invites* the specialized agencies, the International Atomic Energy Agency and other intergovernmental bodies to co-operate fully with the Ad Hoc Committee in the implementation of the present resolution.

1639th plenary meeting,
18 December 1967.

2467(XXIII). Examination of the question of the reservation exclusively for peaceful purposes of the seabed and the ocean floor, and the subsoil thereof, underlying the high seas beyond the limits of present national jurisdiction, and the use of their resources in the interests of mankind.

A

The General Assembly,

Recalling the item entitled "Examination of the question of the reservation exclusively for peaceful purposes of the seabed and the ocean floor, and the subsoil thereof, underlying the high seas beyond the limits of present national jurisdiction, and the use of their resources in the interests of mankind",

Having in mind its resolution 2340 (XXII) of 18 December 1967 concerned with the problems arising in the area to which the title of the item refers,

Reaffirming the objectives set forth in that resolution,

Taking note with appreciation of the report prepared by the Ad Hoc Committee to Study the Peaceful Uses of the Seabed and the Ocean Floor beyond the Limits of National Jurisdiction,[1] keeping in mind the views expressed in the course of its work and drawing upon its experience,

Recognizing that it is in the interest of mankind as a whole to favour the exploration and use of the seabed and the ocean floor, and the subsoil thereof, beyond the limits of national jurisdiction, for peaceful purposes,

Considering that it is important to promote international co-operation for the exploration and exploitation of the resources of this area,

Convinced that such exploitation should be carried out for the benefit of mankind as a whole, irrespective of the geographical location of States, taking into account the special interests and needs of the developing countries,

Considering that it is essential to provide , within the United Nations system, a focal point for the elaboration of desirable measures of international cooperation, taking into account alternative actual and potential uses of this area, and for the co-ordination of the activities of international organizations in this regard,

1.   *Establishes* a Committee on the Peaceful Uses of the Seabed and the Ocean Floor beyond the Limits of National Jurisdiction, composed of forty-two States;

2.   *Instructs* the Committee:
(a)   To study the elaboration of the legal principles and norms which would promote international co-operation in the exploration and use of the sea-bed and the ocean floor, and the subsoil thereof, beyond the limits of national jurisdiction and ensure the exploitation of their resources for the benefit of mankind, and the economic and other requirements which such a régime should satisfy in order to meet the interests of humanity as a whole;
(b)   To study the ways and means of promoting the exploitation and use of the resources of this area, and of international co-operation to that end, taking into account the foreseeable development of technology and the economic implications of such exploitation and bearing in mind the fact that such exploitation should benefit mankind as a whole;
(c)   To review the studies carried out in the field of exploration and research in this area and aimed at intensifying international co-operation and stimulating the exchange and the widest possible dissemination of scientific knowledge on the subject;
(d)   To examine proposed measures of co-operation to be adopted by the international community in order to prevent the marine pollution which may result from the exploration and exploitation of the resources of this area;

3.   *Also calls upon* the Committee to study further, within the context of the title of the item, and taking into account the studies and international negotiations being undertaken in the field of disarmament, the reservation exclusively for peaceful purposes of the seabed and the ocean floor without prejudice to the limits which may be agreed upon in this respect;

4.   *Requests* the Committee:
(a)   To work in close co-operation with the specialized agencies, the International Atomic Energy Agency and the intergovernmental bodies dealing with the problems referred to in the present resolution, so as to avoid any duplication or overlapping of activities;
(b)   To make recommendations to the General Assembly on the questions mentioned in paragraphs 2 and 3 above;
(c)   In co-operation with the Secretary-General, to submit to the General Assembly reports on its activities at each subsequent session;

5.   *Invites* the specialized agencies, the International Atomic Energy Agency and other intergovernmental bodies including the Intergovernmental Oceanographic Commission of the United Nations Educational, Scientific and Cultural Organization to co-operate fully with the Committee in the implementation of the present resolution.

1752nd plenary meeting,
21 December 1968.

B

The General Assembly,

Recognizing that it is in the common interest of all nations that the exploration and exploitation of the resources of the seabed and the ocean floor, and the subsoil thereof, should be conducted in such a manner as to avoid infringement of the other interests and established rights of nations with respect to the uses of the sea,

Mindful of the threat to the marine environment presented by pollution and other hazardous and harmful effects which might result from exploration and exploitation of the areas under consideration,

Desiring to promote effective measures of prevention and control of such pollution and to allay the serious damage which might be caused to the marine environment and, in particular, to the living marine resources which constitute one of mankind's most valuable food resources,

Recognizing the complex problem of ensuring effective coordination in the wide field of environmental pollution and in the more specific area of prevention and control of marine pollution,

Noting with satisfaction the measures being undertaken by the Inter-Governmental Maritime Consultative Organization to prevent and control pollution of the sea by preparing new draft conventions and other instruments for that purpose,

Recalling, in this regard, the progress achieved towards such concerted action by intergovernmental bodies and the establishment, by the Food and Agriculture Organization of the United Nations, the United Nations Educational, Scientific and Cultural Organization and its Intergovernmental Oceanographic Commission, the Inter-Governmental Maritime Consultative Organization and the World Meteorological Organization, of a joint group of experts on the scientific aspects of marine pollution,

Recalling further the competence and continuing valuable contributions of the other intergovernmental organizations concerned,

1. *Welcomes* the adoption by States of appropriate safeguards against the dangers of pollution and other hazardous and harmful effects that might arise from the exploration and exploitation of the resources of the seabed and the ocean floor, and the subsoil thereof, beyond the limits of national jurisdiction, notably in the form of concrete measures of international co-operation for the purpose of realizing this aim;

2. *Considers* that, in connexion with the elaboration of principles underlying possible future international agreements for the area concerned, a study should be made with a view to clarifying all aspects of protection of the living and other resources of the seabed and the ocean floor, the superjacent waters and the adjacent coasts against the consequences of pollution and other hazardous and harmful effects arising from various modalities of such exploration and exploitation;

3. *Considers further* that such a study should take into consideration the importance of minimizing interference between the many means by which the

wealth of the ocean space may be harvested, and that it should extend to the examination of the circumstances in which measures may be undertaken by States for the protection of the living and other resources of those areas in which pollution detrimental to those resources has occurred or is imminent;

4.   *Requests* the Secretary-General, in co-operation with the appropriate and competent body or bodies presently undertaking co-ordinated work in the field of marine pollution control, to undertake the study referred to in paragraphs 2 and 3 above and to submit a report thereon to the General Assembly and the Committee on the Peaceful Uses of the Seabed and the Ocean Floor beyond the Limits of National Jurisdiction.

1752nd plenary meeting,
21 December 1968.

C

The General Assembly,

Having considered the item entitled "Examination of the question of the reservation exclusively for peaceful purposes of the seabed and the ocean floor, and the subsoil thereof, underlying the high seas beyond the limits of present national jurisdiction, and the use of their resources in the interests of mankind",

Reaffirming that exploration and exploitation of the resources of the seabed and the ocean floor, and the subsoil thereof, should be carried out for the benefit of mankind as a whole, taking into special consideration the interests and needs of the developing countries,

Recalling that international co-operation in this field is of paramount importance,

Bearing in mind its resolution A above establishing the Committee on the Peaceful Uses of the Seabed and the cean Floor beyond the Limits of National Jurisdiction, and the mandate entrusted to it,

1.   *Requests* the Secretary-General to undertake a study on the question of establishing in due time appropriate international machinery for the promotion of the exploration and exploitation of the resources of this area, and the use of these resources in the interests of mankind, irrespective of the geographical location of States, and taking into special consideration the interests and needs of the developing countries, and to submit a report thereon to the Committee on the Peaceful Uses of the Seabed and the Ocean Floor beyond the Limits of National Jurisdiction for consideration during one of its sessions in 1969;

2.   *Calls upon* the Committee to submit a report on this question to the General Assembly at its twenty-fourth session.

1752nd plenary meeting,
21 December 1968.

D

The General Assembly,

Convinced that the nations of the world should join together, with due respect for national jurisdiction, in a common long-term programme of exploration of the ocean as a potential source of resources, which should eventually be used for meeting the needs of all mankind with due recognition of those of developing countries and irrespective of the geographical location of States,

Recalling also that in its resolution 2172 (XXI) of 6 December 1996 the General Assembly requested the Secretary-General to prepare proposals for ensuring the most effective arrangements for an expanded programme of international co-operation to assist in a better understanding of the marine environment through science, and for initiating and strengthening marine education and training programmes,

Recalling further the proposals made by the Secretary-General in his report,[2] pursuant to resolution 2172 (XXI), as well as the various views expressed during the consideration of this subject by the General Assembly at its twenty-third session,

Noting that the Bureau and Consultative Council of the Intergovernmental Oceanographic Commission of the United nations Educational, Scientific and Cultural Organization considered the proposed international decade of ocean exploration a useful initiative for broadening and accelerating investigations of the oceans and for strengthening international co-operation,

Endorsing the objectives expressed in Economic and Social Council resolutions 1380 (XLV), 1381 (XLV) and 1382 (XLV) of 2 August 1968 and recalling particularly the invitation to the General Assembly to endorse the concept of a co-ordinated long-term programme of oceanographic research, taking into account such initiatives as the proposal for an international decade of ocean exploration and international prgrammes already considered, approved and adopted by the Intergovernmental Oceanographic Commission for implementation in co-operation with other specialized agencies.

Aware of the consideration given to the proposal in the Ad Hoc Committee to Study the Peaceful Uses of the Seabed and the Ocean Floor beyond the Limits of National Jurisdiction, arising from the contribution which the international decade of ocean exploration would make to scientific research and exploration of the seabed and ocean floor, as an important part of a co-ordinated long-term international programme of oceanographic research,

Seeking to enrich the knowledge of all mankind by encouraging a free flow of scientific information on the oceans to all States,

1.   *Welcomes* the concept of an international decade of ocean exploration to be undertaken within the framework of a long-term programme of research and exploration, including scientific research and exploration of the seabed and the ocean floor, under the aegis of the United Nations on the understanding that all such activities falling under the national jurisdiction of a State shall be subject to the previous consent of such State, in accordance with international law;

2. *Invites* Member States to formulate proposals for national and international scientific programmes and agreed activities to be undertaken during the international decade of ocean exploration with due regard to the interests of developing countries, to transmit these proposals to the United Nations Educational, Scientific and Cultural Organization for the Intergovernmental Oceanographic Commission in time to begin the decade in 1970, and to embark on such activities as soon as practicable;

3. *Urges* Member States to publish as soon as practicable the results of all activities which they will have undertaken within the framework of the international decade of ocean exploration as part of a long-term co-ordinated programme of scientific research and exploration , and at the same time to communicate these results to the Intergovernmental Oceanographic Commission;

4. *Requests* the United Nations Educational, Scientific and Cultural Organization that its Intergovernmental Oceanographic Commission:

(a) Intensify its activities in the scientific field, within its terms of reference and in co-operation with other interested agencies, in particular with regard to co-ordinating the scientific aspects of a long-term and expanded programme of world-wide exploration of the oceans and their resources of which the international decade of ocean exploration will be an important element, including international agency programmes, an expanded international exchange of data from national programmes, and international efforts to strengthen the research capabilities of all interested nations with particular regard to the needs of the developing countries;

(b) Co-operate with the Secretary-General, in accordance with paragraph 4 of the General Assembly resolution 2414 (XXIII) of 17 December 1968 on the resources of the sea in the preparation of the comprehensive outline of the scope of the long-term programme of oceanographic research of which the international decade of ocean exploration will be an important element, making available its views as to the appropriate relationship between the several international programmes already considered, approved and adopted by the Intergovernmental Oceanographic Commission for implementation, the decade, and the long-term programme;

(c) Keep the Secretary-General informed of all proposals, programmes and activities of which it is informed in accordance with paragraphs 2 and 3 above together with any comments it may consider appropriate;

(d) Report through appropriate channels to the General Assembly at its twenty-fourth session on progress made in the implementation of the present resolution.

1752nd plenary meeting,
21 December 1968.

---

[1] Official Records of the General Assembly, Twenty-third Session, agenda item 26, document A/7230.

[2] E/4487 and Corr.1-6, and Add.1.

2574 (XXIV)   Question of the reservation exclusively for peaceful uses of the seabed and the ocean floor, and the subsoil thereof, underlying the high seas beyond the limits of present national jurisdiction, and the use of their resources in the interests of mankind

A

The General Assembly,

Recalling its resolutions 2340 (XXII) of 18 December 1967 and 2467 (XXIII) of 21 December 1968,

Having regard for the fact that the problems relating to the high seas, territorial waters, contiguous zones, the continental shelf, the superjacent waters, and the seabed and ocean floor beyond the limits of national jurisdiction, are closely linked together,

Considering that the definition of the continental shelf contained in the Convention on the Continental Shelf of 29 April 1958[1] does not define with sufficient precision the limits of the area over which a coastal State exercises sovereign rights for the purpose of exploration and exploitation of natural resources, and that customary international law on the subject is inconclusive,

Noting that developing technology is making the entire seabed and ocean floor progressively accessible and exploitable for scientific, economic, military and other purposes,

Affirming that there exists an area of the seabed and ocean floor and the subsoil thereof which lies beyond the limits of national jurisdiction,

Affirming further that this area should be used exclusively for peaceful purposes and its resources utilized for the benefit of all mankind,

Convinced of the urgent necessity of preserving this area from encroachment, or appropriation by any State, inconsistent with the common interest of mankind,

Noting that the establishment of an equitable international régime for this area would facilitate the task of determining the limits of the area to which that régime is to apply,

Noting further the continuing efforts of the Committee on the Peaceful Uses of the Seabed and the Ocean Floor beyond the Limits of National Jurisdiction to elaborate such a régime in accordance with paragraph 2 (a) of resolution 2467 A (XXIII),

1.   *Requests* the Secretary-General to ascertain the views of Member States on the desirability of convening at an early date a conference on the law of the sea to review the régimes of the high seas, the continental shelf, the territorial sea and contiguous zone, fishing and conservation of the living resources of the high seas, particularly in order to arrive at a clear, precise and internationally accepted definition of the area of the seabed and ocean floor which lies beyond the limits of national jurisdiction, in the light of the international régime to be established for that area;

2. *Requests* the Secretary-General to report on the results of his consultations to the General Assembly at its twenty-fifth session.

1833rd plenary meeting,
15 December 1969.

B

The General Assembly,

Recalling its resolutions 2340 (XXII) of 18 December 1967 and 2467 (XXIII) of 21 December 1968,

Having considered the report of the Committee on the Peaceful Uses of the Seabed and the Ocean Floor beyond the Limits of National Jurisdiction,[2]

Expressing its satisfaction to the International Atomic Energy Agency, the International Labour Organization, the Food and Agriculture Organization of the United Nations, the United Nations Educational, Scientific and Cultural Organization and its Intergovernmental Oceanographic Commission, and to the Inter-Governmental Maritime Consultative Organization for their participation in and contribution to the Committee's work, as well as to the Secretary-General for his assistance,

1. *Takes note with appreciation* of the report of the Committee on the Peaceful Uses of the Seabed and the Ocean Floor beyond the Limits of National Jurisdiction;

2. *Invites* the Committee to consider further the questions entrusted to it under General Assembly resolution 2467 (XXIII) with a view to formulating recommendations on these questions, in the light of the reports and studies to be made available to it and taking into account the views expressed in the General Assembly at its twenty-fourth session;

3. *Notes with interest* the synthesis at the end of the report of the Legal Sub-Committee,[3] which reflects the extent of the work done in the formulation of principles designed to promote international co-operation in the exploration and use of the seabed and the ocean floor, and the subsoil thereof, beyond the limits of national jurisdiction and ensure the exploitation of their resources for the benefit of mankind, irrespective of the geographical location of States, taking into account the special interests and needs of the developing countries, whether land-locked or coastal;

4. *Requests* the Committee to expedite its work of preparing a comprehensive and balanced statement of these principles and to submit a draft declaration to the General Assembly at its twenty-fifth session;

5. *Takes note* of the suggestions contained in the report of the Economic and Technical Sub-Committee;[4]

6. *Requests* the Committee to formulate recommendations regarding the economic and technical conditions and the rules for the exploitation of the resources of this area in the context of the régime to be set up.

1833rd plenary meeting,
15 December 1969.

C

The General Assembly,

Recalling its resolution 2467 (XXIII) of 21 December 1968,

Noting with appreciation the report of the Committee on the Peaceful Uses of the Seabed and the Ocean Floor beyond the Limits of National Jurisdiction,[5]

Noting with satisfaction the study on international machinery prepared by the Secretary-General, which is annexed to that report,

Bearing in mind the recommendation of the Committee that the Secretary-General should be requested to continue this study in depth,

1. *Requests* the Secretary-general to prepare a further study on various types of international machinery, particularly a study covering in depth the status, structure, functions and powers of an international machinery, having jurisdiction over the peaceful uses of the seabed and the ocean floor, and the subsoil thereof, beyond the limits of national jurisdiction, including the power to regulate, co-ordinate, supervise and control all activities relating to the exploration and exploitation of their resources, for the benefit of mankind as a whole, irrespective of the geographical location of States, taking into account the special interests and needs of the developing countries, whether land-locked or coastal;

2. *Requests* the Secretary-General to submit his report thereon to the Committee on the Peaceful Uses of the Seabed and the Ocean Floor beyond the Limits of National Jurisdiction for consideration during one of its sessions in 1970.

3. *Calls upon* the Committee to submit a report on this question to the General Assembly at its twenty-fifth session.

1833rd plenary meeting,
15 December 1969.

D

The General Assembly,

Recalling its resolution 2467 A (XXIII) of 21 December 1968 to the effect that the exploitation of the resources of the seabed and the ocean floor, and the subsoil thereof, beyond the limits of national jurisdiction, should be carried out for the benefit of mankind as a whole, irrespective of the geographical location of States, taking into account the special interests and needs of the developing countries,

Convinced that it is essential, for the achievement of this purpose, that such activities be carried out under an international régime, including appropriate international machinery,

Noting that this matter is under consideration by the Committee on the Peaceful Uses of the Seabed and the Ocean Floor beyond the Limits of National Jurisdiction,

Recalling its resolution 2340 (XXII) of 18 December 1967 on the importance of preserving the seabed and the ocean floor, and the subsoil thereof, beyond the limits of national jurisdiction, from actions and uses which might be detrimental to the common interests of mankind,

Declares that, pending the establishment of the aforementioned international régime:

(a) States and persons, physical or juridical, are bound to refrain from all activities of exploitation of the resources of the area of the seabed and ocean floor, and the subsoil thereof, beyond the limits of national jurisdiction;

(b) No claim to any part of that area or its resources shall be recognized.

1833rd plenary meeting,
15 December 1969.

---

[1] United Nations, *Treaty Series*, vol. 499 (1964), No. 7302.

[2] *Official Records of the General Assembly, Twenty-fourth Session, Supplement No. 22* (A/7622 and Corr.1) and Supplement No. 22A (A/7622/Add.1).

[3] *Ibid., Supplement No. 22 (A/7622 and Corr.1), part two.*

[4] *Ibid., part three.*

[5] *Ibid., Supplement No. 22 (A/7622 and Corr.1), and Supplement No. 22A (A/7622/Add.1).*

[6] *Ibid., Supplement No. 22 (A/7622 and Corr.1), annex II.*

2749 (XXV) Declaration of Principles Governing the Seabed and the Ocean Floor, and the Subsoil Thereof, beyond the Limits of National Jurisdiction

The General Assembly,

Recalling its resolutions 2340 (XXII) of 18 December 1967, 2467 (XXIII) of 21 December 1968 and 2574 (XXIV) of 15 December 1969, concerning the area to which the title of the item refers,

Affirming that there is an area of the seabed and the ocean floor, and the subsoil thereof, beyond the limits of national jurisdiction, the precise limits of which are yet to be determined,

Recognizing that the existing legal regime of the high seas does not provide substantive rules for regulating the exploration of the aforesaid area and the exploitation of its resources,

Convinced that the area shall be reserved exclusively for peaceful purposes and that the exploration of the area and the exploitation of its resources shall be carried out for the benefit of mankind as a whole,

Believing it essential that an international régime applying to the area and its resources and including appropriate international machinery should be established as soon as possible,

Bearing in mind that the development and use of the area and its resources shall be undertaken in such a manner as to foster the healthy development of the world economy and balanced growth of international trade, and to minimize any adverse economic effects caused by the fluctuation of prices of raw materials resulting from such activities,

Solemnly declares that:

1. The seabed and ocean floor, and the subsoil thereof, beyond the limits of national jurisdiction (hereinafter referred to as the area), as well as the resources of the area, are the common heritage of mankind.

2. The area shall not be subject to appropriation by any means by States or persons, natural or juridical, and no State shall claim or exercise sovereignty or sovereign rights over any part thereof.

3. No State or person, natural or juridical, shall claim, exercise or acquire rights with respect to the area or its resources incompatible with the international régime to be established and the principles of this Declaration.

4. All activities regarding the exploration and exploitation of the resources of the area and other related activities shall be governed by the international régime to be established.

5. The area shall be open to use exclusively for peaceful purposes by all States, whether coastal or land-locked, without discrimination, in accordance with the international régime to be established.

6. States shall act in the area in accordance with the applicable principles and rules of international law, including the Charter of the United Nations and the Declaration on Principles of International Law concerning Friendly Relations and Co-operation among States in accordance with the Charter of the United Nations, adopted by the General Assembly on 24 October 1970,[1] in the interests of maintaining international peace and security and promoting international co-operation and mutual understanding.

7. The exploration of the area and the exploitation of its resources shall be carried out for the benefit of mankind as a whole, irrespective of the geographical location of States, whether land-locked or coastal, and taking into particular consideration the interests and needs of the developing countries.

8. The area shall be reserved exclusively for peaceful purposes, without prejudice to any measures which have been or may be agreed upon in the context of international negotiations undertaken in the field of disarmament and which may be applicable to a broader area. One or more international agreements shall be concluded as soon as possible in order to implement effectively this principle and to constitute a step towards the exclusion of the seabed, the ocean floor and the subsoil thereof from the arms race.

9. On the basis of the principles of this Declaration, an international régime applying to the area and its resources and including appropriate international machinery to give effect to its provisions shall be established by an international

treaty of a universal character, generally agreed upon. The régime shall, *inter alia*, provide for the orderly and safe development and rational management of the area and its resources and for expanding opportunities in the use thereof and ensure the equitable sharing by States in the benefits derived therefrom, taking into particular consideration the interests and needs of the developing countries, whether land-locked or coastal.

10.   States shall promote international co-operation in scientific research exclusively for peaceful purposes:

(a)   By participation in international programmes and by encouraging co-operation in scientific research by personnel of different countries;

(b)   Through effective publication of research programmes and dissemination of the results of research through international channels;

(c)   By co-operation in measures to strengthen research capabilities of developing countries, including the participation of their nationals in research programmes.

No such activity shall form the legal basis for any claims with respect to any part of the area or its resources.

11.   With respect to activities in the area and acting in conformity with the international régime to be established, States shall take appropriate measures for and shall co-operate in the adoption and implementation of international rules, standards and procedures for, *inter alia*:

(a)   The prevention of pollution and contamination, and other hazards to the marine environment, including the coastline, and of interference with the ecological balance of the marine environment;

(b)   The protection and conservation of the natural resources of the area and the prevention of damage to the flora and fauna of the marine environment.

12. In their activities in the area, including those relating to its resources, States shall pay due regard to the rights and legitimate interests of coastal States in the region of such activities, as well as of all other States, which may be affected by such activities. Consultations shall be maintained with the coastal States concerned with respect to activities relating to the exploration of the area and the exploitation of its resources with a view to avoiding infringement of such rights and interests.

13.   Nothing herein shall affect:

(a)   The legal status of the waters superjacent to the area or that of the air space above those waters;

(b)   The rights of coastal States with respect to measures to prevent, mitigate or eliminate grave and imminent danger to their coastline or related interests from pollution or threat thereof or from other hazardous occurrences resulting from or caused by any activities in the area, subject to the international regime to be established.

14.   Every State shall have the responsibility to ensure that activities in the area, including those relating to its resources, whether undertaken by governmental agencies, or non-governmental entities or persons under its jurisdiction, or

acting on its behalf, shall be carried out in conformity with the international régime to be established. The same responsibility applies to international organizations and their members for activities undertaken by such organizations or on their behalf. Damage caused by such activities shall entail liability.

15. The parties to any dispute relating to activities in the area and its resources shall resolve such dispute by the measures mentioned in Article 33 of the Charter of the United Nations and such procedures for settling disputes as may be agreed upon in the international régime to be established.

1933rd plenary meeting,
17 December 1970.

---

[1] Resolution 2625 (XXV).

2750 (XXV). Reservation exclusively for peaceful purposes of the seabed and the ocean floor, and the subsoil thereof, underlying the high seas beyond the limits of national jurisdiction and use of their resources in the interests of mankind, and convening of a conference on the law of the sea

The General Assembly,

Reaffirming that the area of the seabed and the ocean floor, and the subsoil thereof, beyond the limits of national jurisdiction, and its resources are the common heritage of mankind,

Convinced that the exploration of the area and the exploitation of its resources should be carried out for the benefit of mankind as a whole, taking into account the special interests and needs of the developing countries,

Reaffirming that the development of the area and its resources shall be undertaken in such a manner as to foster the healthy development of the world economy and balanced growth of international trade, and to minimize any adverse economic effects caused by the fluctuation of prices of raw materials resulting from such activities,

1. *Requests* the Secretary-General to co-operate with the United Nations Conference on Trade and Development, specialized agencies and other competent organizations of the United Nations system in order to:

(a) Identify the problems arising from the production of certain minerals from the area beyond the limits of national jurisdiction and examine the impact they will have on the economic well-being of the developing countries, in particular on prices of mineral exports on the world market;

(b) Study these problems in the light of the scale of possible exploitation of the seabed, taking into account the world demand for raw materials and the evolution of costs and prices;

(c) Propose effective solutions for dealing with these problems;

2. *Requests* the Secretary-General to submit his report thereon to the Committee on the Peaceful Uses of the Seabed and the Ocean Floor beyond the Limits of National Jurisdiction for consideration during one of its sessions in 1971 and for making its recommendations as appropriate to foster the healthy development of the world economy and balanced growth of international trade, and to minimize any adverse economic effects caused by the fluctuation of prices of raw materials resulting from such activities;

3. *Requests* the Secretary-General, in co-operation with the United Nations Conference on Trade and Development, specialized agencies and other competent organizations of the United Nations system, to keep this matter under constant review so as to submit supplementary information annually or whenever it is necessary and recommend additional measures in the light of economic, scientific and technological developments;

4. *Calls upon* the Committee on the Peaceful Uses of the Seabed and the Ocean Floor beyond the Limits of National Jurisdiction to submit a report on this question to the General Assembly at its twenty-sixth session.

1933rd plenary meeting,
17 December 1970.

B

The General Assembly,

Recalling its resolutions 1028 (XI) of 20 February 1957 and 1105 (XI) of 21 February 1957 concerning the problems of land-locked countries,

Bearing in mind the replies to the inquiries made by the Secretary-General[1] in accordance with paragraph 1 of resolution 2574 A (XXIV) of 15 December 1969, which indicate wide support for the idea of convening a conference relating to the law of the sea, at which the interests and needs of all States, whether land-locked or coastal, could be reconciled,

Noting that many of the present land-locked States Members of the United Nations did not participate in the previous United Nations conferences on the law of the sea,

Reaffirming that the area of the seabed and the ocean floor, and their subsoil, lying beyond the limits of national jurisdiction, together with the resources thereof, are the common heritage of mankind,

Convinced that the exploration of the area and the exploitation of its resources must be carried out for the benefit of all mankind, taking into account the special interests and needs of the developing countries, including the particular needs and problems of those which are land-locked,

1. *Requests* the Secretary-General to prepare, in collaboration with the United Nations Conference on Trade and Development and other competent bodies, an up-to-date study of the matters referred to in the memorandum dated 14 January 1958, prepared by the Secretariat, on the question of free access to the sea of land-locked countries[2] and to supplement that document, in the light of the events which have occurred in the meantime, with a report on the special problems of land -locked countries relating to the exploration and exploitation of the resources of the seabed and the ocean floor, and the subsoil thereof, beyond the limits of national jurisdiction;

2. *Requests* the Secretary-General to submit the above-mentioned study to the enlarged Committee on the Peaceful Uses of the Seabed and the Ocean Floor beyond the Limits of National Jurisdiction[3] for consideration at one of its 1971 sessions, so that appropriate measures may be evolved within the general framework of the law of the sea, to resolve the problems of land-locked countries;

3. *Requests* the Committee to report on this question to the General Assembly at its twenty-sixth session.

1933rd plenary meeting,
17 December 1970.

C

The General Assembly,

Recalling its resolutions 798 (VIII) of 7 December 1953, 1105 (XI) of 21 February 1957 and 2574 A (XXIV) of 15 December 1969,

Recalling further its resolutions 234 (XXII) of 18 December 1967, 2467 (XXIII) of 21 December 1968 and 2574 (XXIV) of 15 December 1969,

Taking into account the results of the consultations undertaken by the Secretary-General[4] in accordance with paragraph 1 of resolution 2574 A (XXIV), which indicate widespread support for the holding of a comprehensive conference on the law of the sea,

Conscious that the problems of ocean space are closely interrelated and need to be considered as a whole,

Noting that the political and economic realities, scientific development and rapid technological advances of the last decade have accentuated the need for early and progressive development of the law of the sea, in a framework of close international co-operation,

Having regard to the fact that many of the present States Members of the United Nations did not take part in the previous United Nations conferences on the law of the sea,

Convinced that the elaboration of an equitable international régime for the seabed and the ocean floor, and the subsoil thereof, beyond the limits of national jurisdiction would facilitate agreement on the questions to be examined at such a conference,

Affirming that such agreements on those questions should seek to accommodate the interests and needs of all States, whether land-locked or coastal, taking into account the special interests and needs of the developing countries whether land-locked or coastal,

Having considered the report of the Committee on the Peaceful Uses of the Seabed and the Ocean Floor beyond the Limits of National Jurisdiction,[5]

Convinced that a new conference on the law of the sea would have to be carefully prepared to ensure its success and that the preparatory work ought to start as soon as possible after the conclusion of the twenty-fifth session of the General Assembly, drawing on the experience already accumulated in the Committee on the Peaceful Uses of the Seabed and the Ocean Floor beyond the Limits of National Jurisdiction and using fully the opportunity provided by the United Nations Conference on the Human Environment, to be held in 1972, to further its work,

1.   *Notes with satisfaction* the progress made so far towards the elaboration of the international régime for the seabed and the ocean floor, and the subsoil thereof, beyond the limits of national jurisdiction through the Declaration of Principles Governing the Seabed and the Ocean Floor, and the Subsoil Thereof, beyond the Limits of National Jurisdiction, adopted by the General Assembly on 17 December 1970;[6]

2.   *Decides* to convene in 1973, in accordance with the provisions of paragraph 3 below, a conference on the law of the sea which would deal with the establishment of an equitable international régime - including an international machinery - for the area and the resources of the seabed and the ocean floor, and the subsoil thereof, beyond the limits of national jurisdiction, a precise definition of the area, and a broad range of related issues including those concerning the régimes of the high seas, the continental shelf, the territorial sea (including the question of its breadth and the question of international straits) and continuous zone, fishing and conservation of the living resources of the high seas (including the question of the preferential rights of coastal States), the preservation of the marine environment (including, *inter alia*, the prevention of pollution) and scientific research;

3.   *Decides further* to review, at its twenty-sixth and twenty-seventh sessions, the reports of the Committee referred to in paragraph 6 below on the progress of its preparatory work with a view to determining the precise agenda of the conference on the law of the sea, its definitive date, location and duration, and related arrangements; if the General Assembly, at its twenty-seventh session, determines the progress of the preparatory work of the Committee to be insufficient, it may decide to postpone the conference;

4.   *Reaffirms* the mandate of the Committee on the Peaceful Uses of the Seabed and the Ocean Floor beyond the Limits of National Jurisdiction set forth in General Assembly resolution 2467 A (XXIII) as supplemented by the present resolution;

5.   *Decides* to enlarge the Committee by forty-four members, appointed by the Chairman of the First Committee in consultation with regional groups and taking into account equitable geographical representation thereon;[7]

6.   *Instructs* the enlarged Committee on the Peaceful Uses of the Seabed and the Ocean Floor beyond the Limits of National Jurisdiction to hold two sessions in Geneva, in March and in July-August 1971, in order to prepare for the conference on the law of the sea draft treaty articles embodying the international régime - including an international machinery - for the area and the resources of the seabed and the ocean floor, and the subsoil thereof, beyond the limits of national jurisdiction, taking into account the equitable sharing by all States in the benefits to be derived therefrom, bearing in mind the special interests and needs of developing countries, whether coastal or land-locked, on the basis of the Declaration of Principles Governing the Seabed and the Ocean Floor, and the Subsoil Thereof, beyond the Limits of National Jurisdiction, and a comprehensive list of subjects and issues relating to the law of the sea referred to in paragraph 2 above, which should be dealt with by the conference, and draft articles on such subjects and issues,

7.   *Authorizes* the Committee to establish such subsidiary organs as it deems necessary for the efficient performance of its functions, bearing in mind the scientific, economic, legal and technical aspects of the issues involved;

8.   *Requests* the Committee to prepare, as appropriate, reports to the General Assembly on the progress of its work;

9.   *Requests* the Secretary-General to circulate those reports to Member States and to observers to the United Nations for their comments and observations;

10.   *Decides* to invite other Member States which are not appointed to the Committee to participate as observers and to be heard on specific points;

11.   *Requests* the Secretary-General to render the Committee all the assistance it may require in legal, economic, technical and scientific matters, including the relevant records of the General Assembly and specialized agencies for the efficient performance of its functions;

12.   *Decides* that the enlarged Committee, as well as its subsidiary organs, shall have summary records of its proceedings;

13.   *Invites* the United Nations Educational, Scientific and Cultural Organization and its Intergovernmental Oceanographic Commission, the Food and Agriculture Organization of the United Nations and its Committee on Fisheries, the World Health Organization, the Inter-Governmental Maritime Consultative Organization, the World Meteorological Organization, the International Atomic Energy Agency and other intergovernmental bodies and specialized agencies concerned to co-operate fully with the enlarged Committee on the Peaceful Uses of the Seabed and the Ocean Floor beyond the Limits of National Jurisdiction in the implementation of the present resolution, in particular by preparing such scientific and technical documentation as the Committee may request.

1933rd plenary meeting,
17 December 1970.

[1] See A/7925 and Add.1-3.
[2] United Nations Conference on the Law of the Sea, *Official Records*, Vol. I: *Preparatory Documents* (United Nations publication, Sales No.: 58.V.4, Vol. I), document A/CONF.13/29 and Add.1.
[3] See resolution 2750 C (XXV), para. 5, below.
[4] See A/7925 and Add.1-3.
[5] *Official Records of the General Assembly, Twenty-fifth Session, Supplement No. 21* (A/8021).
[6] Resolution 2749 (XXV).
[7] See *Official Records of the General Assembly, Twenty-fifth Session, Annexes*, agenda item 25, document A/8273.

2881 (XXVI). Reservation exclusively for peaceful purposes of the seabed and the ocean floor, and the subsoil thereof, underlying the high seas beyond the limits of national jurisdiction and use of their resources in the interests of mankind, and convening of a conference on the law of the sea

The General Assembly,

Recalling its resolutions 2340 (XXII) of 18 December 1967, 2467 (XXIII) of 21 December 1968, 2574 (XXIV) of 15 December 1969 and 2750 (XXV) of 17 December 1970,

Having considered the report of the Committee on the Peaceful Uses of the Seabed and the Ocean Floor beyond the Limits of National Jurisdiction,[1]

1. *Notes with satisfaction* the encouraging progress of the preparatory work of the Committee on the Peaceful Uses of the Seabed and the Ocean Floor beyond the Limits of national Jurisdiction towards a comprehensive conference on the law of the sea, in conformity with its mandate contained in General Assembly resolution 2750 C (XXV), in particular with regard to the elaboration of the international régime and machinery for the seabed and the ocean floor, and the subsoil thereof, beyond the limits of national jurisdiction;

2. *Notes also* the consideration by the Committee of the reports submitted by the Secretary-General[2] pursuant to resolutions 2750 A and B (XXV) and of the study of possible methods and criteria for the sharing of benefits derived from the exploitation of the resources of the area,[3] undertaken in accordance with the Committee's request of March 1970;

3. *Decides* to add to the membership of the Committee China and four other members to be appointed by the Chairman of the First Committee in consultation with regional groups, with due regard to the interests of under-represented groups;

4. *Requests* the Committee, in the discharge of its mandate in accordance with resolution 2750 C (XXV), to hold two sessions, one in New York during March and April and one at Geneva during July and August 1972.

2029th plenary meeting,
21 December 1971.

---

[1] *Official Records of the General Assembly, Twenty-sixth Session, Supplement No. 21* (A/8421).
[2] A/AC.138/36 and A/AC.138/37 and Corr.1 and 2.
[3] A/AC.138/38 and Corr.1.

3029 (XXVII) Reservation exclusively for peaceful purposes of the seabed and the ocean floor, and the subsoil thereof, underlying the high seas beyond the limits of present national jurisdiction and use of their resources in the interests of mankind, and convening of a conference on the law of the sea

A

The General Assembly,

Recalling its resolutions 2467 (XXIII) of 21 December 1968, 2750 (XXV) of 17 December 1970 and 2881 (XXVI) of 21 December 1971,

Having considered the report of the Committee on the Peaceful Uses of the Seabed and the Ocean Floor beyond the Limits of National Jurisdiction on the work of its sessions in 1972,[1]

Noting with satisfaction the further progress made towards the preparations for a comprehensive international conference of plenipotentiaries on the law of the sea, including in particular acceptance of a list of subjects and issues relating to the law of the sea,

Reaffirming that the problems of ocean space are closely interrelated and need to be considered as a whole,

Recalling its decision, in resolution 2750 C (XXV), to convene a conference on the law of the sea in 1973,

Expressing the expectation that the conference may be concluded in 1974 and, if necessary, as may be decided by the conference with the approval of the General Assembly, at a subsequent session or subsequent sessions no later than 1975,

Reaffirms the mandate of the Committee on the Peaceful Uses of the Seabed and the Ocean Floor beyond the Limits of National Jurisdiction set forth in General Assembly resolutions 2467 (XXIII) and 2750 (XXV), as supplemented by the present resolution;

2.   *Requests* the Committee, in the discharge of its mandate in accordance with resolution 2750 C (XXV), to hold two further sessions in 1973, one of five weeks in New York, beginning in early March, and the other of eight weeks at Geneva, beginning in early July, with a view to completing its preparatory work, and to submit a report with recommendations to the General Assembly at its twenty-eighth session and, in the light of the decision taken under paragraph 5 below, to the conference;

3.   *Requests* the Secretary-General to convene the first session of the Third United Nations Conference on the Law of the Sea in New York for a period of approximately two weeks in November and December 1973, for the purpose of dealing with organizational matters, including the election of officers, the adoption of the agenda and the rules of procedure of the Conference, the establishment of the subsidiary organs and the allocation of work to these organs;

4.   *Decides* to convene the second session of the Conference, for the purpose of dealing with substantive work, at Santiago, Chile, for a period of eight weeks in April and May 1974 and such subsequent sessions, if necessary, as may be decided by the Conference and approved by the General Assembly, bearing in mind that the Government of Austria has offered Vienna as a site for the Conference for the succeeding year;

5.   *Further decides* to review at its twenty-eighth session the progress of the preparatory work of the Committee and, if necessary, to take measures to facilitate completion of the substantive work for the Conference and any other action it may deem appropriate;

6.   *Authorizes* the Secretary-General, in consultation with the Chairman of the Committee, to make such arrangements as may be necessary for the efficient organization and administration of the Conference and the Committee, utilizing to the fullest extent possible the resources of staff at his disposal, to render to the Conference and the Committee all the assistance they may require in legal, economic, technical and scientific matters and to provide them with all relevant documentation of the United Nations, the specialized agencies and the International Atomic Energy Agency;

7.   *Decides* to consider as a matter of priority at its twenty-eighth session any further matters requiring decision in connexion with the Conference, including the participation of States in the Conference, and to include in the provisional agenda of that session the item entitled "Reservation exclusively for peaceful purposes of the seabed and the ocean floor, and the subsoil thereof, underlying the high seas beyond the limits of present national jurisdiction and use of their resources in the interests of mankind, and convening of a conference on the law of the sea";

8.   *Invites* the specialized agencies, the International Atomic Energy Agency and other intergovernmental organizations to co-operate fully with the Secretary-General in the preparations for the Conference and to send observers to the Conference;

9.   *Requests* the Secretary-General, subject to approval by the Conference, to invite interested non-governmental organizations having consultative status with the Economic and Social Council to send observers to the Conference;

10. *Decides* that the Conference and its main committees shall have summary records of their proceedings.

2114th plenary meeting
18 December 1972

B

The General Assembly,

Recalling its resolution 2749 (XXV) of 17 December 1970, containing the Declaration of Principles Governing the Seabed and the Ocean Floor, and the Subsoil Thereof, beyond the Limits of National Jurisdiction,

Noting that, in the said Declaration, the General Assembly, *inter alia*, declared that the exploration of the area of the seabed and the ocean floor, and the subsoil thereof, beyond the limits of national jurisdiction (hereinafter referred to as the area) and the exploitation of its resources should be carried out for the benefit of mankind as a whole, and that an international régime applying to the area and its resources and including appropriate international machinery should be established,

Realizing that the economic significance of the area would depend on its final delimitation, as stated in the reports of the Secretary-General,[2]

Considering that there is a close relationship between any decision concerning the activities and functions of the international machinery and any decision concerning limits,

Convinced that information and data on the economic implications and significance for the area of the various proposals for limits would be helpful to the participants at the forthcoming United Nations Conference on the Law of the Sea, particularly to developing States, many of which are not members of the Committee on the Peaceful Uses of the Seabed and the Ocean Floor beyond the Limits of National Jurisdiction,

1. *Requests* the Secretary-General to prepare, on the basis of data and information at his disposal, a comparative study of the extent and the economic significance, in terms of resources, of the international area that would result from each of the various proposals on limits of national jurisdiction submitted so far to the Committee on the Peaceful Uses of the Seabed and the Ocean Floor beyond the Limits of National Jurisdiction;

2. *Further requests* the Secretary-General to submit his study as soon as possible, but no later than the opening date of the summer session of the Committee on the Peaceful Uses of the Seabed and the Ocean Floor beyond the Limits of National Jurisdiction in 1973;

3. *Invites* States, the United Nations Conference on Trade and Development, the specialized agencies and other competent organizations of the United Nations system to co-operate with the Secretary-General in the preparation of such a study;

4.   *Declares* that nothing in the present resolution or in the study shall prejudice the position of any State concerning limits, the nature of the régime and
machinery or any other matter to be discussed at the forthcoming United Nations
Conference on the Law of the Sea.

2114th plenary meeting,
18 December 1972.

C

The General Assembly,

Convinced of the importance to coastal States, for purposes of economic
development and social progress, of the ocean resources adjacent to their coasts,

1.   *Requests* the Secretary-General to prepare, on the basis of the information at his disposal and in connection with the study to be submitted pursuant
to resolution B above, a comparative study of the potential economic significance for riparian States, in terms of resources, of each of the various proposals
on limits of national jurisdiction presented so far to the Committee on the Peaceful
Uses of the Seabed and the Ocean Floor beyond the Limits of National Jurisdiction ;

2.   *Further requests* the Secretary-General to submit his study as soon as
possible, but no later than the opening date of the summer session of the Committee on the Peaceful Uses of the Seabed and the Ocean Floor beyond the Limits of
National Jurisdiction in 1973, simultaneously with the study to be prepared under
resolution B above;

3.   *Declares* that nothing in the present resolution or in the study shall prejudice the position of any State concerning the limits, the nature of the régime and
machinery or any other matter to be discussed at the forthcoming United Nations
Conference on the Law of the Sea.

2114th plenary meeting
18 December 1972.

---

[1] *Official records of the General Assembly, Twenty-seventh Session, Supplement No. 21* (A/
8721 and Corr.1).

[2] A/AC.138/36, A/AC.138/73.

3067 (XXVIII). Reservation exclusively for peaceful purposes of the seabed and the ocean floor, and the subsoil thereof, underlying the high seas beyond the limits of present national jurisdiction and use of their resources in the interests of mankind, and convening of the Third United Nations Conference on the Law of the Sea

The General Assembly,

Recalling its resolutions 2467 (XXIII) of 21 December 1968, 2750 (XXV) of 17 December 1970, 2881 (XXVI) of 21 December 1971 and 3029 (XXVII) of 18 December 1972,

Having considered the report of the Committee on the Peaceful Uses of the Seabed and the Ocean Floor beyond the Limits of National Jurisdiction on the work of its sessions in 1973,[1]

Recalling in particular paragraph 2 of resolution 2750 C (XXV),

Considering that the Committee has accomplished, as far as possible, within the limits of its mandate, the work which the General Assembly entrusted to it for the preparation of the Third United Nations Conference on the Law of the Sea, and that it is necessary to proceed to the immediate inauguration of the Conference in 1973 and the convening of a rabstantive session in 1974, in order to carry out the negotiations and other work required to complete the drafting and adoption of articles for a comprehensive convention on the law of the sea,

Recalling further its resolutions 2480 (XXIII) of 21 December 1968, 2539 (XXIV) of 11 December 1968, 2736 (XXV) of 17 December 1970 and 3009 (XXVII) of 18 December 1972 concerning the composition of the Secretariat, as well as the general dispositions on the same matter recommended by the Fifth Committee and adopted by the General Assembly at its twenty-sixth and twenty-seventh sessions,

1. *Expresses* its appreciation to the Committee on the Peaceful Uses of the Seabed and the Ocean Floor beyond the Limits of National Jurisdiction on the work it has done in preparing for the Third United Nations Conference an the Law of the Sea,

2. *Confirms* its decision in paragraph 3 of resolution 3029 A (XXVII) and decides to convene the first session of the Third United Nations Conference on the Law of the Sea in New York from 3 to 14 December 1973 inclusive for the purpose of dealing with matters relating to the organization of the Conference, including the election of officers, the adoption of the agenda and the rules of procedure of the Conference, the establishment of subsidiary organs and the allocation of work to these organs and any other purpose within the scope of paragraph 3 below;

3 . *Decides* that the mandate of the Conference shall be to adopt a convention dealing with all matters relating to the law of the sea, taking into account the subject-matter listed in paragraph 2 of General Assembly resolution 2750 C (XXV) and the list of subjects and issues relating to the law of the sea formally approved

on 18 August 1972 by the Committee on the Peaceful Uses of the Seabed and the Ocean Floor beyond the Limits of National Jurisdiction[2] and bearing in mind that the problems of ocean space are closely interrelated and need to be considered as a whole;

4 . *Decides* to convene the second session of the Conference, for the purpose of dealing with the substantive work of the Conference, for a period of ten weeks from 20 June to 29 August 1974 at Caracas and, if necessary, to convene not later than 1975 any subsequent session or sessions as may be decided upon by the Conference and approved by the General Assembly, bearing in mind that the Government of Austria has offered Vienna as the site for the Conference in 1975;

5. *Invites* the Conference to make such arrangements as it may deem necessary to facilitate its work;

6. *Refers* to the Conference the reports of the Committee on the Peaceful Uses of the Seabed and the Ocean Floor beyond the Limits of National Jurisdiction on its work and all other relevant documentation of the General Assembly and the Committee;

7. *Decides*, having regard to the desirability of achieving universality of participation in the Conference, to request the Secretary-General to invite, in full compliance with General Assembly resolution 2758 (XXVI) of 25 October 1971, States Members of the United Nations or members of specialized agencies or the International Atomic Energy Agency and States parties to the Statute of the International Court of Justice, as well as the following States, to participate in the Conference: Republic of Guinea-Bissau and Democratic Republic of Viet-Nam;

8. *Requests* the Secretary-General:

(a) To invite to the Conference intergovernmental and non-governmental organizations in accordance with paragraphs 8 and 9 of resolution 3029 A (XXVII);

(b) To invite the United Nations Council for Namibia to participate in the Conference;

(c) To provide summary records in accordance with paragraph 10 of resolution 3029 A (XXVII);

9. *Decides* that the Secretary-General of the United Nations shall be the Secretary-General of the Conference and authorizes him to appoint a special representative to act on his behalf and to make such arrangements – including recruitment of necessary staff, taking into account the principle of equitable geographical representation – and to provide such facilities as may be necessary for the efficient and continuous servicing of the Conference, utilizing to the fullest extent possible the resources at his disposal;

10. *Requests* the Secretary-General to prepare appropriate draft rules of procedure for the Conference, taking into account the views expressed in the Committee on the Peaceful Uses of the Seabed and the Ocean Ploor beyond the Limits of National Jurisdiction and in the General Assembly, and to circulate the draft rules of procedure in time for consideration and approval at the organizational session of the Conference;

11. *Invites* States participating in the Conference to submit their proposals, including draft articles, on the substantive subject-matter of the Conference to the Secretary-General by 1 February 1974 and requests the Secretary-General to circulate the replies received by him before the second session with a view to expediting the work of the Conference;

12. *Decides* that the provisions of paragraph 11 above shall not preclude any State participating in the Conference from submitting proposals, including draft articles, at any stage of the Conference, in accordance with the procedure adopted by the Conference, provided that States which have already submitted any proposals and draft articles need not resubmit them;

13. *Dissolves* the Committee on the Peaceful Uses of the Seabed and the Ocean Floor beyond the Limits of National Jurisdiction as from the inauguration of the Conference.

2169th plenary meeting,
16 November 1973.

---

[1] *Official Records of the General Assembly, Twenty-eighth Session, Supplement No. 21* (A/9021 and Corr.1 and 3).

[2] *Ibid., Twenty-seventh Session, Supplement No. 21* (A/8721 and Corr.1), para. 23.

37/66.　　Third United Nations Conference on the Law of the Sea

The General Assembly,

Recalling its resolutions 3067 (XXVIII) of 16 November 1973, 3334 (XXIX) of 17 December 1974, 3483 (XXX) of 12 December 1975, 31/63 of 10 December 1976, 32/194 of 20 December 1977, 33/17 of 10 November 1978, 34/20 of 9 November 1979, 35/116 of 10 December 1980 and 36/79 of 9 December 1981,

Taking note of the adoption, on 30 April 1982, of the United Nations Convention on the Law of the Sea[1] and the related resolutions[2] by an overwhelming majority of States and of the decision of the Third United Nations Conference on the Law of the Sea, on 24 September 1982, to accept with appreciation the invitation extended by the Government of Jamaica for the purpose of adopting and signing the Final Act and opening the Convention for signature at Montego Bay from 6 to 10 December 1982,[3]

Taking special note of the fact that the Conference decided to establish a Preparatory Commission for the International Seabed Authority and for the International Tribunal for the Law of the Sea and that the Commission shall meet at the seat of the Authority if facilities are available and as often as necessary for the expeditious exercise of its functions,

Taking note of the extensive functions entrusted to the Preparatory Commission, including the administration of the scheme governing preparatory investment in pioneer activities relating to polymetallic nodules,

Recalling that the Convention provides that the seat of the International Seabed Authority shall be in Jamaica,

Taking further note of the timely measures being taken at considerable expense by the Government of Jamaica to construct an adequate administrative building and conference complex for housing the secretariat of the Preparatory Commission and providing meeting facilities for the purpose of enabling the Commission to function from Jamaica,

Recognizing the urgent need for the Preparatory Commission to be assured of adequate resources to enable it to discharge its functions efficiently and expeditiously,

Recalling also that in General Assembly resolution 35/116 the Secretary-General was requested to prepare and submit to the Conference, for such consideration as it deemed appropriate, a study identifying his future functions under the proposed Convention and that such a study was submitted on 18 August 1981,[4]

Noting that, in a letter dated 7 September 1982 to the President of the General Assembly,[5] the President of the Conference drew attention to the responsibilities which the Secretary-General was called upon to carry out under the Convention and the related resolutions and to the need for the Assembly to take the appropriate action to approve the assumption of these responsibilities by the Secretary-General,

Recognizing that, in accordance with the third preambular paragraph of the Convention, the problems of ocean space are closely interrelated and need to be considered as a whole,

Recognizing the need for the Secretary-General to be authorized to assume his functions under the Convention and the related resolutions, including in particular the provision of the secretariat services required by the Preparatory Commission for its effective and expeditious functioning,

1. *Welcomes* the adoption of the United Nations Convention on the Law of the Sea and the related resolutions;

2. *Calls upon* all States to consider signing and ratifying the Convention at the earliest possible date to allow the effective entry into force of the new legal régime for the uses of the sea and its resources;

3. *Appeals* to the Governments of all States to refrain from taking any action directed at undermining the Convention or defeating its object and purpose;

4. *Accepts* with appreciation the invitation extended by the Government of Jamaica for the purpose of adopting and signing the Final Act and opening the Convention for signature at Montego Bay from 6 to 10 December 1982;

5. *Authorizes* the Secretary-General to enter into the necessary agreement in this regard with the Government of Jamaica;

6.   *Reiterates* its gratitude to the Government of Venezuela for the hospitality extended to the Third United Nations Conference on the Law of the Sea at its first substantive session, held at Caracas in 1974;

7.   *Approves* the assumption by the Secretary-General of the responsibilities entrusted to him under the Convention and the related resolutions and also approves the stationing of an adequate number of secretariat staff in Jamaica for the purpose of servicing the Preparatory Commission for the International Seabed Authority and for the International Tribunal for the Law of the Sea, as required by its functions and programme of work;

8.   *Authorizes* the Secretary-General to convene the Preparatory Commission as provided in Conference resolution I, of 30 April 1982,[2] by which the Commission was established, and to provide the Commission with the services required to enable it to perform its functions efficiently and expeditiously;

9.   *Approves* the financing of the expenses of the Preparatory Commission from the regular budget of the United Nations;

10.   *Requests* the Secretary-General to report to the General Assembly at its thirty-eighth session on the implementation of the present resolution.

91st plenary meeting,
3 December 1982.

---

[1] *Official Records of the Third United Nations Conference on the Law of the Sea*, vol. XVII, document A/CONF.62/122.

[2] *Ibid.*, document A/CONF.62/121, annex I.

[3] *Ibid.*, vol XVII, Plenary Meetings, 184th meeting. See A/37/441/Add.1.

[4] *Ibid.*, vol. XVII, document A/CONF.62/L.76.

[5] A/37/441.

49/28.   Law of the Sea

The General Assembly,

Conscious of the fundamental importance of the United Nations Convention on the Law of the Sea[1] for the maintenance and strengthening of international peace and security,

Recognizing the universal character of the Convention and the establishment through it of a legal order for the seas and oceans which will facilitate international communication and promote the peaceful uses of the seas and oceans, the equitable and efficient utilization of their resources, the conservation of their living resources and the study, protection and preservation of the marine environment,

Considering that, in its resolution 2749 (XXV) of 17 December 1970, it proclaimed that the seabed and ocean floor, and the subsoil thereof, beyond the limits of national jurisdiction (hereinafter referred to as "the Area"), as well as the resources of the Area, are the common heritage of mankind, and considering also that the Convention provides the regime to be applied to the Area and its resources,

Welcoming the adoption on 28 July 1994 of the Agreement relating to the implementation of Part XI of the United Nations Convention on the Law of the Sea of 10 December 1982[2] (hereinafter referred to as "the Agreement"), aimed at facilitating universal participation in the Convention,

Recognizing that the entry into force of the Convention on 16 November 1994 marks an historic event in international relations and in the development of international law,

Welcoming also the holding of the first meeting of the International Seabed Authority at its headquarters in Jamaica,

Noting with satisfaction the convening, on 21 and 22 November 1994 in New York, of a meeting of States Parties to the Convention concerning the establishment of the International Tribunal for the Law of the Sea,

Noting that the Agreement provides that the institutions established by the Convention should be cost-effective,

Noting also that the Agreement provides that the International Seabed Authority shall have its own budget and that the administrative expenses of the Authority shall initially be met from the regular budget of the United Nations,[3]

Acknowledging that the International Seabed Authority is an autonomous organization under the Convention,

Emphasizing the principle stated in the Convention that the problems of ocean space are closely interrelated and need to be considered as a whole,

Convinced, therefore, of the importance of the annual consideration and review of the overall developments relating to the law of the sea by the General Assembly, as the global institution having the competence to undertake such a review,

Conscious of the strategic importance of the Convention as a framework for national, regional and global action in the marine sector, as recognized also by the United Nations Conference on Environment and Development in chapter 17 of Agenda 21,[4]

Aware of the importance of the effective implementation of the Convention and its uniform and consistent application, as well as the need to promote harmonious interaction in the uses of the ocean and to create favourable conditions for peace and order in the oceans,

Recalling that in its resolution 37/66 of 3 December 1982 it approved the assumption by the Secretary-General of the responsibilities entrusted to him under the Convention and related resolutions of the Third United Nations Conference on the Law of the Sea, as well as the functions resulting therefrom which were subsequently elaborated in the report of the Secretary-General and approved by the General Assembly,[5]

Noting the additional responsibilities of the Secretary-General arising from the entry into force of the Convention,

Recognizing the impact on States of the entry into force of the Convention in the light of the rights and obligations arising therefrom and the increasing needs of States, especially developing States, for advice and assistance in the implementation of the Convention and to develop and strengthen their capabilities in order to enable them to benefit fully from the legal regime for the seas and oceans established by the Convention,

Conscious of the need to promote and facilitate international cooperation, especially at subregional and regional levels, in order to ensure the orderly and sustainable development of the uses and resources of the seas and oceans,

1. *Recalls* the historic significance of the United Nations Convention on the Law of the Sea as an important contribution to the maintenance of peace, justice and progress for all peoples of the world;

2. *Expresses* its profound satisfaction at the entry into force of the Convention;

3. *Calls upon* all States that have not done so to become parties to the Convention and the Agreement relating to the implementation of Part XI of the United Nations Convention on the Law of the Sea of 10 December 1982 in order to achieve the goal of universal participation;

4. *Expresses* its satisfaction at the establishment of the International Seabed Authority;

5. *Welcomes* the first meeting of States Parties to the Convention concerning the establishment of the International Tribunal for the Law of the Sea;

6. *Expresses* its satisfaction also at the progress being made in the establishment of the International Tribunal for the Law of the Sea and the Commission on the Limits of the Continental Shelf;

7. *Reaffirms* the unified character of the Convention;

8. *Calls upon* States to harmonize their national legislation with the provisions of the Convention and to ensure consistent application of those provisions;

9. *Requests* the Secretary-General to implement its decision contained in paragraph 8 of resolution 48/263 of 28 July 1994, taking into account the decisions and recommendations of the Preparatory Commission for the International Seabed Authority and for the International Tribunal for the Law of the Sea (hereinafter referred to as "the Preparatory Commission");

10. *Also requests* the Secretary-General to provide, from within existing resources, such services as may be required for the meetings of States Parties to the Convention and for the Commission on the Limits of the Continental Shelf;

11. *Further requests* the Secretary-General, from within existing resources, to convene a meeting of States Parties relating to the organization of the International Tribunal for the Law of the Sea in New York from 15 to 19 May 1995 and, pursuant to the recommendations of the Preparatory Commission and the decision of the meeting of States Parties of 22 November 1994, to designate before 16 May 1995 a United Nations staff member with secretariat support to be charged with making preparations of a practical nature for the organization of the Tribunal, including the establishment of a library;

12. *Decides* to undertake an annual review and evaluation of the implementation of the Convention and other developments relating to ocean affairs and the law of the sea;

13. *Expresses* its appreciation to the Secretary-General for his report of 16 November 1994,[6] prepared pursuant to paragraph 24 of Assembly resolution 48/28 of 9 December 1993, and requests him to carry out the activities outlined therein, as well as those aimed at the strengthening of the legal regime of the seas and oceans;

14. *Notes* with appreciation the functions and role of the Division for Ocean Affairs and the Law of the Sea of the Office of Legal Affairs of the Secretariat, which has contributed to the wider acceptance and rational and consistent application of the provisions of the Convention,

15. *Requests* the Secretary-General to continue to carry out the responsibilities entrusted to him upon the adoption of the Convention[7] and to fulfil the functions consequent upon the entry into force of the Convention, in particular by:

   (a) Preparing annually a comprehensive report, for the consideration of the Assembly, on developments relating to the law of the sea, taking into account relevant scientific and technological developments, which could also serve as a basis for reports to all States parties to the Convention, the International Seabed Authority and competent international organizations, and which the Secretary-General is required to provide under the Convention;[8]

   (b) Formulating recommendations for the consideration of, and for action by, the Assembly or other appropriate intergovernmental forums, and undertaking special studies, including through the convening of meetings of groups of experts, aimed at a better understanding of the provisions of the Convention and facilitating their effective implementation;

   (c) Preparing periodically special reports on specific topics of current interest, including those requested by intergovernmental conferences and bodies, and providing secretariat services to such conferences in accordance with decisions of the Assembly;

   (d) Strengthening the existing system for the collection, compilation and dissemination of information on the law of the sea and related matters and developing, in cooperation with the relevant international organizations, a centralized system with integrated databases for providing coordinated information and advice, *inter alia*, on legislation and marine policy, taking into account chapter 17, paragraph 17.117 (e), of Agenda 21,[9] as well as establishing a system for notifying Member States and relevant international organizations and bodies of information of general interest submitted by States and intergovernmental bodies;

   (e) Ensuring that the institutional capacity of the Organization can respond to requests of States, in particular developing States, and competent international organizations for advice and assistance and identify additional sources of support for national, subregional and regional efforts to implement the Convention, taking into account the special needs of developing countries;[10]

(f) Establishing appropriate facilities, as required by the Convention, for the deposit by States of maps, charts and geographic coordinates concerning national maritime zones and establishing a system for their recording and publicity as part of an integrated programme on the law of the sea and ocean affairs, distinct from the usual depositary functions of the Secretary-General;[11]

(g) Preparing for and convening the meetings of States Parties to the Convention and providing the necessary services for such meetings, in accordance with the Convention;[12]

(h) *Preparing* for the meetings of the Commission on the Limits of the Continental Shelf and providing the necessary services to the Commission, in accordance with the Convention;[13]

16. *Also requests* the Secretary-General to make the necessary arrangements within the integrated programme for administering and supporting the conciliation and arbitration procedures for the resolution of disputes, as required of him under the Convention;[14]

17. *Calls upon* all States and competent international organizations to cooperate fully with the Secretary-General in the discharge of his mandate;

18. *Invites* the competent international organizations to assess the implications of the entry into force of the Convention in their respective fields of competence and to identify additional measures that may need to be taken as a consequence of its entry into force with a view to ensuring a uniform, consistent and coordinated approach to the implementation of the provisions of the Convention throughout the United Nations system;[15]

19. *Requests* the Secretary-General to prepare a comprehensive report on the impact of the entry into force of the Convention on related existing or proposed instruments and programmes throughout the United Nations system, and to submit the report to the Assembly at its fifty-first session;

20. *Invites* the competent international organizations, as well as development and funding institutions, to take specific account in their programmes and activities of the impact of the entry into force of the Convention on the needs of States, especially developing States, for technical and financial assistance, and to support subregional or regional initiatives aimed at cooperation in the effective implementation of the Convention;

21. *Invites* Member States and others in a position to do so to contribute to the further development of the fellowship programme and educational activities on the law of the sea established by the Assembly in its resolution 35/116 of 10 December 1980;

22. *Also requests* the Secretary-General to take fully into account the requirements under the Convention and the present resolution in the preparation of an integrated programme on ocean affairs and the law of the sea, which should be duly reflected in the proposed programme budget for 1996-1997 and the medium-term plan for 1998-2003;

23. *Further requests* the Secretary-General to report, in accordance with paragraph 15 (a) above, to the Assembly annually as from its fiftieth session on

developments pertaining to the implementation of the Convention, as well as on other developments relating to ocean affairs and the law of the sea, and on the implementation of the present resolution;

24. *Decides* to include in the provisional agenda of its fiftieth session the item entitled "Law of the Sea".

78th plenary meeting,
6 December 1994.

---

[1] *Official Records of the Third United Nations Conference on the Law of the Sea*, vol. XVII (United Nations publication, Sales No. E.84.V.3), document A/CONF.62/122.

[2] Resolution 48/263, annex.

[3] See resolution 48/263, paragraph 8, and also Section 1, paragraph 14, of the Annex to the Agreement relating to the implementation of Part XI of the United Nations Convention on the Law of the Sea of 10 December 1982.

[4] *Report of the United Nations Conference on Environment and Development, Rio de Janeiro, 3-14 June 1992* (A/CONF.151/26/Rev.1 (Vol. I and Vol. I/Corr.1, Vol. II, Vol. III and Vol. III/Corr.1)) (United Nations publication, Sales No. E.93.I.8 and corrigenda), vol. I: Resolutions adopted by the Conference, resolution 1, annex II.

[5] A/38/570, paras. 41 and 42.

[6] A/49/631 and Corr. 1.

[7] See resolution 37/66.

[8] Article 319 (2) (a) and 3 (a) (i) of the Convention.

[9] See also chapter 17, para. 17.116, of Agenda 21.

[10] See A/38/570, para. 42, and resolution 48/28, para. 14.

[11] See articles 16 (2), 47 (9), 75 (2), 76 (9) and 84 (2) of the Convention.

[12] Article 319 (2) (e) of the Convention.

[13] Article 76 (8) and Annex II of the Convention.

[14] See Annexes V, VII and VIII of the Convention.

[15] See chapter 17 of Agenda 21, in particular paras. 17.116 and 17.117.

SIGNATORIES OF THE CONVENTION

As at 10 December 1982, when the Convention was opened for signature at Montego Bay, Jamaica

Algeria
Angola
Australia
Austria
Bahamas
Bahrain
Bangladesh
Barbados
Belize
Bhutan
Brazil
Bulgaria
Burma
Burundi
Byelorussian SSR
Canada
Cape Verde
Chad
Chile
China
Colombia
Congo
Cook Islands
Costa Rica
Cuba
Cyprus
Czechoslovakia
Democratic People's
    Republic of Korea
Democratic Yemen

Denmark
Djibouti
Dominican Republic
Egypt
Ethiopia
Fiji*
Finland
France
Gabon
Gambia
German Democratic
    Republic
Ghana
Greece
Grenada
Guinea-Bissau
Guyana
Haiti
Honduras
Hungary
Iceland
India
Indonesia
Iran
Iraq
Ireland
Ivory Coast
Jamaica
Kenya
Kuwait

Lao People's Democratic
    Republic
Lesotho
Liberia
Malaysia
Maldives
Malta
Mauritania
Mauritius
Mexico
Monaco
Mongolia
Morocco
Mozambique
Namibia (United Nations
    Council for Namibia)
Nauru
Nepal
Netherlands
New Zealand
Niger
Nigeria
Norway
Pakistan
Panama
Papua New Guinea
Paraguay
Philippines
Poland
Portugal

---

*   Fiji deposited its instrument of ratification of the Convention on 10 December 1982

Romania	Sudan	United Republic of
Rwanda	Suriname	Cameroon
Saint Lucia	Sweden	United Republic of
Saint Vincent and the	Thailand	Tanzania
Grenadines	Togo	Upper Volta
Senegal	Trinidad and Tobago	Uruguay
Seychelles	Tunisia	Vanuatu
Sierra Leone	Tuvalu	Viet Nam
Singapore	Uganda	Yemen
Solomon Islands	Ukrainian SSR	Yugoslavia
Somalia	USSR	Zambia
Sri Lanka	United Arab Emirates	Zimbabwe

SIGNATORIES OF THE FINAL ACT

The Final Act was signed by all 119 delegations which signed
the Convention, as well as by the following:

Full participants

Belgium	Italy	Spain
Benin	Japan	Switzerland
Botswana	Jordan	United Kingdom of Great
Ecuador	Libyan Arab Jamahiriya	Britain and Northern
Equatorial Guinea	Luxembourg	Ireland
Federal Republic of	Oman	United States
Germany	Peru	Venezuela
Holy See	Republic of Korea	Zaire
Israel	Samoa	

States and territories with observer status

Netherland Antilles

Trust Territory of the Pacific Islands

Intergovernmental organization

European Economic Community

National liberation movements

African National Congress of	Pan Africanist Congress of Azania
South Africa	South West Africa People's
Palestine Liberation Organization	Organization

THE LAW OF THE SEA: A CHRONOLOGY

CONFERENCE ON THE LAW OF THE SEA

1958—First United Nations Conference on the Law of the Sea: 86 States meet in Geneva and adopt four international conventions covering the territorial sea, the high seas, the continental shelf and fishing and conservation of living resources.

1960—Second United Nations Conference on the Law of the Sea fails to produce any substantive agreement on the limits of the territorial zone and fishing rights.

1967—The United Nations General Assembly decides that technological and other changes in the world require the international community to address the matter of laws governing the seas beyond national jurisdiction. A 35-member *ad hoc* committee is set up by the Assembly to study the matter.

1968—The *ad hoc* committee grows to 41 members and is renamed *Committee on the Peaceful Uses of the Sea-Bed and the Ocean Floor beyond the Limits of National Jurisdiction.*

1970—As a result of the Sea Bed Committee's work the General Assembly adopts a *Declaration of Principles Governing the Sea-Bed and Ocean Floor, and the Subsoil Thereof, beyond the Limits of National Jurisdiction.* These areas are declared the "common heritage of mankind". The Assembly also decides to convene the Third United Nations Conference on the Law of the Sea and the Sea-Bed Committee, enlarged to 91 members, is given the job of preparing for the Conference. By 1973 it puts out a 6-volume report.

1973—First session of the Conference (organizational, New York) elects officers, begins work on rules of procedure. Hamilton Shirley Amerasinghe of Sri Lanka is chosen as President of the Conference.

1974—Second session, Caracas. Adopts rules of procedure; 115 countries speak in general debate. First attempt to deal with alternate texts submitted by Sea-Bed Committee.

1975—Third session, Geneva. A "single negotiating text" produced by Committee Chairmen, sets out in treaty language the provisions to be included.

1976—Fourth session, New York. The results of negotiations set out in a "revised single negotiating text".

1976—Fifth session, New York. Further progress in some areas, impasse on how deep-sea mining should be organized and regulated.

1977—Sixth session, New York. An "informal composite negotiating text" marks continuing deliberations.

1978—Seventh session, first Geneva, then New York. Seven negotiating groups created to tackle "hard core" differences.

1979—Eighth session, first Geneva, then New York. First revision of the 1977 negotiating text emerges. Decision taken to complete work on Convention by 1980.

1980—Ninth session, first New York, then Geneva. "Informal text" of Draft Convention produced. Plans to hold final session in 1981.

1981—Tenth session, first New York, then Geneva. First official text of Draft Convention issued. Jamaica and Federal Republic of Germany chosen as seats for the International Sea-Bed Authority and the International Tribunal for the Law of the Sea respectively. United States cites difficulties in sea-bed provisions. "Final decision-making session" set for 1982.

1982—Eleventh session (Part I, 8 March-30 April), New York. All efforts at reaching general agreement having been exhausted, the Conference votes on a number of amendments to the Draft Convention. At the end, at the request of the United States, there is a recorded vote. The Convention is adopted on 30 April by 130 votes to 4 against, with 17 abstentions.

Eleventh session (Part II, 22-24 September), New York. Approves Drafting Committee changes in the Convention, adopts draft Final Act, selects Jamaica as site of signing session.

1982 (6-10 December)—Convention and Final Act are signed at Montego Bay, Jamaica, by 119 delegations.

1983—Preparatory Commission meets in Kingston, Jamaica, to begin work on the creation of International Sea-Bed Authority and International Tribunal for the Law of the Sea.

PREPARATORY COMMISSION FOR THE INTERNATIONAL SEABED AUTHORITY AND FOR THE TRIBUNAL FOR THE LAW OF THE SEA

1983—First session in Kingston, Jamaica (Part I, 15 March - 8 April, Part II, 15 August - 9 September). Election of Mr. Joseph Warioba (United Republic of Tanzania) as Chairman of the Preparatory Commission. Adoption of the rules of procedure. Establishment of four Special Commissions:

•   Special Commission 1 on the problems that could be encountered by developing land-based producer States likely to be most seriously affected by the production of minerals derived from the International Seabed Area.

•   Special Commission 2 for the adoption of measures necessary for the entry into effective operation of the Enterprise.

•   Special Commission 3 for the preparation of rules, regulations and procedures for the exploration and exploitation of the Area.

• Special Commission 4 for the preparation of recommendations regarding practical arrangements for the establishment of the International Tribunal for the Law of the Sea.

Establishment of a General Committee, consisting of the Chairman and other officers of the Preparatory Commission and of the four Special Commissions, to act on behalf of the Preparatory Commission as the executive organ for the administration of Resolution II.

1984—Second session held in Kingston, Jamaica from 19 March - 13 April, 1984. Adoption of the rules for registration of pioneer investors. Composition and functions of the group of technical experts. Examination of the draft rules of procedure for the Assembly of the International Seabed Authority. Elaboration of a draft headquarters agreement, draft agreement on privileges and immunities, draft rules of procedure, and draft rules and regulations for the International Tribunal for the Law of the Sea. Receipt of India's application for registration as a pioneer investor (14 February 1984). Receipt of application from Government of Japan for registration of the Japanese enterprise Deep Ocean Resources Development Co. Ltd. as a pioneer investor (22 August 1984). Receipt of application from the Government of France for registration of Institut Française de recherché pour l'exploitation de la mer (IFREMER)/ Association Française pour l'étude et la recherché des nodules (AFERNOD) as a pioneer investor (23 August 1984). Consideration of procedure for resolution of overlapping claims.

1985—Third session (Part I, 11 March - 4 April, Kingston, Jamaica. Part II, 12 August - 4 September, Geneva). Completion of second reading of draft rules of procedure of the Assembly of the Authority. Examination of draft rules of procedure of the Council of the Authority. Consultations on resolution of conflicts arising from overlapping claims. Continuation of the work of the four Special Commissions.

1986—Fourth session (Part I, 17 March - 11 April, Kingston, Jamaica. Part II, 11 August - 5 September, New York). Adoption of declaration by the Preparatory Commission reiterating its rejection of any claim, agreement or action undertaken outside the Preparatory Commission which is incompatible with the Convention and related resolutions (LOS/PCN/78).

Completion of the first reading of the draft rules of procedure of the Council and the Legal and Technical Commission. Consideration by Special Commission 3 of a draft mining code. Exchange of views in Special Commission 1 on the establishment of a compensation fund and other measures to reduce adverse effects through bilateral agreements between developing traditional exporters and traditional importing States of minerals found in the Area. Completion of second reading of the draft rules of the Tribunal.

1987—Fifth session (Part I, 30 March - 16 April, Kingston, Jamaica. Part II, 27 July - 21 August, New York). Adoption of statement of understanding on the implementation of resolution II (10 April 1987) based on Arusha Understanding reached among France, India, Japan and the former U.S.S.R. Election of Mr. Jose Luis Jesus (Cape Verde) as Chairman of the Preparatory Commission in succession to Mr. Joseph S. Warioba. Receipt of revised applications from the Governments of India, Japan (DORD), U.S.S.R. (Yuzhmorgeologiya) and France (IFREMER/AFERNOD) for registration as pioneer investors (20 July 1987). Completion of second reading of the rules of procedure of the Council of the Authority and first reading of the draft rules of procedure of the Economic Planning Commission. Initial consideration of the issue of subsidization in relation to deep seabed mining. Discussion of issues relating to the training requirements of personnel of the Enterprise and its administrative structure. Examination of draft articles for financial terms of a model mining contract. Completion of second round of discussions on the draft rules of the Tribunal with substantial agreement arrived at on the majority of issues except the procedures for the prompt release of vessels and crews. Progress made on the draft headquarters agreement between the Tribunal and the host country. Registration of Government of India as the first pioneer investor in the International Seabed Area (17 August 1987). Registration of IFREMER/AFERNOD (France), DORD (Japan) and Yuzhmorgeologiya (U.S.S.R.) as pioneer investors on 17 December 1987.

1988—Sixth session (Part I, 14 March - 8 April, Kingston, Jamaica. Part II, 15 August - 2 September, New York). Consideration of matters relating to training of personnel designated by the Preparatory Commission. Introduction by an *ad hoc* working group of draft principles and policies for the Preparatory Commission's training programme. Provisional approval of the draft rules of procedure of the Legal and Technical Commission and of the Economic Planning Commission. Preliminary discussion of implementation of the obligations of the pioneer investors to collaborate in the exploration of a mine site for the Enterprise. First reading of draft regulations on the transfer of technology. Informal consultations on the seat of the Tribunal. Completion of examination of the draft headquarters agreement between the Tribunal and the Federal Republic of Germany. Procedures to ensure the prompt release of vessels and crews adopted.

1989—Seventh session (Part I, 27 February - 23 April, Kingston, Jamaica. Part II, 14 August to 1 September, New York). Chairman's paper submitted to the plenary on the discharge of obligations by the four pioneer investors and their certifying States in accordance with resolution II. Group of Technical Experts submits a proposal for an exploration plan and identifies the priority disciplines for the training of personnel. Special Commission 1 agrees on a provisional list of 66 key recommendations to be submitted to the Authority on the protection of developing land-based producer States. Further consideration of the structure and organization of the Enterprise and of a training programme under resolution II, paragraph 12 (a)(ii). Proposal on the establishment of a training programme for the Enterprise adopted by the Preparatory Commission. Conclusion of the first reading of draft regulations on the transfer of technology for the period of ten years from the date of commencement of commercial production by the Enterprise. Completion of examination of the draft Protocol on the Privileges and

Immunities of the Tribunal. Continuation of informal consultations on matters relating to the seat of the Tribunal. Discussion on universal participation in the Convention. Decision to set the end of 1991 as a target date for the completion of the work of the Preparatory Commission.

1990—Eighth session (Part I, 5 - 30 March, Kingston, Jamaica. Part II, 13 - 31 August, New York). Adoption of a statement of understanding on the fulfilment of obligations under resolution II by the registered pioneer investors and their certifying States (30 August 1990). Completion of second reading of the draft Headquarters Agreement between the Authority and the Government of Jamaica and the draft Protocol on the Privileges and Immunities of the Authority. Completion of first reading of the provisional conclusions that would form the basis of the Preparatory Commission's final recommendations to the Authority on the protection of developing land-based mineral producer States. Continuation of examination by *ad hoc* working group of Special Commission 1 of questions relating to the establishment of a compensation fund, the effects of subsidized seabed mining, and dependency and activation thresholds in respect of applications for assistance. Completion of first reading of draft regulations on production authorization. Consideration of draft regulations on the protection and preservation of the marine environment from activities in the Area. Continuation of consideration of the administrative arrangements, structure and financial implications of the Tribunal and the draft relationship agreement between the Tribunal and the United Nations. Receipt of application from the Government of the People's Republic of China for registration of China Ocean Mineral Research and Development Association (COMRA) as a pioneer investor (22 August 1990).

1991—Ninth session (Part I, 5 - 30 March, Kingston, Jamaica. Part II, 12 - 30 August, New York). Receipt of application from the Governments of Bulgaria, Cuba, the former Czech and Slovak Federal Republics, the Republic of Poland and the former U.S.S.R. for registration of Interoceanmetal Joint Organization (IOM)) as a pioneer investor (8 March 1991). Registration of COMRA (China) as a pioneer investor (5 March 1991). Registration of IOM as a pioneer investor (21 August 1991). Completion of preparatory work for the exploration of one mine site in the areas reserved for the Authority by France, Japan, and Russian Federation. Joint report forwarded for evaluation by Group of Technical Experts. Completion of second reading of the draft relationship agreement between the United Nations and the Authority. Continuation of work on problems that will be encountered by developing land-based producer States and criteria for the identification of land-based producer States actually or likely to be affected as a result of the production of deep seabed minerals. Agreement reached by Special Commission 2 on the purpose and functions of the transitional arrangements for the Enterprise. A joint venture option considered the preferred option for the Enterprise in its initial operations. Completion of the first reading of Part VIII of the draft regulations on prospecting, exploration and exploitation of polymetallic nodules in the Area, relating to the protection and preservation of the marine environment. Continuation of examination of the administrative arrangements, structure and financial requirements of the Tribunal, the draft Headquarters Agreement between the Tribunal and Germany and the draft Protocol on the Privileges and Immunities of the Tribunal. Establishment and composition of the Training Panel. Training programmes submitted by France, Japan and the Russian Federation.

1992—Tenth session (Part I, 24 February - 13 March, Kingston, Jamaica. Part II, 10 - 21 August, New York). Adoption of a statement of understanding on the fulfilment of obligations under resolution II by the newly registered pioneer investors (COMRA and IOM) and their certifying States. Approval of the report submitted by the Group of Technical Experts on the preparatory work undertaken by registered pioneer investors on the exploration of the area reserved for the Authority. Periodic reports submitted by France, India, Japan, and the Russian Federation on pioneer activities. Training programme submitted by Government of India. Consideration of draft Headquarters Agreement between the Authority and the Government of Jamaica, draft Protocol on the Privileges and Immunities of Officials and Experts of the Authority and a draft relationship agreement between the United Nations and the Authority. Completion of the work by *ad hoc* working group of Special Commission 1 on the three "hard core" issues related to the protection of developing land-based producer States. Completion of the study on demand, supply and price of metals contained in polymetallic nodules. Completion of work on comprehensive draft regulations on prospecting, exploration and exploitation of polymetallic nodules in the Area. Completion of review of the draft Headquarters Agreement between the Tribunal and the Federal Republic of Germany. Adoption by Special Commission 4 of draft Protocol on the Privileges and Immunities of the Tribunal.

1993—Eleventh session held in Kingston, Jamaica from 22 March - 2 April. Consideration of periodic reports submitted by the registered pioneer investors. Draft provisional final reports of the Informal Plenary and of Special Commissions 1, 2, 3, and 4. Decision not to hold any further meeting in 1993 but to continue to make provision for the servicing of an annual two-week session of the Preparatory Commission until entry into force of the Convention. Completion of training programme of France.

1994—Twelfth session (Part I, 7 - 11 February, Kingston, Jamaica. Part II, 1-12 August, New York). Completion of the training programmes of India, Japan and the Russian Federation. Consideration of matters relating to the implementation of resolution II, including relinquishment of pioneer areas in accordance with resolution II, paragraph 1(e). Registration of the Government of the Republic of Korea as a pioneer investor on the basis of the report of the Group of Technical Experts and adoption of an understanding on the fulfilment of its obligations under resolution II. Issue of certificate of compliance to the registered pioneer investors. Waiver of the annual fixed fee and the obligations of three registered pioneer investors (IFREMER/AFERNOD, DORD, and Yuzhmorgeologiya) and their certifying States (France, Japan and the Russian Federation) to carry out stage I of the exploration work.

Consideration of matters arising from the imminent entry into force of the Convention, including consideration of provisional agenda for the first session of the Assembly of the Authority, final report of the Training Panel, budget for the first financial period of the Authority and date of the first session of the Assembly of the Authority (16-18 November 1994), report containing recommendations for submission to the first meeting of States Parties to be convened in accordance with annex VI, article 4, of the Convention regarding practical arrangements for the establishment of the Tribunal, final report on all matters within the mandate of the Preparatory Commission to be submitted to the Assembly of the Authority at its first session.

16 November 1994—Entry into force of the United Nations Convention on the Law of the Sea

INTERNATIONAL SEABED AUTHORITY, 1994 - 2000

1994—First session, Kingston, Jamaica (Part I, 16-18 November 1994, Part II, 27 February-17 March). Authority comes into existence upon entry into force of the Convention. First formal session convened by United Nations Secretary-General Boutros Boutros-Ghali. Second part of the first session convened by the Legal Counsel of the United Nations as President *pro tem* of the Assembly. Mr. Hasjim Djalal (Indonesia) elected as President of the Assembly. Adoption of the rules and procedures of the Assembly. Consultations among regional groups and interest groups on the composition of the Council. Identification of eight largest investors. Decision to hold informal consultations on the composition of the Council in New York from 6-8 December 1995. Issue of certificates of compliance by the Chairman of the Preparatory Commission to six registered pioneer investors: COMRA (China), IFREMER/AFERNOD (France), DORD (Japan), Government of India, Yuzhmorgeologiya (Russian Federation), and IOM (Bulgaria, Cuba, the former Czech and Slovak Federal Republic, Poland and the Russian Federation) in fulfillment of their obligations under resolution II.

1995—Third part of the first session, Kingston, Jamaica from 7-18 August 1995. Presentation of the final report of the Preparatory Commission by its Rapporteur-General, Mr. Kenneth Rattray (Jamaica). Decision by the Assembly to continue to use the Kingston Office for the Law of the Sea as the interim Secretariat of the Authority and to authorize the Secretary-General of the United Nations to administer the interim Secretariat of the Authority until election of the first Secretary-General of the Authority. Consideration of organizational matters including the draft headquarters agreement between the Authority and the Government of Jamaica and the draft protocol on the privileges and immunities of the Authority. Preliminary discussion of the priorities of the Authority during its initial phase of work, the decisions to be made in relation to the recommendations of the Preparatory Commission and on follow-up of the Preparatory Commission's decisions concerning the registered pioneer investors, including the training to be provided by them. Discussion of future administrative and budgetary arrangements for the Authority.

1996—Second session, Kingston, Jamaica (Part I, 11-22 March, Part II, 5-16 August). Assembly elects the first Council of the Authority. Mr. Satya N. Nandan (Fiji) elected as the first Secretary-General of the Authority. Assembly elects Finance Committee. Council elects Legal and Technical Commission. Council adopts its rules of procedure. Authority granted observer status by General Assembly of the United Nations (resolution 51/6 of 4 November 1996).

1997—Third session, Kingston, Jamaica (Part I, 17-28 March, Part II, 18-29 August). Approval by the Assembly of the Agreement concerning the relationship between the United Nations and the Authority. Consideration of draft Headquarters Agreement between the Authority and the Government of Jamaica. Consideration by the Assembly of the first annual report of the Secretary-General submitted under article 166, paragraph 4, of the Convention. Legal and Technical Commission begins work on draft Regulations on Prospecting and Exploration for Polymetallic Nodules in the Area. Council decides to extend the provisional membership of Belarus, Belgium, Chile, Gabon, the Lao People's Democratic Republic, Mozambique, Qatar, Solomon Islands, South Africa, Switzerland, United Arab Emirates and the European Union for a period of two years from 16 November 1996 and to extend the provisional membership of the Russian Federation, Ukraine and the United Kingdom of Great Britain and Northern Ireland for a period of one year from 16 November 1996. Requests for approval of plans of work for exploration submitted by the seven registered pioneer investors in accordance with paragraph 6(a)(ii) of section 1 of the annex to the Agreement relating to the implementation of Part XI of the United Nations Convention on the Law of the Sea of 10 December 1982 (19 August 1997). On 28 August 1997 such plans of work are considered by the Council to be approved (ISBA/3/C/9). Assembly adopts 1998 budget and scale of assessments.

1998—Fourth session held in three parts. Parts I and II, 16-27 March, 9-27 August, Kingston, Jamaica, Part III, 12-13 October, New York. Assembly elects one-half of the members of the Council for a four-year term from 1 January 1999. The terms of office of members of the Council and other organs of the Authority are harmonized with the calendar year. Assembly adopts the Protocol on Privileges and Immunities of the International Seabed Authority. Legal and Technical Commission completes work on the draft Regulations on Prospecting and Exploration for Polymetallic Nodules in the Area and submits the text to the Council for consideration. Provisional membership ceases, for all States, on 16 November 1998.

1999—Fifth session, Kingston, Jamaica, 9-27 August. Assembly approves the Headquarters Agreement between the International Seabed Authority and the Government of Jamaica. Council adopts the Financial Regulations of the Authority and continues its examination of the draft Regulations on Prospecting and Exploration of Polymetallic Nodules in the Area.

2000—Sixth session, Kingston, Jamaica (Part I, 20-31 March, Part II, 3-14 July). Assembly approves the Financial Regulations of the Authority. Mr. Satya N. Nandan (Fiji) re-elected as Secretary-General of the Authority for a second four-year term of office. Council adopts the Staff Regulations and Rules of Procedure of the Legal and Technical Commission. The Regulations on Prospecting and Exploration for Polymetallic Nodules in the Area are adopted by the Council and approved by the Assembly.

CONSOLIDATED INDEX TO COMPENDIUM OF BASIC DOCUMENTS ON THE LAW OF THE SEA

This consolidated index to the compendium of basic documents on the law of the sea was prepared by the Office of Legal Affairs of the International Seabed Authority with the assistance of a professional indexer. The index contains citations for the following instruments:

- United Nations Convention on the Law of the Sea of 10 December 1982;
- Resolutions I to IV of the Third United Nations Conference on the Law of the Sea;
- Agreement relating to the Implementation of Part XI of the United Nations Convention on the Law of the Sea of 10 December 1982;
- Agreement for the Implementation of the Provisions of the United Nations Convention on the Law of the Sea of 10 December 1982 relating to the Conservation and Management of Straddling Fish Stocks and Highly Migratory Fish Stocks; and
- Regulations on Prospecting and Exploration for Polymetallic Nodules in the Area.

Nomenclature used in the index

Citations for *articles* in the body of the Convention are preceded by the letters "**LOSC**" and given by article number, paragraph, subparagraph and sub-subparagraph as appropriate, e.g., **LOSC/298(1)(a)(ii)** denotes article 298, paragraph 1, subparagraph (a), sub-subparagraph (ii), of the Convention.

Citations for the *Preamble of the Convention* refer to the operative paragraph number of the Preamble, e.g., **LOSC/Preamble(5)** refers to the fifth paragraph of the Preamble.

Citations for articles in *Annex I to Annex IX* are in the form "**LOSC/A**" followed by the number of each annex in arabic notation **(LOSC/A1-LOSC/A9)** and the article number, paragraph and subparagraph, as appropriate, e.g., **LOSC/A3/17(1)(b)(xii)** refers to Annex III, article 17, paragraph 1, subparagraph (b), sub-subparagraph (xii).

Citations for *Resolutions I to IV* of the Third United Nations Conference on the Law of the Sea are designated by an upper-case "**R**" followed by the number of each resolution in arabic notation (**R1** to **R4**) and the paragraph, subparagraph and sub-subparagraph as appropriate, e.g., **R2/12(a)(ii)** denotes Resolution II, paragraph 12, subparagraph (a), sub-subparagraph (ii). Citation for the *Preambles of Resolutions I and II* refer to the relevant paragraph of the Preamble, preceded by **R1/Preamble** or **R2/Preamble**, as appropriate, and followed by the paragraph number, e.g., **R2/Preamble(4)** refers to the fourth paragraph of the Preamble of Resolution II. In the case of Resolution IV, which contains six annexes, "**R4**" is followed by the number of the relevant annex and the article number, e.g. **R4/A2** refers to Resolution IV, Annex 2.

Citations for the *Agreement relating to the Implementation of Part XI of the United Nations Convention on the Law of the Sea of 10 December 1982* are indicated by the letters "**AGXI**". Citations for its *Preamble* refer to the relevant paragraph of the Preamble, e.g., **AGXI/Preamble(5)** denotes the fifth paragraph of the Preamble. Citations for *articles* in the body of the Agreement are given by article number, paragraph and subparagraph, e.g., **AGXI/7(3)** denotes article 7, paragraph 3, of the Agreement.

Citations for *paragraphs of the Annex to the Agreement* are in the form "**AGXI/A/S**" (section) followed by the number of the relevant section of the Annex in arabic notation and the paragraph, subparagraph, and sub-subparagraph as appropriate, e.g., **AGXI/A/S1(12)(b)(i)** refers to section 1, paragraph 12, subparagraph (b), sub-subparagraph (i), of the Annex to the Agreement.

Citations for the *Agreement for the Implementation of the Provisions of the United Nations Convention on the Law of the Sea of 10 December 1982 relating to the Conservation and Management of Straddling Fish Stocks and Highly Migratory Fish Stocks* are indicated by the letters "**UNFSA**". Citations for its *Preamble* refer to the relevant paragraphs of the Preamble, e.g., **UNFSA/Preamble(11)** refers to the eleventh paragraph of the Preamble. Citations for *articles* in the body of the Agreement are given by the letters "**UNFSA**" followed by the article number, paragraph, and subparagraph, e.g., **UNFSA/47(2)(a)(ii)** refers to article 47, paragraph 2, subparagraph (a), sub-subparagraph (ii), of the Fisheries Agreement. Citations for the two annexes to the Agreement are indicated by the letters "**UNFSA/A1**" and "**UNFSA/A2**" respectively.

Citations for the *Regulations on Prospecting and Exploration for Polymetallic Nodules in the Area* are indicated by the letters "**RPE**". An upper-case "**R**" followed by the number refers to a regulation and is followed by a reference to a subregulation and, if appropriate, sub-subregulation, e.g., **RPE/R3(4)(d)(i)** refers to regulation 3, subregulation 4, sub-subregulation (d), sub-subparagraph (i) of the Regulations. Citations for *Annexes 1 to 4 to the Regulations* are indicated by the letters "**RPE/A1**" to "**RPE/A4**" respectively. Reference to each relevant provision of these four annexes varies, depending on the way each annex is structured. For instance, **RPE/A1/17(a)(i)** denotes paragraph 17, subparagraph (a), sub-subparagraph (i), of annex 1 to the Regulations; **RPE/A2/S3(23)(c)** refers to annex 2, section 3, paragraph 23, subparagraph (c) to the Regulations.

The expression "use of term" is used to represent the definition of that term as used in the aforementioned instruments. The expression "occurrence of term" is used to denote instances where a specific term, such as the name of an international organization, appears, and where there is no practical need to have the term classified into substantive subentries. The expression "other occurrences of term" is used under certain index entries to denote instances where the term appears but, unlike other instances where the same term appears, does not need to be classified into substantive subentries. The word "**Title**" also appears in certain locators when a relevant entry occurs in the title of a section or an article

Agenda 21
UNFSA/Preamble(5)
Agreement
(*see also* arrangements; cooperation;
World Trade Organization)
application of: UNFSA/1(2)(b);
UNFSA/1(3); UNFSA/3(1);
UNFSA/3(2); UNFSA/3(3);
UNFSA/41
between archipelagic States: LOSC/
47(6); LOSC/51(1)
by Authority: AGXI/A/S8(1)(c); AGXI/
A/S8/1(e); LOSC/151(1); LOSC/
151(3)
bilateral, regional, subregional:
LOSC/51(1); LOSC/69(2);
LOSC/70(3); LOSC/70(3)(b);
LOSC/125(2); LOSC/243;
LOSC/247; LOSC/282; LOSC/
298(1)(a)(iii)
commodity: LOSC/A3/7(1); LOSC/A3/
7(2)
conferring jurisdiction: LOSC/A6/
20(2); LOSC/A6/21
by consensus: LOSC/155(3); LOSC/
312(2)
between contractor and Authority:
RPE/A4/S24(2)
and Convention: UNFSA/4
by Council of the Authority: 162(2)(f)
on delimitation between opposite or
adjacent States: LOSC/15;
LOSC/74; LOSC/83; LOSC/
134(4)
on enforcement of laws and
regulations: LOSC/73(3)
by Enterprise: LOSC/A3/5(3)(a);
LOSC/A3/5(6); LOSC/A3/6(n);
LOSC/A4/13(a)
establishing an organization: LOSC/
A9/4(6)
fisheries and access to living
resources: LOSC/62/2; LOSC/
66(3)(a); LOSC/66(3)(c); LOSC/
66(3)(d); LOSC/67(3); LOSC/
69(2); LOSC/69(2)(b); LOSC/
70(3); LOSC/70(3)(b); LOSC/
297(3)(e)
free trade and custom union: AGXI/A/
S6(2)
free zones: LOSC/128
for Implementation of Provisions of
the United Nations Convention
on the Law of the Sea of 10
December 1982 relating to
Conservation and Management
of Straddling Fish Stocks and

Highly Migratory fish Stocks:
UNFSA/Title; UNFSA/
Preamble(9); UNFSA/
1(chapeau); UNFSA/1(1)(b);
UNFSA/1(2)(a); UNFSA/
1(2)(b)(ii); UNFSA/1(3); UNFSA/
2; UNFSA/3(1); UNFSA/3(3);
UNFSA/4; UNFSA/8(2); UNFSA/
14(1); UNFSA/15; UNFSA/17(1);
UNFSA/17(4); UNFSA/21(1);
UNFSA/21(3); UNFSA/21(4);
UNFSA/21(7); UNFSA/21(15);
UNFSA/30(1); UNFSA/30(3);
UNFSA/30(4); UNFSA/30(5);
UNFSA/31(3); UNFSA/33;
UNFSA/34; UNFSA/35; UNFSA/
36; UNFSA/37; UNFSA/38;
UNFSA/39; UNFSA/40; UNFSA/
41; UNFSA/42; UNFSA/43;
UNFSA/44; UNFSA/45; UNFSA/
46; UNFSA/47; UNFSA/48;
UNFSA/49; UNFSA/50
international: LOSC/23; LOSC/280;
LOSC/288(2); LOSC/297(3)(e);
LOSC/303(4); LOSC/311; LOSC/
319(2)(c); LOSC/A6/22; LOSC/
A6/32(2)
on marine scientific research: LOSC/
247; LOSC/249
multilateral trade: LOSC/151(8)
non-parties to: UNFSA/33
objective of: UNFSA/2
others: LOSC/A6/22
between parties to a dispute: LOSC/
281(1); LOSC/282; LOSC/290;
LOSC/298(1)(a); LOSC/299(1);
LOSC/A5/3(g); LOSC/A5/7(1);
LOSC/A5/10; LOSC/A6/36(2);
LOSC/A7/3(d); LOSC/A7/3(g);
LOSC/A7/12(2); LOSC/A8/3(d);
LOSC/A8/3(g)
protection and preservation of marine
environment: LOSC/237(1)
special: LOSC/126; LOSC/A4/13(1);
LOSC/A4/13(7); LOSC/A4/37;
LOSC/A6/24(1); LOSC/A6/24(2)
between States Parties: LOSC/311(3);
LOSC/311(4); LOSC/311(6);
LOSC/319(2)(c)
technology: LOSC/269(b)
on transit and access to and from
sea: LOSC/124; LOSC/125(2);
LOSC/126; LOSC/132
between user States and States
bordering a strait: LOSC/43
Aids
navigational: LOSC/21(1)(b); LOSC/
43(a)

to reaching a decision: LOSC/A7/8
Baselines
(*see also* territorial sea)
archipelagic: LOSC/47; LOSC/48;
LOSC/49(1)
bays: LOSC/10(5); LOSC/10(6)
charts or coordinates: LOSC/5;
LOSC/6; LOSC/16; LOSC/47(8);
LOSC/47(9)
continental shelf: LOSC/76(1); LOSC/
76(4)(a); LOSC/76(5); LOSC/
76(6); LOSC/76(7); LOSC/76(8);
LOSC/82(1); LOSC/246(6)
environmental: RPE/R31(4); RPE/A4/
S5(2)
exclusive economic zones: LOSC/
7(6); LOSC/47(5); LOSC/48;
LOSC/57
method of determining: LOSC/5;
LOSC/7; LOSC/9; LOSC/10(5);
LOSC/10(6); LOSC/13(1);
LOSC/14; LOSC/35(a); LOSC/
47(1); LOSC/47(2); LOSC/47(3);
LOSC/47(4); LOSC/47(5)
reefs: LOSC/6
Bays
baselines of: LOSC/10(5); LOSC/
10(6)
"historic": LOSC/10(6); LOSC/
298(1)(a)(i)
mouths of: LOSC/10(2); LOSC/10(3)
use of term: LOSC/10
Benefit of mankind
LOSC/Preamble(6); LOSC/140(1);
LOSC/143(1); LOSC/149;
LOSC/150(i); LOSC/246(3)
Best scientific evidence
(*see also* scientific evidence)
UNFSA/5(b); UNFSA/6(7); UNFSA/
10(f)
Bigeye tuna
LOSC/A1
**Binding decision/binding force of
decisions**
(*see also* arbitration; Tribunal)
by a court or tribunal: (*generally see*
Part XV, Section 2); LOSC/282;
LOSC/296(2); LOSC/A3/
18(1)(b); LOSC/A6/31(3);
LOSC/A6/32(3); LOSC/A6/33;
LOSC/A6/33(2); LOSC/A7/11;
LOSC/A8/4
on limits of continental shelf: LOSC/
76(8)
**Binding procedures for settlement of
disputes**
LOSC/296; UNFSA/29

Biodiversity
occurrence of term: UNFSA/5(g)
preservation of: UNFSA/Preamble(7);
UNFSA/5(g)
Biological characteristics of the stocks
(*see* stocks)
**Biological information supporting stocks
assessment**
UNFSA/A1/3(2)(b)
Biological unity
UNFSA/7(2)(d)
Biomass
occurrence of term: UNFSA/A2(7)
surveys: UNFSA/A1/3(2)(c)
threshold of: UNFSA/A2(7)
Blackfin tuna
LOSC/A1
Bluefin tuna
LOSC/A1
Board
(*see* Governing Board)
Boarding
delay of: UNFSA/22(4)
and inspection: UNFSA/21(2);
UNFSA/21(3); UNFSA/21(4);
UNFSA/21(5); UNFSA/21(10);
UNFSA/21(14); UNFSA/22(title);
UNFSA/22(1)(b); UNFSA/22;
UNFSA/22(4)
prompt and safe: UNFSA/22(3)(a)
of ship or vessel: LOSC/27(1); LOSC/
27(2); LOSC/27(5); LOSC/28(1);
LOSC/73(1); LOSC/105; LOSC/
110(1); LOSC/110(2); LOSC/
110(3)
Bolívar, Simón
R4/A3
Bond or other financial security
LOSC/73(2); LOSC/218(4); LOSC/
220(7); LOSC/226(1)(b); LOSC/
228(1); LOSC/292(1); LOSC/
292(4)
Borrowing power
of Authority: AGXI/A/S1/14; LOSC/
171(d); LOSC/174
of Enterprise: LOSC/A4/6(m); LOSC/
A4/11(1)(c); LOSC/A4/11(2)
Breadth
(*see also* territorial sea)
of contiguous zone: LOSC/33(2);
LOSC/48
of continental shelf: LOSC/48; LOSC/
76(1); LOSC/76(1); LOSC/76(5);
LOSC/76(7); LOSC/76(8);
LOSC/82(1); LOSC/246(6)
of exclusive economic zones: LOSC/
48; LOSC/57

Chambers for voting in Council
    (*see also* Seabed Disputes Chamber;
    special chambers of the Tribunal;
    Tribunal)
    AGXI/A/S3(5); AGXI/A/S3(9); AGX1/
      A/S3(10)(a)
**Characteristics of fisheries exploiting
the stock**
    UNFSA/A2/3
Charges
    (*see also* fees; production charges;
    taxes)
    LOSC/26; LOSC/127; LOSC/183(1)
Charter of the United Nations
    LOSC/Preamble(7); LOSC/19(2)(a);
      LOSC/39(1)(b); LOSC/138;
      LOSC/279; LOSC/298(1)(c);
      LOSC/301; R3/Preamble(2)
Charts
    archipelagic baselines on: LOSC/
      47(8); LOSC/47(9)
    of Area: LOSC/134(3)
    on board a ship: LOSC/94(4)(a)
    of continental shelf: LOSC/76(9);
      LOSC/84
    depositary: LOSC/16(2); LOSC/47(9);
      LOSC/75(2); LOSC/76(9);
      LOSC/84(2); LOSC/134(3)
    of exclusive economic zones: LOSC/
      75
    large-scale: LOSC/5
    officially recognized: LOSC/5; LOSC/
      6
    publicity to: LOSC/16(2); LOSC/
      22(4); LOSC/41(6); LOSC/
      47(9); LOSC/53(10); LOSC/
      75(2); LOSC/84(2); LOSC/
      134(3)
    scale of: LOSC/16(1); LOSC/47(8);
      LOSC/75(1); LOSC/84(1)
    of sea lanes and traffic separation
      schemes: LOSC/22(4); LOSC/
      41(6); LOSC/53(10)
    of territorial sea: LOSC/5; LOSC/6;
      LOSC/16; LOSC/22(4)
Civil jurisdiction
    LOSC/28; LOSC/229
Claims
    (*see also* settlement of disputes)
    Area: LOSC/137(1); LOSC/137(3);
      LOSC/155(2)
    disputes: LOSC/189; LOSC/229;
      LOSC/294(1); LOSC/A5/6;
      LOSC/A6/28; LOSC/A7/1;
      LOSC/A7/9; LOSC/A8/1
    non-recognition of: LOSC/89; LOSC/
      137(1); LOSC/241

    overlapping: R2/5(a); R2/5(c)
    third party: RPE/A4/S16(4)
Closed areas or seasons
    UNFSA/21(11)(c)
Closing lines
    archipelagic waters: LOSC/50
    bay: LOSC/10(4)
Coastal States
    (*see* applicability; archipelagic States;
    arrangements; artificial islands;
    baselines; cables and pipelines;
    Commission on the Limits of the
    Continental Shelf; consent of a
    Coastal State; continental shelf;
    contributions; cooperation; damage;
    discretion; discretionary powers; due
    publicity; dumping; enforcement;
    exclusive economic zones; facilities;
    fishing; flag States; harvesting
    capacity; innocent passage;
    installations; internal waters;
    international law; islands; joint
    ventures; jurisdiction; land-locked
    States; laws and regulations;
    legitimate interests; living resources;
    marine scientific research;
    notification; opposite or adjacent
    coasts; pollution; ports; remuneration;
    sea lanes; security; settlement of
    disputes; sovereign rights;
    sovereignty; superjacent waters;
    territorial sea; violations; warships)
    conservation and management
      measures applied by: UNFSA/
      16(1)
    cooperation among: UNFSA/20(6)
    dependence on fishing: UNFSA/
      7(2)(e)
    jurisdiction over dumping: LOSC/210;
      LOSC/216
    rights of: LOSC/142; RPE/R33;
      UNFSA/7(1)
    and States fishing on high seas:
      UNFSA/8(1)
Coasts
    (*see* opposite or adjacent coasts)
Cobalt
    (*see also* minerals derived from the
    Area; polymetallic nodules)
    LOSC/151(7); LOSC/A3/13(6)(e);
      LOSC/A4/11(3)(a); R2/1(d);
      RPE/R1(3)(d)
Collection of data
    (see also data)
    compilation and analysis: UNFSA/A1/
      1(1); UNFSA/A1/2
    and dissemination: UNFSA/A1/7(2)

and compilation/exchange, principle
of: UNFSA/A1/2(title)
and provision of information: UNFSA/
14
and sharing: UNFSA/A1(title)
standards for reporting, verification
and exchange: UNFSA/10(e)
Collisions at sea
(*see also* incidents of navigation;
safety at sea)
LOSC/21(4); LOSC/39(2)(a); LOSC/
94(3)(c); LOSC/94(4)(c); LOSC/
97(1); LOSC/98(1)(c); LOSC/
221(2)
Commercial arbitration
(*see* arbitration)
Commercial production
(*see also* first period of commercial
production; interim period of
commercial production; production
authorizations; second period of
commercial production)
Authority revenues derived from:
LOSC/A3/13(1)(a)
beginning of/earliest: LOSC/151(2);
LOSC/151(3); LOSC/
151(4)(a)(i); LOSC/151(4)(a)(ii);
LOSC/155(1); LOSC/A3/7(3)(b);
LOSC/A3/13(3); LOSC/A3/
17(2)(c); LOSC/A3/17(2)(g)
commencement of: RPE/R5(2)
by Enterprise: LOSC/A3/5(7); LOSC/
A4/10(3)
expenditures after commencement of:
AGXI/A/S8(1)(d); LOSC/A3/
13(3); LOSC/A3/13(4); LOSC/
A3/13(5); LOSC/A3/13(6)(a);
LOSC/A3/13(6)(d)(i); LOSC/A3/
13(6)(h)(ii); LOSC/A3/13(6)(k);
LOSC/A3/13(6)(n)(iv); LOSC/A3/
13(9)(a); LOSC/A3/13(11)
expenditures prior to commencement
of: LOSC/151(2)(b); LOSC/A3/
13(6)(d)(i); LOSC/A3/13(6)(h)(i);
LOSC/A3/13(6)(h)(ii); LOSC/A3/
13(6)(h)(iv); LOSC/A3/13(6)(j);
LOSC/A3/13(6)(n)(iv); LOSC/A3/
13(9)(a); LOSC/A3/13(11);
LOSC/A3/17(2)(b)(iii); LOSC/A3/
17(2)(c)
pioneer investor's relationship to: R2/
7(c); R2/9(b); R2/9(c); R2/9(d)
revenues for the Authority derived
from: LOSC/A3/13(1)(a)
use of term: LOSC/A3/17(1)(b)(xiii)
Commercial terms
(*see* fair and reasonable terms and
conditions for transfer)

Commercial value
RPE/R15; RPE/R16(1); RPE/A2/
S2(19)
Commission
(*see specific commissions below*;
conciliation; Economic Planning
Commission; Legal and Technical
Commission; Preparatory
Commission)
Commission for the Enterprise (Special)
(*see also* Preparatory Commission)
R1/8
Commission on sustainable development
UNFSA/24(1)
**Commission on the Limits of the
Continental Shelf**
decision-making procedure of: LOSC/
A2/6(2)
duty of coastal States to: LOSC/A2/4;
LOSC/A2/7
elections and membership of: LOSC/
A2/2
establishment of: LOSC/76(8); LOSC/
A2/1
expenses and Secretariat of: LOSC/
A2/2(5)
functions of: LOSC/A2/3
nationality of members of: LOSC/A2/
2(1); LOSC/A2/5
natural resources of: LOSC/77;
LOSC/79(2)
quorum of: LOSC/A2/2(3)
recommendations of: LOSC/A2/6;
LOSC/A2/8; LOSC/A2/9
sub-commissions of: LOSC/A2/5;
LOSC/A2/6
terms of office of: LOSC/A2/2(4)
**Commission on the problems which
would be encountered by developing
land-based producer States (Special)**
R1/9
**Commission on Transnational Corpora-
tions of the United Nations**
LOSC/A3/13(9)(b)
Commodities
loading or unloading of: LOSC/
19(2)(9); LOSC/42(1)(d)
produced from minerals derived from
Area: AGXI/A/S3(15)(a); AGXI/
A/S6(1)(d); LOSC/150(j); LOSC/
151(1)(a); LOSC/161(1)(a)
Commodity agreements
LOSC/A3/7(1); LOSC/A3/7(2)
Common heritage of mankind
AGXI/Preamble(2); LOSC/
Preamble(6); LOSC/125(1);
LOSC/136; LOSC/150(i); LOSC/

Design

    of installation or devices: LOSC/
        194(3)(c); LOSC/194(3)(d)

    of mining equipment: LOSC/A3/14(2);
        LOSC/A3/17(2)(b)(ii); R2/1(b)(ii)

    of ships or vessels: LOSC/21(2);
        LOSC/194(3)(b); LOSC/
        211(6)(c); LOSC/217(2)

Detention

    (*see also* arrest; foreign ships or
        vessels; imprisonment)

    of crews: LOSC/292(1); LOSC/292(3);
        LOSC/292(4)

    illegal acts of: LOSC/101(a)

    of vessels: LOSC/73(4); LOSC/97(3);
        LOSC/220(2); LOSC/220(6);
        LOSC/292(1)

Developing States

    (*see also* countries)

    ability of: UNFSA/25(1)(a)

    activities in the Area: AGXI/A/S5(1);
        AGXI/A/S1(6)(a)(i); LOSC/
        140(1); LOSC/143(3)(b); LOSC/
        144(1)(b); LOSC/144(2)(a);
        LOSC/144(2)(b); LOSC/148;
        LOSC/150; LOSC/150(d);
        LOSC/151(10); LOSC/152(2);
        LOSC/155(1)(f); LOSC/155(2);
        LOSC/173(2)(c); LOSC/273;
        LOSC/274; LOSC/276(1);
        LOSC/A3/5(3)(e); LOSC/A3/8;
        LOSC/A3/9(2); LOSC/A3/9(4);
        LOSC/A3/13(1)(d); LOSC/A3/15;
        LOSC/A3/17(1)(b)(xi); LOSC/A4/
        12(3)(b)(ii); LOSC/A4/13(4)(d);
        R1/9; R2/1(a)(3); R2/3(b); R2/
        12(a)(i); R/5(i)

    application for approval of plan of
        work with respect to a reserved
        area: RPE/R17(1); RPE/R17(3)

    Assembly of the Authority: LOSC/
        160(2)(f)(i); LOSC/160(2)(k)

    assistance to: UNFSA/25(1)(b);
        UNFSA/26; UNFSA/A1(2)

    assistance to, in implementing
        Agreement: UNFSA/26

    assistance to, scientific/technical:
        LOSC/202; LOSC/203(a)

    cooperation with: UNFSA/25

    Council of the Authority: AGXI/A/
        S3(9)(a); AGXI/A/S3(15)(d);
        AGXI/A/S3(15)(e); LOSC/
        161(1)(c); LOSC/161(1)(d);
        LOSC/161(2)(b); LOSC/
        162(2)(o)(i)

    development and transfer of marine
        technology: AGXI/A/S5(1);

        LOSC/144(2)(a); LOSC/
        144(2)(b); LOSC/66(2); LOSC/
        268(d); LOSC/269(a); LOSC/
        271; LOSC/272; LOSC/273;
        LOSC/274(a); LOSC/274(b);
        LOSC/274(c); LOSC/274(d);
        LOSC/276(1); LOSC/A3/
        5(3)(e); LOSC/A3/17(1)(b)(xi)

    economic assistance: AGXI/A/
        S7(1)(b); AGXI/A/S7(1)(c);
        AGXI/A/S7(1)(d); LOSC/
        164(2)(d); UNFSA/25(2);
        UNFSA/25(3)

    Economic Planning Commission:
        LOSC/164(1); LOSC/164(2)(b);
        LOSC/164(2)(d)

    fisheries: LOSC/61(3); LOSC/62(2);
        LOSC/62(3); LOSC/62(4);
        LOSC/119(1)(a)

    indigenous people in: UNFSA/
        24(2)(b)

    interests of: UNFSA/11(f)

    involvement of: UNFSA/A1/1(2)

    marine pollution assistance: LOSC/
        202; LOSC/203; LOSC/207(4)

    marine scientific research
        assistance: AGXI/A/S5(a)(c);
        LOSC/244(2); LOSC/275(1);
        LOSC/276(1)

    participation of: UNFSA/25(1)(c)

    payment and contributions by: LOSC/
        82(3); LOSC/82(4)

    preferential treatment for: LOSC/203

    provision of assistance relating to
        human resources: UNFSA/25(2)

    provision of financial assistance:
        UNFSA/25(2)

    provision of technical assistance:
        UNFSA/25(2)

    provision of transfer of technical
        technology: UNFSA/25(2)

    requirements of, special: UNFSA/24

    requirements of interests and needs:
        LOSC/61(3); LOSC/62(4);
        LOSC/69(4); LOSC70(4);
        LOSC/140(1)

    as a single chamber: AGXI/A/
        S3(9)(a)

    small islands: UNFSA/24(2)(b);
        UNFSA/25(1)(a); UNFSA/
        25(1)(b)

    training of personnel of: RPE/R27(1);
        RPE/A4/S8

    vulnerability of: UNFSA/24(2)(a)

Development

    of living resources: LOSC/63(1)

    of mineral resources of the Area:

A2/S4(24)(b); RPE/A2/
S4(24)(c); RPE/A3(C); RPE/A4/
S5(2)
Area allocated to the Contractor for:
RPE/A3(B)
of area covered by the contract:
LOSC/A3/7(3)(c); LOSC/A3/
13(6)(h)(i); LOSC/A3/13(6)(l)
area of: RPE/R34; RPE/A3(B); RPE/
A3(C)(1); RPE/A3(C)(3); RPE/
A3(D)(1); RPE/A4/S1(1)(a); RPE/
A4/S2(2); RPE/A4/S2(4); RPE/
A4/S3(1)(a); RPE/A4/S6(1); RPE/
A4/6(1)(a); RPE/A4/S6(3); RPE/
A4/S10(1); RPE/A4/S11(1); RPE/
A4/S11(2)(a); RPE/A4/S11(2)(c);
RPE/A4/S11(3); REP/A4/S13(1);
RPE/A4/S14(1); RPE/A4/S14(8);
RPE/A4/S21(7)
commencement of: RPE/A4/S4(1)
conduct of: RPE/R26(2)
by a contractor: RPE/A4/S1(1); RPE/
A4/S13(1)
contracts for: RPE/R3; RPE/A3; RPE/
A4
data relating to: AGXI/A/S1(5)(j);
AGXI/A/S1(6)(a)(ii); AGXI/A/
S2(1)(c)
duration of: AGXI/A/S1(9); LOSC/A3/
17(2)(b)(ii)
equipment for: RPE/A4/S10(1)(b);
RPE/A4/S11(2)(d)
estimated cost of the proposed plan
of work for: RPE/A2/S3(21)(a);
RPE/A2/S3(21)(b)
expenditures for: RPE/A4/S9; RPE/
A4/S10(2)(c); RPE/A4/S14(6)
expiration of a plan of work for: RPE/
R26(1); RPE/R26(2)
expiration of the contract for: RPE/
R35(3), RPE/R35(4)
extension for the plan of work for:
RPE/R26(1), RPE/R26(2)
fees related to: R2/7(a); AGXI/A/
S1(6)(a)(ii); AGXI/A/S8(3)
geological, of the seabed: LOSC/
277(a)
not pursued by a contractor: RPE/A4/
S14(8)
phase: RPE/R30
by pioneer investor: AGXI/A/
S1(6)(a)(ii); R2/12(a)(i)
plan of work for: RPE/R12(6)(b); RPE/
R16(3); RPE/R18(a); RPE/
R21(5); RPE/R21(7); RPE/
R21(10); RPE/R23(1); RPE/
R24(1); RPE/R24(2); RPE/R28;

RPE/R31(4); RPE/A2/
S3(21)(c)(iii); RPE/A2/S4(24)(a)
plan of work for non-reserved area:
RPE/R16(2)
proposed exploration programme:
RPE/R18(a)
proposed plan of work for: RPE/
R12(1); RPE/R21(5); RPE/
R21(6)(d); RPE/R21(7); RPE/
R21(9); RPE/A2/S3(23)
stage: LOSC/A3/17(2)(c)
by State or entity other than pioneer
investor: AGXI/A/S1(6)(a)(i)
use of term: RPE/R1(3)(b)
work: RPE/A4/S11(1)(b)
Exploration and exploitation
(*see also* continental shelf;
exploitation; exploration; living
resources; marine scientific research;
mineral resources; natural resources)
of Area: LOSC/Preamble(6); LOSC/
1(1)(3); LOSC/151(8); LOSC/
153; LOSC/155(1); LOSC/
155(2); LOSC/155(1)(a); LOSC/
155(4); LOSC/160(2)(f)(ii);
LOSC/162(2)(o)(ii); LOSC/
163(8); LOSC/165(1); LOSC/
168(2); LOSC/314(2); LOSC/A3/
3(3); LOSC/A3/3(4)(c); LOSC/
A3/6(3)(c)(i); LOSC/A3/
6(3)(c)(ii); LOSC/A3/10; LOSC/
A3/13(1)(b); LOSC/A3/17(1)(a);
LOSC/A3/17(2)(a); LOSC/A4/
11(3)(a); R2/7(a); R2/7(b); R2/8;
R2/9(a); RPE/Preamble
of non-reserved areas: LOSC/A3/
6(3)(c)
of reserved areas: AGXI/A/S1(10);
AGXI/A/S2(5)
system governing the Area: LOSC/
153; LOSC/155(1); LOSC/
155(1)(a); LOSC/155(4); LOSC/
160(2)(f)(ii)
technical cooperation: LOSC/269(a)

Facilities
(*see also* off-shore facilities)
for arbitral tribunal: LOSC/A7/6(a)
communication: LOSC/19(2)(k)
custom: LOSC/128
Enterprise: LOSC/A4/8; LOSC/A4/
11(4); LOSC/A4/13(3)(a)(i);
LOSC/A4/13(5)
mineral processing: LOSC/A3/
17(2)(b)(iii)
navigational: LOSC/21(1)(b)
pollution reception: LOSC/211(6)(a)

and regional observer
programmes: UNFSA/18(3)(g)(ii)
protection of the marine environment:
LOSC/209(2); LOSC/211(2);
LOSC/211(3); LOSC/212(1);
LOSC/216(1)(b); LOSC/217(1);
LOSC/223
registration: LOSC/94(2)(a)
request to, for investigation: LOSC/
217(6)
request to the coastal or port State:
LOSC/27(1)(c); LOSC/27(3);
LOSC/218(3); LOSC/218(4);
LOSC/292(1); LOSC/292(2)
responsibility of: LOSC/31; LOSC/
42(5)
rights of: LOSC/90; LOSC/228(3)
warships or ships on government
service: LOSC/95; LOSC/96;
LOSC/110(1)(c) LOSC/110(1)(e);
LOSC/110(2)

**Food and Agriculture Organization of the
United Nations**
expert list maintained by: LOSC/A8/
2(2)
occurrence of term: UNFSA/18(3)(d);
UNFSA/24(1); UNFSA/A1/3(b);
UNFSA/A1/7(2)
standard specification for marking and
identifying fishing vessels:
UNFSA/18(3)(d)

Force , use of
LOSC/19(2)(a); LOSC/39(1)(b);
LOSC/301

Force majeure
LOSC/18(2); LOSC/39(1)(c); RPE/A4/
S17

Foreign ships or vessels
(*see also* investigation; non-
discrimination; ports)
archipelagic passage of: LOSC/53(1)
arrest or detention of: LOSC/28(3);
LOSC/73(4); LOSC/111(6)(b);
LOSC/111(7); LOSC/111(8)
charges which may be levied for
passage through the territorial
sea: LOSC/26
civil jurisdiction in relation to: LOSC/
28
criminal jurisdiction in relation to:
LOSC/27; LOSC/73(4)
design, construction and manning:
LOSC/21(2)
enforcement against: LOSC/224;
LOSC/225; LOSC/228(1);
LOSC/231; LOSC/233; LOSC/
234

equal treatment: LOSC/131; LOSC/
227
hot pursuit of: LOSC/111
innocent passage of: LOSC/19(2);
LOSC/21(4); LOSC/22(1);
LOSC/23; LOSC/24(1); LOSC/
25(3); LOSC/26; LOSC/27(1);
LOSC/27(2); LOSC/27(5);
LOSC/28(1); LOSC/28(3);
LOSC/52(2) LOSC/211(3);
LOSC/211(4)
nuclear-powered: LOSC/22(2);
LOSC/23
penalties against: LOSC/73(4);
LOSC/228; LOSC/230
re pollution: LOSC/211(3); LOSC/
211(4); LOSC/211(6)(a); LOSC/
211(6)(c); LOSC/224; LOSC/
225; LOSC/226(1)(a); LOSC/
228; LOSC/230; LOSC/231
right to visit: LOSC/110
transit passage: LOSC/40; LOSC/
42(2); LOSC/42(4); LOSC/223

**Formal confirmation by international
organizations**
AGXI/4(1); AGXI/4(3)(a); AGXI/
4(3)(b); AGXI/4(4); AGXI/4(5);
AGXI/5(1); LOSC/306; LOSC/
319(2)(b); LOSC/A9/3(1); LOSC/
A9/4(1); LOSC/A9/5(1); LOSC/
A9/5(2); LOSC/A9/7(1); LOSC/
A9/8(a); LOSC/A9/8(b)(ii);
LOSC/A9/8(b)(iii)

Freedom
of high seas: RPE/R1(4)
of scientific research: RPE/R1(4)

Freedoms of navigation and overflight
over continental shelf: LOSC/78(2)
in exclusive economic zones: LOSC/
36; LOSC/38(2); LOSC/58(1);
LOSC/297(1)(a)
on high seas: LOSC/36; LOSC/38(2);
LOSC/58(1); LOSC/87; LOSC/
125(1); LOSC/297(1)(a)

Free zones
LOSC/128

Frigate mackerel
LOSC/A1

Functions
(*see* powers and functions)

Fundamental terms of contract
RPE/A4/S21(1)(a)

Funds
(*see also* compensation fund;
contractors; economic assistance;
expenditures)
of Authority: A3/13(4)(b); A3/13(6);

referral of proposals or reporting to:
LOSC/41(4); LOSC/53(9);
LOSC/205; LOSC/297(3)d;
LOSC/319(2)(a)
responsibility and liability of: LOSC/
139(1); LOSC/139(2); LOSC/
139(3); LOSC/263(3); LOSC/
A9/6
settlement of disputes: LOSC/265;
LOSC/A7/3(e); LOSC/A9/7
signature of Agreement on Part XI
by: AGXI/3
signature of Convention by: LOSC/
305(1)(f); LOSC/A9/2
technical or financial assistance
from: LOSC/72(2); LOSC/
151(10); LOSC/254(4); LOSC/
275(2)
use of term: LOSC/A9/1
International peace and security
UNFSA/Preamble(9)
**International regulations, procedures
and practices**
on safety at sea: UNFSA/22(4)
on safety of vessel and crew:
UNFSA/21(10)
International rules and standards
LOSC/211; LOSC/213; LOSC/214;
LOSC/217; LOSC/222; RPE/A4/
S15(1)
International Seabed Authority
(*see* Authority)
**International Tribunal for the Law of the
Sea**
(*see also* Tribunal)
UNFSA/31(3)
Interpretation of awards
LOSC/A7/12(1)
Interpretation or application
of a contract: LOSC/187(c)(i); LOSC/
188(2)(a); LOSC/A3/13(15);
RPE/A4/S28
of Convention: LOSC/187(a); LOSC/
188(2)(a); LOSC/264; LOSC/
279; LOSC/280; LOSC/281(1);
LOSC/282; LOSC/283(1);
LOSC/284(1); LOSC/286;
LOSC/287(1); LOSC/288(1);
LOSC/295; LOSC/297(1);
LOSC/297(2)(a); LOSC/
297(3)(a); LOSC/298(1)(a)(i);
LOSC/A6/32(1); LOSC/A8/1;
LOSC/A8/5(1); LOSC/A9/7(1)
of an international agreement: LOSC/
280; LOSC/288(2); LOSC/
297(3)(e); LOSC/A6/22; LOSC/
A6/32(2)

Intervention
(*see* proceedings)
Investigation
cooperation in: LOSC/94(7); LOSC/
217(5); LOSC/226(2)
by flag State: LOSC/94(6); LOSC/
97(6); LOSC/217(4); LOSC/
217(5); LOSC/217(6); LOSC/
218(3)
of foreign ships: LOSC/27(1); LOSC/
27(2); LOSC/27(5); LOSC/97(3);
LOSC/217(4); LOSC/217(5);
LOSC/218(1); LOSC/218(3);
LOSC/218(4); LOSC/226(1)(a);
LOSC/226(1)(b)
by port State: LOSC/218(1); LOSC/
218(3); LOSC/218(4); LOSC/
226(1)(a); LOSC/226(1)(b)
Investment/investors
(*see* contractors; pioneer investors)
Irreversible effects of fishing operations
UNFSA/Preamble(7)
Islands
(*see also* artificial islands;
installations; structures)
and archipelagic States: LOSC/46;
LOSC/47(1); LOSC/53(5)
atolls: LOSC/6; LOSC/47(1); LOSC/
47(7)
and baselines: LOSC/6; LOSC/7(1);
LOSC/13; LOSC/47(1); LOSC/
47(4); LOSC/121(2)
and bays: LOSC/10(3)
in contiguous zone: LOSC/121(2)
installations or equipment not
possessing the status of: LOSC/
60(8); LOSC/80; LOSC/
147(2)(e); LOSC/246(5)(c);
LOSC/259
limestone: LOSC/47(7)
reefs around: LOSC/6; LOSC/47(7)
regime of: LOSC/121
rocks: LOSC/121(3)
and straits: LOSC/38(1)
use of term: LOSC/121(1)
Island States
AGXI/A/S3(15)(d)

Joint Ventures
assistance in: UNFSA/25(2)
of Authority: AGXI/A/S2(1)(f); LOSC/
A3/9(3); LOSC/A3/11(1); LOSC/
A3/13(1)(f)
cooperation through: UNFSA/25(2)
of Enterprise: AGXI/A/S2(2); AGXI/A/
S2(3); AGXI/A/S2(5); AGXI/A/
S5(1)(a); AGXI/A/S5(1)(b);

Land-based sources of pollution
LOSC/194(3)(a); LOSC/207(1);
LOSC/207(4); LOSC/213

Land-locked States
(*see also* fishing; geographically
disadvantaged States; living
resources; neighbouring States)
activities in the Area: LOSC/140(1);
LOSC/141; LOSC/148; LOSC/
152(2); LOSC/160(2)(k); LOSC/
274(a)
freedom in exclusive economic zones:
LOSC/58(1)
freedom of high seas: LOSC/87(1);
LOSC/90; LOSC/131
membership in the Council: AGXI/A/
S3(15)(d); LOSC/161(1)(d);
LOSC/161(2)(a)
right of access to and from the sea:
LOSC/125(1); LOSC/126
right of innocent passage: LOSC/17
right of neighbouring land-locked
States *re* marine scientific
research: LOSC/254
right to participate in the exploitation
of the exclusive economic
zones: LOSC/69(1); LOSC/
69(2)(b); LOSC/69(2)(c); LOSC/
69(3); LOSC/69(4); LOSC/69(5);
LOSC/70(3)(c)
transfer of marine technology: LOSC/
266(2); LOSC/269(a); LOSC/
272; LOSC/274(a)
and transit States: LOSC/124(1)(c);
LOSC/124(2); LOSC/125;
LOSC/127(2); LOSC/128;
LOSC/129; LOSC/130
use of term: LOSC/124(1)(a)

Land territory
LOSC/2(1); LOSC/76(1); LOSC/
121(2); LOSC/298(1)(a)(i)

Law of the Sea Conference
(*see* Third United Nations Conference
on the Law of the Sea)

Laws
(*see also* applicability; international
law; laws and regulations; regulations)
applicable: LOSC/A3/21; RPE/A4/S27
to determine in accordance with the
laws of a State a vessel's
involvement in the commission
of a serious violation of
conservation and management
measures: UNFSA/19(1)(e)
to institute proceedings in accordance
with the laws of a State: UNFSA/
19(1)(d)

internal: AGXI/7(2); AGXI/A/S1(12)(c);
LOSC/27(2); LOSC/28(3);
LOSC/94(2)(b); LOSC/217(6);
LOSC/220(2); LOSC/220(6);
LOSC/228(3); LOSC/A4/13(6);
LOSC/A7/6
national: AGXI/7(2); AGXI/A/
S1(12)(c); LOSC/210(6); LOSC/
220(8); LOSC/223; LOSC/
230(1); LOSC/230(2); UNFSA/
20(5)
nationality of a ship: LOSC/104
occurrence of term: LOSC/A5/7(1);
LOSC/A6/28; LOSC/A7/9
of salvage: LOSC/303(2)
of State or entity: UNFSA/43

Laws and regulations
(*see also* applicability; international
law; laws; regulations; violations)
on archipelagic sea lanes passage:
LOSC/54
on cables and pipelines: LOSC/113;
LOSC/114; LOSC/115
on contiguous zone: LOSC/303(2)
customs, immigration, fiscal and
sanitary: LOSC/19(2)(g); LOSC/
21(1)(h); LOSC/33(1)(a); LOSC/
42(1)(d); LOSC/60(2)
enforcement of: LOSC/73
on exclusive economic zones: LOSC/
58(3); LOSC/234
on fishing: LOSC/21(1)(e); LOSC/
62(2); LOSC/62(4); LOSC/62(5);
LOSC/73(1); LOSC/73(3);
LOSC/297(3)(a)
on innocent passage: LOSC/21;
LOSC/30; LOSC/31; LOSC/
211(4)
on marine scientific research: LOSC/
249(2); LOSC/255
occurrence of term: LOSC/111(1);
LOSC/111(2); LOSC/297(1)(b);
LOSC/310; A3/4(4); A3/21(3);
A4/13(4)(c)
on pollution: LOSC/201; LOSC/
207(1); LOSC/208(1); LOSC/
208(3); LOSC/209(2); LOSC/
210(1); LOSC/210(3); LOSC/
210(6); LOSC/211(2); LOSC/
211(4); LOSC/211(5); LOSC/
211(6)(a); LOSC/211(6)(c);
LOSC/212(1); LOSC/213;
LOSC/214; LOSC/216(1);
LOSC/217(1); LOSC/217(8);
LOSC/220(1) LOSC/220(2);
LOSC/220(3); LOSC/220(4);
LOSC/220(8); LOSC/222; LOSC/

danger in: LOSC/24(2); LOSC/44;
LOSC/225
in exclusive economic zones: LOSC/
58(1)
in high seas: LOSC/87(1)(b)
settlement of disputes over: LOSC/
297(1)(a)
in straits: LOSC/36; LOSC/38(2);
LOSC/44

Overlapping claims to pioneer areas
(*see also* nationality)
R2/5(a); R2/5(c)

Participation by international organization in UNFSA
UNFSA/47

Participation of a developing State
UNFSA/25(1)(c)

Parties to a dispute
(*see also* settlement of disputes)
UNFSA/31(1); UNFSA/31(2)

Partnership or consortium
application for plan of work for
exploration by: LOSC/A3/4(3);
LOSC/A3/6(4); RPE/R10(4);
RPE/R11(1); RPE/R13
financial and technical capabilities of:
RPE/R12(8)
occurrence of term: R2/
1(a)(ii)(footnote)
previous contracts with Authority:
RPE/R13

Passage
(*see* aircraft; archipelagic sea lanes
passage; archipelagic States;
archipelagic waters; due
publicity; exclusive economic
zones; foreign ships or vessels;
innocent passage; land-locked
States; laws and regulations;
navigation; noxious substances;
overflight; regime; straits;
tankers; transit passage)

Payments
(*see also* contributions; economic
assistance)
arrears in: LOSC/184
by or to Authority for operations in
Area: AGXI/A/S8(1)(a); AGXI/A/
S8(1)(e); LOSC/162(2)(p);
LOSC/A3/11(3); LOSC/A3/13(5);
LOSC/A3/13(6); LOSC/A3/
13(12); R2/7(b)
by Authority to Secretary-General and
staff: LOSC/183(3)
to compensation fund: LOSC/171(f);
R1/5(i)

of corporate income taxes: LOSC/A3/
13(6)(p)
by developing States: LOSC/82(3);
LOSC/82(4)
by Enterprise to Authority: LOSC/A4/
10(1); LOSC/A4/10(3)
equitable sharing of: LOSC/82(4);
LOSC/160(2)(f)(i); LOSC/
162(2)(o)(i)
for exploitation of continental shelf
beyond 200 nautical miles:
LOSC/160(2)(f)(i); LOSC/
162(2)(o)(i)
of share of net proceeds: LOSC/A3/
13(4)(b); LOSC/A3/13(6)

Peace and security
(*see also* good order and security;
security)
LOSC/Preamble(7); LOSC/138;
UNFSA/Preamble(9)

Peaceful purposes
marine scientific research for: LOSC/
143(1); LOSC/147(2)(d); LOSC/
240(a); LOSC/242(1); LOSC/
246(3)
reservation of Area for: LOSC/141;
LOSC/155(2)
reservation of high seas for: LOSC/88

Peaceful settlement of disputes
(*see also* settlement of disputes)
LOSC/279; LOSC/280; LOSC/281(1);
LOSC/283(1); UNFSA/27;
UNFSA/28; UNFSA/29; UNFSA/
30; UNFSA/31; UNFSA/32

Peaceful uses of the seas
LOSC/Preamble(4); LOSC/301

Penal jurisdiction
LOSC/27(1); LOSC/97(1)

Penalties
(*see also* monetary penalties)
against foreign ships or vessels:
LOSC/73(4); LOSC/228; LOSC/
230
against pirate ship or aircraft: LOSC/
105
for pollution violations: LOSC/217(8);
LOSC/228; LOSC/230(1);
LOSC/230(2); LOSC/230(3)
for violation of fisheries laws and
regulations: LOSC/73(3); LOSC/
73(4)

Performance requirements
LOSC/151(2)(c); LOSC/A3/
17(1)(b)(iii); LOSC/A3/17(2)(c)

Periodic review
of international regime of Area's
operation in practice: LOSC/154

Registrar of the Tribunal
(*see* notification; Tribunal)
Registry
of aircraft: LOSC/42(5); LOSC/
212(1); LOSC/216(1)(b); LOSC/
222
change of ship registry: LOSC/92(1)
of installation or structure: LOSC/
109(3)(b); LOSC/209(2); LOSC/
262
port of: LOSC/98(1)(c); LOSC/220(3)
of vessels: LOSC/209(2); LOSC/
211(2); LOSC/211(3); LOSC/
212(1); LOSC/216(1)(b); LOSC/
217(1); LOSC/217(2); LOSC/
217(3); LOSC/222
Regulation
of fishing activities: UNFSA/18(3)(i)
of transshipment: UNFSA/18(3)(h)
Regulations
(*see also* Agreement; applicability;
communications; enforcement;
exclusive economic zones;
general acceptance;
interpretation or application;
laws and regulations; manning
regulations; marine
environment; maritime traffic;
pollution; rules, regulations and
procedures of the Authority;
stocks; violations)
LOSC/21; LOSC/24; LOSC/42(1)(b);
LOSC/223; UNFSA/30(5)
Related interests
(*see* interests)
Relation of UNFSA to other agreements
UNFSA/44
Release
prompt: LOSC/73(2); LOSC/292
of vessels and ships: LOSC/73(2);
LOSC/111(7); LOSC/226(1)(b);
LOSC/226(1)(c); LOSC/292
**Relinquishment of portions of the
pioneer area**
R2/1(e)
Remuneration
of arbitral tribunal members: LOSC/
A7/7
of Authority staff: LOSC/167(3)
of Governing Board members:
LOSC/A4/5(5)
of scientists of coastal States: LOSC/
249(1)(a)
of Tribunal members: LOSC/A6/18
Renunciation of areas
LOSC/A3/17(1)(b)(v); LOSC/A3/
17(2)(e)

Reports
(*see also* Council; Governing Board)
access to: UNFSA/12(2); UNFSA/
18(3)(c)
conciliation commission: LOSC/
297(3)(d); LOSC/298(1)(a)(ii);
LOSC/A5/7
Enterprise: LOSC/160(2)(i); LOSC/
162(2)(g); LOSC/A4/9
occurrence of term: LOSC/205;
LOSC/206; RPE/R5; RPE/A4/
S10; UNFSA/18(3)(f)
on pioneer investors: AGXI/A/
S1(6)(a)(ii)
Preparatory Commission: R1/10; R1/
11; RPE/R10(1)(footnote 2)
by Secretary-General of the Authority:
RPE/A4/S5(4)
by Secretary-General of the United
Nations: LOSC/309(2)(a)
Representation
(*see also* equitable geographical
distribution, representation,
basis)
of coastal State in a marine scientific
research project: LOSC/248(f);
LOSC/249(1)(a)
of principal legal systems: LOSC/A6/
2(2); LOSC/A6/35(2)
of special interests: AGXI/A/S3(15)(d);
AGXI/A/S9(3); LOSC/161(1)(d);
LOSC/163(4)
Reproductive capacity
UNFSA/A2/3
Research projects
(*see* marine scientific research)
Reservation of areas
LOSC/A3/8; LOSC/A3/17(2)(a)
Reservations and exceptions to UNFSA
UNFSA/42
Reservations to the Convention
LOSC/309
Reserved areas
(*see also* non-reserved areas)
activities in: LOSC/A3/9
data disclosure to Enterprise: LOSC/
A3/14(3); RPE/R16(3)
designation of: LOSC/A3/5(3)(e);
LOSC/A3/8; AGXI/A/S1(10); R2/
3(b); R2/12(a)(i); RPE/R16(2);
RPE/R17(4); RPE/R21(7); RPE/
A2/S2(19)(chapeau); RPE/A2/
S2(19)(a)(i)
Enterprise activities in: AGXI/A/S2(5);
LOSC/A3/3(2); LOSC/A3/9;
RPE/R17(3)

to fish on the high seas: LOSC/116
of flag States: LOSC/90; LOSC/228(3)
and freedoms of States: LOSC/55;
  LOSC/78; LOSC/87(2); LOSC/
  297(1)(a); LOSC/297(1)(b)
of geographically disadvantaged
  States: LOSC/70
of hot pursuit: LOSC/111
of innocent passage: LOSC/8(2);
  LOSC/17; LOSC/21(4); LOSC/
  22(1); LOSC/23; LOSC/24(1)(a);
  LOSC/52; LOSC/211(3); LOSC/
  211(4)
to lay submarine cables and pipelines:
  LOSC/51(2); LOSC/112; LOSC/
  297(1)(a)
of navigation: LOSC/53(3); LOSC/
  78(2); LOSC/90; LOSC/297(1)(a)
of new members of subregional or
  regional management
  organizations or arrangements:
  UNFSA/11
of parties to agree upon or to modify a
  procedure: LOSC/299; LOSC/A5/
  10
to protection of coastal States: LOSC/
  25
of States to exploit their natural
  resources: LOSC/56(1)(a);
  LOSC/73(1); LOSC/77(1); LOSC/
  77(2); LOSC/79(2); LOSC/193
traditional fishing: LOSC/51(1)
of transit passage: LOSC/38; LOSC/
  39(1); LOSC/42(2); LOSC/42(4)
of visit: LOSC/110
voting: LOSC/184

Rises
  LOSC/76(3); LOSC/76(6)
Risk
  of pollution: LOSC/162(2)(x); LOSC/
    165(2)(h); LOSC/165(2)(l);
    LOSC/200; LOSC/204(1); LOSC/
    225
  of serious and unfair economic
    prejudice: RPE/R35(3)
  of serious harm to marine
    environment: RPE/R2(2); RPE/
    R2(3); RPE/R21(6)(c)
Rivers
  (*see also* islands)
  mouths of: LOSC/9
  and sustenance of economic life or
    human habitation: LOSC/121(3)
  and thickness of sedimentary rocks:
    LOSC/76(4)(a)(i)
Roadsteads
  LOSC/12

Routeing systems
  (*see also* sea lanes; traffic separation
    schemes)
  LOSC/211(1)
Routes
  (*see also* exclusive economic zones;
    high seas; sea lanes)
  air: LOSC/53(1); LOSC/53(2); LOSC/
    53(4); LOSC/53(5); LOSC/53(12)
  archipelagic: LOSC/53(1); LOSC/
    53(4); LOSC/53(5); LOSC/53(12)
  through exclusive economic zones:
    LOSC/36; LOSC/38(1)
  on high seas: LOSC/36; LOSC/38(1)
  for international navigation: LOSC/36;
    LOSC/53(4); LOSC/53(12)
  shipping: LOSC/261
  systems: LOSC/211(1)
Rules
  (*see also* amendments; applicability;
    damage; duration of operation;
    general acceptance; government
    ships; implementation;
    international law; interpretation
    or application; marine
    environment; rules of procedure;
    rules, regulations and
    procedures of the Authority;
    rules, standards and
    recommended practices and
    procedures regarding pollution;
    UNCITRAL Arbitration Rules;
    violations)
  accounting: RPE/R12(5)(b); RPE/A2/
    S3(21)(c); RPE/A4/S10(2)(c)
  Economic Planning Commission:
    LOSC/163(10)
  Legal and Technical Commission:
    LOSC/163(10)
  occurrence of term: UNFSA/30(5)
  Preparatory Commission: LOSC/
    308(4); LOSC/A4/11(3)(a); R1/4
Rules of procedure
  applicable: LOSC/294(3)
  of Assembly: LOSC/159(4); R1/5(b)
  of Authority's organs: LOSC/169(2)
  of Council: AGXI/A/S3(11)(a); LOSC/
    162(2)(e)
  of Enterprise: LOSC/A4/6(b)
  of Preparatory Commission: R1/4
  of Preparatory Commission's
    subsidiary bodies: R1/7
  of Tribunal: LOSC/A6/16
**Rules, regulations and procedures of the
Authority**
  (*see also* Authority)
  financial: AGXI/A/S9(7)(a); LOSC/

Secretary-General of the Authority

(*see also* Authority; candidates; depositary functions; geographical coordinates; payments)

access to books, documents, papers and records of a contractor: RPE/A4/S14(6); RPE/A4/S14(7)

annual report to Assembly: LOSC/166(4)

application for approval of plan of work for exploration: RPE/R10 (1)

application for approval of plans of work in reserved area: RPE/R17(1); RPE/R17(2)

appointment/dismissal of staff: LOSC/167(3); LOSC/168(3)

appointment of interim Director-General: AGXI/A/S2(1)

and archaeological/historical objects: RPE/R8; RPE/R34; RPE/A4/S7

arrangement for immediate notification to: RPE/A4/S6(b)

arrangements for consultations with international/non-governmental organizations: LOSC/169

candidates for: LOSC/160(2)(b); LOSC/162(2)(b); LOSC/166(2)

confidentiality of data and information: RPE/R6; RPE/R35(1); RPE/R35(2); RPE/R35(3); RPE/R36(1); RPE/R32(2); RPE/R32(4)

contingency plan submitted to: RPE/A4/S6(1)

continuing flow of full information to: RPE/A4/S6(d)

contractor's annual report to: RPE/A4/S10(1)

contractor's supplement of annual report to: RPE/A4/S10(3)

contracts for exploration: RPE/R23(2)

convocation of special sessions of Assembly: LOSC/159(2)

data and information to be submitted upon expiration of a contract to: RPE/A4/S11(2); RPE/A4/S11(3)

depositary functions of: LOSC/84(2)

drafting of proposed annual budget of Authority: AGXI/A/S9(7)(c); LOSC/172

election of: LOSC/160(2)(b); LOSC/162(2)(b); LOSC/166(2)

emergency orders of: RPE/R32(1); RPE/R32(2); RPE/R32(3); RPE/R32(7)

functions of: LOSC/166(3)

immediate, temporary measures issued by: RPE/A4/S6(3)

incidents of contractor harm to marine environment: RPE/A4/S6(2)

informing of Authority of prospector and general area of prospecting: RPE/R4(5)

informing of proposed prospector: RPE/R4(3)

notice to: RPE/R37(1); RPE/R37(4); RPE/A4/S26(5)

notification by contractor of non-pursuance of exploration:RPE/A4/S14(8)

notification of incidents causing serious harm to the marine environment: RPE/R7

notification of prospecting acknowledged by: RPE/R4(1)

notification of prospecting addressed to: RPE/R3(2)

notification of prospecting recorded by: RPE/R2(1); RPE/R4(2)

notification of suspension and termination of contract by: RPE/A4/S21(2)

notification to contractor of projected time and duration of inspections by: RPE/A4/S14(2)

notification to prospector by: RPE/R2(5)

periodic review of implementation of plan of work for exploration: RPE/R28

privileges and immunities of: LOSC/182; LOSC/183(3)

processing of applications for approval of plan of work for exploration: RPE/R20; RPE/R21(1); RPE/R21(8); RPE/R21/Footnote(8)

prospector's annual report submitted to LTC by: RPE/R5(1)

protection and preservation of marine environment by: RPE/R31(5)

report on implementation and results of monitoring programme: RPE/A4/S5(4)

request by a registered pioneer investor for approval of plan of work for exploration: RPE/R21/Footnote(8)

responsibility and duty of: LOSC/168

review and act on notification of prospecting: RPE/R4(2)

review of implementation of plan of work for exploration: RPE/A4/S4(4)

of operation of Convention provisions:
LOSC/311(3); LOSC/311(4)
of operations in Area: LOSC/
162(2)(w); LOSC/165(2)(k)

Sustainability
(*see* long-term sustainability;
maximum sustainable yield)

Swordfish
LOSC/A1

Symposia
(*see also* training)
LOSC/269(c); LOSC/277(d)

Tankers
LOSC/22(2)

Target reference point
UNFSA/A2/2

Target stocks
UNFSA/6(5)

Taxes
(*see also* Authority)
on corporate income: LOSC/A3/
13(6)(p)
on Enterprise: LOSC/A4/13(5)
on traffic in transit: LOSC/127
on Tribunal: LOSC/A6/18(8)

Technical assistance
(*see* assistance; cooperation;
development)

Technology
(*see also* agreement; arrangements;
Authority; contracts; cooperation;
developing States; Enterprise;
equipment; equitability; fair and
reasonable conditions for the transfer
of technology; fishing; international
organizations; joint ventures; land-
locked States; plan of work for
activities in the Area; training; transfer
of technology)
access to: UNFSA/13(3)(c)
for deep seabed mining: LOSC/A3/
17(2)(a); LOSC/A3/17(2)(c)
fishing: LOSC/62(4)(a); LOSC/
62(4)(j); LOSC/A3/5(8)
holders, suppliers and recipients of:
LOSC/267; LOSC/274
marine, development of: AGXI/A/
S1(5)(i); AGXI/A/S2(1)(d);
LOSC/268(b)
marketing of: LOSC/277(h)
pollution from use of: LOSC/196
use of term: LOSC/A3/5(8)

Technology research centres
LOSC/275; LOSC/276; LOSC/277

Termination of a contract
(*see* contracts)

Term of office
(*see also* Authority; Commission on
the Limits of the Continental Shelf;
Council of the Authority; Enterprise)
of Assembly of the Authority President
and officers: LOSC/159(4)
of Director-General of the Enterprise:
LOSC/A4/7(1)
of Economic and Planning
Commission: LOSC/163(6);
LOSC/163(7)
of Finance Committee: AGXI/A/S9(4);
AGXI/A/S9(5)
of Governing Board members: LOSC/
A4/5(3)
of Legal and Technical Commission:
LOSC/163(6); LOSC/163(7)
of Seabed Disputes Chamber of the
Tribunal: LOSC/A6/35(6)
of Tribunal members: LOSC/A6/5;
LOSC/A6/6(2); LOSC/A6/18(5)

**Terms and conditions for fishing rights
and conservation measures**
(*see also* contracts; fair and
reasonable terms and conditions for
the transfer of)
LOSC/51(1); LOSC/62(2); LOSC/
62(4); LOSC/66(3)(a); LOSC/
297(3)(a); LOSC/297(3)(b)(iii)

Terms of contracts
(*see* contracts)

Territorial integrity
LOSC/19(2)(a); LOSC/39(1)(b);
LOSC/301

Territorial sea
(*see also* air space; artificial islands;
baselines; breadth; cables and
pipelines; charts; conservation
and management of living
resources; delimitation; due
publicity; foreign ships or
vessels; historic title; hot
pursuit; islands; jurisdiction;
laws and regulations; marine
scientific research; opposite or
adjacent coasts; outer limits;
sea lanes; tankers; traffic
separation schemes)
air space over: LOSC/2(2); LOSC/
212(1); LOSC/222
artificial islands in: LOSC/11; LOSC/
60(8)
baselines for/breadth of: LOSC/3;
LOSC/4; LOSC/5; LOSC/6;
LOSC/7; LOSC/8(1); LOSC/9;
LOSC/10; LOSC/13(1); LOSC/
13(2); LOSC/14; LOSC/15;

Made in the USA
Columbia, SC
22 February 2023

12807427R00309